ON MUSIC

Essays and Diversions

ROBIN HOLLOWAY

ON MUSIC

Essays and Diversions

1963-2003

The right of Robin Holloway to be identified as the author of this work has been asserted by him in accordance with the Copyright, Designs and Patents Act 1998.

Claridge Press Ltd
Sunday Hill Farm, Brinkworth, Wilts SN15 5AS
www.claridgepress.com; info@claridgepress.com

Typeset by Kathryn Puffett, Cambridge.

Printed by J. H. Haynes & Co. Ltd. Sparkford, Britain.

CIP data for this title is available from the British Library.

ISBN 0-8264-7629-5

Essays, Music.

to my pupils —
past, present, to come —
in gratitude for all they've taught me

Contents

Part II The Others

Part III 'Think pieces'

Preface

This selection of my reviews, essays general and particular, occasional pieces, polemics, pensées, etc. is drawn from a much larger total body and represents around four decades of reacting to and writing about music. The earliest dates from my last year as an undergraduate (1963–4); the most recent could well, save for the exigencies of book-production, date from last week.

Their level is various, ranging from dense contributions to academic symposia for which, in some bits, technical terms are employed and scores needed, to epitomes, cameos, diversions (almost all taken from the music column in the *Spectator* that I've contributed monthly, with a few exceptions, since late 1988). The balance of tone and length has been deliberately considered, for contrast, complement, relief.

It has been hard not to interfere with inconsistencies, changes of mind and the expression of opinions that strike me now as jejune, stupid or plain wrong. I've not bowdlerised such moments: nor in general changed things beyond stylistic retouching, correction of obvious mistakes and the omission of inevitable overlaps (except when the re-used idea, quotation, illustration is also being re-thought) and ephemeral paragraphs from some of the reviews. I have rewritten when I perceived a tangle or a smudge in the original (there will of course remain tangles and smudges I've not noticed); and many items have been provided with a headnote, usually just factual, now and again giving a more detailed context; some have gained a retrospective/corrective afterword too. But I felt that by and large the contents should stand or fall as they were and are, without the mitigations of hindsight.

*   *   *

In earlier years this sort of writing was infrequent for me. My principal effort went into a doctoral thesis whose nature precluded the lighter touch and shorter fuse of what I've mainly done since. When eventually this thesis, completed for the doctorate in 1971, was published as a book,[1] its style if not its content had been leavened and lubricated under the stern eye of the series general editor, William Glock, who pencilled in a large fierce T whenever he found the prose smacked of academe—meaning, get rid of it! As with the more or less contemporaneous experience of writing for Hans Keller (see p.410), a lesson I've never forgotten.

The late 1960s were for me a period of radical insecurity as an aspiring but untried composer. There's no question in my mind that concentration for about five years on the thesis (albeit intermittent; I recall getting down to it

---

[1] *Debussy and Wagner* (Eulenberg, 1978).

when an urgent grant-application or research-fellowship deadline loomed, each one eliciting a new chapter) was a substitute for creative work. They ran alongside each other; the thesis then took over when composition completely dried, and was eventually edged aside as it tentatively revived. By the time of finishing the long fantasia with which *Debussy and Wagner* ends (for the last deadline of all, submission of the thesis for the degree), composition was ready and able to resume.

Such direct substitution has recurred now and again over the years. When stuck or blocked, some composers simply wait. Those who can, perform, teach, talk, organise, run things. Other therapy can consist of further assimilation of music, further study of its technicalities, or arranging, transcribing, orchestrating, even just copying out an admired master's work. I've had recourse to all these, but the most consistent solution to a recurring inability to write music itself has been to write about it. Sometimes *both* forms of expression are closed off; at others, the protracted difficulty of a literary piece actually resembles that of a recalcitrant composition (and *both* can be abandoned, too, as insoluble); sometimes a period of exuberance opens up both together, as if they flowed from the same source.

Whatever their complex interrelationships in the unknowable 'weather' of one's internal resources, the balance is fundamentally simple. I'm deeply interested, writing about music I love (or indeed deplore), in expressing as clearly as I can the reactions and emotions it arouses, because I'm deeply involved in writing the stuff (as in Wagner, the *Stoff*, or, as we say, *material* or *fabric*) itself, which by definition also involves discovery, elicitation, elucidation of what lies within. With both, the surface—styles or idioms, intentions, intonations—is pretty eclectic, perhaps bewilderingly; but I sense the presence of a hard core, unifying the heterogeneous directions into an integrated viewpoint, which might even be called a vision, of how music is, was, might still be. Though I'd not want to put *this* into words, and probably couldn't even if I did.[2]

* * *

I'm more grateful than I can gracefully say to the patient editors who over the years have commissioned, borne with, in some cases helped to shape, this book's contents: Tom Sutcliffe, editor of the then *Music and Musicians* (long defunct), who gave me my first sizeable break; John Casey and the *Cambridge Review*; David Drew, then Malcolm MacDonald of *Tempo*; Anthony Bye and Nicholas Williams of the *Musical Times*; Nicholas Spice of the *London Review of Books*; the successive arts editors of the *Spectator* ever since at the fruitful suggestion of Noel Malcolm it first took me on as a monthly commentator; and the editors of the several other journals detailed in the acknowledgements.

---

[2] Another collection, almost as large as this one, could be made of my writing about composition, and perhaps will be one of these days.

I'm greatly indebted too to colleagues at Cambridge who have twisted my arm into contributing to their symposia—Paul Wingfield's *Janáček* volume, Dean Sutcliffe's *Haydn*, the late Derrick Puffett's pair on Strauss's *Salome* and *Elektra*. The pattern here was always avid yet apprehensive acceptance, followed by work-shy reluctance, turning into blood, sweat, tears and curses, then in two cases such a total blank that I begged for merciful release which was mercifully not granted. Once out of the tunnel one's pleased to have been tried so hard. But not during!

The principal debt, and least expressible of all, is to friends who have encouraged, endorsed, helped to formulate, sometimes literally with scribbled annotations, sometimes simply through conversation wherein their influence has been more general and unwitting. Keepers of the conscience, like Graeme Mitchison, Jehane Kuhn, Bayan Northcott, Alexander Goehr, Caroline Elam, Oliver Knussen, John Kerrigan—friends whose insights, felicitous phrases, clarifying contentions linger in the mind and enrich its native endowment. I'd like to name many more, but these are maybe the most consistent as they are surely the longest in duration.

And also Frank Miles, my English master in my teens, who inculcated, in a severe Leavisite accent that still remains my fundamental speech (though mitigated by promiscuous eclecticism and an attempt to write 'for fun') the seed of critical thinking. And Roger Scruton, who picked up a proposal that several 'reputable publishers' (as they say) had turned down. And Edna Pilmer, who typed the great bulk of the articles, and many other things, in their original form; and Kathryn Puffett, who has so skilfully set this new whole. And the Master and Fellows of Gonville and Caius College Cambridge, who, over and above a generous grant to help towards publication-costs, have for some three decades given me the peace and quiet within which to play, listen to, reflect on, write, and write on such a range of music.

Robin Holloway
1 May 2003

Part I

The Austro-German Mainstream

1

Two on Bach-performances

i   Bach betrayed

One of my earliest Spectator *columns, early rubbing in the lesson that readers with few exceptions only react with indignation rather than endorsement. This little piece, which now seems to be describing a phase of performance style as distant as the 'Victorian' Bach it affectionately evokes, fluttered a dovecote or two and roused a small waspnest.*

*   *   *

Eighty-two down, one hundred and sixteen to go; I am slowly fulfilling a long-held wish to listen to all the church cantatas of J. S. Bach.

When I first began to explore this supreme body of work, recordings were few and performances almost non-existent. I recall the excitement with which the project for issuing them all on disc was announced and the eagerness with which, back in 1971, I rushed to buy the first releases from Telefunken. But for me, alas, they remained the last. Even then the unmusicality of the performances was unbearable. Nikolaus Harnoncourt presides over a wasteland right at the neglected heart of Western music.

Swallowing the chagrin, I returned to patient waiting for the occasional performance that still lay within what appears to have become a superseded realm of style and sound. The situation for a lover of this music resembles a royalist's under Cromwell, longing for the tyranny of the saints to end and normality to resume.

Bach has suffered far more than any other composer who is subject to the whims of authenticity. Coinciding, as it happens, with the last lap of Harnoncourt's vast enterprise, the BBC rebroadcast in the interval of the B minor Mass from the Proms the other day a thirty-nine-year-old talk by Ralph Vaughan Williams which included his reactions to the nascent drive towards fidelity as they arose out of a lifetime's devotion to Bach. A principal point was Bach's unique timelessness—'he belongs to no period or style'. This belief was the basis for a sympathetic performer's freedom with the known historical circumstances of Bach's church music—the choir and band puny alike in numbers and talents to cope with music of such technical difficulty and wealth of content.

Naturally this viewpoint has dated: things have greatly changed since 1950, when Vaughan Williams was already aged seventy-eight. Insufferable at any time and whatever one's opinion was the jejune patronage with which his modest and deeply held words were dismissed by the BBC introducer. As it was, the performance of the Mass that evening, under John Eliot Gardiner (who also does Debussy and Chabrier) well exemplified the virtues that the authentic movement has by now made almost a matter of course. So when I say point-blank that Harnoncourt is unmusical, what exactly is meant?

There is the sense that the Bach cantatas are, under his hands, being cut down to size. An affectation of 'no nonsense' where architectural grandeur or spiritual expressivity is concerned ensures that the one is denied breadth and the other depth. These negative results are achieved by fast speeds, sharp attacks and a dry, detached sound-quality, thus eschewing warmth of tone and subtlety of phrasing (indeed any phrasing whatever). The benefits and occasional delights of clarity are diminished by the fundamental flaw, a rhythmic instability that vitiates every speed from largo to presto. Whatever the character of the music, Harnoncourt cannot sustain its tempo: he is at once mechanical yet unreliable; there is no real strength, nor the strength to be supple. Dislike of the singing—the chorus fierce without sustaining power, the soloists dull (the men) or hapless (the boys)—would not matter if the priorities were in good order.

Since Vaughan Williams's talk recalled his adolescent discovery of Bach and the BBC twit recalled being bored as a child by a Vaughan Williams Bach performance, I shall also wander down memory lane. I used to take part, as a chorister there, in the annual *St Matthew Passion* in St Paul's Cathedral. Church choirs from the diocese assembled to fill the transepts, bouncing the stereophonic double-choruses ('Look!' 'Look where?' 'On our offence!') with astonishing effect, and massing together for the chorales like a great ocean. The Cathedral choir clustered under the middle of the dome. The soloists, drawn from our midst, included male altos and boys for the bit-parts (maids at Herod's court, Pilate's wife). This much, anyway, was authentic; but the soprano arias were sung by thirty boys in unison even when, in 'Have mercy upon me, O Lord', they were pitted against a solo violin obbligato! A grand piano was used for the recitatives, and the grand organ, suitably tamed, for continuo in choruses and arias. But the mighty monster showed its claws in the 'Thunder and Lightnings' chorus, and full-throatedly roared at other likely places. The individual moment of fullest power was the answer to Pilate's question, 'Whither of the twain will ye that I release unto you? The gigantic cry of 'Barabbas!' and the fifteen-second reverberation as the sound cleared into the dome will remain to the end of my days as an image of brute power, stupidity, magnificence and perfidy.

Monstrous maybe; but every note of the work must be etched upon the minds of all those who participated as something of enormous significance and value. What Harnoncourt has done to Bach is more monstrous: he has drained this music of its meaning.

ii *Mengelberg's* St Matthew Passion

I have just [April 1992] heard the year's seasonal Bach Passion; this time the *St Matthew*, a live recording made on Palm Sunday 1939 in the Amsterdam Concertgebouw under William Mengelberg, and without question the most inspired that has ever come my way. It is disconcerting to realise that virtually every aspect of it would be panned by today's critics and, sadder, cause it to be laughed from the platform by today's brainwashed audiences.

What it conveys above all is a sense of immense significance and sublimity. Those who dislike it will find this portentous; those who admire it do so for its endeavour to be worthy of the sacred narrative and its musical setting. For Bach the events of Holy Week were 'the greatest story ever told'; he manifestly gave to his Passion music the best of which he was capable; and it is difficult to imagine that the result will ever fail to stir its listeners to their utmost, irrespective of the ebb and flow of the sea of faith. Mengelberg's annual performances of the *St Matthew* (the atmosphere of a solemn social fixture is clearly audible) are a symptom of the ethos whereby the concert hall replaces the church service, taken here so far that art has positively become religion. The aesthetic and the entertaining are transcended, to concentrate upon the naked essence; the work has returned to its origin, an impersonal ritual, a disinterested act of faith.

Yet this conductor's most ardent apologist can hardly claim that he practises self-effacement! His commanding presence is ubiquitous—for instance in the extravagant pulling around of speed in the aria about weeping tears, and in the monster Hammer Horror organ chord at the startling key-change in the chorus of thunder and lightning. The chorales are all individually interpreted with extreme slowness and a dynamic range between triple-soft and triple-loud that belies their communal simplicity. But such licence always serves the intended purpose: each gear change in the aria produces, each time, a renewed stab of grief; the brazen organ reproaches nature for failing to protect him as Jesus is abandoned and led captive to face the trumped-up trial; while the super-heightened treatment of the chorales opens up the infinite richness of expression within the four-square tunes and their pietistic words. Less exceptional features are the performance's masterly dramatic pacing and a forward momentum and oceanic balance of tension and repose as required in Wagner; a complete grasp of architectural articulation from the most gigantic (the opening *via dolorosa*) to the tiniest; clarity of texture in spite of large forces; and the quality of the six soloists led by the astounding Evangelist of Karl Erb. The total result raises the back hair rather than the eyebrows. To the purist, for whom all this suffices already to make the very idea grotesque, further details of anachronistic performance practices could only add disgust to distress; and it is also heavily cut, as though a too-long opera, thus offending the modern fetishisation of completeness.

The reason why the whale-sized subjectivity and flagrant inauthenticity that prevail from start to finish are not offensive, or even obtrusive, is the passionate desire to elicit its utmost from music so moving that coolness and objectivity become bogus goals. Every lover of this work knows that Christ's institution of the Eucharist is beautiful in Bach's setting beyond creed or sacrament, that 'Have mercy upon me' (the soprano aria of meditation upon Peter's betraying his master) is the supreme expression anywhere of contrition and self-reproach, that the tiny chorus testifying, after Jesus' death, 'Truly this was the son of God' encapsulates in a few simple chords an utterance as profound as religion itself. Mengelberg is concerned to ensure, with all his charisma, brilliance, waywardness and genius, that such moments (there are many others) not only do not go for nothing but are, on the contrary, significant beyond momentary *frissons*, intense beyond anything normal, absolutely unforgettable, because of what they *mean*. Too bad for us if the *St Matthew Passion* is simply another of the world's 'supreme fictions' alongside the *Oresteia* and the *Iliad*, *Lear*, *Faust*, the *Ring* and comparable cultural icons. And too bad if our costive current notions of what is proper in Bach performance makes such interpretative *grandezza* impermissible. The truth is not so much that no one would dare nowadays as that no one can.

iii (Appendix) Absurdist Bach

The avant-garde composer Mauricio Kagel, who had impishly celebrated in 1970 the bicentenary of Beethoven's birth and in 1983 the 150th of Brahms, reserved his wittiest effort for Bach's tercentenary in 1985. Claiming that music-lovers, for all their discrepant beliefs or varieties of atheism, are united by faith in Bach, he took the composer's life, as documented both officially and domestically, and presented it in the Lutheran format—recitative, aria, chorus, chorale—as the *St Bach Passion*. The result is more than a *jeu d'esprit*. Unwinding as interminable monotone, it develops the irritating allure of a radio serial which cannot be relinquished in spite of one's wry contempt. Eventually Satie's observation that 'boredom is mysterious and profound' is vindicated once more. In its very prosaicness and lack of uplift this cod-homage succeeds where all versions of the gospel-proper since Bach's time fail in greater or lesser measure, be it hassocks and harmonium like Stainer's *Crucifixion*, a high-tech modernist con completely divorced from devotional use like Penderecki's *St Luke*, or something between the two, like Arvo Pärt's *St John* (a piece of mock-humility that has, for the moment, inherited the earth). The greatest responses, in music as in painting, to this subject come from the masters of epochs when the passion narrative was universally acknowledged to be holy writ, of immediate and intimate concern to every living soul.

2

Haydn: the musicians' musician

This long-considered and effortfully-composed essay, written to conclude a volume of Haydn Studies edited by my Cambridge colleague Dean Sutcliffe (CUP, 1998), was an attempt to write about pure music with no helpful handle from its composer's personality or the text/story content of his work. The whole text is an implicit extension of Tovey's brief note on 'Haydn the Inaccessible': if his own moving tribute to the composer he ultimately valued above all others had been available yet (see p.422) I'd certainly have included it here to join the long line of great musicians for whom Haydn is 'the composers' composer'.

*   *   *

One is rather embarrassed at having to call him original; it is like saying that a Cheshire cat smiles.

Randall Jarrell on William Carlos Williams

Natural utterance did not come naturally: it was a quiet triumph of sustained artifice.

Clive James on Kenneth Slessor

The current picture of Haydn is something like this: a great inventor, intelligence, humanist, wit, who works with juvenile diligence to master every available old technique while simultaneously eager to embrace and advance every new, forced by the isolation of his employment to 'be original', quivering for a time to strains of emotional turbulence which immeasurably deepened his art, then learning to wear it lightly with tropes and timing from *opera buffa*, before broadening with maturity and age into the expression of social, ethical, religious values with genuinely popular appeal—all held together in a balanced synthesis that embodies to its fullest in music and perhaps in all the arts the concept of Enlightenment. The musical character is perceived as sunny, energetic, impersonal, normative, unbowed by angst, cheerfully pious, a life-enhancer: *Laus Deo*.

Such a 'Haydn the Accessible' is certainly not wrong. It is the basis of the affection in which he is held, especially in the country which took so immediately to him and his music in the 1790s. Yet he is not, and probably never will be, a wholly popular composer like Mozart, Beethoven, Tchaikovsky, and now Mahler and Shostakovich. Not even an ampler grasp of his true size and scope will bring this about. There is something inherently unembraceable.

Even in minuets his good humour can frequently not be quite what it seems; the *innocentamente* of variation themes and finales is definitely not to be trusted; the unmistakable *affettuoso* of slow movements can also be austere, even chilling; and the cerebration of sonata-allegros is sometimes so urgent as to drive out immediate musical pleasure. 'Haydn the Repellent'? There is also, alongside the up-front straightforwardness, an emotional reserve or veiling which invites another sobriquet: 'Haydn the Withdrawn'.

Such qualities have never alarmed professional musicians—performers, connoisseurs, academics, analysts and perhaps composers most of all. From the discriminating appreciation of his middle life and the wide dissemination of his old age, Haydn has enjoyed the praise of fellow practitioners. Testimony from the greatest of his immediate successors is more in works than words: Mozart and Schubert, very different kinds of composer from him and from each other, are audibly saturated in Haydn as source and example; Beethoven, audibly the same kind of composer, owes enormous and quantifiable debts (which are fully repaid). The early Romantic generation had little regard, as they had no use, for Haydn's particular mastery. But even as the Romantic century advanced and his repertory was contracted and his style patronised, his stature for the chosen few remained unimpugned. To the avid creativity as well as the nostalgic historicism of Brahms, Haydn stood in parity with the other three Viennese masters. 'I want my ninth symphony to be like this!' he exclaimed, playing the Andante of Symphony no.88 'with wallowing enthusiasm'.[1] More surprising is the cordiality recorded by Cosima in Wagner's conversation: a few favourite symphonies and quartets were often piano-duetted or played live, eliciting joy and reflection (sometimes profound). What must surely be the same Andante ('of Haydn's G major symphony') 'is one of the loveliest things ever written; and how wonderful it sounds!'[2] On 19 October 1873 R. takes 'infinite delight' in the 'masterly art' of the 'London' Symphony: 'Haydn, spurred on after Mozart's death by Mozart's genius, became the true precursor of Beethoven; varied instrumentation, and yet so artistic; everything speaks, everything is inspiration.'[3] On 3 February 1874 R. 'plays the Andante (G minor) from another [H.] symphony, explaining its beauties, above all its concision—everything expresses something, no arabesques, the two themes circle around each other like sun and moon'.[4] (I think Cosima might mean the C minor/major Andante of no.103; there is no G minor slow movement in the Paris, Oxford or London sets likely to have been available at the time.) 'How wonderful it sounds':

---

[1] See Donald Francis Tovey, *Essays in Musical Analysis* (London: Oxford University Press, 1931), vol. 1, p.142.

[2] Cosima Wagner, *Diaries* (New York: Harcourt, Brace, Jovanovich, 1980), vol. 2, p.31 (26 February 1878).

[3] *Diaries*, vol. 1, p.689.

[4] Ibid., p.730.

another master of the large up-to-date orchestra, Rimsky-Korsakov, actually placed the 'primitive' Haydn at the summit of this branch of the art.

The last Romantics, like the first, felt least rapport. For a Delius, a Debussy or a Rakhmaninov, such music has nothing beyond dead formulae. Mahler, notoriously contemptuous of eighteenth-century development sections, invoked Haydn for association in the principal subject of the Fourth Symphony's first movement and, still more, its accompaniment. Strauss's feeling for the epoch was confined to a periwigged and chocolated Mozart—Haydn's lack equally of sensuality and dinkiness had no appeal. And for Schoenberg the evolutionist, Haydn is merely the first in a Viennese Classical package that awards him no distinguishing features. But his progress with moderns and postmoderns has been triumphal. In his old age Stravinsky's listening included the quartets and symphonies in its very select company;[5] Britten used to curl up in bed with pocket scores of the quartets. Their attitude can characterise at the highest level the prevailing view. As appreciation has widened, from Tovey (who as usual implied it all) into Rosen and Webster, with Robbins Landon for vociferous documentation, and the advocacy of performers like Brendel and Schiff, rather than sloggers like Dorati and the Aeolian (though some old-stagers—the feline Beecham, the granitic Klemperer, the sinewy yet singing Rosbaud—remain unforgotten, and Britten's *Creation* from the 1966 Aldeburgh Festival is the single most inspired Haydn performance I've ever encountered), his standing in general has never been higher. And in particular among composers, there is scarcely a dissenting voice.

Yet even here, amidst his loyal subjects, Haydn remains oddly shadowy and elusive. Acknowledged by all, he is still without influence. Of the Viennese package, Beethoven hung like a thundercloud over his progeny from Schubert to Schoenberg, emphatically including Brahms, Bruckner and Wagner. Mozart's influence has been a complementary rebound all the way from *Mozartiana* to *The Rake's Progress* and beyond; but more often he has been made to embody an attitude rather than a style, as in the ideal posited by Busoni's 'Young Classicism' or the very different versions invoked by Ravel in his two-hand concerto, Strauss in his wind sonatinas, Messiaen in his *Sourire*. Whereas, apart from Robert Simpson, possibly Elliott Carter and a facetious tootle from Vaughan Williams ('Haydn to the rescue' from a temporary impasse in composing *his* ninth symphony), Haydn has had no progeny and has received only a few rather cursory *hommages*—from a distinguished French handful (including Ravel and Debussy) for the centenary of his death in 1909, from six British composers (including George Benjamin) for his 250th birthday in 1982. He appears to be unsusceptible to 'recomposition' *à la* Stravinsky (except, appropriately, for certain Haydnesque features of Stravinsky's Symphony in C): no doubt because he has already done it all himself.

For no composer before, and none again till modern times, has been so self-conscious. The former image was one of innocence, unaffected simplicity,

---

[5] Igor Stravinsky and Robert Craft, *Conversations with Igor Stravinsky* (London: Faber, 1959), p.127.

cheeriness, whether of a 'Papa' or childlike ('Haydn is like a child, for there is no knowing what he will do next' was Keats's reaction when his friend Severn played him symphonies on the piano in Rome in 1820). It accompanies a sonorous stereotype of C major openness, music of clear outline and definite goal, unsullied by self-expression, stilted heroics, lachrymose pathos: music in a pristine state. This picture has now been enormously amplified, and partially reversed. Haydn is now seen as a sort of scientist or doctor of music: knowledge is explored and exploited, experiments are undertaken, both these things sometimes without the alleviation of aesthetic charm. There is little reliance upon moulds or self-evident formulae ('for heaven's sake, a new minuet!'): despite the fertility there is great care not to do the same thing twice, which can produce dryness but never routine like Mozart on an off-day or sleepwalking like Schubert, let alone the trickle or gush of a Vivaldi, Raff, Martinů, Henze. Rather than childlike and spontaneous, Haydn is 'artificial' —deliberate, quizzical, critical; even (dread word) 'ironic'[6], inasmuch as he can achieve his complex ends with hackneyed material of no intrinsic worth.

This expanded view of him fulfils a modernist dream of the composer as craftsman, an impersonal maker of functioning objects. So conspicuous a devotion to the craft of composition is valued both for itself and as a stick with which to knock expressionist splurge and impressionistic haze, equally with avant-garde pseuderie and the blackmail of 'commitment'. Further aspects yet are so alien to previously received notions of him that they are still coming into focus: Haydn the mannerist, the whimsical, the Shandyan; Haydn who teases—not always in fun, less cat-and-mouse, more tigerish— his material, his forms, his players, his listeners. Just as he leavens his learning with 'obsequious' acknowledgement of licentious infringements on the local scale, so, on the large, whole movements, whole works even, can be sarcastically subversive—not with the tedious doctrinaire 'absurdity' of Dada and surrealism but, rather, within the synthesis and integration that remain so paramount that he has always to be called one of their greatest exemplars.

All this could make him into a somewhat forbidding icon of 'the right attitude' to the materials of music and their proper deployment—the master of small points in a comprehensively cogent musical speech so well understood that allusions, jokes, surprises, ambiguities, subversions, ironies become normative too, and confounded expectations as expected as straightforward fulfilment of the rules of the game. Which suggests not so much an icon as a sacred cow ruminating the cud of every correct notion in cultural studies at large; the composers' composer or musicians' musician yielding to the analyst's, the academic's, the historian's. Which is as boring as Dada without the fun. If there is an angle from which this complex figure can be seen steadily and

---

[6] Most debased of critical terms, requiring forcible retirement. 'Saying one thing to mean another' produced profound effects from Greek tragedy to Jane Austen, Henry James and beyond. In music, so masked by Mahler, Shostakovich, Stravinsky (cheap material carrying genuine emotion, or playfully inverted) that it has worn threadbare. In general connotes little beyond 'sarcastic', 'piquant', 'coincidental'.

whole, it must surely be in the idea of music's intrinsicality; whatever else might or might not be present, music as music, unsullied or compromised by extraneous matter, autonomous. Haydn leads more directly than any other composer to this easily uttered but endlessly slippery idea.

He is the purest of all composers; his art has the fewest external referents, is more completely about itself than any other. Bach is rightly regarded as the supreme celestial mechanic; but possibly the most characteristic, certainly the deepest, aspect of Bach is his weaving a tissue of messages and meanings soaked in *Affekt* way beyond the norms of his epoch, evincing a personality of morbid inwardness wholly compatible with his robust functionality, vigorous physicality and learned 'science'. Mozart is always opera *manqué*, his articulation and phrasing vocal, his setting theatrical, his forms and processes not organic but, rather, whisked on and off like prefabricated flats. His great instrumental genres are concertos or chamber works with eloquent protagonists—the soloist in the Clarinet Quintet; the amorous duetting of first violin and first viola in the Andante of the C major String Quintet, K.515; the two right hands in that of the F major piano duet sonata, K.497; the trio of first oboe, clarinet and basset horn in the Adagio of the thirteen-wind Serenade, K.361; all four winds in the Larghetto of their quartet with piano in E♭ major, K.452. He doesn't argue, or build, or grow; he sets out the sections in finely judged symmetry/asymmetry and sends them through a constellation of closely related keys. Interest derives from the fine draughtsmanship which distinguishes high calibre from routine; sensuous pleasure, from his perpetually fertile melodiousness.

Beethoven is music made from music for sure, supreme in the processes of development as argument and journey, and also in extracting the ultimate potential from his thematic material. As Wagner remarks, he is, in this, the fulfilment of Haydn. He raises the temperature and the voice, enlarges the durations and the difficulties; the strain waxes heroic–pathetic, with a rhetoric of struggle and victory aimed at more people, in bigger rooms, aimed at Humanity *en masse*. He has something important to tell them. Put in words this message tends towards inert abstractions like 'brotherhood', the 'ideal feminine', 'freedom', etc.; but what he really has to show that is so important to him as to compel audiences ever since into feeling that it is also important to them, is of course his *notes*. And sonata's greatest victor has imbued his actual notes with a new tone—ethical, moralistic, idealistic, 'improving'. Music, as it were, returns to church (secular, non-denominational: First Church of God Pantheist) after a few generations at court, at the theatre, in the market place.

Schubert, by contrast, is all voluptuous hedonism and 'amorous propensity', driven by a libido which is wholly compatible with such complements as great stillness, great radiance, or temper-tantrums of extraordinary violence, and severity pushed towards unsurpassed extremes, as in the *Winterreise* songs which so signally disconcerted his circle of friends. And so to the first Romantics, to Wagner, late Romantics, Expressionists, Degenerates: a tale of degradation—the wholesale invasion of music as a medium of sociability and intellectual exchange by subject-matter, story-telling, atmosphere-painting, message-bearing, capable of gushing over into autobiography both lubricious and spiritually ostentatious, the confessional quadruple *forte* and sextuple *piano* (both are to be found in the first movement of Tchaikovsky's *Symphonie Pathétique*) which have become for its average lovers what music is expected to be. And so to the modernist reaction which gleefully topples the rotten tree.

Haydn alone gives no handle: there is nothing to latch on to, biographically or in subject-matter. *Sturm und Drang* of course; 'Farewell', *La Passione*, the *Lamentatione*. But what are they beside a Bruckner Ninth, a Mahler Tenth, an Elgar Second or Sibelius Fourth? Nor do any quartets reveal the secrets of sickroom and convalescence, let alone an *Aus mein Leben*, an *Intimate Letters*, a *Lyric Suite*. His operas, for all the musical value, do not apparently live as drama, nor is he, like Mozart, an instrumental dramatist via the concerto. When he does produce an instrumental *scena* the result is stilted or parodic, or both. The primal archetype for his melody is often neither vocal (like Mozart again) nor instrumental, but rather a sort of fabrication which can cope equally well with values from a semibreve to a demisemiquaver in one long line, throwing in plentiful turns and graces, with triplets and other divisions *en route*. Haydn the Artificial.

Onomatopoeia *does* figure of course, both early—*matin, midi, soir*—and in the two late oratorios: whether juvenile or mellow the result is so one-dimensional and pantomimic as to seem naïve even when manifestly sublime—a classic instance of naïve as opposed to sentimental art. Unlike the, in some ways, comparable Brahms there is no body of secular vocal music to suggest by analogy any interpretation of his favourite turns-of-phrase (but who could find Brahms abstract or impersonal anyway? The character is almost palpable in his textures, harmonies, contours, procedures). Neither affects, nor onomatopoeia, nor a clear projection of personality (though they are not exactly lacking) provide the clue to his core, as they can with every other composer, even when, as with Stravinsky, such things are deliberately eschewed. Even while practising with consummate perfection the art of music as amicable intercourse, the doors are closed. Haydn the Impenetrable.

This music is pure because it cannot be translated. Despite one's ready recognition of a ragbag of tropes and types—snippets of nonsense from *opera buffa* and pathos or elevation from *opera seria*, tags from textbooks, snatches of folksong 'from Croatia's woods and fields' or urban serenade from Vienna's back alleys, opening and closing gambits from contemporary cliché—it owes less than any other to metaphor, simile, association. Haydn doesn't seem to invest his artistic capital in such stock; he does not fully ally himself with it. Other composers inhabit; Haydn is aloof. Then to proceed to build entirely from such material, and entirely upon points of grammar and proportion, would seem a flagrant courtship of dryness. 'Music as music', upon which he is so single-mindedly fixed, is, artistically, a dead letter—mere grids, blueprints, engineers' working-drawings.

He is music's supreme intellectual. Yet every lover of Haydn recognises within the cerebral power many characteristics difficult to name without absurdity, so wholly are they musicalised. But the risk is worth taking. The range is enormous. High spirits, all the way from physical brio and athletic bravura (Tovey makes the connection with the cerebral power: 'his forms become the more subtle as his animal spirits rise'[7]) to jokes, puns, games of sometimes surprising intellectual and even expressive weight, profound in their ambiguity, exploratory in their paradoxes, witty like the metaphors in metaphysical poetry, touching on rarified places which no other means could reach. (When unambiguously farcical, as in *Il distratto* and other mid-period symphonies the effect is quite different—*simply* silly; it's a pity that this side of Haydn receives disproportionate emphasis.) There is serenity and hymn-like calm; Enlightenment openness, sage and humane; radiance without shadow-like tempera, pure colours on a white base. Their opposite—twisting strangeness, contortion, mannerist extremity—is almost as frequent, and this too is shadowless in that it is never morbid. Compare Bach with his worm-gnawed chromatics of sin, guilt, corruption; the hectic consumptive flush of Mozart in G minor; the driven *Tod*-tarantellas of Schubert (to go no further than composers who overlap Haydn's life at both ends). Rather it is part of his unceasing exploration of yet another aspect of music's extent that fascinates him for a moment or a movement, something he can *use*, as he *uses* stale old contrapuntal routines both for earnest and for effervescent purposes. Then there is deep still contemplation, simultaneously remote and glowing, giving utterance to an extreme of inner solitude paralleled only in Bartók and possibly Kurtág: a bare space wherein something exceedingly quiet, intense and private is apprehended with a nudity beyond sensuous beauty, making music an object of both meditation and solace, worked out in a dream realm of punning harmonic labyrinths. Into this, cheerfulness is always breaking, for these pools of loneliness are always adjacent to the body-rhythm of a minuet or appear within the tearing energy of a finale.

The tone of voice ranges similarly from such confessional impersonality to the late development of a successfully common-touch *lingua franca* in the oratorios and last Masses, whether raptly devotional or ceremonially jubilant, with a repertory of moods between the two that satisfactorily renders whatever it sets out to and wisely evades characterisation (those three Archangels! that Hanne, Lukas and Simon!!)—though the birds, beasts and insects are vivid, and the injunction to the whales to multiply touches the depths. But a further secret side of him gives tongue with extraordinary passion—such places as the wild improvisatory gypsy flourishes of the first violin above the chorale on the other three strings in the second movement of the String Quartet op.54 no.2; or, in the misleadingly titled Allegretto of the Piano Trio no.44 in E major, the uncurling of the melody above and then below the gaunt stealthy bass, in octaves then thirds and tenths, till the tension is so great that the movement literally breaks apart before snapping shut like a slap

---

[7] Tovey, *Essays*, vol. 1, p.147.

in the face. Utterance of such unsullied-by-*espressivo* intensity makes the Romantics seem extrovert, showy and babyish, whatever the higher pitch of their anguish or the urgent pressure of their engagement. Just as startling is Haydn's mastery of the primeval, not so much in *The Creation* itself as in the powerfully pregnant slow introductions to eleven out of twelve London symphonies, and most particularly the 'London' itself, no.104. When the *fortissimo* tutti falling fourth of bar 2, answering the rising fifth of the opening, is replaced in bar 15 by a *pianissimo* falling fifth on strings alone, the space and mystery evoked are as vast as such effects in Bruckner, though the actual duration is tiny.

Mendelssohn's famous declaration that music sets up resonances more definite than words receives a supreme testing in Haydn's instrumental works. A couple of further concrete instances might extend the sense of a language in use, of which both arts partake. The first is comparatively early—the *Affettuoso e sostenuto* movement from the String Quartet op.20 no.1. What is it? Certainly not a melody: rather, a themeless continuum, momentum, texture, not quite homophony; not quite polyphony either, making a dense serious sound, sometimes close-spaced, sometimes wide, often peculiar, with perverse interlocking and crossing of parts, arbitrary doublings, passing chords that if lingered on would be solecisms or even Stravinskyisms. Everyone plays all the time almost without exception, in even quavers almost without exception; the only rests come with the first-violin solos which also produce the only decoration, at the double bars and for the three bars in the second 'half' which lead to the 'return'. For 'half' it is not: despite the impression of unbroken tranquillity, the larger structure and the smaller phrasing are asymmetrical and unpredictable (except for the movement's one weak link: the sequential repeat, in the second 'half', of bars 52–3 as 54–5, though the compensating descent in bars 58–9 seems to rectify in retrospect). From start to close the listener glides on an imperturbable loop of endless melody, renewing itself out of its own motion—a gentle, modest ancestor of the *Tristan* Prelude and the *obbligato recitative* from Schoenberg's op.16. In *mood*, however, this movement achieves an encapsulation of largo religioso feeling without any hint of 'religioso' sanctimony: everything inheres within the notes.

Next, a middle movement from the end of Haydn's quartet-writing life: the Andante from the String Quartet in F major, op.77 no.2. Again it is a matter of an ongoing momentum: but here textures, spacing and density are perpetually changing and the whole movement is melody-led and propelled by a walking bass; their combined impulse is so strong that both continue to be felt even when either surprisingly ceases. The melody (essentially 'three blind mice' with twiddles) is a sort of *faux-naif* Lego, whose every link can be used to make a different thing. It is at once genuine-simple and true-complex in its tone—how serious? how light?—as in the apparently artless, actually ultra-experienced, twists and turns of its perpetually reinterpreted harmonisations. The crunch comes from bar 74 on, where it makes its most elaborate reappearance. The spacing is marvellous—low viola on the march-bass, high cello on the melody, first violin delivering a decorative descent of arpeggios and scales in staccato demisemiquavers (with second violin confined to occasional help filling out cadences). Instead of rounding off, it opens out. Taking up the bars of bare minims earlier in the movement, all three lower strings hold broad chords, but violin I continues its brilliant *essercizi* as the accompanying trio become explicitly military, even peremptory ♫♩♪♫♩, then urgent ♪♪♪♪, then *pesante* ♪♪ in crescendo to *fortissimo*, as the solo violin flourishes cadenza-like on D major triads then scales, the last being joined by the second violin and viola in an upward rush of parallel first-inversion chords. It ought to be commonplace; in fact it is tense and electric, creating an effect of extraordinary liberation—a tethered eagle unleashed. Yet the great bird is left in mid-air, and the movement's only silences follow (still perceived in measure), with one slashing dominant, brutally banal; then the resumption of the opening melody, richly harmonised *à 4* in sonorous low-position *pianissimo*, winding down via its internal self-recycling in ever-new textural subtleties and harmonic/rhythmic inflections, to close in a brief coda-ish extra. The feel of the movement altogether is haunting yet ordinary, obsessive yet open, short-circuiting yet free: persistent in dogged stoical trudge, genial but not wholly amiable, as much defiant as cheerful.

How are we to take music that seems to evoke such ambiguities and contrarieties as these, but that certainly supersedes their merely verbal expression—that offers, in its own intrinsic terms, a play of mood, as of material, simultaneously so straightforward and so ungraspable?

Things as remarkable, and extremely various, could easily be multiplied[8] from the quartets between op.20 no.1 and op.77 no.2, as well, of course, as from his other greatest genres—mid-early and very late piano sonatas and symphonies, and the fascinating treasure-house of piano trios. But how would such adjective-laden prose-poems as they might well elicit square with the claim that Haydn is concerned more purely than any other composer with music's intrinsicality? Painting can more obviously than music be at once abstract and concrete. In the landscapes and still lifes of William Nicholson

[h]orizons fall at endlessly surprising intervals and angles across the canvases; objects are unexpectedly aligned or misaligned with each other, placed with odd centrality, or half-dropped off a canvas's edge. Viewpoints are often unusually high, or low; boldly frontal or oddly oblique. As purely formal arrangements of tone and colour, the works have great individuality and sonorous beauty. These very formal and perceptual paintings are also, of course, highly metaphoric.[9]

It would be idle to ask further: metaphors of *what*? This is the area at the heart of all the arts where structure and process fuse inseparably into expres-

---

[8] I wrote many such in the course of preparing this essay.

[9] He might actually be writing about Haydn! Merlin Ingli James reviewing the landscapes of William Nicholson, *Times Literary Supplement*, 17 May 1996, pp.18–19.

sion; the total result is an emanation, however direct or oblique, from the life of the unique individual who is doing the making and summoning into being.

Music is about notes, whether the upshot is Tristan's delirium, Tchaikov-sky's floods of passion, cardiac convulsions in Mahler and Berg, or any sona-ta, trio, quartet, symphony by Haydn. If it's not good composing, neither is it good expression of an emotion, or depiction of a character, or evocation of sunlight playing on the waves and all the rest. If 'words, not ideas, make a poem', how much more true for the relatively unconnotational art of music. Not passions, neuroses, concepts, pictures or any other extraneous intentions make a piece of music, but pitches, rhythms, durations, timbres, in all their infinite potential for organised combination.

Yet music does render all those extraneous things. If it were indeed just 'pure music', something—the main thing—would be missing (as in Mon-drian, or Nicholson *fils*, when the viewer hankers to see apples, boughs, faces). So what is abstraction, and how can unmitigated concentration upon the process of composition be at the same time a quest for what Debussy called 'the naked flesh of emotion'? It must be that the materials of music themselves not only convey passions, pictures and so forth, but that they actually *are* passionate and pictorial—intrinsically, of their nature. The 'extras' inhere; they are of the essence too. The problem is to reconcile music's natural tendency towards extramusical content with the impulse to make pattern, argument and structure that are equally intrinsic to the art. And Haydn is poised right at its centre: because of the exceptionally nice balance he strikes, he compels one more than any other composer to ask what music actually *is*.

If there is, fortunately, no answer, further parallels from painting can again shift the ground. 'Significant form' was the once-familiar phrase coined to indicate the composition of a picture to be its own subject in the teeth of its ostensible replication of a nude, a landscape, a still life.[10] Music as its own subject produces for Haydn a representation of itself—the disinterested exploration of compositional possibilities, the posing of difficulties, the pleasure and astonishment of their resolution—with 'sonata', 'double-variation' and all the rest of his composing-kit for playground or chessboard. Its material is the mass of sonorous actualities available to him—clarinets here, no trumpets in Lent (etc., etc. *ad nauseam*)—together with, of course, shapes and gestures that have been used over and over again and are dense with associations. The rest is all specific and particular: invention, resource, experience and experiment, intelligence focusing hard and fantasy flying free, the dispassion and involvement, amusement and interest, the piety and warmth of heart, the essential strangeness and solitude, and all the other traits of personality and character with which this individual human being will perforce infuse almost every one in the succession of musical objects he makes.

---

[10] That this stiff idea can be made supple, sensitive, attractive is beautifully borne out by James's review in full (see previous footnote).

Confronted by this *œuvre*, discrepancies between abstract and concrete seem factitious. One could even sophistically claim that Haydn's very concreteness makes him so abstract, and vice versa. Moreover, his awareness of such sophistries is a part of his genius. He is as consummately in control of such questions about how music is doing what it is doing as he is of the materials and processes of a particular piece. There is an omniscience to his art that surpasses even Bach's, who knew everything about the science of music but was, one senses, unconscious of what his music was saying through its extraordinary transcendence of its sylistic norms and ostensible aims. Bach is the profounder artist; Haydn is the greater realist. None of which renders him any more graspable. To the last, Haydn the Ambiguous.

And how appropriate for Haydn the Ambiguous that his most inspired movement, *The Representation of Chaos*, should be simultaneously the representation of Order in a perfectly formed introduction–sonata, the weird contradiction expressed in sounds that sometimes come from some chuckling Biedermeier serenade (bars 28–31), sometimes grope into Bruckner at his creepiest (bars 32ff), sometimes heave and pant with the sheer physical strain of giving birth (bars 26–7, 48–9), touch upon the metaphysical without strain throughout, and for the final ten bars (till the cadence) stray into the 'music of the future' fifty years before time. But Haydn is the music of the future still. The true extent of his greatness is for the connoisseur a well-kept secret, for the larger public a ticking time-bomb that has yet to go off. When its hour comes, the explosion, rather than a Big Bang, will be a still small voice telling of the strange within the normal, the vast within the modest, the dark within the bright and vice versa: the essence of human experience in essentially musical terms.

3

Mozart: redundant genius

A tart riposte to the squelchy bicentenary in 1991 of his death.

* * *

Mozart died almost exactly 200 years ago. The celebrations have been so neon-lit as to make the Bach/Scarlatti/Handel tercentenary in 1985, even the Beethoven bicentenary of 1970, seem by contrast pale and tasteful. But the great masters do not need round-figure birthdays; their reputation no longer fluctuates and their music requires no arbitrary boosting.

Nonetheless Mozart's present universal popularity would have surprised the taste of 1891. Early in the century he was taken by Hoffmann as a harbinger of romantic daemonism, but as the romantic epoch blossomed (with Hoffmann one of its key sources) Mozart was seen rather as an island of innocence before music realised its full powers. Between the summits of Bachian polyphony and Beethovenian symphonism came Papa Haydn and the infant Mozart. Schumann's well-known view (incomprehensible to us) of the G minor Symphony's carefree gaiety reaches a climax in Mahler's notorious contempt for classical formulae. Though his supremacy in opera was never doubted, vicissitudes of taste lost *Idomeneo*, *Così fan tutte*, even *The Magic Flute*, for many decades. These works, unsurpassed in their respective genres, all had to be revived in this century.

In fact, Mozart is a stranger composer than his apparently complete centrality would suggest. He lies athwart the main lines. On one hand there are the affect-and-image-makers—Bach, Schubert, Wagner—with their baroque continuity of texture and primacy of expressive meaning. But his native place would appear to be on the other—the thematic development and tonal argument whose focus is in the Viennese classical style and the sonata principle. At bottom, though, Mozart is not really like his two peers Beethoven and Haydn. He is not by nature an arguer or a developer. His starting point is the conventions, routines, *données* of material and form that make the going commonplaces of his time. His instrumental works 'go through the motions', shifting prefabricated musical units across highly formalised perspectives of key and texture; construction and proportion are what concern him, not logic, or journey, or organic growth. They are at their greatest when most is in play, above all in the mature piano concertos with their extraordinary abundance of themes (far more than required by Haydn and Beethoven, whatever the genre). But in symphonies and chamber music the result is often neat and dry. Only when these genres are infused with a vocal/dramatic element does he take off as an abstract composer.

For what stirs his depths is virtuosity and display, wowing the aisles and bringing the house down. Though this also accounts for the quality of the piano concertos and those movements in chamber works which seem to be rendering an operatic scene, it reaches its native land in music for the human voice. Everything in Mozart needs to be vocally phrased, never more so than when it actually *is* vocal. And vocal means the gamut of human expression, placed in an operatic context. Church music only comes to life when charged, sometimes flagrantly, with theatrical fervour. Mozart's religious and ethical aspect lies altogether elsewhere, in pieces for masonic rituals that culminate in the sublime Funeral Music, and only reach a larger public, as it were surreptitiously, via *The Magic Flute*.

Another difference between Mozart and his classical peers is that his catalogue is full of oddments—bits and bobs that he touches with the highest flights of fantasy. Who but Mozart, commissioned to write something for a glass harmonica or a clockwork organ, would have bothered to turn these unappealing tasks (we have his word for it) into one-off masterpieces, or lavished his genius upon arias for insertion into other composers' operas, or transformed routine serenades and divertimentos (sometimes) into inspirations that belong with his greatest work? Uninspired pieces are also, of course, numerous. Glenn Gould compared Mozart on an off-day to an interdepartmental communication. That such music shares the same lucidity and command as his greatest makes his greatest vulnerable to easy-listening muzakisation, as invited by not much of Haydn's, and almost nothing of Beethoven's. A high percentage of Mozart's bicentennial popularity is fuelled by the wallpaper quality which can debase him into a rococo successor to Vivaldi.

This bicentenary! Its blatant commerciality can only be compared to present-day Christmas: exploitative greed with a saccharin veneer of quasi-religious observance. Its main message is not so much the undying glory of Mozart as a reminder, lest we forget, that since the end of ecclesiastical, then royal or aristocratic patronage (at which turning-point his unhappy career is poised), the creative musician lies at the bottom of the pile. In whatever current present ever since, he is always dispensable and redundant, in glaring contrast with the perpetual demand for singers, pianists, conductors, impresarios who actually keep the mills churning. He becomes (if he makes it) necessary and 'classicised' only after his death, when the benefits are too late. The living composer, unless he pushes or is pushed, is superfluous. There are exceptions, but this with all its clichéd pathos is the norm. Cultured society ignores the innovative creator, then venerates him and creams the profits, spiritual and material—symposia, conferences and concerts, equally with the CD editions, the coffee-table books, the Mozart chocolates. Death by overkilling the vital essence is the awful warning of 1991, just as death by neglect of the mortal individual remains that of 1791.

4

Schubert's songs recorded

i Near the start (March 1990)

Recording a long succession of sizeable works in the same genre—Haydn symphonies or quartets, say—virtually necessitates ordering by number and chronology. But this simplest of groupings is inimical to miniatures (except those deliberately gathered by their composers to make a collection). It is particularly fatal for songs, and for none more than those of Schubert.

His lieder have always been recorded item by item. HMV's fascinating anthology *Schubert Lieder on Record* covers the 78 era, from 1898 to 1952, reaching back to a singer who grew up in Biedermeyer Vienna not so long after the composer's death. The LP era tended towards single-record recitals by individual artists. Inevitably favourite songs predominated. One became used to flipping through the contents of new releases, weighing the proportion of much-duplicated Trouts and Heidenrösleins to songs hitherto unavailable and reluctantly declining, in most cases, to purchase. Every singer of note left his or her stamp upon thirty or so standards, leaving the other 480-odd songs (not including the forty-four in the two great cycles) untouched.

There have been honourable exceptions: Janet Baker's two-record recital for HMV included beautiful accounts of some unfamiliar songs; the young Fischer-Dieskau and later the young Peter Schreier roamed well outside the routine. Half of a BBC record (the other being devoted to Wolf) is especially precious, a recital by Pears and Britten compiled from broadcasts made in 1959 and 1964, all but one of the songs rare in every sense, with performances unequalled for interpretative inwardness.

The chronological approach was monumentalised in two forbidding boxes made by Fischer-Dieskau with Gerald Moore for Deutsche Grammophon. Vol. 1 covered 1817–28 on twelve LPs; vol. 2, on thirteen, filled in the earlier songs from 1811–17. This is an heroic achievement: the supreme calibre of the two artists is unquestioned, but the sense of dutiful trundle is unavoidable—especially, for obvious reasons, in the mass of work from Schubert's teens. Brahms said that something could be learned from each single Schubert song, however naïve, to which Tovey sensibly added that often enough one would have to be a Brahms to learn it. But the main point is that this is not an opus like a Bach organ-mass, nor even a loose bouquet of Songs without Words or Lyric Pieces. These hundreds of songs represent hundreds of separate lyric or dramatic occasions, whose merely chronological proximity (even when several were composed on the same day) has no particular meaning and is often positively contradictory.

Thus Hyperion's project to record all the Schubert songs would be welcome even if its results were not so satisfying artistically. Graham Johnson, its architect, annotator and accompanist, divides the vast field into well-balanced CD-length recitals, sometimes linked by a common theme (though this is not laboured), sometimes by subtle inner sympathy. Juxtapositions, both congruous and contrasting, are sensitively moulded to ensure an overall musical coherence that also extends to key-relationships (often inexcusably jangled in the past, even within song-cycles where the composer clearly intends them to tell).

Each recital is intelligently suited to its different singer. Thus for the first, Janet Baker, with night-thoughts of longing and fulfilment, is all calm exaltation; for the fifth, Elizabeth Connell is all pantheistic grandeur, whether it tends toward Greek mythology or Enlightenment Catholicism. Elsewhere, other organising principles are at work, for instance the close-knit creative friendships within Schubert's intimate circle, or his respectful treatment of the distant frowning Olympians Schiller and Goethe. Every one is imaginatively complete and happily represents its singer's vocal type and artistic temperament.

Only the accompanist need be protean, and Johnson's volatility here is beyond praise. He has the exact expressive and pianistic weight of each song just right, from a tinkling little thing like 'Taglich zu singen' ('Daily, daily, sing the praises') to a crashing anthem like 'Die Allmacht'. Where called for, he is orchestral—in 'Der Zwerg', for instance, that Poe-like tale of obsession and murder (superbly sung by Anne Murray) aboard a mysterious ship on a desolate *Tristan*-ocean. And in such feats of sheer stamina as the half-hour ballad of 'Der Taucher', Johnson is tireless where poor Stephen Varcoe shows understandable signs of going under. Yet he can also be gentle and unobtrusive, as for the most part of the recital with Philip Langridge.

The end result is to enhance, if possible, one's sense of the range of Schubert's genius. Apparent dead ducks—prattling ditties in 6/8 or ramshackle scenas from *Ossian* and Greek drama—come to life both in themselves and alongside famous masterpieces which every singer performs and scarcely inferior treasures which are hardly ever visited. The series will be completed, on some thirty-five discs, in time for the composer's bicentenary in 1997. Even after only five, the project is already a source of delight that can only deepen as its riches accumulate and its gaps gradually close.

ii Journey's end (December 2000)

Earlier this year [2000] one of the most important and handsome undertakings in the century-old history of recorded music reached its not-overly-trumpetted completion.

But I'll abandon circumspection and say outright that the Hyperion edition of Schubert's complete songs on thirty-seven CDs, with its flotilla of distinguished singers, masterminded, extensively annotated, piano-accompanied throughout by Graham Johnson, simply *is* the handsomest and most important achievement in the gramophone catalogue.

Its value lies firmly in the calibre of its contents: performances are never less than worthy and sometimes touch great heights of interpretative skill; recordings are absolutely unexceptionable (i.e. you don't notice them, until with some discs so generously filled the outer limits can skitter out of control). But the whole project is focused upon the genius of Schubert: its importance lies in the revelation of this extraordinary body of work, its handsomeness in the intelligence and imagination with which the corpus is laid out, like a great love feast, a loving garden, a country, a continent, a world, for its listeners to gratefully devour, explore, populate.

For despite the high standing of the two great cycles and a handful of celebrated individual songs the vast majority of Schubert's output in this genre still remains if not absolutely *terra incognita*, largely undervalued by music lovers in general. This is partly because of the essential quietness of the genre itself. 'Not overtly trumpetted'—unlike symphony cycles by Mahler or Shostakovich, Beethoven or Tchaikovsky, unlike flights of instrumental virtuosity whether solo or in concertos, unlike 'completist' collections vaunting their virginal authenticity, most of all unlike grand opera, the art-song with piano remains intimate and special: it can never make a big noise and be hot news.

Then there is the problem of its remoteness in sentiment and sensibility. It can seem as remote as the way of life, copiously discussed by Johnson, that gave it birth and saw it to maturity. The comparison lies with the other twin peak of nearly subterranean musical achievement, the 200-odd church cantatas of Bach, where the ideology, spirit, language in which the texts are couched, to which the music is bound however much it transcends them, are still further removed; whose conventions, once normative, are still further lost beyond any possibility of retrieval. Perhaps both these half-lost domains can only be rediscovered nowadays in ambitious recording ventures like Hyperion's.

Johnson's booklettes do their utmost to help.Sometimes too much: he can weary the willing reader not by his exhaustiveness so much as by his frequent self-indulgence in whimsical punning, personal interventions, touches of fulsomeness. Yet the sugar of enthusiasm coats a wealth of hard fact whose assiduous amassing amounts to a work of scholarship more interesting than most doctoral theses.

But Schubert is his own best interpreter. The music shines bright through foreign languages, lost conventions, alien sensibilities. Also, it must be said, through much fustian, bombast, tacky sentimentality and naff narrative, insipid prettiness, poetic corn, didactic prosiness. Amongst all this loom lyrics and ballads by accredited masters of German letters as well as translations from, *inter alia*, Shakespeare, Pope, Scott, Byron (alongside inevitable reams of Ossian). In effect this makes little difference, for it should go without saying that great poetry by no means guarantees great setting, and a polymorphous amorist like Schubert is likelier to be aroused into full bloom by verse that doesn't intimidate, cow, inhibit.

So through all this literary matter, occasioned by it and consuming it utterly, burns the compelling intensity and unlimited beauty of—I'm throwing caution to the winds!—the most original, fecund, inspired composer who has ever existed. Original because so unbeholden: no composer before or since has had in his gift a larger admixture of absolutely new things that music can embody and express. Fecund because so frequent, with such protean variety (obviously not every one of the 600 will be equally new, beautiful, profound, but the proportion of quality is high, there is plenty to cherish on the lower slopes of Parnassus, almost nothing is wholly untouched by his powers). Inspired because he is the composer closest to music's intrinsic nature; he combines consummate purity of grammatical usage (even when such usages had scarcely been touched on, or touched off, before) fused with an unprecedented reliance upon total expressiveness; objective and subjective are held in such equipoise that they lose their customary polarity.

Whereas in instrumental forms the ouput, however treasurable or astonishing, remains with his death at thirty-one understandably 'unfinished', in songs he is from his mid-teens onwards the flawless master of a hitherto unsuspected realm. There were *Lieder* before, but the genre was minor, even puny. With Schubert it becomes for all its brevity and the humbleness of its performing resources and domestic circumstances as significant as symphony, concerto, sonata, opera, oratorio, mass. This is major art with modest means: not water-colour as opposed to fresco or oil-painting; because the emotional range is so wide and so deep.'All human life is here'; within this lyric/narrative genre any and every shade and degree of feeling can be contained, uttered with comprehensive psychological penetration, breathtakingly direct in the physical appeal of its sheer loveliness, in its workmanship subtle and far-reaching beyond analysis or any other description. 'Size matters': the actual dimensions (together with the lurking cosiness of the mere genre, the remoteness in culture and sensibility, and the frequent triteness of the mere words) are subsumed in the grandeur of the *real* content.

Hyperion's thirty-seven discs provide a thoroughly coherent and artistic organisation of one of the supreme treasure-caves in all the annals of humanist achievement. A lifetime three times as long as its creator's will barely suffice to explore and know it to the uttermost resonance. But the means lie to hand!

5

A noble nature

One hundred and fifty years ago, still under forty, of overwork and premature exhaustion, died Felix Mendelssohn, music's eternal representative of youthful gaiety and grace. How was sunniness so ineluctably transformed into dutiful killer routine? Materials for an answer are gathered into Roger Nichols's new *Mendelssohn Remembered*[1]. This excellent format, drawing widely upon the testimony of friends, family, colleagues, observant strangers, obviates the need for formal biography, sometimes stodgy, often prurient. Every reader can draw his own portrait with what the editor has so skilfully provided.

Felix was felicitously named: blessed by the good fairies with every talent, social, personal, artistic; born into enlightenment, affluence, comfort; unthwarted by struggle with circumstances, unbruised by struggle within the temperament. Descriptions of him as a boy, from the family circle right up to Goethe himself, sound an angelic chorus: 'That beautiful youth, with his auburn hair clustering in ringlets around his shoulders, the look of his brilliant clear eyes, and the smile of innocence and candour on his lips.' But also a proper boy; after serious grown-up music-making, the twelve-year-old makes for the garden, 'clearing high hedges with a leap, running, singing or climbing up trees like a squirrel—the very image of health and happiness'. When not composing, or playing, or drawing, or writing very intelligent letters, he was a vigorous and skilful gymnast, a tirelessly enthusiastic swimmer (inventing little songs for his chums to sing while actually ploughing the water), an accomplished horseman, a winner at chess.

The lovable best of the music, mostly from the younger end of his life, beautifully fits these characteristics. More than any other it embodies youthful grace, freshness, eagerness; it is high-spirited, yet refined, elegant without over neatness, impeccable yet intoxicating. The string Octet, its outer movements buoyant and fiery, the brio at once physical and intellectual, the slow movement with its shy blushful tenderness, the scherzo with a speed, effervescence, weightlessness never heard before, nor recaptured by any composer since. In the *Midsummer Night's Dream* overture two years later, the eighteen-year-old's new sensibility expands into congenial romantic territory. The eager listener is entranced by the acute delicacy with which the stiff bright ceremonial strains, and the rustics with their braying donkey, equally

---

[1] Faber and Faber, 1997.

with the fairy flickering and pattering, are perceived at a distance, overheard, overseen down the wrong end of a telescope, populating crystal-clear yet unfathomably deep forest vistas. Through a glass lightly, uncanny but without shadow.

A few years further on, the *Hebrides* overture and its perfect fusion of romantic picturesqueness into classic form, with a watercolour precision very different from the oil painting to come—Berlioz, Wagner, Strauss, for all their debt to this prototype—and quite unrelated to the exactly contemporary Turner in seascapes where a maelstrom or haze of texture all but obliterates the subject. Mendelssohn preserves shapely exactness in which every phrase, purposely busy or masterfully empty, is embued with mysterious power of suggestive evocation. And on then to the large-scale triumphs—The *Scotch* and *Italian* symphonies that take the classic-romantic art of landscape to its peak, and the violin concerto which eschews pictorialism altogether.

Work of this order is not achieved without enormous expenditure of nervous energy, however invisible. We *see* it as the youthful shine begins to dull, and composition becomes a matter of conscience: the finesse slackens, to be replaced by finicalness. All but the best of the chamber music, the church music, the numerous songs with and (preferably) without words, convey a touch of the production line, and the truism that the pure gold with which he'd set out is only fully recovered later in the additional numbers for *A Midsummer Night's Dream* is surely true.

Discipline had been inculcated early. From his mother the boy learnt 'the unceasing activity which became a way of life to him', from his father 'the conviction that our life is given us for work, for usefulness and constant striving'. This heavy work-ethic nurture, as well as the lovely pieces where the effort doesn't show, produces the exhortatory pew-filling side of his output which exactly fulfils, and indeed resembles, the gravity of the early instruction. Life isn't all fairies and Hebrides, there is the 300th anniversary of Luther's *Augsberg Confession* to be celebrated (*Reformation Symphony*) and the 400th of Gutenberg's invention of printing (*Hymn of Praise*). Hard on his glorious resurrection of Bach's *Matthew Passion* after a century of neglect come his own sacred choral monuments: a New Testament oratorio (*St Paul*) for the Germans, and Old Testament (*Elijah*) for the British; and six organ sonatas for the *cognoscenti*.

The serious aspect, despite occasional moments of inspiration, tends more often to set up amidst the prevailing sweet unction a desperate hankering for what he's not doing, that he does elsewhere, that is so much truer to his genius. Only one of these 'nobler efforts', the still early *First Walpurgisnight* (a bold confrontation between Druids and Christians, prefiguring and superior to the contest between Jehovah and Baal in *Elijah*) breathes this freer, fresher air.

Vanished for good is the unfettered subject of a story retold in Nichols: returning with friends late at night down the empty Paris boulevard deep in earnest conversation: 'Mendelssohn suddenly stops and calls out: "We *must* do some of our jumps in Paris! Our jumps I tell you! Now for it! One ! Two !

Three!'" Elsewhere throughout these pages we follow what happened. The angelic boy and omni-gifted youth grows up into 'the Prophet David'—all the descriptions agree as to his fineness, distinction, the expressive mobility, the sweetness, intensity and power of the mature man. Behind the face lies infinite tact and address, charming the high society of three countries emphatically including 'our own dear Queen', and not averse to elegant misbehaviour in the best circles. Domestic Mendelssohn, loving and simpatico, devoted to his beautiful wife and five beautiful children. More important still, Mendelssohn the indefatigable performing musician, organiser, musical educator, establishing foundations and principles in concert hall and conservatoire that remain intact to this day.

But even such superhuman indefatigability must tire. Later reports speak of growing 'irritability', 'distrustfulness', 'fretfulness', 'morbid conscientiousness'. One lifelong friend, writing in February 1846, says frankly 'I thought he did not discriminate between his impulse to work and to create.' By August of the following year Mendelssohn says to a visitor three times in as many days, 'I shall not live to see it' ('and the glow faded from his face, and the sad, worn look came back which it pained the very heart to see'). Early that November the most attractive human figure amongst all the great composers was dead—victim of a noble nature, instinct with generosity, a highly-strung nervous constitution, and a code of work-till-you-drop-to-the-glory-of-God.

6

Some thoughts about Tristan and abstract nouns

A written-up version of some impromptu remarks contributed to a day-long conference on Transcendence held in Tilburg January 2001 by the Nexus Institute, later printed in Dutch in vol. 29 of their proceedings.

* * *

I think it extremely important to try to rescue great artworks from the ideas and beliefs that helped them into being—and by extension, from their creators' character and biography. Naturally there is much music from all epochs to which this caveat does not apply; in earlier times especially, the sheer lack of biographical information, let alone any ascertainable aesthetic or ideology; in modern times, too, the fundamental irrelevance of life, character, career in composers so different as Bruckner, Debussy, Sibelius, Ravel (I'd like to list most, if not quite all), despite our appetite for anecdotes and our fascination with every aspect of the individual creative personality.

But Wagner somehow always seems different! There are three temptations that commentary on him finds hard to resist: to be seduced by the altogether extraordinary personality and biography; to become enmeshed in the coils of his published theorising and reported opinion on a wide range of subjects whose extreme sensitivity shows no sign of diminishing; and then, even if the artworks undoubtedly born from his life and thought as well as from the springs of imagination are kept 'clean', to be hung up on the 'issues' they raise, which can obscure, even obliterate, concentration upon the meaning inherent within the narrative, situation, character, utterance, and—paramount—the actual facture by which the poet/dramatist/composer brings all this into being.

Precisely because their invitation is so apparently ample, we shouldn't be overawed or beguiled by big abstract nouns like Love, Death, Renunciation, Redemption, Transfiguration, Transcendence. 'When I hear such words I reach for my gun.' Or, as F. R. Leavis said in relation to Dante Gabriel Rossetti's splurgy poetic vocabulary, it is 'beggar's largesse'. Or as Philip Larkin said of some of his peers, 'I am not going to fall on my face every time someone uses words such as Orpheus or Faust or Judas'. Or—ultimate purist—Mallarmé's celebrated injunction to Dégas when the painter turned poet, 'poems are made with words not ideas'. Paintings are made of painted paint, music of composed sounds.

Which is not to say that the music of Wagner is not, also, inspired by and saturated in such large abstract concepts—more so perhaps than any other composer of major stature, never more so than in *Tristan*. But they'd be as nought—beggar's largesse—if he'd not succeeded in imbuing them deep into the actual stuff of his musical invention, the opposite of abstraction, conceptualisation, woolly vagueness; the specific notes.

How he did this, how these sounds *work*, remains the boldest individual achievement in the entire culture of Western music. It also remains contentious still, long after the Wagner wars are over and the *œuvre* become a recognised cornerstone of operatic repertoire as well as common intellectual and cultural 'heritage'. Whether superficial or deeper, anti-Wagner polemic on the technical level has always been concerned with an abuse against the very nature of music itself (as I said, I'm keeping the artworks 'above' all ideological and biographical consideration). From whatever position of purism—classic ('a harmonic hooligan'), neo-classic ('shapeless, formless, without measure'), or postmodernist *blasé* ('too Freudian, too knowing, too explicit; everything underlined and **hammered home**')—the objection focuses implicitly upon the way that this composer, through claiming somehow to be more than merely a composer, compels music to attempt matters that music intrinsically cannot do—or if it can, shouldn't. At its simplest this is the endeavour to represent objects, places, persons, psychological impulses; at its worst (or at least, most tendentious) the desire to express the big abstractions—the words like Transcendence that make even so ardent a Wagnerite as myself reach for his gun—concepts that move beyond the social/familial/amorous/ambitious preoccupations of humanity at large (and so comprehensively understood or explored within the microcism of the music-dramas) into a sphere that should properly pertain only to religion. Yet Wagner of course *does* succeed in imbuing his actual unmetaphysical notes with resonances from such woolly matter. He musicalises the so-called extramusical. Which oughtn't to be possible either as an undertaking, or technically—but there it is; he's done it. What we'd all like to know is, *how*: if this can be answered we might perhaps be able to say *what* it is, and what it *means*. I'd like to concentrate simply and briefly on the problems and solutions of Wagner the *composer*, thence Wagner the dramatist-in-music, rather than add to the confusion and hot air of Wagner the metaphysician (let alone the dangerous ideologue). But this is by no means to deny that these 'other' Wagners do get in eventually, and that to get them in might have been a main, even a primary, aim (though if it were, I would have to claim that the art works need protecting from it).

The nub of Western music is harmony—journey, argument, arrival, tension-and-release; how to open, to continue, to interrupt, develop, to close; the balance of suspension and resolution. By common consent *Tristan* is pivotal within this tradition of exploiting music's powers of inhalation and exhalation, intensifying them beyond anything imaginable before (and very little since, most of it by Wagner too, or in his wake). The opera's initial moves set up huge implications, of size, of trajectory, of emotional expression—impulses with consequences, causes requiring effects. The entire fabric of the ensuing three acts can be heard as the realisation of these opening moves—a complex, richly ambiguous cadential idea spread wide over a structure lasting a whole long evening, that needs this amount of sonorous time-and-space for its full purport to be unwound, then resolved.

Is the prelude to Act I in A minor, or C; or even A major? Its *ultimate* goal is none of these; untransposed, it heads with surprising yet consummatory conviction for B major. But its immediate resolution, at the start of the first act, is C minor; the act's eventual harbour is C major (with a powerful penultimate A minor too). Simply to measure this one main journey through it, charting the delays, extensions, interruptions, evasions, frustrations, feints, whereby C is dangled, denied and finally achieved, with all their mastery of musical grammar and their range of expressive nuance from irony and scorn to wild excitement, would show the inextricable linking of compositional prowess with dramatic pacing and human utterance of the highest order. Then there'd be all the further subsidiary strands in all their interwoven complexity (even though Act I is far the most 'straightforward' of the three). With such grasp of the composition in one's hands—whether intellectual/ analytic, or as in the theatre by sheer intuitive gut-response—it might then be permissible to begin on the abstractions and conceptualities.

Just to make this chart would be sufficiently interesting. To elaborate it to its fullest reaches of significance would take years of labour. Fortunately, neither is necessary: Act I of *Tristan* has already done it for us in the most succinct and elegant manner imaginable.

And so with Acts II and III. A first, practicable line through II might again centre in concentration upon its breathing. The enormous span of love duet is articulated around some five perfect cadences (sometimes vulgarly given a more carnal name). Their effect is extraordinarily powerful, at once reposeful and arriving, yet opening up new larger vistas, after the normative language of I in which expectation and closure are constantly thwarted, and before the delirium of III in which tonal usage is strained, dissipated, exploded. After such conspicuous perfect-cadencing, the cadential interruption when the lovers are discovered and ecstatic night yields to cold dawn is overwhelming; an aching bruise only pacified in the closing stretch of the *Liebestod* at the end of III, whose whole course recapitulates the final stage of the love duet, sweeping grandly on over the place which had been so painfully cut off.

Another Act II exploration could focus on the beautiful and profound effect of the exchanges between the lovers after King Marke's reproachful monologue. After the ocean of a-periodic music with its amazing spans of free-prose and apparent improvisation (derided by Stravinsky as 'the slag-heap of art' but more justly characterised by another Wagner-derogator, Nietzsche, as the precious jewellery of a musical miniaturist 'who compresses an infinity of meaning and sweetness into the smallest space'), elements from it are drawn in, re-aligned, combined with material from all the cognate Wesendonck-settings save one, to fashion another stanzaic, almost strophic, *song*. Formality is made from flux, absolutely with formalism, in this almost courtly *invitation au voyage* which plumbs the depths without seeming even to try to. Then, again, it doesn't full-close, opening out instead upon yet another interrupted cadence, gentle as the cut-off of the duet was violent, when the lovers' shared private ritual lifts its eyes, via their kiss, to face the consequences of their action in its wider social context.

The two most important architectural features of Act III are self-evident: the emblematic combination at Tristan's death of material from crucial previous places—the three signals with which Isolde summoned him to join her near the start of Act II, the 'death-devoted heart' motif, and the opening moves in the Act I prelude; and the massive symmetry already mentioned set up by the *Liebestod* recapitulating the close of the Act II duet under guise of contrasting mood, tempo, texture, then sweeping it over into fulfilment and quietus. What this 'means' is Transcendence (*hélas!*). But the big woolly concept cannot be actualised without the meticulously-planned and flawlessly-executed mechanics of the compositional small print (which, sometimes, can be so fluent that it seems to run on auto-pilot: Wagner himself scribbled on the rough sketch of the *Liebestod* 'now the children can finish this!').

The other most conspicuous feature of Act III, however, is complexity incarnate, requiring bar-by-bar description/analysis, and occasionally note-by-note, to do it justice. This is the interweave of motifs from all over the opera, from recent bleeding or ecstatic past and distant painful buried childhood past, penetrated with the shepherd's ubiquitous present-tense piping which elicits all the traumatic matter of Tristan's delirium in all its mesh of interconnection, tight and loose. The impeccable control with which extreme states are rendered with extreme means—x-ray, fragmentation, pulverisation, cross-copulation, disintegration and reintegration—make evolution audible, even visible—a sonorous/verbal fusion over the edge of sane utterance, laid out with uncanny lucidity.

Some processes in Act III would be easier to illustrate; for instance showing the stages whereby its four-note opening motif derived directly from the third Wesendonck setting, so completely different in effect from the four-note shape at the opera's very opening, nevertheless eventually merges indissolubly into it. This too would be a demonstration of evolution in action, interestingly different from its sources equally in Beethovenian development and Bachian spinning-out. And here too the purpose of the exploration would be to show how the conceptual, abstract, 'extramusical' is achieved by purely musical means. And this in turn suggests another whole field for fruitful investigation, concerning the nature of the utterance-potential innate in all musical patterning with or without texts or subject-matter; the quality whereby melodic contour, rhythmic propulsion, harmonic direction, timbre and all the further interlinked parameters of composition contain and convey meaning. But this would take more than a lifetime! And, again, is not in fact necessary: great works of music time without number achieve this already, with precise exactness combined with the highest degree of expressive com-munication.

7

Motif, memory and meaning in Twilight of the Gods

Contributed to the Royal Opera House / English National Opera guide to the opera, edited by Nicholas John (1985).

* * *

No artist has attempted a task more intimidating than Wagner's in writing the last and largest instalment of the longest musico-dramatic work yet completed. Coherently but not laboriously to tie up all the threads, to synthesise without artifice, to get the ending absolutely right, required almost superhuman powers. He also made huge demands of his performers in terms of understanding and stamina, of his theatre in technical resources and illusion, and not least of his audience for long-distance concentration upon a drama that unremittingly fuses emotional intensity with dense intellectual argument. Yet he was at pains to make what he is doing at all points self-elucidating. Wagnerian music-drama is mass-communication rather than arcane secret; there are no meaningless ciphers or inexplicable mysteries; the complex entity glares out with comprehensive exhaustiveness, offering, whatever the depths, a surface that shows everything needed for its own apprehension. It invariably gives the listener a foothold, and sometimes the emphasis of a didactic finger. Tovey's 'first article of musical faith'—that 'while the listener must not expect to hear the whole contents of the piece of music at once, nothing concerns him that will not ultimately reach his ear, either as directly audible fact or as a cumulative satisfaction in things of which the hidden foundations are well and truly laid'—applies as well to Wagner as to the wordless forms which prompted it. How this huge structure works in the small and in the large, how we take in what we hear, how we hear it in the first place, and how we make sense of and interpret it: these are the questions this essay will consider.

They boil down to one: how does Wagner interfuse his music and his meaning? In the large, by his manipulation of musical memory by recapitulations and other formal symmetries, familiar from the music of other periods (though never before so extensive nor so complex); in the small by the leitmotif. Large and small are, of course, closely related. The function of the leitmotif is to build, to describe, to recall. First it gives something a name and sound; every subsequent incidence is a reminder; at the point when the sound becomes the thing named and we have learned to think in this language, the leitmotif becomes a building-unit from which the structure is formed.

Even at its most straightforward this is not simple. The most purely demonstrative motifs are not one-dimensional, and as the work advances most of them accumulate a web of associations that makes any one name inadequate. An activity (smithying) becomes the whole race of Nibelungs or an individual Nibelung of particular importance (Mime); an object (his horn) becomes a character (Siegfried). That his sword also comes to 'be' Siegfried is a yet more complex development because we have seen its history—its discovery by his father, the fight in which it was shattered and the father killed, the forge in which it was remade. With Wotan's spear, the history (slowly divulged, though not seen on the stage, throughout the tetralogy) is such as to make the equation Wotan/spear/authority/contracts/restraints a drastic short-hand whenever the motif is heard. Thus when sword splinters spear in the third act of *Siegfried*, the cycle reverberates from beginning to end. *Twilight* contains the subtlest example of this process: Alberich's use of the Tarnhelm in *The Rhinegold* is simply to become invisible and to transform himself into serpent and toad; in the first two acts of *Twilight* this fairy-tale device (almost forgotten meanwhile) comes to represent deception, becoming the means whereby deception can be manipulated to play upon an inner weakness. As such it is indispensable to the meaning as well as the mechanism of the plot.

From the most onomatopoeic (the waters of the Rhine) to the most abstract (the motive often simply labelled 'destiny', 'renunciation of', or 'redemption by', 'love'), the leitmotifs always do their work successfully because they are musical objects of great distinctness. Not only things—objects, places, types, individuals—but activities and ideas are rendered in brief, memorable *musical things* which scarcely ever change and, when they do, always remain recognisable. As Wagner's paragraphs grow longer, the harmonic usage more supercharged, the motivic combinations (whether fluent or 'yoked together by violence') more bold and subtle, the range of reference further-flung, these essential nuggets can always be apprehended and identified.

Since leitmotifs are memory-containers as well as building-units, the vital facts come to mind whenever the sound is heard. Without this constant reminder of things past we would not be able fully to understand the present. Moreover with leitmotifs memory works forward too; the present is made omniscient by this commentary from fore and aft. 'It takes a sound realist to make a convincing symbolist', as D. J. Enright once wrote; the wealth of interpretation *The Ring* attracts would not be possible without its strong basis in specifics.

Take the ring itself. This crucial object has a motif that for once is deliberately not distinct, because the ring is of its nature volatile, amenable to anyone's cupidinous fantasy. But the gold is always present in the ring, and the Rhinemaidens' primal cry of 'Rhinegold!' —

— is remembered whenever the ring motif is heard, whatever the associations and distortions pressed upon it later. By contrast, the motif of the curse placed upon the ring—

— never alters; rather it pulls other motifs into its highly distinctive musical quality, just as it influences everyone's behaviour; equally it recalls at every recurrence what it is, what was said, and how it came about. A curse was pronounced upon a ring made of gold stolen from the Rhine; all this is embodied in musical motifs, distinct in themselves yet capable of so inter-twining as to make an image-cluster that is finally indissoluble. So much for symbolism! This is the work of a sound realist. It also embodies the drama. The plot could be told from one point of view by following the whereabouts and ownership of the object itself, just as all the occurrences of the curse motif could be joined up to make an 'invisible picture' of Siegfried's death and the fall of the gods. The focus of intense drama in *Rhinegold*, the ring sleeps throughout *The Valkyrie*, comes sharply to mind in the first act of *Siegfried* and into the action of the other two; while in *Twilight* its ownership and whereabouts (whose finger? when? how?) make the machinery of the story.

Wagner's usual way of working our musical memory hard is intensified in *Twilight* by his extraordinary pains to make salient motifs recur at the same pitch. Sometimes this can even jeopardise musical grammar, though more often it is the stuff of which his grammar is made. Either way there is some-thing almost fetishistic about it, as if the motifs would not have their full sig-nificance when transposed. Score-readers and perfect-pitchers will respond to the precision with which the Tarnhelm seems to work its treachery only when it moves from G♯ minor through E minor to the bare fifth on B—

—but this (and the many comparable manipulations with other motifs throughout the work) will probably be lost on the great majority of listeners. It is the only aspect of Wagner's method which requires his listeners to hear more than they can reasonably be expected to take in, even while it does form another level, significant because so concrete, in the work's articulation of its meaning. But no-one will fail to recognise what *is* essential: the individuality of each motif's harmony, melody, rhythm, timbre. And the same goes, in a looser way, for Wagner's use of key. Again this is often 'symbolic'—would Siegfried's passing be properly celebrated if his sword were not in C and his horn in E♭? Is Gutrune quite herself except in G? But the main difficulty here comes from the fact that the tonal architecture of *The Ring* is too big to measure. Our key-sense, impressionistic enough even for Haydn and Beethoven, cannot be expected to cope with the more complex tonal activity of Wagner's late style. Yet Tovey's 'first article of musical faith' still applies; we sense that we are in good hands even though it cannot be proved. The broad structure is both simple and rock-hard; within it we concentrate moment-to-moment on the improvisatory riot of detail produced by the leitmotifs and the vagabond modulation to which they are subjected.

The combination of local- (the perpetual play of leitmotivic recall) with memory-architecture on the broadest possible scale (actual recapitulation, developing recapitulation and parallels of other kinds) together accounts for the return of all three earlier evenings during the fourth of the tetralogy. By *Twilight*-time our memory is long, and has moreover to accommodate new characters and events, complex and rapid beyond those in any other opera by Wagner, with all the new musical material they necessitate. Its past is richer, its present more intense, and from the very first two chords its end is approaching, inevitable and magnetic, at once louring like a cliff and drawing everything towards it like a cataract. This essay will follow the story as it unrolls forward and refers backward, hanging fast to the means whereby narrative and meaning are fused into music.

The opening chords are taken from Brünnhilde's awakening in the last act of *Siegfried*; the scoring (a massive wind *tutti* yielding to the soft second chord on flutes and low brass) is significantly similar, the effect entirely so; and though we can hardly *hear* that this unforgettable sonorous image now moves from E♭ minor to C♭ major rather than from E minor to C major, we at once connect its two appearances. Moreover the next sound is equally recognisable as a dusky echo of the waters of the Rhine at the very start of the cycle. It is not yet clear what is signified by this gesture that yokes the depths of *Rhinegold* with the summits of *Siegfried*; but it indicates from the start that in *Twilight* our memory of the whole work will be stretched to the limit. It is repeated, using the second pair of chords from Brünnhilde's awakening. At the third, when formerly the light shone brightest, the blast of E♭ minor sinks into the fate motif and what follows is not the river again but a cobweb of soft shifting dissonance—the Norns, a trio of nature-daughters as old, withered and wise as the Rhine-maidens are young, fresh and foolish. Their scene is built around the refrain spinning the rope of fate which functions as a kind of ritornello while they tell by question-and-answer of events already known and events hitherto unheard; thus many old themes are called to mind in ashy guise (particularly the strange slowed-down version of the fire music, formerly so volatile), as the basis of their look into the future.

We learn for the first time the history of the World Ash Tree: how Wotan violated it to win his wisdom and his spear by paying an eye, how the deed wasted the tree and dried up its spring of wisdom. We learn again of the hero who splintered the spear and every treaty it upheld; we learn newly of Wotan's consequent command to fell the dead tree and pile its logs around Valhalla ready for razing should the moment come. We discover new angles of Wotan's relation to Loge, and how the god will command the fire to ignite the logs as once he compelled him to encircle Brünnhilde. Seeking to know what happened to the stolen gold the Norns hear only the echo of Alberich's cry for revenge; a bright horn-call cuts through their cobwebs, the rope connecting past and future snaps, and, as the curse sounds for the first time in *Twilight*, they sink from sight, their wisdom spent.

The curse always suggests a cadence into B minor. The famous dawn music that follows lingers suspiciously long upon the dominant, but the F♯ inaudibly turns to G♭, which descends to F, over which Siegfried's horn-call sounds forth, soft, but with grand full harmony like a chorale, in B♭ major. The new dominant bass also lasts too long for credibility: as a new motif flowers (of Brünnhilde's fulfilment in love) the tonality turns decisively towards E♭ major, though even now there are still seventeen more bars of dominant preparation before the sun rises with the sun-god's horn theme in full splendour. The lavish radiance of the duet that follows it makes maximum contrast with the shadowy impotence of the Norns by the simplest of all key-relationships, major to minor. Yet it, also, is a reworking of old themes in a new light, built upon a ritornello figure —

— which frames and punctuates the lovers' almost formal apostrophes to each other before pervading everything in the rapturous close. This technique of building a scene around a ritornello motif seems to be unique to the later *Ring* style: the first instance—using the second half of

— is the dialogue between Erda and the Wanderer that opens the third act of *Siegfried*; it is employed throughout *Twilight*, whether as explicit refrain as with the Norns, or subtly incorporated into a texture of continuous development.

Siegfried, going out into the world as a man has to, innocently gives Brünnhilde the ring as a love-pledge. She gives him Grane in return. The scene ends in a blaze of E♭ major glory which links across the intervening space to the next 'mountain-top', the climax of the interlude describing his journey, the marvellous moment of liberation when he sees the Rhine lying broad and clear in its valley far beneath. This is no less a *coup-de-théâtre* even if the curtain is down. We have not seen the river after *The Rhinegold*. The motifs of its waters and its treasure have become steadily more smirched, and the most recent re-hearing, in the Norn scene, had rendered them thin and lacklustre. So the thrill of this restoration of the river's motifs to their pristine freshness and their primal key is achieved purely by sonorous means, which then ramify into broader interpretative significance. Siegfried is in the flower of his youth and innocence; he won the ring in fair fight, not lusting for it, and ignorant of its possibilities; he has given it to his lady to pledge his love. These twin peaks of Eb major are the work's high-points of optimism. The darkening of the Rhinegold cry as the interlude ends, and the way it turns subtly but purposefully into the first Gibichung motif, tell us unmistakably that the rest of the journey will be ill-fated.

The Prologue has been made almost entirely from familiar material richly reworked. The main action is set in a new place among new characters, the Gibichung court and its troubled first family. This necessitates new material, whose chivalric cast reminds us that *Siegfried's Death*, the *Ring* project as first mooted, would have been Wagner's next opera after *Lohengrin* rather than, as it turned out, the sixth. But this new material is permeated by the old, just as the new characters have inherited old memories and desires.

The basic key is B minor, into which the curse that ended the Norns' scene would have cadenced were it not deflected by dawn, duet and Siegfried's journey. And just as the Rhine runs alongside the action for the rest of the work, so is the curse motif never far from the music, because Hagen knows that Siegfried holds the woman who holds the ring that holds the curse. (How does Hagen know? With hindsight we understand that his everwatchful father keeps him in touch in the way we will overhear for ourselves in the first scene of Act II.)

The way the old motifs function in new situations shows the possibilities raised by Wagner's methods at their boldest, achieving complex dramatic expression that words have to labour to explain. Hagen's newly-planted idea takes root, that the Gibichungs use Siegfried to solve their troubles: he can marry Gutrune and win Brünnhilde for Gunther. 'How can we bring him here?' asks Gunther, and the curse arises from the orchestra pit intertwined with Siegfried's horn-call from down the river. A moment later Hagen describes his progress—'with a powerful stroke, / yet with leisurely ease, / he drives the boat, / braving the stream.' The music is now the Rhinegold cry and the flowing river itself, crossed with Siegfried's horn, the whole image-cluster fused into a graphic description of the hero's muscular prowess ('such strength in his arms / ... it is he who destroyed the dragon. / Siegfried comes, he and no other'). Another moment, and Siegfried is near enough to hear and answer Hagen's call; another, and he appears, lands, and is greeted by name with courteous words. But they are set to a lurid, rhetorical statement of the curse motif, with upbeat drumstrokes and climactic cymbal crash, the loudest sound in the work so far—though its presentation is the reverse of those twin peaks of sustained brilliance, the end of the love duet and the climax of the river-journey: it arises rapidly out of *pianissimo*, diminishes immediately after maximum impact, and soon collapses into complete silence when Siegfried, his future bride, brother-in-law and slayer confront each other in electric embarrassment. The implication is so large as to make this moment architectural rather than local, a turning-point in the drama as a whole. Siegfried's arrival is desired, brooded upon, broached, agreed; at just the right moment the music brings him up the river in person; and here he will meet his death because the music says so. The words here are simply the necessary formalities; the leitmotif tells the truth. Although the ring itself is distant, such musical emphasis compels us to remember the curse's origin (often forgotten as the motif comes and goes on less crucial occasions) in the words Alberich burned into his treasure as he lost it; they have never failed so far, and they will not fail as the decisive first move is made in the game by which its noblest victim will be taken. Here the motif denotes the fulfilment of Alberich's ultimate ambition, the downfall of the gods, and names Siegfried as the instrument of this fulfilment. The importance of this conjunction is confirmed by the emphatic move back into the temporarily forgotten B minor effected by the curse motif's being at its usual pitch.

This mighty moment is followed by its echo, as Siegfried asks Hagen how he knows his name (whose two syllables are again set to the curse's falling octave). This time the crucial dissonance ([2], fifth bar, always over a pedal F♯) alters and the music moves into the unctuous warmth of the Gibichungs' deceptive cordiality. The curse's next occurrence confirms that events are indeed moving with dream-like ease. Through the reverse-side of his innocence and courage—his inexperience of men and their ways, his ignorance of himself—Siegfried is easily tricked into drinking Gutrune's magic drink. Within minutes he has agreed to fetch Brünnhilde for Gunther in exchange for that standard item of barter, the sister; and his new cunning suggests how the Tarnhelm can help.Before Hagen explained, he didn't know what the Tarnhelm was for. Now—another instance of the rich compression of meaning made possible by the leitmotif—he has drunk self-deception with the potion of forgetfulness that represents it in a stage-prop (here the original Tarnhelm motif is extended musically in conjunction with the expansion of its meaning to encompass betrayal of others and self). So when the curse begins and ends the oath of blood-brotherhood between Siegfried and Gunther we understand quite explicitly that this brew of heartiness and harshness provides permission and justification for Siegfried's death, when occasion offers, uttered freely by his own words—'If one friend should betray, / then not drops of blood, / all his life blood ... / shall flow in streams from his veins; / traitors so must atone!'

Doped and duped, Siegfried sets off eagerly back the way he came, to win for his new blood-brother the woman he has already won for himself. Hagen keeps watch, developing the dark choked harmony peculiar to *Twilight* into a brooding set-piece that, with the Rhinegold cry in a piercingly dissonant harmonisation—

— makes a transition to Siegfried's goal, Brünnhilde's rock, where she awaits his second coming. We hear the curse now entwined with fragments of her new love theme as the action again nears the accursed object, worn on her finger. Instead of what she wants to hear, 'sounds I once knew so well steal on my ears from the distance' as her Valkyrie sister Waltraute approaches. *We* know them too; the sisters' scene together brings back the essence of Act III of *Valkyrie*, Wotan's rage at his errant daughter, together with the music from Act II when, while she was still obedient, he told her his dilemma. It moves on to Waltraute's full-scale description of what the Norns have already touched on: the Ash Tree cut down and piled in logs around Valhalla and the vast hall thronged with silent heroes awaiting the unknown outcome. This superb set-piece gives the basis for the apotheosis of Valhalla in the closing pages of *Twilight*; while the music for the description of Wotan speechlessly clutching his shattered spear, for the raven-messengers who will return with good news or ill, and for the words eventually wrung from him as he remembers his love for Brünnhilde ('If once the Rhine's fair daughters / win back their ring from Brünnhilde again, / then the curse will pass; / she will save both god and the world!')—all separated here by Waltraute's account of the frightened gods deprived of Freia's apples, the Valkyries cowering at their father's knee, and her own temerity in persuading Wotan at last to speak—are worked into the sublime continuous stretch of the last scene where Brünnhilde, at last understanding everything, tells the ravens what they need to know and grants the god his quietus. Here is another turning-point of the work, requiring references backward and forward and marked by a fusion of gold, curse and ring motifs, working towards a full-close in the Valhalla music in its first and last key of D♭. If Brünnhilde had not been told *now*, when she is least likely to yield it, what ought to be done with the ring, she would not know what to do with it after the catastrophe.

But *now* she holds fast to her love-pledge, Waltraute rushes off in despair, and Brünnhilde remains alone surrounded by flames as at the end of *Valkyrie*; except that she is awake, her rescuer has come, and the music tells her of his unexpected return. Siegfried's second ascent through the flames is an exact repetition of his first in *Siegfried* Act III; where it diverges, in the horrible dissonant chord at the climax, it points the crucial difference: that it is not Siegfried. The chord is the dominating harmony of Hagen's Watch (still in progress, of course); Brünnhilde sees Gunther's form, and we (as Hagen's chord collapses onto the start of the Tarnhelm motif) see a Siegfried who is directed by Hagen and no longer his own man.

Both its legitimate owners are close to the ring. Brünnhilde cries that so long as she wears it she is safe (if only she could heed the *music* to which her own words are set, she would know they couldn't be true—but, unlike Siegfried, she is still unaware of the Tarnhelm's power to deceive). Siegfried, singing the curse as a melodic contour (unusual in itself) says 'from you I shall take it / taught by your words!' and a scuffle ensues, beginning with Hagen's hideous version of the Rhinegold cry, then fought out between her own motif and the curse. She wins as Siegfried gains his own love-pledge; again a raucous sound collapses into the Tarnhelm motif, through whose miasma she unconsciously looks into and recognises Siegfried's eyes. He, having done this foul deed as blithely as he once dispatched a dragon, now calls upon his sword to lie between them in the cave, keeping his new bride inviolate for his brother.

[7]

It is important that Brünnhilde, in all the wretchedness of her betrayal, *hears* this music; in her final monologue she will return to this unwittingly false oath sworn upon a true touchstone, explain it, and put it right. The act ends with the Tarnhelm motif *con tutta forza* at its usual pitch: the note B runs through all its three chords, grounding the entire Gibichung act in a B minor whose sway has been potent though its periods in office have been brief.

The prelude to Act II is the continuation of Hagen's Watch from Act I, making from the same ingredients the harshest music in all Wagner (using [6] again). The scene it introduces, between Hagen as he sleeps and his never-resting father Alberich, is another prologue, like the Norn-scene both retelling old matters and glimpsing future events by now equally familiar. But whereas the Norn music had moved slowly enough to be grasped readily, the motifs are here broken down and recombined in a style of rapid allusive lightness that makes this the most difficult area of *The Ring* to assimilate. Furthermore, Alberich's angle on the familiar makes it different. Wotan's defeat at Siegfried's hands, and his preparations for the end, the hero's blithe lordship of the ring making its curse ineffective: this well-covered territory is now whispered in hectic consternation—only Siegfried's undoing can win it for them: 'he's a fool, the real enemy is the wisdom of the woman he's won—if she has the wit to return ring to Rhine our hopes are ended.' Between these flustered utterances come Hagen's stolid assurances that, he, too, works what his father desires.

We learn the history of Hagen (already hinted in *Valkyrie* Act II) from its source—how Alberich begot and reared his son in hatred to accomplish what his father could not do for himself. Thus we understand why Hagen looms so large in the meaning as well as the mechanics of the plot. Hagen is far closer to Siegfried than he is either to Gunther (respectively half-brother and relation by oath and, later today, marriage): both have been conceived to fulfil the aims of others, have grown autonomous and revolted against their manipulators; they are brothers under the skin. As the scene closes with both phrases of the curse (in honour of him who first uttered it) Hagen tranquilly quietens his father's anxiety with the assurance that he swears to himself, and to no other, that he will gain the ring. Here too he stands apart; the cupidity in the ring breeds betrayal even when father and son share a mutual end. For Alberich is clearly not up-to-date, and Hagen has made no attempt to tell him that what he desires is already in motion, that his shadow-brother, though defying dragon and Wotan head-on, can be manipulated from behind. Hagen works what his father desires; but for no one's benefit save his own.

Twilight had begun with a re-creation of the opening of *Rhinegold*. Now comes a second, a dawn over the Rhine which, like the dawn dissolving the remnants of the Norns when their rope broke, dissolves the memory of Alberich, making the colloquy seem like Hagen's dream before the day that will see the fruition of his plans. This 'dawn-chorus' evokes the opening of *Rhinegold* by sonority and texture; over a B♭ pedal a flowing canon for the eight horns rises, with a new thematic contour that provides material for the first part of the main action.

Most of the other Act II music is familiar, but the curse motif undergoes a striking evolution. Hitherto it had been the quintessential 'musical thing'; now its separate elements, so tightly locked into each other, pull apart and go against each other, the musical grammarian in Wagner working with the dramatist to elicit the full extent of its latent power. Hagen's set-piece summoning the Gibichung vassals shows soon enough the enormous musical charge released when the curse is detonated. His uncouth epic jocularity stems on the surface from his saturnine humour ('Glad times have come to our Rhine, / when Hagen, / grim Hagen, / with laughter can shine!') and underneath from his satisfaction at the speed with which his purpose is ripening. Having seen to it that Brünnhilde is already wronged, he can vindicate the deed that he does for his own interest as if it were a communal good. 'Honour your lady, / come to her aid; / if she is wronged, / you must revenge her.'

These dark strains are temporarily forgotten in the magnificent chorus of welcome, its B♭ major answering the B♭ minor of the Hagen/Alberich scene just as the E♭ major of Brünnhilde, Siegfried and the Rhine illuminated the Norns' E♭ minor in the Prologue to Act I. Those who remember Brünnhilde's vulnerability after her first rapture of awakening in *Siegfried* Act III will catch its momentary reappearance here as she stands mute, with eyes downcast, between the first huge burst of greeting and Gunther's ceremonial words. After a second blast of vassals, Gunther continues in warm, florid periods somewhat reminiscent of old Nuremberg, culminating in the four names of the participants in the double wedding. Last comes Siegfried, and Brünnhilde is galvanised. A motif first heard in the wretched manoeuvres at the end of Act I, then worried in and out of Alberich's anxiety at the start of this act, now assumes great prominence for the rest of the action. She nearly faints—'My eyes grow dim ... ' and Siegfried, who once kissed them awake, rushes to support her. She looks into his face, as when he was disguised by the Tarnhelm; he betrays no recognition; but on his finger she recognises what betrays him—'Ha! The ring— / upon his hand! / He ... Siegfried?' (and its curse rises in the orchestra). 'Now mark her words', says Hagen when the squalid and inexplicable muddle is exposed. To music first heard in *Rhinegold* as Alberich conceived the curse, which then returns as, having uttered it, he spells out its inevitable consequences, she presses her bewilderment—'A ring I see / upon *your* hand; / that ring was stolen, / it was taken / seized by *him*! / So how did *you* gain / that ring from *his* hand?' Siegfried remains unperturbed: 'absorbed in distant thoughts while contemplating the ring', his fuddled memory permits a beautiful glimpse into his past, when he fought the dragon and gained the ring—briefly the gold motif is heard pure as the time of his boyish valour is recalled. Then, in a fine motif-pun, Hagen takes the 'dragon' tritone away from territory where Siegfried might remember too much, and forces confusion into confrontation: 'Brünnhilde, are you sure / you recognise the ring? / For if it is Gunther's ring, / then Siegfried is false to his friend; / he must pay then for his treachery!' He is premature; even if true this would be too petty a misdeed to justify to the onlookers the vengeance he wants; he cannot understand that Brünnhilde's betrayal is on a higher plane than a wrangle for a ring. She cries out to the gods at the outrage (Hagen's version of the Rhinegold cry ([6] again), and the ubiquitous ring motif itself)—let them teach her such vengeance as never was, let her heart be broken, so long as he who broke it atones.

A sudden phrase of conventional rant, cadencing a paragraph of high inspiration, occurs as she makes her cataclysmic announcement that she is already Siegfried's wife. This creaking flaw is soon forgotten in the battle of wits that now begins. It is her words against his; the details of their night together emerge; Gunther realises the extent of his shame if she is not refuted; Gutrune, Siegfried's; the men take up the cry to resolve it by oath. 'Which of you warriors will lend me his spear?' asks Siegfried. This is now the right moment for Hagen; the killer and his weapon are ready for the hero to confirm his unknowing falseness and assure his own death. This vital moment in the plot is not articulated by the music as a great turning-point like Hagen's first greeting to Siegfried in Act I—which, we now realise, is powerful enough to reverberate on to the moment of its fulfilment in Act III. Here the pace is so fast that we sail straight into the next set-piece: rival oaths sworn on Hagen's willing spear. Siegfried says 'If I am to be slain for treachery, let this be the weapon.' Brünnhilde says 'Let this be the weapon by whose point he dies, for he has broken all his vows.' Their vocal contours are almost identical but the rhythmic values differ greatly, and her orchestra, as well as a fierce Valkyrie fizzing, produces an echoing trumpet-line only hinted at before. Her version expands, and finally she sings more than he, and more vehemently. He is merely drugged; but she has lost everything worth having and can only desire his death. Now they have both uttered this thought, Hagen only needs to work it round to word, then deed. The crazed intensity of the whole scene erupts as the men call upon the gods' thunder to drown the disgrace. This diffuses the turmoil; Siegfried manages to pass the events off lightly, promising a good outcome and leading everyone off to the wedding-feast.

The curse, silent since Brünnhilde saw the ring on the wrong hand, closes a scene of maximum turbulence with architectural punctuality, as if to guarantee that it governs what has been witnessed and what will now follow. Hagen, Gunther and Brünnhilde join forces to activate it (the ring is still on Siegfried's finger as he carouses nearby). Even at the height of the turmoil Brünnhilde was able to unscramble part of the confusion; now her mother-wit shows her further that Siegfried was disguised, that Hagen was somehow responsible, that Gutrune was the bait. But this partial realisation only exacerbates, and Hagen is able to elicit from her rage and grief what her love would never admit: that Siegfried can be struck down from the back. Another vital hinge in the mechanism, this time not sailed over, but instead deliberately underplayed and even contradicted. For the music here recalls him as the 'child of delight' from their duet in *Siegfried* Act III —

— and the love music from the Prologue of *Twilight*; her pride in his courage that will never turn its back to a foe is the first intimation that by the end of the work her love for him will have ousted her hate. These ambiguities do not interest Hagen, who now has all he needs—'My spear knows where to strike!'—and turns to the next item, taunting Gunther till he too will acquiesce. Brünnhilde also rounds upon him. His cry for help in an anguish of shame at last provokes the *words* for what has been fixed by the music since Hagen hailed Siegfried with the curse. *Siegfried's Death*, Wagner's earliest title, remains a more accurate focus upon the work's central event than the mythological distancing of his final choice. Hagen dares utter them; Gunther dully questions; Brünnhilde flares up in confirmation—'So the death of one / now must content me: / Siegfried's death / atones for his crime, and yours!' So Hagen has to tempt Gunther with the ring. Gunther sighs over his new blood-brother's fate and his sister's unhappiness, but the curse's poison ('all who see it shall desire it, and it shall give them no joy') quickly works. Brünnhilde, thus reminded of the poor creature, spits out her hatred of Gutrune; Hagen devises the details of how Siegfried may plausibly be killed; and when Gunther next speaks he has agreed—'It shall be so! / Siegfried dies!' All three sing together to their various gods of their common aim; Gunther and Brünnhilde to Wotan that he witness the broken oath and the just revenge, Hagen to the lord of the Nibelungs that the oppressed race shall soon once more obey their ring-master. The music is a riot of the new material in Acts I and II, especially the two oaths, that of the first act as prominent as that of the second, permeated by the dissonance released by splitting the curse motif. When the smouldering trio yields to the marriage festivities that end the act, this split creates its most powerful effect since the vassals were summoned; the C major triad of its fifth bar makes loud specious merriment, but its tonic and dominant are assaulted simultaneously with tritonal and semitonal clashes from F♯ and D♭—Alberich and Hagen uniting to overthrow consonance and stability.

Act III is based entirely upon familiar material and, as the work moves towards its end, explicit evocation of its past increases, amounting in one instance to a section of pure repetition, though wonderfully recast for its new context. Almost at once, after Siegfried's and the Gibichungs' hunting-horns have resounded from all sides and the curse harmony has recalled the hunt's secret purpose, comes the third and most direct return to the start of

Rhinegold; eight horns rise from the depths in canon on their fundamental notes, crowned in the tenth bar by the Rhinegold cry in its freshest diatonic form. What had originally taken 113 pages of orchestral score is here encapsulated in fifteen bars! When the Rhine music resumes after a further salvo of horn-calls, it is different, coloured by delicate, melancholy chromaticism as the girls sing of the dark waters that were once bright with their gold. They cheer up at the prospect of the hero who will restore the ring, knowing who he is and that he is near. As his horn sounds closer they dive down to take counsel, and Siegfried appears on the bank, puzzled, led astray by an elusive quarry. The gold's feckless guardians reappear, and it is clear from their words that they have arranged the encounter. They try to tease him into giving them the ring, but fail; he refuses them what they long for too much. Left alone he reflects—they had called him miserly, teased him for being too answerable to his wife; he takes off the ring, holds it high, and calls to them that they can have it. But they also have changed their tactics; he can keep it, and taste the ill fate that it carries. Unafraid, he returns it to his finger, asking them to tell what they know. And now their solemn warnings are useless; no more than they could tease it can they force it from him, though they screech his name to Hagen's piercing version of the Rhinegold cry. They tell him what we know so well but he not at all. Singing the curse in unison they become portentous as Norns, and when he is not swayed they almost turn into their faded sisters, reproducing, to frighten him, first Erda's warning from *Rhinegold,* then the Norns' web of fate. Siegfried is contemptuous and superb—'My sword once shattered a spear; if a curse is woven into the web of fate, I'll cut the Norns asunder!' This accidental reference to a point where his memory is blocked elicits from the still-callow Siegfried, who has only the day before rushed into false relations and sold his true wife up the river, a moment of reflective gravity: 'Though Fafner once warned me / to flee the curse / yet he could not teach me to fear. / The world's wealth / I could win me by this ring: / for a glance of love / I would exchange it; / if you had smiled the ring would be yours. / But you threatened my limbs and my life: / now though the ring / had no worth at all, / you'd still not get it from me. / My limbs and my life!—/ See! So freely I'd fling it away!' (as he 'picks up a clod of earth, holds it high over his head, and throws it away behind him').

By their ill-judged babbling, the Rhinemaidens have lost their treasure all over again when it was so close to home. Their consternation at his astonishing words shows that, for all their prescience, they have not foreseen the outcome their behaviour has ensured, though they know what will happen after he has decided so wrongly. But is he wrong? It is not clear whether this is a moment of supreme freedom for Siegfried, or whether he is still bound, for all his brave words, in the web of fate. The rules of the story say that he is not free to return the gold; the ring is not yet cleansed, and he who wears it carries its curse. But Siegfried, uninterested in the ring's limitless powers, using it only as a love-pledge for Brünnhilde, is untouched by the causes that animated the curse. And it is not until this scene that he has ever understood what he was playing with. Fafner told him of the curse as he died by it, but

Siegfried was hot from the fight and longing to learn from the dying creature only about himself. The woodbird told him that the ring would make him master of the world. Neither dragon nor bird connected ring with curse; and when Siegfried emerged from the cave bearing ring and Tarnhelm on the bird's advice, one of the most beautiful passages in the cycle described his regret that these pretty toys were useless in teaching him to fear.[1]

The truth is that Siegfried's guilt with regard to the ring is of a different kind from everyone else's. He has never desired the power and wealth it bestows. On the contrary he is 'the world's treasure' who makes power and wealth seem paltry. But he has wrested it by force from the woman to whom he gave it freely as the symbol of their love, and so negated that love. Where Siegfried is concerned, the intertwined curse and ring come to *mean* something different. What Alberich had renounced to get the gold, Siegfried had placed in the gold; what Alberich had 'sublimated' shines forth in Siegfried as pure libido. The gold has Siegfried's life-force within it; the ring freely given is his loving virility, the ring forcibly wrested destroys both Brünnhilde and himself. The scene where he teases the Rhinemaidens with the gold makes a titillating echo of these high themes. In this way the curse applies to a hero who, although innocent of greed, is inherently vulnerable. Hagen knew his man's weakness before Brünnhilde confessed to his unprotected back, when he induced Siegfried to desire Gutrune. 'Dayspring mishandled cometh not again.' The ring comes to stand for what in Siegfried can so readily betray Brünnhilde.[2] It is therefore accursed for him too, and Alberich's words on it must still come true: 'To death he is fated, doomed by the curse on the ring!' (The symbolism of the ring and its curse is at its most complex here, so Wagner, sound realist that he is, ensures that for once the object itself can be seen quite clearly by everyone, on stage and in the theatre!)

Moreover it would be out of character for Siegfried to give the ring back to the Rhine. It would be weak, prudent, ignoble, rather than impetuous, youthful, proud. Alternatively, it would be more 'grown-up' than Siegfried has shown himself so recently to be. He is still something of a bold booby like Parsifal at his first appearance, with a long journey towards full humanity before him, cut off almost before it has begun. That it *has* begun, this vacillation over the ring and the gravity that underlies the bravado of his words attest. Though overflowing with life (especially on this his last day) he seems not to mind dying, and will of course face it fearlessly. 'I value myself little and freely fling away this valueless thing'—there is profound complexity in the image-cluster of the 'finger's-worth' of his life: the ring on his finger, the

---

[1] When we remember what *did* teach him fear we realise that this is a delicate moment in the mechanism, as well as the meaning, of *Twilight* as a whole. If Siegfried can recall breaking Wotan's spear, why not also what he was so impatient to reach when the spear barred his way to it? Perhaps, the main deception-work being done, his memory is beginning to return even before it is prompted.

[2] And Brünnhilde recognises this too: 'Gutrune is the magic that rapt my man away.'

life-force in the ring, the clod of earth that like himself he can freely cast into extinction, and the gold that, whatever it means, he holds up high yet does not fling away. Irrespective of what he now chooses to decide with the Rhinemaidens, his death is already sealed: the oaths on Hagen's spear, the trio with the declared aim of Siegfried's death, and assassin, weapon and occasion all worked out. There is moreover a death-premonition and acquiescence in Siegfried himself that resonates remarkably with the wider course of the cycle as a whole.[3] It is the death-wish of the unmorbid animal in full flush of youth and spirits: a fair animal hunted by a black shadow that finds the one place which is weak, soft, rotten, connected with what first taught fear—'My spear knows where to strike!'—and how to bait his trap.

The answer from the *music* is that this is not one of the work's secret but mighty hinges. It is certainly dense and elliptical in its combination of leit-motifs: Siegfried's most complex musical moment, in striking contrast to the directness of the narrative in the following scene. His words to the Rhine-maidens are best taken as generous overflow, like his still grander bravado, still closer to death, when the wine he drinks with his murderers spills over onto the earth and he hails the universal mother—that earth which he threw over his shoulder and into which his blood will soon soak in a still more generous libation. Ardent, abundant, glorious even when technically both traitor and dupe, he amply justifies Brünnhilde's final exoneration of his heroism.

Apart from this, what would become of the rest of the story if he returned the gold to the Rhinemaidens? And Brünnhilde? He is caught in the mesh of past and future, as he is caught in the flaws of his own character. Still a mix-ture of Rhinemaidens and old Norns, the girls thrash the waters in violent agitation, seeing present ('He thinks he is wise, / he thinks he is strong, / but he's stupid and blind as a child!') and future ('your ring returns to Brünn-hilde, / by her, our prayer will be heard') for what they are and will be. 'To her!' they cry in turn, their last intelligible syllables. Suddenly the music turns radiant and stable again; they sing their perennial *Weialala* tinged with *Twilight* melancholy, but fresh as if they had not a care in the world. Sieg-fried too is happy. He smiles as he sings of the ways of women. Were it not for his troth to Gutrune he'd surely have enjoyed one of these delicious water-creatures! As their voices, then their music, disappear, the curse closes the scene with architectural punctiliousness, restoring 'Hagen harmony' [6], above which the Gibichung horns approach and Siegfried answers with his own. The next time we will hear the curse motif is the moment when Hagen strikes him down.

The hunting-party now joins him beside the river. The music is made of lusty diatonic materials—Gibichung music and Siegfried's horn-calls—presented with bucolic roughness; but its latent unease sounds in 'Hagen harmony' when Siegfried tells them that his death has been foretold for that very day. He alone remains blithe and genial.

---

[3] Compare his first salutation to the Gibichung king in Act I: 'my only birthright my sturdy limbs, consumed as I live my life'.

The course of *Twilight*, while moving fast through a new and complex story, has managed to bring before us the events and music of almost every salient part of the three preceding operas. Now comes the simplest and most wonderful return, of the long epoch when Brünnhilde was asleep; the boyhood of her deliverer, covering the action of the first two acts of *Siegfried*. It comes neither in the form of a web of allusion like the horns, nor a reiteration of old obsessions like Alberich; appropriately for Siegfried, it is pure narration. But his memory is blocked. We have heard him recall how he gained the ring, and that his sword once shattered a spear. Between these and beyond them his memory has to be prompted and stage by stage unlocked. A beautiful three-note motif—

— does this; it is Siegfried's *madeleine*, a horn motif, turning upon itself over tenderly shifting harmony, speaking of nostalgia for time lost, showing that this 'overjoyous' man of action, as Gunther calls him, begins again to reflect and look within himself as he had as a boy when his life lay still before him. Thus it is also the motif of his dawning awareness: as more of his experience is allowed, he possesses himself more fully; land reclaimed from the drugged past and understood for the first time. Finally he repossesses Brünnhilde too. He has grown again to his full stature, a man as great as the woman he awoke or the god he pushed aside. But by the same token this self repossession also means his death, since in his progress towards illumination he will inevitably reveal what will lead to his murder.

It begins simply. When Siegfried says lightly that some waterbirds have told him he will be killed today, Gunther and Hagen exchange dark looks. Hagen passes it off—'A cruel and evil hunt, / if the bear should get away, / and then a boar should kill you!'—and Siegfried passes on; 'I'm thirsty', and the memory motif makes its first appearance. Hagen prompts 'Can it be true you understand birdsong?' but Siegfried is not yet tempted; he boisterously exchanges drinking horns with his downcast blood-brother, mingles the wine so that his overflows, and dedicates the offering to mother-earth. Gunther gloomily calls him 'overjoyous'[4] and Siegfried jokes aside to Hagen that Brünnhilde must be causing trouble. Hagen keeps him to the point—'Her voice is not so clear / as the song of birds to you!' But Siegfried does not react; the memory motif as yet only recalls waterbirds and woodbird—'Since women have sung their songs to me, / I've cared for the birdsong no more.' Hagen and motif persist—'Yet once you knew it well?'—and though he does not immediately get what he pursues, his insistent hints surely contribute to the overflow when it comes.

---

[4] Compare also the way that all through Acts I and II the fire music has come to represent Siegfried as he burns himself into his life-force. Once he's conquered and possessed it (by traversing it to reach Brünnhilde) it becomes identified with his own fiery masculinity, which eventually burns him out ('consumed as I live my life').

Immediately, however, Siegfried attempts to enliven Gunther and the gloomy party with tales of his boyhood. Here there is no ban; his memory has been gently stirred, making it natural enough for him to begin at the beginning and continue till he can advance no further. The nostalgia motif turns its contour towards Mime's forging music as formal introduction. Once started, Siegfried moves quickly to recall the 'starling song' of the dwarf's self-pity at the boy's ingratitude, how he was reared to achieve Mime's ambition—to kill the dragon and gain the gold for him who couldn't, how he forged anew from its splinters his father's sword, how they found the place, and how with the sword he killed Fafner the foe. It is quite uncanny how Wagner in two pages of vocal score captures in fluent flashback the audible essence of enormous tracts of previous music. Now the pace slows. 'Now you must hear / what happened next: / wondrous things I can tell you.' They all return: the dragon's blood ('and when the blood / had but wetted my tongue', the motif is there, now on oboe and English horn, prompting both memory and understanding, hinting at the thematic contour of the sleeping woman, in anticipation of what cannot yet be *licitly* recalled); Mime's self-revealing plot, his death, and Siegfried's wondering possession of ring and Tarnhelm. Such is the spate of recall he has not needed prompting; he relives his past in the present, as if the bird spoke to him now or even spoke through him, making clear again things that have since become opaque. But after Mime's death there is the expected hiatus; Hagen's coarse jest ('unable to forge it, still he could feel it!', exactly reproducing his father's Nibelung-laughter at the moment the dwarf had been killed) nearly breaks the spell. Now two vassals take up the narrative—'What heard you then from the woodbird?' and again the *madeleine* (now restored to the French horn) gently insinuates its three notes and a very expressive fourth. It is this subtle musical elicitation that makes his access to the next events of his adventures so credible, rather than the mere mechanics of the new potion squeezed by Hagen into his wine. 'Drink first, hero, / from my horn. / I have here a noble drink; / let its freshening power wake your remembrance.' Siegfried looks deep into the horn and drinks slowly; the besottedness in Act I is audibly reversed; strangled sounds of Tarnhelm yield to a tender, infinitely remote memory of Brünnhilde, not as he first knew her in *Siegfried* but in their rapture at the start of *Twilight*. This tiny glimpse of the later work in what is otherwise a recall only of the earlier has an effect moving out of all proportion to its size.

He has freed himself to release what happened next. 'In grief I watched / the branches above'; the woodbird's comforting advice for his loneliness— the glorious bride sleeping surrounded by flames, and how she can be won— out it all comes. Once Brünnhilde's name is uttered, Gunther listens in horrified astonishment. Hagen's next cue ('and did you take / the woodbird's counsel?') is scarcely needed, for Siegfried's rapturous recollection cannot be curbed. It sweeps him over the edge of the second act of *Siegfried* into the third, and over Wagner's relinquishment of the work that left it suspended here some twelve years. 'Yes, I arose / and went on my way, / till I came to that fiery peak' (having touched upon it in the scene with the Rhinemaidens, he now obliterates altogether the episode with the Wanderer and his spear); 'I passed through those dangers, I found the maid ... / sleeping ... my glorious bride!' The excitement of the ascent, the long pages of utter stillness at the mountain-top, his bafflement, his fear at last, seeing a woman for the first time, his efforts to wake her, the fearful kiss with which he did so, and its eventual outcome—all this is compressed into three pages.

His conclusion ('Oh, then like burning fire I was held by lovely Brünn-hilde's arms!') takes us to the end of *Siegfried*, the consummation of the lovers' long and tortuous courtship, but leaves us musically poised upon the cadence that ends their duet just after Brünnhilde's awakening. Here the present intrudes for the second time. The first reminiscence from *Twilight* itself had been intimate, known only to Siegfried and played only by four clarinets; the second is public, violent, horrible. The cadence hangs in the air; Gunther springs up in horror; the harsh Hagen dissonance (hideously scored—eight stopped horns, low oboes, English horn, clarinets, a stab of four trombones, a blanket of strings) slithers up in parallel as the watchful ravens, knowing the moment, circle over Siegfried and fly off towards the river. He turns to follow their flight; Hagen, even here cracking a black joke ('and can you tell / what those ravens have said?'), thrusts his spear into his exposed back; and night begins to fall. The curse, silent since the end of the Rhinemaiden scene, is thrust harshly up against Hagen the manhunter. Siegfried swings his shield high as if to crush his shadow-brother; but his strength fails, and his motif ends on a dissonance, the same that crowned his ascent through the flames disguised as Gunther. That had collapsed onto the Tarnhelm motif, by which the disguise was done; now there is no more deception, it is 'Siegfried, no other' who is felled, and his motif falls onto the rhythm that will dominate his funeral music—

[10]

—heard here four times as its anticipatory upbeat. Hagen turns calmly away and walks off through the twilight, having answered the vassals' appalled question with a snatch of the blood-brotherhood oath ('falsehood is punished'). The 'fate' motif sounds twice, separated by funeral-rhythm drum-taps, prophesying a passage still further ahead, in Brünnhilde's final scene. The sympathetic vassals and grief-stricken Gunther gather round to support the dying man. The intrusion of present horrors into rapt reliving of the past has lasted only thirty-two bars. Now Act III of *Siegfried* resumes.

The rate of recapitulation has become steadily slower—one and a half acts in two pages—the next events (bridging the *Tristan–Meistersinger* expedition) in three, slowing always towards the original broadness. After the thirty-two bars of violent action and shocked reaction, it broadens still further. Siegfried, continuing his tales of boyhood even as he expires, goes back to the most wonderful of all his adventures. As he 'opens his eyes radiantly', the music returns exactly to Brünnhilde's awakening gestures when *her* eyes were opened. Only the words are different, painfully intermittent as he struggles to hold the vision. The shortened repeat as she greeted sun, light, day, is not needed; thereafter the recall of the music is again total. At first the words are poignantly different: Brünnhilde's 'Long was my sleep; / but now I wake: / Who is the man / wakes me to life?' becomes Siegfried's 'Who has forced you / back to your sleep? / Who bound you in slumber again?' One crotchet's-worth of major triad *not* in *Siegfried* illuminates the pathos of his questions. In the next section, still musically identical, he dislocates his own former words: in life he had answered her question thus—'I have braved the dangers / blazing round your rock; / from your head I unclasped the helm; / Siegfried wakes you, / brings you to life.' In dying this becomes: 'Your bridegroom came, / to kiss you awake; / he frees you, again, / breaking your fetters. / He lives in Brünnhilde's love!' The third section, however, begins to elide as his strength ebbs. It begins identically, but whereas Brünnhilde, hailing gods, world, Erda, rose to a climax of glory, Siegfried gutters out —

— with their love motif declining all the way, and a more and more exquisitely tender version of the 'child of delight' (whose first appearance was as bright and fierce as the light they had welcomed together). 'Ah! See those eyes, / open for ever!' Though what has gone wrong and why he is struck down is never untangled for him, as he dies he too sees clearly; his deception, duplicity, treachery are washed away by the music. Siegfried's death (again we recall the emphasis of Wagner's first title) links two turning-points in the tetralogy: its hero's greatest moment when he wakens Brünnhilde, and his lowest when he has betrayed her and she has brought about his killing; they are united in the farthest-flung arc of memory-architecture ever achieved in music. Between them comes almost the entire action of *Twilight*, and only as the great span reaches its farthest extent do we see clearly why the work opens with the fusion of Brünnhilde's awakening, Siegfried's death, and the waters of the Rhine. The tetralogy's highest and lowest points are united here with what began *The Rhinegold* and what will end everything: the waters of the river, enclosing their gold, purged of its curse. Wagner's two titles fuse; *Siegfried's Death* intermeshes with the *Twilight of the Gods*.

The funeral music is recapitulation of a different kind, working together many related motifs into a self-contained structure, a threnody in C minor marking the hero's passing, recalling his ancestry, celebrating him in both tonic and relative major, all hung upon the rhythm first heard just after he was toppled. Its early stages set out Siegfried's family-tree. This necessarily returns to the part of *Valkyrie* not yet revisited in *Twilight*, i.e. Act I. First comes the Volsungs' theme; during its second strain the moon illuminates the receding funeral procession, perhaps recalling the Volsungs' only moment of happiness, its spring dawning in the first act of *The Valkyrie*; then comes the theme of their destiny and the love music of Siegmund and Sieglinde, then a huge build-up to the apotheosis of their son, the Volsungs' noblest scion. All these themes are presented in diatonic splendour: his sword, in the C major inseparable from it since it first shone gently for Siegmund in the tree; Siegfried's own theme; then the grandiose elevation of his horn-call, confirming E♭ as his heroic resting-place, and forged into the rhythm of the tattoo which has also made the gigantic chordal flourishes separating his three themes. Tovey deplored this transformation as bombastic and forced; but it is surely, and appropriately, the boldest instance of an attribute becoming a person. The very crudeness of the transformation makes the contrast more telling as, in the subtle transition which follows, Siegfried's horn-call again represents the living man in Gutrune's frightened imagination, while the procession returns with his corpse.

This change of scene is punctuated by the curse, in close conjunction with Hagen's version of the Rhinegold cry. Our dazed attention is drawn to *things* again; the gold and its curse still lie on Siegfried's finger. We hear the curse only three times more. The first is almost immediate: Gunther and Hagen squabble over possession of the ring (recalling Fasolt and Fafner, Mime and Alberich); Gunther is killed, Hagen claims his own from the dead hand but the whole arm rises threateningly, and at this moment Brünnhilde, absent from all this pettiness, comes forward to take control. She has been in communion with the Rhine and its maidens: they have reached her as they said they would, and completed the information Waltraute gave her when telling her what to do with the ring.

Her final scene is the most important and elaborate area of developing recapitulation in *Twilight*; to untwist every strand and relate it to its origins would involve revisiting most of the tetralogy. Everything she knows is here; what she does not, we have heard again from those who do. In the spacious opening paragraph, introduced with fate motif and drumbeats from the silence after Siegfried's death-blow (which recalls the solemn portents when she appeared to announce Siegmund's death), she calls upon the vassals to raise a pyre upon which she will also die. That this music grows directly out of the Norns' scene in the prologue and Waltraute's narration in Act I makes a purposeful identification of the two final fires, here and at Valhalla. Lofty command yields to intimacy as she contemplates Siegfried's body and puts the paradox of the truest friend and lover who yet broke his oaths and betrayed his love as never before. The third stage resolves the paradox; to music taken directly from Erda's denunciation of Wotan's falsehood in the last act of *Siegfried*, she tells him, through the attendant ravens, that she now understands clearly how it came to be, how it had to be so; and to music taken directly from her scene with Waltraute (with one sublime addition) she dispatches the ravens with the god's repose vouchsafed him at last.

The curse has been heard here for the second time since Siegfried's death, but its power is nearly gone. Just for a little longer she holds the accursed object, drawing the ring off the dead man's finger and reflecting on what it has done—'I claim my inheritance—accursed ring—I grasp your gold, and cast you away'—word and deed for which the whole work has waited. Only once has anyone wanted other than to keep it, and the other times it has been yielded are both recalled here: Wotan, with intense reluctance and only when compelled by a *dea ex machina*; and Siegfried himself, who gave it willingly to Brünnhilde with an ardour conspicuously unmarked by the curse motif, but who then couldn't part with it quite so easily to the Rhinemaidens, in that crucial scene which makes a clear parallel with what Brünnhilde does now. As she dons it again, it is clean. She is not a victim of the curse; her action is voluntary, for the benefit of all as well as herself. The fire will consume her lover's dead and her living body; from its ashes the river-daughters will claim their own and guard it better. She knows that when she ignites the pyre, Loge will start the bigger blaze that marks the end of the gods. The ravens have stayed to see the first brand cast, before flying off to the Valkyrie rock to summon Loge for the congenial task of razing Valhalla. They thus miss Brünnhilde's final ecstasy, the reunion with Siegfried in a consummatory blaze of his theme, her Valkyrie music and the motif of 'redemption by love'.

The curse is active to the end for those who think in its terms. Cupidity still drives Hagen. As the Rhine rises to receive its gold, the curse and Rhinegold cry fuse for a final embrace as he lunges wildly after the Rhine-maidens and is dragged to his death, shadow following substance to the last. The maddened waters, having extinguished the earthly fire, return to their bed, and the girls are seen playing with their trinket. The gold and the curse have counterpointed each other throughout *Twilight* because their meaning is intertwined; the waters have been ravished of their treasure which thereby becomes unclean; its restoration to them cleanses it and restores what is right. But this apparently simple act involves a complex tangle, every thread of which has to be sorted out. As part of this an old order has to disappear, and now comes the second fire, promised by the Norns, rehearsed by Waltraute, implicit in Loge's final words in *Rhinegold*—the destruction of Valhalla. Its music is intercut with lilting strains of primordial river music, and the apotheosis of love and womanhood swells warmly above. Just before the flames seize upon the gods themselves, Siegfried's theme rises up for the last time; then as flames obscure them, their end, *the* end, the twilight of the gods itself, makes a vast neapolitan cadence onto all that remains—the eternal feminine in the skies, the clear golden river beneath, and, perhaps, Alberich in its depths awaiting for ever his next opportunity.

8

Experiencing music and imagery
in *Parsifal*

Contributed to the Royal Opera House / English National Opera guide to the work, edited by Nicholas John (1986).

* * *

Parsifal is the supreme instance of music-drama realised by means of a sonorous image-cluster: a central complex of metaphor expresses at once the story and the characters whose story it is, and the broader subject-matter that lies within character and event; all this is caught or borne by the music, everything fusing together into an indivisible whole. There is nothing like it in any other composer; indeed the only comparison is with the relationship of plot and character with verbal imagery in mature Shakespearian tragedy.

The sonorous image-cluster grows from the more direct though not necessarily simple leitmotivic usage in *The Ring*. It is special to *Tristan* and *Parsifal* and can more easily be described in the earlier work. All the central material in *Tristan* is manifestly related to the melody, chord, progression of the opening. Its unmissable recurrences, carefully placed at hinges in the story which are also crucial in expression of both subject and psychological theme, project local meaning into large-scale aural architecture. For each further reference to the opening recalls and includes those before, requiring the listener to remember and compare, to make intelligible and therefore to interpret, its ever-wider-ramifying implications. The opening also generates endless detail that gradually aligns itself and merges with material at first apparently quite distinct. And so it can eventually gather together the whole enormous span, being at once its outer limits, its principal junctions, and its core. It is not a leitmotif; its use is far too rich and pervasive to be named. It is all-comprehending—what the work is made of and what it is about. The sonorous image-cluster is the nucleus that gives life to the work's expressive and musical substance.

This, together with the altogether different *Meistersinger*-technique of building huge diatonic paragraphs that unfold quasi-polyphonically on a minimum of leitmotivic material, is *Parsifal*'s starting point. In some ways it is simpler, as if after the overwhelming abundance and complexity of the last four acts of *The Ring* Wagner is not so much returning to basics (though there is an element of this) as refining and quintessentialising all his discoveries, concentrated in a chalice rather than spilling forth from a cornucopia. Indeed this final simplicity can sometimes seem calculated to *demonstrate*, as well as to explore, a close area of tight interconnections. Every character in *Parsifal* can be identified by a thematic tag as if we were back in *Rhinegold*. Hearing a major triad with added sixth (i), or a minor triad with strong augmented colouration (ii) we know at once who is meant and how they are related. Have the minor triad rise rather than fall, diminish then expand its fifth, and a whole physiognomy and psychology come instantly to mind (iii). Take the same phrase but lower the octave from the third note and continue in sequence (iv) and we have an equally recognisable character, related significantly to the one before.

Such demonstrativeness might seem like a reversion to the earliest phase of leitmotivic technique. But *Tristan* has intervened, where the lovers are merged into the central sonorous image to such a point of cross-identity (even interchangeability) as neither to possess, nor to need, individual themes. And what is new to *Parsifal* is the small differentiation of the character-tags. The motifs just shown are for the four principal characters—Parsifal, Amfortas, Kundry, Klingsor—but what they have in common is as important as what makes them distinct.

Their common ground lies ultimately in their relation to the six-bar melody whose quadruple statement so unforgettably opens the entire work.

First it comes in the major [1] in subtly-scored unison, and is at once reiterated, surrounded by a fleecy nimbus of repeated chords and arpeggios, trailing off into the heights. After a long pause the melody returns in the minor, rhythmically, intervallically and orchestrally intensified; again the fully-scored and harmonised presentation follows and disappears into silence. This wonderfully fertile melodic shape, in its diatonic and chromatic versions, gathers in or gives out all the central material of the work. In the major mode it is sometimes used complete, as during Communion in Act I, and can be broadened into the sweeping melodic arcs of the choruses that follow. All the motifs bracketed within [1] are in play throughout (the version of (a) reserved for two moments of special fulfilment is important enough to be called [2]). And this major-mode version also contains the multitude of simple diatonic fragments that make up the work's imagery of goodness, innocence, holiness, purity in nature and in the human heart: from the Dresden Amen—

—the motifs of dove

, swan

(borrowed from *Lohengrin*)

, and Monsalvat bells

, to the music of Nature's healing in Act I—

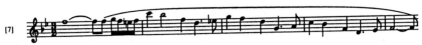

—and its full flowering in the Good Friday baptism—

—and meadows—

—in Act III; from the most gigantic diatonic sound in the whole work, the long-sustained alternations of tonic and dominant in the whole orchestra when Parsifal is crowned Lord of the Grail, to the serene terraces of consonance upon which it closes.

All these interconnections are summarised in the following slightly tongue-in-cheek ideogram (which puts all the music into the work's opening and closing key of A♭ for ease of comparison). It can be read left to right for musical line and story-line; and up and down for the vertical parallels that support the sense one has when listening that all this material is made out of the same diatonic shapes.

The Dresden Amen

and the Opening Theme (climactic version) for the

Baptism

of

Parsifal,

in the

Good Friday Meadows,

près de

Monsalvat

built upon the

Rock of Ages

(silent role – and often lost to sight and sound)

The minor-mode or chromatic version of the opening melody is more a source from which grows, rather than a synthesis of, the work's imagery of guilt, suffering and the uncleanness that yearns for purification and redemption.

[10]

Amfortas' theme is made from (x) inverted followed by (y) the right way up (given here in C and simplified to facilitate comparison—and see also the continuation of ii from p.54):

[11]

Kundry's theme

[12]

derives from a conflation of the first bar with the chromatic intensification of the second; while the dissonant harmony associated with her uncouth laughter is taken from the crucial chord in Amfortas' theme (its third bar), spelling out by sonorous means the connection that binds them. Klingsor's theme

[13]

is a further filling-out of the Kundry-shape, as shown more simply in iii and iv (p.54); and many other chromatic motifs and fragments associated with guilt and suffering derive from the same fertile six bars of the prelude.

The major and minor versions of the opening ([1] and [10]), taken together, focus the sense that the whole enormous work is mainly made out of a surprisingly small web of closely-related motifs not very greatly distinct from each other. This would seem to make the central core a contrast, or series of connected contrasts, set up in the basic musical material itself, which embodies those in the story and its characters: between purity and impurity, innocence (or 'foolishness') and guilt, chastity and carnality, spiritual health and spiritual sickness, selfless compassionate suffering for others and suffering that indulges its torment in remorse and self-pity. Not that these contrasts are peripheral, or that their presentation is in any way muted. I have rather diagrammatically indicated their raw musical constituents; in the opera itself they are rendered with an immediacy that raises psychological excruciation to a pitch unlikely to be surpassed in a work on this scale. But beyond this it is Wagner's extraordinary achievement in *Parsifal* to show the oppositions that apparently make up his very subject-matter to be deeply interfused and interdependent, utterly ambiguous, in the end not opposed after all. From this fusion at the centre, and the sonorous imagery that embodies it in music, spring story and character, music and meaning, reaching outwards to the work's extremes of differentiation. The nucleus is more than a dynamic equilibrium of tensions: it is reconciliation and accord.

On a straightforward level the apparent opposites begin to meet and mingle from the very start of Gurnemanz's narration. These early stages of Act I, sometimes held to be monotonous even by those who admire *Parsifal* 'once it gets going', seem to me one of the summits of Wagner's art (all the more so for being so little a set-piece), unrolling with an apparent randomness that conceals the utmost mastery all the prior events and all the thematic relationships that will be needed to follow action and music when they advance into the present.

After the vast diatonic spaces evoked by the prelude and, when the curtain rises, the still more motionless morning prayer that seems to close the work before it has begun, comes the first intimation (as Gurnemanz falls into his narrative) of Amfortas and his never-ceasing pain, and a hint of the prophecy of the innocent fool who will heal it. The first flicker of faster music, describing Kundry's wild ride, is built out of her driving ostinato rhythm and culminates in the piercing discord and plunging descent of her laughter. This temporary momentum and volume collapse into soft stasis as in exhaustion she delivers the balsam to ease the man whose suffering she has caused. (So far, then, vast diatonic calm with little scuds and flurries of the disturbances to come.) Amfortas is borne in on his litter, and the earlier intimations of his music grow into a big slow paragraph combining the chromatic music of his pain-racked exhaustion with the pentatonic evocation of the waters that might quench it. He takes further the hint of a prophesied deliverance, but it still remains incomplete and he equates its fulfilment with death. Enquiring the origin of the balsam he actually talks with Kundry, thus bringing his music of pain into proximity with her painful laughter as she spurns his thanks and hurries him off to temporary assuagement, for which the pentatonic strains take over again. (Does Amfortas know who she is and how he encountered her before? Gurnemanz obviously does not; and Kundry obviously *does*—her silent presence throughout this exposition, being who she is, having done what she has done, is a powerful part of its total effect.)

The young squires talk ill of her as she lies on the ground like a troubled beast. Gurnemanz's sober reproof uses only what of hers we have heard already, the driving rhythm and the laughter, to describe further her paradoxical impulses of humility and hatred. Their querulousness subsides into questioning: by now a sufficient base of information has been unobtrusively divulged for him to embark on the almost casual reminiscences that their questions elicit. And only now, as he describes how Titurel found her in deathly sleep when the castle of the Grail was built, do we hear her actual motif for the first time. The narration alludes in passing to 'the evil one over the mountains', neither naming him nor giving him his theme. Kundry's contact with him is still as unknown to us as it will forever remain to Gurnemanz, which makes an unbearable irony when he addresses her directly—'Where were *you* then / When by our Lord the spear was lost?' (to a full exposition of her theme, together with the chord and plunge of her laughter).

First mention of the spear and its loss signals a return to fragments of motif from the opening melody of the prelude. As the tale turns towards Amfortas and his fall the now completely familiar Kundry theme is much in evidence: listening, we make the connection that is painfully well-known to one person on stage—if not at the first time of hearing, then (with hindsight) at every subsequent one. Gurnemanz's description of the fatal far-distant kiss casts a long look forward towards the kiss we will actually witness in Act II, upon which the entire story and music are centred. Both kisses are made with a powerful pun by which the upward semitone in Kundry's motif is dwelt upon, intensified, and transformed into the motif from bars 2–3 of the opening melody:

Fleshly pleasure audibly turns to fleshly anguish as, at the moment of delight, Klingsor (now named for the first time) seized the spear from its neglectful guardian, pierced his side and escaped with it, laughing.

The evil one's name is dropped rapidly and in passing. The third squire catches it and uses it to prompt the old man into more story. But here the present impinges again: Amfortas' litter bears him back from lake to castle; as it passes offstage the music of sickness and healing is briefly encapsulated. Our interest, caught before because we saw him and because the music carried such a weight of unexplained suffering, is now heightened by the narrative's interruption at such a point, even though we do not now see him again. Gurnemanz, after asking how the King fares, falls into sad brooding over the past. But the third boy insists upon knowing about Klingsor. The answer is at first oblique, consisting instead of an account of something still further back, Titurel's vision that led to the erection of the sanctuary to guard the sacred relics, spear and chalice, and the foundation of the Knighthood of the Grail. This is set to an enormous paragraph interwoven *à la Meistersinger* out of the Dresden Amen—hitherto always separated from the musical flow and, anyway, not heard since the offstage brass that extended the prelude beyond its ending into the stillness of the morning prayer, the opening melody and the chorale-like music that evokes the vision. Only after this, the most continuous movement heard since the curtain rose, makes a full Amen-close does Gurnemanz get round to answering. (We learn to enjoy the affection as well as the art which employs throughout the whole narration an old man's dogged slowness that gets around to everything eventually, but in its own good time.) Now, as he tells fully the story of Klingsor, the moment has at last come to hear his motif. We learn of his longing to achieve holiness; how it was denied him because he could not deaden his lusts; his drastic self-mutilation that gained mastery over magical powers able to win what his failed sanctity never could, lordship of the relics; of the perfumed garden of earthly delights (again a vignette of forepleasure that will blossom for us in full actuality as an intermezzo on the journey towards the kiss that has been already anticipated); of Amfortas' expedition, armed with the spear, to raze the evil place over the mountains.

What there became of it and him has already been recounted; the narration peters out in gloomy inconclusion. But we are nearly up-to-date, and this (Gurnemanz continues) is how things stand: Klingsor holds the spear and the means to seduce the guardian knights into gaining him the Grail too. (Kundry listens to all this mingling of sacred and profane in a writhing fury of agitation.) The deadlock is illustrated with a full exposure of Klingsor's motif. But a gleam of hope survives in another vision, vouchsafed to the guilty lord himself, and built upon the 'Amen', at first in tortuous chromatic distortions that clarify into complete diatonic purity for the return of the opening melody (major mode) with a beautiful enharmonic change on its climactic note. The prophecy of the chaste fool made wise by pity, twice hinted at, is now repeated by Gurnemanz with its hitherto unheard second half (which comes complete in only one other place, at the end of Amfortas' monologue just before the Grail is revealed and the sacraments consecrated). Its already-known first half is taken up by the four squires; the pregnant stillness is interrupted by cries of outrage, the flight of the wounded swan, and the precipitate entry of the prophecy's unlikely embodiment, not named for a long time yet and not recognised for far longer, though his motif rings out brave and clear. And so the action of the opera begins.

This remarkable exposition has presented the work's opposite musical poles in subtle alternation and shown them to be, at the very least, highly interdependent. But the nucleus where opposites are fused has still not been reached. It comes in the extraordinary sound that summons up *Parsifal* to anyone who has ever heard it, as surely as *Tristan* is summoned up by its opening bars—the work's central sonorous image as heard thrice in the transformation music that shifts the scene from forest exterior to the interior of the sanctuary:

This music is not even thematic, let alone leitmotivic. It comes as a slab of orchestral texture, of processional movement, of harmonic suspension, that puts the bowels into heat. Or, technically speaking, it is simply a segment of sequence, indefinitely extensible and indestructible and useful—musical material in the abstract, like something baroque.[1] It is baroque also in its *Affekt*—a conventional icon of weeping and sighing, weighed down with grief, thrust against a mighty bass that bears its load gladly and if not checked will pound on for ever round the cycle of fifths. Together these two functions produce the central sonorous image of *Parsifal*: the baroque *Affekt* that burns expression into sound, making a symbol actual, that then gathers up ever more resonance by altered contexts and further associations until it achieves a satiety of expressive utterance, while the baroque usefulness of this sturdy material that can do anything and go anywhere provides a norm of continuity and cadence that can be extended all the way from local *frisson* to large-scale structure. The combination is powerful enough to carry the complex and contradictory meaning of the whole work.

Here is how this overwhelming plangent final result grows, via a few hypothetical intervening stages, from the opening melody. Its minor version ([10]) placed a new emphasis on the penultimate bar—it is sharper in rhythm and more dynamic in volume, being turned towards a second climax on the low B♮ rather than the dying away of the major mode version. It is this

---

[1] Compare two places in Contrapunctus XI from *The Art of Fugue* where, known to Wagner or not, Bach has hit upon the same sonority and sequence—bars 118–19 and more particularly 142–5.

penultimate bar that contains the seed of the sound that surfaces in the transformation music. The major version, in A♭, ended on its third, C; the chromatic version, in C minor, ends on its tonic, C; the sense implicit even in this unharmonised line that the last bar might, after all, cadence into A♭ is the kernel:

This colouration of an interrupted cadence where both bass and third move up a semitone to resolve, but not together, making a rich major-minor poignancy, becomes the norm of resolution for the whole work.

It has already been fully discovered in the closing stages of the prelude, where a series of sequences grows from the expiring end of the opening melody in a pattern whose prototype might be

Three possible stages in its growth towards full complexity might be below— though of course there is nothing so formulaic as these, and what Wagner

actually *does* do towards the close of the prelude, and then in the earlier stages of the transformation music before this material reveals its full power, is worth looking at with these crude prototypes in mind.

The surest way to give meaning to this music that works above all by intense unspecificness, is to take it first at its most explicit and then follow it back and forward into the different contexts that extend its range. It breaks out with Amfortas' words when, the company assembled, Titurel asks to see the Grail again before he dies. Guilt and suffering are the keywords here; at its next appearance Amfortas tells of the 'unequalled punishment borne by the tormented Lord of mercy', and at its next, of the spear that 'inflicted the sacred wound / In pity's holiest yearning'. This sound can thus conflate Amfortas' pain-racked guilt with Christ's guiltless agony. That it is not just private to Amfortas we have already heard when the knights' procession used the same music in turning from solemn festive diatonicism over the bells' ostinato, to allude to the Redeemer's blood-sacrifice for sinful mankind. This in turn is a mere echo of its huge use in the triple climax of the trans-formation, where sinful mankind *en masse* treads the same sequential steps weighed down with the same groaning burden.

Later, as the Eucharist is celebrated despite Amfortas' attempts to stop it ('How radiant God's greeting today!'—another instance of Wagner's grandiose slow-motion irony), the sonorous image returns in a mystic shimmer as of sexuality transfigured into spirituality, which while still echoing its intensest and most visceral usages (all of them heard by Parsifal himself), takes us back to the final stages of the prelude (as the Communion itself had repeated its four-fold opening) where the sonority first grew into being. After the distribution of bread and wine the knights process diatonically from the hall, cleansed by the ceremony, leaving the disturbing music behind with Parsifal. Here it renders his puzzled incomprehension: Amfortas' suffering, and every-thing it contains, is refracted through Parsifal's ignorant and unconscious identification with it. When the sanctuary is empty save for the old man and the young fool, pure C major is reached, rudely interrupted by another use for the image, to accompany Parsifal's wordless answer (he can only repeat the convulsive clutch of hand over heart that first seized him when hearing Amfortas cry for mercy) to Gurnemanz's ill-humoured cross-examination. After Gurnemanz pushes him out as a goose the soft repetition of the prophecy tells us again that this is indeed the long-desired swan, and the music resumes its celestial C major with chorus and bells, in which the interruption seems scarcely to have happened.

From this catalogue of its occurrences in Act I we realise that the crucial sonorous image of *Parsifal* is quite different from its equivalent in *Tristan*. There it is the first, unforgettable music we hear, returning unmistakably at all the crucial places, and sublimely resolving at the end. In *Parsifal* the nucleus slowly comes into being; it has to be uncovered and found; though all-permeating it can disappear for long stretches, and its eventual course is gradual assuagement and elimination rather than a grand final integration. In Act II its increased versatility allows it to encompass and connect more and more meaning. It produces at the climax of the prelude an obscene parody of the Act I transformation for the comparable entry into Klingsor's anti-Grail castle, showing his impotent mockery of holiness to be imbued with a suffering of its own. In another guise it accompanies Kundry's ascent into wakefulness from the timeless void she inhabits when between two worlds; it accompanies her moan of 'Sehnen' ('longing') that Klingsor can only interpret sardonically. A little later she tells us, to the same strains, what it is she longs for—sleep, release, salvation. Her longing is already tinged with eroticism, for Klingsor has now galvanised her almost completely into her other role—at first unwillingly, then avidly, pitifully compliant—as seductress. Far further on, after the seduction has failed, her explanation to her victim/ victor of *why* she longs for sleep and release, the laughter at Christ on his cross that condemns her to wander the earth's surface down the centuries in crazed hilarity, is again set to the same musical image.

And, of course, it permeates Parsifal's outburst immediately after the kiss, realising its full baroque potential in a modern re-creation of the ritornello, the one stable element in the astonishing *mélange* of motifs that accompany his astonishing words (in bold where it is used).

PARSIFAL[2]

Amfortas!	Amfortas!
The Spear-wound! — The Spear-wound! —	Die Wunde! — Die Wunde! —
It burns here in my heart!	Sie brennt in meinem Herzen!
Oh! Torment! Torment!	**Oh! Klage! Klage!**
Fearfullest torment,	**Furchtbare Klage,**
the cry of anguish pierces my heart.	aus tiefstem Herzen schreit sie mir auf.
Oh! — Oh! —	Oh! — Oh! —
Keen anguish!	**Elender!**
Piteous sufferer!	**Jammervollster!**
The wound that I saw bleeding	Die Wunde seh ich bluten,
is bleeding now **in** me	nun blutet sie **in mir**!
Here — here!	**Hier — hier!**
No! No! Not the Spear-wound is it.	Nein! Nein! Nicht die Wunde ist es.
Freely the blood may stream from my side!	Fliesse ihr Blut in Strömen dahin!
Here, a flame in my heart!	Hier, im Herzen der Brand!
The yearning, the wild fearful yearning	Das Sehnen, das furchtbare Sehnen,
that fills my senses and holds them fast!	das alle Sinne mir fasst und zwingt!
Oh! — pain of loving!	**Oh! — Qual der Liebe!**
How all things tremble, quiver and shake	Wie Alles schauert, bebts und zuckt
in sinful, guilty yearning!	in sündigem Verlangen!

While Kundry stares at him in fear and wonder, Parsifal appears to fall wholly into a trance.
He continues calmly.

This gaze is fixed now on the holy Cup —	Es starrt der Blick dumpf auf das Heilsgefäss —
The sacred blood now glows:	Das heill'ge Blut erglüht:
redemption's rapture, sweet and mild,	**Erlösungswonne, göttlich mild,**
To every heart brings all its healing:	**durchzittert weithin alle Seelen:**
but here—in this heart will the pain not lessen.	nur hier—im Herzen will die Qual nicht weichen.
The Saviour's cry is stealing through me,	**Des Heilands Klage da vernehm'ich,**
lamenting, ah, lamenting	die Klage, ach die Klage
for the profaned sanctuary:	um das entweih'te heiligtum:
'Redeem me, rescue me	'Erlöse, rette mich
from hands defiled and guilty!'	aus schuldbefleckten Händen!'
Thus rang his lamentation,	So rief die Gottesklage
fearful, **loud, loud to my spirit.**	furchtbar **laut mir in die Seele.**
And I, a fool, a coward,	Und ich—der Tor, der Feige,
to childish deeds of daring fled away!	zu wilden Knabentaten floh ich hin!

---

[2] This uses Andrew Porter's translation rather than an absolutely literal version of the German.

He throws himself despairingly on his knees.

Redeemer! Saviour! Lord of grace!	**Erlöser! Heiland! Herr der Huld!**
Can I my sinful crime efface?	**Wie büss ich Sünder meine Schuld?**

In Act III, fitting the trajectory of the work as a whole, this central musical image is distanced; though what it represents is still unassuaged, its recurrences seem to echo from a remote past. Its overlapping interrupted cadences are first heard again as the mysterious black-armoured knight approaches, and are given their most beautiful treatment of all when Gurnemanz eventually recognises him and the spear he carries; the descending major thirds follow at once as, at the height of the pious old man's exaltation, Kundry is compelled to avert her gaze from what she recognises all-too-poignantly. It thrice shadows the Good Friday meadows as a brief reminder of sin and suffering long ago. The pastoral episode first emerges from its decline after Kundry is baptised; it returns as Gurnemanz tells of the Cross that this day perpetually memorialises (she was there), then recedes as he tells of the purification of nature effected by Christ's sacrifice; and is heard again at the pastoral's close, when Parsifal juxtaposes magic flowers of evil with natural flowers of good, chastely returns Kundry's kiss and absolves her of her curse—a ghost of what had once been the most powerful noise in the opera, soon to be succeeded by sounds from the still remoter past, the Monsalvat bells stealing across the meadows, not heard since Act I.

It remains ghost-like in Amfortas' second monologue; after the huge impact of the second transformation music and the communal outcry against him, it barely flickers into life just before his first words of exhausted sorrow. It is heard for the last time as the 'pure fool made wise by pity' touches the racked body of his predecessor and reunites spear with chalice: 'This holy weapon that has healed you / Upon its point fresh blood is flowing / And yearning to join the kindred fountain / That darkly in the Grail is glowing'.

So the central sonorous image in *Parsifal* is a sort of virus, that contaminates everything it touches, sates itself, and works its way out—more like a far more complex and loaded version of the curse motif in *The Ring* than the progression in *Tristan*, whose goal is its integration into the work's final cadence. And its use is so wide-ranging that what it eventually stands for would seem to be uncontainably contradictory. Its ubiquity and omnipurposefulness indicate more than the fusion of opposites: they show the fusion to express an experience of communal rather than individual import. The characters overlap; each is a version of the other, undergoing the same trial according to his lights. If the words and story are considered in isolation, this is explicit to the point of formula (which excites the pleasure of symbolists, allegorists and symmetry-lovers, and the disapproval of those who find such things manipulated and frigid). It is obvious that Klingsor is a spoilt Amfortas; that Kingsor's self-willed abstention mirrors Parsifal's involuntary temptation and restraint; that Parsifal relives Amfortas' adventure but emerges unscathed; and that Kundry is the unchanging instrument of their various progresses.

But, as always with Wagner, it is the musical realisation of such symmetries that saves them from stiffness, making them not merely more intelligible and interesting, but flexible, significant, profound beyond the power of unaided words. This is why these four principal characters' individuating motifs are less important than their interrelationship and common origin in the work's opening theme. This is why the work's central sonority, also growing out of the opening theme, impartially expresses them all, melting black/white, good/ bad, diatonic/chromatic into a fermenting elixir where truth resides, for all that the formal layout of the story itself, from the largest massing to the smallest details, is built around these stark polarities.[3]

The clearest indication that the principal characters overlap is the music of their main monologues. These are all fashioned from the same ingredients, and their identifying motifs, which in *The Ring* would be paramount, are scarcely present. To be sure, Amfortas' Act I monologue begins aria-like with his motif in the orchestra, to which he then sings his first two lines of verse [11]. But thereafter his own music is present in just two references, lasting four bars in all, the augmented-triad motif (see ii, p.54) that represented his pain as he was borne to the waters of the lake. The monologue is otherwise made of many contradictory motifs writhed together in desperate *mélange*— the Amen and the opening melody, Kundry's motif and Klingsor's that grows out of it, the dissonance and plunging descent of her laughter, and the ubiquitous ritornello of the basic sonorous image. In Klingsor's briefer passage of self-expression in the first scene of Act II, the first two lines are again sung to his own musical contour (though it is also Kundry's) and the rest is the mixture as before: Amfortas' augmented triad is used more here than by Amfortas himself, Kundry's laughter is given the spitting orchestral sharpness unique to this scene, one Amen is well-aimed at a dissonant rather than consonant climax, and the whole is framed by the basic sonority.

Parisfal's outburst upon being kissed uses neither his motif nor the prophecy that pertains to him. The kiss itself begins as an exact replica (though more solemnly prepared, richly-scored, and lingered-over) of the kiss between Kundry and Amfortas already described by Gurnemanz in Act I. But it goes horribly wrong. The memory of Amfortas' guilty agony comes between the youth and the woman, he clutches his heart as twice before and cries out the unforgotten name to an intensification of the unforgettable cry for mercy. Thereafter the music is a still wilder *mélange* of exactly the same ingredients again, thrown together in a rush of free-association that defies grammatical analysis even while it captures a psychological reaction with horrifying precision and the utmost intensity. At the end of Act I he had been dumbstruck and uncomprehending like a fool. Before, we had seen his first uncouth actions, his bashful gormlessness about his name and origins, and his dangerous vulnerability over his mother. And we have followed almost every step in his action since, from the boyish love of wild adventure that has

---

[3] As shown with fearful and fascinating symmetry in Wieland Wagner's *Parsifal-Cross*.

brought him to Klingsor's castle, and bloody encounter with Klingsor's knights (described by their master from his ramparts), to amorous encounter with Klingsor's girls (as enjoyed in sight and sound on stage) and seduction above and below the belt by a Kundry now young, beautiful and calling him by the name his mother once used. As she kisses him all this experience fuses: Wagner's power to yoke opposites in powerful symbiosis is never more daring than his hero's substitution of a burning in his side after such build-up to a burning somewhere else. The conflation of sexual excitement kindled by Kundry with the guilty compunction she had aroused for his mother's death produces a total identification with Amfortas and his torment. It is presented in an inextricable tangling of opposites—base and exalted, carnal and spiritual, painful and pleasurable[4]—that fuse into one overwhelming meaning-filled sound.

It is overwhelming also because we have been through it before and know its every element. All the music for the central characters' crucial places is made from the same cluster of motifs. It is a game with three chances. By the time Parsifal's turn comes round it is ours too. His version of the experience is incomparably more protracted and intensive than his predecessors'; it is indeed the main event in the opera. Every sign has indicated him to be the one who does not fail where the others failed, who breaks the pattern. But though he is clearly from the start the chosen one, he is not distinct and individual. As the music shows, he is a generality, a composite of his predecessors, a representative man, elected to carry our burden and undergo initiation into an understanding that connects and integrates high and low.

Parsifal the character may be of necessity something of an identikit or cut-out figure. *Parsifal* the opera is anything but; it is indeed quite unique. At its centre is an excruciatingly vivid exploration of the blackest and bloodiest places of carnal psychopathology and their intimate connection with every aspect of the personality. This is caught and expressed in the physical and psychological power of the work's sonorous imagery, fusing its subject and meaning into the musical materials from which it is made. This red-hot central matter burns its way out of the work; assuaged and eventually rendered harmless, it completely disappears. And in doing so, it puts right old wrongs; the goal of the work is restoration, refreshment, revivification.

So the *Bühnenweihfestspiel* is not so much an allegory of Everyman, nor a Passion-play, as a rite of purification. It is presented as something of gigantic significance and elevation, absolutely not normal or realistic. No one could exactly call it a comedy—and there is certainly no double-wedding in sight at the end, nor any intimation of generation even at Tamino level (let alone Papageno!)—yet the sense as the prophecy is fulfilled, the spear touches the wound and rejoins the chalice, and the music settles down into A♭, is very much that of 'happy ever after'.

---

[4] He has not forgotten Amfortas' words, nor their music, that he heard in Act I, when 'transfixed by rapturous and joyful pain' at the flow of sacred blood from Jesus' side and the sullied blood from his own.

Perhaps the work is best understood as a super charged fairy-tale. Klingsor, Amfortas and Parsifal—they are like the three wishes where only the third, restoring the *status quo ante*, gets it right; or the three sons, where only the youngest is wily (in this case dumb) enough to avoid his elders' mistakes and win the girl (in this case Grail). This is not so silly as it sounds. Concentration upon the liturgical element and the perfervid language of guilt and redemption that has from the start provoked on the one hand such derision and on the other such misplaced religiosity, tends to direct the communal hero along a *via dolorosa* or at least a pilgrim's progress. But a truer parallel is with Wagner's previous hero, Siegfried. It would be interesting and illuminating to open up the comparison between his pagan and his Christian paragons; for all the immense difference of context, manner, story and imagery, there is more in common between them than there is separation; and the principal adventure for both lies in their discovering who they are, and what they can do about it.

9

Humanising Wagner

How is anything new about Wagner possible? The most voluminous composer outside music—acres of theoretical, polemical, autobiographical writings, an estimated thirty volumes of letters, drafts of projects unrealised, as well as works completed—Wagner is also the centre of rivetting reminiscence, most notably the 2,000-odd pages of his wife Cosima's diary; and he has notoriously occasioned more commentary than any other artist.

Yet *Wagner Remembered* (Faber, 2000) manages to inflect the image. Within a chronological framework whose clarity is already a help in encompassing the volcanic life, its editor, Stewart Spencer, by intelligent selection, avoiding the hackneyed and coming up with some genuine *trouvailles*, has produced an impartial, fully rounded portrait—brief yet suggesting stature—in the words of family, friends (and foes), peers, colleagues, employees, disciples—of the most protean century's most protean creator.

Childhood traits—relish for spooks and japes, passionate love of nature, addiction to storytelling in paint, drama, words, music—permeate the adult. Whatever the depths scraped in his early career, particularly the cringing penury of the first Paris years 1839–42, Wagner's native boisterousness, volatility, madcap high spirits, survive intact, sweeping all before them when his fortunes turn. Despite its heavy programme of nationalist regeneration, and its upshot in colossal debts, the Bayreuth venture emerges infectiously from these pages as *adventure*. The sheer brio of fulfilling fantasies, solving problems, dressing up, playing parts, inform the most daring artistic gamble ever attempted.

That he was a born leader is shown most directly in accounts of his conducting; its complete control yet spontaneous fluidity rendered music's essence as never before. Such genius for getting what he wanted is attested in less obvious areas.

> How well he understood the art of spurring on his men, of getting his best work out of each one, of making every gesture, each expression, tell! These rehearsals convinced me that RW was not only the greatest dramatist of all time but also the greatest of directors, and a marvellous actor as well.

The organiser, the fundraiser, the solver of practical problems, are all exemplified in telling anecdote: 'Tears come into my eyes [recalls the movement-man for the Rhinemaidens in their underwater gambols] at the fact that it all worked, something which all of us (with the exception of W.) had doubted.'

Also the revolutionary, the theorist, the philosopher, the sage and the domestic paragon (a charming recollection from the family governess, a poignant one from the young Siegfried, aged fourteen, of the unforgettable day when Cosima played Schubert a few prescient moments before her husband's fatal seizure). And the wily man of money, 'a favourite subject with him' according to his publisher to whom he pointed out the lavish *objets d'art* in the Villa Wahnfried at Bayreuth: 'You like my new home?' (said the composer); 'God, if only you knew!' (and proceeds to give him a rundown of the parlous position).

Wagner the talker is well-represented, mesmerising believer and agnostic alike with the charisma of his readings, airing with torrential velocity his political, racial, social, cultural opinions—or, over a beer in a London chophouse, convulsing congenial compatriots with 'stories about the German Jews, told in their peculiar jargon'. Nor is Wagner the *composer* forgotten, with vivid glimpses into his wild yet methodical workshop.

And the man himself? In 1845 'slightly less than average height ... with staring eyes, pinched mouth, a curved nose, a strikingly broad and powerfully developed forehead and protruding chin'. Queen Victoria ten years on confirms with different emphasis '... short, very quiet[!], wears spectacles, and has a very finely developed forehead, a hooked nose, and projecting chin'.

And his apparel? The most vivid evocation dates from the second, equally disastrous Paris residence 1849–51: 'rigged out in a blue jacket with red frogging and a yellow smoking cap trimmed with green torsades' (changed after vamping through half of *Tannhäuser* for a yellow jacket highlighted in blue, capped with a red bonnet decorated with yellow braid). Beneath such garish externals the underwear had to be of silk because of the composer's susceptible skin condition. Later in life he was able to indulge fully the luxuriousness necessary for spirit as for body. His favourite milliner recalls her efforts for his private closet:

... the walls were lined in silk with relievo garlands all the way round. From the ceiling hung a wonderful lamp with a gentle beam. The whole floor was covered in heavy, exceptionally soft rugs in which your feet literally sank.

She did his boudoir in Vienna, again in Munich, again in Triebschen (Lucerne). No doubt Wahnfried was just as lavishly appointed. 'He was boundlessly affable,' she adds, and her bills were all paid, picked up by the bounty of King Ludwig of Bavaria.

Theirs are not the only happy voices in this book. By dozens of individual variegated touches, Wagner is humanised without being denigrated. Against all the odds this unattractive, unappealing man attracted and appealed. We are left with an abiding impression of his capacity to inspire not just self-sacrificial devotion, unwavering loyalty, unstinting work, but also life-enhancing astonishment, delight, fun—even humour of a sort—and, above all, love. 'The companionship of that great, era-making man was so fascinating that all who had the good fortune to be able to gaze upon him in the last few remaining years of his life agree that in him God created one of his greatest sons.'

10

Two on Bruckner

i *Short*

When the impossible question 'Who is your favourite composer?' comes up, my instant unthinking answer is 'Bruckner'. When compelled actually to think *why*, I'm at a loss for words. What can be said about music which in its every detail, whether normative or idiosyncratic, so exactly reaches the places that seek sustenance and irrigation; that discloses the potential heights that daily life never touches, even as it similarly plumbs the depths; that seems to say Carry On Living, the earth is firm, the heavens secure, God is good.

The centenary of his death this month (11 October 1996) tempts me to try. And Bruckner has never been more available. His standing in this country is at its zenith. Four of the symphonies were heard at this year's Proms, and Radio Three has launched into an admirably comprehensive series covering them all, in most of their puzzlingly complicated alternative versions. Yet not even this centenary has produced a complete cycle in the concert-hall; whereas the 1995 Proms covered virtually every note of Mahler without benefit of anniversary.

Perhaps linking their names, a commonplace before either composer was well known outside Austria, still bugs the older. They are polar opposites. Mahler is a Modern: from the sixties onwards the ambiguous friction of virtuosity, histrionics, hysteria, heartache, searing lyricism, nostalgia, undercutting irony has accorded with the *Zeitgeist* and moved into centre-consciousness. In characterising Bruckner every one of these words could be reversed. He has no hysteria or histrionics—whatever the psychopathology of the man (notorious in endlessly recycled anecdotage), the symphonies and sacred choral works that form the great bulk of his output are impersonal and non-self-expressive, monumentalised almost into implacability. And though he can convey angst, irrupting above all in the searing lyricism and still-startling dissonances of the Ninth Symphony, it is monumentalised. The pang of personal feeling is burnt out from them; their emotion is set in stone not in the deliberated manner of twentieth-century objectivity, *à la* Stravinsky, but because this is how they are. And there is absolutely no irony, no nostalgia, no world-weariness.

Nor, of course, virtuosity. He is utterly not a wizard or a showman. No one would now accuse Bruckner of deficiency in technique. Virtually every passage of every work bristles with his hard-won learning, displayed with naïve pride and open mastery. His singularities of structure and procedure—the stops and starts, the reiterations, the self-interruptions, the colossalism so repugnant to early hearers, not only those duty-bound to hostility (Like Brahms and his henchman Hanslick, who termed Bruckner 'a symphonic boa constrictor') but moving even the sympathetically disposed to make huge cuts in the composer's supposed better interests—all these are now understood, and valued as the very constituents of an astonishing originality which, overcoming outward diffidence, had no choice but to be Itself with a granitic inevitability that can still, for all its manifest mental power, be fairly called primitive.

Equally, there is no call now to 'correct' the wonderful orchestration, once routinely castigated as 'organistic'. An obvious resemblance remains in the way that ranks of woodwinds, strings and especially brass (in single families and as a full chorus) are juxtaposed in antiphony and combined in mass. But far more striking is the way he eschews mixing, concentrating instead upon bold naked purity of timbre, a sonorous ideal at the other end of the range from the Wagner orchestra to which he also owes so much.

The influence of Wagner can be misrepresented. That he didn't miss what he *needed* from Wagner, the audacity of theme, size, volume, space, harmony, is audible enough. What is not so often said is that, as with Wagner's orchestration, the use of what he took could hardly be more different from his hero's. *Chez* Wagner, the musical speech is nothing if not emotive. It raises the temperature for love, pain, yearning, baleful broodings, heroic exaltations, and all the rest. It is always libido-driven, erotic, even carnal. Bruckner takes over and indeed intensifies the language, but, like any self-expression, Eros and *Sehnsucht* are burnt out as if by the purging fires of the Holy Ghost. The contrast of musical imagery from below the belt and above the forehead propelling the story and subject of *Parsifal* so grossly that it can still sicken the unattuned admirer simply doesn't arise for the non-dramatic, non-psychological, essentially meditative and architectonic symphonist.

His true ancestor in both largest and smallest is that other quintessential Austrian, Schubert. Not, naturally, the Schubert of songs, nor even of such few atypical symphonies as the young Bruckner might have known. I've long been intrigued by a reference in Hans Redlich's pioneering Master Musicians study (*Bruckner and Mahler*, that eminently non-attached couple) saying that the nineteen-year-old rustic 'played Schubert's piano duets with Karoline Eberstaller, who had played them 20 years before [this is now 1843] with the composer himself'. For it is in these freest and most widely ranging of Schubert's works, written for the essentially private, intimate medium of the drawing-room, where the connecting links to Bruckner leap to ear and even to eye. Try the first movement of the *Grand Duo*, then the scherzo of the F minor Fantasy!

But not even Wagner is more imbued, in every phrase, than Schubert, with Eros and *Sehnsucht*! The clue to Bruckner's perfect chastity of expression even when, as a mature artist, he handles the most tumescent musical materials, can perhaps be found in the same paragraph from Redlich: 'On an old piano ... Bruckner practised Bach day in, day out.' And every town or village in the region had an organ in its church at which he mastered his impulses and learnt his nature.

ii Long

Fifty years ago, Bruckner and Mahler were virtually unknown to audiences outside their native Austria (save for their popularity in Holland), and could still be widely dismissed by the cognoscenti. They were bracketed together as symphonic mastodons, inordinate in length, loudness, portentousness and tedium. Such distance from the truth now seems unbelievable in itself. Mahler, the more variegated and seductive composer, in tune by the prescience of his electric nervous sensibility with the anxieties and confusion of modern times, came well ahead in the race: from the 1960s onwards, his music has swept the world like a great apocalyptic wave. Bruckner's present popularity, which will probably never be so extravagant, is possibly built on solider credentials. His high position is less dependent upon a particular phase of Zeitgeist. He is the tortoise who stays the course. As the Mahler wave now ebbs, the dry land of Bruckner emerges confirmed and defined.

Though they overlap both biographically and in some shared ancestry (Wagner, Schubert, Beethoven), they could not be more different as artistic types. And while the astonishing growth of Mahler's fame has been inseparable from the vehement and passionate inner life to which each song and symphony added a further instalment, Bruckner's œuvre—confined equally to a handful of genres (in his case, symphonies, religious choral music and one glorious string quintet)—is adamantine in its impersonality, never more freed from programmatic or self-expressive narrative than when he absurdly tried to claim its presence.

Indeed, it has always with Bruckner been exceptionally difficult to understand the discrepancy between 'the man who suffers and the mind that creates'; and harder yet to imagine what might be contained in the spaces between. These two books[1] assail the unknown with complementary means. The first is academic, a barrage of manuscript study, historical and technical perspective, hefty analyses relieved by a single slender glimpse of the composer's character and nothing whatsoever more broadly critical. The second concentrates upon personality and circumstances to a fault. A good fault, though, and well within the nature of a series which has already resulted in composite prose-snapshots of, *inter alia*, Mendelssohn, Ravel, Satie, Bartók that entertain more, even as they cast more light, than many a weightier effort.

Bruckner Studies gets off to a stolid start with a thorough haul through the multifarious revisions of the F minor Mass. After a biographical interlude come four interrelated historical chapters of no intrinsically musical concern

---

[1] *Bruckner Studies* (CUP, 1997); *Bruckner Remembered*, ed. Stephen Johnson (Faber, 1998).

—indeed, not about Bruckner as man and artist at all—but quite interesting as cultural and political contexts for this notoriously unworldly figure. The first places him within his lifetime against a backdrop of Viennese Wagneism. The other three explore his posthumous fate as compatriot of Hitler, who wanted to make the monastery of St Florian, the composer's spiritual home between choirboy years and ultimate interment there, into a special Foundation under his personal patronage.

Other highlights of these chapters are the speech by Goebbels demonstrating the legerdemain by which Bruckner was groomed for Nazi iconography, so much so as to fulfil the at first sight surprising claim that 'no other great artist of the past became so unconditionally and totally occupied by fascist ideology'. In evidence, an evocative photograph, risibly solemn, shows the Führer, cap humbly doffed, before the composer's bust on its elevation to the marble halls of the Regensburg Valhalla in 1937. More suggestive still is the brief account of the 'Dunkelkonzerte' phenomenon in wartime Vienna: the programmes were heard in darkness and religious silence, a deliberate exercise of patriotic and spiritual uplift in grim times; and always culminated in a Bruckner symphony.

Half-way between history and technicality comes a useful discussion of harmonic theory *chez* Josef Schalk, one of the two brothers who so freely 'corrected', with his own concurrence, Bruckner's alleged blunders, thereby, in substituting safe conventionalities for dangerous audacities, obscuring his true stature for several decades. The remaining four chapters are set in the lotus-lands of hard-going music analysis, all fetishistic gratification for all their slog. Simplest and least disheartening is the last, Joseph Kraus on 'Phrase rhythm in Bruckner's early orchestral Scherzi', not so dull as it sounds, and recognisably about what it says, covering in dogged detail the rhythmic play that gives, sometimes violently energetic life to the work of the young Bruckner, before being stultified by his own revisions or smoothed out into the bigger machines of his middle-to-late manner.

One would welcome, too, the affect-laden, sometimes openly emotive language of Timothy Jackson's sixty-eight-page 'Bruckner and Tragic Reversed Sonata Form', were it not so extravagant and silly. The inordinate length is the result of Schenkograms from Haydn and *Idomeneo*, via Cherubini and Beethoven, Brahms, Schubert, Liszt, dented with excitable exclamation marks at crucial corners. Bruckner's 'tragic reversed sonata form' (the finale of the seventh symphony—most unsatisfactory of his many disappointing last movements) appears only after forty-seven pages. But the wait wasn't worth it, nor the coda beyond Bruckner into Mahler, Sibelius, Schoenberg. This is seminar material, fine as a starting point for class discussion, tedious and redundant when 'written up' as a 'contribution to knowledge'.

The two remaining analytical chapters are still less readable. The mind jibs at the passionate intensity of such pseudo-scientific substitutes for the creative original. Warren Darcey ('Bruckner's Sonata Deformations') does it with words alone. His 'seven hermeneutic concepts' turn out to be new complications for straightforward old functions, and, when he gets going, the difficulties are compounded by tables of letters and numerals with never a note in sight. Behind this reader-hostility lies naivety so unguarded that one almost sympathises with the defences after all. 'The whole sonorous fabric [of the coda? the finale? the particular symphony? the *œuvre* as a whole?] may be interpreted, as statement of the inadequacy of merely human activity and the necessity of redemption from outside. And having uttered this statement of faith, Bruckner throws himself into the mercy of the silence that follows.' Perhaps Darcy has access to 'Dunkelkonzerte' unbeknown to the general music-lover.

Edward Laufer ('Aspects of Prolongation in the Ninth Symphony') invests his entire capital in visible notes symbolising audible sounds, page upon page of 'engineer's drawings', beautifully presented and so little devoid of detail (Schoenberg's famous complaint against Schenker's *Eroica*-gram, that all his favourite bits had been harassed into the small print, does not apply) as almost to substitute for the original score. Such intricate labour makes this chapter a masterpiece of perverse ingenuity. Its putative usefulness—to underline the supreme competence and inspiration with which in this work Bruckner composes—would be pre-empted anyway by listening with absorption to an adequate performance. But one's flicker of sympathy with Laufer as he toils to fill his sieve to the brim, is alienated when the feebleness of his basic impetus is uncovered—to see that Bruckner might be vindicated in Schenkerian terms, in the teeth of Schenker's denigration of Bruckner's 'defective' equipment; then to say that he should be thus vindicated; then to effect this noble aim. It amounts to pleading the cause of the Goddess of Dullness against an erring Pope. (For an analytic account of the Adagio from this work that truly illuminates its structure and processes see the brilliant diagrammatic précis by Derrick Puffett in *Music Analysis* 18/1, pp.5–99.)

All in all, then, *Bruckner Studies* represents state-of-the-art, spirit-of-the-age academic musicology in all its artistic and critical nullity. Fulsome tributes to the sublimity of this music would of course be otiose. But one has no sense that such reverence lies implicit within these 'studies'. The prevailing impression is, rather, that the wonderful body of work, with all its problems of text, dating, language, provides mere grist for dull ostentatious virtuoso 'études' leading towards conference-time, shelf-space, promotion. Though the intention is quite other, Bruckner is traduced here, a century after his death as he was in life.

The aforementioned biographical chapter is no exception. Elisabeth Maier tries hard to elicit an 'inner biography' from the composer's twenty-three surviving pocket diaries. Which, as one would expect, are completely inexpressive: neither the daily résumé of a Pepys, let alone the introspective searchings of a Woolf; simply engagement books jotting down appointments, times of classes, accounts, records of private devotions, in which the occasional red-letter-day, such as an interview with the Emperor, receives no special emphasis. She objects that the death of his mother 'is recorded in only two words'. Does she look to Bruckner, of all people, for a Proustian release of memory? The well-meaning crassness, subterranean throughout, surfaces with the 'hermeneutic connection' between the unwonted entry in one of these engagement books of a quotation from a famous anatomist (a meaningless query concerning the location of the soul) and current work on the Ninth. 'In both cases we can detect existential questioning and wrestling with final statements.'

And so to the avowedly character-based anthology of recollections and pen-portraits made by Stephen Johnson, *Bruckner Remembered*. Here, too, though the absorption is this time intense, I have to register ultimate bafflement; Bruckner as man and artist remains unreadable. His life is notorious for a profusion of anecdotes emphasising the unlettered naif. Johnson claims to supersede this somewhat gormless figure with somebody 'complicated, sometimes tormented'. So most of the well-loved stories have disappeared. I miss especially Bruckner's exclamation on opening his eyes (preferring Bayreuth in the dark) to the closing scene of *Walküre*—'Why are they burning that woman?'—which, even if apocryphal, suggests so much with such economy. But the equally notorious aspects of morbidity and compulsion remain and are even enhanced in this collection. Positively twisted is the character that emerges from the account of an unholy fascination with a sex murderer. Bruckner avidly attended the trial (where his excitement embarrassed his well-wishers), failed in eager efforts to witness the execution, but succeeded for compensation in ordering from a restaurant close to the courthouse a schnitzel off the same veal that provided the murderer's last earthly meal—after which the composer stayed up all night to pray for his soul. Elsewhere, Johnson documents with plentiful illustration another trait straight out of *Psychopathia Sexualis* (first published 1886, between the Seventh and Eighth): the tragicomedy of Bruckner's indefatigable infatuations with young girls, often enough nearly resulting in marriage. One might ask, repressively, what light this shines on the music, only to be confuted in the simplest way: 'He was always ripe for infatuation and his emotions caught fire very quickly ... many melodic passages in the symphonies owe their inspiration to some pretty face that took his fancy'; or more directly, 'Come, sit down [he said to a beautiful sixteen-year-old whom he'd pursued around the town of St Florian], and I'll tell you about the Ninth.'

Everything, yet nothing, is 'explained' by such equations as these and, elsewhere, anecdotes recalling numerological and other fixations. Such a colossal drive to create will find a way, though the culverts be never so cracked, crooked, cramped, curious, crabbed. Another reminiscence makes quite clear what is anyway pretty evident, that, despite taking precautions in this late sixties against his wet dreams being found out, his physical chastity was unimpugned. And still there is no connection. E. M. Forster's little tag does not apply: the mind and the man, though certainly in communication, do not add up. Within a droll little oddity, girt about with textbook psychoses, lies one of the mightiest music-machines ever known. One has to leave it at that. Neither of these books can open the mystery, to which in a sense they are both irrelevant. But whereas the one is a bore as well—and, inasmuch as it substitutes for the works, bogus to boot—the other, on the man, is intriguing, piquant, compelling, deeply touching, for page after page of its modest length.

11

Two on Brahms

i *Love abideth foremost*

A reply to a Spectator *piece on the centenary of Brahms's death (April 1997) where Michael Kennedy mildly deplored the composer's 'ridiculous elevation to a Trinity with Bach and Beethoven'.*

* * *

Brahms's reputation is so secure as not to need the factitious advantage of an anniversary. Moreover, unlike Schubert, Bach, Mozart, his *œuvre* on the whole lacks nooks and crannies of fascinating unfamiliarity: only a handful of choral works and a majority of songs and partsongs remain relatively neglected. But he still has his surprises, and is certainly great enough to merit a second tribute in this month of the centenary of his death, especially since the angle is largely different.

Like Michael Kennedy (Arts, 22 March) I took a long, devious route to reach anything like a fair view. As an enthusiastic teenager drunk on Debussy, Mahler and modernism, I regarded the classics as simply boring. As teens turned to twenties, the classics marched in in full regimentals, followed by the metal-clad romantic heavies Bruckner and Wagner. Brahms had no place with either; he fell between the intellectual energy, social grace, physical vitality of classical Vienna and the mythological–heroic sublimity and sheer sonorous magnificence of his contemporaries. He appeared merely stodgy, muscle-bound, without wit, *brio* or charm; sentimental in expression when not, unconvincingly, uplifting.

To the stiff priggish Leavisite that I was, wholesale appropriation of Nietzsche's gibes—'he cannot exult'; he reveals 'the melancholy of impotence'—was all too easy. And I recall a spasm of genuine prudishness when first hearing the celebrated *Four Serious Songs*, the master's penultimate opus. The first three seemed dull brown as usual, but the last was positively offensive. It sets the famous passage from I Corinthians. First comes plenty of beefy twenty-fingered piano-writing, rendering tongues of men and angels, sounding brass and tinkling cymbal (etc.) with singular ineptness. Then when apostle and composer see through a glass darkly, looking forward to full face-to-face knowledge, the speed and mood change completely: over gentle piano ripples the voice swells out into a waltz melody whose character—oleaginous yet beery—becomes more and more pronounced, culminating in a saucy little barmaid twiddle in the final phrase. After briefly returning to full speed to set up the three cardinal virtues, Love (Charity) is awarded the palm to a return of the slow waltz, piano now crooning along with voice, oozing with unction—'the Grease of God'.

The callow ear, attuned to the neon-lit alienation of Mahler and Strauss's purposeful vulgarity, missed out on the tone of this typical passage of Brahms (written when both his juniors were getting into their stride). For him, strains of salon and beer-hall can express exaltation, idealism, piety, absolutely without irony. As the *jongleur* juggles before the Virgin because it's what he does naturally and best, so Brahms hymns Love in a waltz. He'd long before bound them together in two sets of *Liebeslieder-Waltzes*, composed for drawing-room pleasure and set (with one exception) to *vers-de-societé* of amorous triviality.

As an ex-chorister, I should have trusted appetite and scorned supercilious superiority. Like most cathedral choirs, mine did a few numbers from the agnostic master's *German Requiem*, unsuitably masquerading as Anglican anthems. All three were keenly relished, and they all contain waltzes. One, 'How Lovely Is Thy Dwelling Place', could go alongside the *Liebeslieder* in style though of course longer, more various and elaborated). It portrays the delights of the celestial mansions with unabashed worldliness—one seems to tread on carpets, sit on sofas, glance through the potted palms at Johann Strauss and his band—though strenuous counterpoint cannot be kept out of the middle section.

In the other two the waltz-nature is not explicit. Indeed, 'Behold All Flesh' is no dance, but a funeral march in triple-time. Yet a lilt gets in at the sighing figures later accompanying the words 'and lo, the grass withereth, and the flower thereof fadeth'. The central section, concerning the patient husbandman, is a gentler, subliminal *Liebeslied*-waltz. And then, after the march's full-scale return, the Lord's word blows away soldier-trudge or ballroom-lilt in a vigorous common-time fugue. But they return when the Last Trump sounds, again in triple-time after a spooky march ('Here on earth have we no abiding place'). It certainly doesn't sound like a waltz to start with, nor yet for 'Death where is thy sting?'; but when it reaches 'Hell, where is thy victory?' there's a hoofy lurch to the triple-time that brings connotations of rustic rather than urban dance-floors.

All this is by way of indicating that Brahms, though one of the safest pillars of concert-life, is by no means set in stone. Michael Kennedy is right to say 'routine Brahms is somehow worse than routine anybody else' (possibly routine Verdi, or a routine *Swan Lake*, can be worse still). The thick veil of classical sobriety and emotional reserve conceals some surprises. It is, of course, a metaphor: the disguising beard (actually grown quite late in life), the cigar, the coarseness, the brusque ill-humour with which he fended off interference and, possibly, the urges of Eros: in musical terms the muscular effortfulness, the unconcealed cerebration, the Old Masterishness. Beneath all this beats a maiden's tender heart, a vulnerable openness to feeling that, so often thwarted, dignifies without hardening over the decades into autumnal stoicism which, disdaining equally the consolations of religion and the high-noon apotheosis of Wagnerian redemption-by-love, can yet declare to strains of sublimated beer-hall that, of the three virtues, Love abideth foremost.

Paradoxically it was when young in years, and fully beardless, that his composition was most heaven-storming. One pities the audience, the piano and the pianist, when the three early sonatas are undertaken, let alone the colossal first concerto. But there is a magnificent bravado to the ambition here that later retreats as if it had singed its hands; and, in the concerto at least, the themes and their deployment are so inspired that what for Michael Kennedy is ham-tragedy inclines me sometimes to call it his greatest work. The First Symphony, originating in this period, completed in maturity, still reveals fissures that are not so much healed as evaded in its triumphalist finale. Other pieces athwart the same biographical fault-line resolve it with marvellous powers of integration—the Piano Quintet with its struggle to find the right format (the 'interim' two-piano version best realises the physical weight), and the Third Piano Quartet with its turbulent emotional resonances from Goethe's *Werther*—and in its inspired material and its fascinating handling, its absence of lapses, its perfect balance of medium and content to medium, by far the greatest..

And, meanwhile, the true Brahms, lyrical and Schubertian rather than Beethovenian and dynamic, had come into being; first in such enormous but non-barnstorming works as the other two piano quartets (though it's true that Schoenberg felt compelled to make his glorious Technicolor orchestration of the first because it was usually played so clumpingly); and then in the long catalogue of instrumental masterpieces both chamber and (once the First Symphony was out of the way) orchestral. And the point about the true Brahms is his ability to subsume the mental power and physical muscle—his heritage from the other two 'great Bs' from whom Michael Kennedy would detach him—into a stream of songfulness learnt from his two adored Schus (-bert and -mann). Brahms's formidable synthesis of B and B enabled him to achieve what neither Schu had managed—the wholly successful fusion of lyric song and structural argument.

Michael Kennedy and I are on the whole in happy accord over the heart of the matter, the corpus of mature masterpieces. Our ways part when he 'dares' to suggest that they are 'small-scale'. This is an illusion based upon mere duration and (in orchestral works) forces that by Bruckner/Wagner standards are relatively modest. Brahms's very different mightiness lies in his compression: these works are terse and compact in a way that abhors slack. This can sometimes result in crabbiness and impaction; far more often, one is left in astonished admiration at the distances covered, and the sense of songful expansiveness, within such brief lengths.

Mentioning song leads to my only serious disagreement. 'Sentiment in hob-nailed boots' is a grand phrase for van Gogh, but won't do for Brahms's songs at their frequent best. Surely 'Venus in furs' or 'Masoch in Sachertorte' would be nearer he truth?

For in this largest part of his output (one wouldn't credit it from the same old handful endlessly repeated in recitals and recordings), as in the precious late harvest of piano miniatures with which he withdrew from the world, Brahms the beardless is revealed with touching frankness. Sometimes it's direct—there's a song about a girl's rosy cheeks which almost brings a blush to one's own. More characteristic, however, is obliqueness, even evasion, under whose cover he can give voluptuousness, flirtatiousness, or longing and despair, or melancholy acquiescence in disappointment (a sort of written-out detumescence) their various voices.

This music could be called repressed were it not for juicy *jouissance* of the actual notes. For all his self-abnegation Brahms is almost visible in these densely sonorous yet delicate, elusive, ambiguous intimacies, with or without words. He yields nothing in confessional confidences to those composers who bare their privates in public as a way of life. Yet the mighty brainpower, suitably subtilised to work on the smallest scale, is still at work, in play. His treatment of the only high-calibre text in the *Liebeslieder,* its epilogue from Goethe, can crystallise everything. While the four voices sing its long arching lyric phrases, the accompaniment sets up a typically complex waltz *à deux temps* over that most intellectual of devices, a ground-bass, taken straight from the composer's most directly personal work, the *Alto Rhapsody,* whose text (also by Goethe) begs a merciful dispensation from the Father of Love to the misanthrope lost and alone in the barren wasteland.

I'm glad we no longer see Brahms as a Titan, and have overcome the temptation to decry him because our illusion has been exploded. What he actually is is so much more lovable, interesting, complex; and, in the end, great enough to put him up there with the Bs, Ss and Ws, not on their terms but on his own.

ii   A world of private meanings

This more serious piece was a response to academic studies whose Philistinism and pedantry (with honourable exceptions) are the real enemy.

*   *   *

What every lover of Brahms's music would like explained, unless they're happy simply to swim in it, is the particularity of what it is and how, why it is good, and how it produces its emotional effect. Universal questions; the answers specific to each composer should be an attainable goal. But if not, the attempt has perhaps the value of a Grail in inspiring adventurous voyages of discovery.

Take the Clarinet Trio op.114 as example. The score itself is a completely accurate notation (Brahms was an unusually scrupulous proofreader) of complex conventions by which the compositional organization of pitch and duration are transmitted as instructions to its three performers. The stringed instrument is the cello, maternal yet passionate in high tessitura, masculine, lyrical and powerful on the bass. The wind instrument is the clarinet, the most strongly characterised yet best able to blend, widest in compass and dynamic range, supplest in figuration, velvety in tone. The piano is the composer's own instrument, where all ten strong fingers (all twenty, as Clara once thought, hearing him practice from outside the room) exercise their tactile mastery of harmony and counterpoint.

This first of the last works is in places richer and darker in sonority than ever, but sometimes in the outer movements spare to the point of severity, even didactic, were technical mastery not so interfused with a lifetime's emotional utterance. In the middle movements, different lifelong aspects of the composer reign uninhibited: the slow movement's warmth, and the feline *Liebeslied-waltz* of the third with its rustic second trio—salon and farmyard faces of 'Fräulein Klarinette', as he called the instrument which seduced him out of premature retirement (after the Second String Quintet) into renewed creative life.

All such observations make a starting-point. From it come more fanciful ramifications of metaphor and intuition, things dreamt by the free-floating imagination while the ear concentrates, reveries entirely shaped by the music's nature and course. Two instances are Nietzsche's attribution to Brahms of impotent melancholy and the inability to exult, and the reaction of a six-year-old girl of my acquaintance to this same work, her face gloating with knowing delight—'knickers!'

Many such matters, from the most concrete to the most fugitive and subjective, mysteriously blossom when the players obey the exactly notated score to project Brahms's op.114 in actual time and acoustic space. Something stirs into being—the piece's purpose and meaning, its expressive existence. It is made out of the life of the person who wrote it: of course from his craft and from the particular *données* of this particular piece, but also from his physical person—brain, body, blood, memory, experience, feeling—the fusion of physiognomy and soul that is uniquely his own personal self and at the same time overlaps with communal human experience.

Responsible and sensitive exploration of the inseparability of 'the man who suffers and the mind that creates' is what one wants most from any book on music that is more than a simple chronicle. These two recent collections for the most part turn their efforts resolutely elsewhere, producing the usual unillumination, reducing a palpitating and chalorous artistic achievement to a further few inches of library-space, bibliography and renewed academic tenure. *Brahms and His World,* edited by Walter Frisch,[1] is the less acceptable. Under guise of 'reception and analysis', ancient writings that should for the most part be left to moulder are resuscitated (the exception, Tovey's essay on Joachim's *Hungarian Concerto,* is not especially relevant and can anyway be easily found in Volume Three of his programme notes).

A 'memoirs' section is inconsequential save for a few austere utterances remembered by Brahms's pupil Gustav Jenner. The new material ranges from journeyman (a study of Brahms's pianos) to frankly rudimentary (on Clara Schumann) or perverse (on the Third Symphony).

---

[1] Princeton, 1991.

The book is partially redeemed by its first two essays. Leon Botstein piquantly transforms the 'former' Brahms (boorish bachelor comforted by greed and deprivation, or, in artistic terms, stoic discipline sweetened with glutinous waltzes and autumnal melancholy) into a thoroughly modern man, poised between the physiology of Helmholtz, the physics of Einstein and the temporal speculation of Husserl. Peter Ostwald's study of 'Brahms the Solitary Altruist' (later, 'the Transitional') makes a welcome change from the nowadays routine invocation of 'Brahms the Progressive'. Both essays, scarcely top-notch, afford a glimpse of the creator's inner life. But there is no exploration of the 'other' Brahms that one knows to exist—the Brahms of eager acquiescence in Max Klinger's fascinatingly dreadful etchings inspired by his music, of ardent youthful romanticism via Schumann out of Hoffmann and Jean-Paul, gone rancid and weird beyond the dreams of the French, Belgian or Norwegian *fin de siècle,* the Brahms who is deathwards turned with purpose as grim as Tristan's wildest ravings, all this somehow compatible with an unwavering commitment to the musical language of German folksong and Viennese classics.

Nor is this to be found in *Brahms Studies,* edited by George Bozarth,[2] the belated result of a conference held for the composer's 150th birthday in 1983. There is modest sustenance here in the first two contributions, though career-analysts may find them belletristic. The opening address by the then eighty-four-year-old Karl Geiringer comes from the lost world of the composer's own culture. In unpretentious fashion it says by implication everything needed for background to the music itself. Christoph Wolff's exposition of conflicting ideas of historicism in Brahms and Wagner, though not entirely free of waffle, is also fundamentally civilised.

The wilder shores of phoniness are in fact only represented here by one contribution: John Rahn's 'D-Light Reflecting' refers to the key of the Second Symphony and the Violin Concerto. Aaron Copland might simply have said 'that sure makes a lot of Ds'; for Rahn it produces intellectual indigestion. A crass metaphor of D's edibility on his first page is followed on his next by jejune sprightliness in Plato's Cave, and on the next by galumphing play with 'holistic' examination of the 'elephant' of the two works' 'intermodulation'. Just as one thinks one's in for twenty more, the piece rushes to a premature climax in a clatter of Greek prefixes.

But the book's prevailing texture is pedestrian—undemanding tasks, worthily fulfilled. Right at the bottom comes a dull account of all Brahms's slow movements and an exceedingly futile piece on his edition of Schubert's dances (so he arranged them in a certain order!). Almost as feeble are dogged accounts of his early songs and a paper concerning the gathering of songs into opus-numbered groups. A long final essay on sonata form laboriously rehearses the already well known. Walter Frisch superfluously re-bars passages from the Piano Quintet and the A major Piano Quartet to demonstrate with complications what in the originals is perfectly lucid, as if the power of

---

[2] OUP, 1991.

syncopation were not felt by every listener whether or not he has heard the term.

Only three contributions are really worth reading. David Epstein on 'Brahms and the mechanisms of motion' provides a convincing study of related tempos within single movements (for example, both the overtures) and the complexities of *tactus* that unobtrusively relate and unite the diverse speeds and characters of the entire First Symphony. By means of substantive hard work Epstein earns the right to his closing remarks, simple but not crude, on the composer's secretive husbanding of his privacy. James Webster's contribution similarly appeals by its evidences of aesthetic evaluation amid the necessary fiddlesomeness of its tables and numbers. For he has measured the internal proportions of every sonata first movement in the *œuvre* from the op.51 quartets to the final clarinet sonatas, and by arranging the figures around a common standard is able to discuss the norms and deviations (of weight and treatment as well as of length) that one senses instinctively, while listening and particularly while playing, with a precise yardstick to refer to. The very facts thus revealed are in themselves suggestive. Handled with such sense and sensibility, this approach seems to me the only palpable advance in analytic description since the deceptive straightforwardness of Tovey (though by no means so graceful to read). Best and briefest, Charles Rosen's witty piece that, emerging from behind a mistaken key in an analysis by Dahlhaus of the Piano Rhapsody op.79 no.2, ends up with wide-ranging hints towards a subtler understanding of Brahms's simultaneous exploitation and subversion of the classical heritage he wore so heavily yet with such fitness.

Rosen is suggestive through intelligence, observation, compression. It is one of the long-winded drudges, none the less, who opens up the desirable wider view. Bozarth's essay on the poetic content (or 'suppressed vocalization') in the early piano sonatas, though turgid in itself, undoubtedly takes the bull by the horns and *interprets*. The fact that the results (see particularly the detailed programme for the F minor Sonata op.5) are raw does not mean that they are untrue.

Every sympathetically attuned lover of his music recognises that Brahms of all composers 'speaks in the language of music'. Later, the interdependence is as much more complex as the works themselves surpass op.5 in quality. This first clumsy attempt to translate should fire the ardour of scholars and commentators for greater accuracy, rather than their superciliousness and scorn. This endeavour is fraught with difficulty, but failure to make it is a failure of imagination and nerve. It is worth risking the obvious dangers of vagueness, gush, tastelessness and absurdity. The kind of apparently valuable work represented for the most part by such books as these is an evasion. Even when good of its kind, it fails to match up to the substance of its subject.

Brahms is all one, from the young artist convinced that even to conceive, let alone write, such a piece as Bach's D minor Chaconne would drive him mad with 'extreme excitement and emotional tension', to the early-old man who could pen such a piece as the Eb minor Intermezzo op.118/6, at once

abashed yet shameless in the unguardedness of its psychological and physiological self-portrait. His entire *œuvre* offers such points of entry. Behind the
impersonal lies confession, just as his angelic youthful face lay behind his
shapeless and aggressive beard. His music is as charged with implicit meanings, private but scarcely hidden, as Wagner's is with explicit meanings
brazenly trumpeted forth. In the refusal of the 'professionals' to talk about all
this, the familiar fable is reversed: we are given the emperor's robes only; it
is the man to whom they belong who has been erased.

12

Gingerbread artistry

Every musical child used to be taken to Engelbert Humperdinck's *Hansel and Gretel* for his or her first opera. I can recall after over thirty years the old Sadler's Wells production and Anna Pollak's Witch. I have never seen the piece since and am looking forward with childish anticipation to the same company's seasonal update of the hardy perennial in their present huge theatre.[1]

But what can present-day children think of it? Surely the Witch is no longer scary nor her gingerbread house seductive for those born to *Star Wars*, computer games and Indiana Jones? The pokerwork homeliness, the dream-pantomime of guardian angels, the Sandman and Dew Fairy, even the clapping game, the atmosphere so homely, cosy and cultured: all this must nowadays seem so remote as to be virtually incomprehensible.

Above all, the music's sheer complexity makes it seem suitable for adults only! Its combination of elaborate artistry with simple sentiment fascinates the musician. The score is wonderfully composed; and as a meeting-point and reconciliation of so many strains in Austro-German music its importance—indeed its greatness—is difficult to overstate. *Hansel* used to be called 'Wagner for beginners'. Humperdinck did indeed hail from the Bayreuth powerhouse. He was so closely involved with the first production of *Parsifal* in 1882 that when its Act III transformation music proved too short to cover the elaborate scenic effects devised to accompany it, he was given the job of padding it out in his Meister's voice.

Though his own fairy-tale opera is soaked in unmissable Wagnerisms, the paradox remains that *Hansel* is a key work in a tradition that avoids Wagner's radicalism altogether. This music flows from the well-springs of German diatonic folksong, both direct and as elaborated through Schubert, Weber, Mendelssohn, Schumann and Brahms, to end in the Mahler of *Das Knaben Wunderhorn* and the simpler aspects of Wolf, Strauss and Pfitzner. Two extremes of style mingle here in happy union. The first is lowbrow—for instance, the luscious waltz-tune that evokes the house of sweeties and the exuberant one for the Witch's downfall, which do a Johann Strauss *in excelsis* (nor was the message lost on Richard, who conducted *Hansel*'s première in 1893 and audibly never forgot it). The other is the 'sanctified' style, which

---

[1] The wonderfully inventive and moving production by David Pountney.

with less unaffected treatment can easily become sanctimonious. The closing phrase from the children's prayer, so sweet and demure in its piety, becomes merely bombastic and insincere as blown up in the Resurrection chorus of Mahler's Second Symphony.

Most obviously Wagnerian is the Witch scene, the only stretch that tends slightly to outstay its welcome. Its source is mainly in *Mastersingers,* where the same reservation applies, on an enormously larger scale. Wagner's comedy invents at a stroke the golden busyness without which *Hansel* wouldn't be possible. Dare I say that I believe Humperdinck's is the better composed of the two? Not just in the obvious superiority of its tunes (never Wagner's strong point, even here where he actually needs them), nor in its better balance between length and musical content, but above all in its degree of finish, the extraordinary high level of the craftmanship, that links him to Wagner's arch-enemy Brahms.

Hansel shows that Wagner can be well-written according to academic tenets that are far from stultified; that his harmony can be classicised, his orchestration rendered positively Dvořák-like in euphony; above all that the frequent uncouthness of Wagner's polyphonic leitmotivic coupling can be done with counterpoint so felicitous that one sometimes blinks in aural amazement. I yield to none in admiration for Wagner's achievement, the greatest of its kind; but one can see how, from the grammarian's point of view, he might be thought to have 'ruined the art of music', as well as, from another, to have tastelessly exploded music's expressive decorum. *Hansel and Gretel* provides an unlikely as well as a delightful resolution of the notorious rift between conservative and progressive in late nineteenth-century German music, and in doing so shows it to be factitious. Long before Schoenberg, with mighty labour and dubious consequences, reconciled Brahms and Wagner, Humperdinck's so-called children's opera had done the same with easy grace.

13

Unobtrusive conservative

Franz Schmidt is the most complete instance since J. S. Bach of a historically uninevitable great composer whose legitimacy is denied by the progressive party line. Born in Bratislava in 1874, the same year as Schoenberg (whose father came from the same city), he lived from his fifteenth year in Vienna, where he died fifty years ago last month [this piece appeared to mark this date, March 1989]. Together the two composers make a textbook illustration of complementary radical and conservative artistic types.

In middle life Schoenberg, his expressionist fervour spent, returned to the mainstream armed with his new twelve-tone technique, in the pious delusion that this was the chosen instrument of that mainstream's perpetuation. Schmidt had meanwhile continued composing as before and was now ready to fly high. The constituents of his mature style are unmistakable: the symphonies of his older contemporary Mahler and their common teacher Bruckner; the orchestral and chamber works of Brahms and, behind all three, rather than the tersely argued Beethoven, the ruminative lyric processes of Schubert's largest works. Schmidt was also an organist, linked via Reger to the endless fertility of Bach The leaven within this blameless pedigree is the Hungarian gipsy music—swaggering, gorgeous, opulent without turgidity— that appears somewhere or other in virtually everything he wrote..

It is not a large *œuvre*. There are two operas, *Notre Dame* and *Fredegundis*, whose lurid plots and sensual coloration are surprising in this musician of organ-loft and conservatoire until one remembers his fifteen years as cellist in the pit of the Vienna Hofoper. They are packed with marvellous things. The handful of organ works includes some gems but would not in itself suffice to keep his name alive in a wider sphere. His centre is the four symphonies and the strongly symphonic variations for orchestra on a Hungarian hussar song. These masterly and very varied pieces deserve to enhance the ever-diminishing run of standard classics still to be heard in concert-halls; and the Fourth Symphony, at least, appears to be breaking into this charmed circle.

The Book with Seven Seals, Schmidt's massive oratorio completed in 1937 to a text condensed from the Apocalypse, partakes of all these genres. It is symphonic in scope, baroque in its grand architectural fugues and its prominent solo organ part, and dramatic in depiction of successive world-engulfing cataclysms. Here the Hungarian flavour surfaces in an exultant

Hallelujah chorus just before the meditative close. His last work, finished by another hand, was a second oratorio, *Deutsche Auferstehung*, whose embarrassing text (ending with a resonant 'Sieg! heil!'), understandable in the circumstances, calls for a tactful whitewashing. But this composer's genius can be heard at its happiest in the three enormous piano quintets written for Paul Wittgenstein, one with strings, the other two adding a clarinet. Wittgenstein's disability (he lost his right arm in the First World War) compels a lucidity of sound unique in German chamber music with piano after Mendelssohn. The fusion of Brucknerian size, Mahlerian expression and Brahmsian texture is enlivened by a transparency more akin to Fauré. The result, whether elegiac, serene or sparkling, has a luminous ease and buoyancy, a molten honey quality, quite special to its composer, however explicit his sources and conservative his language.

Revolutionary achievement, if good, speaks for itself (though not always at once). It is much harder to estimate music of calibre that alters nothing. The rhetoric of our times, still hung up on romantic uniqueness and geared to 'making it new', tends to favour only the sharply distinct artistic profile. Yet the unobtrusive mastery with which Schmidt continues his inheritance will ensure him an important place as the music of the twentieth century is in retrospect better known and understood. Boulez, the voice of the undying avant-garde, proclaims in a recent interview that history will forget those composers who do not follow its dictates. But who wants to be remembered by *history*! Schmidt's music will come into its own when its power to give pleasure reaches those who are best endowed to receive it—everyone who loves the Viennese classics from Haydn to Mahler. And everyone else too (unless they're deaf).

14

Mahler's tragic friend

The single completed symphony by the obscure and tragic Hans Rott has recently been issued on an excellent Hyperion CD, no doubt its final resting-place. It is a fascinating document.

Rott, like his contemporary and close friend Mahler, was a favourite pupil of Bruckner at the Vienna Conservatoire in the late 1870s. The first movement of his Symphony was written in 1878 when he was twenty. In spite of official discouragement he went on to complete it by spring 1880 and that autumn played it over to Brahms. The not-so-old master (forty-seven that year) was so brutal that within a month Rott's delicate mental balance had collapsed. Enforcing at revolver point the extinction of a fellow-passenger's cigar he explained that through Brahms's malign cunning their train was packed with dynamite. The diagnosis after a year in an asylum was that 'his recovery is no longer to be expected'. He lived on into spring 1884.

Another friend and contemporary, Hugo Wolf, had already in early 1879 been cruelly snubbed by Brahms. Then in 1881 Mahler's teenage cantata *Das Klagende Lied* failed ignominiously to gain a prize from a committee on which Brahms was the luminary, a decision that, as Mahler saw it, sentenced him to the 'treadmill' of a conductor's career. Some twenty years after, now at the top of his profession (and well into his Fourth Symphony), Mahler re-read the score of Rott's Symphony with a view to including it in his Vienna Philharmonic concerts. His reaction was ardent. 'What music has lost in him is immeasurable.' Rott's juvenile Symphony soars to such heights as to make him the founder of the form as Mahler now understands it. 'His innermost nature is so much akin to mine that he and I are like two fruits from the same tree ... we would have had an infinite amount in common.' Thus Mahler to his confidante Natalie Bauer-Lechner, in the summer of 1900.

After hearing Rott's work their musical commonality seems more like appropriation than empathy. That summer Mahler completed his Fourth Symphony, whose first movement virtually reproduces one passage intact. But countless moments from the earlier symphonies show that in the intervening years his friend's work had sunk deep into his memory—the resemblances of Rott's scherzo to that in Mahler's *Resurrection* Symphony are only the most obvious. The influence is not confined to details: the astonishing originality of Rott's ways of filling out an hour-long symphonic canvas has not been lost. Nor does the resemblance cease after 1900. The best music in Rott, the elaborate slow introduction to his finale, constantly recalls its equivalent in Mahler's Sixth of 1904 and thence that of the unfinished Tenth of 1910, where some of these new ways of integrating and articulating a large structure achieve their boldest realisation. And Mahler's middle-period scherzos are even more 'Rottian' than ever.

Of course Rott's work is immature and sometimes downright callow. It too is 'full of quotations', most specifically from the chorale in Bruckner's Fifth and the finale tune from Brahms's First (itself—'as any ass can see', according to its blunt composer—derived from the joy theme in Beethoven's *Choral*); and the whole is swathed in Wagner—mystic shimmer, sounds of nature and a curious composite of festive exaltation from the *Siegfried* love duet and old Nuremberg. In spite of its high promise and occasional moments (even, in the scherzo, a whole movement) of genius, it does not yet show the ability to fuse and synthesise. Whereas Mahler's contemporaneous *Klagende Lied* is so utterly itself—himself, rather—that it cannot be called simply promising. The briefest excerpt from the first four symphonies and their adjacent songs so proclaims its composer that it is hard for us to understand how they could have been widely dismissed as 'conductor's music', even as Mahler's wide eclecticism becomes more apparent as the years go by.

Since Stravinsky brought it out of the closet such creative rapacity is (perhaps) better understood. Only the other day Thom Gunn was saying, 'Talent has to be remorseless in the way it gets its nourishment: it eats and runs.' Maybe his very avidity for his friend's work explains why Mahler failed to promote it after all. And we remember that Brahms himself was a greedy devourer of more than sardines, though presumably his beastliness to young composers stemmed from detestation of artistic tendencies quite unthreatening to his own achievement.

Meanwhile the actual *sound* of Rott's work—a 'Mahler symphony' before the event, but doomed to be heard for ever with hindsight—suggests two parallels, one sublime, one ridiculous. It recalls Mahler's Tenth in its half-realised sketchiness: a latent scheme of enormous scope is imperfectly embodied in music that, *chez* Rott, is simply not yet up to it, and, in the case of the mature master, has not yet been worked up to full compositional pitch. The other parallel recalls an aspect of the musical scene at Cambridge a few decades back. A well-placed official at one of the nearby US military bases was writing 'one-finger' Mahler symphonies which were transformed into the real thing by a fluent undergraduate, copied, and recorded by an orchestra of student performers. *Ersatz* Mahler, written with hindsight and knowingness, sounds astonishingly like the half-formed striving of his tragic friend exactly 100 years before. Except, that is, for the occasional touch of genius.

15

A Dutch Mahlerian

My first experience of the great Continental concert halls London so woe-
fully lacks was a visit to the Amsterdam Concertgebouw for an all-American
orchestral programme.[1] The whole structure vibrated to the massive onslaught
of Ruggles's *Sun Treader*, and the glistering knife-across-glass textures of
David Del Tredici's *Adventures Underground* seemed calculated to scrape the
gold-embossed names of old masters off the dowdy décor. Among those
names, Zweers, Dopper and Diepenbrock stood out for incongruity as well as
intrinsic oddness. I ignorantly mocked them as small-culture pieties of a
particular epoch—the equivalent might perhaps be Barnby, Parry and Bantock stencilled upon a frieze in the Albert Hall. I could not have foreseen the
intense pleasure that would a few years later be afforded by the music of one
of the funny Dutch names. Alfons Diepenbrock, thanks to some recent
recordings for Chandos by the Residentie orchestra of The Hague, has come
into focus as a distinct voice of singular beauty amidst the ebb and splurge
left in the wake of Wagner.

Distinction is hardest to recognise when the generalities of a style are
already well received. In renaissance polyphony, in baroque concertos and
classical symphonies, individuality is indistinguishable from convention,
even routine, except by excellence, that palpable but wordless *sine qua non*.
By now the same goes for the vernacular of late Romanticism where Diepenbrock belongs. When the idiom is so familiar the critic always tends to
describe resemblances rather than try to measure differences which, albeit
crucial, are often minute. Subtle inflections within well-known norms only
reveal themselves with repeated hearing.

Born in 1862, and thus coeval with his favourite Mahler and Debussy,
Diepenbrock made his living (he died in 1921) by teaching Latin and Greek.
Musically he was self-taught; his passion for composition rapidly won its
place, *primus inter pares* in a wide range of cultural, religious and political
involvements. Though only one work was published in his lifetime he was
performed, with recognition, and his music holds a distinguished place in his
native repertory, though making little headway beyond. A body of religious
choral music is central to his output. The *Missa in die festo* of 1891 sounds
intriguing in its attempted fusion of old Netherlands polyphony with late-

---

[1] See p.380.

romantic harmony (I imagine a cross between Bruckner's motets and the angel-dictated Mass in Pfitzner's *Palestrina*, but at once more cerebral and more juicy). This side of him is completely unknown to me; I can only go by what the records contain. On their evidence his purely instrumental work is attractive but not exactly arresting. The *Hymn* for violin and orchestra is wrought with mild sweetness in a style perilously close to Ketelby without the tunes. The music for *Marsyas* noodles amiably around somewhere between Delius's *Paradise Garden* and the sunburnt landscape and shaded hollows of Debussy's *Faun*. That for *Elektra* is miles removed from Strauss's shrieking score; it resembles more closely the restrained incidental music of Fauré and Sibelius.

I'm falling into the resemblance game. Diepenbrock's claim to substantiality rests upon a handful of orchestral songs which stand outside such facile parallels. Some are called *Hymn*, all are hymnic in manner—rapt and elevated—and symphonic in scope, the voice merging into the orchestra, which often takes over altogether for extended interludes and postludes. His poets are German romantics on the edge of mystical experience: Novalis and Hölderlin at the turn of the nineteenth century and their late re-echo in the dithyrambic side of Nietzsche. Night, darkness, self-abandonment, oceanic love-death-wish: these well-worn themes, so conducive to turgidity and afflatus as German romanticism passed its noon, receive in Diepenbrock's treatment an expression that refreshes them through delicacy and restraint. His orchestration in particular is astonishingly transparent—tempera not oil—with no loss of fullness. The combination can stand for the musical substance itself, a distillation from the idiom of the day that makes most of it seem rather gross.

This composer *believes* in the high romantic values of his texts, with all the fervour of his Catholic upbringing. His Nietzsche does not spit and rave; his Hölderlin achieves without friction a synthesis of Greek, Christian and pantheist; his Novalis draws back into itself the destructive blackness which had swollen into Tristan and Isolde's passion and Tristan's madness. The ecstasy is unruffled by agony; there is no doubt or *diablerie*, and the only irony is that the occasional false touches in one of the *Hymns* derive from a too-undigested reminiscence of Franck, the composer above all others of blameless religious faith! Everything is smooth, gentle and beautiful. So one is immediately wary of blandness and on the alert for the approved signs of disquiet. They are not to be found; the unearthly tranquillity remains perfectly still.

Difficulties in accepting this are all our fault. If a composition aims to be radiant and even, it behoves it to be so to the fullest extent its maker can make it; half-loveliness or mitigated calm would be feeble. The question of 'self-indulgence' on composer's or listeners' part—because Diepenbrock's music so wholly lacks abrasion—melts away with realising that this is the means whereby it is so true to itself.

16

Mahler 10

For reasons never divulged the editors of Tempo *rejected this review of the first publication of the Deryck Cooke realisation of Mahler's Unfinished Symphony (Faber / Associated Music Publishers, 1976) even after it had been set up in type, so this is its first appearance. The potted course of the genre after Beethoven and Schubert at the start does overlap with other writing reprinted here (albeit written later) but I've let it stand, first because a context for Mahler's last work is helpful, second because a longer account of Schumann and the symphony has not been included.*

* * *

Mahler's Tenth Symphony must be set in its long-term context and then in the immediate context of his own *œuvre* for full realisation of its importance.

The spacious background is the course of the symphony after its classical summation. Already before Beethoven's death Schubert, with a characteristic combination of tightness and looseness, gave the sonata a different emphasis, with melody and melodic-style development that would seem to contradict the classical idea altogether. That it does not is demonstrated by Brahms, who worked Schubert's new procedures back into the older procedure of motivic development. Bruckner however took the new expansion and tightness to their extreme. Whether he knew the Schubert works that so amazingly forecast his own forms is uncertain; his direct inspiration came from a profound saturation in the feeling as much as the actual workings of the greatest classical symphony, Beethoven's Ninth. Even in the composers who conserve the old forms there is much play with closer unification than the classical scheme ever needed, from simple linking which keeps the movements intact (Mendelssohn's *Scotch*) to a simple interpenetration of all four movements (Schumann's D minor symphony). There are motto themes (Schumann C major, Brahms 3); reproduction of one movement in another (Schumann C major, slow movement into finale) or transformation of one into another (Bruckner 5, scherzo and adagio); and thus the work that seems, explicitly or implicitly, to derive all its movements from a common source (Brahms 4, Bruckner's last three).

The non-conservers dissolve the classical symphony by more radical means. First, by programmes and unstaged dramas; these impure genres run from Berlioz and Liszt into the symphonic poem, which, after its extravagant apogee, is finally restored to its source in the two greatest specimens,

Falstaff and *Tapiola*, both written by masters of the symphony pure. More seriously undermining is the early romantic penchant for the miniature, and for joining miniatures together in a new kind of big form, one of context—the juxtaposition of mood and type. Nothing could be less compatible with the tonal developmental unity of the classics. But these works—the song and piano cycles of Schumann above all—are genuine unities, not just collections. Tchaikovsky's three ballets, on a much bigger scale and with the help of an explicit rather than a covert story, do just the same—build loose-knit but genuinely architectural structures out of a succession of self-contained lyrics and dances; his last three symphonies are at once programmatic, suite-like, and attempts at classical form. While Schumann never crossed the genres like these other composers, he is in detail a bolder dissolver of form than any before Wagner in the way the overall structure flows across double barlines, through the different tempos, keys and characters of the component parts.

Wagner of course enriches and complicates everything. After him a new texture appears in symphonic writing. The themes work together as they do in music-drama, and the forms enact a kind of abstract scenario whose high-points are like the exceptional moments in Wagner, where the main strands fuse or are forced together (the clearest example is Tristan's death). The normal leitmotivic texture will keep many themes in constant play, in a manner not mainly, or not at all, governed by classical procedure (the clearest examples here are Acts III of *Meistersinger* and II of *Götterdämmerung*).

Mahler's symphonies inherit all these developments, extend them, and mix and overlap the genres more boldly than anyone before. Thus there are suite or cycle-symphonies (a gathering together of contrasting, sometimes interrelated, movements)—1, 3, 5, 7, 9; programme symphonies (not so much outlining a plot as illustrating a poetically conceived idea)—2, 3, 4. All of them are 'episodes in the life of the artist' in a generalised sense; 1 and 6 are explicitly scenes from a spiritual autobiography like the later Tchaikovsky symphonies. There is an intimate song-cycle symphony, *Das Lied von der Erde,* and a grand public affirmation symphony (oratorio first part, operatic second), the Eighth.

Considering the greatness and importance of this symphonic *œuvre* it is surprising to realise how few are indubitably successful as wholes. There are isolated movements of the highest quality, in totalities that do not tell, aesthetically, and sometimes verge on the preposterous. The spirit of *Lélio* is not absent from Mahler's *Titan* and *Todtenfeier,* the spirit of Lisztian religiosity from his 'Auferstehung'. While the huge bombastic sprawl of the outer movements holds up less and less well, such things as the ländler and scherzo of 2, and above all the minuetto and scherzo of 3, perpetually renew astonishment at their range, of expression and of compositional power. In the ostensibly more 'classical' symphonies of the middle period the divisions lie deeper and more troubling than in the *Wunderhorn*-works. 7 is the most peculiar; its overall scheme is nonsensical. If only Mahler had relinquished it as a *symphony* and cut the work up! The extraordinary first movement,

Mahler's closest approach to his great opposite, Strauss, could stand by itself as a tone-poem self-portrait: *Don Gustavo*. The middle movements (the march and scherzo even surpassing those in the earlier symphonies) are part of a suite, a cycle, a set. The big pomposo finale, which in context so signally fails to make any sense of what precedes it, could be rescued by standing alone as a sort of '1812' or *Meistersinger*-prelude concert-piece; and though one wouldn't want to hear it so often as the first movement, there would be no lack of recognition for its mastery. But if 7 would benefit from being split up, 5, 6 and 8 manifest their symphonic unity all too laboriously. Of course they are full of marvellous invention, including passages where the overall scheme really tells; but it is symptomatic that the most successful individual movement in them is an island of lyricism—the Andante of 6. And 9 is the most disconcerting of all. Its first movement is so perfect and complete that the others are rendered intolerable even if they weren't such a mixture of good and bad anyway. However clearly they can be *shown* to belong, they *feel* as redundant as some epilogue to the *Ring* or third act for *Moses und Aron*.

So in almost every symphonic work of Mahler the whole is less than the sum of the parts. The perfect wholes—4 and *Das Lied von der Erde*—come when the poetic scheme is in harmonious alignment with the forms used to embody it. 4 is extremely unclassical, but the movements do really belong to each other in an all-embracing unity; their order, their keys, their material and its treatment, their variety of style, tone and genre, are really expressive as an entity; and this poetic rightness shows greater formal mastery than the striving will-to-unity of 6. And even so, the impression left by 4 is of four perfect movements that 'beautifully belong' to each other; the same goes for the six songs of *Das Lied*. The unity is still of the same kind as in Schumann's early song cycles.

Why was Mahler so given over to the symphony as a genre? This obstinate adherence to it seems retrograde in the face of its wholescale and brilliant dissolution at his hands! One senses that his authentic genius lay in an altogether other direction. *Das klagende Lied*, that marvellous production of his late teens, is a hybrid that fuses rather than implodes: cantata, song-cycle, narrative ballad, latent opera that precludes 'naturalistic' or practical stage exigencies to allow dreamy protraction with play of layered time-dimensions, as suggested by the interlocked mingling of past and present in *Tristan* and Act I of *Parsifal*. The result, particularly when *Waldmärchen*, the first panel (later dropped when Mahler revised the other two on and off throughout the 1880s and 90s, publishing it in 1898 and giving the première in 1901) is included, manifests greater conviction in its marriage of material, method, content, to genre than any of the symphonies except 4 and (as I'm trying to argue) 10.

The importance of 10 is that it would promise to be the one work where the whole is greater than the sum. At first sight its scheme seems to be another hopeless attempt to 'be like the world and contain everything'. But, rather, it is a synthesis and crowning glory of the symphony as extended and dissolved in all the ways already described: a cycle is embraced within a symphonic frame; there are motto motifs and material is reworked from movement to movement; there is song-like material and leitmotivic development; elements of programmatic and poetic meaning; 'the world everything', but within the artistic bounds of what a symphony can hold. There are imperfections, of a very unusual and circumstantial kind; but the work is rescued by a plan that is extremely strong without being imposed like a grid upon material that seems ideally not to call for it.

The handsome score[1] enforces a full sense of the work's inherent greatness, and of the extraordinary skill of the late Deryck Cooke's realisation of the sketches. Its layout is indispensable but complicated. The first two movements and the first twenty-seven bars or so of the third are given in Mahler's own sketch full score, the editorial additions and amendments in small type. Thereafter, Mahler's short score is transcribed in small type under each system, the full score being entirely editorial. Thus the movements that show most clearly the editor's unobtrusive mastery are iv and v; and it implies a criticism of the composer that he took ii so far as this sketch full score without altering or cutting. No praise is too high for Cooke's work; its devotion and mastery are evident throughout, and the debt to his labours so far exceeds the usual gratitude to a good editor as to approach the sort of admiration felt for the creator himself.

The following examination of the work, with some details of its realisation, tries to account for the very high evaluation I place on some music that, considered intrinsically, can hardly deserve it. The point is that the circumstances of the work's incompletion rule out an intrinsic view; and the overall conception is so coherent that it can carry the patent weakness of some of the material and the deficiency in its treatment. It is another five-moment scheme: i Adagio; ii first Scherzo (half march, half ländler); iii *Purgatorio*; iv second Scherzo (wild and impassioned) fading, then cut short, direct into v—slow introduction—Allegro—slow epilogue.

In the Adagio the tortuously criss-crossing material on the strings, with the very full harmony needed to render it bearable and beautiful, is interbroken by the dispassionate *Stimme aus der Ferne* of the opening viola melody, and with material whose relative friskiness can turn febrile within a few bars. It is full of extraordinary touches, and the climax is in a class of its own for its power to singe and terrify. The viola melody tails off under long wispy violin notes; suddenly an immense chorale-like block of common chords rears up, then the main theme's first phrase collapses onto a single

---

[1] Published jointly by Faber Music Ltd., and Associated Music Publishers, with introduction and notes by Deryck Cooke. The input of three composers closely concerned with the project must also be mentioned: Berthold Goldschmidt, who conducted its memorable complete première at a Prom during the 1964 season; and the Matthews brothers, David and Colin, with their enormous orchestral skills and fraternal involvement with Mahler's music since their early teens.

high trumpet note, around which a horrible dissonance builds up on the full orchestra, layer by layer. It is cut off as if by a switch leaving the trumpet alone, like a voice from a cloud. Then the chord, now simultaneous, rams down again, all the violins enter screaming at the top of their range; and the cloud slowly disperses, revealing a land of lost content into which the movement gently subsides. The dissonance, though it has a long ancestry (back through *Erwartung*, *Salome* and *Elektra*, the Adagio of Bruckner 9, Kundry, the *Tannhäuser* Bacchanale, *Tristan* Act III, the *Faust-Symphony*, poignant stabs in Chopin, Schumann and Schubert, the frightful outburst before the recitative in Beethoven's choral finale), is in context perhaps the most painful moment anywhere in the orchestral repertory. What horrifies is, first, its seeming gratuitousness—a mere scream, out of all proportion, imposed upon the movement rather than, as in the Bruckner, growing inevitably out of a grinding progress which is bound to end in a terrific unresolved dissonance—and then its sadistic deliberation: blow by blow the noise is built up as if the constituent ingredients of anguish were being meted out and analysed.

But it makes more sense now that its place in the total scheme can be shown, even while its impact is slightly dulled just because it was so exceptionally striking without its full setting. The total scheme gives meaning and vindication to what had seemed uncalled-for. But on the other hand the relaxation that follows now seems too long for the work as a whole. A beautiful concert-ending for the Adagio by itself (though there are some decidedly wonky moments: bars 238–40 especially, just about saved by an unexpected move—the horns at 242, the key-change at 244), it detracts from the long-drawn-out F♯ major end of the whole symphony. But the uniqueness and quality of this movement have never been in doubt. Cooke's edition effects some important corrections and cleaning-up.

Serious trouble starts with the second movement. Its character is a *pastiche-et-mélange* of 6's scherzo, 7's finale, and the middle movements of 9; there is even a flicker of 3's scherzo (bars 471f.). The material is poorish (on p.57 the 'symphonic waltz' from *Intermezzo* raises its ridiculous head only to be snubbed by the harp glissando from the rondo-burleske of 9), the working patchy. What is really required is something Cooke quite properly denied himself—manipulation and excision. The thinness of 39f. and 54–5 can just about work if one strains one's sympathy; but the idea of the gaps in the ländler theme is ill-executed (pp.47–9—though followed on p.50 by a very good return of the scherzo); 55f. is *kapellmeisterisch*, and thence to the end of the movement altogether the weakest part of the work, barely rescued by the overall scheme however much it requires a movement of this character. Presumably Mahler would have worked it hard into something resembling the scherzo of 5 for exuberance of detail. It needs all that the editor and performer can give it. Some of Cooke's little touches seem to me unsuccessful (e.g. the timpani, pp.44f.) and from 46 or so to the end Mahler's score surely requires more filling-out. More can be heard on Ormandy's record than appears in the score as printed. I regret the loss, for example, of the cymbal in the penultimate bar and wish that the realisation could bubble up like this more often.

The *Purgatorio* seems when first heard to act as an intermezzo between the two scherzos: a *Wunderhorn*-song-without-words—a lyrical episode like *Blumine* in the earlier version of 1. This comparison, however, shows how the *Purgatorio* is in fact (unlike *Blumine*) the indispensable hub of the whole scheme. The seemingly insignificant little lyric should be compared rather with 'Urlicht' in 2 and 'Das himmlische Leben' in 3 and 4; it is great with meaning too big for its modest scale and requires an enormous area for its potential to be fully deployed. To find it trivial misses its purpose as well as its poignancy. For this 'intermezzo' colours and pervades everything subsequent: a ubiquitous presence in the second scherzo, it provides the main theme of the introduction and the thematic substance of the allegro in v; even the return of the climax of i as the finale is now *Purgatorio*-facing, and the passionate upcry and downsinking of the last pages, are absolutely direct from the source in iii, though the transfiguration also is absolute. The source necessarily gives the simplest statement of the simple material, in order that its manifold transformations can make an immediately telling impact.

The editor's task was relatively straightforward here. I find too great a contrast between the tutti outbursts and the chamber-orchestra texture of the enclosing treadmill; but this, like so much else in works fully realised by their composers, can be adjusted in performance. The fourth movement, though, brings the first of Cooke's triumphs: e.g. pp.94f., this realisation as a parodistic fiddle solo of Mahler's instruction *Tanz*; 100–1 the wispy strains of ländler (a fine bit of genuine compositional invention); and from about 113 to the end all the aspects of the realisation, particularly the orchestral colour (a good cymbal was heard at p.115 in the broadcast by the BBC Northern SO recently—in general the best performance I've heard[2]—but isn't in the score; the master of Bruckner's cymbal-cruxes has left one of his own!). He has added surging quavers underneath the theme on p.85 and subsequent appearances,

---

[2] Of the two available recordings Ormandy is almost invariably more convincing, even when Morris is patently deeply felt. Ormandy can be perfunctory and downright crude; but he lets the work alone. Morris fusses and cannot be straightforward—nor *fast*! The abandon needed to get ii and iv off the ground is absolutely lacking; all *ritenuto* is overdone, the end of iv especially is absurdly too slow (winding down all the way to the tempo of the introduction of v). The strings are messy, the brass coarse, the phrasing lumpy. Praiseworthy features (the slowness of i) or good moments (the start of the allegro in v) go for nothing in the overall earlier indecisiveness. But both versions are interim, and it's surely about time conductors worthy of the work waived their scruples and gave it the weight and diversity of interpretation it deserves.

This note can now (2003) be updated. While the older Mahler conductors understandably remained chary of the Cooke completion (and indeed of others that have appeared since), a younger generation has taken it up, sometimes to convincing and moving effect—notably Simon Rattle. Now that its place in the greater whole is so overwhelmingly apparent it is rare, and seems wrong, to hear the opening Adagio alone.

and elsewhere too; they sound so well that one wishes he'd done still more (the one failure is the xylophone: an authentic idea, but completely unconvincing in sound). One query that perhaps can't be resolved with so many different 'states' of the score—should there be a trumpet on p.88 and again on 102–3—is it an accidental or a deliberate omission?

The idea of this movement is marvellous: the three sharp chords again and again punctuating its course, setting it different, while clearly connecting it to the unforgettable dissonance of i. In itself the material is not of the first quality. So closely made from the *Purgatorio*, and with strains 'von der Jammer der Erde' running through it, it is almost a parody movement, with the 'Rondo Burleske' from 9 as immediate prototype for shape and character, until the wind-down fade-out ending whose prototype is that of the scherzo in 6. But the thing lives a life of its own, unlike ii; the only bad sag is from p.101 onwards (after Cooke's excellent ghostly ländler); and from around 111 to the end is very good. The last note, the sudden thwack on the big unstrung drum, obliterates the double bar, hanging the music open-ended over the silence before the next thwack, the first note of the finale. This is tremendous; thereafter the thwacks come too often, too predictably when not expected (though admittedly this deflation of hope is part of Mahler's rhetoric). This introduction plainly recreates that to the finale of 6; the fascination here is in the completely different use made of the *Purgatorio* motifs already so brilliantly exploited in iv.

It raises itself out of the depths for the famous flute melody, and so into the Allegro on the same themes from iii, whose realisation, with the ending, is Cooke's greatest triumph. Glancing from the pitiful small print sketch to the living full-score above, the constant reaction is, just so!—he's so clearly done the right thing as to make it seem, after the event, that there'd been no choice. The *feurig* passage, pp.136–7, can serve as one illustration among many. But from p.139 or so right up until around 145 the texture is too slack. Thereafter the trouble lies in the sketch's actual length; there is not enough allegro, the movement seems to run into the sand, so that the climax comes from nowhere—an accidental rather than a deliberate surprise. The dissonance from the climax of i is as unnerving as it was there, but in a different way. There it was an unprepared outburst, extremely theatrical no doubt (like the similar gesture in mid-iii and start of v in 2) but authentically terrifying. As the shudder died down one asked why, and had to wait four movements for the answer. Here the moment unnerves because the sketch is still such a blueprint of a Wagnerian 'great-moment' or 'turning-point' combination of themes. The music to which the opening viola melody evaporated just before the outburst in i (p.19) is now given *tutta forza* on all violins, against which the horns blare the main rhythmic tag of the *Purgatorio* material. Now the dissonance comes back wedge by wedge, each sharpened with the same rhythmic tag. The single trumpet is left hanging, while two others snarl out the Allegro's main motif in its form closest to the *Purgatorio*. The entire chord rams down and again the single trumpet is left hanging; under it, the horns give out the opening viola melody (complete, rhythmically more

emphatic, and no longer a distant murmur but beginning as powerful summons—*à4 forte*—then fading gently until only the first plays *p diminuendo);*
the hanging trumpet simultaneously descends as the violins did on p.10 and
tutta forza on p.151. All this is effective indeed, and there can be no doubt
whatever that fearful symmetry is established across five movements. But the
apocalyptic character of these pages cannot conceal the fact that the execution of the idea is painfully bald. The sound is so *dangerous*: the scaffolding will be removed and the walls will not hold; the plaster will crack and the
wound will not be healed.

Danger of another kind threatens the resolution of these crucial thirty-two
bars. In i the opening melody led into the main theme in F♯ major; in v the
same melody now leads into B♭ major. The work originally ended in this
key; it is surely one of its simplest and greatest inspirations that F♯ major
finally became the ultimate goal here as well as in i. The change necessitated
the insertion of sixteen bars whose fat banality resembles the Strauss of the
late wind works—a loveable quality there, but *here!* (bar 313)—and a very
shaky modulation into the F♯ ... by 315 it's really there; and by 316 it's
clearly safe home. These first eight bars in F♯ major somehow reproduce the
character of the main theme of i without employing its material. Then at 323
the music turns gently back to the flute melody from the introduction to v.
Danger is close again in the contour and harmony of this melody (see especially its appearance, the cowboy-style of bars 34–7; here the main lurch is
given in bars 326–31). Its accidental near-banality is a sort of revenge on
Mahler for his lifetime of successful skirting around deliberate near-banality.
Here is another disconcerting quality in this symphony, that having been
taught by this same composer rightly to distrust the sentimentally easy flow
of feeling, one then has to accept it head-on in his last testament. For this
flute melody and its later flowering is not 'ironic'—it is heartfelt, evidently,
and this is stylistically almost disastrous. The only solution here is to take
such *simplesse* at its face value and turn it sublime. This had already begun
even before the Allegro, and the characteristic interruption by the drum
(pp.124–7); now in the epilogue with no drum to cut it short it flowers gorgeously then fades out, flames up in a last cry of passionate ardour, then fades
richly and fully away in the right key; no desolation—a happy ending. Once
bar 331 is safely past there are no more lurches, or only comfortable ones and
the second return to F♯ major (bar 347) is as beautiful as the first was
awkward. From here all the rest is elevation—the Tchaikovsky/Mahler 9/iv
climax (with a couple of bars—363–4—of *Lulu* thrown in) and the long
descent, are all realised with firm assurance and beauty by Cooke. Page 162
is a wonderful page, and even so potentially dubious a detail as the three solo
violins on p.163 is right and beautiful. The use of both *Purgatorio* motifs, so
recognisable but by now transcendentally transformed, in the last sixteen
bars, is really inspired; very simple, no *simplesse*, all falseness purged from
notes that, without the spirit, would indeed be rather banal.

*   *   *

If a composer himself has forced on his listeners the feelings which over-whelmed him then he has achieved his object. The language of music has then approached that of the word, but has communicated immeasurably more than the word is able to express.

The significance of the *Purgatorio* in Mahler's Tenth, its place at the centre, its powers of pervasion and transformation, its ability to gather the scheme together as a whole; all this is at once deeply poetic and symbolic, and quite undefined. Herein lies its expressive power; the *Purgatorio* is vital just where the 'burial' and especially the 'resurrection' of 'the hero' or the hammer-blows that 'fell him as a tree is felled', creak. In the Tenth Mahler has got poetic and formal scheme, *Wort und Ton*, into just balance. The musical fabric acts as carrier of the poetic idea—he no longer has to *resort* to the word to realise the music's full suggestion; the music is complete without it, but completely upholds it and contains it as a vital but inexplicit (indeed inexplicable) element in the total significance. ('And Mahler took up his glass and emptied it with a cry of "Death to programmes!"')

And yet its greatness *is* ultimately inherent rather than actual; for of course its greatness could only be fully embodied in its detailed execution. *Pace* everything, for long stretches this score doesn't sound like real music; compositional foreground and background are in the same plane. The overall scheme and its great focal points are a thrilling conception, yet as the climax of v shows, there is a painful absence of flesh. The different state of this movement and i is clear, yet even the Adagio, comparatively often played and recorded as it is, has an indefinable aura of unrealisation. Yet there is something special about this sketch-bareness: the naked exposure of the lines, particularly on the quadruple woodwinds; the 'unnatural' distinction between lines and supporting harmonic masses—such accidental features have authen-tic aesthetic quality, and open up possibilities excluded in works of high compositional finish. It would he absurd, in normal circumstances, to take this the way of Henry Moore and actually *prefer* the pregnancy of incom-pleteness to the barren perfection of the fully-worked end-product. In music the sketch as such has no aesthetic value; but occasionally through some accident value is forced upon it. Mahler's Tenth is one such; the loss of its full-working seems to me the most crucial in modern times—the only comparable incompletion is Bruckner's finale to his Ninth. Act III of *Lulu* appears to be a case of realising an already-worked intention,[3] and while the continuation of the *Jakobsleiter* must obviously remain mysterious, the enor-mous torso we possess is, again, in substance fully worked. It has been absorbing and moving to study in this edition both what one hears and what Mahler left; admiration for Deryck Cooke's achievement, formerly general-ised, is now specific, gratitude constantly renewed, as point after point is rescued from the void. My wish that here and there he'd chanced his arm further is also a tribute, because I'm certain such risks would have justified

---

[3] See pp.137–72: this was written before the première of Cerha's orchestration.

themselves. But I realise that this was not the intention of the enterprise; it was bold enough to have undertaken what is here so nobly achieved.

Mahler's remark about programmes (at a party in October 1900) is one of the items in Kurt Blaukopf's new *Documentary Study*.[4] This form is especially effective for Mahler, for whom the sources are so varied, interesting and self-expressive. He has suffered much in recent years from authorial imposition; Blaukopf restricts himself to annotation, introductions and linking, leaving this rich collection of photographs and documents public, sociable, and intimate, to speak for itself. Its evocative power is extraordinary—not just the man, but the circumstances and settings of his profession within his epoch stand vividly before one, most notably the life of the provincial theatres through which Mahler flashed on his way to the top, over and out. The very piquancy of the contrast between all the outward circumstances and the documents of his inner life, the *œuvre*, brings him vividly before the imagination. Suddenly the whole phenomenon is rounded-out and homogeneous; and this extra dimension slips easily into one's understanding of the art without needing laborious explanation and 'interpretation'. The middleman's middleground of 'Mahler Scholarship' is tasteless and superfluous. We have the documents, inner and outer: these two publications, both works of self-effacement, complete all we need to know. Only one more thing is needful: the score of *Waldmärchen*.[5]

---

[4] *Mahler: a Documentary Study* by Kurt Blaukopf (Thames and Hudson, 1976, £12.50).

[5] This too had been available even at the time of writing (from Belwin–Mills).

17

Strauss: two pieces on the fiftieth anniversary of his death (September 1999)

i Some thoughts

The British problem with Strauss, since it's a problem of our own self-definition or self-understanding, will never end. Who was it said 'I never feel happy about pleasure'?—some famous or nameless genius of the national character. Yet this ambiguous discomfort about Strauss isn't merely prudish, priggish, prissy. Something in it isn't wrong, though not exactly right either. But—for our good and to our loss—such crashing plenitude of grossness and vulgarity sticks in our Pre-Raphaelite maw.

Take *Schlagobers*. What could be more utterly dreadful than this tasteless ballet about sweet-tasting goodies, this preposterous celebration of conspicuous consumption set in an all-too-*haute-bourgeoise* patisserie: completely lacking in the aristocratic finesse, and the romantic splendour, of its unacknowledged source in *Casse-noisette* Act II, temporarily culminating in a girlie-routine *à la* Busby Berkeley for the 'Waltz of Whipped Cream' before setting down with a comfortable porcine grunt to its true dialectic: class-warfare between privileged pralines and proletariat buns, located in the lugubriously overstuffed stomach of a greedy schoolboy? Could tackiness go further? Tactlessness too, as inflation loomed in the countries for which it was written, where even a humble gobstopper could cost a million Marks.

But Strauss always surprises and disconcerts. *Schlagobers* doesn't fulfil any prim expectation that such an awful project has *got* to be bad. One listens (following the full score in the deluxe Imperial purple-and-gold of the collected edition of all the stage-works), positively aghast at the upsplurge of unchecked stomach-churning all the way down the alimentary canal. *Positively*, though. As well as predictably copious, easy, 'wonderful' etc., it is so *inventive*. Not a masterpiece, not even all that good, just very emphatically *itself*. Up to the minute, too. Strauss is odd, wary, curious. Janáček, Hindemith, Weill, Stravinsky are cunningly assimilated up to a point—then one recalls the date (1921–2) and realises that, more likely, they've been pre-empted. Compare the now-so-ascendant Korngold—e.g. *Das Wunder der Heliane*, still closer to the edge of the collapse of the culture that produced it, still more luxurious in story, emotion, musical language, stage and vocal and orchestral demands, even than Strauss's not-1000-miles-distant 1920s megakitsch *Die Aegyptische Helene*. *Heliane*, despite its unimpugnable idealism and manifest technical prowess, is 'music of a bygone aesthetic'. It creaks; it reeks late Wagnerism plus early Strauss gone rotten and ridiculous. Strauss himself had had the wit to steer clear of that mistake well before World War I. Now, after it, he has modernskified himself—and before *Intermezzo*, commonly held to be the cue for *neue Sachlichkeit* accommodating itself to old expressionism—according to his lights (which of course remain pretty heavy).

Strauss's tastelessness and tedium remain stumbling-blocks. The first is all-permeating, inseparably part of the very definition of his genius. The second is less forgivable: would-be sublimity (*Die Frau ohne Schatten*), sweetness (*Arabella*) and fun (*Schweigsame Frau*) are accompanied by stretches of note-spinning routine that sometimes almost engulf the whole work. But let us continue to indulge, forgive and explore him, to be open to the amplitudes of a composer who can no more be taken for granted in 1999 than in 1949, or indeed in 1921–2 or any other point along his confident trajectory.

ii The songs with orchestra

In 1964, for the centenary of Richard Strauss's birth, his publishers issued the complete songs with piano in three volumes, completed by a fourth containing some twenty orchestrated versions from the master's hand, together with the four sets with opus numbers and the 'Four Last Songs' without opus, making another fifteen in all that were from the start written for voice and orchestra. In 1999, the fiftieth anniversary of his death, they are for the most part as neglected, even unknown, as in 1964.

Down the intervening years I've pored over the 600-odd pages of this volume, longing to hear more than the handful that are recorded over and over. All are rarities in concerts save, of course, the Last Four, rightly celebrated as the crown of his achievement in lyric writing and perhaps of his *œuvre* as a whole. On disc the usual suspects are rounded up again and again: one has to accept duplication—quintuplication—for the sake of an occasional previously unavailable number. Since this involves singers as distinctive and distinguished as Schwartzkopf, Norman, Heather Harper, Lucia Popp, the accumulation can be a pleasure. Not so pleasant, surely, as to hear the missing music. But gradually the gaps are filling. Only one orchestral song remains that I've never encountered live, on disc, or broadcast.

The song with orchestra, one of the loveliest concert genres imaginable, has a small but choice repertory. Romantic predecessors include Berlioz's *Nuits d'été* and Wagner's Wesendonck set; the heyday comes with Mahler, Diepenbrock, early Schoenberg, Chausson's *Poème de l'amour et de la mer* and Ravel's *Scheherazade;* after-comers include Berg's *Der Wein*, Barber's *Knoxville*, Schoeck's *Lebendig begraben*, Britten's *Nocturne* and *Serenade*—not a dull or duff moment.

Strauss's contributions are well up to this standard. In his songs with piano the threads of tinsel amidst the gold can be off-putting. Accompaniments tend to be sufficient but routine: the endless inventiveness of Brahms or Wolf, let alone Schubert, simply doesn't form part of Straussian economy, except in that fascinating anomaly *Krämerspiegel*—Mirror for Shopkeepers—where he lavishes ideas both tart and lyrical on a *jeu d'esprit* lambasting grasping publishers, in a project doomed from birth to be only circumstantial. He rescued only its closing arc of melody to form the orchestral interlude in his last and most perfect opera, *Capriccio*. Elsewhere, too, the sketchy keyboard textures audibly cry out for the orchestration that often followed, sometimes immediately, in some cases many decades later.

Here he, of course, is a consummate master. Not just perfunctory keyboard parts but musical ideas themselves that can seem hackneyed and lazy take on richness and resonance, realising compositional potential in such a way as to give new meaning to a term like threadbare. Take the *Die Heiligen drei Könige*. On piano the slow sustained background is ineffective, the onomatopoeia of bellowing bullocks and crying child obvious: on orchestra the illustration is naïve rather than cheap, and the final transfigured processional has a fairytale shimmer that transports everything to a higher plane.

This is Strauss almost wholly purified of dross and slag. Not of kitsch, vulgarity, sentimentality, erotic exhibitionism, stylistic provocation: if these too were purged, what would be left of him beyond Mendelssohn and Schumann doused with attar of Wagner and Liszt? If we've learnt anything in the years between his anniversaries about this puzzling composer whose well-knit surface conceals paradoxes as glaring as those his contemporary Mahler reveals, it is that *chez* Strauss vulgarity, banality and all the rest, are fused into creative powers of a high order, for manifest unambiguous benefit all round. A harder lesson than unadulterated genius, however 'difficult'. He himself realised this and said as much with the same blunt realism that informs the music: 'Must one become seventy years old to recognise that one's greatest strength lies in creating kitsch?' (though many years earlier he'd already adumbrated a future for 'sentimentality and parody' as his prime urge after the first World War).

The range of the songs is broad and contains surprises. Erotic lyricism predominates, together with tender domesticity, parenthood, a famous and tacky hymn to mutual marital masochism (*Befreit*), songs of nature in storm and repose, and the consummation of all these themes, bound into nostalgia and farewell in the Four Last. But there is also *Der Arbeitsmann,* a grim piece about the working man under the hoof of capitalism whose harsh, almost Weillish orchestration was only rediscovered and published after the 1964 collection. There are the three Hölderlin Hymns, ecstatic pantheistic/patriotic utterances calling for a superhuman combination of radiance, delicacy and blockbuster power in the doughty soprano who takes them on. The pagan element, revealing the dionysiac furor beneath the Bavarian phlegm, appears in several songs culminating in the marvellous *Frühlingsfeier*—rites of spring—admittedly another orchestration of a piano original, though it's hard to believe, hearing the orchestra's seething frenzy, that the piano was anything more than a stopgap.

Unwonted excursions from soaring soprano to the deeper voices produces the best of all (always excepting the Last Four): a pair for deep bass, op.51, studies in introspection, weariness, ageing, touching on facets of his style untried elsewhere. And, still finer, the pair of songs for low voice (male or female) op.44. The first, *Notturno,* explores (for around fifteen minutes) a death-haunted psychological landscape of alarming desolation, anxiety, morbidity—all expressionism is here, latent and actual, in the last year of the nineteenth century. The second, *Nächtlicher Gang,* is the one I've never heard from any source. It *looks* fantastic—nearly forty pages of orchestral score, boiling up and over with fiery intensity.

It is most regrettable that, *still,* the wobbly stature of Richard Strauss is not more securely anchored by the availability and wide dissemination of a genre in his enormous output set consistently at top notch. There is no room in his songs with orchestra for the longueurs and lapses of the operas, or the legerdemain, persiflage and bombast of the symphonic poems and programmatic symphonies. Let's hope that by his next round-figure anniversary in 2014 the balance will be improved. [In fact for this very anniversary a handsome three-CD set of the complete songs with orchestra, beautifully shared between seven different singers, came out on Nightingale Classics.]

18

Salome: art or kitsch?

This and the companion-piece on Elektra *(see p.122) were written at the request of the late Derrick Puffett for inclusion in the two studies he edited, devoted to each of Strauss's fin-de-siècle blockbusters (both CUP, 1989). Some passages of detailed discussion, particularly of the fine-tuning in the scoring of* Elektra, *are fully intelligible only with reference to the orchestra scores (Boosey and Hawkes: also reprinted by Dover). But I hope the general sense will communicate even without.*

* * *

... people who are most strongly imbued with an instinctive taste for bad music and for melodies, however commonplace, which have something facile and caressing about them, succeed, by dint of education in symphonic culture, in mortifying that appetite. But once they have arrived at this point, when, dazzled—and rightly so—by the brilliant orchestral colouring of Richard Strauss, they see that musician adopt the most vulgar motifs with a self-indulgence worthy of Auber, what those people originally admired finds suddenly in so high an authority a justification which delights them, and they wallow without qualms and with a twofold gratitude, when they listen to *Salomé*, in what would have been impossible for them to admire in *Les Diamants de la Couronne*.

Proust, *The Guermantes Way*[1]

... there is not a character whose physical individuality, whose morality (or immorality), whose thoughts and acts are not minutely translated, almost to the point of naiveté. Atmosphere and colour are portrayed in their finest nuances, all by means of mediocre themes, it is true, but developed, worked, interwoven with such marvellous skill that their intrinsic interest is exceeded by the magic of an orchestral

---

[1] *Remembrance of Things Past*, trans. C. K. Scott Moncrieff and Terence Kilmartin (Harmondsworth: Penguin, 1981), vol. 2, pp.465–6.

technique of real genius, until these themes—mediocre, as I said—end by acquiring character, power, almost emotion.

Fauré, reviewing *Salome* in 1907[2]

I really like this fellow Strauss, but *Salome* will do him a lot of damage.

Kaiser Wilhelm II[3]

i

I am impatient both with the piety that can unquestioningly place Strauss among the great composers, and with the dismissive distaste that, pleased with its good taste, deprives itself by banishing him to 'whichever purgatory punishes triumphant banality'.[4] *Salome*, just because it is one of his strongest and most characteristic works, poses the problem at its centre. If it were classic art in whatever mode (*Orfeo, Figaro, Tristan, Ballo, Wozzeck*) or if it were masterly kitsch (*Butterfly, Die tote Stadt, Troilus and Cressida*) the position would be unanxious; there would be no problem, and the various appetites would agree to differ. That it is at the very simplest a mixture of both is clear from Fauré's direct and Proust's oblique comments. A work that can at such voltage hold the mediocre in suspension with the inspired has a fascination of its own. It is precisely with such pieces, where just estimation is trickiest and it behoves the admirer equally with the carper to try to work out exactly what they mean, that new ways of seeing and understanding can come into being; new definitions of taste adjudicating more subtly, more in accordance with how a listener actually vibrates, than the blanket endorsement or discredit of good or bad.

Which, nonetheless, still makes the best starting-point for a preliminary survey. *Salome* does contain some unambiguously great music. *Pace* Fauré there is one superb theme whose beginning is worthy of Bruckner at his most primeval, though it always tails off into inconsequence: the motive in fourths (first appearance nine bars after fig.65, biggest statement six before 141) that suggests the spiritual stature of the Baptist and his irreducible integrity. From fig.298 into the final scene is perhaps the work's greatest stretch and certainly its most 'advanced'—even the meanest historicist view would have to acknowledge that this music is astonishing in every parameter: timbre, gesture, quality of emotion and, above all, harmony. The writing is cleaner here than earlier (even without considering for the moment the famous solo double-bass note); Strauss explores the excruciating sonorities that render Herod's frenzy and Salome's anticipation with an essentiality and intensiveness quite different from the often routine textures earlier on. The remarkable harmony

---

[2] *Le Figaro*, 9 May 1907, translated in *Composers on Music*, ed. Sam Morgenstern (London: Faber, 1958), pp.283–4.

[3] Quoted in Michael Kennedy, *Richard Strauss* (London: Dent, 1976), p.45.

[4] Stravinsky, in Igor Stravinsky and Robert Craft, *Conversations with Igor Stravinsky* (London: Faber, 1959), p.75.

as Herod sinks in despairing defeat—at figs 299 and 303–4—is not lost on the Schoenberg of *Die glückliche Hand* or the Mahler of the Tenth Symphony. Between these two places the texture makes the starting-point for the Schoenberg of Op.16, no.4 and especially no.1—the low D-centred cluster (D in octaves on bassoons, horns and timps, B♭ and C on trombones, G trilling with A♭ on bass clarinet and two low clarinets, the whole reinforced by the whole-tone tattoo on the four drums) underpinning an all-hell of shrieks and yelps in high woodwinds, horns and strings. The creepy music of Salome's panting impatience, from fig.307 to 313/8 when the gigantic black arm brings up the head, curdles the blood as previous thunderings from Jochanaan fail to (it even succeeds in partially redeeming his other motive, the far-from-superb one, in the two bars before 309). And the music from fig.314, when the head is hers and she addresses it in ecstatic triumph, makes one of the greatest passages of orchestral exaltation in the repertoire. Not every note is audible in these wonderful pages, either before or after C♯ minor is decisively reached (see especially the celeste at this very moment—the three bars beginning two before fig.316—vainly *undoubled* on the work's opening theme!); but the overall effect could have been achieved no other way. These millions of notes are not merely fun for the eyes; they make a teeming froth of multiform textural invention, equal or superior to contemporary parallels in Mahler, Schoenberg or Berg for which it is anyway the prototype, and far more intense than anything comparable in Scriabin, early Szymanowski etc. The inspiration continues to burn hot and bright throughout most of the heroine's final scene (the four bars before fig.341 lapse into the Marschallin, and the twenty-odd bars that follow are distinctly weak; but by 344 Strauss is on course again). The passage from 348 to just after 350, and the extraordinary juxtaposition of murky bitterness as she broods on what she has tasted (figs 355–8) with (358–61) ecstatic abandonment to what she has done, sustain a pitch of intensity not unworthy of Wagner.

Nor are the manifest successes of *Salome* always a matter of exaltation and extremity. There are at least two devices where 'less is more' as surely as in the music of Webern or Stravinsky. The first is the brilliant use of woodwind trills (which Stravinsky surely remembered in the 'Rondes printanières' from the *Rite*). They begin to figure in the crucial moments where, before deigning to dance, Salome extorts from Herod the promise of whatever she will ask, and persist intermittently till the work's final climax.[5] At the opposite

---

[5] Four bars before fig.228 ('Will you indeed give me whatsoever I shall ask?') the first clarinet trills on A♯; Salome's voice and harmony convert it into B♭; Herod takes it back to A♯. At fig.229 ('You swear it, Tetrarch?') the same clarinet trills on the same B♭; his answer takes the music to E♭ minor, converting it to major; she is inexorable ('By what will you swear?'), and the B♭ melts into A major. Trilling resumes at fig.230/3 as she bores on ('You have sworn, Tetrarch'), now on F♯ (= G♭ in E♭ minor) and transferred from the A to the B♭ instrument. His ardent answer restores E♭ major, but the F♯ trills on (both clarinets now) with a crescendo over the arrival at C minor with which he vouches half of his kingdom. All this is held in suspense through a gust of uncanny wind, a few routine words from Jochanaan and the entire

extreme is the famous high-pitched solo double-bass note (well-taken by Webern both early and late) as Salome peers down into the cistern trying to make out what is going on after her desire has been granted. Notwithstanding the elaborate instructions for its execution (see full score p.294: Strauss's punctiliousness of detail is worthy of Ligeti!) it is nonetheless a simple idea, whose result is the most unnerving, and understated, sound in the entire operatic repertory.

Turning to bad music, the choice is embarrassingly wide. A recurrent low-point is the unctuous strain that usually characterises Jochanaan, heard first at fig.66 and in its full flatulent flower from fig.132 to c.134. But perhaps the worst single moment is the duet for the two pious Nazarenes (fig.210 onwards), with its pat conclusion at fig.212, where in answer to Herod's question they sing together ('Jawohl. Er erweckt die Toten') as if a Savoy

---

'Dance of the Seven Veils', to be resumed with chilling effect to dog Herod's ever-increasing regret for his rash generosity. Having concluded the 'Dance' itself (fifteen bars of freeze before the five of precipitate wildness that end it) the trills needle on— the very sound of her steely will—throughout her inexorable insistence on her rights. At fig.249/5 she teases him ('I would that they presently bring me in a silver charger ...'), and two clarinets (E♭ and A) trill an octave apart. The oboes continue their D dissonantly against Herod's infatuated interruption, but when at 254 he is back to the point ('What, in a silver charger?') so is she, and the trill slithers up till it makes a sharp dissonance (G and A♭) with her motive in B major, resolving into the major and minor thirds of E as, at last, she voices her *real* object.

Trilling resumes three bars before fig.256, now below the voice but soon returning high, in octaves (and always on the clarinets) as she keeps him to his word. Every wriggle of would-be escape ends with a cessation of tempo but a prolongation of the maddening oscillation. At two before 261 it is again high on a solo clarinet, then in octaves as she becomes more emphatic; at two before 271 it is low on a solo oboe, the voice (doubled by trumpet) a tritone lower still; but it then veers upwards and back to the clarinet. At 279 and 284 four clarinets trill in two octaves, dissonant with her voice. At 297/7 nine woodwinds trill up on the high open fifth of the D major with which Herod concludes his final desperate extravagance, the Veil of the Sanctuary. Salome sings against this fifth, in E♭, of the one thing only that she craves; and so follows the music from fig.298 that has already been discussed. Notice that two low clarinets and the bass clarinet trill uninterrupted (though the pair, at least, is mercifully staggered) for no less than thirty-three bars (!) before their G yields in a sudden spasm to the low E♭ of the back desks of the basses, creating with the bass drum the chasm of low vibration from which the solitary high bass will sound so uncannily.

Trilling recommences at fig.354/6. Here the dissonance implicit in any semitonal trill is made explicit by the upper strings, tremolandos on both notes. The strings soon disappear, but the A/B♭ tingle continues on flutes and clarinets against her motive in piercing E minor (oboe and piccolo) and the murky blur, miles beneath, of C♯ minor (plus F♯ and A♯). This evocation of the taste of her ambiguous *Liebesmahl* persists for some twenty-eight very slow bars. Even as (at fig.358) the harmony begins to clear and glow through F♯ major, then A major, the A/B♭ continues; C♯/D joins it; and the climax of the whole work (from fig.359 to Herod's cry, fig.361/5), including its most celebrated scrunch, is swathed in a halo of trills involving sixteen wood-winds, timps, suspended cymbal, tambourine, side drum and—again—both hands of the sonically hapless celeste, sanctifying the unclean act in a nimbus of quasi-mystical joy.

refrain had strayed into *The Martyr of Antioch*. Equally bad but very different music is employed for Jochanaan to denounce the corruption of Herod's court (from four before fig.70 to fig.76), to rave away at Salome herself (*ca*. figs 81–5) or to foretell (figs 220–2) the dreadful end of the world. Piling on the dissonances and the orchestral *frissons* to make our flesh creep is as vain as the oleaginous appeal to 'higher things'. Indeed they appear in close juxtaposition in the first passage cited: at fig.73 the prophet exhorts Herodias to arise from her incestuous bed ('Green Horror' music)[6] to heed the word of the Lord at fig.74 (churchy strains) and repent her of her sins (fig.75, back to the shivers and shakes). We know about Strauss's difficulties with religious emotion that is not broadly pantheistic/erotic from his reluctance to depict the 'goody-goody' hero of *Josephslegende*;[7] it is no surprise that baleful imaginings from the Apocalypse should produce an equally stock response. Onomatopoeia and mimicry just cannot render such things.

But give him a *wind* (fig.164, again at 167, a third gust at 168, and finally up, away and over the top from 233 to 241) and his virtuosity with straightforward orchestral depiction can flourish unchecked by the creaking stilts of spiritual content. As we shudder with Herod and with him grow hot and cold, the physical force of it almost lifts us from our seats. This is neither good nor bad in itself, it is merely breathtakingly *successful*. And within a few bars of the last, extremest gust—bars in which Herod has exhaustedly asked Salome for the last time to dance for him and she has, this time, knowing his oath, agreed—the Baptist is at his pious exercise again (fig.243).

Juxtapositions like this, of materials indifferent or even positively bad, can be the source of some of *Salome*'s most telling moments. Thus to take two simple instances first, the 'Green Horrors' of the prophet's warning of doom set off by extreme contrast Herod's lavish gesture, just as impoverished in musical substance, of Invitation to the Dance (three bars before fig.224); while the chorus of Jews (from five before fig.189 to fig.207) with its thousands of notes zipping past, composed by rote with unflagging skill upon indifferent material, makes its full effect, as a well-aimed comic scherzo, by placement against, at one end, the angry jitterings of Herodias, Herod's waxing *voluptas* and Salome's indifference, and, at the other, the bland duet of Nazarenes which I have already singled out for its special awfulness.

---

[6] 'At that time [Strauss's] music reminded me of Böcklin and Stuck, and the other painters of what we then called the German Green Horrors.' *Conversations with Igor Stravinsky*, p.75.

[7] 'The chaste Joseph himself isn't at all up my street, and if a thing bores me I find it difficult to set it to music. This god-seeker Joseph—he's going to be a hell of an effort! Well, maybe there's a pious tune for good boy Joseph lying about in some atavistic recess of my appendix.' Strauss to Hofmannsthal, 11 September 1912 (*The Correspondence between Richard Strauss and Hugo von Hofmannsthal*, trans. Hanns Hammelmann and Ewald Osers (Cambridge: Cambridge University Press, 1980), p.142. See Hofmannsthal's shocked and high-minded response two days later! Strauss so realistic, Hofmannsthal so airy-fairy: little doubt, surely, who has the truer grasp.

But the crucial instance is of course the 'Dance of the Seven Veils'. Here there is an additional stratagem involved: cunning use of the audience's expectations. Both Herod's previous invitations—to the dance already mentioned (three bars before fig.224) and to 'trink Wein mit mir' (fourth bar of fig. 172)—launch generously into a tune that never comes, foundering equally upon Salome's indifference and Herod's short concentration-span. Disappointment at such withholding as to seem like an incapacity for delivering the wished-for goods is amply assuaged when the 'Dance' at last comes (thus deftly aligning the audience at once with Herod's desires and Salome's knowledge that she possesses the means of steering them towards the realisation of her own). After its flurried introduction it is all tunes from beginning to end. All of them are 'vulgar' (Proust) or 'mediocre' (Fauré), if not frankly bad. But we know how strangely potent cheap music can be.[8] The bargain-basement orientalism at letter F is both blenchmaking and stirring; at letter V we continue to be stirred even when we realise we are being taken advantage of—the oriental knicknack is a palpable fake. Are we stirred against our better nature, or do we gratefully acquiesce in our true baseness? Strauss is very clever at raising such puritanical teeterings upon the verge of the ocean of kitsch. They should already have been banished by letters K to P, where we have perforce to give in, submitting to the experience for what it is worth, for what it has cost, realising that it couldn't and shouldn't be otherwise. This sense of the music's quality and character as inevitable enables it to survive the glimpse into the wrong chamber three bars before letter O (where a peruked bourgeois gentilhomme makes a tiny accidental appearance some seven years, or seventeen centuries, before his due time), because our goal, now so sure, is the thirty-two-bar slow-waltz tune that commences eight bars before letter Q, where all this 'genius for bad taste' is clinched with 'triumphant banality' indeed. Sustained, masterly, deeply-thrilling kitsch here comes into its own as the absolutely right level and intonation for this particular situation in this particular work. 'Good taste' would involve a loss of face, even a chickening out, and therefore be artistically fatal. This defence is not offered as a sop to the allure of a camp aesthetic whose ultimate wriggle says 'it's good *because* it's awful'. Much more straightforward: if it weren't what it is it wouldn't come off; it succeeds within the same stylistic area as the 'wind', already discussed, that has Herod crying ice and fire in almost the same breath.

The fact that the 'Dance of the Seven Veils' is so maligned shows the difficulty of defining this area and evaluating it fairly. In one sense it *is* cheap, mediocre, vulgar music. But this is *Salome*, not *Les diamants de la Couronne* (nor yet *Tristan*), and Strauss as always provides exactly what is needed. What do people *expect* otherwise, who complain of its tawdriness? What do they *want*?—the perfumed garden and calls-to-erection of the *Poème d'extase*, the ultra-elegance of amorous soft porn *à la Daphnis et Chloé*, the small print of sensuality refined and spiritualised *à la Jeux*? The *donnée* is Strauss,

---

[8] Noel Coward, *Private Lives*, Act I.

adapting as opera Wilde's play on Salomé and the Baptist with the artistic aims and resources of a thoroughly up-to-date German master in the prime of life, *anno* 1905. Get it right!

The questions raised here will have to be sorted out later. For the moment, before continuing the exploration of *Salome*, it is enough to see how quickly consideration of the work's purely musical character leads in to central questions about its composer in the large. The norm of the work, far more frequent than high exaltation, vigorous vulgarity or cunning mediation of different levels of badness, is the 'perpetual dazzle' of which Fauré's review goes on to speak, 'which tires not only the spirit but also—does this seem absurd?—the eyes'. And above all the critical faculty; for it is an essential part of Strauss's technique to produce such a copious and detailed rush of sound as not to grant time for its examination. Or even assimilation; there isn't time to stop and reflect—he has contrived that we cannot distinguish good from bad, tiring us into an unresisting acceptance of whatever happens next. The clearest examples are the orchestral interludes where Jochanaan is brought out of the cistern (figs 59–66) and, still more, when he is taken back down (from six bars before fig.141 to just after 151): astonishing in their audacity of raw excitement and extreme compositional crudeness, the protagonists' motifs juxtaposed or superimposed any-old-how, jacked up and down in sequences, at once insouciant, importunate and mechanical—ice and fire at the turn of a knob, as if in a well-practised and knowing improvisation. Thus if we reflect; as we hear it at the speed with which it seems to come into being before our very eyes like a carpet unrolling before our feet, this music is, again, 'exactly what is needed' in these particular places; it is as totally efficacious as the ungraspable rushing of the Jews' chorus or the wind, or the readily assimilable slow-waltz tune in the 'Dance'. Strauss's technique *holds* like good luck: his indifferent mastery is such that we are able, as we listen, to play off almost unwittingly the improvisatory scurry of the work's norm of texture against the underlying simplicity, definiteness and slow-motion of the structure as a whole.[9] Thus the drastic slowing-down for the final scene, so that it can actually be taken in at the same speed at which it comes out, both mitigates the audience's anxiety at not quite having caught the earlier events as they flashed by, and gives them the comfort, and the satisfaction, of having worked hard to earn such expansion, ease and warmth. All this being in perfect accord with the composer's saving his greatest inspiration for this final scene as if all the earlier stages were the improviser's warming-up, trying over his material, getting into gear, working up the heat that at last, extruding all this slag and fuss, leaves only the gold, red-hot and more or less pure.

---

[9] Compare Glenn Gould: '... at every moment—regardless of the breadth of the score, regardless of its metric complexities, regardless of the kaleidoscopic cross-reference of chromatic tonality—the bass line remains as firm, as secure, a counterpoise as in the works of Bach or Palestrina.' From 'An Argument for Richard Strauss', in *The Glenn Gould Reader*, ed. Tim Page (London: Faber, 1987), pp.87–8. As always, Gould (writing about Strauss in general, not any particular work) overstates.

ii

The phrase 'exactly what's wanted' is a portmanteau enclosing a number of possibilities. They range from the most practical exigencies of the opera's stage-craft and timing (as it were Petipa's instructions to Tchaikovsky) to what will be required of the music by way of matching, interpreting, enhancing, trans-forming the original play (as it were Boïto to Verdi); from the lively sense that this practical type of artist always shows for just what his performers will seize on (the Strauss of the *Ariadne* Prologue, at home backstage, intimate with his prima donna, his tenor, his soubrette) to the vital business of what the audience wants (the Strauss of the Producer in *Capriccio*, sticking to his philistine guns amidst the pretty salvoes of the poet, the composer, the ele-gant man of the world and his sensitive sister)—all its desires from the most elevated to the most debased, all its reactions whether communal or covert. What Strauss himself wants is seemingly lost in the gratification of accom-modating all these prior commitments with the successful outcome of his endeavours. After 'exactly what's wanted' has been handed out all round, it might begin to be possible to see what *he* might want in composing *Salome* (apart, with hindsight, from the income that paid for his villa in Garmisch); and thence to define him a little more closely. He seems to set out only to give, not to get, satisfaction, as if irrespective of his own predilections, or indeed as if he had none. That this is not true is clear from the remark already quoted: 'If a thing bores me I find it difficult to set it to music.' Yet, in the epoch of unprecedented self-expression and larger-than-life artistic profile, in spite of such grandiosity of self-presentation as *Heldenleben* and *Domestica* (not to mention the potent sorcerer in *Feuersnot*), he is curiously absent from all his richest creations, as if *Salome* and *Elektra* were not so different from a *Taillefer* or a *Festliches Präludium*.

Stravinsky said that Strauss 'didn't give a damn';[10] Hans Keller that he had 'a hole in the heart'.[11] But these negatives fail to describe the kind of artist who is the opposite of self-expressive and passionately engaged in his every utterance; equally the opposite of the mediumistic, the chosen vessel through which a divine message passes. He could say, 'I want to put myself to music';[12] and he could say, 'I want to give music as a cow gives milk'.[13]

---

[10] 'Strauss may charm and delight but he cannot move. That is partly because he was never committed. He didn't give a damn.' Stravinsky, after *Der Rosenkavalier* at Ham-burg, 2 May 1963, quoted in Robert Craft, *Chronicle of a Friendship* (New York: Vintage Books, 1973), p.215.

[11] Frequently in conversation; and see also 'Unmade History', Part 2, *Music and Musicians* 23/11 (July 1975).

[12] 'What I'd like best of all, time and again, would be to put myself to music.' To Hofmannsthal, 12 July 1927: *The Correspondence between Richard Strauss and Hugo von Hofmannsthal*, p.436.

[13] At the final rehearsal before the first performance of the *Alpine Symphony*: 'At last I have learned to orchestrate. I wanted to compose, for once, as a cow gives milk.'

He manages both: the apparent megalomania of the first actually comes out as a kind of young-bullish boastfulness and selfishness miles removed from typical late-Romantic *Angst* and introspection; while the self-effacement and homeliness of the second allows him to get inside a Juan or a Till, a young superman or deluded old Quixote, a lustrously indifferent Salome and her lust-besotted stepfather, or to depict from the outside himself routing his enemies and taking off to the mountains with his mate, or, a few years later, the selfsame couple plus infant son, rioting over the breakfast table in a positive bacchanal of bourgeois domesticity. Above all, these pieces are so entertaining!—hilarious and exhilarating, if not always intended in quite the same spirit as we now take them—and so greatly adding to the gaiety of nations as to make his desire later in life to be 'the Offenbach of the twentieth century' not such a *volte face* as it at first seems.[14]

Strauss is neutral. He is a kind of emporium, whose rich, well-stocked and widely diversified wares are all produced on the premises by reliable craftsmen. Whether humdrum or exalted, everything is a job of work, planned and executed with business-like efficiency. Strauss is protean in his own enterprise, being at once the craftsman who makes, the merchant who sells, and the middleman who ascertains (even creates) demand and links up the various separate departments. He is also the genial provider, the cornucopian source who fuels his company and keeps it fed. As with so many of the big nineteenth-century producers, it is as much a matter of machinery as of Art[15] (though something very similar in spirit is already present in descriptions of the workshops of the great painters and sculptors of the Renaissance). When everything functions with such manifest smoothness, copiousness and success, it seems not so much churlish as irrelevant to ask for something else, something 'more'. What would it be? No one with a sense of what's what in matters of style and artistic nature would demand sublimity, severity, spirituality, intellectual grappling, philosophical profundity from Strauss at his most characteristic and best—and therefore from *Salome*. We know where such qualities are located, and go there to find them. He gives us what he's got, gold and dross, poured out like milk.

How does 'exactly what's wanted' actually work in all its various meanings? The 'Dance' requires (say) at one point a long, slow thirty-two-bar waltz-period. The exigencies of the stage require (say) just such-and-such a length to raise Jochanaan from his cistern and get him back into it, or for the soldiers at the end to rush forward and crush Salome to death before the curtain falls. Herod and Herodias (say) require to be memorably and effectively characterised; and the wind that he feels and she does not will need to be

---

[14] Letter to Hofmannsthal, 5 June 1916: further, 'sentimentality and parody are the sensations to which my talent responds most forcefully and productively'. *The Correspondence between Richard Strauss and Hugo von Hofmannsthal*, pp.250–1.

[15] Compare Busoni: 'Richard Strauss who (even in his art) is a cross between an artist and an industrialist...', in *The Essence of Music and Other Essays*, trans. Rosamund Ley (New York: Dover, 1965), p.52.

rendered in music. The subject itself, and its time and setting, require the sheen of opulent near-Eastern depravity in which all its events are swathed. When we turn to the details of the text and its musical matching, such general needs become more precise and well-defined. In itself Wilde's play is a poor thing, the ingrown child of a whole line of literature evoking antiquity in its decadence. Closest behind it stands Flaubert's late *Hérodias*, of which Wilde's play is indeed a virtual plagiarisation, sensationalising its treatment of the same story and trifling with its underlying theme.

But it all suits Strauss down to the ground; it is the native soil of his most avid fecundity. The operatic *Salome* is a perfect match of genius and talent. Wilde's poetic language, at once hyped-up and debased, covers a void that cries out for Strauss's descriptive powers to fill. Such period-piece poetastery as '[The moon] is like a woman rising from a tomb' (from the first scene) or 'Thy hair is like clusters of black grapes' (etc. *ad nauseam* in Salome's attempted seduction of the Baptist) releases true gorgeousness in the music. The bankrupt's largesse, in the accumulation of treasures Herod offers her if she but desist from the only prize she really wants, finds its perfect complement in Strauss's well-heeled literalism; the composer who prided himself on being able to distinguish in music between silver and silver-gilt is here given the richest opportunity in all his *œuvre* (until the late shower of gold in *Danaë*) to exercise this freakish gift. Such pseudo-sublimity as 'The mystery of love is greater than the mystery of death' (from the final scene) becomes in this composer's hands, not profound for sure, but a genuine and expertly-posed shudder, rendered in the external manner which we have seen to be his way with everything, through which we, like the heroine, may kiss the dead lips of a severed head.

So Strauss can flesh out Wilde's flashy insubstantiality, provide gold and dross to redeem his paper money, animate his languid literariness. What he cannot do is ennoble or deepen the treatment of the subject itself. Something that might in more thoughtful hands be subtly disturbing and genuinely subversive remains decorative and, for all its apparatus of lust and violence, extraordinarily *comfy*. There is, moreover, a vein of opportunism in Strauss's appropriation of what for Wilde had been an *exercice de style;* the lurid treatment of a Gospel episode (however peripheral) would inevitably scandalise authority both ecclesiastic and civic, to the work's enormous initial advantage till, the honeymoon over, it settled down, like all erstwhile shockers that turn out to have staying-power, to become 'fun for all the family'. And thus, in the end if not at once, 'exactly what's wanted' by the audience too: a whipped-cream panto with strip-tease and an improving moral. In its day the combination was irresistible of outrageously advanced but fundamentally recognisable music with a quasi-sacred story which, pretending to treat the anyway thoroughly corny but tolerably serious theme of sensuality's head-on conflict with asceticism, was really all set to yield a below-the-belt thrill. What survives of it now for us who see so clearly how the machinery works, and why does the appeal remain so potent? Strauss's worldly wisdom concerning his audience's desires, how it goes about gratifying them, and how it squares the gratification with the demands of heavy-duty high culture, is as infallible for nowadays as for 1905. *Salome* neither invites nor needs tendentious new interpretation to remain perennially 'relevant'.

The word 'invites' opens up another large metaphor. If Strauss the artist can be compared to an emporium, *Salome* the artwork is something of a *grande horizontale*. This metaphor of the opera's meretriciousness, in thoroughly bad taste, is closer than any other to the way it remains so successfully and perennially enjoyable; it can be exploited for what it's worth and so far as it will go. Where low pleasures meet high culture we tend to be hypocritical and devious. We want a bit of a thrill, a touch of danger, a whiff of the exotic; but decent appearances must be kept up, and elevations and ticklings must be legitimised. We want to be excited and stirred but not disconcerted, disturbed, singed or seared. *Salome*, so well-made, efficient, comfortable and safe, is the perfect answer: a night on the side for the assiduous spouse of great art. An important element is the willingness and habituality of both parties-in-pleasure. Embarrassment and vacillation, whether over the function or the payment, have long since disappeared. The opera knows what it is for, does it well, enjoys it, flourishes on the proceeds; general satisfaction all round.

Such directness about why Salome and her client have come together overlays another kind of knowingness, that what they are doing is wrong. This is not *sin;* it doesn't fan 'the fire i' th' blood', let alone open a peephole upon the sublime knowledge of evil of which Baudelaire speaks in his *Intimate Journals* in words which truly make us tremble.[16] That would not be *Salome*: it would be *Parsifal* Act II or *Lulu* Act III. The area of misbehaviour is, rather, the domain evoked by such clichés as 'naughty but nice' or 'a little of what you fancy does you good', a brief self-indulgence as we abandon for a moment 'the straight and narrow'. We know this and it is part of the attraction. We cannot live with Parsifal and Lulu all the time, any more than with Hänsel and Gretel, or with the in-laws and the next-doors. Our desire for a package-debauch is perfectly understood and used: our need to be thrilled and our willingness to spend to obtain it are in exact collusion with the work's very being. There is no evil in it, and its horrors are dangerous only so much and so little as Belgian chocolates are dangerous. Indulgence in *Salome* is more like the smoker's habitual ignoring of the government health warning than the bravado of 'unsafe sex'.

The metaphors of the emporium and of the 'good-time girl' both operate in a thoroughly bourgeois/consumer way to render the nexus between artwork and audience completely grateful. Bouvard and Pécuchet would purr over *Salome*. Conspicuously well-crafted, its materials ostentatiously the best that money can buy, with notes like sequins stitched on in their millions by expensive specialised labour, it is not cheap in any material sense. Nor is it

---

[16] 'For my part I say that the unique and supreme pleasure in love-making lies in the certain knowledge that one is doing *evil*. Men and women know from birth that in evil lies all pleasure of the sense.' Charles Baudelaire, *My Heart Laid Bare*, ed. Peter Quennell, trans. Norman Cameron (London: Weidenfeld and Nicholson, 1950), p.157.

mere entertainment. It has pretensions to serious presentation of deep matters—a thoroughly modern study of the psychopathology of crazed pubescent sexuality deflected from one aim to seize morbidly upon another, gaining its own way by flagrant will-power till suddenly and satisfactorily crushed like a poisonous snake; it is set in the East, with its well-known mysteriousness and ungoverned abandonment to unnatural appetites, where the air is heavy with perfume and blood; and to dangerously advanced music by a notorious modernist. Yet all these potentially explosive ingredients are defused and turn out to be *entertaining*, with no need to furrow the brow or search the soul: scratch the modernity and you have *Liebeslieder* waltzes, scratch the exoticism and it is 'made in Birmingham', scratch the psychological profundity and you get sensationalised stereotypes in a stock situation. Finally, Strauss draws no moral. *Salome*, contrary to the early reactions of outrage, is not immoral in the slightest. Nor is it 'improving': a moralist wants to teach, exhort, reform, change lives, and for such modes Strauss indeed 'doesn't give a damn'. In short the whole thing is predigested, processed and (so to speak) served up on a plate.

iii

Commercial, meretricious and shallow! But, evidently, something that, like sugar, we want and even need. Generous indulgences are called for, rather than denunciation and contempt. We willingly bend our severe standards to admit such a grossly pleasurable intrusion into our ordinary lives. For *Salome* is powerfully enough itself to permit a grateful defence of its supremacy in a category where it is not necessary to reproach its composer or ourselves for confusing art and kitsch; where their mingling together produces not only the cheap thrill and the naughty chocolate but an emotion too—fugitive but genuine—the warmth of the work's response to what in us, its listeners, is always able, willing and indeed longing to be taken for a ride. Its peculiarly satisfying quality lies in the surprisingly substantial depth of feeling induced by the frankness of the reciprocal arrangement made so easily once our hypocritical, hypercritical hang-ups are overcome. There is an aesthetic realm of rich cheapness, sufficient shallowness, genuine corn: the bargain-basement below the belt, the rag-and-bone shop of the heart, where such art as Strauss's comes into its own. *Salome* is surely its principal ornament; manifest high inspiration works with supreme technical accomplishment, in a spiritual void, to raise kitsch to *Kunst* by sheer genius. Its sense of its own success is so convincing that we have perforce to share it. We are not so much convinced as convicted, partners in a guiltless relinquishment of our supposed better nature, mown down like grass before such energy, inventiveness, headiness, an overall *Schwung* that not only mends the insouciance as to larger absences but melts away all qualms as to what is present, be it ever so vulgar or mediocre. He knows how to get a stage to vibrate, a girl to sing, an orchestra to seethe, erupt and incandesce. He knows how to rouse his audience to a frenzy. Later, with the Marschallin, he begins to manipulate tears and heart-strings; in *Salome* he is still content if (as Bernstein says) 'there's not a dry seat in the house'. Nobler things had been done supremely well; this is Strauss's thing; it is new aesthetic territory even if he and his admirers after him persuade themselves into thinking that he is still in line with the great tradition. Only if we forget the damaging absurdity of taking *Salome* and *Die Frau ohne Schatten* to be Wagnerian, and *Der Rosenkavalier* and *Capriccio* to be Mozartian(!),[17] can Strauss come into his own, a category apart. His denigrators, equally, are missing something unique and extraordinarily interesting.

These genre-mistakes arise because Strauss, unlike the comparable Puccini, is complicated by cultural striving, a sort of do-gooding which remained a weak point all his life, from *Macbeth* to *Metamorphosen*, well before and after Hofmannsthal nagged and rebuked him into airy-fairy-land. Admiration for his serious aspiration has inevitably to place *Die Frau ohne Schatten* at the head of the operatic output and the *Alpine Symphony* at the summit of a series of increasingly profound symphonic poems (the succession regrettably lapsing with the *Domestica*). The 'earthy' riposte would urge the claims of *Don Juan* and *Till*, the most vital music in *Feuersnot*, *Der Rosenkavalier* without the massive longueurs, and *Intermezzo*. In fact at his best he exploits the comic and expressive potential of juxtaposing high and low.[18] Latent in *Till*, this becomes the actual substance of *Don Quixote*, and when after his Expressionist excursion Strauss discovers his native Bavarian rococo with Viennese trimmings, it lies at the core of his style. The *seria* of *Ariadne abbandonata* is not particularly inspired in itself; the *buffa* of Zerbinetta and her troupe seems rather middling once we spot its origin in that masterpiece of confectionery *Hänsel und Gretel* (whose première Strauss had conducted); the heroics and erotics of Bacchus are distinctly saggy. But the juxtapositions and tentative comings-together of these diversely undistinguished strains give *Ariadne auf Naxos* a unique flavour; thereafter the differences do not need such emphasis, and by the time of *Capriccio* their fusion is harmonious and total.[19]

The fascination, and the quality, lie in the mixture.[20] *Salome* is the best instance of this in his entire *œuvre*. Her sister *Elektra* overdoes both the horrors (leaving the audience half-saying 'go on, do it again, do it more', and half-stunned into indifference) and the beauties (in the voluptuous hedonism, quite

---

[17] Overheard during the supper-interval at a Glyndebourne *Rosenkavalier* (answering the question 'Who wrote the music?'): 'It's Mozart, dear; you can tell by the costumes.'

[18] This was well-taken by Hofmannsthal. In his letter of 15 May 1916 he speaks both of 'the contrast between the heroic ideal and its denial' in *Ariadne* and of the 'spicing of the sentimental with its opposite' (for Zerbinetta) that 'is quite in your spirit'. *The Correspondence between Richard Strauss and Hugo von Hofmannsthal*, pp.246–7.

[19] See 'Strauss's Last Opera', p.142ff. Some of the notions here are taken from this earlier attempt, some are carried further, some controvert it.

[20] Hofmannsthal again (to Strauss, 12 February 1919): '… both my art and yours derive so effortlessly, so naturally from the Bavarian–Austrian Baroque with its mixture of different elements and their fusion in music.' *The Correspondence between Richard Strauss and Hugo von Hofmannsthal*, p.324.

wrong for its context, of the Recognition Scene). Moreover in *Elektra* the true seriousness of the subject is traduced by Strauss's being his most natural self, so that in order to enjoy the high inspiration of its best music we have to divorce it from its relationship to the situation, and take it for itself alone.[21] *Salome* is not beset by such problems: high and low are tellingly juxtaposed or else rub down well together; the high scrapes the depths and the low is exalted to the heights (as it says in the Bible), with Strauss in the prime of his energies, superbly indifferent to good and bad, generously covering the trashiness of characters and situation with the fruit of his copious cornucopia.

   Salome is of course a crucial work historically. Taken one way, it opens up important aspects of early Schoenberg and later Mahler; *Wozzeck* and *Lulu* are inconceivable without it. Taken another, it facilitates more colouristic sensationalism by smaller talents, from the relative distinction of *Die Gezeichneten* and *Eine florentinische Tragödie*, via *Violanta* and *Mona Lisa*, to the pure low-grade kitsch of the film scores of Hollywood's palmy days. But for Strauss himself these 'German Green Horrors' are an excursion. Being a master of mimicry, costume-change and ruses, he is 'trying it on'. After *Salome*, and as *Elektra* is already under way, he is begging Hofmannsthal for further sensational subjects—'a really wild Cesare Borgia or Savonarola would be the answer to my prayers'.[22] Fortunately he was diverted via the huge success of *Der Rosenkavalier*, and its sense of stylistic homecoming, into more fruitful paths; so that, as we have seen, he can by 1916 claim that his principal gift is for sentimentality and parody and that he feels called to be the modern Offenbach. Surely this master of the quick change of mask is responsible for *Salome* too? Everything in it stems, as shown, from 'what is wanted'; which turns out to be, 'what to wear that will suit the occasion'. Like his own *Till* he is seeing what he can get away with, how far he can exploit this particular vein. In the end his best-fitting fancy costumes are the 'rococo' (eighteenth-century in setting, with heavy admixture from the mid-nineteenth-century Viennese waltz, the whole as unmistakably of its epoch as the pastiche Mansart of the Edwardian Ritz Hotel) and the neo-Greek (somewhere between Schinkel, Böcklin and the 1936 Olympic Stadium). And his easiest undress is the skat and slippers of the homely husband of Garmisch. Underneath Salome's seventh veil, or the bitchiness of Herodias, or the bittersweet of the Marschallin, or the hefty ordinariness of Barak's wife, lies Pauline.

iv

Strauss as we have seen him to be, Strauss *au naturel*, provides in setting this particular story at this particular time everything that might be expected; the

---

[21] See 'The orchestration of *Elektra*: a critical interpretation', p.122ff..

[22] Letter of 11 March 1906 (*The Correspondence between Richard Strauss and Hugo von Hofmannsthal*, p.3). They both agree upon a *Semiramis* (see Hofmannsthal's detailed description of 22 December 1907, pp.10–11), and Strauss also mentions a *Saul and David* and a *Dantons Tod* in these early days of their collaboration.

work fulfils its promises to the utmost and, tenderly stripped of its illusory pretensions to depth or sublimity, stands naked before us as itself—'ich bin Salome'. So the earlier comment that 'what he cannot do is ennoble or deepen the treatment of the subject itself', if uttered as a complaint, puts the emphasis wrong. Understanding Strauss aright, we should neither require this of him nor blame him that he does not do it. And the same goes for reproaches or denunciations of the sharply inconsistent calibre of his musical materials.[23] These are questions that simply did not occur to him. No artist would *choose* to be patchy or shallow; it is manifestly involuntary. Strauss, as properly seen, would no more labour for the purity of his gold (*à la* Webern) than he would be capable (*à la* Stravinsky) of ironic play with inverted commas around the debased coinage. *Salome*, unlike his more serious subjects, is enhanced by this rather than traduced.

He trusts himself totally, thoughtlessly, to what his fertility yields him. Such unabashed naiveté is surely vindicated, for greater discrimination in the part would have inhibited the whole; 'sentimental' self-consciousness would not have allowed *any* of this red-hot mix of gold and slag past the censor. The vindication lies in *Salome*'s serendipity; not only of incidental wonders all the way, but in the fact that the whole *kitsch suprème* lives in spite of every objection that can be raised. It's not 'good *because* it's awful': on the contrary, it is the best, by far, of its own kind.

---

[23] Compare Debussy: 'In the cookery book, under Jugged Hare, will be seen this wise recommendation: "Take a hare." Richard Strauss proceeds otherwise. To write a symphonic poem he takes anything.' Quoted in Edward Lockspeiser, *Debussy* (London: Dent, 1951), p.241.

19

The orchestration of *Elektra*: a critical interpretation

(See headnote for Salome, *p.107.)*

* * *

i

The problem in considering the orchestration of *Elektra* is to reconcile Strauss's instruction to play the work 'as if [it] were by Mendelssohn: fairy music'[1] with the largest forces required by any opera in the repertory. Its starting-point is the orchestra as constituted for the *Ring*, but the aesthetic goal is very different. Wagner deploys his vast forces to produce homogeneity, rounded-ness and warmth; contrasts of colour and weight are gradual, as befits his scale and speed, and even when the sonority is at its maximum (*Götterdämmerung*, Act II) there remains a fulness that is always built up from a powerful bass. Strauss's use of the same forces plus some extras comes after *Salome* and all but one of the symphonic poems, whose tendency has been to break up the homogeneity, splash on the colour, raise the tessitura and take brilliance of detail to the very edge of virtuosity. He can be more brutalistic and more brilliant, heavier and lighter, all with an electricity and a rapidity of change that would be out of place even in the more extravagant reaches of *Parsifal*, where the sources of *Elektra* mainly lie.

Brass is exactly as in the *Ring*: eight horns, of which four double two pairs of Wagner tubas whose bass is the contrabass tuba; three trombones and a contrabass; for normal purposes three trumpets and a bass trumpet, strength-ened in the heftiest climaxes by three extra players (and thus overtopping Wagner's demands). The woodwinds are basically in fours: piccolo and three flutes (first also doubling piccolo), three oboes (third doubling cor anglais) and heckelphone, three bassoons and contrabassoon. Strauss alas did not follow up the somewhat gingerly experiment with an optimal saxophone choir in the *Symphonia domestica*, but clarinets are expanded with typical turn-of-the-century

---

[1] 'Ten Golden Rules for the Album of a Young Conductor' (1925), in *Recollections and Reflections*, ed. Willi Schuh, trans. L. J. Lawrence (London: Boosey and Hawkes, 1953), p.38.

generosity to eight in all: four ordinary clarinets (B♭ and A), one small in E♭, one bass (B♭) and a hapless couple of basset horns strayed out of their native eighteenth century. Here, then, there is a far wider spectrum of timbre than in Wagner (as well as four more players). But the more specifically colouristic aspects of *Elektra* are modest by some contemporary standards (*Rapsodie espagnole*, *Firebird*, Mahler 8, *Gurrelieder*): though the two harps may be doubled from p.353[2] to the end, the celeste is optional. Two timpani players are required, and the percussion is straightforward; the list at the start of the score omits the *two* pairs of castanets that clack four times on p.11 and the switch (*Rute*) that spurs Klytämnestra's procession into motion on pp.75–91 ('a confused noise of trampling beasts, of whips, of muffled screams'[3]). The latter had first been heard on p.23 when the young servant-girl was beaten.

More seriously incomplete, or at least ambiguous, is this list's breakdown of the strings. Violins are divided into firsts, seconds and thirds, eight of each, making twenty-four in all, eight less than the thirty-two in the standard *de luxe* turn-of-the-century division of sixteen firsts and sixteen seconds. Do the missing eight help swell the violas up to the eighteen mentioned on the first page of music (as opposed to the list, which only requires six)? No, because almost from the start and unmistakably by pp.20–1 all three viola parts (6 + 6 + 6) are well below violin range. (Strauss is notoriously cavalier about notes off the bottom of the violins: in *Elektra* he gives all twenty-four violins just six crotchets' rest to retune the G-string down to encompass the three low F semiquavers on p.26.) In fact it is the other way about: the top third of the eighteen violas has twice to become fourth violins, for the recognition scene and Elektra's hymn before action (pp.272–98) and from p.342 to the end (Elektra's apotheosis and death). The score says 'muta in IV. Violinen'; whether this is a change of *function* for players who still remain playing their violas, or involves a change of actual *instrument* is not made clear. But the result is in effect the standard firsts/seconds division of the violins. The twelve cellos are divided into firsts and seconds almost throughout, and there are eight double basses. (For comparison, the *Ring* asks for 16:16:12:12:8.) The 'house feature' of *Elektra*, strings laid out in nine parts—vl. I, II, III; vla I, II, III; vcl. I, II; cb.—is more frequent throughout the work than any standard layout.

With an orchestra of twenty woodwinds, twenty brass, heavy battery and sixty-two strings, 'fairy music' would seem to be an unobtainable goal. Whereas one's instinctive sense-impression of *Salome* is shimmer and spice (albeit quite thickly laid on), *Elektra* reverberates in the mind with its weight; its animal bloodiness; its screams, tearings, axings; its nightmares and proces-

---

[2] Page references are to the miniature orchestral score and are used only when the rehearsal numbers common to this and the piano score cannot suffice to make the location clear. Many of the points will of course be meaningless without an orchestral score.

[3] Quotations from the libretto are given in the translation that accompanies the Solti recording (Decca SET 354-S).

sions; above all, the galumphing and colossal dance-motions with which it ends. The paradox can be evaded: perhaps it is just one of Strauss's notorious 'shrugs'—'don't bother *me*; I don't know'—designed half-embarrassedly, half-teasingly, to put questioners off the trail and escape culpability for his own excess. Or it can be circumvented by an exceptional performance, such as the *Elektra* under Carlos Kleiber that I saw at Covent Garden in 1977, where finesse and hairsplitting detail produced something quite different from the usual all-stops-out blow to the solar plexus. Or it can be laboriously explored by the commentator to yield what fruit it may.

What Carlos Kleiber missed was the normative in the work: the straight tutti usage which provides a gauge by which to measure its extremes. Its most and its least inspired sections are equally atypical of the special internal balance whereby hyperstrain becomes the norm. Least inspired by common consent is the long outburst for the 'normal' sister Chrysothemis (figs 75–114) and its varied return much later when Elektra plays upon this very normalcy to get Chrysothemis to act with her after the false news of Orestes' death (figs 52a–82a).[4] Though in *Elektra* these passages jar, in the context of Strauss as a whole they are typical enough—the Strauss who produces music 'as a cow gives milk', all the way from the genial banalities of his teens to the wind-band Sonatinas of the 1940s. The orchestra is so classically used that we forget its hugeness—that, for instance, all eight horns are in play from fig.102 till just after 112. It is like a turn-of-the-century solution to the problems of balance when the post-Wagnerian orchestra plays Beethoven: simply double (or even quadruple) all winds. Since the 'house feature' of the nine-part string texture is also retained, the result is a golden churn of Happy Workshop ease, as undistinguished in substance as it is masterly in its layout for maximum warmth and flow.

The recognition scene (figs 148a–155a) is also characterised by this golden strings-and-horns sound. The strings are given melody and flowing accompaniment figures; the halo of divisi and solo players does not conceal the basic layout as vl. I and II, vla, vcl. I and II, cb., simplifying by fig.153a into only three parts. A few woodwinds are sparingly used to double and intensify; all eight horns provide a glowing core of organ harmony, at its most ardent at fig.154a, where the paragraph's point of climax simultaneously begins to droop. The whole scene sounds like the work of a Mantovani of genius. Utterly gorgeous in sonority, it yet remains what Busoni would call 'transcribed'.

So the centre of Strauss's orchestra in *Elektra*, in its supreme passage and in its two dullest and most dutiful stretches, is the combination of horns and strings. In *Elektra* an abnorm in its very normalness, this kind of sound relates to the basis of Strauss's orchestration throughout his life. I want to stay with strings and horns separately for a moment before moving on to the less absolutely

---

[4] Excepting, in the first, the more acrid bars when Elektra's pitying contempt turns Chrysothemis' music unwontedly baleful, and, in the second, Elektra's brief Salome-like blandishment of her sister's womanly charms

quintessential instruments. Even here, at the heart of his orchestra, there are usages that are typical and usages that are special: usages and abusages of the heart.

Pretty normative is the passage from fig.18a: here the strings in four parts (all vls, vlas, all vcls, cb.) would *look* like an advanced turn-of-the-century string quartet (as it might be Schoenberg op.7 or Zemlinsky no.2)—four busy independent thematic lines (the bass with long sustained notes as well)—were it not for the wind and brass doubling the lines, the usual horn/organ part (anything from one to eight) and the more massive wind harmony towards the climax at fig.22a. More straightforward still is the first appearance of the Orestes-recognition theme, in its native A♭ (from bar 9 of fig.45): all violins unison, all cellos an octave below, harmony on violas *à3* and double basses *à2*, doubled by light low woodwinds and horns; horn 1 also doubles the tune in the lower (cello) octave; and the poignant A♭ minor phrase at its end is joined by a solo oboe in the upper (violin) octave.

From such instances of strings-as-foundation-of-the-orchestra I move to places where they are anything but. At fig.47 (through to 50) the violins split into their three, first joining with the three-part violas for skirls and banks of parallel chords in three, four and six parts, then doubled by low woodwinds, with four horns, also in parallel, pulling away in contrary motion, as also, well below, the basses, contrabassoon and contrabass tuba. Pure eye-and-ear onomatopoeia in the eight-part whirl for strings that for six bars at fig.233a drenches the ongoing beat of Elektra's final dance in 'the ocean, the twenty-fold vaster ocean' which in the very moment of revenge keeps her from rejoicing. More complex the string textures at figs 135–8, where the banks of unrelated triads spaced thus—vl. III + vla I + vcl. 1; vla II + vcl. 1; vla III + vcl. II, all three lines doubled by three muted horns—are set against soft but penetrating chords on six solo violas. Such description makes heavy weather of an extraordinary effect which could not have been achieved more simply.

So to usage and abusage of the heart's other half: the eight horn players, including the four Wagner tubas taken up, after the fashion of the *Ring*, by the second quartet of hornists. Their norm, as we have seen, is a warm mass of organ-harmony. There are of course solo passages, but almost nothing of that highly individuated writing for the whole section which makes some of Strauss's later scores (above all *Capriccio)* look like the Schumann *Konzert-stück* (a brief, partial exception comes in the six bars centering on fig.143a). *Elektra* is also the classic place for 'dreadful horn-writing'—unidiomatic if exciting whoops and runs (for example, fig.188 to one after 196; figs 1a–4a), signalling the horn-player's son in his furthest revolt against nature.

The previous history of the Wagner tubas, in the *Ring* and Bruckner's last three symphonies, is one of exalted sublimity with elements of the bucolic (and a touch of the grotesque for Fafner). Their sublimity is used early in the scene between Elektra and the stranger before he is recognised as her brother (figs 123a–126a). Though the four trombones join them (on p.250 the names of contrabass tuba and contrabass trombone are mistakenly reversed in the score), the timbre is tuba-ish in the most normative way, and all five of the family retain this low-horn organ-harmony foundation in the superb fourteen-bar sentence beginning at fig.126a. As against this, well within the intention for which Wagner invented the instruments, there is writing that pushes them to an extreme. Their first significant entry (figs 48–51) had been unobtrusive; from fig.123 they are warming up (à la Elgar); from 127, the start of Klytämnestra's entry procession, they begin to be fully characterised, with the big yawps (heraufschleifen) sticking out like an animal in pain; and from just after 130 the bullocky sound of their unison is a powerful ingredient in the general mêlée (their part coming in to 132 actually looks like Fafner's motive). The first stretch of the Klytämnestra scene (fig.135 to fourth bar of 141) extends this new character and colour for these big noble horns, a kind of hormone-charged alto-tenor throb, suggestive of her sexuality, her guilty bed redolent with memories and nightmares, her diseases of body and mind. (It seems a bit silly that three of them have to change back for only one chord at fig.145 before resuming their tubas just after 152.) Nothing else the Wagner tubas play is so striking as here, though this new colour and character are indispensable to the music beginning at fig.177, when Klytämnestra describes her bad nights, right through to the end of the scene and Elektra's premature triumph (fig.260), and thence into the orchestral interlude reversing that triumph, which will be considered later.

ii

Strings, horns and Wagner tubas are the melody, base and core of the Elektra orchestra. The mass of the woodwinds, even the heavier or more brilliant brass, are extra to this basic sound, and their parts are more a matter of notable individual moments and sometimes extended stretches, than ongoing background with an occasional sense of patient routine. I should like now to consider Strauss's orchestra as a tutti; again the idea of 'normal' and 'abnormal' can be useful, recognising always that, within the claustrophobia of this work, the two tend to be reversed.

Three interconnected examples will show the Elektra-tutti at its most usual. First, the end of Elektra's monologue, with its foretaste of the triumphal dance that will succeed righteous revenge. This passage (fig.53 to just after 64), the most sustained continuity in the work so far, is in musical substance as in orchestration a magnificent blow-up of the Johann Strauss waltz, with singing strings and emphatic rhythm-marking harmony on the brass, the whole sound underpinned by a 'continuo' of two timp.players, triangle, cymbals, bass drum (though not the ubiquitous side-drum of the Viennese dance-bands) and two harps (always in unison). Particularly successful as the dance gets under way is the combination of dry pounding dance-rhythm with sostenuto melody. From five after fig.58 the recognition theme in $^2/_2$ is placed across the dance in $^6/_4$, whose principal figure ($\downarrow. \flat\downarrow$) is at fig.59 bounced with heavy lightness across the entire orchestra, while the melody is passed among the upper strings (with unobtrusive woodwind doublings); the holes in this aerated texture are imperceptibly plugged by soft sostenuto whole-bar chords on (mainly) trumpets and trombones. The totality, made up of layer upon layer each incomplete in itself, leaves space for the harps' arpeggios to come through, subsidiary though they be, together with the delicious little flourish on two flutes in the third bar of fig.59. All this by way of contrast with the onslaught of the tutti from four before fig.62 to its fade around 64 as Chrysothemis appears.

The passage from the seventh bar of fig.172a to the sixth of 180a, when, at the end of the recognition scene, Elektra hymns the deed that is now about to be done, takes up and extends the lyric strain of the first waltz-dream. The texture is now open, singing, surging, basically on strings. The previous $^6/_4$ galumphing is replaced by the organ-like sostenuto chords, on all five tubas, that characterise Orestes; the percussion (all present except triangle) is used in occasional strokes and tingles rather than for rhythmic underlining—which is transferred to the tattoo motifs derived from the Agamemnon theme ♪♪♪ crackling across the texture in $^4/_4$ on aggressive brass (trombones, trumpets) but very softly. The mastery of Strauss's fluency in getting up heat, exaltation and shine on pretty indifferent musical materials can ride even the appalling eight bars at fig.177a, when the recognition theme is smeared across the texture by the first four horns in unison—a moment as crude as the comparable moment at figs 58–60 was subtle.

The second dance-episode, from fig.236a to just after 260a, completes this strain in the work, taking up both its singing and its strenuous aspects into a kind of dance-'Liebestod', a hymn of ritualised motion more psychological than physical. Its first stages (after the initial racket of arriving at C major dies down) are entirely lyrical, with singing strings and surging inner parts derived from the passage just discussed, and its sostenuto harmony now on the eight horns and the four trombones alternately. The festive percussion gradually joins, this time including a glockenspiel (after fig.244a)—and from this point the Agamemnon-tattoo is transformed into a hoofy downbeat from which is launched each bar, then each half-bar, of the powerful dance-motion at fig.247a. Two bars after fig.248a this turns into the ♩ ♪♩ motive, not at once obliterating the cantabile but predominating more and more till from around 252a it sweeps all before it to the four climactic bars at 254a. Thereafter it retreats to the bass (the double basses are actually marked *leicht)*, and by fig.257a is only kept up on the two harps and triangle (the clarinets doubling the harps do not count, since this motif when played legato loses its character), while soprano and orchestra sing with *Arabella*-like lyricism. From the seventh bar of fig.258a it grows suddenly and gigantically; seven bars suffice to achieve maximum volume (all eight horns, all seven trumpets and a proper cymbal crash) at 260a.

These three episodes taken together make a 'Dance of the *Überweib*'-cum-'Liebestod' whose athletic aspect evidently grows from the 'Ride of the Valkyries' and whose lyric aspect, less evidently but demonstrably, derives from the flowing $^6/_4$ of Mendelssohn's *Schöne Melusine* and her warmer-blooded descendants the Rhinemaidens (see the eleven bars from the key-change just after fig.255a—the timps in particular are straight out of the first scene of *Das Rheingold*, the musical substance out of the Mendelssohn). The whole is swathed in a vastly exploded Viennese waltz, updated to the Palm Court of the Ritz Hotel *c*.1908. It is a tribute to Strauss's panache that he can carry off such a *mélange* with complete lack of self-consciousness: confronted with this triumphalism, 'tis folly to be wise!

By contrast with such gigantism, what Strauss might mean by 'fairy music' begins to become a little clearer. Two outstanding passages come to mind; though neither is exactly gossamer-like, they both have a speed and fluency that derive ultimately from Mendelssohn's scherzo-types. The fleet $^6/_8$ of the interlude, from five before fig.261 to the work's halfway break before 1a, is the first really fast music in the opera; its sharpness and apparent gaiety render at once the unholy exhilaration of Klytämnestra's joy at the news of Orestes' death and the lighting of torches to banish the nightmares she has just divulged. The starting-point is the scherzo from *A Midsummer Night's Dream*, given weight, grandeur and length by Loge's big set-piece in Nibelheim, then restored by Strauss to the original quicksilver movement while retaining something of the Wagnerian weight (the ♩ ♪♩♪ figure on seven low clarinets and cor anglais, and then on the four Wagner tubas, even on the first page). The virtuosity has been learnt from his own *Till* and the $^{12}/_8$ section of *Zarathustra:* the scales and arpeggios on woodwinds and strings (always at least doubled—he is not so reckless now as earlier—and more conveniently disposed for the instruments).[5] The passage is not lightly scored—the result is more tumultuous than delicate—but the writing is both fool-proof and absolutely transparent.

The second Mendelssohn scherzo-type—the $^2/_4$ scurry—comes when, abandoned by her sister, Elektra goes it alone, scrabbling dementedly for the axe and watched towards the end by a silent, unrecognised and unrecognising brother (figs 110a–123a). The lower strings scurry around in staccato semiquavers, articulated with gruppetti on low slithery woodwinds (basset horns, bass clarinet, bassoons single and double); the texture works rapidly up to yelps for the upper strings and woodwind, and the Agamemnon triplet theme pierces through on four muted trumpets and side drum; as all this sinks back to earth, Agamemnon's repeated-note theme rises up to die on one soft, high, muted trumpet note. Motion starts up again at fig.114a; at a second lull, the theme that spells out Agamemnon's name is heard on lugubrious oboe and bassoon in octaves, weirdly spaced between the high violin repeated semiquavers and the single-note interrogation, held now on two muted trumpets. For the third resumption of motion at fig.116a, both top and bottom of the texture retain the semiquavers, gradually coming down to meet in the middle occupied at first only by occasional spasmodic jerks on solo horns. From fig.118a sustained heavy brass begin very softly to fill out the bass registers as Orestes appears; they make a sudden lunge into fig.120a as Elektra perceives the stranger who watches her frenzied activity. As she questions him and bids him move on, the little scherzando episode gutters out into the Wagner tuba chords that begin the recognition scene (fig.123a). Behind all this is, surely,

---

[5] Cf. also the bassoons' 'scale-practice' passages from four before fig.115 to fig.122.

another, very distant, fairy-Mendelssohnian source: the centre of the *Midsummer Night's Dream* Overture, where 'things go bump in the night'—sudden holes in the texture, alien blasts on horns or ophicleide, but distant and muffled, the delicate perpetual motion constantly set off-course, only to resume again in another place. This distant source, greatly strengthened and muddied by its recreation in the first scene of *Das Rheingold* when Alberich scrambles to reach the treasure (grotesque wind gruppetti and flailing lower strings), is recreated by Strauss with a repossession of the Mendelssohnian transparency and speed to depict the thoughts as well as the motion of the demented soil-scrabbler; the next, surprising, stop on this line, the ultimate in this kind of animated freeze of suspense, is the 'Danse de la terre' from *The Rite of Spring*.

From these two 'fairy tuttis' it is possible to extend the scope of the word to cover something rather different: the music, in which *Elektra* abounds, of split hairs, screaming nerves, nightmare hallucinations, visceral obsessions of blood and shame. The paradox *here* is, rather, that Strauss the easy-going, none-too-thin-skinned 'good chap' is such a master of these discomforts, rendering them with the physical immediacy of a nettle-sting or a mosquito at your ear. Or perhaps only someone so at ease in his own skin could do such things at all, with the sort of externalised brilliance of a master-mimic or hallucinator. Questions like this, where the orchestration seems to point straight to the composer's innermost qualities and failings, will be taken up at the end of this essay.

Meanwhile, *black* fairy-music: nightmares, curses, enthralments, obsessions, horrors. Fig.64: as Elektra's first waltz-dream fades on to a single *pianissimo* woodwind octave (first harp and triangle all that's left of the percussion 'continuo'), Chrysothemis timidly utters her sister's name, snatching her from her reverie (one quaver *sehr stark* on thirteen brass instruments and timps with wooden stick) and bringing forth words of wounding contempt. The texture is instantaneously turned into a thing of horror. High F minor is sustained on three solo violins doubling a flute and two piccolos, simultaneous with four muted horns on B minor. As the first harp tremolandos on the F minor, a pungent bank of two low oboes, cor anglais and heckelphone, supported by bassoons, basset horns and solo unmuted violas and cellos, swells up from the B minor triad in a distorted fragment of the preceding dance music. An abrupt Agamemnon-gesture across a widely-spaced B minor for the tutti muted strings is overlapped by three trumpets and one trombone, all muted, entering on the low B minor; their crescendo, obliterating the slide of the three solo violins to a C major triad, precipitates a new spasm of the distorted dance, now pitched around a low F minor triad, and set sharply off by the tutti string pizzicato as well as the four muted brass. One soft chord underlies Chrysothemis' words ('Ist mein Gesicht dir so verhasst?')—the dominant seventh on B♭, hinting at the E♭ of her big outburst beginning a few pages later at fig.75, and warmly scored on two bassoons and two unmuted horns. During this the solo strings quickly mute and the whole body, with that choked quality of muted strings played with violence, gives the heavily-accented chords that break up Elektra's harsh reply: in between the two last, well under her unsupported voice, the Agamemnon theme in octaves on two clarinets and bass clarinet (helped at first by basset horns) begins hollow and soft, swelling to a reedy *fortissimo*.

After such punctilious exactness in orchestral layout as this, the passages of flesh-creeping sound-effects that follow can seem, arguably, a little cheap.Elektra's laugh at fig.71, and the diverging streams of parallel diminished fifths, weirdly spaced, that evoke 'the strangled breath, the death-rattle of murdered ones' in the palace's unhallowed walls (though the spacing at fig.73—two flutes, bass clarinet, contrabassoon—anticipates late Janáček, Birtwistle, Colin Matthews) are on the edge; over it, the moment at fig.89 when 'storms shake the hut' and Strauss feels obliged to break the golden flow of Chrysothemis with five bars of bad onomatopoeia. Another dubious place is the passage beginning eighth bar of fig.114; yet within a few seconds of these routine scarifications, we have the four bars at 119 which in their naked exactitude of imaginative detail (the passage for four bassoons; the fourth on the timps and the third on low trombones; the semiquaver run up a B♭ clarinet, the E♭, the piccolo; the trumpet solo so unusual in contour) are worthy of the *Survivor from Warsaw* which they acutely resemble.

Around fig.157 comes the basset horn's moment of glory, recalling this time the fantastical decorative Schoenberg of *Pierrot* or the *Serenade* op.24, and followed at fig.158 by arabesques on a solo violin straight out of Kundry's seduction of Parsifal; at 159 the brass attack produces a remarkable effect, simultaneous *sforzandi* on one horn and one trombone, and *piano* on the second players (all four muted). The grotesquely high pizzicatos on violins II/III here, doubled by piccolo and E♭ clarinet, seem to have been recalled from the second movement of Mahler's Fourth Symphony. Going further into Klytämnestra's scene, the pages from just before fig.170 are particularly rich in such detailed instrumental inventiveness. The dispersal here of the dark *Tristan/Wozzeck* poison into *Parsifal/Arabella* healing is quite brilliant. The twelve or so bars from fig.175 are extraordinary: the seven clarinets (including basset horns and bass) lurch in almost *Wein*ian drunkenness, against light staccato repeated notes ascending chromatically on flute and piccolo in octaves, and the whirring triplets, creepily legato, of a solo violin and solo viola; the whole over deep sustained contrabass trombone notes disappearing into the low brass B minor as mother and daughter are left alone together at fig.177.

We have reached this chord once before, in talking of Klytämnestra's bullocky Wagner tubas. They are muted, and the top note of the four-note chord is doubled by two muted horns, the other three by three muted trombones, the whole underpinned by the muted bass tuba. Above this, Klytämnestra's bad nights unfold in dully-bright chords on string pizzicato double and triple stops, the two harps, a glockenspiel catching the top part, and one flute 'spreading' the chord with the plucked sound, a very successful idea. The contrast just before Klytämnestra's first words of clear soft woodwind F minor and low dim plucked B minor is equally telling, as also the succession of tiny obbligato accompaniments (bass clarinet, oboe and first horn, over four trombones and timpani) that accompany Elektra's first words, 'Träumst du, Mutter?' ('Do you dream, Mother?'). The wind chording over deep trombones *ppp*doubled by harps *forte* at fig.180, the contrabassoon's moment of glory at 181—this is writing of classic simplicity, without a hint of the cheap effects which come so easily to Strauss the orchestrator or Strauss the composer: best is the barest moment of all, the solo trumpet (now *not* muted, which is its genius) tattooing softly on low D, doubled by harp, an octave below Klytämnestra's sudden long-held D on 'eine *Kraft*' (the *power* that lies within each one of her amulets). At fig.186 there is another brilliant adaptation of Wagner, when the two lower Wagner tubas, doubled at the unison by contrabass tuba and at the lower octave by contrabassoon, for eighteen bars convert Fafner the mighty monster into some appalling tape-worm, spiral bacillus, or horror of the imagination. The timbre of the orchestral tutti from fig.188 onwards is astonishing in its evocation of choking claustrophobia— the four muted horns (doubled by muted cellos in four parts) running a band of parallel close harmony, in the strangulated top of their register, against a similar band of the three violin groups and first violas (doubled by three flutes and the first clarinet), emptying out into great steam-choked chords around fig.192, where high trumpets *pianissimo* interlock with flutes and piccolo.

It would be possible to continue at this level of detail for the rest of this extraordinary scene. Just one more example will suffice, the wonderful use of the cymbal to reintroduce Elektra's festive dance music, stealing over her as she engineers her mother's incipient collapse (fig.205). Much more effectively does this simple stroke suggest her 'secret smile' than did the elaborate onomatopoeia of her laughter (fig.71); the powerful pull of the returning dance-jubilation in the pages following is all the stronger for their restraint, culminating in the magical arrival at a *ppp*C major at fig.212 (which will return all-stops-out at 236a), with soft cymbals and triangle, and ♩. ♪♪ just touched in by the brass.[6]

No accident that the most part of such details come in the work's first half: *chez* Strauss there is always a sense of routine later on, even in a work like this, which depends upon maximum intensity. Once he has found his habits, he does not tax them overmuch, lets things go with their own momentum, then pulls himself together for the final stretch. It had been so with *Salome* and was to persist, through *Der Rosenkavalier*, *Intermezzo* and *Arabella*, right up to *Capriccio*, irrespective of style or subject-matter.

---

[6] Many further points of detail exemplify the same acuity of ear. How well Strauss understands that difficult instrument the bass clarinet (compare Schoenberg, who always gets it so wrong). Not least at the very opening; the big D minor chord dies away leaving only bass clarinet and timp.on the low tonic, together with a bass drum, so that when the timp.disappears too the bass clarinet and bass drum fuse into a kind of bass timp.in D over which the maid's first muttered words link daughter's name with father's theme. And how he understands the bass tuba in its tiny solo five bars after fig.39, when she thinks of her parents' royal bed, now so outraged.

iii

It is interesting to return, via a passage like figs 188–93, to reconsider the orchestra of *Elektra* not as a tutti but rather as a corporate multiplicity of such details as I have described. Strauss is not by instinct a 'chamber' orchestrator like Mahler and Schoenberg; as with Wagner his is always a tutti conception. His erosion into detail is the result equally of his lively response to dangerous subjects and of the spirit of the age which saw in the large orchestra both an organism evolving ever upwards and a machine capable of ever more complex precision. I want therefore before concluding to look at a few further tutti passages which show why he still remains the principal master of a particular epoch and manner of composing.

First the passage from fig.32 that takes us from the young servant girl's whipping to Elektra's first entry, with its brilliantly clear delineation of a V–I cadence in D harshed and excruciated by F minor. The whip is represented by the *Rute* (switch) doubling sharp F minor attacks on two oboes and high violas. Against this a three-note ostinato on four trumpets alternating the triads of F minor and F♯ minor is twice heard (♪ ♫ ♪ | ♫); the instant it stops (second crotchet of second bar of fig.32) there is one more stroke of the whip (high cellos and three bassoons); on the next quaver comes the entry, up high, of the sinuous theme, made out of Agamemnon, foreshadowing Elektra (loud, penetrating, but not harsh—all violins, plus two flutes, a clarinet in E♭ and one in A); on the bar's fourth crotchet F minor enters powerfully on four muted trombones (discreetly helped by two low clarinets and the basset horns) underpinned by a low D on bass clarinet and four bassoons (including the contra, at the same octave); on the eighth quaver the four trumpets begin their ostinato again, overlapped this time at a quaver's distance by the timp.on the A♭ lower than that in the trombones' F minor, and at the next quaver by cellos and basses (unison, not an octave apart) with their same three-note rhythm emphasising the low D. All this is reproduced in the next three bars, but less loud and an octave lower, with modifications as required by the change of tessitura (the whipping is now on violas and cellos doubled by cor anglais and heckelphone, the trumpets' figure goes onto four horns and bass trumpet, the sinuous melody onto violas doubled by first oboe and two B♭ clarinets). The next four bars see a drastic simplification of this hectic activity, simply alternating sundry blows in F minor with woodwind writhes and grimaces in D major, all over the lowest D in the orchestra, until the full presentation of the sinuous theme in D minor, cadencing at fig.34.

The next of these passages, the entry of Klytämnestra's procession (figs 126–32), has already been noted for its use of the Wagner tubas. Indeed the quality and sonority of the orchestra as a whole is bullocky: the main motive itself, obstinately set across itself, stylises the groan of the beast of burden (♪ ♪ | ♪ ♪ | ♪), and the placing, low but loud on all the strings, *muted*, colours the whole texture with a veil of powerfully thwarted energy. From fig.129 bright but equally strangulated sounds cut through (a figure on flutes and piccolo, oboes and cor anglais, and four muted trumpets), and the strings demute over the next seven bars to present the diminution of the main motive with maximum tone. From 130 the orchestra starts to heave; the trombones (hitherto growling at the bottom) begin to surge up in triplets, the bass wood-winds in semiquavers; by 131 the entire orchestra is abandoned to a sea of scales in contrary motion, across the bullock-groan high and low; and in the final three bars all this is rent asunder by three eruptions of Agamemnon triplets from the bottom to the top of the heaviest and most cutting brass. The prototype is evidently the piling-up of the Nibelheim treasure in Scene 4 of *Das Rheingold;* characteristically, Wagner depicts from within, making an unforgettable spiritual image of oppression, bondage, tyranny, while Strauss brilliantly depicts the externals—the cracking whips, the groans, the sweat, the weight. The final stages of the procession resemble a crazed version of Fricka's entry in Act II of *Die Walküre,* but with Wotan's consort replaced by Kundry. (Incidentally, while we're onto this kind of thing, the closeness to Wagner's fate motive at fig.135, as the haunted queen cries out to the gods against her daughter's presence lying so heavily upon her, must surely be deliberate.)

From these oppressive places to the exaltation of the recognition scene, in particular figs 128a–130a. This, arguably the greatest passage in the work, shows Strauss's powers of lyric paragraph-building at their height. Its orches-tration consists (as Piston would say) of three 'elements'. The first is the ♪♪ figure that persists throughout. In the first four bars (beginning at the second of fig.128a) it is in octaves, on the upper the tutti violas and the cor anglais, on the lower the tutti violins and a bassoon; a pair of clarinets binds the two octaves by playing both. From the fifth bar the upper octave goes to two flutes and an oboe, with solo violin, the lower to the first basset horn with solo viola, the pair of clarinets coming in and out, showing, in these five bars where the figure has become a motion rather than a theme, their division, according to the phrasing of the voice part and its harmony, into 2 x 2½. After fig.129a the second woodwind players alternate on the figure (now melodic again) with the first, and the tutti violins and violas with the solo players, making these three bars into 2 x 1½. The heckelphone reinforces the lower octave, and a solo cello detaches itself from the internal melody to join the other two solo strings for the closing four bars of the phrase (the four into fig.130a), where the line is now in unison (parallel with, when not actually duplicating, the soprano) on these three, plus all three flutes, first oboe and first basset horn.

The internal melody also is doubled at the octave, on a pair of horns and tutti cellos divided *à2;* the lower octave is further reinforced by the bass clarinet. This full but potentially stolid sound is marvellously brought to life by being doubled throughout by both harps, a simple idea with unsimple results. When from the sixth bar of fig.128a the phrases become antiphonal, the answers are given to the second pair of horns, muted, and two bassoons, the cellos leaving only one solo player on the top octave, and the harps play-ing (at this same octave) in harmonics. The dialogue lasts for the five bars before fig.129a, when all the instruments that have been involved on the part (but omitting the pair of muted horns and the solo cello) and some that are new to it (the heckelphone, the second basset horn, the double basses) join to play what proves to be its final bar before coalescing into the passage's harmony.

The harmony has been spaced with economy and simplicity. In the initial four bars D minor is given in semibreves on lowish flutes and oboes, and two clarinets and two basset horns in their dullest register, brought to life by two soft high trombones doubled by two solo violas (who renew their sound every other bar, thus binding the chords together). There is a soft drum-stroke D on each first beat. When the harmony moves and the phrasing becomes more complex, the drum is silenced, the chords are sustained only by four woodwinds (flute 3, cor anglais, heckelphone, second basset horn) and the bass trumpet takes on the function of the two trombones. The tutti violins and violas also, with the voice and the clarinets, divide these five bars into two halves. The paragraph's climax, at the middle of the three bars beginning at fig.129a, is one of the most memorable and finely-placed of all Strauss's innumerable $^6/_4$ chords, good, bad and indifferent. Not even Stravinsky could scream at this one,[7] so asymmetrically placed in the phrase, and making D major with such sure harmonic timing the unexpected climax of a D minor paragraph. The inner-melody lines meet here and are reinforced by two trumpets, three trombones and the soft return of the drum gently rolling on the low A. For the closing four bars the descending line shadowing the voice is supported by minim chords allotted equally to mixed woodwind, brass, harps and strings, as if to tie everything up before proceeding onwards.

The last of these tutti passages comes a little later, when Elektra at last recognises the dark stranger (figs 144a–148a). In this vast wild upbeat to the principal lyric stretch of the work the orchestra seems to be vomiting itself up; yet the layout is rational, lucid, clean, without redundancy or sensationalism in its enforced combination of so many clashing lines. Noteworthy is the control of the overall diminution of volume after the climax at the fifth bar of fig.146a, by means of thinning the score as well as by individual diminuendos. As in the three bars before fig.132 the Agamemnon triplets cut through from bottom to top of the heaviest brass. After the first thrust, third and fourth trombones are heard no more, after the second the bass trumpet, after the third, trumpet 1. At this point horns 6 and 8 take a short, then a long break, to reappear only *mezzoforte* on the low E♭ preparing the first, still uncertain, arrival of A♭ at fig.148a. The first two trombones reach *piano* and cease one bar before fig.147a; the remaining two trumpets (2 and 3) reach *piano* and cease three bars later. The timp.survives till 147a and thereafter gives only two soft isolated strokes; the tuba dies four bars later. Also at 147a the E♭ clarinet is taken off, the first pair of clarinets and the two basset horns a bar later, and two bars later horns 1 and 3, and 5 and 7 stop; but the first of these pairs now doubles the first pair of clarinets (the second having been taken off

---

[7] 'I cannot bear Strauss's six-four chords: *Ariadne* makes me want to scream.' Igor Stravinsky and Robert Craft, *Conversations with Igor Stravinsky* (London: Faber, 1959), p.75.

meanwhile), in alternation with the basset horns and the second and third bassoons, on the rocking sixths (played in full by the strings) that wind down to Elektra's gentle re-entry on the word that, at the start of this passage, she could only cry out: her brother's name. The two lower flutes, the second oboe and the heckelphone are also severally lost during these bars; and of the other pair of horns, 2 loses his mate 4.

The mastery of such manoeuvres as these is a matter at once of machine-like exactness, an experienced technique in good practice and a lively imagination for the humble human functions by which the result is actually effected. This mastery imbues everything Strauss wrote for orchestra, however perfunctory the musical substance. When, as here, the musician in him is thoroughly charged with his material, which moreover comes from the top drawer and not the bargain basement of his copious store, there is no discrepancy between technique and creation. If the whole of *Elektra* were at this level, my essay could stop here. But as I said earlier, there are places in the work where even its most masterly aspect seems to invite larger definitions of its composer's achievements and limitations.

iv

In *Elektra* a Greek drama is 'nervously' reinterpreted with all its period's mod. cons of psychology and decadence, and clothed in music of peerless onomatopoeia that renders its every spasm and bloodfleck with naïve efficiency. The work's *obvious* lapses concern Elektra's siblings: the all-too-homely effusions of Chrysothemis have already been described; the measly part for Orestes is equally contingent upon Strauss's besottedness with the soprano voice and inability to imagine fully a man's part, even when every-thing, from truth to Elektra's father/brother-dominated psychology to the sheer need for her to rest a bit before the final scene (and ours for relief from the work's almost-all-female tessitura), cries out for the man's music that should go with those brass chords. The two stretches when invention flags— towards the end of Elektra's long coercion of her sister, and towards the end of the duet with her brother—are pretty clear (and of course reflect the same weakness). Not for nothing are most of the standard opera-house cuts made in these two areas.

The treatment of Aegisthus, though related, marks a different kind of lapse. It is positively surreal to hear these voluptuous Viennese waltz-strains, as if a Sachertorte had been delivered to the Royal Palace of Mycenae by a flunkey from M. Jourdain's entourage.[8] Though the intention is to make an obvious

---

[8] Cf. Romain Rolland:

> ... I am in the process of reading the score of *Elektra*, by Richard Strauss, which has just been performed in Dresden. The materials are, as usual, rather (or very) vulgar; but one is swept along by the torrent. The libretto is much more beautiful than that of *Salomé*. That legend of the Atridae is in any case unfailingly moving; it exudes horror and a tragic pity which grip one irresist-

dramatic irony, the hand is so heavy and the incident so prolonged (figs 204a–212a) that the opera is all but ruined at a crucial point. The surefooted bad taste by which Strauss convinces us that his heroine *must* waltz her way to her apotheosis has here deserted him.

But these lapses are incidental. There is something subtly wrong about the work as a whole; something missing, or askew, that needs to be explored further.

It is glorious, but it is not Greek! Why should we worry about this here when other instances (*Daphnis et Chloé* and *Oedipus rex*, to take the opposite ends of the 'Greek' spectrum) raise no doubts? It is surely because, though the chastity and elevation of the original are relinquished, the work still purports to be exceedingly serious, and thus inevitably invites damaging reminders of the real thing. As always this is Hofmannsthal's fault, here in substituting neurosis and naturalistic slaughter for religiously and morally sanctified revenge. Strauss being Strauss can only respond to this, as to everything similar, with onomatopoeia. With what remains of the original's sublimity he is ill at ease and out of his depth; whereas in the shallows that suit him he is without parallel. He can be relied upon, like a sky-ride, always to give his audience a thrill; we have to admire the generosity so eager to please, as well as the cold-blooded manipulation to which we willingly submit; together they sweep all before them. But in *Elektra* still more than in the comparable case of *Also sprach Zarathustra* we cannot miss, even while lost in admiration, the discrepancy between goal and aim that simply does not arise when his prodigious gift for music-making is attached to the completely appropriate subject. His genius for virtuosity, decoration, sumptuousness, energy and easy voluptuousness that suits *Salome* to a T can in *Elektra* seem, on a bad trip, rather appalling; and even on a good, just a shade *disappointing*—so much labour, so much skill, such resources ('the largest forces required by any opera in the repertory'), all signally failing to touch the core or sound the depth of the emotions portrayed. The cheap thrills of *Salome* are certainly more successful, perhaps more elevated, because everything about the work is wired for cheap thrills. *Elektra* is wired for sublimity, and has a long way to fall.

But if not Greek, it *is* glorious! If we can once forget the subject, it is possible to enjoy Strauss at the height of his powers, using the medium he supremely understands—the orchestra (with soprano voice)—with a mastery

---

ibly from the beginning to the end. Strauss himself has been caught by it (in spite of his nonchalance and Bavarian bantering which I, who know him well, come across endlessly in his ambling phrases and his eternal waltz rhythms, which he trails about everywhere with him, even at Agamemnon's: it's a very odd thing to see these German waltz rhythms transformed in his hands, and gradually translating with frenzied passion the transports of Elektra or of Clytemnestra).

Letter to Paul Dupin, 13 February 1909, in *Richard Strauss and Romain Rolland: Correspondence, Diary and Essays*, ed. and annotated with a Preface by Rollo Myers (London: Calder and Boyars, 1968), p.159.

and fulness of expression that can stand by itself as its own subject. It is disinterested, detached from causes; it is the story and character and subject-matter that are beside the point. *Elektra* is an '*orchestral* masterpiece', as Stravinsky said of *Jeux* (for '*trop* Lalique' we might say 'ein bisschen zu Klimt').[9] I think that for its full appreciation the heavy subject-matter and bloodiness should be made to become as diaphanous as the silly scenario of Debussy's ballet.

We could go further, and listen to *Elektra* as if it lay in the aesthetic of *L'heure espagnole* or *Petrushka*. These works do not *pretend*; unlike *Jeux* they present no ambiguity, and can be apprehended with Latin directness. But with Strauss such detachment has to be fought for (though we see that he possesses it already), battling through the impediment of psychological profundity and other traditional pieties whose true place is elsewhere, to reach his essential content, which is authentic indeed if much simpler than appears at first sight. He is a wizard, a conjuror, a puppet-master, a charlatan even, in the special sense whereby the charlatan in *Petrushka* brings his creatures to life for astonishment and delight, if not for pity and terror; he is the greatest master there has ever been of the *means* of music; and his vehicle is the most highly-developed machine yet produced by musical culture—the turn-of-the-century orchestra at its highest pitch of efficiency and pride.

---

[9] 'I still consider *Jeux as* an orchestral masterpiece, though I think some of the music is "*trop* Lalique".' *Conversations with Igor Stravinsky*, p.50n.

20

Die Frau ohne Schatten

Originated as a review of the much-vaunted superstar recording for Decca under Sir Georg Solti: the purely review-part has been dropped.

*　　*　　*

The music-lover's desire to take the will for the deed has never been more acute than in recent decades, with all the great humanistic themes devalued after global horrors actual and potential on a hitherto unimaginable scale, and in the microcosm of music itself, the very bases called into radical question. Such success-stories as Britten's guilt-and-atonement *War Requiem* and Shostakovich's suffering symphonies, or such signs of the times as Penderecki's Hiroshima threnody, Tippett's *Knot Garden*, Bernstein's Mass, and the work of Schnittke are symptomatic. The recent spate of deeply sincere but artistically *ersatz* religious work (Pärt, Gorecki, Tavener), the heart-on-sleeve compassion of James Macmillan, the militant-sentimental Leftism of Steve Martland show a more specialised development of the same nostalgia. Such tendentiousness—music 'about' matters more 'important' than mere music—reveals in its broad appeal the ubiquity of the desire and its genuineness. It also shows how easily mass audiences (and those who promote and depend on them) can be swayed.

In this sensitive area it is difficult to avoid charges of cynicism, hardheartedness, frigid or namby-pamby aestheticism. Yet in the end all musicians know in their heart of hearts that music is made out of notes, not concepts however ethical, mythologies however grand or moralities however elevated; and that by the quality of these notes alone do the extramusical aspects live. When making matches intention then indeed the miracle occurs whereby the one becomes inherent in the other, abstract musical processes bearing messages as naturally as they interfuse with depiction, evocation and the expression of emotion. Maybe 'miracle' is too strong; it is as intrinsic to music to be extramusical as it is to be purely itself, and this has happened so often and for so long that we come, rightly, to expect it. The highest instances—the *St Matthew Passion*, say, or *Die Zauberflöte*, *Winterreise*, *Parsifal*—are not exactly the norm. Rather such pinnacles set a standard by which every subsequent oratorio, or fairy-opera, or song-cycle, or solemn mysterium is implicitly measured. Especially when an aftercomer actively courts the comparison!

Die Frau ohne Schatten all too obviously sets out to take the heights and depths by storm. But when musical inspiration manifestly fails to equate with sublime aspiration the result is cold, even when executed with flawless technique, boundless energy and millions of notes. This aesthetic area where will is required to pass for deed, after its relatively ingenuous beginnings in Liszt and Berlioz, becomes disingenuous where the last romantics cross with the early moderns. Especially with Strauss and Mahler, the language is mined with parody, irony, deliberate banality; alienation and dislocation lie just round the next bend. But the problem is larger, located in the overlifesized ambitions of the entire post-Wagnerian generation except for Debussy and Fauré. One judges such high-flying curate's-eggs-of-genius as Mahler 8, Delius's *Mass of Life*, Scriabin's *Prometheus*, and indeed *Die Frau*, by the fairest and most precise criterion possible—work by the same artists that *is* perfectly achieved, e.g. Mahler 4, *Sea Drift*, *Le poème d'extase*, *Salome*. There is vitality enough in *Die Frau* to ensure that it will always be revived. Not the vitality of Grieg's Piano Concerto or *Rhapsody in Blue* (to name but two)—bad pieces, crammed with howlers, which nevertheless come up forever unquenched because of their naïve generosity. Strauss's own *Don Juan* and *Till Eulenspiegel* (though far from naïve) are of this order; but his operatic blockbuster is for the most part a mere discharge of duty, albeit with staggering energy and expertise. In Auden's words (from another part of the famous letter to Britten,[1] not quite so hackneyed as the rest) it is a 'large unfeeling corpse' whose infallible technique emanates from the bourgeois side of an artist's make-up—the part subject to the pull of Convention and Order in its deadening sense.

Strauss himself said as much, with characteristic directness, in his equally-quoted letter wearying of the task, longing for characters of flesh and blood like Ochs and the Marschallin, longing to be released back into the world of rush and send-up he's so happily stumbled into, interrupting his labours to write the new prologue to *Ariadne auf Naxos*. 'I'm toiling really hard, sifting and sifting—my heart's only half in it, and once the head has to do the major part of the work you get a breath of academic chill (what my wife calls "note-spinning") which no bellows can ever kindle into a real fire' (to Hofmannsthal, 28 July 1916). Perhaps he was wrong, as Tchaikovsky was so often about some of his very best works. But Strauss isn't the type to be lacerated by self-destructive diffidence. He speaks here as confidently and knowledgeably as when he's proud of his efforts.

I think he was right. So why do so many Strauss-lovers fall for the opera's credentials rather than exactly appreciating its actualities? It is a perfect example of the wishful thinking that arises when a work's subject-matter is so all-significant as to transcend manifest deficiencies in its realisation. If Strauss's own claim that he responded best to parody and sentimentality is true, so be it. He should be allowed to work within this range and *be* his best.

---

[1] See pp.212–13.

Die Frau is a mausoleum of high intentions, in which its apologists find what they need rather than what it holds.

As always, the chief culprit is Hofmannsthal. An inspired poetic vision, clothed in strong, lucent language, is then forced with difficulty into plot and people that cannot adequately carry it. The mythology is *nouveau pauvre*—fabricated and lacking resonance: this Keikobad, this Upper and Lower World, what are they to us? Unlike the gods, demons, superhumans and cosmology of *The Ring*, these inventions have no substance. The symbolism, so eloquent in the poet's account of his story, doesn't speak in the story itself; and wholly lacking is the experienced manipulation of the state that can carry an audience willingly through a maze in spite of obscurities and incredibilities, as evinced by *Zauberflöte* supremely, and many a successful opera before and since. The 'selling-point' is a sublime allegory of human fertility set to Strauss's greatest score. The actuality is a pretentious and overwrought mishmash by a composer of genius who is self-confessedly tired and bored.

If he'd not said so we would know it from the music anyway. Exhaustion and boredom are shown above all in the flogging-to-death of the two poor, short, unpregnant main themes, and then in the endless stretches of what Pauline 'very rightly' called note-spinning (it would be apt and piquant if this familiar phrase originated with her!). There is a lack of fresh ideas, alongside heavy dependence upon things done with greater zest in earlier pieces—e.g. the long cello solo preceding then continued within the Emperor's big number in Act II (a diluted replay from *Don Quixote*) and the orchestral interludes where the vast forces seem to vomit themselves up (so much more thrilling in *Salome* and *Elektra*). The use of extreme intervals, in Act III especially, can epitomise the discrepancy between will and deed. They are literally an attempt to soar out of the habitual, but they don't sear and hurt like comparable places in Bruckner 9, Kundry's music and late Mahler (to say nothing of early Schoenberg) because the harmony is basically bland. Contrariwise, the mixture of blandness and surprise so magical in the late Strauss is also missing as yet.

Oddly enough, some of the most unlikely places seem to me to work best. The early part of Act III, when the story is at its most contrived, produces an extraordinary atmosphere of busy, churning, frighteningness with elements both cosy and solemnly hymnic. One really feels the 'play of higher powers' the Nurse invokes so often. And the early stages of the liberation of the Unborn towards the work's end are ravishing: the music really does 'lift' here as Strauss hoped, in a fusion of celestial Humperdinck, the end of *Ariadne* (quoted, no doubt by accident, several times) and the halcyon children's choruses from the Goethe-part of Mahler 8. The much-put-upon goodness of Barak elicits from Strauss a long-sustained arc of pure D major that holds one astonished at its span and ease. And there are, of course, moments of daring the depths and riding the heights, superb inspirations from a master of musical means. They are associated most often with the opera's most compelling character, the Nurse, and her wholly malevolent view of mankind. Her opening 'speech' is electric, and quite a lot of Act I retains this level, and its solemn *serious* closing stretch really does justify some of the idealistic hype. Then routine and boredom set in, an inexhaustible supply of notes from an exhausted imagination. Not until he was out of Hofmannsthal's clutches did Strauss fly free again, as his own librettist, celebrating domestic sentiment and parody in *Intermezzo*.

21

Strauss's last opera

I want loosely to elaborate an interesting line of intertwining connections behind Strauss's last opera. He writes to Hofmannsthal (16 June 1927): 'The other day I heard *Meistersinger* again—a tremendous work. Ever since I've been unable to shake off the urge to write a work of this type some day—unfortunately, needless to say, at a respectful distance.' Hofmannsthal replies to his request for a '*Meistersinger* No III'[1] with one of the finest letters in the correspondence (1 July 1927), an evocation of Nuremberg as celebrated in romantic literature, and the culmination of this celebration in *Meistersinger*, whose 'indestructible truth' is that it 'brings to life again a genuine, complete world which did exist—not ... imaginary worlds which have never existed anywhere.' He claims *Rosenkavalier* as a descendant of *Meistersinger*: 'Just as in the former opera the Nuremberg of 1500 is the true vehicle of the whole thing and that which gives life to the characters, in the latter it is the Vienna of Maria Theresa—a complete and real and therefore convincing city-world composed of a hundred living interrelations ... from the palace through the backstairs ... to the peasant in the farmyard.'

Hofmannsthal's letter contains two points which extend the connection to cover subject-matter. First, resignation: Sachs, 'the ageing artist between desire and resignation', must surely recall the Marschallin; for all the differences between her poignant renunciation of her young lover and Sachs's noble relinquishment of his hopes for a young bride, the motif is the same. Second, class: 'the fine intermingling of the world of the knight with the world of the burgher' is as true, *mutatis mutandis,* of *Rosenkavalier*—compare the nuptials of Junkers Walther and Octavian with merchant-daughters Eva and Sophie.

A more general connection, concerning the artist's appearance in his own work, can be made between *Meistersinger* and Strauss at large (although not now including *Rosenkavalier*). One can take Walther and Sachs as self-portraits of the artist in fiery youth and rounded maturity: Walther routing his critics; Sachs teaching Walther how, by combining their prescriptions with respect for the traditions, to shape his visions into art. The analogues in Strauss are *Ein Heldenleben* (self-portrait of the artist as virile musician routing his

---

[1] 'There can be no "second *Meistersinger*"—freely adapted from H. von Bülow who called me Richard III.'

critics), *Sinfonia domestica* (self-portrait of the artist in virile maturity), *Intermezzo* (scenes from married life). In old age Strauss's tendency to self-portraiture is diffused into such character-pieces as the 'convalescent' and 'merry workshop' Sonatinas; something of a specific self-portrait (the artist as man of energetic *savoir-faire)* is seen in the heroic Theatre Director in *Capriccio. Capriccio* also provides idealised (not self-portrayed) creative figures in its poet and composer, both of them derived from the composer in the Vorspiel of *Ariadne.*

The fault of *Meistersinger* and its descendant *Rosenkavalier* is disproportion between form and content. In both a slender story is mercilessly prolonged, and musical invention better suited to a number-opera is given relentless music-drama treatment with the result that romantic comedy and operetta, respectively, become inflated beyond what these genres can properly take. This is not to deny the wonderful beauty and resource of Wagner's score, nor the gorgeous opulence and affecting poignancy of the best things in the Strauss. The disproportion is unacceptable only in their would-be comic aspects, the unfunniness of Ochs's and Beckmesser's discomfiture and the exaggerated crudity of its depiction in music.

Hofmannsthal realised something of this. He expresses it in a remarkable letter to Strauss (11 June 1916) which, perhaps regrettably, was never sent. Strauss, he says, had in *Rosenkavalier* 'wholly failed at certain points to enter into my ideas, and treated quite a few things in the wrong style altogether ...' He instances the chorus of Faninal's servants in Act II, 'written only to be rattled off in burlesque fashion, i.e. in the transparent Offenbach style. What you did was to smother it with *heavy* music and so to destroy utterly the purpose of the words ... The fun of this passage has simply ceased to exist.' He complains similarly of the end of Act I and of the Baron's exit in Act III. In only one work, he says, has Strauss achieved the right style—the incidental music for *Le bourgeois gentilhomme.*

This music and *Ariadne*, the opera which originally formed the conclusion to the same project, have this *Meistersinger–Rosenkavalier* nexus as their background. Strauss to Hofmannsthal (September 1916):

> Your *cri-de-cœur* against Wagnerian 'note-spinning' has deeply touched my heart, and has thrust open a door to an entirely new landscape where, guided by *Ariadne* and in particular the new *Vorspiel*, I hope to move forward wholly into the realm of un-Wagnerian emotional and human comic opera. ... An amusing, interesting plot, with dialogue, arias, duets, ensembles or what you will, woven by real composable beings *à la* Marschallin, Ochs, Barak. ... I promise you that I have now definitely stripped off the Wagnerian musical armour.

Capriccio seems just round the corner with this prescription, although the path there was long and arduous.

Meanwhile the final version of *Ariadne*, like *Salome* before and *Capriccio* after it, is a happy instance of subject, tone and style exactly fitting its composer's capabilities and predilections at the time (this only if one thinks, as I do, that the 'higher content' of Hofmannsthal's idea, although beautiful and thrilling, remains incompletely realised in his text). The enforced juxta-position of *buffa* and *seria* at once suits Strauss's extraordinary cleverness and touches his true warmth. Taken separately the exalted-style music would be 'cheap and poor', as Stravinsky says, while the *buffa* parts are not in them-selves exactly top-level (unlike the *Bourgeois gentilhomme* music, his most perfect in this vein); but when both are understood to be equally parodistic, their relationship produces fascination and a sort of greatness.

Capriccio is a second brew from this rich mixture. The *Meistersinger-Rosenkavalier* nexus is still behind it, both as modified by *Ariadne* and directly, as in the letter of July 1927, which made the nexus clear. What *Capriccio* has lost from its prototypes is their sense of the larger social whole—'a genuine, complete world which did exist', 'composed of a hundred living interrelations'—and the wider class ramifications, 'the fine inter-mingling of the world of the knight with the world of the burgher', 'from the palace through the backstairs world of the footmen to the peasant in the farmyard'. It replaces these by unity of class and place; the rich specificities of Nuremberg in 1500 and Maria Theresa's Vienna have now shrunk to a country château, with Paris in the 1770s (Gluck *versus* Piccini, the new fashion for chocolate, old Goldoni etc.) indicated by a skilfully suggestive sketchiness. A complex structure of social interconnection is no longer implied; instead we have the polite mingling of those socially 'possible' or plausible in an aristocratic salon. Of course authenticity of detail is not here of primary interest. This setting in time and place has been chosen because of its suitability to sustain a sentimental fantasy of aristocratic elegance and refinement, justifiable because it will elicit from its composer what he is able to do and wishes to.

Capriccio returns to *Meistersinger* for a feature which the altogether more full-blooded and straightforward *Rosenkavalier* had no place for: the disputa-tion upon art-forms, the public, tradition *versus* innovation etc. One feature among many in *Meistersinger*; in *Capriccio* this has come so far to the fore as to embrace both plot and subject-matter, which have no existence outside it. The work is a Conversation-piece, a disputation upon a question moved, whether *Wort oder Ton* should take priority. The characters are both allegori-cised and reduced to typical expressions of a point of view, so that the events, such as they are, count as allegory and as argument as well as plot. Compari-son of *Capriccio* with the allegory-disputation aspect of *Meistersinger* produces these interesting points of contact:

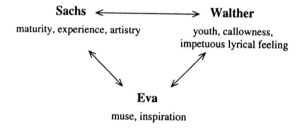

Sachs ⟷ **Walther**

maturity, experience, artistry   youth, callowness,
                                        impetuous lyrical feeling

Eva

muse, inspiration

(Prize Song, inspired by Eva and composed by Walther for the purpose of winning her hand; helped and given justification by Sachs. Wagner identifies both with Sachs and with Walther, as his youthful and his mature selves; they combine to put pedantry to rout and conquer the heart of the people.)

Capriccio

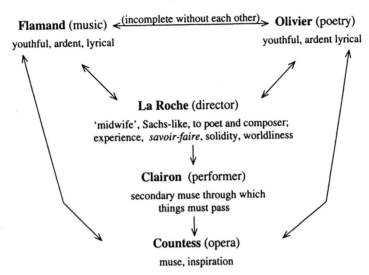

('Prize Song' (the Sonnet) inspired by the Countess as muse of opera, composed by poet and musician, both seeking her love, in an unwilling collaboration which makes an involuntary unity greater than either taken separately. Indeed after it is written, they can no longer be separated. Strauss's identification is rather with the director than with the poet or composer—the man who speaks of 'human beings ... who resemble us and speak in our language ... Let their sorrow move us and their joy fill us with gladness.')

Thus *Capriccio* flowers from *Ariadne* and *Le bourgeois gentilhomme* in musical style, and in subject from Strauss's wish to do a '*Meistersinger* No.III', and, obliquely and at a great distance, from *Meistersinger* itself. The deficient form-to-content balance of *Rosenkavalier* is resolved; *Ariadne* had been on the right lines, but in spite of Strauss's promise the 'Wagnerian musical armour' only gradually fell from his later operatic ventures. In *Intermezzo* he took the direction indicated by the Vorspiel towards lightness, dexterity and conversation, but after it *Die Aegyptische Helena* reverts to heaviness. The best parts of *Arabella* advance further towards parlando and lyricism, while *Daphne* almost overdoes the latter, ending with a soprano concerto closer to Glazunov than the *Liebestod*. These, and the other operas of the thirties still more so, are tired in inspiration in spite of passing beauties. In *Capriccio* quality is restored, and these two characteristics allow lyricism and parlando to flourish throughout, while lightness, whose lack Hofmannsthal had so deplored, is achieved and sustained. It says 'Open Sesame' to the grace of the last concertos and songs.

After this prehistory of Strauss's last opera, some features of the work itself. There is something fascinating and elusive about it; I think a clue towards defining its very special character can be found in its lack of distinction, using the word in several senses. At first acquaintance the music seems undistinguished, lacking quality and fineness. When with familiarity what had seemed boring is no longer so, the music is undistinguished because lacking differentiation, everything merging into everything else, nothing separately and distinctly descried.

This happens through the idiosyncrasies of Strauss's 'late-style', which had been touched on as early as Sophie's music in *Rosenkavalier* and hinted at in his music from the start: soaring arches of vocal cantilena; rhythmic ambiguity over a fundamental four-square solidity; accompaniments flowing and aerated, although always richly-upholstered; shifting, almost punning, harmony over a fundamentally simple tonal usage. It will be seen that I am describing something which has an urge to disguise itself—it might have been said as justly of Strauss as of Prokofiev, that 'first he writes his music like everybody else, then he Straussifies it'.

Undistinction is also achieved by the use of leitmotifs, the last survival of Wagnerian usage in *Capriccio*. Wagner's motifs delineate and distinguish; Strauss's tendency was always towards indistinction. Hence the possibility of such thematic combinations as the 'Works of Peace' in *Heldenleben*. This blurring was a weakness earlier on; in *Capriccio* it is a felicity.

The central thematic mesh concerns music and words (Flamand and Olivier) and their losing their differentiation in opera. Words and music are brother and sister, as the composer tells us very early on: so are the Count and Countess, he representing the rationality of words ('Opera is an absurd thing'); she, music as the language of the feelings ('Secret emotions rise in my heart, though their meaning evades me'). These characters' motifs lack distinction in both senses—they are tired little scraps of tune, and they are extraordinarily undifferentiated one from another—and the result is that Strauss can effect with them a continuous state of reference, light, easy-going, lacking 'identity card' denomination, and corresponding perfectly to the subtleties of the situation.

So undistinguished are these motifs that the work has a curious technical similarity to *Pelléas* (which it also resembles in the skill of its parlando convention, although of course the works are miles apart in style and idea). In Debussy's opera 'every motif shares the same intervals with every other motif ... can be fragmented into accompaniment or ostinato, every ostinato or accompaniment can emerge as a motif ... either everything, or nothing, is happening at any particular moment'. However, Debussy never attempts Strauss's superimpositions. The twenty-four bars between octet and sestet of the Sonnet as sung in the last scene, and the twelve bars immediately preceding the final horn-calls provide the most complete and compendious examples of the whole work's textural norm: the effortless merging into masterly indistinction of themes, interconnected by leitmotivic connotation, which had at first seemed flaccidly undistinguished.

This norm would not be enough to sustain a whole opera by Strauss. Vigour and variety are provided by the Italianate and French elements—the harpsichord dances; the Italian duet (inferior to the aria in *Rosenkavalier*); Clairon and the Count; *buffa, seria (al'Ariadne)* and *bourgeois gentilhomme* in La Roche—and two sustained melodies give the work body, the Sonnet with its stiff five-bar phrases, and the easy flow of the song theme which runs through the texture at various points and finally flowers in the interlude before the last scene.

Thematic undifferentiation provides a clue to another of the opera's felicities—the contrast between formality and flow. The three dances, the Italian duet, the contrived shapeliness of the Sonnet are played off against the spontaneous shapeliness of the ensembles, the so-called Fugue and the Laughing and Quarrelling Octet. The sparkle of these ensembles puts them in a class of their own in Strauss's output. It is wonderful how, so late in a lifetime of bad habits, he could suddenly concentrate himself like this to produce real energy, not just an inexhaustible spinning of notes, and real wit, not just rib-tickling fun, yet lose nothing of his genial expansive flow.

Between these opposites comes the 'shapely sprawl' of the undifferentiated thematic norm, which seems a blur of unpunctuation until familiarity brings out its subtleties. And finally the superior powers of spontaneous shaping over a larger scale, which we see in La Roche's harangue, and (after the slight tiredness of inspiration which ensues is overcome) the triumphant succession of pleasures, from the goodbyes, through the servants' chorus, the scene with the prompter, the interlude, to the last scene. In this succession all vestiges of Strauss's rather factitious 'music-drama' are abandoned. It is virtually number-opera.

The last scene, however, restores symphonic flow to build the most perfect of his soprano monologues. The end of *Rosenkavalier* Act I surpasses it in richness and intensity of content, but such 'red corpuscles' (Strauss's own phrase) would be out of place in *Capriccio*, whose essence is that it presents everything diluted and muted. The familiar sentimental treatment of time passing, beauty fading, the mirror, the uncertain heart and the great lady in the rococo décor are here given a final exquisite refinement.

Further felicity is found in the unforced pointedness of many little touches of characterisation and structure; the three beginnings, the sextet for the audience, the 'real' sextet for the stage and the final start as the director wakes up; the skill of the diversified entrances; the cleverness whereby the conversation-piece builds up by twos and threes until an ensemble is called for, after which a big monologue shows to best advantage; the delights of the characteristic exits, Clairon and her couplets, Flamand's last words to be 'Prima la musica', the Poet's 'Prima le parole'; the director's leave-taking. 'See that I get effective exits in my part ... a really striking exit makes a great success ... the last impression a figure can make ...', as he fades out for Paris.

These unsophisticated and charming touches are continued in the servants' scene—'They'll shortly be bringing domestics into their operas'—and the Prompter, who has, it seems, controlled the whole performance up to now in his sleep, but must wake to leave the final decision to the Countess. And, of course, the famous trivial ending as she yearns for an ending which will not be trivial—a delicate version of the close of *Ariadne* whose tongue-in-cheek suited Strauss so much better than exaltation or gravity: 'Supper is served'; no decision made; the only possible decision. These things are pure poetry, in the tradition of the Nightwatchman at the end of *Meistersinger* Act II, and a worthy appendix to that supreme touch.

The most successful joke is the central one, that of making the events we see into the work we are seeing. The initial idea, to make the opera they plan be Strauss's own *Daphne*, would have been an echo of the idea of *Ariadne* without its point. The eventual solution, that from the very beginning the whole work has been bringing itself into existence without our realising it, is in a different category from those painfully excogitated 'works of art about themselves' and other comparatively frigid self-reflexities, which have provided so much gratuitous tedium in the arts of the twentieth century. In *Capriccio* the idea is so spontaneous and natural, its execution so easy-going and unpretentious, that there is no temptation to force upon it what it clearly eschews. It's simply a good idea, the happiest of the work's countless felicities; *c'est cela*—it's simple, charming and right, with no labour and nothing to investigate.

Another much vexed problem of modernism is solved for himself by Strauss with the ease that comes, perhaps, from sheer unreflection. This is the question of style, as it concerns pastiche and re-creation of the past. Here Strauss is just as much a 'stylist' as any composer since. His basic manner is Mendelssohn–Schumann with Brahms for thickening; very fluent, pretty commonplace, but with lots of dash and extraordinary skill. He turned to Liszt and Wagner for his symphonic poems and early operas, with an excursion into 'Green Horrors' from which he plunged precipitately into *Rokoko* (the eighteenth-century Bavarian and Viennese elements in his style, summed up in his love of Mozart) and *galant* (the French elements: Lully, Couperin and Rameau). He employs his Wagnerian armoury for mythologies, historical and classical; for 'period' pieces he wears his *bourgeois gentilhomme* outfit. Even at his most *Rokoko* or *galant*, music-drama keeps breaking in; even at his most Wagner-plated the native Mendelssohn–Schumann–Brahms is never far to seek.

On top of all this, the Waltz; whether in *Elektra* or *Le bourgeois gentilhomme* (to take the extremes of each style), the Waltz is bound to emerge sooner or later. The contemporary analogues—Debussy's interest in the *clavecinistes* and Palestrina; Elgar's Handel orchestration; Busoni's, Schoenberg's and Webern's Bach; Stravinsky's Pergolesi and everything else— would make an interesting comparison. Strauss's 'time-travelling' seems to me as idiosyncratic as any. Superficially it is a question of a deliberate *simplesse* of pastiche (as in the final duet in *Rosenkavalier*) and in *Ariadne* and the other *Rokoko–galant* works a venture into the antique trade—high-class 'period' fakes, expensive, superbly done, and with remarkable individuality, so that we value them *as such*, not for what they imitate. Yet it is never right to be put off by what *seems* to be the case with Strauss.

It is in this context of style that the elusive fascination of *Capriccio* should finally be seen. Its internal felicities have already been discussed; now it appears just as happy in its place in Strauss's output, as a refinement and synthesis of elements originally heterogeneous and crude. Music-drama heaviness is refined to a delicate leitmotivic usage (in which undistinction of invention ingeniously corresponds to the undifferentiations and ambiguities of the set-up), and the *Rokoko–galant* strain now reaches its most delicate and sustained flowering. These borrowed stylistic elements are now in a completely natural equipoise with the native beer-hall vein. Add to this the final triumph of the lightness and speed discovered in the *Ariadne* Vorspiel; the resolution in a homogeneous flow of the deliberate antithesis of *seria* and *buffa* in *Ariadne* itself; and the elegances of story and its management already indicated; and we have the constituents of the perfection of *Capriccio*. And he has at last managed to conquer and expel those once-ubiquitous Viennese waltzes! (There's only one more to come—the revised *München* of 1945.)

To call *Capriccio* Strauss's most delightful and perfect opera is not to make a false claim. The 'Green Horrors' and the early *Rokoko-galant* works are obviously altogether more vital, but with his vitality went all his faults—the price of the ravishing perfection of his last opera is that it is undoubtedly a little lymphatic. While *Rosenkavalier* has the multiplicity, richness and directness of its greater ancestor *Meistersinger*, *Ariadne* is already something of a speciality, a self-indulgent conceit about opera, carried out with a combination of sophistication and vulgar gusto. *Capriccio* is still more tangential and rarefied. It would be wrong not to acknowledge this however much one loves the work; but that we can know this and still love it shows just how worthy of love it is.

22

Strauss—Stravinsky—Schoenberg

A review from 1977 of three then-newish volumes in the Master Musician series: Michael Kennedy's Strauss (1976), Francis Routh's Stravinsky (1975), Malcolm MacDonald's Schoenberg (1976); included here because it unconsciously touched off for the first time what I now see to be one of this collection's main underlying themes, the erosion of the Austro-Germanic mainstream of music by a Franco-Russian counterthrust aimed at its most deliberate and lethal by Stravinsky (see pp.330–41).

* * *

Strauss is the last composer who, as he wished for himself, 'gave music as a cow gives milk'; lived at ease (though a prodigious worker) in his native culture; felt no compulsion (for all his outrageousness) to make it new; and fed off the fat of the land, living in the present so long as it was congenial, and in the past when the present no longer supported him in the style to which he was accustomed. Stravinsky is the lean kine, undernourished and disaffected, at home nowhere, whose bottomless emptiness can swallow up whole fields of plenty and still leave him fretful for more. The one composer he absolutely couldn't swallow was Strauss.

An utter contrast; yet what parallels and complements the two throw up. The conventional pairing of Stravinsky with Schoenberg has its uses in ticking off the main polarisation of twentieth-century composition, but it is not 'expressive': it can't be used to advance understanding of either composer. This is just what can be done with a Stravinsky–Strauss connection. Obviously it must not be pressed further than it can bear; but that far, just because it is picturesque it can show more sharply what is distinctive to both sides than a reasonable, historical connection. As time elapses, Strauss emerges as an unthinking specimen of what Stravinsky is consciously: a stylist, complementing (within his all-nourishing tradition) Stravinsky's more radical (because his soil is so thin) kleptomania and 'fitting-out of old ships'. In both, a certain absence has to be filled out, and a stylistic *donné* is needed to set them off. Strauss at first finds it to hand in the music around him; Stravinsky from the start takes possession of what he wants. Later, Strauss also turns to 'reproduction'; *Ariadne* and the *Bourgeois gentilhomme* are as much epiphanies as *Pulcinella* and the Octet, and the old cliché that Stravinsky makes everything he takes inimitably his own applies just as well to Strauss. But in the differences—super-taste and super-vulgarity (*chic* and

Schmaltz with their attendant dangers); austerity and opulence; music by the centimetre or by the yard; music as merchandise, spiritual or fleshly; tight set-forms or music-drama prose; classical subject-matter *à la* Picasso or *à la* Böcklin—lies the relationship that can define the particularity of each with the greatest sharpness.

Schoenberg of course is in direct, non-fanciful relation to Strauss; they are extremely different, to be sure, but within the unifying embrace of a common tradition. Born within a decade of each other, they share the same culture, antecedents and artistic ethos, and what they share is the best starting-point to describe their divergence. Think of their curve toward and away from their respective radicalism into their respective versions of baroque and rococo, or their attitudes towards and uses of their native popular dance-styles. *Mutatis mutandis* they belong together, and Stravinsky is outside. Put in tabloid form, Strauss is the vestigially-genuine but now hollow centre; Schoenberg, the eccentric who would urge that his idiosyncrasy is a new centre, or the same as the old 'but only badly played'; Stravinsky, flourishing best when in opposition, the ironic destructive-creative attitude to the centre (wherever it lies), pulling its leg and exposing its feet of clay. They do not invalidate each other, and we can love them all. Think for instance of the gorgeous sugar-plum celeste in the Presentation of the Rose, its weird but equally luscious use in *Herzgewächse*, its total negation in the celeste-part of *Threni*, and the sublimation of sugar-plum to crystalline coldness at the end of the *Requiem Canticles*.

The Master Musicians volumes vary in quality. A few are real contributions to knowledge and understanding; most fulfil a modest but genuine function; one or two are deplorably bad. Francis Routh's *Stravinsky* lies towards the bottom of the middle range; not deplorably bad, but not greatly to be commended. Routh's norm of comment is exemplified in this remark about the end of the *Symphony in C*: 'Of all Stravinsky's coda-sections, this one has a more intense poignancy than the other comparable ones, such as *Apollo* or the *Symphony of Psalms*, because it has a personal as well as a musical and structural meaning.' (p.95) How many important questions lurk latent here! Unless they're explored the remark is pointless; Routh lets them all go begging. Discussion of the music is minimal, but the brevity is not that of concentration, for Routh singularly lacks the *mot juste* except when, usually unacknowledged, he employs Stravinsky's own phrases. The original is so memorable that it acts as a burglar-alarm. The most flagrant instance is the paraphrase, on p.99, of the composer's notes on the *Symphony in Three Movements*. Better to give the source direct—no shame in that—or else to transform completely.

Routh is dumbfounded by the late works; he virtually gives up the attempt to describe, and simply gives note-rows for every piece from the *Canticum Sacrum* to *The Owl and the Pussycat*, all helpfully punctuated by a caesura between the hexachords. There is no comment or evaluation, only a few banalities about Stravinsky's 'sense of order' which is presumed, in the very existence of these rows, to speak for itself. 'In his studied avoidance of the ordinary, the expected, the cliché, he never repeated himself; each work is unique.' For confirmation see list of rows! The most important composer of the age deserves better than this, in his elevation to Master Musician.

Michael Kennedy's *Strauss* is much more pleasing; the biography is fuller and better told, the discussion of the music usually sound and occasionally illuminating. His sympathy for Strauss the man (see especially the chapter 'Under the Nazis') is matched by his generous indulgence of Strauss the composer's weaker pieces. There is, in fact, a general tendency to overvalue; though he draws the line at *Schlagobers*, Mr Kennedy cannot see that scores like *Intermezzo*, which excite his enthusiasm, are not all that different. Sometimes he frankly recognises that there are conspicuous gaps in Strauss that it is not merely 'puritanical' or 'anti-hedonistic' to insist on. These joyless attitudes are deplored in Mr Kennedy's warm defence of the *Symphonia domestica*; yet his appetite for the coarser side of Strauss brings out a certain crudeness in his own appreciation, most clearly in his continual derogation of Hofmannsthal—*Die Frau ohne Schatten*, for instance, is 'a forest of obscure and pretentious symbolism' (p.162). The Strauss–Hofmannsthal collaborations are a complex mixture of subtle affinities and incompatibilities, and it is surely not possible to adjudicate so starkly. Philistinism like this seems to be an ineradicable trait of English writing on music, especially when it exhorts relish of works for their robust vulgarity. It produces a temptation to its opposite, shown for instance in Donald Mitchell's exhortation *not* to enjoy *Verklärte Nacht* or the *Gurrelieder* or Strauss since they encourage self-indulgence and spoil the listener for tasks which, because sterner, are apparently more proper.

Malcolm MacDonald's *Schoenberg* is by far the most accomplished and interesting of the three. The sometimes brusque, even schoolmasterly tone can be forgiven for the quality of which it is a part: a heartfelt defence of the musicality of Schoenberg, and a concern to rescue it, for the common listener, from the academic technician. The eloquent Preface and the discussion on p.86f. will do this if anything can.

MacDonald plunges straight into deep hot water with an account of the 'scandalous' première of the Second Quartet. This extends into the composer's current marital and compositional crisis; and only when the full complexity of his situation is established do we return to the childhood and early life that help explain it. If only more biographers could be intelligently free from chronology! 'We live life forwards and understand it backwards'—the chronological order of events will not necessarily reveal their full significance. The sensitive biographer must anticipate and flashback, follow up themes, and elicit or even impose sense-making patterns. The strict truth remains intact, after all; all the Master Musicians volumes give as their first appendix a resumé of dates and events, and their authors could easily use the resulting liberation to good purpose. But usually they prefer to perpetuate the banal 'life-and-works' formula. MacDonald interpenetrates them more richly than usual: and his account of Schoenberg's death, murmuring 'Harmony ... harmony' amidst a cluster of real and symbolic thirteens, 'leaving an artistic legacy whose real complexities the commentator should not obscure by mere playing with numbers', unifies his main preoccupations with some subtlety.

The chapter called 'Heart and Brain' shows him to be as sympathetically attuned to Schoenberg's tortuously-intermingled aggression and paranoia as Kennedy is to Strauss's easy-goingness (the books' cover photographs give each character at a glance!). The discussion of individual pieces abounds in good ideas (e.g. *Erwartung* as 'the most astonishing written-out improvisation in the history of music') and some eccentric evaluations (the dances in *Moses* greater than *Le sacre*? the Second Chamber Symphony such a masterpiece?), but is most valuable for its determined unfogging and demystifying of atonality and serialism. 'Tonality is the key', he says, exemplifying with complete conviction that this music is 'essentially an extension, not a negation, of the ear's previous experience', and how tonal and serial can infiltrate and fertilise each other. This is not new, of course, but it needs to be spelt out until everyone can hear it for himself. And there is a real surprise—a reinterpretation of Schoenberg's remark about his technique renewing a century of supremacy for German music:

> Could not Schoenberg's remark have made an ironic dimension? He had lighted ... on a highly versatile compositional device ... which any other real composer might take, leave or adapt at will. But his awakening reidentification with the Jewish race enabled him to view dispassionately his own deep Austro-German culture. He may have recognized that in the Germanic mind, with its love of system and authority, this device was fatally easy to misinterpret as a law to be obeyed rather than a tool to be applied: as a magic formula which would take the place of hard and true creative work.

And so the speculations ramify—why Schoenberg never formalised a theory nor taught twelve-note technique, why he protested too much about twelve-note *music*, not twelve-*note* music. This view of Schoenberg's notorious remark (hitherto understood only as arrogance) genuinely extends understanding of the composer's predicament, even if as an interpretation of his *tone* it remains implausible. For Schoenberg's *avowed* irony is so unmistakable; blundering and laborious, glancing off its object to wound only himself with its witless laceration. A typical example is given (p.102) from his preface to the *Satires* op.28. Satires! Schoenberg satirical is like Schoenberg ironical, contradictory through and through.

But then Schoenberg-apologists can persuade themselves of anything. 'For my part, I shall continue to whistle Schoenberg's tunes whenever they come into my head' (p.xi). Brave words; but *listen* to people as they whistle! All the time their whistling is supported by an innate understanding, usually quite unconscious, of the harmony that gives the tune its meaning, whether it be a snatch of Beethoven, *Jerusalem,* or something off the hit-parade. Why don't the committed 'plain-man' Schoenbergians start from the truth that his harmony is no longer in gear with the melody it underlies, that the melody therefore is out of focus, that something absolutely simple and absolutely fundamental has gone wrong, and that from this central fault every aspect of his later music is riven with chaos and distress? Realistic, surely, to work from the truth towards what can be rescued, rather than to assert an Ideal which continues to elude the common listener still more than the academic technician. If Schoenberg really longed so intensely as he said to be taken for a 'better sort of Tchaikovsky' why did he not act on it? The means so evidently lay within his gift. If people are to 'know his tunes and whistle them', they have to be not merely 'a bit better' than Tchaikowsky but *as good*! Perhaps Schoenberg's final words were a death-bed reconversion to the faith he had lost round about the period he sketched the symphonic interlude in the *Jakobsleiter*. Yet the last, also uncompleted, work, has a quality of recrudescence, as if harmony were coming back into its metaphorical as well as its technical dimension. Extraordinary to realise that only a couple of years before, the aged Strauss had recharged his glancing, shifting triadic usage in the first two of the *Four Last Songs,* and that Stravinsky was just on the point of remaking his own compositional bases for his last and richest (because most minimising) stylistic reassumption.

23

The great mutilator

In keeping with the permanently unquiet spirit of its subject this little piece (earnest of a full treatment that I still hope to write one day) from the earliest phase of my Spectator *columns (it was only the third) elicited more vociferous reaction than anything in the so-far fifteen years subsequent, either pro or con. Which certainly didn't foretell the 'frigid tranquillity' to which, like every journalist, I've grown accustomed!*

* * *

This weekend the South Bank's four-month festival of *Arnold Schoenberg—his Works and his World* reaches its climax with the 'Hymn to the Dawn' that concludes his gigantic early *Gurrelieder*. The Centre's resources have been skilfully coordinated. A galaxy of international superstars has presented a wide range of concerts, fringed by an exhibition, films, even a series of 'Viennese Teas' recreating in the unlikely ambience of the Festival Hall's function room something of the atmosphere of the turn-of-the-century coffee houses where so many radical ideas were argued out. Altogether, a decisive stand against long years of wasteful mediocrity.

But the problem of Schoenberg remains. The festival was subtitled 'the Reluctant Revolutionary'; the main reluctance where Schoenberg is concerned has always been the audience's. Obviously *Verklärte Nacht* with the Berlin and Karajan, or *Gurrelieder* with Rattle and Birmingham presents no problem: everyone loves these gorgeous late-Romantic masterpieces which Schoenberg relinquished so soon. Though the next stages in his amazingly rapid evolution are not exactly popular, one feels that they could easily become so. The lurid depths of the two expressionist one-act operas, the elegant black wit of *Pierrot lunaire*, the grandiose mystical aspiration of *Jacob's Ladder*, the fervency and ravishing beauty of the *Five Orchestral Pieces*—these and other works of his 'free atonal period' (c.1909–17) would seem in their mix of sensual and spiritual, luxuriant and refined, fin-de-siècle and futuristic, perfectly gauged for the eclectic, thrill-avid taste of our own day.

But the invention of the dreaded twelve-note method casts a blight over all that preceded it. And his output subsequent to this 'historically inevitable' move still falls between two stools. For the sophisticated modernist (spokesman: Pierre Boulez) Schoenberg failed to realise his invention's potential, falling instead into fustian academicism. Yet for the average music-lover

Schoenberg's apparent conservatism remains the very type of 'nasty modern music'. An in-between position is hard to formulate. The problem in brief is the complete discrepancy here between horizontal (linear, melodic) and vertical (harmony, both accompaniment and overall architecture). In tonal music the two were absolutely fused. Schoenberg's twelve-note music is still composed upon tonal premises, but the notes no longer make sense except in mere rationality of construction, and their actual sound is excruciating, with constant overloading and tension without resolution, and a new coarseness in the instrumentation that had once been so rich and delicate.

Our equipment for measuring lucidity and pleasure in music, equally with incoherence and ugliness, is our ears. The only criterion, when the tonal framework we virtually take for granted is withdrawn, is their individual acuity and sensitivity. Anything new or difficult tweaks our ears and we resent it. But willy-nilly their receptivity expands and alters. Throughout the course of music, what was first perceived as senseless cacophony comes in the end, by hard application or passive seepage, to be a further prospect in the garden of delights.

On the whole this course has been one of increasing complexity, a complexity which evolves from within the intrinsic processes of music itself. Schoenberg's 'reluctant revolution' gets this the wrong way round: grammar before speech, a body with skeleton and organs on the outside. It is the blue-print for a grammar only deceptively related to the actual language of music, however much he protested that it was its inevitable outcome. The scientism and pseudo-rationality that have hobbled the more recent avant-garde (together with the arrogant credulity that theirs is the one true way forward) stem from Schoenberg's attempt to renew an 'exhausted' tonality. What he failed to see was that tonality itself is but one current in the more universal stream of musical possibility.

Schoenberg invoked the great tradition of German composers from Bach to Brahms in an unsuccessful attempt to mend what he had blown up. But in that explosion he had unfortunately lost his ears. And the result was the mutilation of a whole epoch of music. He was the first of many to say that what he did was 'necessary'. But it wasn't: it was uncalled-for, artificial, idiosyncratic, arbitrary and not a little crazy. All we like sheep have dumbly concurred in the rightness of his stance, against the evidence of our senses and our instincts. No subsequent composer of stature is unharmed. Yet the irony is that pursuits so sterile in his own hands have since proved fruitful in all sorts of unpredictable ways. 'We are all Schoenbergians now', and have been since around 1951, when the Master died and Stravinsky began his great leap forward. The difference between his 'reluctant revolution' and the upheavals produced by Beethoven, then Wagner, is that their work gained popular acceptance, however great the initial hostility. Schoenberg's music has shifted the earth's crust without actually being widely played or greatly loved—merely *studied*. Like Moses he leads the way to, but cannot enter, the land of milk and honey (which is also the land of lost content), where music both makes sense and sounds beautiful.

24

Lulu

This account of the first-night of the world-première production to include Friedrich Cerha's implementation of Act III (Paris Opéra, 24 February 1979) conflates a sort of diary of the occasion which first appeared in the Cambridge Review with a shorter more musicologically-directed notice for Tempo. In running them together I've tried to eliminate repetition but can't completely disguise the two clients' different requirements.

* * *

i A parallel with Wagner

Imagine trying to make sense of *Tristan* lacking its third act. We would have two acts whose very intensity of feeling and complexity of detail would compound the frustration of being so rudely cut off. Our frustration would not be resolved by knowing the continuation of the story. The more important incompletion would be the absence of resolution in broader terms. Gigantic architectural symmetries and gigantic emotional tensions, spiritual and psychological, have been set up, which remain incomprehensible, unbearable, in-artistic until understood, eased and rendered into significant form. There is a romantic quality of all-or-nothing; any missing detail threatens the sense of the whole. 'In the lost Act III Tristan is transported across the sea to the house of his childhood; he lies there in delirium, his life sustained only by the hope of Isolde's arrival; when at last she does arrive he is unable to sustain the excitement and dies in her arms; she remains oblivious while events are unravelled and explanations are offered, then comes round to sing her lover's death-chant.' A bald outline like this shows just how little the plot matters in the total effect of the completed work. For this isn't story, it is music; the symmetries and asymmetries, the balance of forward symphonic momentum with returns and re-workings—these are the *raison d'être* of the work, for which there is no equivalent in words or events. Words and events are carried by the music, and fused into inseparability from it. It is in the music that we find the meaning of the story and text, and it is the music that gives them their timing, weight, interpretation and depth of meaning.

Without it, the interlocking and fulfilment by Act III of the other two would seem highly artificial if not absurd. In fact it would be impossible; without the music as *raison d'être*—source and goal—all these things would be mere ghosts. Through the working of countless significant compositional details these schemes and correspondences are brought to life in themselves, to become the focus for the expression of the meaning. Every lover of the work understands this intuitively; its profound unity does not have to be spelled out in order for it to be experienced as what it is. The work is complete and completely self-integrated.

And now the same is true of *Lulu*. The two-act version already familiar is as rich musically, and as meaningless, as a two-act *Tristan*: the release of the third act is a comparable restoration of significance. Knowledge of the rest of the action has never helped, while knowledge of Berg's elaborate intentions for parallels and symmetries has been downright repellent. This last has seemed heartless and contrived, a denial of the evident expressive quality of the familiar music, reducing the work to another Culture-Monument of modernism, deliberately impenetrable, made for no audience except Joyce's 'ideal insomniac', and consequently to be feared and avoided by everyone except analysts and commentators. *Lulu*, as intended, seemed like *Ulysses* in diagram form, stripped of all its richness of artistic surface, a mere container for artfully-worked but non-expressive contrivance. In fact the complete work comes over as spontaneous and telling. Complex intentions are realised through significant surface detail, and manipulatory schemes are vindicated by their unforeseen emotional directness. The boldest opera ever written from the viewpoint of daring subject-matter and intellectual demands on its audience justifies itself almost completely. And oddly enough, though there is about an hour's worth of additional horrors and demands, the work is less fearsome now that it is complete; the increase of scale gives them both room to breathe; the intellectuality broadens out into explicit affect-making, the horrors are bound in to cause and effect, and their weird liaison becomes altogether more assimilable.

There is a strong sense of the three acts, so densely intervolved with each other, having been written simultaneously. We experience a whole, and many aspects of it whose schematic value before was dubious, are now palpable as expressive architecture. The main symmetry that can now be felt rather than read about is the division of the three-act whole into two halves, separated by the celebrated palindrome in the middle of Act II. On the one side, based on *Erdgeist*, the first of Wedekind's Lulu plays, we have the heroine's ascent through two husbands and their sticky ends to a third marriage which gives her at last who and what she wants. On the other, after Wedekind's second Lulu play, *Die Büchse der Pandora*, we have her decline and horrible end. The other big symmetry now clearly revealed is the device imposed by Berg upon the original plays (which are by and large used very straight), whereby in the final scene, with Lulu at her lowest ebb as a prostitute, her three clients should be played by the same singers who represented her three husbands in Acts I and II. This gives Berg the opportunity for extensive recapitulation; such musical tying-up is the most telling aspect of the symmetry and seems to me the truest reason for it.

So two overall shapes are superimposed: the advance/retreat of Lulu's fortunes, with the forward and forward-again pattern of her marriages becoming her pick-ups. In addition several other new parallels strike the listener without being far-fetched. The role of Schön, Lulu's third husband and 'the only man I really loved', whose death is the immediate event before the halfway division, parallels the role of the Countess Geschwitz (absent from Act I as Schön clearly must be from Act III), Lulu's faithfullest and, in her necessitated pureness, most disinterested lover. Schön the weak strongman, prey to his passions (including his passion for respectability), is also shadowed by Schigolch, the true strong man for all his asthma and apparent decrepitude, unafraid of his wishes and highly practical in disposing of unwanted bodies. Lulu's second husband, the Painter who produces the all-important portrait of her, shadows Alwa the composer, Schön's son and Lulu's first lover in the downhill half of the opera. The Painter—soft, weak, devoted—killed himself after his innocent eyes were opened by Schön to Lulu's true nature. Reappearing as client number two he is in every respect the opposite—Negro, mad, illiterate, brutal. Almost unprovoked he murders his counterpart the composer, also soft, weak and devoted (if not exactly innocent, being very much the son of his father though without Schön's forcefulness). Their ends are the most painful and gratuitous in the whole range this work offers of horrors unattached to causes and unattended by any normal sense of the terribleness of death by violence. Shadowy parallels like these are none the less telling even if unmasked by full-scale symmetry-making musical devices.

ii Wonders and difficulties of Act III

The first, Paris, scene of Act III contains some marvellous new music, including passages that change our overall view of Berg. Outstanding are the three ensembles for the fatuous demi-mondaine gaming and drinking party, through which run sordid undercurrents of pimping and blackmail. Though they are built on the animal-trainer music heard at the start of Act I—the only explicit amplification of this metaphor—their effect is unlike anything else in the opera or indeed in Berg's output. The third, fastest and longest, is the most vivid and unexpected stretch of hitherto unheard music, and achieves a kind of vertical take-off of excitement. More remarkable still is the earlier *Pantomime*. The whole company moves around the room not singing for once (a welcome respite), their movements choreographed by their various musical motifs, linked and superimposed in a sort of composition-by-free-association, in the masterly fluidity and richness of Berg's latest manner, liberated from note-counting or scheme-filling.[1] More beautiful still, the ravishing strains to which Lulu uses her hold over the Geschwitz to persuade her to plead with the loutish Athlete for his favours—she to pay him in

---

[1] Not so! Once George Perle's comprehensive study appeared, one read that this apparent spontaneity was as symbolic/schematic as anything and everything in the opera.

exchange the 20,000 marks for which he is blackmailing Lulu! (There will be more to say on the tendency of the music to soar into ecstasy the more repulsive the plot becomes.) All the same it cannot be denied that there is still a certain amount of the old Bergian jungle in this scene, and that one very important moment goes for nothing. This is verse two of the 'Lied der Lulu'. She had sung its first verse in Act II; the Earth-Spirit's apologia, superb in its female frankness, as Schön stood over her demanding that she admit the guilt she cannot feel. In verse two she is threatened by the pimping Marquis, who offers her a choice between a luxury brothel in Cairo or denunciation to German justice. Here is her further instalment of self-defence:

> I might have liked the brothel at fifteen ... but then I spent three months in hospital never setting eyes on a man for my pleasure. And in that time it's as if my eyes were opened at last and I saw myself plain. I used to dream, fantasising every night on the ideal man who was made for me alone; and when they let me out, I wasn't such a goose. Since then, when any man approaches me in the blackness of night, I can tell a hundred yards off whether he's right for me. And when I have gone against what I know to be my sort, I come the next day to hate myself, besmirched in body and soul.

These words, vital for the last scene as well as for understanding Lulu aright, are simply lost in the welter of surrounding activity; and, as so often, including stanza one, familiar from the *Lulu Symphonie*, as well as Act II, the main inspiration doesn't seem to be vocal, for all that it is meant to be a *song*.

Which reminds one that obfuscation, by multiple cross-references as well as by innate moment-to-moment complexity, does remain a problem in all Berg's music until the Violin Concerto. Here his work liaises with a general issue in modernism   is difficulty intrinsic to it, even indispensable to its quality? The dense texture of *Lulu* corresponds to that in an icon of impene-trability contemporary with it, *Finnegans Wake*, destined by its author mostly for 'the ideal reader with the ideal insomnia'. But if obfuscation were all, *Lulu* wouldn't have the direct effect it manifestly has. Berg's adoption of Schoenberg's serial technique at first gave further ammunition to his ten-dency to camouflage himself in a jungle: yet in the works that follow he gradually moves towards a victory over obfuscation for lucidity. From the nightmare finale of the *Kammerkonzert*, via the alternation of 'free' and 'strict' in the *Lyric Suite* (where as we now know, 'free' is as disciplined by private associations, lovers' knots and favourite numbers, children's ages, quantity and meaning in Baudelaire as by serialism) to *Der Wein* and *Lulu* itself, he succeeds   even, perhaps, against a native tendency to secrecy   in progressively imbuing the actual sounds with the comprehensible audible evidence of the processes by which they are chosen. The perfect balance in the Violin Concerto of public/private content, 'alchemical'/recognisable con-struction, serial/tonal language is the outcome. (It is a matter of temperament, and ideology, whether one finds this brilliant compromise a wonderful master-piece or a cop-out.)

Lulu is three-quarters there, but it's certainly possible still to be lost among or hung up on a mania for organisation exercised at the cost of expressivity and, sometimes, intelligibility. Of the big symmetry-making recapitulations in the London scene of Act III, one serves, in its comparative straightforwardness, to show the bizarre nature of the other. The simpler one comes after Lulu's first client has left. Footsteps are heard; it is Geschwitz, her devotion undaunted, bearing from Paris Lulu's portrait, reminder in its unchanged appeal of Lulu on her upward path. When she would destroy it, Alwa intervenes; he 'feels his self-respect is restored'; he 'understands his fate'. 'Who stands before these lips with their promise of pleasure, before these eyes innocent as the eyes of children, before this white and rosy ripening body, and still feels safe within his bourgeois book of rules, let such a man cast the first stone at us' (unusually tendentious words in this elaborately amoral work). A quartet develops out of his paean to Lulu's beauty and sexuality that ended Act II, in which his voice remains prominent. We are stirred by this glowing re-creation of past raptures in the midst of present squalors—one client gone, two more, and three deaths, still to come. We are moved, all the more so as the original was cut short by Lulu's devastating curtain-line whereas this re-creation surges on to achieve the climax hitherto denied (compare the 'Liebestod' in its relation to *Tristan* Act II). Our emotion is completely explicable; this is Alwa's noblest moment, and very soon he is going to come to an ignoble end; his corpse will be shoved out of sight so as not to offend Lulu's clients and put them off their stroke. Strange and repulsive maybe, to have such an extravagantly radiant outpouring in such circumstances; but not meaningless.

Genuine dislocation of meaning, though, seems to be the intention (as it certainly is the effect) of the final and easily most extensive pattern-making recapitulation, the identification of Lulu's three clients with her three husbands. The first client, doubling her first husband, elderly Dr Goll, is a Professor; silent, by his gestures a crackpot, by the pamphlet found in his pocket a bit of a religious maniac; but he pays well. Lulu's reaction when he has gone is a weary 'He gave me such a thrill'—much like the good Dr Goll, presumably. The musical return is confined to her playful little song over his body (he had died of a stroke brought on by catching her and the Painter fooling around); recast, and with curious stops and starts that articulate it differently and produce an effect of emotional distancing.

As already indicated, the second client reincarnates the Painter who had married Lulu soon after they had caused the death of her first husband. This symmetry is more complex. The Painter's suicide had been preceded by a confrontation with Schön opening his infatuated eyes to a carefully-angled selection of his wife's past, musically rendered by one of Berg's most staggering technical/expressive inventions, a 'monoritmica' that gradually permeates the whole texture in a perfect image of intolerable pressure. When the scales at last fall from his eyes, the Painter rushes off 'to have a few words with her'. Schön mops his brow with relief—'that was hard work'; but within seconds we hear the horrible sound of the wretched man in his death-agony, having cut his throat.

Though these Act I events are illustrated in an extremely graphic way, their full violence remains unexpressed, defused as always by the hectic rush to cover up and move on. Expression is deflected into the scene-changing interlude that soon follows, a fervent Mahlerian adagio growing out of the decline of the same monoritmica that has just served so painfully to turn the screw. It expresses Lulu's only emotion, love for her protector Schön. Thus the Painter's death in Act I makes no impact; its latent feeling explodes with terrifying effect in Act III, where the monoritmica returns and is given its head as never before to accompany the Negro's brutality with Lulu and his murder of Alwa. This is horrible, but not gratuitous; it satisfies the frustration caused by the pent-up refusal to let go in Act I. Yet even now something remains unspent. With the first client there was intercourse, with the second, murder; only the third, the reincarnation of Schön himself in the guise of Jack the Ripper, releases both blood and sperm.

This is the most elaborate of the symmetries and the most inexplicable. It is clearly the emotional climax of the work, and its effect is overwhelming, yet it is still very difficult to understand what is really meant by it. The above-mentioned adagio returns, and to its passion and heartache are added the various strains of Lulu's earlier, uncommercial seductions; to music which formerly had Schön beguiled around her little finger, she now begs the alluring but frightening stranger to stay with her till the morning. She abjects herself for his favours; he cannot pay what she asks, nor even half—never mind, she'll give herself for nothing and even give him the bus-fare so he can return the same night to his family. In a voice full of suffering (Berg's direction) she says 'I'm really drawn to you. Please don't keep me waiting longer'—and we recall the words of her song about the man made for her alone. But the music reworked here is the deliriously vulgar 'kiss-me-quick' phrase by which she incited Alwa to make love to her at the end of Act II, which now miraculously blossoms out into a return of the most rapturous moment in all this disconcertingly rapturous opera, the cry of 'Freiheit!' when, rather earlier in the same act, she was at last released from prison into her native world of men. Their ultimate context gives an extraordinary resonance to these returns.

'I'm quite ready,' says Jack. While they're in her room the former barrel-organ music is replaced by Geschwitz's haunting 'Nocturnal'—she can't take these people any more—she'll return to Germany and equip herself to fight for Women's Rights. A horrible scream is heard; Jack emerges bloody-handed, stops to knife Geschwitz too, mutters 'that was hard work' as he wipes his hands (heavens knows what *this* little recapitulation means!) and rapidly leaves as the orchestra furtively recalls the animal music from the prologue. The opera ends with another passage of seraphic beauty (also well known from the concert-suite); the dying Geschwitz sings her elegy for Lulu and herself, joined in death as never in life ... 'I will remain by you ... for ever ... accursed.'[2]

These large-scale returns appeal to our sense of neatness: nothing is wasted and some superb music receives a welcome second hearing. Our feeling for musical architecture is used to resolve the incomplete expression of the first two acts, whose claustrophobia is at last given breathing-space, and whose accumulation of tension receives first its full utterance and then its ultimate repose. Yet at the same time the imposed symmetries dislocate our sense of the relationship between music and characters (to say nothing of our sense of these characters' initial separate identities). We hear music of intensely expressive content, always requiring an explicit musical response, in contexts that make such a response peculiar at the least, and at the worst impossible. If we are concentrating on action and characterisation, the music is inapt. If (more likely) we are seized by the richness and urgency of the music, we will obey its instructions as to how to take it, irrespective of their denial by the composer's enforced re-associations. The process in Mahler whereby emotion becomes detached from its utterance and is parodied, producing laceration, is taken much farther by Berg and stylised into a convention. Yet it is also different. Mahler's deepest emotion trembles on the brink of hollowness, and awareness of this produces mockery and pain. In Berg the deep emotion is intact, and rendered at full intensity, but dislocated from what has caused it and what it ought to be expressing, to be deflected on to something else that remains unclear and produces an effect impossible to define.

Wozzeck is on the cusp: and indeed it has often been objected that the famous interlude before the final scene gives its hearer, however sympathetic, no escape from an over-explicit instruction-kit as to what to feel and how to feel it. *Lulu* appears to reverse this aim. Maybe the simple reason is that an expressionistic *Lulu*—the emotional and onomatopoeic rendition in music of all those horrible events—would be so profoundly inartistic. Instead we find detachment, inconsequentiality, even a surrealistic abandonment of responsibility towards meaning which allows characters and events to be manipulated like pieces in a game. Yet in Act III, where this tendency is most marked, the music glows with ever-greater intensity of direct emotional expression; the old gibe that Berg is 'the twelve-note Puccini' (properly understood, a compliment to both composers, of course) is never so true as here. So while there is no doubt that the restoration of Act III has vindicated the whole work and put it into an altogether different order of creative achievement, there are nevertheless serious problems in understanding just what it is doing. However this is hardly surprising. It will be a long time

---

[2] '*Verflucht*': the dying word in the last two bars of Geschwitz's part and the work as a whole appears in the vocal score, not in the orchestral, and is present or absent in subsequent performances according to taste. We still need a complete *apparatus criticus* for Act III such as the Cooke realisation of Mahler 10 provides, and the 1994/9 edition of the finale to Bruckner's Ninth.

before the complete *Lulu* is as familiar as *Tristan*, and able, as Wagner is, to be experienced for what it is without the meaning having to be spelt out.

The complex history of Act III's release (moving from confident expectation of a complete première within a year or so of Berg's death, through refusal to allow access to the manuscript, to an eventual blank denial of the music's existence) is of great interest in itself, both for the psychopathologies involved and for the legal wrangle between individual and public possession of works of art; but is not necessary for its artistic estimation. The three other major incompletions in modern music are dissimilar one from another, but Act III of *Lulu* is in a category of its own in that Berg's composition is complete. It is neither a sketch like Mahler's Tenth Symphony nor a torso like the *Jakobsleiter* of Schoenberg; nor, like his *Moses und Aron*, an ostensibly uncompleted project which in fact is fully realised as it stands and would have been spoiled, even betrayed, by the fortunately-never-composed final act. The further course of *Jakobsleiter* is completely unimaginable; though the text is published, there is no basis on which its setting could be predicted. Maybe even Schoenberg was daunted by the prospect of so many more pages of clotted amateur theosophy (except that the hefty portion actually composed suggests that he boggled at nothing). This music, containing passages the equal of anything he wrote, is complete in its notation but not scored; and though no one could have done the job so well as the master, it *is* a feasible job, with adequate parallels in the comprehensive instrumental details of such closely-allied works as *Die glückliche Hand* and the *Four Orchestral Songs*. (The actual performing version has not taken full advantage of these incomparable models.) Realisation of Mahler's Tenth is different again: two movements are in a nearly final state; the rest varies from comparatively detailed sketching to a bird's-eye view that has concentrated on getting things down as fast as possible without losing time by struggling for quality. The patent inadequacy of the details cannot conceal an overall conception whose greatness has to contend with the inevitable embarrassments of what is actually on the page.

Act III of *Lulu* suffers from none of these various forms of incompleteness; it is complete and fully composed with only the tiniest lacunae; but it is not orchestrated. There is a surer guide for realising this missing dimension than in any comparable case: the full-score of the first two acts (especially since Act III contains so much recapitulated music—though actually I think Berg might have changed its colouring rather drastically); the two movements orchestrated for the concert-suite; and the commencement of a full-score of the act, which reached approximately 250 bars. Friedrich Cerha has let himself be guided, and his reward is that it is impossible to tell where Berg takes over and the rescuer yields. None the less if by mischance the legal action against the publishers were successful and Cerha's orchestration banned, the horse has bolted and nothing will ever get him back again into confinement..

iii Production and performance

Like any great theatrical work *Lulu* may be seen in many different ways, though there are certain immutable obligations which every production must respect or flout only with good reason. Thus, for instance, period need not be laid down, but Schön's interior in Act II must always have plenty of chairs and curtains for Lulu's troupe of lovers to conceal themselves behind, and a sofa to receive its mortally-wounded owner's collapse. Seen live, M. Chereau's quirky production and the baleful sets of Richard Peduzzi did not appear to be trying very hard to fulfil the basic requirements. A subsequent viewing of the television relay has modified the bad impression without fundamentally changing it.

They certainly were very different experiences. At the Opéra the sets were so huge and the lighting so dim that it was often hard to know just what was happening. Distances were too great in this monumental setting; the all-important doorbell throughout Act I necessitated scampering that barely managed to fit arrivals and exits into the music provided; the Painter's studio and home, and Lulu's dressing-room, were all so big that the perpetual proximity of the few characters became absurd. In Act II Schön's drawing-room was like the interior or even the exterior of a fascistic People's Palace, with walls of gleaming marble-substitute, a huge sweep of stairs, and a virtual absence of domestic furnishings. Here, as well as an even more annoying sense of the distances being too great for the movements, a new and more serious fault obtruded—there were so many supernumeraries (waiters and houseguests) that the activities of the principals, difficult enough to take in even when only they (there are eight) are involved, became hopelessly obscured. Since the lighting was too poor to distinguish faces, and since the colour was virtually monochrome, point after point was lost, both the macabre and the farcical elements going for nothing. It was easy to recognise the ladies (Lulu *petite*, Geschwitz tall and stately in her decidedly feminine-style clothes—a minor transgression of the directions that in the circumstances was just as well). The men however were hard to tell apart, except for the Athlete's unfortunate fatness. The Paris scene of Act III was more successful since what is needed here is bustle, the eager crowd of variously fatuous and/or repulsive guests streaming in and out from gaming-room to dining-room, against which the squalid duets of blackmail and bribery stand out. Here the big space was well-used for the first time, the complex movements well choreographed, and the witty curtain deftly handled.

In the London scene M. Chereau revealed that sensitive rapport with the composer's truest intentions already famous from his *Ring* for the Bayreuth centenary. We were to understand that Lulu, Alwa and Schigolch had somehow set up their sordid domesticity not in a high attic (on whose roof the rain audibly patters in the score) but in an underground public lavatory, with a row of gleaming basins all-too-conveniently expecting Jack's need to wash his hands. He and the Negro were, sure enough, played by the singers of Lulu's second and third husbands; but her first client, the gentle religious maniac who pays so well, was played not by her first husband, but by the

Dwarf who had been seen hours before as the Animal Trainer's assistant in the Prologue to Act I. As well as being confusing in a part of the work whose parallels are difficult enough even when faithfully carried out, this was gratuitous, adding a kinky touch to a scene whose depiction of excentricity is already assured. After Jack had done his bloody work, washed his hands and dried them on a strip torn from Lulu's petticoat, the performance continued with the curtain-calls. Because, for the first time since the Prologue, the footlights were on, we could at last distinguish *faces*, including M. Chereau himself, jogging on in flip defiance of his audience and ostentatiously chewing gum.

The television showing complemented all this, sometimes with an emphasis so changed that it hardly seemed like the same work. It concentrated on close-ups, to such an extent that the viewer who didn't already know about the vast spaces in which these intimate scenes were played could probably not have realised their existence; and the lighting either had been improved or was necessitated by the cameras, for general visibility was much better. This double concentration on individuals revealed the action clearly and showed what was impossible to see in Paris, that there was intelligence at work and some very striking image-making. After a confusing Prologue that fudged the chance to make explicit for the first time the animal and human parallels, virtually every scene made better sense—the very first moments, of prowling men (Alwa and his father sharing the same predatory stare) gathering in on the innocently-seductive female, can exemplify the whole. (Incidently the Painter's studio now sported academy nudes and portraits, very different from the blown-up Pop-image of his Lulu-portrait, that were not in evidence on the first night; one of many small changes all for the better.) Even the biggest nuisance of the stage version, the confusing extras, now had a generalised effectiveness: the procession of waiters bearing loaded trays through Schön's marble halls and the crowds of silent shuffling guests idling up and down his Valhalla stairway gave an air of surreal grandeur, though the actual scripted characters and events of this scene were as muddled as ever. The idea presumably is to present these private domestic embarrassments before a stage audience, at once shocked and indifferent, intermediary between the principals and the true audience, and thus to build towards the crowd of actual singing characters, intent on their Jungfrau shares or their gains at gaming or dining tables and oblivious of the hideous realities, in the Paris scene of Act III. But the loss in clarity is greater than the gain in stage-picture. The idea only works once, at the end of Act I. We have already caught a glimpse of Schön's fiancée as he arrived backstage with her after Lulu's jealous fainting-feint during her performance. Then in the tussle that ends the act the same large silent blonde reappears staring unmoved through the glass with the Prince (another of Lulu's suitors) at the scene within, as Lulu dictates the letter by which Schön breaks off his engagement. They stare, they implicitly judge, they show him to be trapped, and gradually a crowd of stagehands and chorus-girls accumulates, all impassively gawping at the strong man's total humiliation. None of this is in the score, but though tendentious it is not without point. It was repeated with equal effect, in the Paris scene of Act III where another Lulu-flouting fiancée appears as a dumb extra, this time the Athlete's intended; he being another shadowy counterpart to Schön, a powerful bully, vain, loutish and completely unimportant to her.

The television close-ups and lighting also revealed the male members of the cast to possess distinguishing features, and that some could act and some couldn't. Of those who could, Franz Mazura's Schön/Ripper was outstanding, a real tiger as indicated in the Prologue. Robert Tear's Painter/Negro was also good; and since these two were also the best male singers the hardworking monoritmica turn-of-the-screw was intensely gripping. Alwa (Kenneth Riegel) was plump and undistinguished; the Athlete (Gerd Nienstedt) fat and better; Schigolch (Toni Blankenheim) corny. The best pure singing came from those of indeterminate sex, Hanna Schwarz in the two trouser-roles of the Schoolboy and the Groom, and Yvonne Minton's Countess Geschwitz. Her presence was statuesque and almost maternal; not quite right, but moving, and very beautifully sung. Turning to the one, primeval, woman, Teresa Stratas was also not quite right—too intelligent, too nervy, too fastidious to be an *Erdgeist*. But she is fascinating: every gesture is volatile and full of interest, most particularly during the duet with Alwa that ends Act II. Rarely have I seen such an uninterpretable expression. At first it was pure contemptuous impatience with Alwa's rhapsodising—here she is, free again after prison and cholera, and here is a man—why does he go on so instead of getting down to it? Then as he launches into his 'Hymne' her expression registers dumb, insolent, puzzled animal blankness—an extraordinary sight, promptly effaced by the appalling curtain-line ('Isn't this the sofa on which your father bled to death?'), a failure and embarrassment at every performance, largely through Berg's own underlining emphasis, which not even Stratas's subtlety could mollify. In Act III she was wonderful again; anxiety and anguish suit her best. The tableau of her pleading with Geschwitz, embracing her, promising her the love for which she has waited so long, if she will pay off the Athlete by pretending to desire his favours, was the most touching moment in the work.

The Opéra orchestra is not the world's most supple band, and the brass in particular provided some unintentionally searing moments; but the general sonority was good, the all-important obbligato instruments (vibraphone and saxophone, 'the very apple of *Lulu*'s fascination', as Stravinsky said) admirable, and the big piano part outstanding. The direction was always competent and occasionally distinguished. Warmth was on the whole absent; Boulez's view of the work was characteristically hard-driven. Everything it owes to Mahler, everything spacious and voluptuous, its norm of *Ausdruck* and rubato, was rather tight. But there were marvellous things, where his equally characteristic lightness and precision had full scope—the first interlude in Act I, that frothy resumé of everything in the previous scene; the delectable 'jazz' overheard in Lulu's dressing-room at the end of the same act; a hair-raising palindrome at the opera's newly-focused dead-centre; a radiant return of Lulu to her 'Freiheit'; and an unwontedly eloquent account of the opera's closing moments. Subsequent performances will no doubt be more fully realised, but meanwhile the credit as well as the *réclame*, are entirely deserved.

The whole experience was incredible at the time and now seems so remote as hardly to have happened: dashing off in the middle of a crowded term—a rapid succession of small culture-shocks—London, Heathrow (Age of Austerity), Charles de Gaulle (Things to Come), métro—barely time to find the hotel and a meal before rushing to the Opéra—first-ever sight of that sublime and ridiculous interior, the wonderful staircase, the gilded salons (stolidly fence-sitting between opulence and coarseness), the absorbing circus of an international first-night audience—then the crimson plush grotto of the amphitheatre itself, the charms and dangers of the lady seat-guardians—then, once safely seated, the production itself with its dreary sets and its frustrating action, so indistinct after the brilliant unambiguity of the audience promenading the galleries or rushing to the bars. Yet perhaps its studied neutrality helped focus the mind on the music: after all the opera itself has separated its musical expression from its narrative content. And as the second half of the expedition unwound itself palindromically backwards (hotel, métro, Charles de Gaulle, Heathrow, London, Cambridge) one was permeated by a sense of significant occasion. In fact this first complete *Lulu* joins the première of the completed Mahler Tenth Symphony and the first London performance of Schoenberg's *Jakobsleiter*-torso as events which for all their attendant dissatisfactions remain among the profoundest artistic impressions of my life. A very great and seminal work is now an inviolable unity (for a performance without Act III is as inconceivable now as a Wagner opera without its third act). A *Ulysses*-like complexity of contrivance is now vindicated; and, like *Ulysses* (or for that matter like Wagner), *Lulu* is at once a culmination and dead-end, yet paradoxically pregnant, in its disintegration, with a thousand new possibilities. Above all, in spite of that red plush of the auditorium and that fake marble onstage, there was the unmistakable sense of a great composer—perhaps the century's greatest simply in terms of natural endowment if not in range or quantity—taking off into his amplest, freest creative flight. The wasp whose sting, causing Berg's fatal illness, prevented that flight from achieving its full span of years must have come straight out of *Die Büchse der Pandora*.

iv The complete Lulu

In *Lulu* the combination of *music* (ranging from the most refined elegance to the extremest emotional utterance) plus *action* ('sordid', 'degraded', 'animal' etc.) plus *contrived symmetries* (creating strange barely-explicable correspondences and non-correspondences), equals *dislocation* of musical affect from its normal workings. We are already accustomed to dislocation in the first two acts, where horrible events flash meaninglessly by without being registered for what they are (as if seen through Lulu's own moral sensibility). For instance the huge emotional expenditure of the Schön Adagio in Act I, when the doctor's death and the painter's have passed unmourned, is 'balanced' (though perhaps the word should be 'unbalanced') by the emotional void at the death of Schön in Act II, where there's nothing but animal panic. Berg hasn't stinted himself on 'expression'; but there is both displacement of cause and effect, and sometimes a deliberate rift between them. Act III takes this much further. The discrepancy between stage-picture, music heard, and that music's first context, can be focused in the rebarring of the recapitulated material. It *sounds* identical, but is being beaten (and followed in the score) by a contradictory signature—a symbol of the strange and disconcerting effect of this act altogether.

Berg began in expressionism, a style that tells its listeners pretty unambiguously how to react—onomatopoeia of the emotions. Taken rather further, it contradicts its own intensity and undermines its listeners' instinctive obedience to emotive instructions. But *Lulu*, though retaining some gestures from this style almost in inverted commas (as in Schön's asides in the first scene of Act II when he returns to find his house full of Lulu's lovers), is so different as to amount to a reversal of the expressionist aesthetic. What is it? People are now saying 'surrealistic', on the strength of the new dreamlike inconsequentiality, fluid in the Paris scene and monumentalised in the husband/client symmetry of the London scene. Is it 'redemption by music; *alla* Wagner but in a characteristically subtilised and parodistic re-interpretation? Or is it something as yet undefined that can only be obscured by would-be helpful analogies from other styles? Whatever it is, there is no doubt that the clamour set up by Acts I and II is completely fulfilled by the restoration of Act III; but the new totality sets up its own clamour for definition and meaning.

All this is a confused and interim reaction to something complex that will need familiarity, a long perspective and much rumination before it can begin to come straight. Meanwhile a few more specific comments on the newly-unveiled music.

The big stumbling-block, after several hearings and poring over the vocal score, remains the concertante Chorale-Variations as the Marquis tries blackmail on Lulu early in the first scene. After the lucidity of *Der Wein* and most of *Lulu* itself, this music reverts to the impenetrability of the *Kammerkonzert*—a work crammed with secret games that, unlike the private messages in the *Lyric Suite*, are intended to be heard, and whose inexpressivity therefore makes a failure of the piece as a whole. In this part of the opera Berg still seems to be at the mercy of his facile complexity, and embarrassed with too many notes that one senses are there because he feels they ought to be rather than because he really wants them. The result is opaque and frustrating; and the two enclosed songs bring no relief. The Marquis's 'Song of the Pimp' somehow fails to tell, while the all-important second verse of the 'Lied der Lulu' (whose contour we already know from the similarly crucial *apologia pro vita sua* in Act II) is lost in the tangle of overgrowth. No wonder, in a scene where the words go fast and are vital for comprehension, that the ears can only take in what they know already, the snatches of 'English Valse' from Act I scene 3.

Towards the end of these variations we recognise another familiar Bergian sound. The solo violin, prominent from the start, now begins in arpeggio chords across the strings to sound a pre-echo of the Violin Concerto. Later there is a second unnerving slip into familiarity; a re-do of the duo-cadenza from the *Kammerkonzert* as Lulu's two blackmailers try to outwit each other. Maybe in time the disconcerting effect of these reminiscences will vanish; already the placing of the cadenza (as well as the way it isolates the blackmailers' associated solo instruments) works as contrast to and relief from the normal texture of dense orchestral activity.

An important aspect of Act III is that it vindicates familiar music that has never seemed to work before. The most notable example is the Variations, well known from the *Lulu-Symphonie* where the contents, between the brusque and ugly chords enclosing them, always seem desultory and undefined. In context, on the contrary, they are full of meaning. The chords disappear, and the first variation (we have already heard the theme, admittedly rather lost in the jungle, as the 'Song of the Pimp'; now the Marquis's design for Lulu is about to be realised, though not in a luxury house in Cairo) sails straight in to crown the best curtain in the whole work, and Alwa's escape from the police and the blackmailers. Variation 2 is the barrel-organ music that in primitive form will punctuate the first two of Lulu's three sessions on the streets and will recur as she is on the job with the first client; another Mahlerian idea taken further—banal music to represent life as a treadmill of meaningless dreariness, and sex debased into commerce without joy. Variation 3 is the funèbre in 5/4. The time-signature makes its full point only later when the Hauptrhythmus, in its basic 5/4, explodes with all the fury that was kept potential at the painter's suicide in Act I, for the revenging murder of Alwa the composer by the second client, the Painter's reincarnation as a Negro. The funèbre makes its full point only when it returns as Alwa's epitaph (whose words, sung by Schigolch, make a typical dislocation—'I'd better move him or Lulu's next customer'll have a shock').

Schigolch's part in Act III is another rescue of a character and music that one has always endured rather than enjoyed in Acts I and II. He now becomes important in the plot (for disposing of the Athlete), and interesting in himself, with his touching little begging-scene for his 'not very youthful' girlfriend and his efficacious comfort for the distracted Lulu. Above all the revelation that he is not her father but yet another lover lends a different sense to his scenes earlier in the opera. Moreover his creepy wheezing music really comes into its own here for the first time.

And finally, actual newnesses. The three ensembles in the Paris scene are outstanding among the music never heard before (though an aspect of them is familiar since they are built on the animal-trainer music in the Prologue to Act I—the music of bars 9–16 of I returns exactly as bars 1–12 of III, now barred in 2/4 not 3/4. The ostinato-building is unlike anything in the first two acts (the Film music resembles it only in technical description, not in actual sound); and the combination of the resulting slowed-down harmonic rate with regular rhythmic definition of a kind hardly used elsewhere in the opera produces a forward momentum new in Berg. The first ensemble is only twenty-five bars; the second, at a slower speed, lasts about sixty-five bars; while the third and fastest achieves a vertical take-off that makes its 110-odd bars one of the most exciting passages in the work, and certainly the most vivid and unexpected stretch of hitherto unheard music. No one can speak of Berg's 'habitual languor' after this.

The *Pantomime* just before has already been singled out (p.159). Its concentration upon gesture and movement links it with another of the opera's greatest stretches, also wordless, the film music that stands at exact mid-point of the three-act structure, and in its palindromic reversal symbolises the heroine's ascent and decline as surely as it narrates her equally-symmetricalised adventures in prison and hospital. The astonishing inventiveness of these purely orchestral passages, the one airy and delectable, the other tumultuous and cataclysmic, around its erotically suggestive still turning-point, both written according to mind-bogglingly strict compositional procedures, seems to me to reveal Berg as the century's most richly endowed composer.

Afterword

2003: Well, perhaps not, after all! The excitement that understandably kindled the musical world at such an extraordinary unveiling has now died down. The three-act version has become standard, and has settled down as a classic without growing any more explicable or inevitable. Far the best production (and musical performance) that has come my way was the Glyndebourne version (Glyndebourne? *Lulu*!) by Graham Vick, conducted by Andrew Davis. Unless done with such responsible imagination and *Schwung* the full thing—very long, unremitting in textural complexity, consistently emotionally draining—can overwhelm with sheer metal-fatigue rather than effecting the healthy purgation of tragedy and Wagnerian music-drama.

Then there's been the lucid presentation by George Perle (*The Operas of Alban Berg*, vol. 2, University of California Press, 1985) of the truly awesome mechanics of the composition itself. It must be the most consciously planned and elaborated piece of music ever written—*certainly* of its scope and size.

All this taken together can make its audience feel threatened, oppressed, entrapped by a work in which not a single parameter is impulsive. Everything from the bloodiest murder to the tiniest musical flicker (or silence) is overdetermined, in a work whose most beautiful and moving moment sets the word *Freiheit!* And while Act II is not wholly innocent of note-spinning by the composer himself, Act III, as it now stands, reveals with familiarity some dead patches which one can't imagine him have let stand. All involve recapitulation/*rechauffage*: the second stanza of Lulu's Song, still more unsatisfactory in Act III than its first in Act II; the awkwardly laid-out and texted Quartet developed from the Lulu/Alwa duet; and above all the return of her husbands in the form of her clients. Yet this last, most of all, induces creepiness, then scariness, then sheer horror, then heart-in-mouth apprehension culminating in pity and terror, even as it also fulfils those maddeningly

pedantic games of bar/metronome-mark/note-counting which Berg apparently couldn't compose without.

When it doesn't work one hankers in guilty exhaustion for the incomplete
version; two rich acts and an orchestral epilogue. When it does work, and one
is strong enough not to crack, there is nothing else to touch it (above all its
would-be successors and out-toppers, notably *Die Soldaten*). For all the
shimmering sleaze and gleaming steel mechanics of her context, Lulu is up
there with Isolde, Kundry, Salome, Elektra and the unnamed woman of
Erwartung (though perhaps the comparisons she herself would choose are
Carmen, Delilah, Manon, Lakmé, Mimi crossed with Musetta).

25

Schoeck the evolutionary

The full story of twentieth-century music has yet to be told disinterestedly. Every writer—composer, commentator, historian—has an axe to grind, often unwitting. Time does its work of pure ablution; the merely worthless slowly sinks beneath the horizon. But what then happens, it seems, is that we're left only with the huge grim important Easter Island figures of the great pioneers. Such Academy- or 'History'-hallowed idolatry, tremendously impressive, is difficult to resist, and tends to demote any music that doesn't accord with the accompanying ideology, denaturing a richer understanding of the whole. Art isn't so clear-cut. Any attempts to make it so are simply not true. The *true* story of what is distinctive, valuable, permanent in the last romantics, the moderns, the neo-classicists, serialists, constructivists, folklorists, neo-romantics, minimalists, neo-tonalists, neo-moderns, post-moderns of the past hundred years or so—the huge span remains discrete because we're still so hugely involved in every phase of it; it's still being digested—will need vast efforts of listening and assimilation, evaluation and revaluation to amount eventually by thousands of individual small siftings and shiftings to a complete re-alignment of the field. Probably the main patterns as currently received are not all that far out: certainly we will be able to agree upon some seminal masterpieces without risking the dogmatic claustrophobia of Boulez's recent concert-programming. But what must yield is the very idea of main lines *only*, and *only* the main lines permitted, admirable, right—so deceptively definite, so crudely black/white, so cruelly denuded of detail.

Between the well-lit and -policed guidelines lie wiggly routes left and right of centre: primrose descents and rocky climbs, streams and ponds, waterfalls and lakes, rivers and reservoirs—also bridges, mine-shafts, viaducts, palaces, chapels, follies. There are parks, gardens, orchards, fields, woods, forests filled with curious animals, delicious birds, intricate insects; also marshes, swamps, ravines, deserts, poisonous snakes, fearsome diseases that nevertheless have their role in the balance of nature. Every item of such a list could stand for a type of composer who has lived and worked in the last century. One could go on for ever having silly fun with this game. The serious point is that the fantastic multiplicity of its compositional achievement (second to no other epoch in this, at least) cannot be appreciated if the usual rigid exclusionism prevails. There is no call to lower the sights, embracing it *all* in all its Whitmanesque contradictions just because it's there.

On the contrary, I'm advocating stringency and ears sharpened by their very openness. But our futuristic Utopia must not be confined to concrete walkways between Easter Island idols.

Othmar Schoeck is a perfect example of the sort of composer ironed-out by such factitious 'historical necessities'. It's as if his only fame (or rather, the pale opposite of fame by which he's known at all, if at all) were in balance with the 'redundancy' of the output, its style and stance guaranteeing the hopelessness of any bid for election to the Pantheon of the Chosen Few. Nevertheless his music refuses to lie down and be flattened by the steamroller. As I reflect on him, listen again, reflect further, the fugitive subtlety lodges, the unobtrusive individuality unobtrusively deepens, and even alongside the adjacent giants—sometimes in contradistinction to them—the stature expands.

Clearly the corpus of over 300 songs with piano, a handful of cycles with instrumental ensembles and one masterpiece with full orchestra will remain the touchstone of his achievement. Overall they make a fifty-year journey from fresh tunefulness and relative conventionality into a refined distillation of essentialised simplicity devoted in the main to the exploration of pantheistic nostalgia. His poets earlier on are usually familiar German romantics—Goethe, Eichendorff, Lenau, Uhland, Mörike. Later the Swiss predominate—Gottfried Keller, Conrad Ferdinand Meyer, the all-but-forgotten Heinrich Leuthold, drawn to his attention by his friend Hermann Hesse, whom he also set generously. The themes however remain constant: romantic germanic inwardness, grown sliver-thin with use—love/man/nature/gloom/despair/meditation on faith and doubt/recollection in tranquillity/death. Nothing could be further in matter and manner from the artistic concerns of the 1920s, 30s, 40s that are now seen to represent their times at their acutest. Living and working throughout these decades, his language at first responds in part, then turns gradually another way, a move that is eventually wholesale. Even at his most experimental[1] he never revolutionises or mod-cons. Rather the impress from the modern is a means whereby inherited romanticism, and his innately frugal take on it, can be concentrated yet expanded, yielding a final subtle strangeness audibly evolved from what gave it birth. Compare the gradual invisible growth in Fauré from tickling salon music to mature then late work in the same genres, wherein the musical speech has been transmuted into something utterly strange that yet retains a spectral familiarity.

Not revolutionary then; just radical. Unlike Fauré, whose distilled rarification is always charged with inner intensity, Schoeck's later music can wander dangerously towards *mere* etiolation, in which the pellucid bareness of a generally temperate emotional climate fails to retain the repressed passion, and results in insipidity. In such places one remembers the nega-

---

[1] See the detailed analytic studies of proto-quasi serial organisation in the songs, discussed by Derrick Puffett in his study *The Song Cycles of Othmar Schoeck* (Haupt, 1982).

tives—he was out of touch, with the worst of times, oppressed by a sense of failure, embittered by a sense of neglect. Thus the eventual unreality of the later song-collections, the demands upon performers and listeners alike to distend themselves so long over such thin terrain—though the last, *Das holde Bescheiden*, forty Mörike settings lasting some two hours, composed 1947–9, is also the most beautiful.

But undoubtedly the greater vitality of the interwar output is more appealing, compelling, surprising. First, that this piano-song-based composer could also write so well for instruments. Several cycles employ small ensembles in a fashion all his own. Circumventing the epoch's most influential precedents—Stravinsky's Russian songs from the Swiss period (raucous pungent primary colours that deliberately don't harmonise) or Schoenberg's *Pierrot Lunaire* (fantastical chiaroscuro of dense yet melting polyphony), Schoeck deploys a rich yet transparent harmonic texture growing out of the piano's native resources of figuration, resonance, blurry yet luminous pedal effects. The piano usually remains centre as well as source of the entire sonority, as in the beautiful *Elegie* of 1921–3; with just string quartet the *Notturno* of ten years later is atypically lean and linear.

And there is the masterpiece for voice and full orchestra after the example of Mahler, Strauss, Diepenbrock—*Lebendig begraben* (1926), a sort of *Song of the Earth* taking place six foot beneath. Keller's poems tell the unlucky protagonist's bizarre fate in his own words, from initial horror ('they've made a mistake!') and the panicking desperation of the attempts to attract attention and be released, via gradual acquiescence, to eventual ecstatic abandonment—freedom at last—into a pantheistic compound of ocean, sky, eros and Helvetia. Schoeck's personal melancholy and sense of artistic isolation obviously found expression here: the result is a high pressure in the turnover of marvellous ideas unsurpassed in his output. Such places as the representation of the sound of the church bell resonating through the six feet of earth and a sealed coffin, or the tender piety of the victim's blessing on his pathetic meal (the rose buried with him, eaten in darkness, never to know whether it was a red or a white), or the moment when the confining wood seems to transform into a lordly vessel cresting a warm swelling sea, are among the great well-kept secrets of twentieth-century music.

Still more surprising is that this introspective passivist was so ardently drawn towards the stage (five full-fledged operas, several other slighter or hybrid pieces). Of the three operas I've heard (but of course not seen) only one fulfils the going notion (if there is one) of what might be expected from Schoeck's music. *Massimilla Doni* (1934–5), after the short story by Balzac, for all its play of subtle half-lights might well work more vividly in the theatre than can be imagined from simply listening (it was apparently one of the season's highlights at its first production, Dresden 1937). It can be related in theme and to some extent in treatment and musical idiom with *Ariadne auf Naxos* before (interplay of illusion, convention, real feeling) and *Capriccio* still to come (the opera that infolds itself upon its own making, while debating the nature of the genre), though, naturally, falling short of Strauss's robustness and stage-acumen, as also of his lapses into coarseness or note-spinning. And if something so *recherché* as *Capriccio* can leave the study to enter the repertory, surely so perfectly-realised as piece as *Massimilla Doni* could follow. Lacking Strauss's drive to consummate his subject—the sonnet uniting poet and composer in their shared muse, the clear resolution of the words/music dichotomy that can then allow the equivocating play with 'triviality' and 'depth' in equipoise, prompter and moonlight, rococo mirror and supper served, to end with; as if the shifty shuffle of the Monsieur Taupe scene prevailed throughout, even in moments of undoubted erotic charge. But *Massimilla Doni*'s embodiment of its quasi-philosophical theme and its deeply-felt exploration of the relations between the sexes, more adult, more daring, more ambiguously human than the semi-abstractions of both Strauss works (or indeed the sweeping stereotypes of most standard rep.), inform every page of the score, with its iridescent play of surprise that eschews the perfunctory, the commonplace, the facile, delicately intimating disturbing insights by nuance rather than taking the bull by the horns as in some further comparable works, the eroticised yet literary expressionism of *Der ferne Klang* and *Die Gezeichneten*, not to mention *Die tote Stadt*. *Massimilla Doni* is like late Henry James in music.

Venus (1919–20) intertwines Merimée's famous tale *The Venus of Ille* with elements from an Eichendorff novella where the involvement of living flesh-and-blood with mysterious statuary is lightly handled and happy of outcome. The main thrust from the Merimée—the irresistible allure of the bronze Venus leading towards a terrible human death—is utterly convincing, beyond the obvious thrills, as a rendition of psychological compulsion. As the tale unfolds one senses Schoeck's relative uninvolvement with anything in it that doesn't focus direct upon this emotional core. Sinister undertones amidst the wedding celebrations, later an orchestral storm interlude, are a bit routine, lacking the lurid touch for such things that comes so naturally to Schreker and Korngold, let alone Strauss. But everything that draws Horace towards the uncanny statue is convincing. And the more this basically words-and-voice-centred composer yields to his subject, the more the music, too, takes fire in the orchestra. During the quarrel with his best friend who tries vainly to curb the mounting mania, Horace breaks off to listen to the *sound* of Venus'ss beauty: as they move towards physical fight a wordless chorus *à la* Janáček gives the potentially clichéd scene a deeper resonance; soon after, the *sound* of his wedding-ring, now immovably gripped by the statue's bent finger, is as vivid as anything.

And Horace's passionate *Liebestod* before the living statue crushes him in her embrace is crowned with surprise in a brief, superb orchestral coda to the whole work. Here its strength, the inner frenzy below the decorum and silky orchestral finish, achieves maximal effect: first, the unearthly strangeness of the Venus motif, a quintessence of Schoeck's complex yet undissonant harmonic idiom, opening out into a quiet mesh of searching query, then a smash of tam-tam and a tearing of high violins, closing again into velvet lower strings, to end with a few low elegiac spasms on muted trombones as the bronze arms close around the love-crazed youth. Webern himself could not have done more with less.

The other main element in *Venus* is the pastoral freshness of Simone's music (the Eros-driven hero's innocent fiancée, completely upstaged by the powerful forces resonating from her bronze rival). This is the gentle, pastel-flavoured Schoeck of his usual repute. It might seem bland. But careful attention to passages like her offstage hymn to nature and happiness at the start of Act I, or the chorus at its close looking forward to her imminent wedding, can disarm this charge. There is a simple test for measuring music in styles that appear half-received and on the verge of seeming 'bygone' or used-up. Ask yourself as you listen, 'what will happen next?' at every turn of phrase. As composer, 'what would *I* do?', to a critic, 'what would *you* do?', faced with *these* words (metre, stanza-shape, image), or indeed this *particular* word. Where are we so far in this phrase, sentence, paragraph (both in operatic context and in the purely musical situation)? What *might* this composer do now; what *does* he do? Such games sharpen involvement, intensify observation, enhance one's sense of individual style, in all music, most particularly music with an elusive, low profile personality like Schoeck's, on the fact of it not all that distinct from the general norms of a going idiom. They quicken one's admiration equally for the innate endowments of any composer, and the acquired skills that make the most of them.

So it is with the happy music in *Venus*. Another direct example, Simone's beautiful moment of reflection in Act II when she first confronts the spectacle of her lover's bemused fascination with the unknown woman at her wedding dance. Later places involve discriminating between different levels of realisation: for instance the hero's marvellous first address to the mysterious beauty, then a slightly shop-soiled *espressionismo* as he gives her his wedding-ring, then a slightly *ordinaire* masquerade, then its sudden transcendence as she unmasks. Thus in Act III his first invocation to her is a little dull and lacklustre till the new light cast on it by the superb *dunkel* chord at its end; the touch-and-go character of the rest of this act till the consistent heights of its closing stretches, from the moment he realises the mysterious woman was indeed the bronze Venus come to life, to the cataclysmic close already mentioned.

The biggest surprise of all from this master of the intimate nuance is *Penthesilea* (1924–5), a faithful encapsulation of Kleist's excoriating play. The opera's unleashed violence remains startling even in the epoch's wider context for such expression: on the more local scale it is extraordinary to compare the banked-down ellipses, the civilised compromises, the eventual acquiescent rapprochements with which the war of the sexes will be handled in *Massimilla Doni*, confronted by this all-out rendition of sexual attraction and repulsion carried inexorably to its bloody end.

The obvious prototype is *Elektra*, a one-act trajectory alternating lyric episodes with crazed disturbance, moving swiftly to a crisis, resolved in a hymnic apotheosis-cum-*Liebestod*. But Strauss doesn't loom in quite the way one might expect. *Penthesilea* shares the same general terrain in harmony, melodic contour, rhetoric, but its emotional tone is quite different. It wholly lacks the glowing sensuality, the frank relish of colour, the abandonment to glutiny that can court Khnopff and scupper the vessel even in Strauss's most exalted flights. Though it would be foolish not to acknowledge his superior compositional potency, there are times when even a cordial admirer has to say 'too much'.

Comparison is closest when Schoeck moves to the waltz-rhythms ubiquitous throughout *Elektra*. But one feels *chez* Strauss that this is a trait of idiom to which he is enslaved; Schoeck is its master not its victim. And in the crucial Achilles/Penthesilea duet that soon follows, the passion is inside the notes, not extrovert, explicit, 'on offer'. The music doesn't stint, while completely avoiding any hint of Kitsch or porn—and if this sounds like a prescription for dull tastefulness, just listen! One is continuously asking oneself how something so simple, even austere, can be so rich in sound and high-charged in feeling. The answer lies in the distinction of the long sinuous melodic line—a remote descendant of the Wolf of *Um Mitternacht*; and the marvellous harmonic control, wherein the inheritance of Austro-Germanic romanticism, with just a touch of Puccini, is filtered through Duparc and Fauré. Then listen to the ensuing battle music, the ten clarinets reeling and writhing in the orchestra-pit, the off-stage trumpets in hot chilling bitonal clash, the howling voices of Amazon and Greek soldiery locked in fight-to-the-death sex war mirroring the love/hate of their respective leaders at the heart of the plot. Absolutely sensational: absolutely without sensationalism.

Yet even in *Penthesilea* Schoeck still strikes strongest as master of the consonance as much as of dissonance. His basis is always diatonicism, but the range of his harmony is enormous and his control of it covers every gradation of the expressive gamut. From pure triadic writing, to triads with one extra note, and so up via bitonality, 'tritonality' and the denser 'dominants', to something approaching the full chromatic, *Penthesilea* as a whole embraces the variety and modulation of intensity missing in consistently atonal music save when amplified by expressive necessity *à la* Berg, and from neo-diatonic music save when enriched by alien chromatics. 'Radical diatonicism' and clean yet juicy smudginess, in dynamic equipoise.

And the sound of Schoeck's orchestra is quite different from the late-romantic norm exemplified by Strauss at its apogee of prowess and bravura. Again this is a matter of the piano-centred sonority seen already in the song-cycles and ensemble, now taken far further; piano resonance influences every aspect of the voicing, spacing, and even the harmony itself; pedal-effects and cloudy melt in-and-out of attack and decay lie behind every orchestral texture even when the two pianos are not playing, just as much as, in Schoeck's polar opposite, the *secco* piano lies at the heart of Stravinsky's very invention, as well as timbral sonority, from *Petrushka* and *Le sacre*, via *Noces*, throughout neo-classicism into final serialism. Having the two pianos in *Penthesilea* facilitates ostinatos and figuration, used with lightness and definition, achieving continuum without the need of fussy-to-write-and-play detail on woodwinds and strings (especially in a section of some seventeen pages all on a wide-spaced pattern of only D and E♭, then a further twelve edging up by semitones, like the celeste in Bartók's as yet unwritten *Music for strings, percussion and celeste*, thence the end of the *Peter Grimes* passacaglia, thence the 'gamelan' keyboard-writing in the Act I finale of *The Turn of the Screw*). While those ten clarinets, obviously learnt from the line-up in *Salome, Elektra*, later Mahler and earlier Schoenberg, make another effect altogether—seething many-snake-headed polyphony rather than warm organ-like homogeneity.

Parnassus has so many mansions. Much the same *kind* of case, different only in particulars, could be made for many other names as for Schoeck's alongside or athwart the main traffic-routes of twentieth-century music. If the canon continues to ossify and diminish, anything to left or right will languish undervalued and underloved, however special and—often—unique. Everyone will have his own candidates, and there need never be a full objective consensus. But we must keep everything good in play. At his best Schoeck is more than merely good: whether, most typically, in gentle contemplative beauty, temperate, welling deep and pellucid from music's unsullied springs; or sometimes, surprisingly, welling with equal authenticity from the fundamentals of erotic madness, frenzy, violence, despair, rage, his music can reach and sustain real greatness.

26

Two on Weill

The first of these is a straight review of the letters between the composer and his wife/ex-wife/wife-again. The second conflates two much older efforts, a review of an LP with both the symphonies for Tempo, *and another of a concert in the Corn Exchange at Cambridge where a student orchestra had mangled the Second, which must date from around 1973, but was not published. He must have received a copy though, for I'll never forget being 'phoned by David Drew one evening—'I've got Lotte Lenya with me—we're just along the road in the Blue Boar—she's delighted with your article, and would love to meet you'; and being simply too awed and alarmed to say yes.*

* * *

i The correspondence with Lenya

The correspondence between Kurt Weill and Lotte Lenya[1] is surely, with the Poulenc correspondence,[2] the most charming and humanly attractive contribution to music-and-letters to appear in recent years. It provides an informal double-portrait of two distinctive and distinguished artists, and at the same time affords much insight into the making and sustaining of a memorable working relationship.Nothing could be further from the cat-and-mouse horrors of the double-portrait revealed in the Berg–Schoenberg exchanges than its easy give-and-take, forbearing tolerance, and the solicitude that runs alongside the occasional unhectoring admonition. Though both parties are variously unfaithful (almost from the start in her case), the essential note right to the finish is of mutual devotion, expressed with tender capriciousness and teasing, in a half-private language of endearment and harmless salaciousness that includes snatches of music from him, from her, doodly little drawings; all this cheek-by-jowl with the hopes and fears of showbiz— dancing attendance upon moguls, endeavouring to woo and placate 'the right people', anxiously awaiting contracts. However far apart their lovelife or their professional activities took them (for which we can be grateful, as separation produces the frequency of letters), in their mental and aesthetic

---

[1] Edited and translated by Lys Symonette and Kim H. Kowalke (Hamish Hamilton, 1996).

[2] See p.281.

outlook they see as one. It comes as quite a shock to discover that they were for a time divorced before, realising that it made little essential difference, deciding to marry again!

In the beginning Weill's love for Lenya is love for her voice. A letter tentatively dated July 1926 makes this touchingly clear:

> ... When I feel this longing for you, I think most of all of the sound of your voice, which I love like a very force of nature, like an element. For me all of you is contained within this sound: everything else is only a part of you; and when I envelop myself in your voice, then you are with me in every way.

If Britten could have expressed himself so freely he would no doubt have addressed much the same turn of thought to Pears. And the association of personal happiness with artistic self-discovery is equally clear:

> I'm gradually forging ahead towards 'my real self': my music is becoming much more confident, much freer, lighter—and simpler. This is also linked to the fact that I have become noticeably more independent, more confident, happier, and less tense. Of course living with Lenya again accounts for much of this

(from a letter to his parents of 1925, cited in the editors' linking passage-work).

1927, enter Brecht. Their awkward association, rich in yield, low, even base, in human terms, is only glimpsed between the lines of this volume. The abiding impression is left neither by the German triumphs nor the Paris interlude which in *Die sieben Todsünden* produced the greatest of all their collaborations, but the eventual non-contact or positive evasion during their American years, when the monster declines from voracious bully into a supplicator pleading for projects old or new, needing to be warily fobbed off. But new American associations are covered more fully. Historians of Weill's American ventures will find much information here, together with a day-to-day sense of how it felt to be steering a zigzag course across the minefields of Hollywood and Broadway.

But the $64,000 question, concerning the calibre of Weill's American work when compared with the European that he so decisively relinquished, is not resolved even by implication. Are the later works inferior? and if so is the shift in standard knowing, even cynical (in the teeth of his heart-on-sleeve declarations) or genuinely unconscious?

There is no doubting the ardour with which the New World was embraced. On first arriving, they had both addressed themselves seriously to mastering English, a goal achieved from *ca* 1941, judging by these letters; with admirable success. Her usage remains more idosyncratic, as one would expect—witness the delicious *risqué* story p.301 (which in sober fact concerns learning French)—and is stuffed with such tasty accidents as 'conglamorate'. Whereas his is, equally likely, more correct, an instrument fully up to his demands upon it. But it is difficult to square the eager commitment to Democracy with the *de haut en bas* attitude shown elsewhere. 'I begin to think [he writes to her, 21 Aug. 1944] that we are almost the only ones of all these people [i.e. the emigrés] who have found American friends and who really live in this country. They are all still living in Europe.' And the next month he is urging her to register them both as voters in the forth-coming elections. Yet in earlier days he can report from Hollywood, to Lenya in New York, a party where he has met André Malraux: 'it was exactly as it had been with Chaplin: he talked only to me. That is how people like us triumph here: water finds its own level' (25 March 1937). The latent disdain here has grown more judicious in a letter of 8 May following.

> *Blumi*, we want to be very careful with money, because all I'm doing right now [namely machinating, waiting, hoping] will ultimately be justified only if I can save enough to enable me finally to do something really significant again, by my former standards. I don't want to make the mistake everyone here makes ... to spend all the money one makes and then be forced to take another *job* and little by little become a slave to Hollywood. I know this is your point of view as well.

(He then goes on to paint a picture of the domestic life together, whither all this scrupulousness tends, that recalls the Family's dream in the *Todsünden*.)

Weill's ambition to achieve a 'Broadway opera', inspired by seeing *Porgy and Bess* in 1942, is first realised in part by the Cellini-derived *Firebrand of Florence* (1945), which flopped; and then two years later by *Street Scene*, much more appropriate in its all-American setting and subject. Commercial by necessity, idealistic by choice, they represent the climax of an endeavour that never degenerated into cheapness. The overriding desire to continue working (one tends to forget that he was only thirty-five when he arrived in the States), and the impossibility of hawking around the European corpses (whose life had been so specific to their time and place) are wholly under-standable. But something seems askew in the Broadway shows, even as they are now being revived to great acclaim. Common to both is the cultivated craftsmanship that never disgraces the ex-pupil of Busoni whatever dubious gutter he taps. But the European music burns with an acrid genius so corro-sive to liver, lights and life as to make the later, even at its best, seem synthetic and anodyne. From all the output the voice of Lenya is inseparable.

His written voice has already been sampled—serious, scrupulous, thought-ful, realistic—though he can be a good retailer of bitchy gossip, and grants plentiful glimpses into the solitude of the workroom. Her voice as written can now be sampled to end with. She writes from New York on 10 Aug. 1944 to Weill in LA.:

> oh Darling, what a show that promises to be. Those lyriks really sound like François Villon. I haven't been so excited in a long time ... Boy-oh-Boy—Yes my imagination gives me a slight hint, what kind of music you write and still, it will be a surprise even though. Darling, don't fight too much for me, I don't want you to get too much distract. This all sounds so wonderful, that it will be exciting for me whether I am in or not, ... And, Darling, don't get nervous if Ira [Gershwin] hangs around sometimes. Don't forget that you are an exceptional case on vitality. You have to understand, that Ira is just so much slower ... I don't think Lee [Mrs Ira] has discovered yet, how much fun it can

be, to live in a house alone and read. There books printed for the purpose to be read. Doesn't she know about it? How dreary it must be to see the same people over and over again. To live constantly on the suburb of oneself, leads to utter emptiness ...

And later, as she draws to the end,

I got a very nice letter from Nannerl Huston, with a long paragraph about: how unimportent life is and how wonderful death is. I don't know why, but I get terribly hungry, when I read things like that. So I went to the ktchen and made myself coffee and felt, there is nothing more beautiflil than life.

He writes as he thinks: *she* as (I imagine) she talked—an unchecked stream, vivacious and impulsive, illuminated by fun, mother-wit, and a sure sense of what's what. No wonder he loved and needed her so. And it's not so difficult to sense that she loved and needed him in her very different way.

ii   The symphonies

What a curious work is Weill's First Symphony, with its fervent programme, its equally ambitious formal aims, and its mixture of good and bad (both important for the future)—such inspirations as the *mystisch* passage near the end lying in close proximity to crude climaxes and thematic cross-references that work, if surprising overlap between Mahler and Hindemith, at once acid, clotted, stringy and heartfelt. The wind chorale (p.51) shows the diversity of sources at its oddest, the second strain a rising sequence straight from a Victorian organ-loft, but ending in a surprise-diatonic cadence *à L'histoire du soldat*—the whole enclosed in a slithery Regeresque fugue.

Such unsure eclecticism recalls Weill's teacher Busoni. And the First Symphony brings other music to mind: a prominent cadence (pp.7 and 68) is remembered from *Tod und Verklärung*, the *anmutig* music (pp.44–5) gives a foretaste of *Lulu*; the chromatic 6/8 (pp.30–1) sounds like Delius, the opening (especially bars 10–11) like Ruggles. No doubt it is in such accidental momentary touchings—by very different composers working without connection—upon common usages, that a synthesis of the divergent twentieth-century styles will eventually be heard.

The Second Symphony is quite different: a work of masterly assurance, as certain of its aims and language as the First is not. Weill's Second Symphony seems to me to be the almost solitary representative of a tradition that has gone underground and perhaps disappeared entirely. If one accepts the idea of a norm of musical vernacular, one has to acknowledge that amid the glories of the heroic years of the modernist endeavour, this norm somehow was lost. A central style (which in its palmy days could embrace such extremes as Verdi and Wagner, or Sibelius and Mahler, and contain such 'oddities' as Musorgsky or Janáček) still survived, but blind, hollow, devoid of the inner coherence of its centrality—Soviet symphonies, Hollywood film scores, the weakest works of Richard Strauss. The true achievements of the modern movement belonged to a Babel of individualism, where each spoke in his own tongue and without even an esperanto to close the gap.Instead, strenuous anxiety to demonstrate legitimacy whether by cooking the books, forging a family tree or indulging a rare form of kleptomania. The resulting neo-classicism, though fascinating in itself and conducive to some very great manifestations, must not be confused with the normative language of true classicality. Its exponents are stylists, cuckoos to a man, essentially without land or lineage of their own.

If that putative ideal, a central twentieth-century style, were to exist, what would it be like? Imagine a Strauss without the banality and routine, a Debussy less washy and fugitive, a Bartók without either gypsies or golden sections, a Schoenberg without the unremitting omnichromatic gray, a Hindemith without the unremitting diatonic cardboard. Stravinsky alone among the obviously major figures could not be caught like this in a couple of adjectives. But in spite of (or because of) his multiplicity of sources he is still less of a traditional-holder, still more of a self-solver, even than these others. Berg is the other strongest claimant; and in the works including or subsequent to *Der Wein*, when he had got the twelve-note system into fertile alignment with the subtle workings of his ear, we find the closest approximation the twentieth century can show to a central language and usage. But alas there are only three such works (the most ambitious unfinished); and moreover their expressive ambience is decidedly, perhaps drastically, rooted in its own special culture.

The Second Symphony of Weill is the single instance I can point to as showing the absent centre of a putative twentieth-century musical language. A heavy responsibility   but it is a strong work. It is more concentrated and distinguished (as well as infinitely more attractive) than the 'Brandenburger' works of Hindemith which it sometimes resembles. Unlike Schoenberg's neo-classical works it inhabits the real aural sphere. It has a purposefulness often lacking in Stravinsky's neo-classical scores which it also resembles and often antedates. Its first movement rediscovers long before the *Symphony in C* the cumulative rhythmic and architectural power of an unchanging time-signature; its Adagio reconquers the resources of the eight-bar phrase. In all three movements its use of elements from popular song and dance music exposes the would-be sophisticated *Six* as feckless, even inept, and in the satirical 'wrong-note' march in the finale Weill unerringly achieves what in Prokofiev is hit-or-miss, and in Shostakovich miss-and-miss, with twenty times the ammunition. It does not attempt the refined harmonic subtlety and melodic thrill of the songs, but nevertheless displays an irresistible harmonic and melodic potency, is formally masterly, and scored (apart from a few miscalculations) with brilliant and direct simplicity. No one else could have done it; it is as unique in its time as in Weill's *œuvre*. For comparison one has to return to the true classical style. This symphony practices what Busoni could only preach—Mozartean poise.

Obviously many works by the twentieth-century masters are greater; but a masterpiece by even Stravinsky or Berg bears no *especial* relation to the problem of a central language. Was Weill's symphony only a lucky fluke, or might he have gone on from here to create a true *lingua franca*? We knew already from the songs, and the *Sieben Todsünden* above all, that he was a master; but there is no further context for this unexpected projection into the exemplary. Let us hope that the mainstream of a coherent musical communality, whose continuing possibilities are shown so marvellously by this work, still somewhere flows underground, to re-emerge in due time to make glorious summer of our continued discontent.

Henze's law

The recovery of German composition from the ruins of the Second World War makes a tangled tale. The advanced music proscribed by the Nazis, sweeping into the cultural vacuum, understandably produced, rather than equilibrium, an extreme emphasis upon the merely novel that rapidly froze into an institutionalised avant-garde of unparalleled rarefication. Backed by the authority of Adorno, the instinctive antipathy of the two principal lines of contemporary music in its first half-century—Stravinsky and Schoenberg—widened into an impassable abyss.

Hans Werner Henze, aged twenty in 1946, appeared from the start the only composer from this bad background able to resolve the problem. His intrinsic endowment—fertility, fluency, flair for story and words, subject-matter in general and the stage in particular—seemed infinite in its promise. His unbigoted openness, as a German avant-gardist, to the neo-classic Stravinsky, gave him access to his own much wider field of reference—Tchaikovsky ballet and Italian opera, the late-romantic glories of his own tradition, and its more recent history in Weill and Hindemith as well as the Schoenberg school, together with jazz and the voices of popular music, indigenous or commercial, from many lands. For advocates of the middle road he became the man to get music back on to the rails: after revolution, consolidation; after fragmentation, integration; after alienation, communication. Such pieces of the mid-to-late 1950s as the Fourth Symphony, the five Neapolitan Songs, *Nachtstücke und Arien* seemed like an oasis. A personal favourite of mine, from somewhat later, was the *Cantata della fiabba estrema* with its soaring lyric soprano solo, supported by the small chorus's off-Bach chorale and the dulcet hues of the little guitar-centred ensemble, rendering the title's 'extreme fable' in accents hedonistic, erotic and refined. In the pieces of this time the rush of colour to the head, below the belt, and all the other places that other music of the day didn't reach, or even aim for, was equally inebriating.

Or so it seemed at the time; but these pieces have not worn well. One's need for deliciousness and sensuality made for wishful hearing. Intimations of reality came with the first impact in this country of the oratoria *Novae de Infinito Laudes* (1962). The score had looked as copious in fantasy as the texts, chosen, with Henze's customary sense for the striking, from the writings of Giordano Bruno. Why did it *sound* so anonymous? Maybe the performance, maybe one's ears. One gave it many tries; the unmemorability persisted. Doubts were confirmed even by the three operas of those years that can still be seen as his high-water mark, *Elegy for Young Lovers* (1959–61), *The Young Lord* (1964) and the vast Euripides/Auden *Bassarids* (1965).

Then came the radical chic of the late sixties. Solidarity with the Cuban revolution produced *inter alia* the Sixth Symphony; back in the Fatherland the bourgeoisie were *épatée* most notoriously by *The Raft of the Medusa*, a vast semi-staged oratorio out of Géricault via Che Guevara. The sheerly musical quality of his politically committed phase dropped sharply as the agitprop intensified. Perhaps the low point was reached in an operatic collaboration with Edward Bond, *We Come to the River*: the culinary lavishness of the medium and the poverty of the message remain vivid in the mind long after its Covent Garden première; the music, however, didn't survive the night. In those fifteen years Henze has continued to be enormously prolific in a wider range of media than any other living composer. Courted by the world's top orchestras and opera-houses, guest at prestigious festivals and host of his own, he remains in spite of the radicalism and the pieties about the solitude of the creative artist an establishment figure *par excellence*.

The problems concealed by his general acceptability have been posed anew by the BBC's recently concluded Henze festival at the Barbican [June 1991]. The fact is that never in all his torrential output has Henze achieved a voice of his own. The old joke of 'Henze's Law'—when in doubt, write a cadenza—can be extended to cover everything that matters in musical composition. When in doubt, make for the jungle of complication and drench everything with colour. The fundamental inadequacy of the basic elements— a coherent ordering of harmony, counterpoint, motif/theme/melody, architecture—out of which music in any idiom whatever must inevitably be made is thus disguised for a bit. Time and again one's ear is first beguiled, then bombarded, battered, bamboozled and at last bored. The final reaction is despair—where is the piece behind all this masterly *semblance*?

Sampling the broadcast last summer of his newest opera, after Mishima's *Sailor Who Fell from Grace with the Sea* (another canny choice), one found the same old welter of indiscriminate notes in an orgy of clapped-out expressionist gesturing. The Seventh Symphony of 1984—which I have heard all through, many times—is another version of the same. This large work aims high and sounds, first go, like a million dollars. But it is toy money.

Henze's is the saddest story in post-war music. He is a martyr equally to the need since the deaths of Strauss and Schoenberg in the years on each side of 1950 to find a great German master, and the cultured materialism that has prevailed in that country ever since. The fairies at his cradle gave him every gift, but impishly withheld the indispensable jewel of artistic personality. Sad also are the culture-vultures, who, literary sensibilities a-twitching and cloth ears a-flap, hear only what they're told and not what is actually there.

28

Stockhausen's *Inori*

The second London performance of Stockhausen's *Inori* (BBC Symphony Orchestra under the composer, Royal Festival Hall, 3 March 1982) provided welcome variety from the aesthetic paralysis of playing the records, together with a chance to assess the work's visual aspect. It was a memorable occasion—a feather in the BBC's cap the more jaunty for coinciding with the crushing banality that opened the Barbican Centre. These layman's remarks that follow, though largely sceptical, are not intended to deny the substantial evidence of things heard and seen.

But even to the faithful the first twenty minutes or so must be a trial. Such protracted *Stimmung* exasperates rather than relaxes, and having now seen the Master's solemn stage presence I have no doubt that he could produce the right mood in his audience simply by raising his hands. Yet length is not the worry really; once the orchestra has 'tuned' the audience there is never a dull moment in spite of the economy of events. Stockhausen can inhabit his huge spaces with a real feeling for their size; which is by no means as simple as it sounds, for it takes intrinsic grandeur to make a sizeable emptiness that does not bore. That Stockhausen has the necessary grandeur is obvious; it is the least disputable ot his talents.

While the whole is convincingly huge, the details by which it slowly forms itself are undistinguished. The ear for musical specificities is coarse—in harmony, in rhythm, most disappointingly in the much-vaunted play of timbre and dynamic; for all the elaborate apparatus of tonal organisation the impression prevails that this composer only deals in general effects. The simple-mindedness within the complication (revealed above all in the tedious pings and clunks of the extra percussion) would not matter were it stronger and more purposeful ('if the fool would persist in his folly …'). What *does* matter in this selfconsciously 'renovated' context is the lumbering rhetoric, the conventional approach to climax and repose and thence to overall shape; and the turgid textures. The close proximity of Messiaen (particularly of *La Transfiguration*) serves to show by contrast that master's superb ear for density; while the remoter presence of Scriabin, Debussy, even Ravel, leave one longing for an iota of their radiant lucidity. Our frustration is specific because the intention to ravish or knock for six is patent. Stockhausen is no subtle tickler of his audience's capacity for musical thought; rather, he's an extremely literal and thorough speller-out. As with his processes so with his astonishments—we see it coming a mile off. No harm in the obvious; but it must be terrific!—especially in so religiously 'high' a context. Again and again the arrival is blurred and fudged whose prestigious annunciation proves is not *meant* to be thus.

Thus even the main climax of whirring flutters and grinding upheavals suffers badly from the comparisons it unwisely raises. Not that it is not thrilling. With these huge forces there are bound to be thrills of volume, sonority, activity; but there is never the thrill of 'the right notes'. Nevertheless this stretch genuinely takes off—not a projectile (clean and lethal) so much as a kind of Heath Robinson flying bungalow, bristling with quaint quasi-scientific appendages, celestial tea-strainers and home-made aerials to pick up signals from Astral Beings. All-of-a-piece with Stockhausen's beliefs (touched on in his pre-concert talk with distinct if humourless charm and a surprising lack of grandiloquence): good old nature-worship with an overlay of factitious rigour—pantheism with technological knobs on. *Inori* has found a genuinely artistic musical parallel for a mental realm that perhaps raises too facile a smile (though it is not as amusing as Heath Robinson). But we cannot laugh it away; this music catches it and gives it substance.

The visual aspect of the work is on a far lower level. The interest of the initial coordination of mime and music and their subsequent 'counterpoint' is quickly exhausted. Very soon the two dancers distract, then annoy. The climactic triple jack-in-the-box and the single emission of the sacred syllable are unspeakably ludicrous; and in general the mime (which moreover is not particularly attractive in itself) takes away more from the musical unfolding than it adds. Stockhausen continues here as in everything the German tradition of *inward* music that resists any matching physical motion beyond the vaguely expressive. His new body-language synthesised from the world's great religions brings nothing to mind so much as every eleven-year-old schoolboy's subversive invention of private liturgies with their accompanying rituals.

The 'religion' of *Inori* is the same thing but more grown-up and therefore more faked (proof if needed lies a few yards downstream where the National Theatre's *Oresteia* regularly elevates its audience into a congregation). This is the more regrettable in that *Inori* has elements of sublimity quite detachable from the bathos of its *ersatz* mysticism. To receive it one has to switch off all the more sensitised apparatus for the apprehension of fine points and specific ideas embodied in the music's workings, and go for musical ideas or 'philosophies' in a generalised sense.

Stockhausen is not the first composer who asks this sacrifice. Wagner, however, with all his amateur philosophy and impure aesthetic ends, is of course a superb musician with wonderful inspirations that realise the non-musical thought, and exactly the right technique for actualising his huge spaces with the utmost intensity and efficiency. Nothing about Stockhausen persuades that he cannot be judged by the same criteria; and by standards entirely appropriate to him he will not quite stand. The specific gravity of his inventions is too low even in music that legitimately requires not to be fraught with thought, alert with wit, and overflowing with heartwarming tunes. This low pressure of musical events, when carried out with the imprecision of ear already described, produces something which could not be focused aright by any injection of whatever kind of further content (though, equally, mere dislike of the kind he favours could never suffice as a reason for the music's inadequacy). The fundamental fact is that his musicianship (to which after all the whole compositional activity must ultimately be deferred) is so imperfect as seriously to mar the very definition of his extraordinary energy and fertility, the technical and conceptual boldness for which he is rightly revered as a modern wonder.

His work *needs* what to Wagner's was a delightful bonus—a master who will musicalise the grand crude discoveries and by connecting them to the mainstream indicate their further artistic possibilities. In the absence of a Humperdinck we must continue to take Stockhausen unmusical, raw and inordinate; for though he is not so good as Wagner he is far too good to lose.

Part II

The Others

29

Purcell's diligent muse

This month [October 1992] an important enterprise by Hyperion, to record on eight CDs the first-ever collection of Purcell's *Odes* and *Welcome Songs*, is completed, and crowned by a further record of contemporary tributes after the great composer's premature death. Performances under Robert King are first-class examples of 'second generation' authenticity, where phrasing and sostenuto have been readmitted alongside a less abrasive version of the familiar punchiness. The result is crisp and lively (sometimes too lively), with a bright clarity underlined by the use of chamber forces, the choral sections—except for a few works that need a larger body of voices—being taken by the outstandingly good soloists. These discs are a joy to listen to, and place Purcell yet more surely, with Marc-Antoine Charpentier, as the greatest composer between the dissolution of polyphony after *c.*1600 and its reflorescence in Bach.

There is a comparison with Bach as a matter of mere functionality. These twenty-four Odes are all occasional, to be thrown away (unless frugally recycled) once the date has passed. There was no need for them, any more than for the Bach church cantatas, to be inspired: competence and punctuality sufficed. Instead, because both composers so overflow with musical ideas, they write occasional pieces which we would as little think of throwing away as a Holbein drawing. In a sense, Purcell's is the more remarkable victory for quality. Bach's texts often scrape the depths of lugubrious pietism, but elsewhere he sets fine specimens of German hymnody as well as passages from Luther's Bible. And of course he fervently believes every word. Purcell's Odes not only have in almost every instance texts of McGonagalesque badness but dispiriting subjects too. Six celebrate Queen Mary's birthday (though she seems to have been unfeignedly beloved); five hail Charles II and three James II; and there are one-offs for other royal occasions and a few miscellaneous celebrations. The Mary works say 'Happy birthday' with many a lolloping trope, the Charles/James works say 'Welcome home, great sir'. Grovelling obsequiousness is the mode, with the royal personages regularly hailed as 'Caesar and Augusta' and sometimes compared to the Olympian deities. Topical allusion is sometimes made. The principal intonation is imperative—Come! Rejoice! Hail! Sing! Now cease! The void is total. One imagines Purcell's muse tucking up her sleeves with a groan at yet another loyal injunction, before getting down to duty. No time to wait for celestial fire!

Perhaps the nadir is struck in the verses for the Ode on the centenary of Trinity College Dublin (1694). The subject can have been of no interest whatever to the composer. The verses would tax even the dogged anti-sense of Milhaud setting his list of agricultural implements, let alone a composer concerned with tuneful comprehensibility.

Thy Royal Patron sung: Repair
To Illustrious Ormond's Tomb;
As, Living, He made Thee His Care,
Give him, next thy Caesar's, Room.

All nine vocal numbers are equally uninviting. Yet Purcell's fluency not only copes with such broken-backed presentation of such an unstimulating subject, but makes it the vehicle for yet another display of liberal invention growing directly out of music's central essence: now dainty and elegant, now suave and lilting, now melancholy, heroical, dramatical, or hearty and ceremonial, as needed. Whatever the affect, the musical substance is unfailingly strong, light, perfect in facture, with a technical wizardry (especially in the manipulation of ground-basses, of which he must be the world grandmaster) shot through with shafts of strange, piercing expressiveness aligned more closely with the metaphysical poets than the twaddlesome trumpery which commanded it into being.

But celestial fire always waited for him. It is a measure of his disinterested genius that he, could respond to these fustian occasions with the same enthusiasm he devoted to a subject that undoubtedly did stir his passions, music itself and its Cecilia, whose day was celebrated each year by the Musicians' Company with a specially composed Ode. St Cecilia touches off the sublime every time. Purcell's five odes to music range from a ten-minute miniature, Laudate Ceciliam (uniquely not in English), to the most familiar of these (largely unknown) pieces, Hail! bright Cecilia of 1692, at over fifty minutes the grandest in scale and in orchestra and in generosity of inspiration. The text, hymning music as Nature's Voice, the Soul of the World, tuning the jarring seeds of matter into harmonious proportion, and featuring each instrument in turn as a sort of young person's guide, cannot hold a candle to Dryden's wonderful Ode, from which it obviously derives (would that Purcell had set that!). But it serves well enough; and even the crashing bathos of the last line praising the 'Patroness of Us [i.e. the Society] and Harmony' is transcended in the general splendour that closes a work remarkable among much else for its range of techniques and depth of expression, and the boldness of its joins.

Remarkable but not exceptional. The standard here is so high that I can detect a whiff of routine only in one (Celebrate this Festival—we can hear his muse's groan); and even this has unique beauties and audacities equal to anything in the others.

It is fanciful to hope for this music to be re-attached to living causes— new adaptations of the texts to cover The Queen's Return from Balmoral; or to preface *Prince Charles's Address to the British Architect*. It is probably doomed to remain dragged down for ever by its quaint words for defunct occasions, and heard most widely (apart from the two favourites) on these splendid discs. It is good to know that the same artists are now embarked upon the first complete collection of Purcell's church music, a treasury that will embrace the darker, more introspective sides of his inexhaustible gift.

30

Elaborating Elgar's Third

One of the most stirring operations in the English music of recent years is the rescue of Elgar's Third Symphony. It has been handsomely handled: the BBC, who originally commissioned the work in 1932, laid on a studio try-out last autumn which will not easily be forgotten by those lucky enough to attend. And coinciding with this month's public première[1] comes a score (Boosey and Hawkes) and a recording with the BBC Symphony Orchestra sixty-five years on, directed so idiomatically by Andrew Davis as to sound classic already. The ripples will die down leaving a substantial addition to the orchestral repertory and permanent gratitude to Anthony Payne, whose carefully formulated 'elaboration' of the sketches is, in fact, a practical act of homage of the most fascinating kind.

His brief—to realise Elgar's fragments with the family's approval before their copyright ends in 2005, opening the way to possibly less loving and certainly less skilful hands—might appear straightforward. What he has actually achieved is far more remarkable: a living simulacrum of a large-scale late-Romantic / early-Modern symphony by one of its greatest masters, using that master's own material (for the most part already existent, albeit patchy), and intuiting his forms and processes (which for the most part did not exist) by analogy or likelihood.

Which is quite different from the nevertheless comparable case of symphonic retrieval from the same stylistic epoch, Mahler's Tenth. Mahler left a complete scheme of compelling architectural and rhetorical power, with some sections fully-worked and scored, some bare and rudimentary, and plenty betwixt and between: a draft to be worked up with his usual intensity of detail.[2] Elgar left, however, no overall shape beyond the indication of the four movements, and a mass of material much of whose place and function is unspecified.

Yet, this is how he had always worked. A list of 'ingredients' for both completed symphonies can still be disconcerting; such discrepant sources—thumbnail sketches of friends or pets, landscapes and moodscapes, city lights and shadows, grief personal and ceremonial, a facetious entry in a guest book—in some instances dating right back across several decades. If by

---

[1] 15 February 1998, Royal Festival Hall (same forces on the CD).

[2] See p.ooo.

chance the end products hadn't come about, we would doubt that they *could* have. Elgar's processes are the antithesis of organic growth from germinal cells. His diverse materials fuse and synthesise at final rather than primal stage. In so doing they gather many passing inspirations of detailed working, and also the wealth of internal relationships that such methods would seem to have ruled out: and, incidentally yet inevitably, the most basic element of all, symphonic form.

So it would possibly have been with the Third. Material lay to hand, some comparatively recent (incidental music of 1923 for Laurence Binyon's *Arthur*), some pre-war; and Payne is surely right to sense a renaissance of creative vigour in the attempts to work them together that were cut off by Elgar's final illness. (Hats off for perceiving this so many years back, when the going consensus even among fervent Elgarians, including myself, was negative.) All the same, the symphony's most vital material is its oldest. This is true in a metaphorical sense, because through its every page Payne's (and our) love of the great canonical works constantly shines. And true specifically in that its best music—the very opening, realised in every detail by Elgar himself, including the orchestration—hails from his richest period (1899—1913), being intended originally for *The Judgement*, third in the oratorio-triptych abandoned after *The Kingdom*.

Probably because it is imbued throughout with the granitic memorability of this opening stretch, the first movement strikes me as the most successful as a whole. The purposeful trajectory carries over some wobbly moments; and many places, notably the return of the second subject, and the entire coda, are wholly convincing, indeed masterly.

Payne excels at codas. By far his hardest task, he explains on the disc setting out the sketches and what he has done with them, was to discover, in the absence of indication, how the complete work should end. His finale convincingly realises from the start a full Elgarian texture and momentum, made from the work's sparsest sources. Material from the *Arthur* music touches off a vein of chivalry familiar since *Froissart* back in 1890 and reaching its noblest incarnation to depict Prince Hal in *Falstaff* (1913). Mistress Quickly is also present from that wonderful work; later the fat knight himself unmistakably appears, also a reminder of the percussion motif that characterises his scarecrow army. All this is skilfully woven together without solving the problem of the ending. Payne's answer is to crown the weightiness of the preceding movements by growing darker and more serious. An inspired transition leads to a coda specifically recreating the effect of *The Waggon Passes*, the one strong number in the otherwise tedious Nursery Suite that Elgar had put together in 1931 for the Princesses Elizabeth and Margaret Rose. Payne's adaptation of the obsessive rhythm to the finale's authentic material is a stroke of genius, admirable equally in imaginative boldness and technical address. The concluding gong-stroke, however, seems whimsical, a gesture borrowed from the alien world of Mahler and Viennese expressionism.

The two inner movements raise more difficulties than the two outer, though in very different ways. The second is closest to *echt*-Elgar, extant music from *Arthur* requiring minimal handling: one of Elgar's 'dream children', wistful and fragile, growing momentarily forceful before nearly revealing its elusive heart, then fading out at inconsequential length. The slightly fusty quality is focused by comparison with its siblings in the two *Wand of Youth* suites, vivid material from boyhood springs, touched with the loving mastery of prime. After this, the Third Symphony *Intermezzo* seems droopy, and not really belonging to the total scheme despite some cross-referencing.

Reservations about the *Adagio* that follows are harder to voice. At the BBCSO's try-out last autumn this movement made the deepest impression, and it sounds magnificent still, 'at a distance'. Closer proximity reveals the flaws—the internal weakness of the two principal melodies, a solemn funeral march and a consolatory pastoral vision; their short-circuitings, peterings out, general lack of focus, stand in sharp contradistinction to the confident melodic paragraphing in the slow movements of both completed symphonies. The dithery character is moving in itself, and one would willingly rise to the big elegiac emotion clearly intended, were it fully present. Wholly convincing, though, is the tiny link been the two melodies by the master, which is, in fact, entirely Payne's doing.

Which suggests a wry question that might resonate beyond the admiration and gratitude occasioned by this particular event. Could 'elaboration' like Payne's be achieved in the absence of an actual cause, such as a master's unfinished opus from an epoch of well-loved and understood musical language? Elgar's Fourth and Rachmaninov's, Mahler's Eleventh, a Ninth from Sibelius (since his Eighth, known to have been completed before being disseminated in marginalia then destroyed, is already a candidate for direct rescue) just for a start, before reaching back to Tchaikovsky, Schumann, Mozart, Monteverdi, Josquin.... The uncertain idioms of 'difficult' modern music, together with its palpable failure to gain popular acceptance, have much to learn from the enormous sigh of welcome raised by such essentially nostalgic work of reclamation and replication. It might enable many current composers to come clean and dare to write the music that they, too, have secretly preferred all along. It might liberate embargoed knowledge and unstrangulate expressive gold.

31

Fairest Isle

As Fairest Isle, Radio Three's handsome 'celebration of British music and culture', moves into its last lap to coincide with the actual tercentenary this month [November 1996] of Purcell's death, I have been much occupied with Elgar. He will not enjoy a comparable bonanza until his next centenary in 2034; but in fact he is always with us. His stock has never stood higher and he is more admired and performed now than at any time since his brief, brilliant Edwardian heyday.

Arguably the two greatest musicians England has produced, Purcell and Elgar have little or nothing in common as artistic types. They share a complete grasp of their art, but such a phrase doesn't mean much when material, style and conditions are so different. Purcell is often actually and always incipiently dramatic, a master of rhetoric, projecting words and passions with cunning naturalness or stylised into shapely melody. An enormous range of weird and plangent baroque effects combines oddly yet brilliantly with a supreme gift for manipulating pattern. What he can get out of the simplest groundbass beggars description. He is spare, tight, light, fierce and driven even when he melts the heart. Elgar, too, can be stripped for action, but the more immediate image his music conjures is gorgeous resplendency of sonority even to the point of satiation. And his basic mode is contemplation: behind richness (sometimes very close behind) melancholy prevails; a fugitive vision of love and tenderness, nobility and chivalry, companionship, swathed in nostalgia sometimes golden, often aching with pain and loss.

But this unwieldy complement is not their most interesting point of contact. They have two circumstances in common. The first is relatively trivial: both are unsurpassed in unashamedly providing exactly what's wanted for royal and national occasions. The second is crucial: the cultural climate in which they worked did its best to thwart the most natural expression of their genius. With Purcell it has long been obvious that the frustration is theatrical. The going convention of masque-like 'semi-opera', with its marginalisation of music from the main story to the decorative fringes, simply didn't give full scope to a natural musico-dramatic gift potentially the equal of Britten's. The result is wonderful wrecks, albeit full of gold, like the two *Queens* (*Fairy* and *Indian*) or *King Arthur*; and in *Dido and Aeneas* the one miniature gem that really holds the stage just as it stands. Nowadays, neither producers nor audiences are so hung up on genre, and the semi-opera seems poised for a surprising comeback.

But what can be done for Elgar's choral works? Our Fairest Isle's addiction to the oratorio in the nineteenth century amounted, musically speaking, to a national vice. The predominant provincial institutions of the time—festivals at Leeds, Birmingham, Norwich and other centres, especially northern and midland—were all choral-based. Especially, of course, the Three Choirs Festival with its recurring return to Elgar's native Worcester and adopted Hereford.

The long lists of cantatas, ballads and whatnot at the end of Novello scores (they were principal purveyors) tell a tale of flourishing supply and demand. It is perfectly understandable that in his youth Elgar willingly swelled the pile. This was the ambience in which he learned his mastery—by listening, playing violin in the orchestras, conducting and ultimately composing. Works sacred, profane, patriotic—be it *Lux Christi, King Olaf* or *The Banner of St George*—came copiously from his pen.

His confidence and competence in the genre puts him in a different league from all rivals (the superiority was quickly recognised); and the last, longest and most ambitious of the early pieces, *Caractacus* (a tale of honour and defeat set amongst woad-daubed Druids), positively bursts with the proximity of his very next opus, the *Enigma Variations*. Yet, in spite of their superiority, they remain fustian not just in plot and versification, which needn't matter, but in their very conception. These dead ducks are stilted beyond repair in spite of many stretches of beauty and high imaginative involvement.

The incomprehensible part, though, is Elgar's continuing commitment to the dodo in his prime. *The Dream of Gerontius* must be excepted: like all his greatest music, it is frankly personal, indeed confessional, a mode which almost always brings out the best in him. In spite of broad acres where the hand of oratorio lies heavy, *Gerontius* burns with once-in-a-lifetime fervour. Yet even though his aspirations immediately after it turned towards the symphony, Elgar succumbed utterly to the pious national vice—and on the most massive scale: no longer dead ducks and dodos, so much as sacred cows of enormous amplitude.

Perhaps it is unduly unsympathetic to deplore the waste of time, skill, spirit expended upon the Trilogy (à la Wagner, bound together in a tissue of leitmotivs and intended for cumulative performance) of *Apostles, Kingdom* and *Judgement*. The sincerity is patent, and there are a few flights of superb inspiration. But when one thinks of the symphonies we might have had from this composer who, uniquely in our music, was equally a master of the orchestra, of large-scale construction, and of an utterance at once infused with tender privacy yet simultaneously able to speak in a clear public voice, regret turns to exasperation. We have two symphonic masterpieces, but there might have been nine! It seems like a personal cop-out, a wilful artistic defeat, the victory going to Establishment, Philistia, the *Zeitgeist,* and a God in whom, eventually, he didn't believe.

Whatever the truth, there is poetic justice in the way that when the trilogy toppled of its own over-aspiration, the Third Symphony, upon which Elgar worked keenly, after being long dormant, right at the end of his life, made its powerful opening from music originally intended for *The Judgement*.

32

Walton's centenary

One by one the composers who had been the living icons of one's teens are reaching their centenaries. This month [March 2002] one hundred years ago William Walton was born in Oldham. To whirl the output by in rapid free-association is to realise that he could hardly wait to exorcise the place. The gay nonsense and nostalgia of *Façade* (1922); the metallic cinema-deco of *Belshazzar's Feast* (1930–1); the elegiac introspection of the viola concerto (1929) and the Mediterranean hedonism, amorous or sparkling, of that for violin (1939); the well-upholstered blague of the 1937 coronation march *Crown Imperial*, and the use of such language absolutely straight to crown a Symphony (1931–5) which begins in terrific nervy tension, followed by whiplash scherzo crackling with malice, then slow movement of the most ardent romanticism; the wartime film scores which define our patriotic idiom as surely as Copland's contemporary work does for the United States.

Evidently this artist, unlike his younger rival Benjamin Britten, is concerned, rather than exploring and expressing his native roots, to disentangle himself completely. Yet the very directness of this music, its lack of beating-about-the-bush, shows it not to be a home counties product. This go-for-the-jugular character, peaking in the barbaric razzmatazz of an oratorio where the Babylonians have all the best tunes, is born of a brass band and amateur choral society culture, knows its dynamics to a T, exploits them with bravado and relish whatever the changing contexts.

All the pieces mentioned—by far his most popular—are early. Perhaps his centenary will decide at last the merits of Walton's post-war music, still controversial. Reading his correspondence (reviewed here last month by Fiona Maddocks) confirms the impression made by the suppressed effortfulness of the later work even when its intention is lighthearted, that composition, for him always the reverse of fluent, joyous, natural, eventually became almost impossibly difficult.

But this doesn't fully explain the dispiriting later trajectory, wherein everything seems like a recycling of used-up material in the absence of anything to say. The range was always narrow, sharply focused in idiom, gesture, effect. Outside some brave moments in the two major orchestral works from the post-war years, the Second Symphony (1960) and the Hindemith Variations completed three years after, his was not a style that evolved. Again unlike Britten, his contact with radical modernism was unambiguous and negative. The Schoenbergian element in *The Turn of the Screw* fertilises the native mix, enabling its composer to move into suggestive new territory; but the clunky twelve-note passacaglia on which the finale of Walton's Second Symphony is built sounds wilfully thrust upon his native style rather than organically interpenetrating to the benefit of both. And other pieces from this time suggest dilution and dispersal: the 1953 coronation march a shadow of its predecessor, the Cello Concerto (1956) a second brew from those for viola and violin, the *Gloria* and *Te Deum* pallid offprints from *Belshazzar*, *The Bear* (1967) a laboured, unamusing successor to the evergreen parodies of *Façade*, the later overtures and other divertimenti at once vulgar yet whimsical after the rude robust elegance of *Portsmouth Point* in 1925.

The crunch has to be his single full-scale opera *Troilus and Cressida*, composed 1948–54 in an all-out attempt to succeed on the most ambitious level. The correspondence documents in detail the concern with which Walton modelled timing and pacing upon opera's sure-fire winners, mainly Verdi and Puccini. But the principal model for the music sounds like Hollywood at its most synthetic and meretricious. The tight control whereby irony and subversion learnt from his beloved Ravel, Stravinsky and Prokofiev balances and curbs the romanticism learnt from Rachmaninov, Elgar and Strauss, has slackened: below yawns a sleazy abyss of pure Korngold down which Walton disappears with sickening speed. The only detectable irony here is quite different—that the 'pornographic interlude' for the lovers' long-delayed coming together, so lubriciously dangled in the letters as the warm-hearted heterosexual riposte to the all conquering Britten, let alone the contemptible 'arse-over-Tippett' (both obsessively demonised in these later years), is a flagrant but powerless rip-off of the storm interlude in the despised *Peter Grimes*!

Fortunately, there's no need to dwell on the rancorous attitudes and dubious fruits, shrivelled or squashy, of Walton's later decades, when his handful of pre-war masterpieces remains the most-played and best-beloved addition to the mainstream concert-hall repertoire of all English composers since Elgar.

33

Benjamin Britten:
the sentimental sublime

Far the earliest effort in the present collection, this piece, tidied up, cut down (and somewhat expurgated) from a third-year Cambridge undergraduate essay (1963–4) has been included for two reasons: as a 'historical document', harbinger, in its interconnection of the composer's sexuality with his choice and treatment of his subject matter, of what has subsequently become a major academic industry (the late Philip Brett was still around at the time and certainly picked up the vibes when the piece was printed in the Cambridge Review *to coincide with Britten's visit to conduct the* War Requiem *with university forces; perhaps he even contributed to the subsequent correspondence, predictably if fatuously headed 'Battle of Britten'). Secondly, an expiation: so transparently Oedipal an attack requires atonement rather than concealment. I'd immorately loved Britten's music earlier, and though never able to swallow the* War Requiem *('kleenex at the ready', as the American but not the English edition of one of the Craft/Stravinsky conversation-books put it), gradually returned to a moderated yet ardent admiration over the years, as I hope the later writing gathered here will clearly show. I'm happy that a single exchange of letters in the last summer of his life (1976) sorted the business out with mutual forbearance—'I understand only too well [he wrote] how these things come about'—and the next piece, written so soon afterwards (in response to* Tempo's *request for memorial paragraphs after his death) attempts to lay the ambiguity fair and square.*

* * *

Benjamin Britten is a composer at the height of his powers, and enjoys a popularity and success unique among modern composers. His triumph with the general musical public is undoubted; and Mr Donald Mitchell may be said to voice the view of the educated musician when he writes of 'the prospect of Britten, in the second half of this century, filling the role of a—perhaps the—major European composer'.

What then does Britten offer? First of all, quantity—he is prolific and writes quickly and easily. Secondly his music is easily understandable by audiences to whom most 'modern music' is some kind of ugly joke; it is also easy and enjoyable to play and sing. Above all, his music is strikingly *profes-*

sional, by which I mean that it is clearly imagined and thought out and transferred to paper with admirable competence. In all questions of practicality Britten never puts a foot wrong. In this country (despite the magnificent example of Elgar) such competence is rare, and we were until recently so accustomed to provincial-organ-loft-folksong-and-Tallis amateurism that we are in danger of according Britten too extravagant praise for something that in itself means nothing.

So Britten is prolific, easily understandable, grateful to play and professional. It is difficult to name other qualities that are essentially his; Schubert was prolific, Haydn was easily understandable, and yet these are the least important facts about these composers. Webern on the other hand was unprolific, and Schoenberg is neither easily understandable nor grateful to play, and these, too, are irrelevant considerations. The fact is that Britten is rich in every compositional blessing, convenience and faculty, yet somehow all these combine into a hollowness, an emptiness that nevertheless strikingly presents the appearance of a living organism. Every surface glitters but there is no centre; one senses a fundamental frigidity. To put it as basically as possible his music is not *interesting*, not *significant*; there is nothing one feels to be the product of a profound or interesting musical mind. This is why discussion of Britten is so frequently based only on his texts and opera librettos—there isn't any musical substance that is sufficient in itself.

Britten's reputation as a great composer rests primarily on three operas, *Peter Grimes*, *Billy Budd* and *The Turn of the Screw*, and of course the *War Requiem*. In these four pieces Britten's particular crippling weaknesses can be seen most clearly, though the same inadequacies run through most of the rest of his output.

Peter Grimes is a relatively simple case of artistic falsification. In Crabbe's poem the hero was a straightforward ruffian who sadistically ill-treated his apprentices to their deaths, and eventually suffered hallucinations and died raving and unrepentant—a thoroughly anti-social person whom the crowd did right to persecute. But in Britten's intensely sentimental version Grimes has become the outcast from society, the lonely, sensitive-souled visionary (in itself a romantic cliché) and the crowd the aggressive, destructive force. What I mean by 'sentimental' is the unreality, the falsification of the truth that can only come from the deepest unawareness and lack of self-knowledge. Britten evidently identifies himself with this 'tortured idealist':

> A central feeling for us [himself and Peter Pears] was that of the individual against the crowd, with ironic overtones for our own situation. As conscientious objectors we were out of it [i.e. the War]. I think it was partly this feeling which led us to make Grimes a character of vision and conflict, the tortured idealist he is, rather than the villain he was in Crabbe.[1]

Equally false is the relationship of Grimes to Ellen Orford, who was not in the poem and was brought in evidently to provide conventional love interest. But there is no love scene between them—indeed they are almost

---

[1] *British Composers in Interview*, ed. Murray Shafer (Faber, 1963), pp.116–17.

never on the stage together. Grimes will not marry her until he has *money* and *fame*, and his yearning for her ('What harbour shelters peace') is a companion in banality to 'Tonight' in *West Side Story*. The most poignant music is Peter's nostalgic day-dream (in between bouts of lashing and throwing things at his apprentice) of his life with 'her'—'and a woman's care ... a woman's care'—the nostalgia/yearning to be normal at the very moment when the crowd are on their way to destroy him. Surely *this* is the basis for Britten's feeling of 'the individual against the crowd, with ironic overtones for our own situation', rather than—safely in America after all—his conscientious objection.

Grimes, although false and unobjective in these crippling ways (the glamour of 'Enter Grimes looking wild' or the pathos of the mad scene is particularly embarrassing) has nevertheless enough of conventional Grand Opera material to ensure a certain degree of universal validity. It would be difficult otherwise to explain its popularity. But in Britten's later works his private obsessions take over to such an extent as to make them almost nothing but a 'case' publicly presented—*except* that the objectifying power of Britten's music (learnt in particular from Stravinsky) preserves a certain decorum and even occasionally transforms the inner chaos of sentiment into genuine and realised art.

This does not happen in *Billy Budd*, which, with the *War Requiem*, can be called Britten's most emotionally spurious work. *Albert Herring*, Britten's previous opera, had turned a grim Maupassant short story into a simpering and cosy romp, but *Budd* with its pretensions to tragedy shows a falsity much more deeply rooted. Melville's story is homosexually motivated, and to present the opera as anything other is a failure of frankness that detracts greatly from the dramatic effect. When Claggart sings of Billy, 'Oh, beauty, handsomeness, goodness, I must destroy you', it is absurd to try and explain the plot in terms of Good and Evil, or Compassion (the usual *Budd*-speak), or indeed in any other terms than the erotic. And this, too, is the basis of Vere's delight and interest in Billy—Claggart and Vere, both under the pretty powerful pretext of duty, destroy Billy in their love for him. The sentimentality surrounding the figure of Billy comes out most obviously in his 'Farewell to this grand, rough world', and the latent sadism comes out in the fact that the more innocent and childlike he is the better victim he will make. The march to the scaffold with its eager, excited drumbeats, and the actual hanging with its *fortissimo* so-vicariously indulged cymbal-crash of horror bring out with a clarity innocent in itself the pathological undertones of Britten's response to Melville's tale. Violence in general (there is also a flogging scene in *Budd*) for Britten inevitably provides opportunity for a display of 'compassion'. But the point about compassion ('a quality', as one writer puts it, 'that Britten has made peculiarly his own') is that equally inevitably it provides a decent motive and excuse for a flogging, a hanging, a *Budd* or even a *War Requiem*.

The strong emphasis on children in Britten's music is somehow linked with the innocence of Billy. Children stand for innocence—an innocence that the adult has irretrievably lost. The child world is safe; its un-selfawareness means that all is secure, the terrors and assaults of the adult consciousness have no place. The adult will seek to re-enter the same sheltered world of the child. Hence:

> Composers must always write for people. Young composers ought to write for young people. There are signs that one or two young composers are working with children and that is encouraging.[2]

Indeed it is admirable that work should be done with and for children, that every means should be used to inculcate pleasure in and love for music, but when it means that the adult composer's level of consciousness must be abused to that of *St Nicolas* and *Noye's Fludde*, then music as Beethoven, Wagner and Schoenberg understood it has no more meaning. Children, although charming and delightful (as well as primitive and cruel) are, as far as artistic consciousness goes, non-existent; and any music written especially down to them, touching and valuable as it may well be, will not be interesting at an adult level.

The Turn of the Screw is a further expression of Britten's favourite motif of innocence and corruption, and the fact that it deals actually with children and apparitions rather than anything adult makes Britten's intense absorption in the subject produce a relatively successful work of art—spoilt only by the mawkishness of the ending, as well as the usual deficiencies of all his music, thinness of content barely concealed by the superficial brilliance of invention.

The *War Requiem*—that 'established classic' of eighteen months' standing—displays these deficiencies at their most pretentious and least rewarding. The words (whatever the undoubted feeling behind them) are set mechanically, the Owen no less than the Mass. There is a distortion of text and subjectmatter that we have come to expect from Britten, especially in the final poem, where Britten has to omit Owens's 'I knew we stood in Hell' in order to stage his saccharine 'In Paradisum'—('Let us sleep now'). Is this all that a great composer can say about War—the noisy banal trumpetings of the *Dies irae* and the fatuous 'irony' of the *Quam olim Abrahae*?

Britten will survive, if anything, as a writer of songs. The intimacy of tenor and piano seems to suit his slender talent to its best advantage, and, while deploring the pathetically inadequate *Donne Sonnets*, one can sense a slight but genuine art in *Winter Words*, *Songs from the Chinese* and the *Hölderlin Fragments*. But what a *tiny* art this is, that barely breathes when compared to a few songs by Schubert, for example, or Hugo Wolf! The truth is that Britten's talent is limited both emotionally and musically in ways that make it impossible to number him even among composers of the second or third rank.

This is why Mr Mitchell's claim strikes one as so preposterous! But the cult aspect of Britten's popularity is well under way by now and will no doubt continue for some years. The claims universally made for Britten are

---

[2] Ibid., p.123.

extravagantly out of proportion to the size of his talent; even the tiniest and most threadbare *pièce d'occasion*, like the trivial *Cantata academica* or the wretched little Cello Sonata, is a new opportunity to acclaim his genius. But for all his ambitions, and his country's ambitions for him, Britten remains considerably less than a *petit maître* like Chopin or Webern—a composer in spite of his technique and pretensions essentially local, unprofound and in the deepest sense uninteresting. One shudders at the thought of his prospective *King Lear*.

The cult has inflated Britten into a semblance of a Great Composer. As long as he is thought to be this, musical values are upside down, and one can but wait until they swing round right again.

34

Memorial piece

I met Benjamin Britten only once, when, a teenager almost too shy to speak except in a gush, I screwed up my courage to approach him as he listened to a rehearsal in Dartington Hall, and asked him about his unpublished settings of Hopkins. It soon emerged that I was trying myself to do something with Hopkins, using enormous orchestral forces in an inept struggle to capture equally inept and enormous adolescent feelings. His advice of course was to be modest, practicable, to write what could be realised. But my joy at his kindness only made it more imperative to myself that I increase the noise and complication. Immediate gratification, however, was afforded by the purchase and consumption of the biggest available box of peppermint creams and a score of Mahler's Third; the Hopkins settings ground to a natural halt soon afterwards.

Later I learned to be supercilious about Britten's music. The simultaneous excitements of discovering Wagner's overwhelming psychological profundity and Stravinsky's sublime self-objectivising made an *Albert Herring* or even a *Billy Budd* seem childish and the 'public' manner of the *War Requiem* a betrayal of the authentic voice of the *Serenade*, the *Nocturne*, the *Winter Words*. All this culminated in an outburst of rejection, expressed with the vehement excess that ought to reveal that something is false, except that one enjoys it too much to see. Relished above all was a sense of superior under-standing—a *knowingness* that was in fact ignorant of what was going on, namely that this access of insight was based upon his own.

Naturally it took some years for this to sort itself out, especially after the immediate pressure was removed. But as I gradually got to wnte the sort of music I had in mind, so I realised (even more slowly) that the violently rejected thing was precisely the thing closest to home. If one spends months on end in one's formative years listening to *The Turn of the Screw* and *Peter Grimes*, mixed up with the *Five Orchestral Pieces* and *Jeux*, the *Dream of Gerontius* and the dances from *The Midsummer Marriage*, the *Four Last Songs*, *Agon* and *Le marteau sans maître*, curious transformations will take place that won't allow one to lose any of the elements, whatever the vicissitudes of later taste. One gradually recognises that one is what one assimilates, whether one likes it or not (but one wouldn't have gone for it so wholeheartedly if one didn't like it), and so a revulsion from love to hate won't make any difference to the constituents. Since there is no choice—

these accidental conjunctions are here to stay—one had better knuckle down and cultivate one's native soil, with a due sense of dependence on it for the sustenance of life.

Recognition of this leads to more straightforward acknowledgements, of an indebtedness and gratitude within the public domain to a composer who was also a great performer, a gatherer and disseminator of music in a unique sense (the best Schubert songs and Bach Cantatas and Haydn *Creation* I have ever heard); an 'impresario' of almost Wagnerian infallibility (the Festival, the Maltings, and a whole implicit range of taste and ethos); the inventor and consolidator of English opera and English song. But above all I feel the private debt, to a composer whose intensely personal achievement nevertheless bears directly on the malaise of music at large—the flight to the extremes that leaves the centre empty. I wouldn't want to say that Britten's style is in itself central, but I think it can show the way better than any other to a possible pulling-together. In particular the combination of lucidity, emptiness and tightness in the latter works can reveal common ground between the most unexpected and unrelated sources. This music has the power to connect the avant-garde with the lost paradise of tonality; it conserves and renovates in the boldest and simplest manner; it shows how old usages can be refreshed and remade, and how the new can be saved from mere rootlessness, etiolation, lack of connection and communication to and communication with the culture from which it grows.

35

Strange victory

The going view of Benjamin Britten has changed completely over the decades. In 1952 Hans Keller and Donald Mitchell's *Commentary* presented a Mozartian figure, mercurial and joyous, endowed with every musical facility. Undercurrents of innocence and its corruption, sadism as the counterpart of pacificism, gave no hint of what 'dare not speak its name'. By 1984 and the *Companion* edited by Christopher Palmer, the dark side was out of the closet; its obsessive recurrence in the by-then-completed *œuvre* virtually banished the previous emphasis on bravura and high spirits. In Humphrey Carpenter's fat new biography,[1] the shift is total, with an un-relievedly dismal picture of a composer tormented by guilt, unvisited by much happiness or any fun, racked by ailments psychosomatic, then all-too-real, a workaholic driven by ambition, ruthless in vanquishing rivals, discarding collaborators once they'd served, and artists once they'd slipped. The prevailing impression, in an artist so blessed by the muse and so rapidly successful in everything (not just composing) that he undertook, is of tense frustration and provincial tedium.

There is a paradox in presenting at length the life of an artist or thinker or scientist, since it is by definition largely sedentary. The work is the great adventure. So George Painter tells Proust by counterpointing a populous epic of family and society with a solitary inner pilgrimage of prevarication, illness and creation. So Leon Edel tells at twice the length the tale of Henry James, whose events are far less colourful though his life and works are long. *Chez* Proust, the facts of the life and work are uniquely interinvolved. *Chez* James, this can be shown only by more-or-less plausible biographer's fantasy, whereby the novelist unconsciously lives out his themes even while the conscious life, personally undernourished but rich in reported suggestion, is transmuted into impersonal fictions. A composer's life, if the aim is more than simple documentation, presents greater problems. Dangerous livers like Berlioz or Wagner are a gift with their colourful passions and debts. They are the exceptions. The lives of Beethoven, Bruckner, Brahms are more like a norm. Beyond a bare chronicle, a sprinkling of anecdotes, *mots*, some specu-lations (demure or salty to taste) on the sadness of the *vita sexualis*, there is really nothing to say. *Mutatis mutandis*, Britten's story is similar. Such

---

[1] Faber, 1992.

people's lives are spent entirely in writing music, playing music, making music happen; in some instances, they only fully come to life within music's domain and are incomplete human beings without it. They have no biography, let alone one of nearly six hundred pages.

Naturally there are close connections between the life and the achievement even with the impersonalising artist that Britten claimed to be, let alone the self-expressive one that (as Carpenter rightly says) he actually was. We need a study that puts the important things at the forefront, and the curriculum vitae, equally with the intimacies, in its proper place. An 'intellectual biography' so pure as Gombrich's superb study of Aby Warburg (where the children are relegated to a footnote and a prolonged mental breakdown figures only because of new insights born of it as he recovered) is not feasible for a person so practical and non-conceptual as Britten. Nevertheless, it is the intellectual biography more broadly interpreted—'the growth of a poet's mind'—that one most urgently wants. How was the sensibility formed? Whence the aesthetic of essentiality, the insistence on technical prowess, in a land of heartiness and amateurism? How did the Mahler/ Berg nexus so important from so early receive its ideal home in this gauche product of a dowdy seaside resort and an English public school?

Such questions are more important and more interesting than the ins and outs of sexuality, juvenile and subsequent, and the further mishmash of gossip, testimony and opinion with which Carpenter weaves his text. It is only fair to say that, as a representative example of current 'full undress biography', it is conscientiously done and reads very fluently.

His credentials include sound lives of Pound and (obviously germane) Auden. But these are both men of notions, concepts, intellectual passions even when dubious or actually harmful. They are poets, critics, polemicists, whose medium is verbal. Britten is mainly a vocal and particularly an operatic composer, which appears to provide his biographer with a ready-made entrée not found in composers whose inspiration is primarily abstract. But Carpenter's equation of texts and plots with his victim's life is altogether too facile. Britten, as a composer intensively responsive to words, subjects, characters, situations, will of course reveal personality in every choice, and limitation in what he can't or doesn't do, but his medium is the 'occluded' art of music, at once physically direct yet swathed in the protective arcana of its craft. There can never be the direct relationship between the subject of the work and the medium which it employs, as there always is with a writer. Carpenter, a capable literary critic who has in his literary biographies done homework in well-tilled academic fields, is jejune when discussing music, dangerously at loose with a little knowledge, directed to a view of the works' contents that appals by its reductiveness.

His all-purpose key is the letter that Auden sent Britten just before the composer's return to England (early in 1942) from the United States where both had fled from the war. It has been endlessly quoted since its first publication in Donald Mitchell's *Britten and Auden in the Thirties* (1981), and runs like an ostinato throughout Carpenter's book. Though Auden's opposition of 'Order and Chaos, Bohemia and Bourgeois Convention' is a shade glib, it does nail the crux where Britten's wonderful gifts and his technical brilliance meet the problem area of his sexuality, his frigidity, his need for cosiness and protection, his refusal to grow as artist and as man, with unsurpassed acumen.

Auden was the only person able to effect a deep intellectual dent. The callow twenty-one-year-old musician (whose puerility—all 'gosh' and 'golly' —is often evinced in Carpenter's pages) was bowled over by the poet's cleverness, the breadth and availability of his culture, his spellbinding didacticism. Their collaborations are surprisingly few and not (except *Our Hunting Fathers*) top-drawer Britten. But the contact is central. Auden, a natural shaper, bullied Britten into sensibility with a sophisticated ear-training in English verse, giving a range of sources, a way of grouping and under-standing, which lasted long after the poet had been ditched. That he *was* ditched is surely true. Auden was a challenge and threat to Britten's very existence—a bundle of dirt and exuberance, horrifying the uptight Suffolk virgin with the flagrancy of his domestic and sexual *moeurs*, while at the same time providing a seemingly unattainable target of artistic professional-ism. No one subsequently was allowed to threaten or challenge. Collaborators were docile and pliable (with the partial exception of Forster, much older, distinguished, oddly formidable); performers could be eloquently 'not invited back'; more permanent staff, however loyal, could be goaded out of service, even as they rendered it still more sterling (as in the shocking dismissal of the Aldeburgh Festival's general manager, Stephan Reiss, far the worst of many similar affairs recounted by Carpenter).

Though Auden and his Message were evaded, the prognosis came true, the 'warm nest of love' he foresaw closed in like a prison-fortress; within it, Britten *did* 'develop to his full stature' by 'suffering and making others suffer', by becoming, in one nasty unBritish word, a 'shit'. The evidence in Carpen-ter's scrupulously documented pages is omnipresent. 'I have never met a more ruthless person' (Basil Douglas, producer); 'rather a cold fish' (Howard Ferguson, composer and pianist—echoed elsewhere without the qualifica-tion); 'Cruel? Of course he was' (Fidelity Cranbrook, long a guiding-light of the Festival committee). And more: 'he just used people and he finished with them, and that was that' (Joan Cross); 'there was a great, huge abyss in his soul' (Robert Tear).

Enter Peter Pears—not chronologically; rather as the personal embodi-ment of the prevailing atmosphere of Britten's life after their return from America. In his agreeable biography of Britten's singer and other half,[2] Christopher Headington paints a well-rounded portrait of a happy man, bubbling with sensibility and appetite, enjoying life and living it fully, giving his all, wholly realising his remarkable potential. Just because he was so well integrated, he could render the anguish and strain demanded by his composer with conviction and equanimity. Several people, by the accounts given in

[2] Faber, 1992.

both books, found Pears harder to know, in spite of his urbanity and outgoingness, than the introverted composer. I think that those who found him 'opaque' are puzzled by such straightforwardness in a context of repressive formality. But he has been called a 'Svengali'. 'Ben told me that Peter got him away from Auden' (Beth Welford, Britten's sister). The threat that challenges is replaced by the love which—even while it protects, assuages, fulfils something (though by no means all) of the emotional needs—is also a form of emasculation.

'By no means all.' A second skeleton-key to the closet, used by Carpenter in combination with the Auden letter, is the whisper of childhood sexual traumas. Carpenter urges caution, and his treatment (unlike the disgraceful pre-publication publicity and indeed the audience-reaction it presupposes) cannot be called sensational or prurient. But the very length and care with which he treats, near the start, these storms-in-a-teacup (complete with moralising foghorns) make them resonate throughout the book with a significance they could bear only if they were true. On the evidence of these pages, neither episode is plausible. In the late 1940s, Britten told Eric Crozier (his current librettist) that 'he had been raped by a master at his school', an event he held responsible for his sexual nature. Crozier wrote this down some years afterwards, when his favours were so superseded that his name had been suppressed, Soviet-style, from the booklet of the Festival he'd helped to found. Much later still, the composer asserted to Myfanwy Piper 'that his father was homosexual and that he used to send him out to find boys'. The delicate mother's darling had been frightened of his father whose hooded eyes and withdrawn personality were so like his own. But Mrs Piper's homely explanation—that what his father had said was something like 'why don't you bring your pals home from school?'—surely closes the case. Not that these strange admissions are not expressive in themselves.

Adhering to the uncontroverted, Britten was 'just born homosexual' (Joan Cross), with a strong narcissistic bent towards 'thin-as-a-board juveniles' (Auden), representing the perpetualised youth of an ideal version of himself uncomplicated by conflicts, sickness and the corruption of consciousness. After fumblings, feints and failures he found a stalwart maternal protector in Pears, whose voice, according to a childhood friend of the composer, corroborated by his sister, was 'fantastically similar' to the mother's which he'd so often accompanied as a boy. Artistic partnership came first; by early 1939 they were close enough to escape to America to make a new life together away from the war. Consummation came in a hotel room in Toronto in June 1939 and was confirmed in Grand Rapids, Michigan, a few days later ('I shall never forget a certain night in Grand Rapids'). Britten's was the dominating mind, but in bed he yielded to his partner's masculinity (according to Rita Thomson, nurse first to composer then to singer). They remained closely devoted until Britten's death some thirty-seven years later, and at the end, as Britten was dying at home and Pears enjoying the height of his career across the Atlantic, they exchanged letters whose passionate mutual gratitude is extremely moving. This, on the whole happy, mix of same-sex opposites is made unique by the fact that it could be publicly presented, even gloried in, because the tenor elicited from the composer an unprecedented series of works (roughly twelve operatic roles, thirteen solo song-cycles, and indispensable parts in at least six further concerted vocal pieces) that would not have existed as they stand, and perhaps not at all, were it not for their relationship. But equally there is no doubt that Britten's natural libido was directed towards adolescent boys. There is a long succession of suffocated platonic yearnings, often for the young protagonists in his stage-works. Carpenter chronicles country walks and car rides, swimming and tennis, hands-holding, hair-rumpling, wistful goodnights—*e poi, il nulla.*

Now what does all this signify for the much desired study of the 'growth of a musician's mind' and 'intellectual biography' of his mature artistic achievement? Everything and nothing is the shifty answer. To know for sure that he didn't enjoy himself rhymes with what had always seemed clear anyway from his inability to give his music its head. The result might be a case history, or one of the feebler products of Britten's compulsions like *The Golden Vanity.* But it can equally well be a masterpiece like *The Turn of the Screw,* demonstrably born of personal predicament, rendered altogether larger, deeper, more expressive, more significant than those abject origins by a masterly musical mind shaping with powerful imaginative charge a disinterested artwork, independent of its creator, though bone of his bone, three-dimensional and autonomous, directed outward, at a public, for one of the thousand and one varieties of artistic pleasure.

But Carpenter is always simplistic and reductive. When his approach is vaguely appropriate the touch is clumsy, as for instance the laboured point about the boy's 'fall' in *Peter Grimes* or the awful stuff about 'good' triads and 'evil' chromatics throughout. When not appropriate, the banality and off-centredness are quite unbearable. Take *Gloriana,* one of the few big pieces where Britten *is* reaching beyond his usual range to take on a subject with Verdian sweep. Carpenter sees it only in terms of a commonplace subtext about the artist's difficult balancing-act between public and private. *Yawniana* indeed! For this mode of understanding makes the whole *œuvre* appear a morbid secretion from a maimed personality. Both are demeaned. We are certainly not reading a biography of this man for his life. His life without his work is of no public concern. If his work is merely his life 'composed out', then his work is of no public concern either, which obviously can't be right.

The terms of Auden's letter (plus a *frisson* of childhood outrage for the credulous) can surely act as a starting-point in evaluating this music's limitations and, less surely, its positives. The charge is two-fold: first that Britten was deficient on the Bohemian/Chaos side of the balance necessary to create an artistic whole—his was 'a denial and evasion of the demands of disorder'. The criticism, in varying terms, was expressed from early days. Joan Cross felt that *The Rape of Lucretia* failed to deliver fully what it promised, a view reiterated by commentators on its successor *Albert Herring.* Both librettists of the next, *Billy Budd,* knew that the musical depiction of their villain was dud. Instead of Forster's desired '*passion*—love constricted, perverted, poisoned, but nevertheless *flowing* down its agonised channel; a sexual discharge gone evil', Claggart is in Crozier's words a 'boring black-masked villain', diluted from the incomparably stronger prototype of Verdi's Iago. Peter's suicide in *Grimes* is the first of several fudged emotional high points which arguably include the death of Miles, and certainly the fade-out of *Gloriana* and the dénouement of *Owen Wingrave*. These things ramify in such passages as the orgy in *The Burning Fiery Furnace*, the anaemic view of city vice in *The Prodigal Son* and Aschenbach's nightmare in Act II of *Death in Venice*.

Such consistent limitation tends to endorse Robert Tear's view that Britten 'always stopped. He wouldn't quite go over the top.' He is inhibited by gentility and shame. For clearly Innocence is far from innocent, and his work at its greatest and its most typical is impelled by a clutch of dark matter. Nor is this balanced by a corresponding warmth of libido. (Compare Puccini, who gave both sadism and eroticism their head.) There is no good love music in Britten. The two couples in *A Midsummer Night's Dream* are cardboard; Sid and Nancy in *Herring* are charming cameos, Aschenbach goes on about Tadzio's beauty firing him to new flights of inspiration, but the music remains earthbound. The closest he gets is always weird as well as wonderful—such unforgettable inspirations as the purely orchestral chords during which Vere invisibly and inaudibly tells Billy that he must hang; the Ghost and the Governess comingling their passionate voices as the boy through whom alone they can meet dies of the terror they've between them induced.

The other half of Auden's equation is Order / Bourgeois Convention, which, as guardian of technique, issues only in 'large unfeeling corpses'. This can be amplified by a much later remark of Auden (as relayed by Lincoln Kirstein):

what seemed like Ben's lack of daring, his desire to be the Establishment ... playing it safe for amiability as guard against his queerity, but insisting on the innocence of adolescence as if this was a courageous attitude.

The crucial case here is the *War Requiem*. It's understandable that inspiration might not leap up like a singing bird at the thought of the quincentennial of the University of Basel (though I find the *Cantata academica* marginally the better piece). But the strange truth is that precisely where his conscious convictions were most involved the music falls furthest: in the three pacifist tracts, *Voices for Today*, *Owen Wingrave* and the *War Requiem* itself. The standard is set by Britten's own best work (direct comparisons with the didactic threesome would be the *Hymn to St Cecilia*, *Death in Venice* and the *Spring Symphony*). The critic's danger is of seeming himself cold and unfeeling as he confronts these 'large unfeeling corpses' apparently born of large warm feelings about important issues. They can be opposed with nothing more than Mallarmé's 'not ideas but words make a sonnet' (which none the less says it all). There is an emotive double standard at work in this difficult area, by which people hear what they need to rather than what is actually there. On the evidence of his musical inspiration, Britten was more warmly and feelingly stirred by sadism, sacrifice, and death in many shapes than by peace, goodwill, reconciliation and compassion. This should be no cause for regret. We value artists in the end for what they have done best, not for what they 'ought' to have done, and in many instances dark matter is the source of the brightest value.

If Britten 'evaded', 'denied' and 'stopped'—it is worth asking first what prevented him and second what might have been if he'd flown free. The short answer to what prevented him is the replacement of Auden by Aldeburgh. What might have been is a more fruitful speculation. Carpenter mentions three such chances in the career. In 1955, after *The Turn of the Screw* and its pendant *Canticle III*, he told Edith Sitwell (poet of the latter) that he felt 'on the threshold of a new musical world', and that he'd be taking the next winter off to do 'some deep thinking'. And indeed, the ensuing world tour included the revelatory experience of Bali which fertilised important areas thereafter, and of Japan, source of *Curlew River* and thence of his entire late phase. So this is a growth-point where 'what might have been' actually transpired.

Not so the extended emotional range offered in the mid-1960s by two ambitious operatic subjects which both came to grief, *Anna Karenina* and *King Lear*. The excuses for the termination of both projects do not disguise recognition of artistic incapacity. Instead, back to 'innocence' and its dark underside, with boys' voices to the fore, and the drabbest decade in his output, with gritty cello suites, bleak cycles of Blake and Soutar, the steeply diminishing returns of the two church parables that followed *Curlew River*, the lack-lustre *Voices for Today* and the feeble *Owen Wingrave*. The third window opens briefly amid this dead patch: a projected ballet which he discussed with unwonted freedom with Sidney Nolan while touring Australia in 1970. He was thrilled by the desert, the light, the Aboriginal boys, and planned to contrast the stifled life and tragic death of an English juvenile with the Rousseauesque naturalness 'and a kind of *Magic Flute* ending' of the Aboriginal. Though on returning he mentioned the idea to the Covent Garden directorate, Britten had killed this one himself; as the enchanted plane-flight descended, 'he suddenly said "Well, that's the end of that. When I get back to England I won't be like that any more. My destiny is to be in harness and to die in harness."' Which, indeed, is what happened—harnessed, above all, to longstanding *idées fixes* (*Wingrave* and *Death in Venice* had been in mind since the American years) whose grip was so strong that he could only fantasise, not act, upon anything that transcended them.

But in the end we possess what was caught rather than what escaped. And it is positive. This is a major composer, after all, not quite the fourth 'B' that his mother was determined he should be, following Bach, Beethoven and Brahms, but a gigantic figure in the pluralist jungle of post-war music, who probably gave more pleasure than any—a popularity that gives every sign of lasting. His best period remains the astonishingly fertile decade from *Peter Grimes* (1945) to *The Prince of the Pagodas*, with brilliant flashes before and some shafts of genius even as the language grows etiolated, notably the renovatory *Curlew River* (1964) and the valedictory *Death in Venice* (1973) three years before his own. His ultimate importance is, for us now, uninterestingly unknowable compared with what we have enjoyed already and still do and still will.

Then there is Britten the performer. Studio recordings and (even better) transcripts of live concerts substantiate the copious testimonials from those who were there. The solid tribute of the professional makes one of the few happy strands in Carpenter's carpet. Singers and virtuosos, down to rank-and-file orchestral players, knew that they were working with a great artist. The peak is, of course, the duo with Pears, and whatever one's reservations about the voice's idiosyncrasies, the integrity, musicianship and imaginative insight remain unimpugnable. Pears's voice is self-evidently unique (Headington's book includes some valuable jottings made about questions of technique and interpretation). And Britten's pianism is unparalleled (above all in Schubert). No one seems to touch the instrument in the same way, to elicit so much meaning, wholly without point-making or mannerism. More than with any other player he gives us the music itself: cruelty, ruthlessness and frigidity are replaced by their opposites. His conducting, in repertory that suits him, is also outstanding. One senses that only when making music did he enjoy (once the inevitable pre-concert ordeal by vomiting had been surmounted) his physical being.

In addition, Britten represents at the highest level an attitude to music in society which has slowly infused itself into every aspect of this country's cultural life. A comparison of the great impresario/composers of Aldeburgh and Bayreuth could be fruitfully developed at length, from the sublime (like the achievement of a perfect acoustic) to the ridiculous and indeed the pathetic. Both were sacred monsters at the centre of a self-made quasi-royal spider's web of self-projection for the benefit of the nation. The biggest difference is that Wagner was a life-enhancer, Britten a nay-sayer.

And so in the end one closes the fat book about the thin composer, so compulsively readable but so dispiriting, with not much sense of the positives, nor of any adequate handling of the difficulties that lie behind. The thin book about the plump singer by comparison leaves one serene like himself. Such personal happiness as came Britten's way was provided by his singer. Yet the prevailing note is sad, even wretched, and his downward progression from a Young Apollo with the world at his feet to the premature death from sheer exhaustion, surrounded by the visible fruits of his successful employment of his talents and the more impalpable affection and homage of music-lovers the world over, grinds very small and dry. The book's downbeat final pages seem to end in total defeat.

But of course, Britten has won, as he always did in his life, whether in the ferocious games of Happy Families with which the domestic circle used to 'relax' or in the major business of being 'the best' at composing, planning, playing. And it is a very strange victory. To have made public pleasure—in opera above all—out of the deeply screwed-up places of an occluded personality is a triumph of the will that in a perverse way surpasses Wagner's, just because of the off-centredness of its subjects. To get international audiences in music's most explicit genre willingly to side with the sadistic visionary against the decent norms, to throb with the ganglings of a gormless youth tied to his mother's apron-strings, to be moved to the marrow as a man pretending to be a monk pretending to be a mad woman twitters away over the boy she has lost, or as an elderly writer of untarnished probity goes to pieces in exaltation and degradation over the boy he has found, is an extraordinary achievement. He spreads his obsessions and starvations very wide and very deep. Let the last words be by Auden: 'And children [and not only children] swarmed to him like settlers. He [he was favourably named] became a land.'

36

The church parables:
limits and renewals

Contributed to The Britten Companion, *edited by Christopher Palmer (Faber, 1984).*

*   *   *

'A time there was' when music consisted simply of diatonic melody resonating in sympathetic spaces that gave delicate bloom to its austerity. Unsullied eternity was penetrated by the curious serpent, unbinding music's hitherto dormant power to *move*. Harmony and rhythm, once stirred into life, are both engine and fuel. But it's downhill all the way. As motion and emotion grow ever more comprehensive, innocence is left behind in an age of gold beyond recall. Childish directness is blighted by weary knowingness; deceit, baseness, corruption lay siege to head and heart. The slippery road broadens as it descends. Expression once pristine easily becomes sentimentality, exaggeration, cheapness, coarseness, turgidity. The end is nigh—a maelstrom of total anarchy where every note (there are millions) is simultaneously whipped on by a perpetual extreme or intensity and weighed down with an urgent burden of inherited function. Hence a yearning to be cool and still and quiet; to escape the orgiastic debasement of excess and the excruciating exposure of feeling; to jettison the accretion of layer upon layer of sound and meaning; to recover primeval simplicity and freshness.

Traditionally efficacious to quench and console the exasperated spirit is the sound of the harp. And no one since its emancipation from mere arpeggios and glissandos has understood the genius of this instrument as has Britten, who makes its technical character so influence his compositional thought that the music grows directly out of what the instrument can and cannot do. Total chromaticism is beyond its diatonic structure; the possibility of *these* will always make *those* notes unplayable, which necessitates ingenious choice in planning every harmonic change. Such narrow limits exactly suit an ear exceptionally sensitised to every inflection of every note, and a usage latent in his earlier harp-writing (brilliantly idiomatic from the start) increasingly permeates his later music whether or not the harp is literally present. For harp-tuning is an analogy for the way his harmony moves and a metaphor for the way his mind works.

The other instruments in the church parables are chosen out of exigency: a base of percussion and an organ drone to catch and hold the blur of voices; for characterisation, the Ferryman's horn, the Madwoman's flute; for a special pervasive colour, the trombone in *The Burning Fiery Furnace* and the trumpet in *The Prodigal Son*; for more neutral omni-purpose, the viola and double-bass. In the resulting ensemble the harp is a vital element. It doesn't predominate, however; indeed, with a tone resonant yet fragile and an attack somewhat undefined, it remains rather submerged, its very lack of colour serving to bind the voices and disparate instruments loosely together without heaviness. But the principle of harp-tuning is fundamental to the whole sonority. The harp's 'limitations' allow Britten to control the harmony of the parables as a loom can be threaded to produce different patterns. Their harmonic fabric is woven on the harpstrings.

The result is like a return to the source and a new start. What Stravinsky called 'the brief but brilliant history' of harmonic ascendency seems to melt into a remote past as this music is heard; and, along with harmony, metre and measurement , also dissolves, allowing the fluid eternals of diatonic melody to be rediscovered. The great romantic 'new starts' (from Beethoven and Schubert to Mahler by way of the *Rheingold* Prelude and Bruckner) are invariably harmonic; above the deep fundamental an *Ur*-shape gradually unfolds or boldly sounds forth, outlining an arpeggio with strong tonic–dominant emphasis. But Britten's 'new start' is quite different from such conscious primevalisation; it is rather the natural extension of tendencies implicit in his brilliantly wayward mastery of traditional harmony, which, when pressed, can run quite counter to it though still alongside. His comment during his Far Eastern tour of 1956 that the music of Bali 'makes our tonics and dominants seem like ghosts' has a long ancestry quite apart from his own earlier involvement with Javanese scales. He writes after many decades of what can loosely be called orientalism in western music, from Debussy and the gamelan to Boulez and *Le marteau sans maître*. Tenuous parallels for the aesthetic and sound of the church parables can be made with Satie, late Fauré and middle Bartók. More distinct forerunners come in Stravinsky—*L'histoire du soldat* for the band and *Les noces* (especially the end) for the sonority; in such things in Holst as the bitonal canons and the songs for voice and violin; with the recitatives for voice and flute over a drone bass in Mahler's 'Der Abschied'; while very close, in quality of emotion as well as actual texture, is Debussy's Sonata for flute, viola and harp.

More widely suggestive, though difficult to define, is a comparison with music, of whatever epoch, that goes well in large resonant spaces. This obviously includes the entire era of plainsong to polyphony in up to forty parts. In more modern times instances are rare and special. For during the centuries when harmony and rhythm were hugely expanding into ever more sophisticated possibilities for tonal organisation, only music of limited harmonic movement, basically non-modulating in tendency (even in a strict sense anti-tonal) and of broad rhythmic outline, could survive any degree of complicating acoustic fuzz. After the Venetians only Handel (because of his harmonic plainness) achieved this, until the nineteenth and twentieth centuries, when a few figures outside the central tradition—Berlioz, Musorgsky, Stravinsky, Varèse, Messiaen—once again by accident or design write music accommodated to the capacities and restrictions of enormous resonance. To these can be added certain important aspects of Bruckner and Sibelius, who both belong basically elsewhere. Apart from Bruckner, this is all music where the learned refinements of harmonic function are not of primary importance; apart from Handel, music where tonics and dominants are well on the way towards disembodiment. Generalising further, these composers (to whom Debussy must now be added, though his music would certainly not sound well in a big echoing space) are rootless figures, without much of a tradition before them or after. Their musical character is non-developmental; they build by repetition and ostinato, in blocks, whether large or small, separated or molten together. The warmly expressive is usually avoided; there is a tendency towards formalisation, observance, ritual; they evoke places of theistic awe—Catholic interiors, forests and mountains, seascapes and cloudscapes, deserts, canyons and stars, *atmosphères*, *Sirius*, Judgement Day itself.

Strange though it seems at first glance, Britten's church parables belong with this kind of music. They render unending time and imply vast space and place, by dissolving the bounds of harmony and rhythm until it seems that music itself will drain away, leaving nothing behind. Strange because Britten is by no means an egotistic sublimer or a professional visionary, but on the contrary an artist whose themes are humanistic, and who shows a particular feeling for the prosaic, the deprived, the victimised; whose desire is to be accessible and of service to a community, and whose gifts are in complete accord with this desire. His best and most frequent vehicles are song-cycles and operas, whose time-scales are distinctly less superhuman than sociable. Yet simultaneous with this conspicuous humanity a sort of oriental emptiness has evolved, unconscious or preconscious, 'before good and evil', utterly passive and detached; the nescience so longed for in *Winter Words*. That the two aspects are compatible is easily shown. The church parable time-scale is as slow as possible, granted that this strictly practical composer will not make preposterous demands on his audience's time, attention and comfort, while endless space and place can be successfully evoked without a choir of a thousand, four brass bands and St Paul's or S. Sulpice.

The wherewithal for these works, rather, is astonishingly modest; the still small voice is right on target. The *donnée* is a story, an appropriate plainsong, a troupe of acting singers and a little band recalling distantly the Japanese inspiration and based, more nearly, on the needs of the story in characterisation and colour, and on suitability to the church acoustic for which the parables are intended. The musical substance grows out of the endless variety of closely related melodic shapes derived from the initial plainsong, falling into blurring, echoes, drones and heterophony, and perpetually retuned by the harp (literal or metaphorical). The harmonic series alone would set the space vibrating with natural response. A plainsong will set up a blur of diatonic notes in close proximity that hangs in the air and slowly clears. A single note is retuned; then another and others following. We seem to 'see' the notes in all their relationships from the simplest to the more and more complex, audibly growing in unmissable progression, and always remaining absolutely lucid. Every retuning alters the relationships like an altering magnetic field— even the building seems to change in sympathy. However many the parts, we hear not harmony but intervals forming verticals and horizontals, not chords but 'aggregates' which seem to analyse themselves before our eyes as if for an acoustical demonstration. It is Britten's extraordinary achievement in the church parables to have integrated the discoveries of serial and post-serial pitch-organisation into the fundamental unchangeables of the harmonic series.

In *Curlew River* everything already familiar from Britten's earlier operas is quintessentialised with harsh nakedness. Characterisation in voice and by instrument ranges from the Ferryman with his sturdily agile horn and the Traveller with his trudging double-bass double-stops to the astonishing feat of stylisation (out of Donizetti via Japan) in the ululations, flutters and swoops of the Madwoman and her flute. Sense of place, so fully evoked in the *Peter Grimes* Sea Interludes, is now set with the barest minimum of notes. Just as the acting area gives next to nothing to see, so this music gives next to nothing to hear; but this minimum suffices to render river, marsh and circling birds with startling vividness. Sense of movement—Britten's gift for depicting action (hauling the boat, spinning, laying the dinner-table, plying the lagoon)—is never so basic as here in hoisting the sail and poling across the river.

Though there is precedent too for the ensembles, it is in these that the newness of the church parable style is most striking. They are indeed remarkable; their mixture of fixed and free (always with the scrupulous sensitivity to pitch-inflection already mentioned) unostentatiously resolves the twentieth-century problem of voices moving against each other in anything but triads and scales. The first and most inspired, 'Birds of the Fen-land', opens up a fully realised vision of a kind of music different from anything ever heard before, though its ingredients are all, when separated, extremely familiar and extremely simple. Set against the ensembles are the various 'arias' for the Madwoman; and again the exposure and intensity of such things as 'East, east, east ...'and 'Hoping, I wandered on ...' takes them into a sphere beyond their direct ancestry in Britten's previous portrayals of desolation, anguish and madness. Things that could be mannered to the point of self-parody seem here to enter an area where painfulness no longer gives artistic pleasure; such unclothed excruciation makes one almost grateful that he never composed the *King Lear* of his dreams.

Three moments of harp-tuning genius must be singled out: the flute's last entry in the 'Birds of the Fenland' ensemble, whose final B♭♭ becomes the Ferryman's A♮ as the action resumes; the electrifying effect of the harmonic change from the moment of universal recognition that she is the boy's mother to the Madwoman's own recognition; and the wonderful way the piccolo solo representing the boy's Spirit takes his mother's characteristic dissonance out of A♮ into A♭ regions, the closing ceremonial heterophony then restoring C, and the final plainsong A♮. Such matters are virtually meaningless in words; the point is, they have been so composed as to make them completely audible and affecting to a listener who doesn't know what 'flat' or 'natural' means.

The work gives a beautiful sense of grading its sonorous resources for maximum meaning. The percussion base and the deeper voices set the Mad-woman in relief; indeed we tend to forget that she also has a man's voice, so isolated are she and her flute from the mid-range of other voices and instruments. The motion of crossing the river sets up a feeling of great spaciousness that persists long after the ferryboat completes its journey. Soon before the crisis of the action, the marvellous entry of the deep bell takes this sense of opening space on to a different plane, awakening the deepest and fullest range of reverberation, catching the little bells which in turn sympathetically attract the voice of the Spirit, itself thin and deliberately only just perceptible between the waves of the massed other forces, but none the less forming the 'acoustic climax' as surely as it does the dramatic. After this, the spaciousness is fulfilled; the work's most sonorous passage yields to its least; the boy's voice trails off and up into the piccolo, diminutive of his mother's curlew-flute, and is lost to sight; the echoes die, the building ceases to vibrate.

The importance of *Curlew River* as a crossing-place and synthesis can hardly be overstated. In some dream-conflation of harsh East Coast Anglia and milk-and-honey West Coast America, middle-age Christian culture lies down with ageless Japan and Bali, and native Englishry (folksong, Elizabethans and Purcell, Vaughan Williams and Holst, the earlier Britten himself) nuzzles the European avant-garde. Very difficult, vitally important questions of harmony and rhythm are solved and dissolved with breathtaking ease (the practicality of the performing notation in itself opens up enormous new possibilities for compositional procedure). None of this would signify were the work not also very beautiful, and quite peculiarly affecting. Indeed there really seems to be no parallel for its fusion of narrow concentration with infinite suggestion. This music goes straight to the most painful place in a totally disembodied martyrdom of St Narcissus (Canticle V)—the spiritual groin.

After this, *The Burning Fiery Furnace* is clearly something of a fun piece, sometimes unsuccessfully, as in the arch little riddle scene, sometimes with uncertain results, as with the would-be comic gravity of the young Israelites' reluctance to eat at Nebuchadnezzar's table. Modest fun is made from their three names, outlandish in two languages; and glorious fun with the 'cornet, flute, harp, sackbut, psaltery, dulcimer, and all kinds of music'. By far the best thing in the work is the march inspired by this list of instruments, and there is hardly a better instance in all Britten of his delight in gratifying our desire for a half-expected surprise than the moment when the players transport the delectable little invention all round the church.

But in spite of the brazen trombone and the new colours in the percussion, too much is a pale replay of the predecessor. Everything fresh and inevitable in *Curlew River*—the triple frame of plainsong, address, ceremonial heterophony; the characterisation in voices and by instruments; the big set pieces—is here by formula, because the genre requires it. The twitterings of Nebuchadnezzar and his Astrologer are closer to mannerism than to real characterisation; and during the earnest chanting of the three goodies our ears stray guiltily to the musicians as they prepare one by one for their 'unholy' procession. Dissatisfaction is focused in the other set pieces. The orgy of abasement before 'Merodak' is ice-cold, horrible and completely stunning. But its complement, the miracle in the furnace, badly hangs fire. The greyness of the crowning *Benedicite* recalls Britten's United Nations anthem *Voices for Today* with its equally doleful vision of the age of gold. Even the return, with converted Babylonians joining the goodies and the finely composed instrumental enrichments, cannot ignite it into celebration. The triple frame closes in, but the climax has escaped.

With *The Prodigal Son* the sense of genre has become distinctly dutiful, and the musical impulse tired. The story is again serious, but without the inward concentration of *Curlew River*. In its absence we hanker for something to compare with the pleasure of the intricate and delicious little Babylonian march. The main set piece, the orgy in the City of Sin, goes rather for the coldly disgusting quality of 'Merodak', heightening it into something more complex in meaning, though just as horrid in sound. There are of course inspirations throughout, notably the Prodigal's frisky escape from boredom and the brilliant closer and closer entwining of Tempter and tempted as the city is neared. Also inspired is his homeward journey, an urgent fantasia on the work's germinal plainsong in four free parts over the percussion ostinato of his weary footsteps. But just before it, his lowest hour grubbing with the swine is set to a rehash of incomparably more poignant originals in the Madwoman's arias. And some of the music is frankly perfunctory, especially the elder brother with his landlubbery clusters, and the dance of welcome when the Prodigal returns.

There is a problem of monotony. The deliberate blandness of the father's farm is all too effective; at the reconciliation our strongest reaction to the return of the seraphic unchanging B♭ chord from which the younger son fled is to remember the boredom that impelled him rather than to be moved by his return. More difficult still is the final ensemble. The voices go up and down and round about, repeating 'was dead, and is alive; was lost, and is found' to the densest 'aggregate' in all three parables and the one closest to a discord that needs resolution; but nothing seems to focus or clinch, whether musically or dramatically. As in *The Burning Fiery Furnace* the climax is somehow missed (though everyone knows where it should be); moreover in *The Prodigal Son* the reserve upon which the genre depends for its expressive manner gives way in two crucial places to a direct appeal—to pathos in the father's forgiveness, to reconciliatory warmth in the final ensemble; and in both cases the result is ineffectual.

These shortcomings in *The Burning Fiery Furnace* and *The Prodigal Son* suggest limitations in the church parable convention unraised by *Curlew*

River; moreover they touch upon wider limitations in Britten at large. In the depiction of Babylonian gold-lust and the debaucheries of the Big City a tone can be heard that is not so much ascetic as prim and even priggish. This music renders abandon with monkish distaste; there is no imaginative understanding of the ambiguity within 'sinfulness'. One has only to recall the comparable vignettes in *Mahagonny*—also the work of a moralist whose attitude to what he pictures with such seductive pleasure is unmistakably severe—to see how coldly Britten looks upon the frailty of the flesh. The effect in *The Prodigal Son* of setting the famine the morning after to the same music as the 'dark delights' of the night before is of lofty disapproval rather than spiritual insight. 'Sin' is only joyless, fearsome, loathly; therefore its music is made so; and as the framework closes on each story and the Abbot comes forward to preach, we feel a discomfort different from what is intended. After the story of the miracle in the furnace he tells us that 'God is tried in the fire, and the mettle of man in the furnace of humiliation' and prays that

> God give us all
> the strength to walk
> safe in the burning fiery furnace
> of this murderous world.

The aptness is undeniable; but what the composer's art has so extraordinarily opened up suddenly becomes thoroughly small and dry, and not a little banal. How serious, really, is the tone of this elaborate medievalising? Do the spectators also dress up, in fancy, to become illiterate peasants receiving a 'sermon in sounds'? No answer; the musicians process out, taking their noises with them, leaving their audience too much in the dark.

Worries about the didactic strain in these explicitly moralising works open up wider reservations still. The church parables officially exemplify Hope, Faith and Love, but it is difficult not to find such neatness a little laboured, especially after *Curlew River* had beautifully embodied all three. Faith and Love remain abstractions in their respective parables, giving scant warmth, for all the wagging finger. The same is true of *Curlew River*, but with positive effect. It is far less insistently didactic, working—overwhelmingly—by pity and terror; and it is propelled by something absolutely authentic, a yearning for 'someone ... someone ...' that goes altogether beyond an emblem of Hope in the abstract. If the three parables have a common theme it is the drabbest stoicism: make do, knuckle under, hold fast, carry your burden, forgive and forget, dutifully kill the fatted calf. This is cold comfort at best, and at the worst, not bread but a stone. And artistically the result is a severe impoverishment, even a denial, of the free spirit that could once set Rimbaud and Michelangelo, and write the *Spring Symphony* and *The Prince of the Pagodas*.

And so the very clarity of the renewal in the parables soon serves to expose limitations more clearly than before. The irresolutions that linger on after three ostensibly reconciliatory endings suggest a high degree of disquiet which indeed surfaces in Britten's next stage work, *Owen Wingrave*, with a turbulence, almost an incoherence, unique in this artist. 'Peace' here is certainly not an inert abstraction, but whereas the cardinal virtues fail to quicken their respective parables, 'Peace' has a weight thrust upon it which it simply cannot bear. It is a truism that everyone hates war and wants peace, and equally that a tyrant has never been defeated or a people civilised without the military virtues. Why not write three parables on honour, courage and glory?—for it is another failure of imagination, another deception, to dismiss them as base or hollow. To place all self-deception, brutality and blood-lust on the one side and all humane decency on the other is more than just simplistic and mean; it is *untrue*. And this, in a man of painfully sensitive conscience, must stand at a peculiarly vulnerable place. It is commonplace to pay pious tribute to Britten's pacifism. But Peace and its facile companion Compassion can hardly be reconciled to a preoccupation with subject-matter that sometimes seems closer to a nervous compulsion than to the spirit of 'peace on earth, good will towards men'. And in Owen's monologue praising peace we sense that the word's larger vibrations carry beyond the purely conventional associations invoked. His fervour and the music's glittery warmth amidst so much that is angular and crashing suggest what dare not speak its name in work after work. 'Love is the unfamiliar word'—not love as an abstract, but the individual eros. Peace is the symbol of self-discovery, self-possession, self-realisation: 'in Peace I have found my image'. The private, almost fetishistic quality of this word in Britten's output explains itself—warrants its full warmth—only if it is understood as the pass- or code-word for his sexuality.

The wonder is that he could ever as an artist get beyond this impasse, for the extent of repression that these unresolved tensions indicate is so great as to suggest the imminence of an explosion. *Owen Wingrave* indeed has about it something explosive, though characteristically muffled, for Britten's more fruitful way out is by relaxing, by easing off the tight tense area into a state of mind which in full consciousness can honour, and eventually glory in and die for, its devotion to its own 'sinful' predilections. *Death in Venice* has no sermons about sacrifice to idols, or admonitions to Carry on Hoping or to Love your Neighbour. Here beauty, not peace, is hymned; and beauty's devotee, far from dedicating himself to its destruction or being its unwilling agent, as once in the past, can give himself up to the human body that possesses it; rapt, intent, and relieved even to ecstasy by uttering what has been so long constrained. This explicitness (absolutely delicate, unprovocative, unlibidinous) of Britten's last opera opens up a more humane moral sphere than the moralisings of the church parables. Their sermons appear sour, their presentation of the virtues impoverished. *Death in Venice* is neither mean nor covert; it knows what it is doing, and its moral understanding has put aside childish partiality. Yet the opera would not have been possible without the parables; the strait has contributed generously to the open. The masterly fluidity and flexibility, the minimum of notes and maximum of suggestion, evocation and implication everywhere in *Death in Venice* are a triumphant vindication of procedures that, beginning in the utterly strange and new, had run, in the two later parables, into perilously shallow water.

This extraordinary flowering out of the church parables shows by contrast that they had indeed moved towards the very edge of musical interest. For worse as well as for better they are necessarily thin. Negatively this implies undernourishment—works of art that, as Henry James put it, 'ask more of the imagination than they can be detected in giving it'. Positively it implies 'nothing in excess'; 'less is more'. Britten is obviously an archetypal thin (in modern times the thin have been leaner still in reaction to the preceding epoch of unbridled fatness). The balance can be delicate; there is a point where the paradox of less-because-more becomes strained; pregnant parsimony miscarries; the hungry sheep look up and are not fed. Much in his later music crosses this threshold: the conspicuous loss of sensuous surface in the later song-cycles, the grit and grind of the cello suites, the sourness of *Children's Crusade* and much of *Wingrave*. Such music certainly seems to require more of us than it gives. But the parables are poised at the crux. It is clear that this style's parsimony is its strength; that it wears its starvation like a rose; that renewal is born from a scrupulous and humble attention to native limits. It is hardly surprising that the miraculous fusion of monotony with intensity happens only once.

What thinness cannot do is obvious enough; but positive thinness has the power to have us forgo what it misses, and concentrate upon the special range of effects that it alone can achieve. In the end what Britten can and cannot do are equally conducive to the resulting music. Thus the familiar 'inability to let go' that arguably fudges the climactic emotional moments in *Peter Grimes*, *The Rape of Lucretia* and *The Turn of the Screw* becomes a source of great intensity when not letting go is of the essence. This is why we demur when Britten ventures in the parables to re-allow direct pathos even in *Curlew River*;[1] and the problematically 'sinful' orgies in the other two can be related to the relative tameness of the Dionysiac element (indicating recoil rather than abandon) at the end of the main action in *Billy Budd* and in Aschenbach's nightmare in *Death in Venice*.

Knowing from Nietzsche that 'the degree and kind of a man's sexuality permeate the loftiest flights of his intellect', we read without surprise, in the famous letter to Britten where Auden urges upon his friend the 'demands of disorder',[2] of the correlation of his attraction to 'thin-as-a-board juveniles' with prelapsarian innocence. The mature Britten's characteristic thinness, of which the parables are the crucial examples, is inseparable from the theme that inspires all his most individual work. Their unexampled severity presents with startling clarity the feeling for innocence and the nostalgia to return to simplicity and unconsciousness. Their method enmeshes the theme in the work's very substance, making it possible to hear every troubling element— the Madwoman's anguish, the Babylonians' idolatry, the temptation and fall and humiliation of the Younger Son—as a mistuning, a disturbance of the

---

[1] There is just one, very brief, unconvincing touch—the passionate descending phrase in octaves at Fig.76.

[2] See p.212f.

eternal diatonic drones. As the story unwinds, its crises are sympathetically caught in ever more tortuous distortions; as it comes out well, so alien notes are restored to normal; and thus the rebirth of nescience is woven into the actual sounds themselves, providing the very reason for the notes being the way they are.

37

Britten's tenor-man

A memoir contributed to the Observer *on the great singer's death in April 1986.*

* * *

Peter Pears, because of his association with Britten, became the most remarkable interpretative artist of our time. The succession of solo song titles, from the early *Serenade* (where his voice is built into the subtitle, 'for tenor, horn and strings') to the tenor parts in such bigger works as the *Spring Symphony* and the *War Requiem*, were all directly inspired by his voice.

And, above all, the operas: the title roles in *Peter Grimes* and *Albert Herring*, the male lead in *Gloriana*, *The Turn of the Screw*, and the three church parables, the male chorus in *The Rape of Lucretia*, the main consciousness in *Billy Budd* and that supreme *tour de force* of stamina and intensity, Aschenbach in *Death in Venice*.

The extent to which this music was not only inspired by the singer's artistry but built upon timbre, register, strengths and limits of the voice itself, is extraordinary. The recordings by Pears of virtually all the music Britten wrote for him will always exist to show the degree to which the actual notes grew out of the vocal physiognomy.

The unique relation to Britten apart, the lack of complacency in his repertory was noteworthy. It was large and unhackneyed, and the list of premières in the book published last year to mark his seventy-fifth birthday makes impressive reading. This re-creative urgency survived the loss of his singing voice after his first stroke. I recall the avidity with which he siezed upon the idea of a 'song cycle' for speaker and instruments which I proposed to him in the excitement of hearing his highly musical reading of verse and prose. He always wanted to explore and to work, and my most recent memory of him is his rehearsing and performing this piece last autumn, with all the old alertness and visionary intensity.

The singing voice was strange and not altogether attractive in itself, with an uncomfortable edge (more discernible on record than live); the charge of mannerism, even affectation, could not always be denied. But this edge suited him especially well in the expression of uncomfortable states; in all the Britten roles, of course, but also in such classics of romantic suffering as Schumann's *Dichterliebe* and the two cycles of Schubert. That he possessed comic gifts is shown by his Purcell and Walton's *Façade*; that he could be heroic, by his Handel, or his Oedipus in Stravinsky's opera. Above everything one will remember his spiritual intensity in such music as Wolf's religious song and the surprising but utterly convincing assumption quite late in his career of Elgar's Gerontius.

And his supreme achievement outside the Britten *œuvre* was actually one of plainness, with the Evangelist parts in the two Bach Passions. The most unforgettable sound I ever heard from Peter Pears came not in any Britten operatic role nor in Schubert or Purcell, nor even in the Bach Passions, but in the Evangelist's narrative upon which the St Matthew Passion of Schütz is hung. Music of such nakedness exposes its interpreter completely. From its norm of austere recitative the long-sustained cry of 'Eloi lama sabachthani' emerged as startling in its intensity: wild yet pure, white-hot yet non-subjective, the artist submitting his voice and interpretative powers to the score's modest requirements and producing a moment of visionary incandescence.

My own memories were only of his last decade or so. I was lucky enough to participate in his vocal 'Indian summer', after a period of quavery drynesss, that shone out just before he was forced to cease singing. It was with great temerity that I wrote songs for this famous voice. Anything written for Pears would inevitably have to be some kind of homage, at best *using* all its associations, at worst simply succumbing to them.

Awe and alarm were banished at once by practicality—'suppose I do *this?* … would you like this? … Is *that* right?' He was humble, disinterested, malleable and totally collaborative; we were *making* something, with earnest concentration; I could suggest, correct, or even rebuke, but he gave as good as he got, and was always resourceful in artistic solutions.

There was not a hint of the traditional 'stupid tenor'! He had no time for vanity and nonsense. Above all I was impressed by his acute placing of the emotional core in text and music (always in terms of drama—he was a born projector); his way with what I'd written told me more about it than I knew I knew.

Personally he was a trifle fey and whimsical, even a little insipid, evoking a particular epoch of genteel upper middle-class culture—those pink gins!—long since made respectable and by now impervious to surprise and shock by anything raw. There was a distinct twinkle of humour, much sharp common sense, and a certain purring contentment in the unmitigated success of the enterprise: a great composer and his great interpreter, rendering tortuous themes, yet unsurpasssed in our day for appeal and popularity—and the Queen had made the one a Lord and the other a Knight! I'm sure that old friends who knew him longer and better will recall earlier times of greater exuberance.

The point is that all this blandness had nothing to do with the *artist*. The wild-eyed visionary Grimes, the mellifluously seductive Quint, the anguish-pierced madwoman of *Curlew River*, Aschenbach progressively abandoned to his fatal passion, Captain Vere glimpsing the goal of his life's journey—Pears *became* these things, indeed he had in a sense *made* them; without him as he was, they would not exist as they are.

38

Britten twenty-five years on

Benjamin Britten has been much in concert and on the air this month [November 2001], to coincide with what would have been his eighty-eighth birthday (shared with the nameday of Cecilia, patron saint of music) on 22 November and—the immediate pretext—the twenty-fifth anniversary of his death on 4 December. The music, of course, needs no pretexts. The early flowering of his manifestly outstanding gifts took him instantly to the top after the triumph of *Peter Grimes* in 1945, despite the sneers of the establishment of which (as usual) he imperceptibly, inescapably became a part, to end up, five months before his too-early death in 1976 a peer of the realm. By then it was the young and snooty who sneered. With the general public, popularity was ardent and unfeigned, and his worldwide following twenty-five years on continues to increase.

Yet in this quarter-century the perception of him and his music has drastically altered. The earlier image combined Mozartean comprehensiveness with Mendelssohnian facility and brilliance in a vein of mercurial brio, gaiety and dash, and was expressed in a technique too unselfconscious to be fazed by the 'sentimental' problems of modernity.

Since his death a shift of angle, together with biographical 'revelations' as expected, has elicited a dark side to his work, as with his personality. Britten as seen twenty-five years after is tormented by guilt and angst, revealed most explicitly in the obsessive return again and again to ever-narrowing variants of the same few themes—prejudice, persecution, pacifism and destructiveness, and corruption of innocence even while it is vainly hankered after—culminating in the oblique but unmistakable self-projection of *Death in Venice*, completed in 1973 in advance of major heart surgery after which his further composing was virtually posthumous.

These opposing perceptions are compatible, even complementary. It is obvious that, between the pastoral opening song of the *Serenade* and the deep serenity of the closing sonnet, and alongside the gay vivacity of the hunting scherzo, lie the sick rose with the canker at its heart and the blood-flecked demonism of the *Lyke-wake Dirge*; and we now appreciate *Peter Grimes* as the representative masterpiece of English 1940s romantic/gothic, where Graham Sutherland's thorny forests parted to reveal neo-Grünewald and John Piper was so persistently beset by glowering weather. So to darker matters: exploration of the nexus between desire and destruction in *Billy Budd*, not so much via the stilted villainy of Claggart (recognised hollow by Forster, the opera's co-librettist, to his deep disappointment) as in the ambiguous yet unswerving relish with which Billy's own goodness and Vere's justice, fairness and decency all make as surely, and far more convincingly, for the kill. Above all, the twists and feints by the the erotic glamour that dare not speak its name drowns out the all-too-complicit innocence in *The Turn of the Screw*; and the exposure of pure naked anguish in that unique fusion of East and West, mediaeval and serial, strict and floating, *Curlew River*. That the dark prevails in this complex vision is clear as daylight: that it was always so is confirmed by the higher standing nowadays of such earlier milestones of introspection and pain as *Our Hunting Fathers* and the *Sinfonia da requiem*.

But concentration on this 'sado-masochist' aspect is now so general that there is a real danger of neglecting the earlier perception, all sweetness, lightness, radiance, exuberance and breathtaking technical ease—the Young Apollo (with prominent nose and receding chin) whose last lovely fling was the fairy music in *A Midsummer Night's Dream*. All this remains, and is the more valuable since such qualities were rare in twentieth-century art at large, particularly in most music concurrent with Britten's peak production and (for me and I suspect for most of his lovers) compositional prime, c.1943 to 1958. *Albert Herring*, the *Spring Symphony*, *The Prince of the Pagodas*, as well as many smaller things (for example, everyone's favourite, *Hymn to Saint Cecilia*) are undimmed witness.

I fear that my continuing aversion to the *War Requiem*, his most celebrated success, might seem to put my ardent advocacy of Britten in general at a disadvantage. I would place it with other pieces that don't share its popularity, like the United Nations anthem *Voices for Today* and the pacifist opera *Owen Wingrave*; they are sermons, on pokerwork texts of startling simplism —war is bad, peace is good, we must love one another and/or die. Simply on musical grounds (what others are there?) this public aspect lacks the sharp memorable inspiration and sheer compositional invention of the authentic masterpieces whose ethical credentials might well be seen as 'incorrect'—all the dark matter already mentioned, and plenty more.

The only view to have sunk below the horizon is the middle course that Britten himself hopefully characterised as his purpose: to be useful—local first universal last if at all—an impersonal provider like all pre-Romantic composers and Rossini and Verdi in later times; a sort of superior occasional artist, fulfilling a need with no-nonsense craftsmanship. This has so obviously come true that it hardly seems worth remarking. But however posterity decides, and time winnows grain from chaff in a large output that undoubtedly tends towards self-dilution and self-duplication at its latter end, Britten will surely last through many a further shift of emphasis. The next checkpoint will be the centenary of his birth in 2013. Stay tuned.

39

Fertile masterpiece

I've self-indulgently included this as my first-ever Spectator *column.*

* * *

I looked forward all day to the recent live broadcast [autumn 1988] of Scottish Opera's new production of Tippett's *Midsummer Marriage*. Anticipatory glow permeated the afternoon's fraught meeting of the Music Faculty Board at Cambridge where all its chairman Alexander Goehr's skills were required to calm the troubled waters. Listeners to last year's Reith Lectures will recall his intonation—silky, husky, sophistical. After the meeting he and I repaired with our composer colleague Hugh Wood to my rooms nearby to recover with Scotch and silly jokes. Seven o'clock drew near; I shooed them off and switched on the wireless, to find the same voice, in mid-sentence that had been sounding throughout most of the previous five hours, interviewing Sir Michael about his first opera.

But the apparent continuity contained a time-warp; the conversation had been recorded on the occasion of the work's first revival at Covent Garden back in 1968, years before Tippett was a knight and Goehr a professor. Few could have foretold that, twenty years on, Sir Michael would still be going strong, pushing eighty-three, his fifth opera currently nearing completion—which if his former patterns still obtain will mean a fifth string quartet, symphony and piano sonata before he calms down.

How does *The Midsummer Marriage* sound now, some forty years after its composition? In spite of mediocre singing in the two principal roles (the soprano's cold was announced but the tenor had no such excuse) and a hard orchestral sound in a tight acoustic, the magic still casts its spell. The ambience remains a funny mix of Shaw with something extremely amateur and toga-wearing at the bottom of the garden *circa* 1902, Pan-like presences flitting in and out of the shrubbery behind the tennis court. There is also a brave try at the modern world with the businessman (plus holster and gun!), his sensible secretary and her nice boyfriend from next-door. Underneath lie Jung and *The Golden Bough* and many a Pelican book on comparative religion. World mythology is rifled with abandon, and the resulting mishmash bedecked with figures from *The Waste Land*. The actual story is a highly archetypal affair; though based ultimately on *The Magic Flute* it leaves theatrical plausibility far behind. It is short on flesh and blood; completely flat in moments of crisis (the death of 'King Fisher', the aforesaid business-man); most successful when frankly formalised into the two couples' symmetrical ascents, descents, pursuits, statuesque poses, like its further ancestor the English masque. And it is sung to the composer's own text, sufficiently rich in awful moments to warrant frequent cringing.

So why is the work so good? The answer is of course its music. In Act I the busy grey Hindemith of Tippett's earlier work still shows; yet such minor events as the archaic plainness of the Ancient Dance (an early creative response to the Monteverdi revival) and the daring deliciousness of the secretary Bella's repeated trips to ring the supernatural doorbell, show something already individual and fresh. More substantially, the lyric charge of Mark's big aria, the white intensity of Jenifer's ascent to the heights, the burning urgency of his response in crashing the gates of the underworld, and their subsequent confrontation and reversal of trajectory achieve symbolic profundity without laboured explanation.

And after Act I the All-Bran is out of the system. Here the prosaic couple's dreams of courtship and domesticity provide the frame for three ritual dances whereby woman hunts man as prey, in the form successively of beast, fish and bird, around the seasons from autumn to spring, in the elements of earth, water and air. The domestic scenes are framed, in turn, by offstage choruses mysteriously evoking midsummer rituals of human fertility. Here the different levels genuinely interact: this is no hotchpotch; a poetic meaning without pseudery or dead wood is realised in music of vibrant colour and lyricism.

Act III, which returns to the main story, is rocked by dramatic absurdities, but the music remains on the highest level. Such high points as the fourth ritual dance and love duet, where man, woman, fire and summer fuse into one, the cold dawn that ensues and the altogether extraordinary closing chorale, at once fast and slow, continually cut off and resumed, can make even the best post-war music by other composers (be it advanced, mainstream or conservative) seem not inferior exactly so much as *undernourished*, lacking in physical robustness and spiritual health. The private anguish of Britten, the strident angst of Shostakovich, the saccharine unction of Messiaen, the grating complication of Carter, the manicured exquisiteness of Boulez—to name the most obviously major post-war figures—all lack a vital something that Tippett's *magnum opus* for all its creaking flaws yields with generous abundance.

40

Splendid but silly

I have to begin roundly with a declaration of disappointment. Of all our major composers, Michael Tippett is the one from whom one might reasonably have expected a distinguished autobiography: not so much for its 'literary merit' as for the record of a voyage of inner exploration, an apprehension of thoughts and feelings in their true significance of the same *kind* at least as the great confessors—St Augustine (whose mystical experiences Tippett has strenuously attempted to encompass in music) and Rousseau; self-mythologisers like Yeats (also a key source) and Lawrence; or those artists whose fascination with themselves and their doings communicates itself to others without a sense of eavesdropping, as with De Quincey and the Ruskin of *Praeterita*.

Instead, we have this slack flat volume[1] which presents only a glimmer of the man behind it, and depends for some 130 of its 280 pages on verbatim reproduction of old letters and selections from an extensive 'Dream Diary' kept in 1939. Much of the rest is a lazy recycling of material familiar either because he has printed it already (for example, the recollections of Britten) or has divulged it to his principal commentator Ian Kemp for the biographical chapter that opens his 1984 study. The scanty new material reads exactly as what it is—Sir Michael chatting away at odd moments into a dictaphone, the result transcribed and loosely touched up. The Stravinsky–Craft conversation books began life in a comparable manner, but they didn't end up so. A composer just as old and busy and still more eminent bothered to work away with his Boswell[2] to shape and sharpen, define and refine, until disciplined essentiality emerged out of casual table-talk. A great opportunity has been missed for a man known for his articulacy to dig deep into his memory for the communal benefit.

Tippett's particular aura of vitality and hilarity, though still present, is obscured here by a vapid garrulousness whose principal characteristic is a kind of naïve vainglory. Perhaps such self-wonderment ('having lived to 83 ... enjoying a seemingly endless creativity ... it was tempting to think that I might go on for ever') is indispensable to his artistic functioning. Its origins

---

[1] Those Twentieth Century Blues: an Autobiography, by Sir Michael Tippett (Hutchison, 1991).

[2] See p.315ff.

in his life-story are attractive; the high spirits and affections of childhood are retained into his teens with charming period glimpses of cycling the South Downs and travelling the Continent (the Tippett parents, living peripatetically, would send Michael and his brother money to make their own way in school holidays to wherever they had, for the moment, landed up; one memorable telegram from Italy read, 'Father bitten by a tarantula. Come immediately', but the alarm was false and the story ended happily with the Giottos, and a sexual encounter, in Padua). This zaniness persists through the 1930s, as in the absurd adventure in the Lake District when the friends' sodden clothes and bedding, left to dry on a handy gasometer, were frazzled to a cinder. Even the shadows—the traumatic adolescent experience at Fettes, from which dates his private sense of being a 'loner', a conviction which in the Second World War blew up into public trouble and a term in prison as a pacifist; the turmoil of his closest relationships, culminating, as the war drew to an end, with Francesca Allinson's suicide—rush by in the same giddy whirl. So much so that when he adds at the end of what proved one of his last letters to her, 'Am 40 today', one blinks—the sense of teenage high spirits has been so strong. And the same can be said of his second forty, the energy, eagerness, self-delight have not only ensured his survival but kept him ever young in movements and voice, in mind and, until quite recently, in actual appearance.

All this comes over in Tippett's memoirs with considerable charm. None the less, the story needs rounding out by reference to Kemp's book, indispensable for its far fuller account of Tippett's prolonged and unusual studies and his long path to self-discovery as a composer, its clear account of his politics and how he put his beliefs into practical action, and its absorbing glimpse of Tippett as the inspiring head of music at Morley College. Far from being academically official, Kemp's modest biography actually succeeds in conveying Tippett's unique character better than the composer himself. The combination of high spirits, zaniness and naïve vainglory persists, in his own account, right up to the minute, with breathless international travelogues, with self-recognition when encountering Nietzsche's famous phrase about the internal chaos needed to give birth to a dancing star ('that's me!' and, with less justice, 'it's also this maverick book'). The tone is encapsulated in this account of an adventurous holiday in 1987:

> The Persians used the road to conquer the Greek cities on the Aegean coast; Alexander the Great used it to march his troops down to Egypt, where he founded Alexandria; Mark Antony brought his armies down along to Alexandria and succumbed to the charms of Cleopatra ... the Ottomans ... Napoleon ... Now it was Tippett's turn.

This elicits an indulgent smile. Elsewhere, a similar tone begins to put one off. 'Barely a week after the final rhetoric of *New Year* (one humanity, one justice) had been proclaimed from the stage of Houston Grand Opera, the Wall came down and the frontiers were opened in Eastern Europe; a few months later and Nelson Mandela was released from nearly three decades of imprisonment. Not quite an example of Jungian synchronicity but close.' The chapter-headings reveal portentousness not always justified by their contents—'Spring awakening', 'The wandering years', 'Interpretation and its discontents', 'The world my country', 'The final dream'. All this suggests not so much self-mythologising *à la* Yeats as a life seen increasingly in terms of media cliché. A tendency which perhaps began with the exhibition for his seventieth birthday entitled *A Man for Our Time* here reaches an unlovely plateau. The autobiography's very title, *Those Twentieth Century Blues*— drawn (would he if he'd realised!?) from Noel Coward rather than the Deep Black South—is unconvincingly glossed in a bizarre context: commissioned by the Third Programme to present aspects of Schoenberg in the months after his death, Tippett finds himself, 'as someone committed to singing those twentieth century blues', absorbed in tracing the history of the *Mitteleuropa* intelligentsia and the West Coast.

In places like this one cannot avoid feeling that indefinable *something* that chimes exactly with the false touches in the concepts, and actual words, of Tippett's self-made librettos and other texts, and indeed the false notes in the music itself. Pretentiousness isn't quite the *mot juste*; pseudishness (as suggested by *Private Eye's* 'Sir Michael With-it') is off-centre, and it's miles away from any of the cultural modishnesses that have come and gone in the course of his eight decades. It's not bogus—on the contrary, it stands in close association with vulnerable sincerity and touching candour. It also goes with a determined intellectuality—'as someone seeking to fertilise creative projects with intellectual ideas and perception, I was running very much against the grain of English musical life'; 'I found it perfectly right to accept the example of Shaw and Butler, and deploy the intellect as part of one's creativity.' Plainly Tippett *is* an intellectual, with an exceptionally wide range of reading and an almost fatal receptivity to ideas. But the problem is not one of intellectuality at all. What is lacking is the capacity to assimilate and transform. All the big works to his own texts show in varying degrees the uncooked quality of raw reading that cannot be digested. This has become still more apparent in recent decades when the sources have widened to include movies and TV, resulting in a *brouhaha* of world news-events, popular science and nature programmes, thrillers, documentaries and soap - operas, lying alongside old favourites like the earlier Eliot and the later Yeats; Jung and Frazer; Homer, Shakespeare, Goethe, Shaw and Barrie. And behind it all lies this indefinable *something*—which is vague, ethical, affirmative, high-minded, muddle-headed (for all the 'intellectuality'), warm-hearted and incredibly silly. It's holy-fooling (if you like); or else sheer old British battiness.

Yet in the end it is probably not possible to isolate this vein of silliness (or whatever it can be called) from the moments of fully realised intensity that abound in his work. To take the greatest: if the first idea for *The Midsummer Marriage* (as given in Kemp and again in the present volume) were all one had to go on, one would say 'it's got something but it's completely barmy'. When after some fifteen years of slow and often painful growth the master-piece stands unveiled, its initial absurdity exonerated and the toil vindicated that saw the vision through, one would still have to say that layer upon layer of symbolism and cultural reference have not necessarily produced the desired richness, let alone clarity. That they *sometimes* have is undoubted. Nevertheless, one of the glories of modern music is riddled with ineptitudes, inseparable from its very being, that are the result of an inbuilt intellectual incoherence quite as culpable as the anti-intellectualism that Tippett so deplored, and possibly more harmful to a composer in the long run.

That there was always an element of self-indulgence is shown here by the tedious 'Dream Diary' (it is well known that ingestion of Jung's books produces Jungian dreams as surely as the body excretes its physical waste). But if the reward is a mind cleared for *A Child of Our Time* and the precious handful of songs and instrumental works round it in which at last he found his true voice, then so be it. And the same applies to the far more undiscriminating acceptance of extremely unpromising ideas in recent years, represented here by a few pages concerning his latest opera, *New Year.* Maybe even this preposterous stuff could have ripened with time into something worthy of the first opera with its comparably preposterous start. But in recent years Tippett doesn't seem to have given his creations as much time as he once did.

Which opens up the tricky question of an overall estimation. The earlier critical commonplace, that with the conspicuous and self-conscious change of direction marked by *King Priam* (1958–61) Tippett had gradually gone off, is unusual now in these days of total canonisation. Having got him wrong once, people are anxious not to do so again. My own view is that the watershed lies across *King Priam*, in the two orchestral masterpieces that flank it, the Second Symphony (1956–7) and the Concerto for Orchestra (1962–3). They foretell the future—the incessant energy and busyness, the mosaic construction, the skeletising of the orchestra and the ossification of the rhetoric, the standardisation of the actual musical invention and the decline of its pitch-quality and sonorous exactness, ending up for the most part in something grey, albeit bedizened with bells and gongs, a mechanical contraption out of Yeats's 'Byzantium', the poem Tippett has most recently set. But a backward glance would take one all the way back to the origins in grey, busy, Hindemithisch counterpoint, which is then lured into dance by the English madrigalists, into song by Purcell, into warmth, light, colour, wine and sex by the slow-maturing glory of *The Midsummer Marriage*. If only this book could have been written by the Tippett who gave us *that*.

41

Remembering two composers

Robert Simpson, March 1921 – November 1997
Michael Tippett, January 1905 – January 1998

* * *

To lose its two senior living composers within two months, even if they depart in ripe old age, their harvest all gathered, is heavy for a country to bear. Michael Tippett made a characteristically conscious decision to retire at ninety with an explicit farewell in an orchestral tone poem *The Rose Lake*. And though Robert Simpson the unobtrusive, cruelly smitten a few years back with strokes that prevented further sustained work, lived on in enforced silence, it is possible that he too, without making the deliberate choice, had said his all.

Both had begun, within a recognisable English tradition, to embrace a modernism that could hardly have been more individual. Simpson is far less well known and harder to write about. The body of work is entirely abstract: symphony follows symphony, quartet quartet, without helpful handles—whether incidental, like the nicknames attached to his beloved Haydn, or germinal subtitles (*espansiva*, 'inextinguishable') as with his beloved Nielsen. Even when there is programmatic inspiration, from cosmology, biology, ecology, it is subsumed into a musical dialectic whose severity is without parallel in the last half century. The result is absolutely radical. Eschewing every blandishment of colour, sensuousity, allusion, it takes its stand on pure process, the construction of shape and form out of the grammar of music's materials.

Widely regarded, beginning with himself and his immediate supporters, as conservative, locked in embattled defence of classical tonality, Simpson's music is no such thing. For, paradoxically, his mature work realises with single-minded ferocity what is implied by some of the twentieth-century lines he so excoriated—the tight intervallic organisation of serial music, the obsessive repetitions of simple figures in Stravinsky, even the athematicism of Boulez and the all-system pattern-making of minimalism. His basic urge, however, remains old-style humanism, man-the-measure, aggressively advocating peace, freedom, justice; and the rhetoric that carries it remains old-style musical tropes—especially those tattooing trumpets and drums!—whose conventional and increasingly machine-made nature is redeemed by such purposeful proportion and direction. If all this sounds more rebarbative than attractive, that is its nature and its essence. Which at its best—at a rough hazard the 'middle period' symphonies three to six, before they begin to grow too long and 'indistinguishable'—surely lies alongside the best of Tippett; not so lovable, but impressive in unforgiving integrity.

Tippett's modernity, unlike Simpson's, could be considered willed rather than evolved. The feckless eclecticism and reckless trendiness of his later decades grow out of the early openness to many different sources—old music, new music, folk and urban vernacular—all grafted with intensive labour on to the basic English stock. The labour paid off in the marvellous personal synthesis of the output's heart: two visionary song cycles, two masterpieces for string orchestra, the first two symphonies, *The Midsummer Marriage*. The *volte face* in his next opera, *King Priam*, to a 'modern music' style, all hard, spiky, dissonant, peremptory, juxtapository, grieved lovers of the earlier period at the time (early sixties), and still has the power to disconcert. The years have vindicated the first results of this switch. Most of the *Concerto for Orchestra*, much of the Third Symphony, above all *King Priam* itself, stand well alongside, if a little below, the earlier summits.

Thereafter, though, comes a long slow decline, piquantly counterpoised by the colourful hype of a reputation that had been almost universally undervalued during his richest creative years. It is sobering to hear again the later music in proximity to the earlier. The abundance, radiance, soaring decorative lyricism and tense muscular strength don't disappear so much as coarsen, generalise, turn to habit, thence routine. Whether clipped and telegrammatic like *The Ice Break* or loose and woozy like *The Mask of Time*, essentiality of musical definition escapes, and the musical personality once so ineffable is replaced by mannerism. The end product can be curiously anonymous, what looks juicy and interesting on the page sounding fussy, grey, ineffective—the complete reversal of their earlier relationship.

Of course there are exceptions—flickers of genius, whole good stretches, isolated or sustained moments of beauty or bravado. Passages from the oratorio on texts from St Augustine's *Confessions* come to mind, and from the concerto for violin, viola and cello, and the closing pages of *The Mask of Time*. But most of the later music sounded stillborn from day one. And the home-made texts, for operas especially, grew more and more half-baked, unchecked by any guiding spirit of seriousness, or absurdity. There has never been a better case for the Academy of taste and decorum that Matthew Arnold claimed would be of so much benefit to English culture than the librettos of the later Tippett operas! It will be surprising that any age subsequent to our own could prefer the final oratorio to *A Child of Our Time*, the fourth to the second in quartet and symphony alike, or *New Year* and *The Ice Break* to the numinous first opera.

Time will decide. And Time's judgements can be unexpected. Meanwhile, the fact that the view of the world in *all* this music, whatever Time's decision, is unforcedly, unfeigningly life-affirming, though it can't be in itself a guarantee of calibre, none the less puts it at sharp contradistinction to most of the epoch's greatest productions, and adds a further fervour to the glow of gratitude.

42

Alexander Goehr: towards a critique

Now his singing moves towards a climax and brakes into a dance.
———introductory note to *Nonomiya*

The Piano Trio op.20 can stand for the fully-realised side of Alexander Goehr's art. Its first movement disperses and re-combines his typical punctuation-mark material through an ever-shifting range of possibilities to open up a form of cumulative power and perpetual surprise. And in the Lento his typical parsimony of notes actually produces the effect of abundance; material apparently limp and tentative is isolated in just these qualities until it achieves an extraordinary degree of inevitability—rock-hard yet tender and intimate—something comparable to Debussy's *chair nue de l'émotion*. The *Nonomi a* programme note misprint that fortuitously characterises the limitations of much of Goehr's music here indicates the essence of something extraordinarily beautiful. This movement truly 'brakes' into expression, and its muffled intensity puts it with such forerunners as Debussy's sonatas or Webern's Symphony. The *Metamorphosis/Dance* op.36 is another, and very different, fully-realised piece with a complex structural scheme that really tells expressively, and in addition a delicate warmth of instrumental colour unique in his output.

But there is a price to pay for every unambiguous success. The following thoughts about Goehr's music attempt to schematise what I see to be its limitations, with the object at least of helping to focus and define, and maybe at best of providing a starting point for a less polarised exploration that could touch on the no-man's land of truth.

Bayan Northcott has written, 'Goehr's central concern has been with a concept of music not as mystical stimulation or political exegesis but as a medium of ideas in itself, a human activity like reading a book: "I write music in order that people can follow from bar to bar and know that certain notes follow and that others don't."' I on the contrary see music as fundamentally anti-linguistic—rather, as a representation or embodying of inward emotion and outward motion, reproducing the ebb-and-flow of life. Both definitions are metaphorical. The metaphor of music as rational discourse derives its sustenance from the more fundamental metaphor of music as feeling and movement; reversing this balance produces some of the difficulties discussed below.

The view of music as 'a medium of ideas in itself' commits its holder to seeing composition not just as the manipulation of a range of techniques for ordering sounds but as the elaboration of quasi-linguistic structures. This in Goehr has striking benefits. His endeavour to rationalise the post-serial chaos is admirable. His cross-pollination of series with mode has with lucidity and resource indicated an answer to the crucial problem, how to produce harmonic sense from this kind of musical organisation while retaining for it a genuine *raison d'être*. So far so good, but now the linguistic metaphor begins to become concrete and limiting rather than remaining pliable and pregnant. For even in Goehr's best pieces one asks constantly, why a 'language'? The passage 'speaks' because the ear is excited or pleased. The combination might have been brought about by a note-row, a magic square, a throw of the dice, or the cat running up the keyboard. But its cause is not its reason; the intelligibility lies in the sound itself, and choices which might have been (metaphorically) linguistic for their creator do not have any direct bearing except in at much as the sureness of his choice compels the ear's recognition that they are right.

Goehr seems to have got this the other way round. For him notes need to *prove* rather than to *be* something, and one frequently feels that music is being made with concepts rather than sounds—that the notes are a mere code for something else. And in the end the compositional results of his lucidity and resource are often oddly cursory. Music written to demonstrate 'that certain notes follow and that others don't' has in theory got sound and sense out of alignment.

If the full autonomy of composition is thus curtailed by the metaphor of composition as language becoming too literal, it will need support from external sources rather than from within itself. Hence Goehr's interest in parallels to composing from mathematics, anthropology, linguistics, semiology. Intellectual liveliness is especially attractive when most musicians so stolidly pursue their single furrow. But again the richness of these parallels lies in their suggestiveness as metaphor—indeed as frankly poetic stimulation (Goethe, their greatest exploiter, knew this well). The artist who surrenders himself to the prescriptions of 'scientism' puts at risk his surefootedness on the goatpaths of empiricism.

Factitious models of rigour lead to emphasis upon analysis as the musician's chief means of understanding his art. Goehr's predilection is for the method that begins in the assumption of an alleged deep structure in a work, truer than its obviously apprehensible stylistic surface and its immediate deployment of its affects. Therefore for him preoccupation with style, as with emotional content, trivialises: style is merely decorative, affective content is *belles lettres*. But suppose that such obvious surface features were what the composer had intended the listener to take in? In that case they would be the truest content, to grasp which would make analysis superfluous; mere curiosity to see how the wheels go round. Analysis is how we hear anyway; the composer has taken pains to make things clear for us. There are no deep secrets, for everything significant tells sooner or later. If it does not, the work tends towards being linguistic in the secret and damaging sense—it becomes cabalistic.

Fortunately Goehr the composer does not practise what he seems to believe. The surface of his music at every turn offers its listeners the necessary information for assimilating its processes. Nevertheless his idea of music as *essentially* analysable—as if it were written in order to be studied—results again in a reluctance to yield to sound as such. Relish of 'glorious mud' is surely a *sine qua non* of any musician however austere; we do not have to analyse in order to feel the force of the content; we just have to hear the sounds. The near-incomprehensibility of (for instance) the last page of Schoenberg's Variations op.31 is inseparable from the frightful, temporarily pitch-deaf noise it makes. Goehr is incapable of such a denial of aural truth as this; but there is a certain lack of feeling for the physical basis of composition in sound, and there appears to be a strong reservation about these sounds' direct access to our physiological and psychological bases. The clearest indication is in his instrumental colour and his rhythmic invention, but it gets deep into the melodic and harmonic substance of his music and is shown at its broadest in the reluctance to bring the music to a head or to a definite end. Too often his norm of texture is the nervously-articulated punctuation-mark. This would be Stravinskian except that it so signally lacks Stravinsky's relish and power.

However the composer most suitably evoked remains Brahms; and here again there is a polarity between the admirable 'Goehr-the-Progressive', revivifying and clarifying a creatively backward-looking language full of possibilities for a sane future, and on the other hand the aspects of Brahms that called forth Wolf's fury and Nietzsche's contemptuous 'He is unable to exult'. There is no need to defend Brahms from this! No one would go to him for Wagnerian ecstasy or Brucknerian sublimity; but the *œuvre* from op.1 to op.121 affords ample indication of his saturation in the 'mud' of music—for instance the utter physicality of the way his particular pianists' hands compel certain musical shapes, his almost lascivious delight in filling the strictest, most cerebral forms with rich textures and glutinousness of emotion (those *Liebeslieder-waltzes* in the Fourth Symphony chaconne!). He clearly exults, in his fashion, in the primary ingredients of sound, and his music (with no hint of the subjective self-portrayal of a Tchaikovsky, a Strauss, a Mahler) realises a complex and contradictory personality with exceptional fullness. This is not always true in the case of Goehr. The extremest example is his Doctoral Chaconne for the centenary of the University of Leeds. It wears its learning heavily, yet at the same time defies all sense of occasion. What would ring out in Bangor or Cardiff for such an event can be only too easily imagined; but to be embarrassed by the appropriate has a banality of its own (Brahms of course struck exactly the right tone). This single example can stand for something typical. In a sense, all music-making is an occasion; much of Goehr's music seems to resist its being so, yet half-reluctantly, as if wistful and only wanting a little encouragement to be emboldened to join in.

The more natural musician would not think twice about doing the right thing for the Leeds centenary. He would then take care to make it as good, as clever as he knew. Goehr, being self-examining and full of scruples, produces a tortuous half-private work that will neither please nor outrage nor set officialdom a-thinking. A general picture emerges of a composer, very thoughtful and subtle, too selfconscious quite to trust to his truest intelligence which lies in his intuition. In common with many of his generation he appears to have lost the sense of a 'given' compositional practice that can be employed without being enquired into or even fully understood. One can walk upright without having heard of gravity or the articulation of bones and muscles. Goehr has made a musical 'language' but has not so far acquired the confidence to use it in full freedom.

These limitations appear drastic; but in the end they can be seen as helping to define a quality. Goehr's best work achieves its distinction precisely by his putting his limitations to expressive use. Poignant feeling is rendered through starvation of the medium employed, and scrupulous intelligence can make much out of little while many a more abundantly-endowed talent spills out notes indiscriminately and squanders nature's plenty. Almost *malgré lui* Goehr is a true creator, and every apparent disqualification is in the end worked upon to creative purpose. These laboriously sought-out sounds show the benefits rather than the illusions of his kind of analysis and linguistic parallels. Lacking either the music-making machine of the 'figured-bass'-composer or the sheer 'oomph' of the 'improviser'-composer, Goehr has something rarer: the ability to put together small elements into a larger grammatical order, that makes him, at whatever distance, a true heir of Haydn, Beethoven and Schoenberg.

Goehr's sense of this heritage, and his endeavour to add to it, are the key to his value. For after all he is pursuing a greater goal than any of his contemporaries. Most post-serial composition is arbitrary and egoistic; its base is intellectual caprice frozen into dogma. Goehr has always possessed the common sense to see through the nonsenses, and the humility that serves music rather than the arrogance that uses it for unmusical ends. Rather than the pursuit of pointless complication (and in spite of a few 'scientisms'), he has an authentic yearning to achieve grammatically-articulated classical usage. If Goehr the generous teacher, the eloquent expounder, the sympathetic colleague, the amusing and lovable man, makes no appearance here, it is because—in my view—his music has pursued a somewhat defensive 'objectivity'. But I recognise that my reaction may also reflect the inevitable rebound of the pupil who has benefitted greatly from his master's voice before moving off in his own direction.

*   *   *

For an update on Goehr's distinguished and prolific output since the appearance of the symposium in which this piece first appeared, see my contribution ('Sandy at 70') to the Festschrift edited by Alison Latham (Ashgate, 2003).

43

Knussen at fifty

The tapes made in my unavoidable absence had cut off the broadcast's first couple of minutes: but there was no mistaking the music's voice—lithe, bright, purposeful, wittily concealing yet revealing within colourful elaborations the ghost of the early Stravinsky sparkler to which it pays hommage. It could only be Oliver Knussen's *Flourish with Fireworks*, suitable opener to a concert of his own music only, under his own baton, given earlier this month [November 2002] at the Barbican by way of a late fiftieth-birthday present (the actual month is June) and broadcast on Radio Three the week following. It also opened up the complex question of this richly endowed musician's career and standing as he poises for their next phase.

No young composer in this country 'since Britten' (as journalistic cliché soon said) had started out with such dazzling gifts; indeed Knussen's precocious launch and subsequent difficulties have set something of a mould for several aftercomers. Now, thirty-five years since that well-covered concert when the fifteen-year-old conducted the LSO in his new First Symphony, the achievement as interpreter of new music is consolidated beyond cavil. 'Interpreter' is the *mot juste*: most conductors are glad to get through such fiendishly complex scores as Carter's *Double Concerto*, Ferneyhough's *Carcere*, Birtwistle's *Meridian*, Colin Matthews's *Suns Dance* without mishap.Knussen not only unscrambles such tangles more lucidly than any: he then with a composer's instinct grasps other composers' intentions both formal and expressive, and is able to communicate them with powerful conviction, making persuasive what might before have seemed to be lost causes. This applies also to new music of greater apparent simplicity, where the style and tone are elusive, hence perhaps still more in need of the intuitive sympathy that can make the thing speak, dance, sing: the work of (among so many) Goehr, Turnage, Del Tredici, Lieberson, Lindberg, Anderson, Ruders, Henze and your present columnist. All these, so diverse as they are, would agree on one thing: that OK has either launched their new work to its greatest possible advantage or—maybe more beneficial yet—rescued it from duff initial performance(s) to give the 'real' première.

Nor is this revelatory gift confined to the strictly new. The same ardent precision has lit upon a magnificently non-pigeon-holed twentieth-century terrain from familiar (Bartók, Britten, Berg, Copland etc.) to the unknown or unjustly neglected. Of course, much of this repertoire has been very well played and interpreted before; nevertheless Knussen's attentions can set new standards, as in the glorious recordings of three ballet scores: *The Fairy's Kiss* of Stravinsky, Britten's *Prince of the Pagodas*, Henze's *Ondine*. A more famous Stravinsky work, *Le sacre du printemps*, received another of those quasi-premières (rescuing it from being just another showpiece; restoring the sense of shock) under his direction at this year's Aldeburgh. And in one case, his versions of the last works of Stravinsky, what's been achieved easily surpasses previous contenders (admittedly few in this still-untrodden area).

The main impression given by the Barbican concert (continuing the illuminating interviews that accompanied Knussen as 'composer of the week' at the time of the actual birthday) is, how much creation and performance have nourished eath other. That juvenile symphony has been withdrawn, but we heard its two successors, both conceived and mainly executed within a few years of it, though the second half of the Third was only finished after many vicissitudes and changes of shape, many years later. The Second, however, stands as firm now as it did already in 1971: an extraordinary piece of neo-expressionism, setting for stratospherically high soprano texts by Webern's early favourite Georg Trakl, enclosing an emaciated last word from Sylvia Plath—moonstruck, death-haunted till the roseate bell-hung dawn at the close, yet tinglingly alive in every ravishing detail. It is Knussen's *Midsummer Night's Dream* overture: the complete expression of a sensibility, flawless technically, at a very early age.

The rest is history: the first half of Symphony Three, alongside chamber and ensemble works splintering and disciplining the empirical discoveries, sometimes to enchanting effect (*Ophelia Dances*), sometimes turning the screw too tight for ease (*Rosary Songs*, *Trumpets*, also to Trakl poems and heard in the Barbican concert). Then came their expansion and relaxation in two celebrated fantasy operas for children (and consenting parents), *Where the Wild Things Are*, *Higgledy-piggledy-pop*; the more sporadic output of recent years, wherein not every eagerly awaited new piece is so good as its predecessors. The best of the later Knussen—two song-cycles inspired by Whitman (four actual settings for soprano and piano or orchestra, and *Songs without Voices*, where the texts remain latent); and two *Organa* for chamber orchestra (fabulously intricate and delicious fabrications around a core of mediaeval clockwork) are clearly amongst the loveliest music, and the most cunning technically, of their time.

Another item in the concert suggested an altogether different trajectory. This, too, was virtually juvenilia, the *Concerto for Orchestra*, played by the LSO, again under the composer's direction, in the wake of the earliest symphony; but, unlike it, admitted back to the canon a year or so ago knowingly (as he said with a twinkle in one of the birthday-week interviews) recomposed and divested of its original finale ('a combination of tarantella and Charleston—very 1969'). The resulting *Symphony in One Movement* is an absorbing document. Its up-front exuberance and all-American expertise sweeps all before it. No one in England could have written it at that time, or would have dared! It shows an aspect of this outstanding composer to which, in the pursuit of refinements stemming from the Second Symphony, he has never returned. Far from being tied as perpetual period-piece to '1969', it deserves a place in the repertoire on its own merits, and also as a reminder of what has been and what still might be.

44

Two on Chabrier

i La vie en rose

Emmanuel Chabrier is to be Radio Three's composer of the week [5–9 June 1989]. I can think of no more joyous way, musically speaking, to start or end the day. Chabrier has no peer in the expression of exuberance and gaiety.

Music of such sharply defined character has never lacked discriminating admirers. But they have not necessarily seen him straight. Ravel and Poulenc do; their delight has no axe to grind. For Ravel, modern harmony began with Chabrier, without whom his own mature style would hardly have been possible. Ravel acknowledged his debt without false shame, and Poulenc, whose use of the earlier composer amounts now and again to pillage, shows the same frankness.

But Debussy's praise—'so marvellously endowed by the comic muse'— is disingenuous, as is Stravinsky's a generation later. For both, Chabrier was an instrument with which to beat the dreaded or detested Wagner. Nietzsche had used *Carmen* for the same purpose. Such cultural polemic greatly distorts the artworks employed as ammunition. Chabrier would not have understood; for him Wagner was the biggest treat that music could offer. As a young man he had copied out the full score of the overture to *Tannhäuser* 'to learn the orchestra'. His first *Tristan* ('I've waited ten years for that A on the cellos!') precipitated the determination to abandon the civil service and, aged nearly forty, launch upon the precarious career of a fulltime composer.

The truth is that Debussy and Chabrier are the only French composers individual enough to take on Wagner and survive. But Debussy's secretive nature compelled him to cover his traces and eventually to turn against his early love. Chabrier, however, declares unambiguous affection everywhere, even when he mocks. His quadrilles 'on favourite motifs from *Tristan and Isolde*' (entitled *Souvenirs de Munich* because that is where he saw it) express at once engaging disrespect and genuine devotion to the epiphany that had changed his life, while in the late *Bourrée fantastique* the yearning Wagnerian harmony is completely interfused with the acrid sparkle and pounding rhythmic vitality that are literally all his own in as much as no outside references are needed to set it going. 'Wagner's music belongs to him,' he wrote, 'one shouldn't steal from anyone even if one is the poorer for it.' In the end he gets it both ways; the benefit of the greater richness shines out over an area far removed from the Wagnerian aesthetic.

For Chabrier celebrates in music of unfailing elegance the delights of the vulgar and the sentimental. Relish is paramount; there is no alienation or slumming. He evokes in vibrant colours and pungent flavours the pleasures of the senses, and expresses with tenderness the affections of friendship and love. His vision of the good life (bourgeois version) resembles the achievement in painting of his friend Manet and its continuation in the *plein air* joys of the Impressionists. Like them he is not hung up on fake seriousness or the need to grapple with great subjects. His contribution to the gaiety of nations accords exactly with his gift and how he employs it.

The output is small but the standard is high, and the most apparently trivial item can turn out to be a pearl. All ten *Pièces pittoresques* for piano are charmers (he himself orchestrated four to make the *Suite pastorale*; Ravel later added the splendid *Menuet pompeux*). Better still are the *Trois valses romantiques* with their happy mix of exuberance and lyricism. Of the handful of songs the four devoted to 'natural history' (prophetic of Ravel's cycle, and Poulenc beyond) are best, together with the deliriously sentimental nostalgia of *L'île heureux*. The two original orchestral pieces, *España* and the *Joyeuse marche*, are little masterpieces of colour and verve masquerading (successfully) as lollipops. Quite different is the *Ode à la musique* for women's voices and small orchestra, written to celebrate, in strains tender and refined, a friend's housewarming. An intimate weave of the *Ode*'s tender amorousness, the sublimated salon music of the *Valses*, the wit of the 'bestiary' songs, the bravura of *España* and the *Marche*'s outrageous raffishness runs through all the concert-work of this adorable composer.

His stage works are more problematic. *Gwendoline*, set in an Anglo-Saxon England torn by invading Danes, would seem an obvious invitation to the heavy Wagnerism which, in fact, never comes. A 1983 production of this virtually forgotten work revealed a succession of musical delights. The single completed act of his last serious opera, *Briseïs*, sounds, from pounding it over at the piano, as if he is breaking new and still richer ground. The two masterpieces of his comic muse are *L'étoile* and the cornucopian *Roi malgré lui* (which Ravel would rather have written than the *Ring of the Nibelungs*). The first just about works on stage, but the lavish musical endowment of the second splits the slender vessel of *opéra comique* asunder. Offenbach and Sullivan knew by experience how to be mean. Chabrier's ebullient invention is so copious that the idiotic story is pulverised. Both these latter works have been recorded in recent years, and perhaps all four should be heard rather than seen. But I would like to be proved wrong.

ii His songs

From the very first track of the forty-three in Hyperion's new 2-CD set with all Chabrier's songs [issued in 2002] the idiom and accent are unmistakable. However much he developed over his relatively brief composing life (aged twenty-one in 1862, date of this first song, declining into helpless incapacity a few years before his death in 1894) he was one of those composers who are born fully themselves. It's all here already in potentia—the succinct melodiousness, the wit, energy, high-spirits, the amorousness and underlying melancholy, the idiosyncratic pianism, the piquant and original harmony—not just in dabs and flecks, more a manner of thinking—that so attracted Debussy and so helped Ravel, and after him Poulenc, to achieve their own unmistakable styles.

Not every one of the forty-three is so good as the first: sixteen tracks are devoted to 'les plus jolies chansons du pays de France'—folksong arrangements, pleasant enough, but lacking for the most part the Chabrier flavour and even a little insipid, particularly when every unchanging stanza is remorselessly included. Yet it's good, in our 'completist' times, to have them gathered in too; and the discs are generously filled, and the performances—a varied roster of soloists headed by Dame Felicity Lott under that expert and experienced compère of *lied* and *mélodie* Graham Johnson—are well nigh perfectly inflected.

And the main body of original work is so good! Even its most ardent defenders can be known to groan, if pushed too far, at ritual pieties extolling French culture, so light, gay, refined, yet tough beneath the sparkle, all elegance and clarity, none of that Teutonic bombast, ostentatious brainwork, turgid texture, emotional overstatement. So what! one can say—to hell with *clarté* and *l'esprit français*—I want music that gropes the depths, scorches the nerves, exposes the soul, and brings me to my knees! I've already invoked much of the usual menu for Chabrier: here's some more—adorable, irrepressible, friend and collector of Manet, fanatic at once reverent and irreverent of Wagner; the tragi-comic operatic misventures, the handful of brilliant miniatures wherein he fulfils his high euphoric calling. Resistance to all this would be plain morbid: the felicity is as attractive in this music as in daily life; to deny oneself either would be plain perverse.

Actually the range of the songs is wider than the usual agenda might suggest. Johnson's characteristically voluminous and informative notes explore the sheer unexpectedness with sensitive enthusiasm. Alongside the celebrated *bestiare*—little pink pigs, gross pompous turkeys, silly cloned ducklings, grackling cicadas—come songs of sentiment from flirtatious to passionate, glowing evocations of nostalgia, character-sketches saucy, sexy, wistful, droll; and occasional o.t.t. outbursts of pure delirium like the comedy-duo for the *opéra-comique* Usherette and her young man the Draper from the *bon-marché*, or the crazy waltz-sequence entitled *Ivresses*. Sometimes slight, sometimes rampageous, always vivid and vital.

All these categories have a masterpiece (or several): in the love songs perhaps *Chanson pour Jeanne*, claimed by Ravel to be the precipitate for his mature harmony; which he must also have found in the cicadas' song (*Les cigales*) with its daring aromatic acridity and nostalgia's apotheosis, hymning the earthly paradise that never was and never shall be, *L'île heureuse*.

Some are without parallel. Three stand out in particular. The setting of Baudelaire's *L'invitation au voyage* (originally all three stanzas, cut to two in the song's published version, restored here), enters the same territory as *L'île heureuse*, nostalgia for a land of lost content, based now not on a never-never but the here-and-always of Dutch canals transfigured to a golden ideality surprisingly and beautifully matched by Chabrier's ecstatic cantilena with obbligato bassoon! In prospect absurd, in actuality meltingly tender and infinitely yearning, a rare mood finely nuanced by all three artists. Another unique number is the setting of Hugo's *Sommation irrespecteuse*, a long angry plaint of bitter pain whose protagonist harshly reproaches himself and her who's caused the anguish, set to music that fully captures the complex ambiguity.

The third especial highlight is the last track of the forty-three (it also involves a small back-up chorus of female voices: 'Polyphony'—excellent): the *Ode à la musique* written towards the end of his composing-years for a friend's housewarming. I've known and loved this six-minute jewel for ages in its orchestral version. Though of course missing with piano only many delicate touches of colour (like the exquisite *pianissimo* tingle of triangle at the close—next stop Debussy's *L'après-midi* and its antique cymbals!), one comes closer here to the amorous domesticity and cordial intimacy lying at the heart of this composer, from it coming forth so unstintingly to reach ours.

45

Two on Fauré

Both these were written for the 150th anniversary of Fauré's birth, May 1995.

* * *

i Master of hearts

> Bare simplicity... always the most difficult thing to imagine.
> ——Gabriel Fauré

> Exquisitely, deliciously simple as it was, it was only that because it was founded on infinite cleverness and care.
> ——Patrick Hamilton, *Hangover Square*

Debussy dubbed him the 'Master of charms'; his well-known review of a performance of the early *Ballade* for piano and orchestra compares the music with its pretty performer, straightening her shoulder-straps after each pearly scale. 'I don't know why,' Debussy disingenuously continues, 'but I somehow associated the charm of these gestures with the music of Fauré himself. The play of fleeting curves that is its essence can be compared to the movements of a beautiful woman without either suffering from the comparison.' Feline, but not unfair (as the infelicity of a complementary notice makes plain, Alec Rowley discerning in the *Ballade*'s late counterpart, the *Fantaisie*, 'only the vital points and, if one may say, the musical suggestions and uprightness of a sincere gentleman, whose sentiments are reflected in quietness and culture'!). Other tributes to the man's personal qualities emphasise solicitude, dreaminess, selflessness and empathy. Stravinsky recalled his kind face, Nadia Boulanger the adoration felt by his class at the Conservatoire. And Casella goes further: 'Fauré was an unusually likeable person ... a small man with a beautiful white head and the large, languid and sensual eyes of an impenitent Casanova.'

Artistically, this quality is 'feminine' in its unreformed conventionalised sense—graceful, refined, elegant, poised, supple and subtle; which in turn implies a fitting range of moods and subjects—decorative, amorous, demure. It eschews the harsh, strenuous, uncouth, brutal, preachy, extreme; overkill and o.t.t. are alien; there is neither unseemly display nor *espressionismo*; no plumbing of murky depths or storming of rugged heights. Its watchword is Apollonian and Greek 'nothing in excess'—aud its culture is wholly Gallic.

Fauré fulfils this stereotype so perfectly that if this is your sort of thing you can draw the limit here, and return to a *valse-caprice* or a well-forned *mélodie*. From his youthful flush of self-discovery in the First Violin Sonata and First Piano Quartet through to his ardent and satiny prime in the Verlaine settings of the 1890s, Fauré is the composer above all others of felicity, *bonheur*, the civilised man at home in his own skin. Not even Mendelssohn, his closest rival in it, has hit off this particular mood with such natural ease.

With most composers the word 'feminine' suggests the force of the *ewig-weibliche* or muse-figure, usually embodied in a loving partner, encourager, angel in the house, advisor and censor, nurse, reproachful schoolmarm, domineering task-mistress: Clara, Cosima, Pauline, Alma, Alice and Liszt's two principal women spring to mind. Sometimes the yearning for such a figure can overcome 'the facts', as in the amorous obsessions of Janáček and Berg, where sheer wish-fulfilment provides what is needed to bring the music to birth. But Fauré belongs with those composers whose artistic nature, whatever the sexuality and the biography, contains a large, even predominant, 'feminine' component. Other immediate instances are Mozart, Schubert, Tchaikovsky, Puccini. In all of them the depth of the sensuality, the yielding to utterance of desire and bliss, the empathy with all sorts and conditions of womankind from waif to ice-princess (not excluding normative womanly grace *à la* Susanna or Pamina) speak plainly and unambiguously—especially if they are contrasted (again in rapid free-association) with composers who seem to lack in part or wholly (and again, whatever the exigencies of their life in fantasy and in fact) this feminine strain: Bach, Haydn, Beethoven, Schoenberg, Sibelius, Britten, Simpson. Then there are figures where the balance is askew, like the two great celibates of late nineteenth-century Vienna: Brahms, whose music palpably embodies the tender girlish heart with the prickly beard, gruffness, aggressive cigars that protect it; and Bruckner, a figure out of Krafft-Ebing with his touching sexual longings, their displacement into engines, corpses and paving-stones, and the colossal compositions from which every personal element is purged.

Such generalities are too facile and gamelike for print, perhaps—though in games begin responsibilities, and the huge potential of properly informed psycho-biography has barely begun to be tapped. But as generalities go, Fauré is certainly amongst the flowermaidens in the Land of Smiles. Together with well-being, he is the composer of love with a happy ending, without repression, renunciation or sublimation. Neither rejection, as in lieder from Schubert to Mahler, nor swathing in secrecy like Brahms, nor crying eros from the housetops like Wagner and Strauss, figure in the consummate *œuvre* of Gabriel-Urbain, Master of Charms and Bachelor of Hearts. So what is missing; what is wrong? For his very qualities can seem like charges brought against him, sentencing him for all posterity as a *petit-maître*. The accusation is that he's too neat, too smooth, too bland; is all lilac and lavender; lacks strength and fire; fails to stir the mind, the heart, or the dark forces below the belt.

'People will not believe that Mozart can be powerful, because he is so beautiful', said Edward Fitzgerald. The romantic disposition that pits hairy 'men-and-mountain' composers against 'Dresden-china' daintiness has long-since disappeared. But Fauré still suffers from its muscular vestige; and while his defence must take the same sort of path as that of Mozart, the way is sinuous with twists and turns. Inner strength and mental energy underlie even his slightest *morceau de salon*, nor is the serene surface broken even when ambitious subjects are attempted. This doesn't always work. Everyone who witnessed the open-air spectacle of *Prométhée* set in the rocky amphitheatre of Beziers testifies to the music's powerful impact, but without spectacle and occasion Fauré's preludes and declamations sound flat. Restraint and absence of colour do seem here to be limitation. His other incidental scores yield richer results and a surprisingly wide range, from the Alma-Tadema Rome of *Caligula* and the Watteau of *Masques et bergamasques* to the Allemonde of the heartbreaking *Pelléas et Mélisande* music and the almost mystic elevation of the Venetian nuptials and nocturne for *Shylock*. But it is on his single full-length opera *Pénélope* that the case for Fauré's sheer scope must rest.

The Greek ideal is a persisting and important line in French music of the *bel époque* and the interwar years. Like all such themes it is angled to the predilections of its exponent. *Chez* Debussy the archaic world is languorous and erotic—explicitly so in the two works entitled *Chansons de Bilitis* setting Pierre Louÿs' cod-Greek anthology prose-poems, the famous triptych of songs with piano and the less familiar work for reciter and instruments to accompany 'poses plastiques' suggested by the soft porn of the texts. In other Greek-inspired pieces the eroticism is implicit: 'Danseuses de Delphes' *(Préludes)* I) and the two *Danses* (sacred and profane) for harp and strings evoke bodily motion now grave and ritual, now lilting and suave. And while his masterpiece of pagan hedonism *L'après-midi d'un faune* (once memorably misprinted in the *Musical Times* as *L'après midi d'un fauré*) was not initially written for dancing, it had possibly been intended at one stage to be like the recited Bilitis, going alongside Mallarmé's eclogue spoken and mimed; and it certainly proved compatible with its notorious visual realisation by Nijinsky's choreography, and Nijinsky himself, in the Ballets Russes production of 1912.

Nijinsky's special airborne leap inspired the first musical notations for Ravel's *Daphnis et Chloë*, chief glory of another version of the Franco-Hellenic ideal, where the fundamental eroticism is dissolved in a clear-eyed haze of nostalgia for antiquity as interpreted by Poussin and Claude. Ravel's liquid score lies behind the dryer, stiffer view of a Greek subject in Roussel's *Bacchus et Ariane*. But the real austerity is found in Satie, whose *Gymno-pédies*—dance exercises promoting the physical fitness of nude Greek youth—is quite without hedonistic impulse (though Debussy scored and Ravel imitated them). Then in *Socrate* Satie achieved a tour-de-force of minimalistic *anti-espressivo* whose obedience to the Apollonian motto is so extreme that less does indeed become more and wisdom is born out of folly's persistence.

Fauré is exactly-placed by temperament and talent to realise the full possibilities of this theme in his culture and times, and to strike the golden mean, frugal not starved, blooming but not licentious. There's a symbolic appropriateness in his having produced back in 1894 a harmonisation for the archaic 'Hymn to Apollo'! More germane is the early saturation in plainsong and modality that gives his entire vocabulary from the start a counter-Teutonic slant which is then pursued with increasing boldness throughout his life. By the start of the new century his armoury was entire. *Pénélope*, completed in 1913, conquers just that lavender-tinge in its libretto which his detractors find enfeebling in his music, to achieve noble simplicity, understatement that says everything, and, above all, power and fire. They grow with the mounting certainty of Ulysses' identity, the strength of his dynamic purpose counterpoised with the strength of Penelope's long vigil of 'masterly inactivity', to culminate in the easy prowess of the one arm able to wield the bow that slays the parasitic suitors and re-unites the husband to the constant wife in calm ceremonial joy. Yet all this remains (so to speak) latent not manifest; nothing less Straussian could be imagined. Such purposeful nudity had not been heard in opera since the first *Ulysses*—Monteverdi's nearly three hundred years before. It is Debussy's opera that captures the halflight and the unspoken; Fauré's is clear and hard as crystal. It could be seen, both in story and in manner, as an emblem of his entire artistic stance.

The next stop along this line is the body of Greek-inspired works written by Stravinsky within the few years after Fauré's death—*Oedipus rex*, *Apollo*, *Perséphone*, and such related concert works as the Violin Concerto and the *Duo concertante* for violin and piano. The aesthetic of this music is remarkably close to Fauré's. Both derive strength and beauty from a 'suppressionism' whose keywords are restraint, discipline, subjugation of the personality, submission to the laws. Satie's ideal of 'poverty' is taken by Fauré then Stravinsky as far as it can fruitfully go. Satie really *was* poor; he didn't have much to suppress! Stravinsky with his self-denying artistic temperament is merciless to himself and to his material, inducing miracles of stylisation whose authority cannot be refused. Fauré, with a more fluent technical equipment and a suppler notion of self-discipline than either, alone balances the mean and the generous without grievous loss: nature is pruned to the precise point for ensuring abundance.

All this is obvious enough. But I also feel intuitively that the 'Greek vase' Stravinsky, epitomised by the wonderful 'Dithyrambe' that concludes the *Duo concertante*, as well as sharing, perhaps, the same aesthetic stance, is also indebted to Fauré in language and technique. On the face of it, Stravinsky would have no interest in, no use for, Fauré whatever. But the pellucid linear severity, the cleanness, the 'white-note' diatonic-nontonal sound, can be surprisingly similar. Though Stravinsky did see *Pénélope* during its Paris run in May 1913 (when he met its composer and remarked on his kind face), the similarity is most marked with the songs and chamber-works of Fauré's last years:

Maybe Nadia Boulanger, avid disciple, performer of, and apologist for both composers, is a connecting link. The reference in her *Conversations* to her old teacher's 'supreme sobriety' and 'true classicism' could be a covert dig at her new master's vinous propensity and neo-classicism! Seriously, I still hear Fauré clearly in *Orpheus*, the *Rake*, and the diatonic-non-tonal portions of Stravinsky's crossover works right up to the opening, close, interludes and 'Gaillarde' in *Agon*.

If this is so, then Fauré stands to Stravinsky—and thence to the pole of the Adorno-made dichotomy of which Stravinsky is the icon—rather as Mahler to Schoenberg and thence the alien pole. Which would make him as important historically as he is intrinsically. There is certainly no laying-on-of-hands as with the Austrians; the relationship is tenuous and ideal rather than personal and direct. But the resemblance in actual sound is closer than with Debussy, whose sonority had been crucial for the pre-war Stravinsky and whose mosaic-kaleidoscope construction is retained even after the actual style has wholly diverged. The enormous difference is, to put it crudely, that Fauré never stops, whereas Stravinsky only stops! Late Fauré comes in an imperturbably flowing stream of serenity; Stravinsky can sometimes seem to be all rock and no water (though not in the two works closest in spirit and in sound, *Perséphone* and the *Duo*). But they are linked in obedience to Apollo (though Stravinsky perhaps protests his submission too much).

It is a bad sign when we have to apologise for a major artist's being charming, cultivated, urbane, refined, understated, serene and generally well integrated! It is interesting to try to discover how such qualities come to seem insufficient and even faintly contemptible. The trend of musical appreciation has in modern times moved towards a notion of authenticity whose marks are *angst*, violence, sickness, extremity. Suffering, whether personal or political, has become in itself a guarantee; persecution wins awards; a terrible fate is a good career-move. The communal throb of commitment to big issues runs all the way from *A Child of our Time* and the *War Requiem*, via *Threnody for the Victims of Hiroshima* and *Annotations of Auschwitz* to spasms of protest over Tianamnen Square or laments over Bosnia. Alongside it goes an easy glow of compassion for the individual, with *Lulu* and *Wozzeck* right up at the top, Isabel Gowdie somewhere in the middle, and a phenomenon like the Corigliano 'Aids' Symphony beyond the pale. When the individual is not fictional but real, illness, oddness, deprivation, grotesquerie figure large, be it Schnittke and his strokes, Ustvol'skaya and her coffin-box, Kurtág and his de-voiced *diseuse*, Vivier and his shocking end. And there is the blatant selling of life-styles and personalities, like ... but every reader can fill in this part for himself. He can also fill in the roster of Musical Mystics; as 'organised religion' dissipates, its saccharine substitutes, Eastern or Western, cultivate opium in new guises (and lay up the golden rewards on earth as well as in the life to come).

Undoubtedly amidst this welter of the excessive, the extraneous, the exhibitionistic and the ersatz, there is individual genius and some certain masterpieces. But the frank words that sum it up in general are salesmanship, hype and emotional blackmail. The tendency, so universal as by now to be customary, is for modern music, desperate to seize upon an otherwise indifferent public, to attach its very existence to the proclamation of unmusical content. To hold to purely musical goals is unusual; to have done so and remain blithe-spirited and life-enhancing is rare; to have done so without parody and cannibalism is, in recent decades, and the decades that gave them birth, virtually unknown.

Thus Fauré appears as the still small voice of truth from the bottom of the well. Amongst his contemporaries he alone neither upheaved, disintegrated, nor backed down. It is easy to see what they have that he lacks, harder to appreciate what he retained that was otherwise lost in that uniquely turbulent period. His development is, like one of his first movements, a continuous arc of unobtrusively exploratory refinement so flawless that there is no foothold for picturesqueness, excuse, exegesis. He knew his art and craft, worked within their limits, turning every one into a strength; with him every seed reaches fruition, more maybe than with any other composer except Bach. Yet it would be a mistake to call him a fogey: the late Fauré, especially, is as radical as any music of its time (1914–24). But it is so tranquil and sober that it could seem just a bit boring—from which it is saved by subterranean passion and utter strangeness. And it is this last quality that makes him radical for us now.

Taste swings like a pendulum. When one manner is for the moment exhausted—Strauss, say—another—say Mahler—replaces it, till the world sickens of a surfeit of Mahler and Strauss and swings back, revealing facets and possibilities not discerned under the shock of the immediate impact or the first wave of rejection (like Ligeti eagerly perusing the score of Strauss's *Daphne* 'to see how he does it'). For the moment we have spent every penny of the thrills and spills of early modernism; it will return like a race of giants refreshed; and meanwhile poor Satie has unexpectedly become the father of millions! More substantial—also more comparable to Fauré—is the late-flowering influence of Janáček, still only at its beginning; and the extraordinary shift in the valuation of Sibelius, formerly hailed in Nordic and Anglo-Saxon culture as legitimate heir to Beethoven, then universally decried, and now rediscovered as a revelation of new technical possibilities.

Such surprises lie latent everywhere—again, every reader will have a personal list. I am myself convinced, between the fluctuations of the larger reputations, the gradual recognition of hitherto unperceived stature (Grainger, Enescu, Ruth Crawford) and the as-yet incalculable results as treasures from the ends of the earth and the dawn of human time are slowly assimilated, that Fauré will become more and more important. His account has not yet been squandered; his time-bomb has not yet gone off. It's mainly a matter of harmony—which runs imperceptibly into melodic contour and rhythmic articulation, which all in turn ramifies into procedure and proportion, which, facilitated by his fascinating contrapuntal felicity, determines in a new fusion the entire substance of a whole movement, a whole work, and by implication a whole style. Somewhere, somehow, there lies within this an elixir for the future, an imperishable perfume, a sacred fount of clear spring water from the world's first morning that will help anneal its sleazy evening of litter, weariness, and ennui. A 'Master of Charms' in every sense!

Helpful reading: Koechlin's little book remains touching and stirring. Nadia Boulanger's reminiscences evince devotion and love. The larger tomes by Orledge and Nectoux are useful but stodgy (Nectoux quotes some suggestive material on Fauré's harmony from a 1954 thesis by Françoise Gervais). Bayan Northcott's article in *Music and Musicians* (April 1970) is classic and should be reprinted, as also Wilfrid Mellers' essay in *Studies in Contemporary Music*.

ii *Fulfilling every desire*

A hundred and fifty years ago—12 May 1845—Gabriel Fauré, the supreme composer of felicity, was born. Gentle, polished, radiant, elegant, tasteful— the adjectives come tripping off the pen. They are all appropriate—as is also his rarely heard middle name, Urbain—for this demure yet subtly sensuous darling of Paris and London high society during the years of *entente cordiale*. Yet they imply some reservation, even a slur, which lovers of his music would like to see removed.

It is true that he stands to the side of his time, the headiest in the whole of music. Mahler bared his inner life for all to behold, Strauss stripped Salomé of her veils and exposed Klytemnestra's evil dreams, Schoenberg penetrated the unhinged unconscious, Scriabin flooded the senses with perfumed ecstasy. The most famous of Fauré's compatriots were producing scores of atmospheric evocation and hedonistic shimmer—Debussy's orchestral triptychs, Ravel's *Daphnis and Chloé*—whose sensitivity to colour is unlikely ever to be surpassed. Then came the two hammer blows from the young Stravinsky, *Petrushka* with its mechanised animation and *The Rite of Spring* with its mechanised violence.

From all this Fauré remains aloof. He eschews the *fin de siècle*'s principal medium, the enormous orchestra. Though both his stage works treat heroic classical subjects (extensive incidental music for an open-air Prometheus, and an opera on the return of Ulysses to his faithful Penelope) they are powerful by restraint rather than physical force. His only other sizeable work, the *Requiem* (still his best-known in England, where it has slipped unobtrusively into honorary Anglican citizenship), down-plays, like the genteel prelate in Pope who 'never mentions hell to ears polite', the fire and brimstone, fear and contrition, in favour of sweetness and solace. Its concluding 'In Paradisum' seems to pervade the work from the start.

But the bulk of his 120-odd compositions consists of songs with piano; several series of solo piano works with unrevealing genre-titles like nocturne, barcarolle, valse, caprice, prelude; and chamber music—sonatas, quartets, quintets and a trio with piano, and a solitary string quartet. These ten works pursue purely musical ends over the course of a long lifetime (the First Violin Sonata dates from 1876, the String Quartet, his last work, from 1924, the year of his death) so unruffled by events from the outer world or within the art itself as to seem, to the unsympathetic, not merely detached so much as frigid.

In a time which favours thrills, extravagance, slogans, revelations, explicit radicalism, and general sound and fury, the still small voice can hardly be heard; and if it can, doesn't appear to be saying anything big enough to be worth repeating. Yet the benefits of moderation can be appreciated. Debussy's *Pelléas* with its famous reduction of the love-duet from a bawl to a whisper, once seemed destined to be forever peripheral and special. Now it is almost popular. Debussy is of course part of his epoch's hedonism which accords so well with contemporary taste—Mucha and Monet, Redon and Klimt. Fauré's unmistakable voluptuousness is by comparison frugal and severe.

Perhaps his best hope lies in his songs. Everyone who loves songs loves *Après un rêve* even when it's sung on a cello, a horn, a saxophone. This early flower blooms with mature lustre in two wonderful Verlaine cycles of around 1890—*La bonne chanson*, telling of courtship, love and marriage with a very un-Schumannian happy ending; and the *Cinq poèmes de Venise*, a group linked by mood and motif rather than narrative. In both, Fauré's prime-of-life richness is perfect as a ripe peach. Later cycles carry pellucid economy so far towards austerity as to give hostages to the ill-disposed. And broadly speaking this is the trajectory of the piano *œuvre* too.

But the late harvest of chamber music runs no risk of etiolation. In his seventies Fauré seemed to grow fresher and stronger; the sacred fount bubbles spring-like, and the water is distilled into complete purity. This handful of late works makes an interesting comparison with the exactly contemporary chamber music of Elgar. By 1918 they even looked similar—stoutish old men with white moustaches, survivors from a vanished epoch. But Elgar, though younger by twelve years, is broken in heart and spirit; the older composer remains inwardly youthful and capable of self-renewal. Though apparently recrudescent, Elgar's three chamber works are a last gasp. Passages of deep inward beauty exist, and are milked very hard. But the working-out is conventional, routine and stuffed with padding. And this great master of the symphony orchestra is ill-at-ease with slender forces; he lays it on so thick that one wants to call for the strippers.

Whereas Fauré, who scarcely touched an orchestra in all his life, can produce without strain, from his habit of abstemiousness with concomitant attention to clarity and balance, a complete range of sonority from his two, three, four or five players. Moreover Elgar's works seem still to be trying, for all the turn towards meditation and elegy, to make public clamour. Fauré, unaccustomed as he is to public speaking, is experienced in the art of understatement. He fills some surprisingly large dimensions (the Second Violin Sonata lasts twenty-five minutes, the Second Quintet half an hour) with meditative utterance all the more eloquent for its lack of bombast. Nor does he lack variety: the scherzos sparkle, and the finales can accumulate a calmly gigantic power.

This music appears to drift and ripple effortlessly past. In fact its inner tensility and subterranean fire demand concentrated attention. They also induce it; yet the collaboration has a most unusual nature. One listens in a kind of trance; the effort has been all the composer's; the listener absorbs the result as something dreamlike in its ease. One is drained by an experience consummating, yet also replenished and refreshed. Rarely in all music is the appetite so *exactly* satisfied.

46

Three on Debussy

Obviously most of my more substantial thoughts about Debussy went into the study of his work under the sign of Wagner referred to in the Introduction. These three brief pieces add somewhat; but I recognise the lurking presence of Unfinished Business.

* * *

i An original magpie

There are composers whose music one knows so well that one scarcely gives it a thought or troubles to listen to it any more. It might be an early passion that's lost its lustre—Mahler, Bartók—or simply a totality perfected in one's mind, a secret garden that one doesn't want to disturb. A mix of both has proved to be so with me for Claude Debussy, principal joy of my teens, a joy just rekindled in preparing five scripts for *This Week's Composer* on Radio Three [July 1994].

As a small boy I was entranced with the easier piano-pieces of Debussy that I was (sort of) able to play, and thrilled by more grown-up playing of the harder pieces. Rather later I realised that some of these were transcriptions of orchestral works, and began to hoard every sixpence towards buying them on LP—Toscanini's blazing *La mer* conspicuous among them. The shops' re-opening after Christmas was the best time. Loaded with seasonal cash, I could actually afford two or three records in one go. In January 1959 came an unknown Debussy ballet called *Jeux*. My first hearing of this was like first looking into Chapman's *Homer*. Its entire world—the atmosphere, the swoons and sharpness, the shimmer and glow, the refined incandescence of the harmony, inseparable from the astonishing orchestral luminosity—all that adolescent hankerings had vaguely imagined, was realised fully, at a touch, like a dream come true. For the next few days the turntable never stopped till this life-transforming eighteen minutes had permeated memory and blood-stream.

And at about this time the great Pierre Monteux, already in his eighties when (rumour had it) given a 100-year contract with the LSO, gave some revelatory Debussy concerts in London. They included an unstaged *Pelléas et Mélisande* (though no *Jeux*, not yet a standard), and to my mind remain unequalled by any later interpreter. Nor has any conductor so well as he managed to overcome the Festival Hall's cruel acoustic, bathing it in the gentle effulgence of a Monet landscape. But—as with the Impressionists indeed—one wearies. Somehow, in spite of manifest mastery and manifold delights, a dimension seems to be missing from this music. As teenage taste moved forward into the abrasive wonders of modernism which owe Debussy so much, and back into the endless riches of music before him, the celebration of hedonism in effects of light and colour appeared insufficient, however consummate.

One-dimensional because his repudiations are so comprehensive! Despising symphonic dialectic ruled out the classic core from Haydn to Brahms and beyond; despising romantic subjectivity ruled out the whole epoch from Mendelssohn and Berlioz to Mahler and Strauss; despising tuneful melodrama ruled out Italian opera. He was only interested in early music for its aura, and in Bach for his play of supple arabesque, and in Handel not at all.

A taste so largely defined by negatives leaves precious little with which to build an *œuvre* that is without question major. What is left? A miscellany of highly-flavoured soundbites that attract this thieving magpie with the sensitive ear and the short attention-span. He loves fragments from nearby Franck's voluptuousness, Massenet's suavity, Chabrier's pungency, Satie's frugal weirdness. To these native sources is added over the years a strain of piety for France's musical past, sharpened into overt chauvinism under the impact of the first World War.

Everything else is exotica. Wagner in glowing flecks of colour though emphatically not in the whole; little touches of Weber and Schumann, bigger of Chopin, still more of Borodin, and most of Musorgsky. All these, and the French sources are fused and transformed by a seminal experience, the gongs of Java, encountered in Paris in 1889, that 'make our tonics and dominants seem like ghosts'. Intake from music so crosses over into influence from nature—'the sound of the sea, the outline of a horizon, the wind in the leaves, the cry of a bird' (as he said) that the two cannot be distinguished.

And all this is inseparable too from his absorption in artefacts visual and verbal, and from his astonishing empathy with remote places and rarified states of the spirit. The still water of *Reflets dans l'eau*, the deep clear well in his opera, the stagnant pool in the first of his late Mallarmé songs—these are at once visual images, places of the mind and moments of sonorous organisation. And so it is for the piece evoking a Japanese lacquer of goldfish, or a Spanish. night sultry with perfumes, or a fresh flaxen-haired girl, or a submerged cathedral, or gardens in the rain, or the faun toying with the memory of the nymphs, and all the familiar list of apparently peripheral picturesqueness. Every one is profoundly contemplated in sound, till like Keats's Grecian Urn they attain a quasi-religious significance all the more moving for the absence of emphasis.

With this kaleidoscope of surprises and incompatibles he made a new way of perceiving musical events. He invented nothing; all his material existed already, in its own discrete context. But he is totally original. Jettisoning the residue, he isolated just the colours he liked and presented them as objects for reflection in which the appeal to ear and eye are indistinguishable. The way he heard what caught his imagination has become the way everyone hears. He altered music more completely than any other composer: but the message has been so wholly received as to seem by now rather ordinary. Ordinary; like Bach and Mozart; a classic.

ii Debussy and the theatre

'I have this curious need to leave my works unfinished', wrote Debussy in a letter of 1909. This book[1] shows him throughout his life evading (again his own words) 'the approach of the moment when I shall positively have to write something', documenting the 'compulsive inachievement' of his theatrical ventures in far greater detail than before, and revealing its (and their) hitherto unsuspected extent. Orledge's chronological appendix lists some sixty projects. A famous handful are realised, however unevenly—one opera, three ballets, and the grandiose D'Annunzio *Mysterium*. Some are of course adaptations, usually for dancing, of existing concert-scores (Orledge reproduces three hilariously soppy pictures of *Printemps* as mounted in London, Spring 1914). Predictably, there are passing fancies that flicker briefly and go out for ever ('Debussy's score was never started' becomes a familiar formula). Surprising is the large number of apparently serious propositions upon which energies were expended and hopes built—scenarios drafted, texts written and rewritten, contracts signed, money taken, music commenced—ideas that advanced well beyond the impulsive and some-times, as with the two Poe operas, occupied him to obsession-point over many years, and yet still petered out, *sans issue*.

'Apparently serious'—but for the most part such clear non-starters as to be difficult to reconcile with a Debussy of delicate literary discrimination. There is a remote period charm in the decadent pseuderie of *Les noces de Sathan*, *Le Chevalier d'or* (a 'Rosicrucian pantomime'), the *Drame Cosmo-gonique*, *Siddartha*, *No-ja-li* and so forth. Mixed in with such trash are several themes from great literature—*Eugene Onegin*, *King Lear*, *Don Juan*, *Tris-tan*, the *Oresteia* all figure. Their incongruity for his purposes must have struck the composer, but at least the *Tristan* lingered on for some years, and was publicly announced.

But there *are* some genuine might-have-beens. On the basis of what we know already, the *Axel* project of the late 1880s, the Louÿs collaborations of the 90s, even the Saint-Pol-Roux fantagasm of 1911 (though Orledge doubts this last) would all seem cause for regret. The operatic version of *As You Like It* sounds enchanting (intensest interest 1902–4, but Debussy had considered incidental music back in 1886 and was to again in the last months of his life); while the two Valéry projects, a ballet *Orphée* (c.1895) and an opera *Amphi-on* (c.1900) cause a real pang of regret: beautiful and original in conception, beautifully suited to Debussy's sensibility yet suggestive, unlike the Poe-

---

[1] Robert Orledge, *Debussy and the Theatre* (CUP, 1982).

fetishes of later unhappier years, of drawing from it notes he never otherwise would have sounded. The same goes for the various projects with Victor Segalen.

Orledge's detailed text is a chronicle of almost complete failure; even the successful exteriorisation of *Pelléas* and *Jeux* is shown to be accidental, enhancing these works' aura of fragility and specialness. One senses between the lines what it must have been like, at once blessed and cursed with a vision of some as-yet-intangible relation between music (itself only slowly emerging and of its nature infinitely fugitive) and a stage far removed from the norm of footlights, greasepaint and projection of over-lifesized personality, and then in pursuit of this vision to be caught in a succession of perpetually hopeful collaborations, idealistic, yet ever more devious as free fancy meshes with expectant impresarios, anxious publishers, aggravated performers, as the failed delivery-dates and broken contracts mount up—all this incurred in pressing need of money to sustain a profoundly uncongenial way of life. The great 'normal' theatre-composers—Mozart, Wagner, Verdi, Strauss, Puccini, Stravinsky, Britten—appear almost vulgar by comparison, not in their commercial acumen so much as the way that their theatrical ventures, however visionary and ratified, are so robustly exteriorised to accord with the status quo.

These things are sensed between the lines because Orledge's avowed explorations (especially in a final section awkwardly entitled 'Some reasons for Debussy's lack of theatrical "productivity"') are drastically literal-minded. He gathers in a wealth of fascinating material but doesn't know how best to deploy it, is gullible and credulous, sometimes finds significance in the trivial or absurd, and deals insensitively with difficulties, both personal and critical, that require delicate handling. His 'reasons' come down to women, money, inept collaborators and the composer himself, explicitly deplored on p.300 as 'self-indulgent, self-centred, impulsive and indolent'. True enough, no doubt—aren't we all?—but what is special to Debussy here has escaped, and such simple judgements after such difficult evidence hardly allow him a view as understanding as Debussy's own (which happens to be apropos Massenet): 'In art the person one has most often to struggle against is oneself: the victories thus won are perhaps the most marvellous of all.' Though he quotes this on the very same page, such severe charity doesn't come into the scope of Orledge's common-sense verdict. His book, so rich in documentation, so disappointing when attempting critical estimation or analysis of character, would have been more comfortable as frankly a catalogue, illustrated, exemplified and provided with detailed notes that present all the information and surmise as neutrally as possible. This would have given us in compendious form the benefits of his great diligence; we could revel freely in his extraordinarily interesting *trouvailles*—the best being the music examples for two late projects, *No-ja-li* (1913–14) and *Crimen amoris* alias *Fêtes galantes* (1912–15)—and be spared things like his pedestrian commentary on *Pelléas* or his distressingly jejune attempts to 'sum Debussy up'.

iii The writings of Debussy

The old reaction to Debussy's 'Monsieur Croche', that the occasional delicate perception was hardly worth the perversity and tiresomeness of the rest, is not altered by this collection of the whole body of his journalism. The familiar *idées fixes* seem more trivial the more frequently they are uttered, while the moments of intuition seem less and less to illuminate either Debussy himself or the subject that engages him.

Of course his journalism was produced against the grain even when he was relatively eager to put forward his point of view, for although Debussy is acutely sensitive to words as suggestion, image, mystery, he has no talent for words as argument. Public writing did not come naturally to him, so he wrote artificially, and seemed rarely to get through the banter (feline maybe, but more like a kitten than a panther) to what he really meant. The interviews included here are also largely disappointing. The composer is reserved, even evasive, and one has the impression of a mind rather meagrely stocked—the opposite of a Stravinsky. Only in his letters, where there is no obligation either to be on his best behaviour or to be predictably provocative, does Debussy express himself directly and naturally.

So this collection[2] is more irritating than pleasurable. Yet there are indispensable things here, and it is worth trying to separate the wheat from the chaff. The hack notices could be discarded: Debussy is no Shaw, and cannot make dead concerts live. The *idées fixes*—anti-German, pro-French—could be kept to a minimum. The urgency with which he harps on these interlinked themes shows how serious for him was the threat to native lucidity from Teutonic grandiosity and symphonic dead wood, but time has gained its customary victory over mediocrities oppressive in their brief hey-day, and these polemics now seem self-negating. The final item, an open letter of December 1916, puts his position simply and not without nobility. The rest is tedious.

Yet to lop like this would be too drastic. Even the concert notices produce the occasional sentence too good to lose (on the Dukas Piano Sonata: 'You could even say that the emotions themselves are a structural force'), and the *petit France* anti-German polemic for all its nagging thinness does go straight to the book's true content, Debussy's self-definition by means of what he likes and what he rejects. On any given subject he is uninformative: the interest lies in what his writing enables us to discern about himself. For instance we see in his remarks about Richard Strauss the fascination of the fastidious composer, slow and infinitely painstaking, with one who, to write a symphonic poem, 'takes any old idea'. Yet there is no resonance in Debussy's relation to Strauss. His fascination with Wagner is quite otherwise: a Klingsor enthralment, whose expressive power is revealed by the frequency and intensity of his repudiation. So at the very least the anti-Teutonic line is not as simple as the writer himself would wish.

---

[2] *Debussy on Music*, collected and introduced by François Lesure, translated and edited by Richard Langham-Smith (Seck and Warburg, 1977).

Turning to the patriotic line one senses something enforced in the propaganda for Couperin and Rameau—a determination to align himself with his own culture and make for himself some rather self-conscious roots. Much more authentic is the indulgence he grants to his *recent* compatriots: Franck ('It's all pure music, and what's more, it's all exquisite music ... even the discovery of a beautiful new chord could fill his day with joy'), Gounod ('For all his weakness ... a necessity'), Chabrier ('So marvellously endowed by the comic muse'), Fauré ('The play of fleeting curves that is the essence of Fauré's music can be compared to the movements of a beautiful woman without either suffering from the comparison'), Massenet ('His music is vibrant with fleeting sensations, little bursts of feeling and embraces that we wish would last forever'). All this, taken with Debussy's known delight in Delibes and Lalo, suggests a Frenchness very different from the official endorsement of the eighteenth-century masters and one very close to the origins of his style. Subtract Rameau and Couperin and an *Image* is lost, and a strain in the three sonatas, but *Pelléas* would be very different without Massenet, and without Franck, Debussy would be unimaginable as he now stands.

The interest of these views lies (except with Strauss who hit him after his manner was fully formed) in Debussy's relation to his sources, whether native or 'imported'—(one would hardly turn to him to read an impartial account of Wagner or Franck)—and this remains true of the best things in the book, those passages where Debussy involuntarily helps focus his own aesthetic. On Musorgsky's Nursery cycle ('No question of any such thing as "form"; or at least any forms that there are have such complexity that they are impossible to relate to the accepted forms'); on 'the divine sense of the arabesque' in Renaissance polyphony; on the ornamental curve of melody in Bach ('a wealth of free fantasy so limitless that it still astonishes us today'); on the growth of a motif in the Choral Symphony ('It never seems tired or repetitious ... like the magical growth of a tree that sprouts fresh leaves and blossoms at the same time'); on music out of doors ('a mysterious collaboration between the air, the movement of the leaves and the scent of the flowers—all mingled into music'). And his occasional admissions about composing: 'The sound of the sea, the outline of a horizon, the wind in the leaves, the cry of a bird set off complex impressions in us. And suddenly one of these memories bursts forth, expressing itself in the language of music.' Or, 'let us purify our music! ... let us be careful that we do not stifle all feeling beneath a mass of superimposed designs and motifs ... every time someone tries to complicate an artform or a sentiment, it is simply because they are unsure of what they want to say.' Only in such passages as these (they are few and far between) can we identify Debussy's writings with Debussy the liberator of sounds.

Inclusiveness, although perhaps necessary, is pedantic and militates against quality; the nuggets are lost in the gravel. This material needs to be reduced to its quintessence: *Les idées de Claude Debussy* again but, unlike Vallas, disinterested, uncredulous, unpropagandist, comprehending, comprehensive and up-to-date. His letters, journalism, interviews, reported conversation and all other documentation must be boiled down in an attempt to reach the core of Debussy's beliefs—even (with his reticence and the sheer inability of such things to be adequately verbalised), if the endeavour remains necessarily imperfect. Above all there should be an absolute integration with his compositional practice. Granted that Debussy is a great composer, then hints towards the definition of his very idiosyncratic aesthetic can be found and given their due interpretation even in such marginalia as this. Voluminous triviality could be compelled into a slim volume of golden thoughts.

Richard Langham Smith has done his job nicely, although the tone of his translation wavers in slang and casual usage. He is well travelled in the *rues et chemins* of the background. In fact one senses in the fullness of his annotation (do we really need Colette's reviews of the same concerts that Debussy attended? Her ease at frivolous nothings only points his laboriousness) a certain frustration. Maybe it is he who should produce the necessary out of the redundant, and pare Debussy's thought to a slim volume that really *must* be 'on every musician's bookshelf'.

47

Two on Ravel

i *Artificial by nature*

Fifty years after his death [1987] Ravel is well loved and understood; his stock has never stood higher. His music brings to mind a perfection of elegance, a ravishing precision (with both words weighted separately as well as the surprise of their conjunction); its achievement is so complete that comment seems redundant. The self-possession that would rather have written Chabrier's *Le roi malgré lui* than Wagner's *Ring*, and can speak confidently of the mediocrity of Beethoven's *Missa solemnis* is matched by the music's sure realisation of unambiguous aims. It offers no invitation to any reaction not as exactly controlled as the notes themselves.

Ravel was soon himself. The *Habañera* for two pianos (eventually the third movement of the *Rhapsodie espagnole*) dates from 1895 when he was twenty. The first masterpiece is the triptych of songs with orchestra *Shéhérazade* (1903) and the first that speaks with complete mastery of both technique and tone is *Histoires naturelles*, the song cycle with piano of 1906. The next seven years or so are his richest, producing the greatest and the most varied pieces in his output—the one-act opera *L'heure espagnole*; *Ma mère l'Oye* (the piano-duet original and the ballet with marvellous new linking-passages); the magic, ethereal or malign, of his finest solo-piano work, *Gaspard de la nuit*; the distilled hedonism of the Mallarmé settings for soprano and nine instruments; and *Daphnis et Chloé*, the ballet for Diaghilev and Nijinsky which is possibly, despite its occasional droopiness and one unfortunate dead-patch, his finest achievement, as it is certainly his most ambitious. The orchestral version of *Valses nobles et sentimentales* has all his qualities at their peak—perfection of style and manner, working with distinctive and subtle material, the whole enveloped in a sonorous bloom of felicity. This handful of masterpieces is surrounded by many (by his own high standards) lesser works like the *Introduction and Allegro* for harp and six players, and other songs and piano-pieces.

But after about 1914, things change. Whatever the reasons—physical, psychological, the immeasurable impact of the War—the later years show a gradual decline from a plateau of sustained quality. In 1920 Ravel is forty-five, poised apparently upon the brink of 'the middle years', ready for anything. In the event the harvest is meagre after the opulent spring. *La valse*, first mooted back in 1906, tried over in 1914, completed only in 1920, seems to blow a fuse. After it, composition remains effortful and protracted. The works (fewer, and no longer surrounded by smaller pieces) are still beautifully written but the very nature of their gleaming finish shows that a vital element is missing (quizzically symbolised by the adoption of Saint-Saëns as muse). More is lost than the bloom; the kernel itself is in danger.

L'enfant et les sortilèges, the second one-acter (1920–5), is a special case. It is more brilliantly accomplished even than before, but long stretches are thin both in substance and inspiration (compare its dragonfly, nightingale, bat with the creatures of *Histoires naturelles*): however, a few moments unique in his *œuvre* for their explicit touchingness—the boy and the Princess, the animals' chorus of compassion, above all the final cadential confession of 'Maman'—ensure it a very special place.

Positive in this postwar music is a severity only latent earlier; the strength of his material and the rigour of its working are impressive even when the result is less attractive, and less distinctive, than of old. In particular, the Duo Sonata for violin and cello (1920–2) and the first movement of the Violin Sonata (1923–7) show Ravel (always the disciplinarian and economist) so tight and astute with the notes that it is easy to imagine him, had he lived longer, turning like Stravinsky towards a personal adaptation of serialism. When this stringency combines with a vestige of the bloom and a controlled return of the violence of *La valse* the result in the *Chansons madécasses* (1925–6) is the best work of his later years.

The 'Blues' middle of the Violin Sonata shows another Ravel, chic, naughty, up-to-date. This element, also present in *L'enfant* and the piano concertos (left-hand 1929–30; two-hands 1929–31) has irresistible charm and period flavour; that it was unaffected emerges clearly in some of the stories gathered by Roger Nichols in his invaluable *Ravel Remembered*.[1] But these mitigations run counter to this music's almost provocative triviality, while the frank emptiness of the Violin Sonata's finale and the fast music in both concertos is dispiriting beneath its exhilaration and glitter. The *méchant* foolery does not conceal the black vacancy, whether the content is deliberately minimal as in *Boléro* (1928) or alternates with grand saraband and wistful plangency as in the left-hand concerto, or, as in the two-hand concerto, the tender serenity of the middle movement. In fact the close proximity of these extremes places these last works on an aesthetic knife-edge whose power to discomfort is surely inadvertent.

Even for the listener coming to this music for the first time the personality is unmiskable. Ravel's is one of the sharpest profiles in music. So why should he have needed a stylistic model for everything he wrote? When Stravinsky does this, the metaphors for it are violent—rape, theft, conquest; with Ravel, they are of submission, an almost abject surrender to the dominating influence of each particular moment. His attitude to imitation, that the composer's individuality emerge in his unwitting infidelity to his chosen model, is certainly shown in his own work. His *jeux d'eau* are Lisztian, his *valses*

---

[1] Published for the half-centenary by Faber.

pay homage to the spirit if not the letter of Schubert or project a racial loathing of Richard Strauss, his children's fairy-tales make a series of thumbnail stylistic portraits (Satie, gamelan, Fauré etc.). And so with his 'Pierrot lunaire' (in the Mallarmé and madécasse songs), his 'Saint-Saëns', his 'Spain' (out of Bizet, Rimsky, Chabrier), and with everything in his work. Only with the explicit parodies he contributed to two collections of piano-pieces 'à la manière de ... ' does the touch falter (here the inferior composer with no individual pungency, Casella, makes the defter parodist). Otherwise his entire output is either 'à la manière de ... ' or a sort of game of manipulation, or else a sort of elaborated and only semi-joking fake (mirroring stories of his delight at his friends' astonishment with his collections of Japanese and Greek forgeries). His actual *creation*, as well as his well-known joy in toys, automata, fakes, miniature replications of grown-up life, provides the basis for his famous protest about being 'artificial by nature'. Sheer admiration for his genius compels the attempt to turn this about, emphasising the opposite side of the coin of preciousness which makes him too small. To imagine a defence for *Daphnis* (say) that Ravel himself would have been too self-effacing to offer—'my *Daphnis* is fake Greek maybe (to the disappointment of Fokine, the ballet's first choreographer, who wanted something altogether more archaic), but as a vision of Greece through the eyes of Claude, Poussin, Watteau, Fragonard it is as authentic as it could be'; or, 'yes, the characters in *L'heure espagnole* are automata, but see the skill, precision, love lavished on their every motion ... you'd almost say they were human'.

The most telling image in this intricate balance of natural and artificial is his pleasure in Japanese dwarf trees; he would point out that, though tiny, they retained all the power and detail of the real thing. All Ravel's music (excepting only juvenilia and marginalia) has this sense of latent largeness. Sometimes thwartedness, as if, indeed, natural artificiality had been violated and were taking revenge. Ravel's power is heard unconstrained at the crisis of *Daphnis* where the visage of Pan is revealed; elsewhere it shows only involuntarily, for instance in the over-writing in the finales of the String Quartet and the Piano Trio. Furthermore, there is a dark violence, latent in the hectic exuberance that ends the *Rhapsodie espagnole*, explicit in the later stages of *La valse*. Usually this side of its composer is tightly reined-in, which accounts for the highly deliberated efficacy of 'Le gibet' (from *Gaspard*) and 'Aoua!' (from the *Chansons madécasses*) and in *L'enfant* the automata that get out of hand, the pet cats whose waxing sexuality becomes so alarming, leading to the dwarf trees which expand into their full size and strength, groaning to the naughty child of the wounds he inflicted when they couldn't answer back. Such moments are exceptional; Ravel's norm is an equipoise of tensions, alluring lightness, refinement, delicacy—*le plaisir délicieux et toujours nouveau d'une occupation inutile* (the motto that heads the *Valses nobles et sentimentales*).

If his music is 'à la manière de ... ', is Ravel an instance of the Prokofiev-phenomenon—first writing music like everyone else then Ravel-ising it? His not-so-early assaults upon the Prix de Rome (*Myrrha, Alcyone,*

Alyssa—one each year from 1902) are ordinary enough. But 'Ravelisation' had been going when he was interested since at least 1895. The helpful comparison is again with Stravinsky (whose student-works from the Symphony in E♭ to *Fireworks* include no such rebellious flights as the young Ravel's). At first they are trying to be correct and gain approval; they both have the wit not only to see that their talent is insufficient for this somewhat dreary goal, but that it can be realised only by their doing something fundamentally different. They both need a starting-point, a model that is also a store of material, without which their gift exists in a void, with which, and against which, their manner can define itself and come into its own.

For Stravinsky this involves destruction and reassemblage; he falls upon the given matter, converting it into his own shapes and sizes, and continues to do so when, much later, this process is sanctified as an aggressively-held Apollonianism. For Ravel obedience to law and order is intrinsic. He transforms his matter with a manner so intensely idiosyncratic that it can be felt through a dozen mattresses. Outside *La valse* and *Boléro* he has no urge to destroy (though he does enjoy teasing and a touch of outrageousness); his unwitting infidelity remains true to the model as well as being the indispensable means of discovering his truth to himself.

ii Ravel's struggles

A beautifully performed new CD of Ravel's three cantatas for the Prix de Rome[2] has recalled a droll and entertaining tale of how creativity can entangle with bureaucracy. Winning the prize in nineteenth-century France was to receive the kiss of the establishment; its immediate reward a three-year subsidised residency in the Villa Medici at Rome; once back home, the promise of a direct route, up the system, to fame and fortune. The young Ravel needed both the money and the opportunity, even at the cost of suppressing his dangerously avant-garde tendencies.

For the stipulations were stringent and academic. First the candidates were sifted by a preliminary bout of fugue and short chorus: those successful were then locked away with the text, itself the winner of a separate competition, of a cantata, traditionally involving three soloists and orchestra, rendering some fraught moment of picturesque antiquity: the eventual result would be judged by a jury of established composers, almost invariably of a conservative (not to say repressive) cast of mind.

Ravel's five attempts began in 1900 when he was twenty-five. The first time he fell at the first hurdle. The next year he reached cantata stage, and *Myrrha* took the third position. In 1902 he entered again, and again reached the cantata, but *Alcyone* was unplaced (the first prize going to one Aymé Kunc). In 1903 he tried a fourth time, reaching the finals to produce *Alyssa*, which netted him only one positive vote. In 1904 he desisted, resubmitting in 1905, his last change before the age limit (thirty) prohibited further attempts.

[2] EMI, issued summer 2000.

This time he was again disqualified at the first hurdle (the fugue contained 'provocations') and was denied access to the cantata.

Piquancy is added by the counterpoint of these dead ducks with the simultaneous growth of his living idiom. In 1900 he had behind him a few songs and small piano pieces, with but one sparkle of things to come, the *Habañera* for two pianos. In this year of *Myrra* he composed *Jeux d'eau* and heard Debussy playing at a private *séance* his nearly completed *Pelléas*. In the year of *Alcyone*, *Jeux d'eau* received its première, the string quartet was begun, and he attended every performance of Debussy's opera in its first season. In the year of *Alyssa*, as well as completing the quartet and beginning the *Sonatine* for piano, he composed his first unmistakable masterpiece, the orchestral song-cycle *Shéhérazade*, given its successful première in 1904, year of abstention from the Prix. In 1905, year of his final attempt, he finished the *Sonatine* and wrote the *Introduction and Allegro* for harp and sextet, and the piano collection *Miroirs*, which consolidates the mastery, opening out his style from its previous slight whiff of 'Nineties-ness' into full possession of the rich and utterly distinctive language of his most productive period. The discrepancy between such manifest calibre and the lamentable record of the competition produced a highly satisfactory scandal—'*l'affaire Ravel*': favouritism amounting to virtual corruption was exposed, and the Conservatoire handed over to the enlightened reformist direction of Gabriel Fauré.

All three cantatas have been aired before, as curiosities. These new performances are so loving and lovable as, possibly, to change the standard estimation. Ravel appears willing, with whatever ironical reservation, to collude with the flatulent fustian of his texts and the tired idiom of what was expected or required in their setting; and to do this with what sounds suspiciously like relish.

Myrrha, a scena from antique Nineveh involving Sardanapalus, his beloved (the lady of the title), a storm, a flooding Euphrates, a love-death duet on a blazing funeral pyre, sets the basic style of all three, a generally derivative idiom compounded of Wagner, Russian nationalism, native French music—*à la* Delibes, Massenet, Saint-Saëns and Ravel's favourite Chabrier. Yet all this fuses, and the piece as a whole carries surprising conviction. Only the obligatory trio (involving also a High Priest of Baal, preventing the lovers' escape) is wooden. Whereas *Alcyone* in manifestly dutiful and careful as a whole, despite moments of higher quality than its predecessor. (Scenario: horrified by a dream showing the death of her husband Ceyx—a name that defies musical quantity!—the heroine sings her heart out in duet with his spirit, only to fall dead when some fishermen bring in the drowned corpse.) To the same sources as before are added a touch of Franck and reminiscences of Debussy so close as to be almost citation: Alcyone sings in the very accents of the master's Blessed Damozel, and a phrase from his string quartet permeates the entire score in calm and storm, before being punched out on trombones at the melodramatic close.

Alyssa is Celtic twaddle, out of Ossian via early Yeats. Braïzyl follows the elves through a dark forest to a moonlit lake across which the heroine appears in a crystal boat. His invocation to her beauty strikes a suspiciously genuine note of tender passion—but Ravel is so tongue-in-cheek, here as in his 'real' works! Surmounting some surpassingly awful dialogue (B. 'Que dis-tu?' A. 'Je suis fée, hélas!' B. 'Tu es ma vie'; etc.) they launch into a duet which adds Puccini to the range of audible sources. Which remain mostly the same, however, Chabrier to the fore, closely followed by Massenet and Borodin, with Wagner still surprisingly prevalent. *Alyssa* is superior to its successors in transparency, continuity, melodic material, harmonic control and some enchanting orchestration. The 'real' Ravel is equally absent, but the work is real enough in its own way. Enter a swordbearing Bard, reproving Braïzyl for abandoning his clan in its need. Torn between love and duty he chooses love, till a black cloud appears, within it, a warrior's form, his father, killed this moment in the fight, persuading him to do his duty. Off he goes as Alyssa sorrowfully glides off in her crystal boat.

Ravel also took to a boat and avoided a battle: with *l'affaire* behind, he was cruising the canals of Holland ('viewing this mechanical landscape you could end up believing yourself to be an automaton') and the industial lowlands of Germany ('those great smelting castles, those incandescent cathedrals, the wonderful symphony of travelling belts, whistles, terrific hammerblows, in which you submerge…'). Never again would he or his music need to grovel. Yet this is an artist who flourished on constraints, subversion, mockery, parody; who advocated submission to models even at the risk of losing his own personality. The straightforwardness of these three Prix de Rome cantatas, their open confidence in corny melodrama, passion, atmospherics, equally with sweetness and delicacy, never for a moment remotely original, make so obvious an obverse of his actual musical personality—mordant, *précieux*, provocative, dandyish, hedonistic, pungent, guarded—as to suggest that the absurd saga of his struggles with conventionality masks the absolutely serious saga of his struggles with some of his principal sources in the process of becoming himself.

48

Satie's *Socrate*

It might seem strange to record the vocal score of *Socrate*,[1] but in fact there are many advantages. While Satie must intend his instrumentation to make a sound as carefully neutral as his notes, it doesn't really work; balance is odd, individual timbres will not be repressed, and the overall effect is surprisingly coarse. Whereas the piano is the ideal medium—the accompaniment can all be played without loss of detail, and its solemn simplicities realised with uniformity of touch and rhythm. Colour and dynamics can be graded as sparingly as in the music itself, and, above all, harmony sounds clearer.

Similarly, to use one voice rather than to 'dramatise' the work seems to me entirely in the spirit of its particular stylisation. Also that it is a single man's voice rather than four women's; and that this man's voice is so singular and unsinging! In any work that required vocal bloom to make its full effect, this would be disastrous. But in *Socrate* not a vestige of hedonistic pleasure remains; it is not merely paradoxical to say that the effect is enhanced by the lack of gratification. After all this isn't Delage or Ravel, let alone Richard Strauss! Satie's miracle here, like Christ's at Cana, is to make his listeners' *totalement ivre* on water alone.

He does it by employing a harmonic range entirely without dissonance or suspension. Not *literally* without, of course—he has 'suspended the suspension', frozen anything tense and cadence-needing in his chords so that no move is needed after all, and fixed his added notes so that every chord, whatever its constitution, is 'common'. This norm established, exceptions to it are all the more telling. A simple example is the one touch of acid at the end of 'Bords d'Illissus' when the crickets are mentioned. More complex, the major/minor dissonance towards the end of 'Mort de Socrate' when the jailor, following the course of non-sensation from feet to calves, shows the disciples that their master's body is stiffening. These dissonances are at first registered with a pang; then very soon they too are frozen in their turn, to become 'common chords' with all the others. Similarly the uniformly pedestrian movement and level dynamics become a norm against which any change, however slight, stands out with great intensity. Three times in 'Mort de Socrate' a sudden crescendo to *fortissimo* compels the music out of suppression. When (the second time, pp.56–7) this is combined with the one disturb-

---

[1] Hugues Cuenod with Geoffrey Parsons on Nimbus (1977).

ing rhythm in the entire work, the result is climactic out of all proportion to its constituents, or even to its place in the narrative. Then at once all is calm and blank again—but we can now see beneath as well as above—and the next time, we see beneath from the beginning.

With Parsons all these shades are realised; and with Cuenod every word tells—listen for instance to his extraordinary way with 'extraordinaire' early in the 'Portrait de Socrate'. He characterises the two speakers in 'Bords d'Illissus'—barely, but enough (enough is already almost too much in this of all music). The two artists are in complete rapport: they know how—different from any other—their work moves and breathes. Above all in the 'Mort de Socrate'; the monotony (didn't Satie say that monotony is 'mysterious and profound'?) is varied and alleviated so as to achieve exactly the right balance whereby nothing is actually monotonous, but nothing is exactly interesting either (that too would be wrong); and thus the famous closing pages reach a grave limpid pathos 'beyond human feeling', like a simultaneous lowering of the gaze and opening-out of an endless horizon.

49

Two on Poulenc

i Music and letters

The public's love of Poulenc has never been in doubt; the intellectuals have been slower to catch on. By now it is obvious that he alone of Les Six and its associated culture is destined to last; the apparently slender and silly unobtrusively gains ground by intrinsic quality, concealed at first within pure pleasure, while the portentous, the mediocre, the bogus—*Christophe Colombe*, Tailleferre, Auric and Honegger—sink below the horizon of their time and place. But it has been a long journey from the relative disdain of David Drew's classic study of Modern French Music (1957) to David Wright's shy nomination of 'Poulenc the Progressive' (*Tempo,* June 1994). On the evidence of his review of Wilfrid Mellers' new study,[1] Mr Wright has every qualification to attempt this long overdue but as yet hypothetical essay. Indeed he has pre-empted all my points, and I shall have to think of something different to say!

This latest production of Wilfrid Mellers' fertile pen has fewer felicities and more faults than the study of Grainger he published in the same series in 1992. He calls it 'an act of love'—'the main, if not the only, justification for writing about a creator and his or her creations'. The preface goes on to speak of the need to look for technicalities as well as of love, and the difficulty of attempting to balance the two. The truth is that by far the best of this book is its tender regard for its subject and the biographical and cultural sensitivity by which it is realised. It can be treasured for its affection, and for the apparently artless evocation by means of quotation, allusion and felicitous original writing of, for instance, the strong if fugitive line of quintessential Frenchness to which Poulenc is heir, or the dainty thumbnail vignettes of particular figures with whom he can be affiliated, like Chabrier among composers and Dufy among painters, as well, of course, as the succession of poets from Apollinaire onwards by whose graces he produced his ripest fruit. Whereas the technicalities are often laboured, sometimes far-fetched, and on the whole 'boring', not because of their technicality but because not technical enough. The apparently looser passages of evocation and rhapsody also produce sharper illumination.

---

[1] Wilfrid Mellers, *Francis Poulenc* (OUP, 1993).

Mellers' book is shown at its best in the Prelude, with its convincing presentation of Satie as involuntary revelation to the young Poulenc of what was to be his angle upon composition; and in its brief Conclusion. The chapters between sparkle intermittently with insights born of relish. But they can also be extremely tiresome. One indulges their arty French titles—*Poulenc, la voix, et l 'amour* etc.—together with a tendency toward self-parody, knowing how well the author loves and understands music and how greatly he has contributed down the decades to its dissemination. But much of the writing gives hostages to the enemy, and there is something almost unhinged in the obsessive insistence throughout upon key-characteristics. Even the best-disposed reader will groan as Mellers clocks up yet another 'tragic' B minor, 'Elysian' E, 'deathly' A♭ minor, 'vernal' A major and—most gruesome of all—'horrendous' F minor. Such dependence upon the sheer *accidence* of notation belies the common listener's experience even of classically stable tonality, let alone the radical obliqueness, even evasiveness, of Poulenc's usages. More counterproductive still, the associations come up so pat and often as to underline just how much of Poulenc's music is a self-recycling, as well as a recycling of all his favourites from Scarlatti to Stravinsky. Of course conventions of key, like those of affective expression in the broadest terms, accrue to the point where they can be employed as points of reference. But this is inherent to the art, not extrinsic. The way Mellers writes about key-characteristics makes them sound like a directory or a colour-coding system. No composer thinks 'black', then looks it up and writes 'his or her' B♭ minor. The process is surely more like: 'this piece (or passage, or mood) will focus very nicely upon A major (say)—that'll be a good sound to have in that place, to do that thing—well-reached, well-placed, well-aimed (be it starting-point, *en route,* or goal).' It's not A major because A major 'means' this or that. No doubt a more flexible exploration of Poulenc's remarkable way with triads will be prominent in 'Poulenc the Progressive' when Mr Wright gets round to it. (Though it is potentially a vast subject, ramifying immediately into Copland, Britten, Shostakovich for a start, and thence into virtually every composer after Stravinsky, clearly its *fons et origo.*)

My own love for Poulenc is almost wholly confined to smaller pieces, piano and chamber music and above all songs. Small only in the sense of scale and forces; but the complete appropriateness of talent to medium and material, the perfect marriage of style and idea (to coin a phrase), give this body of work a high place in the music of mid-century. Within it he is virtually infallible. The sureness of touch extends to some larger pieces, especially those involving the stage. *Les biches* and *Les mamelles de Téresias* are, in their different ways, triumphs of outrageous stylisation to go alongside *Façade, Carmina Burana, Cinderella* (the much-admired *Voix humaine* moves too far in the direction of heartfelt sleaze to preserve such a precarious balance). But it is when religion enters that I find it hard to share Mellers' high estimation. The a *cappella* choruses can be deeply touching in their sweet frugal devotions. Problems come with the larger orchestral works—

Gloria, Stabat Mater—and such secular concert works, like the Organ Concerto, as overlap in idiom and intent. The aesthetic vindication is visible and viable—the holy fool juggling his balls before the altar, an authentic game equally or more pleasing to the Madonna as suffering seriousness and exalted counterpoint. But this music seems to lose out on both the joyous riot and the interior passion of the songs, seem to be blander yet also indecorous, vulgar without the tickle, and often coarsely composed and crudely scored. And in the *Carmelites,* the ultra-tackiness of the subject together with the actual poverty (not simply frugality) of its musical material—the mix of saccharine and asperity, black bread of humility with soft eiderdown of hedonistic ease—leave, for once, from this lover of rich food above and below the belt, a really bad taste. There's a particular sickly-religious subdepartment of French Catholicism—the 'Sacré Coeur style'—which can sully even the best composers, believers or no, when they turn in its direction: Franck, the Debussy of *Le martyre,* Messiaen. And in its name, anything goes. Poulenc's almost wilful interweaving of his opera's composition with the principal personal crisis of his life is really shocking in this respect. '... the final copy of *Les Carmelites* completed ... at the very moment the poor boy breathed his last. I got up from the table and said... "I have finished: Monsieur Lucien will die now".' This is far worse than anything comparable in Britten or Wagner (except, possibly, for its frankness); especially as the resulting artwork in the tasteless equation is no *Tristan,* nor even a *Turn of the Screw,* but this soggy-kleenex weepie (except for the sudden glory of its final pages). It is piquant to find Wilfrid Mellers, who once used many years ago to write so severely for Leavis's *Scrutiny,* falling right over the top for this flagrant praline!

Elsewhere the volume of letters[2] (from which the above quotation is taken (letter 269)) is a thing of joy. It is extremely well translated and copiously annotated (the notes sometimes musically naïve but full of good extra material, including the fact that Poulenc fathered a daughter). These must be the most enjoyable composer's letters of modern times for sheer exuberance; in this as so much else Poulenc is a worthy son of Chabrier. Mellers has made intelligent use of this volume in his monograph, and here too, another first-rate review (by Jeremy Sams in the *TLS*) has said everything already. I can only mark out a few highlights; beginning with the warmth of the personal tribute to Pierre Bernac ('I will always be indebted to you for inspiring the best of what I've written'), which underlies the depth of the composer's dependence upon his singer during the Lucien/*Carmelites* crisis, culminating in the fine flower of mature practical insight which helped resolve it (letter 256). When not thus entoiled, Poulenc's self-knowledge is secure—'perhaps the heart of the matter is that the worst of myself is the best of myself' (letter 241). For sustained newsiness the exchange between Poulenc in France and Milhaud in the USA just after the war (letters 172–5) stands out. Very

---

[2] Echo and Source: France Poulenc, Selected Correspondence 1915–63, ed. and trans. Sidney Buckland (Gollancz, 1991).

fetching are his lively curiosity and acute observations concerning the emergent avant-garde in the Paris of the 1950s and later, and his old friend Stravinsky's perhaps too precipitate involvement with it. There is no bitterness at being overtaken by fashion; proper self-esteem prevails, with genuine modesty mitigated by occasional bursts of childlike vainglory. The gaiety, savour, intelligence and sense of affection received and given shine forth throughout. Who else would have dared write to Britten: 'do not forget to send me photos [of *Les mamelles* at Aldeburgh, 1958]. I want to see Peter in a dress' (letter 290)? As with the songs, so in friendship, the touch is sure.

Talking of photos, those in this book are an additional delight. Especially pleasing, the adolescent Poulenc with half-open lips already shyly avid for tasty bad-taste, the many images of fellow composers, poets, performers—above all Denise Duval with her glorious wholly-open laugh, and on the back cover Poulenc between Britten and Pears, arm in arm on the promenade at Cannes in 1954, a great overcoated sea-monster wholly at ease between the two hatless Englishmen amused and bemused, and maybe a bit embarrassed, by their lush catch.

ii Centennial

Having missed his actual centenary in January [1999] I come slightly late to the Poulenc roundabout. But, after all, he is one of the composers whose time is always, rather than artificially inseminated by date and occasion. Despite everything, he has come to stay. If the qualification suggests surprise, surprise is still what one feels. Weightier figures—Schoenberg, Hindemith, Bartók—wax and wane; apparently weighty figures now vastly ascendant—Birtwistle, Shostakovich, Henze—will find their final measure in due course. Poulenc's pendulum is by now stationary—minor but major.

Though not a colossus, his is certainly not a still small voice! Raucous, coarse, vulgar, bourgeois and rich yet reeking of garlic and gutter, café and circus, pissoir and back alley; the touch of incense and stained glass only adds piquancy to the succulent mix.

By the stringent standards of high modernism he's hardly a composer at all. It's not just the cheekiness. A friend's memorable remark that his tongue is always in his cheek except when it's in someone else's neatly insinuates the technique (or lack of) whereby, more than any composer before or since, he fabricates his pieces by outrageous cribbing. Phrases from his favourites, pastiches or imitations or direct quotes from, *inter alia*, Mozart, Schumann, Scarlatti, Musorgsky, Offenbach, Satie, Chabrier, together with popular music and folk music from his native traditions and places, constitutes the entire texture and procedure of his work. This thieving-magpie approach is itself stolen from the Parisian decades of Stravinsky, whose 'kleptomania', by contrast so severe and disciplined, nevertheless gave Poulenc an open sesame to his own unbridled riot.

The miracle is that the collage (for he in no way ever tries to synthesise) could not for a moment be misascribed. Poulenc is always utterly recognisable, 110 per cent himself, even when one is shocked by the frankness of the petty larceny, before learning to adjust one's cultural focus to its frank pleasures (Francis—the man was felicitously christened).

The *œuvre* is quite copious and ranges widely in genre and tone. A ballet, *Les biches*, sums up more easily than many a portentous cultural monument the spirit of the 1920s—frivolous, equivocal, sexy. Several concertos include some incongruous combinations—gothic horror and café gaiety (organ); Mozart and Javanese gamelan (two pianos). But there is not much purely orchestral music and it is not top-drawer. More ambiguous is the stature of the sacred choral output beloved of choristers and listeners alike. The grave sweet austerity of the many unaccompanied motets is moving in its naïve fervour. The concert works with orchestra on religious texts, especially the ubiquitous *Gloria*, can irritate by the very mix of sanctimony and vulgarity that gives them their unique smell. The Puritan disapproval that says this isn't how religious music ought to be is exactly what's being teased and cajoled into a submission that can also be a liberation. It's the tale of the *Jongleur de Nôtre Dame*. Heaven forbid that Poulenc commit ersatz-Bach, cod-*Elijah*, off-Messiaen, to realise his religious goals. The *Matthew Passion* or *La Transfiguration* aren't the only offerings acceptable on high: demotic, sleazy, cheap, can also speak from a full heart. But sometimes it's all just a bit much!

For me this ambiguous feeling becomes definite with his most ambitious undertaking, *Dialogues des Carmelites*, an opera about Catholic scruples and tremors set, amongst nuns, amidst the wider disturbance of the Revolution. Everyone feels the queasy power of the final scene where the nuns' chorus is depleted voice by voice as they reach the clomp of the offstage guillotine. Here deliberate compositional naffness expresses a tacky situation to unforgettable effect. But the long preceding stretches of the *Carmelites* is a bland pious bore for which every lover of Poulenc's true muse would instantly swap the deliriously silly and wholly inspired *Mamelles de Tirésias* ('Tiresias's tits') with its 'message' (not so silly, really) to get going, in a world overwhelmed by total war (it was composed in 1944), on the job of making babies. This sparkling *divertissement* bids fairest for Poulenc's masterpiece. (And he fathered an illegitimate daughter in 1946; imagine a 'Little Miss Britten'.)

Nevertheless the weight lies mainly in the frailer genres: a varied body of solo piano music; a handful of duo-sonatas that almost uniquely in contemporary music can exercise the willing amateur as well as the polished professional; they culminate in the evergreen sextet for piano and winds (strings didn't characterise his idiosyncrasies so vividly). And then there is the large output of songs, far more extensive than those of Debussy or Ravel, let alone the precious handful each by Duparc and Chabrier, to all of whom Poulenc is the deserving heir. Their range of mood, atmosphere, emotion, give him a resonance beyond the *petit maître*.

Above all, the love songs, whose finest hour is the Eluard cycle *Tel jour telle nuit*, a surreal recreation of the Heine/Schumann *Dichterliebe* (with Schubert behind both). It shows heightened erotic utterance to be wholly compatible with a musical speech that remains fundamentally within the spirit of light music—elegant, diaphanous, shop-soiled yet transfigured. Like Britten an inspired accompanist writing for a favoured collaborative artist upon whose distinctive voice every phrase is honed, Poulenc knows his medium through and through. These two have, alone, kept the still small art of lieder alive in songless times.

Humanity: his letters, probably the most attractive of any composer's ever, radiate the intelligence, fun, warmth, generosity, appetite, that can be readily heard in the music. They also quiver with the nerviness, religious superstition, emotional vulnerability that beset and complicate the other qualities, making his music as odd and rewarding as any in an epoch whose greatest artists have tended towards abstracting and impersonalising the human countenance—the *figure humaine* of his finest choral piece, whose title could stand as signature for his life and work as a whole.

50

Sugar and spice

Written for the centenary of Tchaikovsky's death, November 1993.

* * *

What passion cannot music raise and quell?

Tchaikovsky is for some things the greatest of all composers. It's not just his melodic genius in itself so much as the musical utterance brought into being when this gift is given complete primacy in the music's total effect. For this, melody has to be suitably accompanied. He is not like Bellini, with the one element mature and the rest rudimentary. His music is very well-composed in every way required to give melody the lead. His command of form is commensurate in his best works with his demands upon it; he is a sure and individual harmonist; the orchestration is of course flawless and highly original; and indeed his actual *accompaniments* are inventive as well as appropriate. All these supporting roles subserve melody, supreme in every sense.

Melody is the means by which music exerts most immediately its power to 'raise and quell' the passions. More even than Handel, Schubert, possibly Verdi—the other supreme melodists—Tchaikovsky depends upon it, to liberate with incomparable generosity music's emotional potential. Above all he is audacious. He risks everything. But he has the resources—the range, copiousness and sheer genuineness to carry it off.

The risk is greatest where he is most conspicuously at home, with the utterance of passion. The gamut from daintiness and charm, via ardour, yearning, voluptuousness, to uninhibited eroticism is given so wholeheartedly as to sweep all before it. 'He never feared to let himself go,' as Stravinsky said. 'Prudes, whether *raffinés* or academic, were shocked by the frank speech of his music.' But this is by no means his only note; he excels also in urbanity and elegance, with melodies that embody with the utmost distinction an aristocratic *douceur de vivre*. This has its bourgeois level—suave still but not so polished—and its rustic counterpart—healthy, happy, exuberant. Central again, the histrionics, the highly-charged, the reckless abandonment to states of extreme tension, wild excitement, despairing hysteria. But even to denominate his melodic types like this is to simplify and limit (and omit); they interact and cross-fertilise with infinite variety.

The wonder is that he could get such extremes together at all. There is a paradox; his control is so total as to be almost *dis*passionate. The propensity within to violent agitation is belied by the orderly life, the manifold scores, delivered on time, the obedience to the apparent constriction of exacting choreographic measurements, the reverence for the Apollonian equipoise of Mozart. But he has his own saving Apollonism. If the submission to the wilds of passion were technically incoherent, their interest would be psychopathological rather than artistic.

His liberation of music's power to touch and express, indeed to 'raise and quell', the secret life of its listeners, with melody as principal means, is the basis of Tchaikovsky's appeal. Mme von Meck imagined him to speak to her soul alone; the truth is that this intimate singing-out applies to everyone. It is open to obvious abuses. The charm can be and frequently is vapid; the glamour and romance can be debased into corn and cheap thrills, the bravura handling of raw-nerve emotion be done by habit. Whereas an uninspired fugue or sonata is merely dull, fervour and passion by rote are unbearable. So he has to be inspired; when not, he is worse than dull.

More serious than such off-day lapses is the potential for cheapness that actually lies, by their very nature, at the heart of some of his greatest and most characteristic pieces. Take the love theme from *Romeo and Juliet* and the second subject of the *Pathétique* Symphony's first movement, the earliest and latest of their kind in his *œuvre*. These marvellous ideas exemplify all the daring of Tchaikovsky's unprecedented reliance upon ardent expression. The opportunity they offer for sheer tackiness, both in performance and in subsequent imitation, is also unprecedented. Expression can be overdone in plenty of previous music; none before Tchaikovksy (and at his best) can be creamed with such ease. The dubious quality is not exactly 'in the notes'; but something in the notes, if not directly inviting a lubricious treatment, certainly does not decline it. After this the path lies broad and downhill toward sleazy sloughs of awful muzak-making, 'artistic' or commercial, ending up in the bog of Sylvichrino and Masturbani.

So all in all Tchaikovsky opens up a Pandora's box of mingled boons and blains. His reward was to be for long decades the world's most popular composer; his simultaneous punishment, to be disapproved, even detested, for reasons that shift with the shifting sands of fashion. When the Teutonic hegemony still ruled unrivalled—Brahms and the Old Testament, Wagner and the New—his attempts upon the great forms were regarded with suspicion, and his ballet music (*not* a great form) with disdain. Nor was he a hero for the Franco-Slavonic reaction. The new appetite sought exotic colour with a touch of the *outré* Russian nationalists, then French *plein-air* and impressionist, then modern primitivity, thence modernism pure and simple. The anti-romantic spirit of the age had in general no use for Tchaikovsky, in spite of Stravinsky's important defence both in words and music. Nor did the bastions of high seriousness with which anti-modernists bore up the collapse of post-1900 Teutonry give Tchaikovsky an opening: Reger wasn't good enough, Mahler not yet seen to be good, Strauss had let the side down, and the radical advances of Schoenberg were simply beyond the pale. In turn Sibelius, successor to Beethoven in the symphony, then Bartók, successor to

Beethoven in the string quartet, then at last the second Viennese group, were accorded the highbrow's veneration as the embodiment of past glories all set for the future. Plainly Tchaikovsky had no place here (in spite of the Tchaikovskian element clearly audible in the earlier Sibelius and not lost when direct influence is sublimated).

So from various exalted viewpoints he 'wouldn't do' even while he provided unmitigated satisfaction for the average music-lover. And since the sixties this role has gradually been assumed by two rhetorical-confessional symphonists who both owe him an enormous debt. Mahler's is ambiguous, deploring and disavowing; Shostakovich's is direct and grateful (and of course he is gratefully indebted to Mahler too). The deification of this pair as the incarnation of middlebrow anguish and ecstasy has displaced those old warhorses, the last three Tchaikovsky symphonies. Other usurpation includes the enormously expanded popularity and dissemination of Wagnerian music-drama, the ever-rising stars of Strauss and Rachmaninov and the recent revival of late-romantic 'degenerates' such as Schreker and Korngold who, perishing in alien modern times, only now receive the prize for their long sojourn in the cold.

All this is, broadly speaking, an extension and intensification of Tchaikovsky's native area of passionate expression: erotic throbs and thrills, self-exposing self-revelations, traumas and neuroses up on the rooftops in neon. He has been wholly upstaged at his own game. But in the general blow-up the core of his achievement, musical utterance via a genius for melody, has escaped. (Expressionism's means are harmonic, polyphonic, textural, timbral, and sometimes sheer volume.) And justice to the uniqueness and value of this achievement is still not so smiling as his case deserves.

The charges against him that seem to have anything to them are defused if his genre-orientation is not only admitted but respected and loved. Everything in his work truest to his genius aspires to the condition of ballet. Here his central gift finds its exactly-fitting form. It's not solely a question of function and style. It involves clarity of aim, a distinction and focus so physical that one can almost see them. *Atti e gesti*, Michaelangelo's twin inspirations, have never in music been so persuasive—Mozart's powers of operatic characterisation are matched by what Tchaikovsky can evoke through stance and movement. Only Stravinsky (whose every bar Balanchine claimed he could choreograph) can touch him here; but Stravinsky is hardly a wellspring of original melody, and his means are largely rhythmic.

This quality of melody-as-gesture can be found throughout Tchaikovsky's work; in whole intermezzo movements and as elements of developmental movements in the symphonies, tone-poems and concertos; in plenty of songs and character pieces, not always by any means from his top-drawer. Also, more intermittently, in the operas—indeed the greatest music in his most successful opera, the letter-scene from *Eugene Onegin*, is a perfect instance, every phrase making a physiognomic and affective gesture of the utmost precision and sensitivity. The *Serenade* and *Souvenirs de Florence* have it, and that other, much-despised Italian tribute, the *Caprice,* is among the clearest examples. When he's least like this he's at his least pleasurable and interesting; the heavy-duty stretches—mechanised developments, stilted joins, virtuoso display, operatic galley-work.

And naturally when the work is an *actual* ballet, the result is the purest concentration upon what he does best with the smallest admixture of clutter and nuisance. The three ballets, whatever his doubts over the genre and ritual moans in *Nutcracker* over failing inspiration (always a good sign with Tchaikovsky!), are the summit of his work. To write a whole evening's worth of music based on the power of melody requires exactly what he had more than any other composer—a bottomless well of it.

But if this genre is still, even unconsciously, regarded *de haut en bas*, what is its defence? That its three occasions elicited such superb scores is vindication enough; in such hands the genre has a glory of its own. This was hardly true of earlier efforts, which teeter on the edge of absurdity and vacuity. The soppiness of *Les sylphides* and *Giselle* seems to have no possible outcome. Only the full-length works of Delibes (much admired and heeded by Tchaikovsky) have artistic substance and some sort of aesthetic integrity. Then with Tchaikovsky the adequacy of the scenario, the classic status (whether from the start or reached later) of the choreography, and the calibre of the music, together raise ballet onto a different plane, a sort of feminine complement to the big serious genres of the late nineteenth century, with the composer as a sort of 'mistress' to the three most conspicuous late nineteenth-century masters—Brahms for brains and culture, Verdi for broad humanity and Wagner for Wagnerism. There's not much reciprocity between them, but some indications of Tchaikovsky's attitudes and a more extended comparison where fruitful will perhaps help bring his greatness into clearer focus.

He aspired to Verdi's popular touch—the direct access to communal feeling, articulated by tight dramatic pacing, and plenty of good tunes—in as much as he aspired to be above all a composer of opera. Not, alas, the very un-Verdian kind of opera which he essayed but once, with complete success —intimate 'scenes from provincial life', at their heart two creatures of passion with whom he could wholly identify; but Grand Opera about Joan of Arc, etc. He didn't have a chance with this, but the clearcut Italianate gestural character of the style certainly leaves audible traces.

Brahms he simply despised. Hearing the new Double Concerto in Hamburg, his contempt was boundless for the German pedantry that constructs a tune by sticking one fourth on top of another (forgetting that many of his own finest are just as systematic). Nor could he be expected to feel behind the apparent subservience to classical conventions a glow at the core not so different in kind from his own; nor to get through the apparently graceless scoring to appreciate its cross-hatching polyphonic subtleties.

Wagner he predictably loathed though he couldn't afford to despise him. Emerging from *Götterdämmerung* was 'like being let out of prison'. But Wagner's mastery of a very different kind of orchestral sonority was not lost on his avid professional ear, and there are stretches in the ballets (notably the depiction of Beauty's 100-year Sleep) where Wagner's way with time and space shows that the prison-sentence has not been utterly irksome. And it is in comparison with Wagner that the particular character of Tchaikovsky's genius can actually be more closely illuminated.

Wagner's realm is mythology, saga, high romance; Tchaikovsky's is gothic legend, classic fairy-tale and nurseryland fantasy. Wagner's treatment of his stories is superhumanly vast and heiratic, his own texts are weighted with ideas, philosophies and interpretations, psychological exploration is everywhere latent, often explicit. Tchaikovsky's is gestural and mimetic, decorative and formal; there are of course no words, neither concepts or declarations; depiction of character is by type, two-dimensional not in-depth, and interpretation is uncalled for. Wagner's aims bring about his musical substance; his normal texture is a complex, omniscient interweave of nominating and commentating motifs, in themselves short and incomplete, then worked together in quasi-symphonic quasi-polyphonic sequential fantasia to produce unprecedented duration, with an underlying massiness of architecture beneath the improvisatory flux. Tchaikovsky's aims bring about his musical substance, exactly, as with Wagner, commensurate with his compositional proclivities—melodic, formal, shapely, articulated, closed, virtually without polyphony and only in exceptional passages developmental. Wagner creates size by an 'endless melody' of musical prose, Tchaikovsky by effortless extension of the single melodic line—'musical poetry'. Wagner's motivic interweave is a means of bending time; the long reach into past and future brings them together with extraordinarily rich and powerful effect. Tchaikovsky's time is a perpetual present in which listeners can always know their exact whereabouts. So he fills a whole evening by addition—an expansion of what Schumann (a German he really liked!) had achieved with the same kind of short complete song-and-dance-units in his larger piano-cycles. Tchaikovsky makes a mosaic, a cabinet of delights; Wagner an organism which can be exerpted only in painfully bleeding chunks. All in all, his medium is thick, Tchaikovsky's thin (no criticism is intended of either; all this attempts only definition).

Then there is the question of momentum. Wagner's is slow, even sluggish, gradually animating via long processes to a rich convulsive stream, oceanic and all-embracing, a rendition of the inner life. When physical he is primal, energetic, brutal—Mime hammering, Siegfried forging. True, the flower-maids waltz gracefully with Parsifal and the apprentices lustily with their Fräuleins; but the general poverty of body-motion in Wagner can be obliquely adduced from Chabrier's burlesque quadrilles on themes from *Tristan*. Whereas Tchaikovsky of course is always utterly physical. The whole body, not just the feet, wants to move—he's written the instructions, in the imperative and seductive mode! And while Wagner is metrically gallumphing and not very various, Tchaikovsky's range is huge—*The Sleeping Beauty* in particular is a compendium of gestural and rhythmic models. This plentiful endowment is the reason he could fulfil the demand for tight choreographic lengths, and when, as often, he outran Petipa's orders, the invention remains measured and shapely. Imagine Wagner attempting to fit into exact bar-counts obeying specific instructions as to tempos, type, even timbre! And finally, their way with expression itself—after all, their principal goal. Here it is Wagner who issues the imperatives—be elevated! be abased! be overwhelmed! Though Tchaikovsky undoubtedly exerts all his powers to excite in his listeners what excites him, the element of dispassion, even of impersonality, keeps a distance: an Invitation to the Dance, for delight, rather than a Summons to the Temple, for ritual purgation.

A direct comparison where myth and fairytale, thick and thin, actually converge, can help fix the connection. The motif of the 100-year slumber in *The Sleeping Beauty*—a virgin, protected from age and decay by supernatural suspension of time and from casual marauders by a thicket of prickles so that only the Chosen One can penetrate it to wake her with a kiss and claim her as his own—is a clear Double of Brünnhilde on her rock at the end of *Die Walküre*. (The only difference of storyline is that Brünnhilde is insured by flames not thorns, and that her sleep is a personal punishment.) Wagner's handling is reckoned, rightly, to be sublime and deep. The ancient motif is placed as half-way climax in his saga; destiny, with long tangled antecedants and a future perilously uncertain between salvation and destruction, is poised in vast expectation. Its human dimension is equally charged. The God–Father, as one link only of the intricate enmeshings in the consequences of his actions and hopes for their resolution, must sacrifice the part of himself he most loves. The Goddess–Daughter, discovering her own will in an impulse towards compassion that disobeys his, must descend from her pedestal and become a Woman, admitting Life and Love their fullest scope. In the face of such manifest grandeur (which cries out for Archetypal Capitals) how can Tchaikovsky's handling hold a candle?

In *The Sleeping Beauty* the same motif, so close to its composer's inner desires, also makes at the heart of the work whose title it takes an extraordinary vastness and expectation. Life slumbers, waiting to be reborn into love. The apparatus of ballet—busy ceremonial, set-pieces of decorative display—is waived, to be reassumed, after the Prince wakes her, with enhanced magnificence and a wealth of invention that even Tchaikovsky never surpassed. Neither before nor after the crucial event is there much plot; character is the merest type; the simplification and flatness are total. But the overall impact is not small. Poetic meaning and artistic expression are anything but impoverished. And there is an extra dimension, which gives this genre its *raison d'être* as singing does opera (including music-drama) and accounts for the flatness and simplification in character and story—the riveting beauty of complex and demanding motions executed with grace, exuberance, apparent ease, individual physical prowess and disciplined communal pattern-making that fuses into an indivisible unity with the music. If the genre had not been so hidebound and hung-up on *divertissement*, Tchaikovsky might have matched his three actual ballets with further works of comparable quality on themes that appealed to the positive side of his histrionic powers—*Romeo and Juliet, Francesca da Rimini, Hamlet, Man-*

fred, The Tempest for a start. If he had, his theatrical *œuvre* would be comparable to Wagner's in weight as well as value.

But all this is an historical conceit. The only contemporary Tchaikovsky *did* fall for in a big way was Bizet, chief weapon in Nietzsche's anti-Wagnerian persiflage: here the comparison is clearly direct and to the point. And so the summa of Tchaikovsky in his true genre is *The Nutcracker*, where the fairytale fullness of *Sleeping Beauty* equally with the tragic melodrama of *Swan Lake*, falls victim to prettiness. Hardly any story survives this voyage from a Biedermeier Christmas, via a night battle between rats and toy soldiers, to the land of eternal meringues. But *what* prettiness! The music is indefatigably alive and (with one exception) all straight from the top drawer. The battle, for instance, keeps up a prolonged sparky animation with at least as much brilliance as anything in the symphonies. The transformation from domestic parlour to fir-forest deep in snow is one of the great romantic moments, the equivalent in this 'thin' medium of the great scene-changes in the outer acts of *Parsifal*. (The one slightly duff number follows, a snow-flake-valse where tinselly wordless voices gormlessly reiterate a less-than-inspired tune). The total void, once the land of confiture is reached, in such plot and characterisation as have hitherto been vouchsafed, is solaced by the sequence of character-dances familiar in part from the Suite—'light music' so distinguished that the adjective simply drops away. Then there's the celesta; then a glorious *pas-de-deux* fitter for Faust and Helen, or Antony and Cleopatra, then its actual occasion; then the best-ever final waltz. Maybe the 'content' of most of this is akin to the paradise of sweeties and wine and music rendered in the finale of Mahler's Fourth Symphony, which will be patronised by no-one. But that *pas-de-deux*? The sheer hugeness of the emotion released suggests what has perhaps been lost, or rather, not fully realised, in his undertaking as a whole.

A remark from the memoirs of Alexandre Benois (whose sets for the London Festival Ballet's *Nutcracker* gave such delight to so many thousands over many panto seasons at the Royal Festival Hall) encapsulates the Tchaikovskian magic with perfect simplicity: this music 'arouses the tenderest moods and an almost celestial joy'. Admittedly he is specifically recalling *The Sleeping Beauty*; but the application is wide. 'What Passion cannot Music raise and quell?' The phrase can cover every shade, even the most sombre and disturbing, in the endlessly fresh world of exactly-realised fantasy, poetically-responsible escape, and precisely-disciplined self-indulgence, created from Tchaikovsky's frank and audacious exploitation of his unmatched gift for melody.

51

Scriabin's *Poem of Ecstasy*

The most astonishing thing about this masterpiece is its sheer quality! Though Scriabin had written three previous symphonies, he was basically a pianist and piano-composer; even in the *Poème d'extase* it is apparent that the characteristic textures and spacings have been conceived at the keyboard. Yet as well as being the supreme expression in music of a certain cast of mind it is also magnificently written for orchestra.

The first two symphonies are diploma-pieces without distinguishing features. They share a disconcerting leaning towards C major bathos: the first, overall in E, turns to C for a choral fugue glorifying Art; the second, in C minor, ends with a march in the major best described in the composer's own subsequent view—'instead of the translucence I desired, I got only a military parade'. The third, *Le divin poème*, written alongside the *Satanic Poem* for piano (1902–4), doesn't wholly escape the same charges. For all the Franck, Wagner, Strauss, together with a first sprinkling of the notorious passional programmes and self-commending performance-instructions (which already carry Scriabin close to Messiaen), it remains at bottom a well-made conservative product. An all-embracing slow introduction yields three linked movements: 'Luttes' (struggles)—'mystérieux, tragique ... triomphant ... vageux' (etc.); 'Voluptés' (pleasures)—'sublime ... avec une ivresse débordante' (etc.)—the most prophetic movement, and far the best; 'jeu divin' (divine play)—'avec une joie éclatante' (etc.)—before its transformation into another E major apotheosis foreshadowing Stalinist kitsch at its most blatant.

Sampling this *divin poème* is the best way to put the greatness of *Le poème d'extase* in context. It too might fit the same description (even down to the colossal C major close) except for the miracle which lifts it onto another plane altogether. Intended at first as a fourth symphony, it was begun directly after becoming first a *Poème orgiaqie* (*sic*) before the definitive title was reached, late 1906. By then Scriabin had published the *actual* poem which provides the score's overheated theosophical credo. This load of sado-masochistic junk is a period-folly more amusing nowadays than dangerous. Some specimens (from Hugh Macdonald's translation):

The spirit of joy and hope / gives itself to the bliss of love. / Amid the flowers of its creations / It abides in kisses, / In a plenitude of delight / It calls them to ecstasy.

I call you to life / You hidden aspirations! / You, buried / In the dark depths / Of the creative spirit, / You timorous embryos of life, / I bring you / Audacity!

' ... the bites of panthers and hyenas / Have become but a new embrace, / A new torment, / The snake's bite / Is but a burning kiss. / And the world resounds / With the joyful cry: / I AM!

The function of the words was to stimulate the music into being by bites and caresses. They served the purpose. The resulting score transcends dated mystico-erotic tat, embodying these 'godlike/diabolic' impulses in memorable themes, gorgeously harmonised, sumptuously orchestrated, worked into a thoroughly efficient shape, its facture still somewhat overdependent on repetition and sequence, yet wholly convincing every time in strictly musical terms. Which by no means implies that one can't hear just what is flagrantly going on from fore to aft. The score doesn't need its *embarras* of French and Italian instructions/commendations; the entire vocabulary of amorous palpitation, perfumed perfervor, mounting frenzy, culminating coming is never ambiguous, least of all the victorious phallocentric theme played by the first trumpeter. No half-lit hints like *Jeux* or erotic insinuendo as in *Daphnis and Chloë*—for all its refinement the *Poème d'extase* goes naked, erect and proud.

It's built on a succession of ripples, tumescing into wavelets, breakers, surf-splurges, culminating in one orgiastic roller-coaster before the hymnic close. First comes longing (*languido*), dreaming (*suavamente*), skimming (*volando*); and the first imperious trumpet-summons. Then come amorous *délices*, a *très parfumé* passage growing via *ivresse* into *délire*; then the trumpet again, followed this time by a stormy episode of 'dark presentiment' with stabbing horn-chords and lurching trombone plunges, before the trumpet breaks through triumphant against background of campanelli, harp glissandos and fantastical woodwind patterns, to achieve a halfway climax. The second half intensifies and kaleidoscopically re-juggles the same ingredients. The final stretch sets off *allegro molto, leggierissimo, volando*, soon overtaken and engulphed by the trumpet theme, now joined by all eight horns (the other four trumpets keeping up a brilliant high battery of twinkling triplets), the whole massive yet gleaming sonority underpinned by a Grand Organ. (At an early stage Scriabin also contemplated lighting-effects and a choral setting of the poem's climactic spasms—in the end reserving these extras for the next 'symphony', *Prometheus*, completed in 1910.) The climax breaks off *sur le point* for one last caress, before the overwhelming final Amen-cadence, powerfully appropriate for what has to be called a religious utterance in carnal guise.

52

Beware the pitfalls of sincerity

How to ensure a sympathetic reception for a new piece of music? Ideally the subject should combine Ecology (with special reference to tropical rain-forests) with Protest (preferably shrill and futile). It should climax with an ecumenical prayer (in every known language simultaneously) for intergalactic peace. The musical material should include at least three of the following: Jewish cantillation, Catholic plainsong, Tibetan chanting, Aboriginal drumming, whalesong. The idiom should be middle-of-the-road, artfully diguised with mod cons (clusters, glissandos, electronics); there should be a strong pop-music element, plenty of repetition *à la* Philip Glass. When inspiration fails, fill the gaps with ritual gong strokes, prolonged and amplified to the threshold of pain.

But such cynicism will not do; this is a serious matter. A recent first visit to the USSR[1] brought into focus for me the large question of evaluating music whose basis of appeal is grounded in extramusical circumstances. The first problem is the dispassionate judgement of compositions that emerge from, and in some cases directly express, political oppression. The wide current appeal of such music seems to touch a nerve of communal masochism. Audiences yearn to groan under the yoke of suffering they may never have experienced. There is even a kind of envy for the depth of vision this fate is thought to produce.

The conspicuous case is Shostakovich, a composer of enormous gifts and awesome copiousness, the only one to satisfy, if intermittently, both his masters and the West. Ever since the 'just criticism' meted out to his early excesses, then the gigantic success of the Leningrad Symphony in the 1940s, he has symbolised the artist caught in the net of public events. As we now know something of the appalling story of his hounding by cultural officialdom, the raucous irony of the middle works and the bitter blackness of the last become entirely comprehensible.

His is the only post-war body of symphonic and chamber music to achieve genuine popularity. Yet it is drastically imperfect. Impressive inspirations mix with the coarsest triteness; there is an inordinate amount of padding and bombast; the reliance on formulae is the most shameless since Telemann.

---

[1] In October 1989; see p.302. This piece for the *Independent* that same month widens and generalises some long-held reflections on its subject.

Nor did things improve as he grew beyond subjection to state reproof. Some late works, notably the Fourteenth Symphony and the songs on Michaelangelo texts, are among his greatest. But in the succession of late string quartets, poverty of substance and spiritual exhaustion are exemplified rather than expressed.

Shostakovich, obviously pre-eminent among Soviet composers, had to bear the cruellest treatment. Bold spirits in the satellite countries were able to take liberties at home (Lutosławski, Penderecki, Kurtág) when they didn't get away in person (Panufnik, Ligeti). The recent change of policy has unfrozen a flood of music by younger figures who have not undergone similar cultural repression, though the conditions of their work remain poignant and precarious. Recently it has been well-aired in this country through broadcasts and festivals; enough to form an initial overall view. I believe that music-lovers are deluded when they claim to find artistic pleasure in any but a fraction of this music. Here, as with most of Shostakovich, the content they locate is a projection of what they know of its circumstances—by which only a heart of stone would not be moved. Take away this knowledge and the appeal would vanish, for the music is rarely able to stand on its own merits.

The second problem is the evaluation of new music that 'deals' with religious subject-matter, however vague. A nostalgia has become apparent, after an era of aggressive atheism, either for the great organised beliefs or for substitutes chiming better with the would-be freer spirit of the times. In the sixties Gurus and pop music were the thing; the present mood is sombre and apocalyptic. In both, the identification with music that attempts to express any part of this vast area tends to be one of self-deceiving empathy. A spiritual void needs to be satisfied, so what is offered as serious and sacrosanct must be as good as it pretends. Instances would include the St Luke Passion by Penderecki and the St John by Arvo Pärt, Messiaen's *Transfiguration*, Britten's *War Requiem*, Tippett's *Mask of Time* and Birtwistle's *Mask of Orpheus*, Steve Reich's *Desert Music*, much of the output of John Tavener and Jonathan Harvey; above all, Stockhausen's seven-day wonder, *Licht*.

Such religious/humanitarian subject-matter—even the Holocaust, Hiroshima and Aids have not escaped—makes a fortress as unassailable by criticism as the art produced under tyranny. The worth of individual pieces is, obviously, very various; consistent is the appeal to piety, ensuring that the elevated theme produces a warmhearted response. These composers are not coldly exploiting their audiences' kindness; they are all equally the victims of the going ideology. And sincerity is not in question. But the hard truth, nailed with all-time accuracy by the other great composer from Leningrad (the one who got out) is that sincerity does not guarantee quality. 'Most art is sincere,' Stravinsky added, 'and most art is bad'. *Ersatz* emotion replaces musical content. The genuine difficulty of understanding intricate artistic designs is evaded by the factitious difficulty of being exalted or troubled by important messages which have nothing to do with musical worth. Artistic value is not an 'extra' even in a threnody for Chernobyl. Without it, message or vision are wishful thinking. Audiences' large capacities for *ersatz*-importance show

how eager they are to be deeply stirred; how easily gulled; how low the threshold of enjoyment must be set for music of our time. What little appeal it has seems to depend heavily on these impurities.

No one would deny that music can embody great humane and religious themes. That it does so, so profoundly, is a vital part of what it is for. There is spiritual value in the very handling of its primary elements to write a little song or dance, even an exercise; even, as Bruckner used to show his classes, in a fifth or octave struck at a piano. The essence of music's higher flights is transcendental in the highest degree imaginable, in ways that are manifestly intelligible and effectual, and quite insusceptible to verbal accounting. Debussy's answer to a journalist who asked if he was familiar with heaven—'yes, but I don't natter about it with strangers'—is not so silly as it sounds. Evasive certainly, but only to acknowledge what cannot be uttered.

The good composer expresses what he feels and makes what he is making from an essentially musical motivation, by essentially musical means, with all the skill and experience he can command. The ends are various: here a visionary oratorio, there an *opéra buffa*; here a craggy piano *étude*, there a melting *morceau de salon*. The degree of craft, the degree of inspiration, are the measure whereby they can be valued; through these are achieved, consciously or inadvertently, the heights and depths of spiritual expression whereby they are 'a joy for ever'.

Music can only be judged on the basis of an attentiveness to its musical essence as sensitive and discriminating as possible. Above all, as specific—an undogmatic reaction to the details in style and technique of the particular composer, piece or passage. Naturally this will include transcendental subject-matter if it's there, and recognise the moments where this sweeps all before it. All the rest is emotional blackmail.

53

Puzzled by Shostakovich

The frenzy of performances marking the twenty-fifth anniversary of Shostakovich's death [2000] reminds me how awkward it is to be in a minority. The dissident doesn't *want* to be perverse. He wants to enjoy the comfort of shared convictions rather than the vulnerability and paranoia of being out in the cold. Above all, not to miss out on artistic experiences that might enhance mind and spirit. From earliest musical discoveries, through to middle age, I've been puzzled by the enormous reputation of Shostakovich. When excited by the wonderful colourists of the early twentieth century, he seemed drab; when electrified by high modernism, dowdy and conservative; when settling down into sobriety and formalism, so obviously inferior to the intended comparisons—Haydn, Beethoven, Mahler. There simply hasn't been a Shostakovich-shaped niche. Inaudible to me was any allure—the beauty, intensity, depth, content that give an entrée to a creator's particular world. What I heard instead was neutral or indeed repellent: battleship-grey in melody and harmony, factory-functional in structure; in content all rhetoric and coercion, exercises or instructions in communal lament and celebration, rendered by portentous slow music and mirthless fast music, nearly identical from work to work, coarsely if effectively scored, executed with horrifying fluency and competence, kept unflaggingly going long after its natural cut-off point had passed; music to rouse rabbles, to be seen from far away like slogans in letters 30 feet high, music without inner musical necessity.

Thus for the symphonic output which might be said to have been wrung from him unwillingly. So what about smaller genres? I'd been startled by the compositional poverty of the preludes and fugues for solo piano wishfully deemed a contemporary complement to Bach. But what about the string quartets—fifteen works in a medium congenial to intimacy and essence that must preclude the rant and bombast of the large orchestra? Here the horrors are different: a rapid degeneration from innocent cheerfulness via terse grimness to the long-drawn-out torture by excruciation and vacancy of the final works. Astonishing that this cycle is now as a matter of routine compared with Beethoven's; like comparing a housing estate to the Acropolis.

In fact the fifteen symphonies, for all that they contain the worst of him (outside copious commercial/functional jobs), are far more various in range as well as quality. No.1 still remains a perfect product of adolescent genius, setting up all his later routines with effervescent freshness and brevity—

perky, energetic, hectic, sentimental, tragic—before they set in Soviet cement. The wild constructivism of the next two and the sheer bravura excess of the fourth can sweep all before them provided one doesn't look too closely. This early phase now stands as Shostakovich's clear high-point, its twin peaks the two operas, *The Nose*, a masterpiece of zany Dada, and the great but equivocal *Lady Macbeth*. For the problems begin before the official repression. Was Stalin so wholly wrong about this work? The prevalence of parody, 'wrong-note' strains used equally to make frenzied murder and incompetent policemen look absurd, and above all the massed bands accompanying the guilty adulterous bed, *are* deeply subversive and offensive and are *meant* to be. *Lady Macbeth* knocks us for six, but humane it is not, till in the closing scene the defensive grimace subsides and such overwhelming pity is evoked that reproach is abashed (unfortunately Stalin had long since left the theatre in disgust).

Now comes trouble: the central bulk of the output, where toeing the line in fear while inwardly demurring in coded protest, and genuinely representing populist patriotic fervour in times of desperate struggle become indistinguishable in the churning mills of compulsive mass production. Light glimmers again with No.11, which relinquishes argument in favour of loose-weave atmospheric fresco depicting scenes and moods from the 1905 Revolution with the resources, and the mastery, of a good film score. The next landmark is the Fourteenth, frankly a song cycle after Mahler and its dedicatee Britten. Shostakovich had always excelled in songs, with piano alone, with small instrumental forces, with orchestra. I believe that some of these— among them settings of Jewish folklore, of Blok, of Michelangelo—will remain potently expressive when efforts like the Fifth, the 'Leningrad' or the Tenth Symphony have sunk without trace. Supreme among them is this Fourteenth Symphony. A good performance 'in the flesh' vindicates every jot of Shostakovich's habitual harshness, meanness, over-emphasis. The nakedness of its desolation, the ferocity of its anger, truly 'make the flesh creep'; they could not have been effected by any other means. Here, at least, is necessity and a Shostakovich-shaped niche. Once only: a triumph of purposeful exiguity; but to do it again and again, as in the subsequent late works, exploits the audience's willingness to endure a hairshirt for the good of the soul, just as much as it demonstrates the artist's compulsion to repeat himself with an ever-decreasing formal and expressive range.

The terrible nature of Shostakovich's circumstances mustn't prevent a balanced response to his actual notes. If it does, emotional blackmail is committed, which for all its rewards involves illusion and delusion—a flattering identification with suffering heroism, a holier-than-thou priggishness in the rush to empathise with oppression. To deplore this is to risk appearing stony-hearted. But what else is there to go on, in works of art, but their artistic workmanship—in music, the actual notes? All human experience can be encompassed and expressed in music's actual notes, when they show themselves to be capable of containing what's entrusted to them. *Chez* Shostakovich I submit that the intrinsic quality of most of the *œuvre* is not strong enough to carry the weight currently put on it—which suggests in turn that what is required of it is lightweight too, underneath the heavy appearance to the contrary.

54

Appalled by Schnittke

I write still reeling a fornight later from the all-out bombardment of the BBC's Schnittke Weekend earlier this month [January 2001]. Even as spaced more widely on Radio Three the concentration was intensive, with some twenty-five works, mostly substantial, running from the Friday to the Monday. Live in the Barbican and St Giles it must have been shell-shocking.

Perhaps unsurprisingly I uncordially detest this music; and moreover, can see in it little of value. With Shostakovich I sense (sometimes) that something which most people find stirring is passing me by. With Schnittke I'm sure it is not. The time and money spent, the care and skill also expended, the gifted intelligences misled, the corporate emotions spilled are saddening. One even had the feeling that the mighty resources involved—two BBC orchestras, the London Sinfonietta, a trio of notable conductors, the BBC Singers, a handful of fine instrumentalists including some of the world's outstanding string players, a committed commentator, authoritative interval talks by such specialists as Gerard McBurney and David Fanning, reminiscing interviews with an aura of high piety and pathos—were taking this composer more seriously than he took himself. Why should these highly intelligent, talented, sensitive folk all without a dissentient whimper unquestioningly condone anarchy over order, destruction over construction, frivolity, portentousness, arid vacuity over genuine content and palpable significance? Why—to end with old-fashioned words only apparently relegated to the lumber-room— prefer ugliness to beauty?

Why do they want to suffer so? What is the Schnittke-shaped wound into which he fits so perfectly? I ask in genuine perplexity!

One work stands out as different in kind: the astonishing First Symphony. Born of an all-time extreme of repression and stultification, its reaction is correspondingly extreme. This long blast of polystylistic raving blows the top off the suppurating cistern of its circumstances with maximum efficiency and intoxicating bravura. If ever a piece *had* to be written just-so, exactly as it is, driven by compulsion, inevitability, necessity, this is it. Its 'historical importance' alone ensures it a permanent place, the dead phrase brought to life by the gigantic physical and emotional impact.

Thereafter, though. Schnittke seems to be following its same trajectory over and over again. The ground had been cleared for gardens and landscapes. Instead, splinters and segments of the explosion become habitual and formulaic. Work upon work sounds as if it obeyed the compulsion of neurosis rather than the *rappel à l'ordre* of art. They begin tense, strained, dissonant (though not notably individual); break off for desultory doodles on harpsichord or celesta or out-of-tune piano; a fragment of cliché baroque figuration twitters away till suppressed (recalling the guinea-pigs in *Alice*) by gong-tormented apocalyptic dissonance, clearing to the sound of Eternal Mother Russia—tolling bells, with or without a glimpse of religious chant. Throw in a sardonic yet arbitrary snatch of Haydn, Beethoven, Johann Strauss, subvert with more baleful rent-a-crowd expressionism, juggle all these ingredients for half-an-hour or so till everyone is convinced that they've undergone a deeply pulverising and meaningful experience and can depart grateful, yet unsatisfied, ensuring that they'll return.

'Little more is needed to write such music than a copious supply of ink' was Stravinsky's wonderfully merciless and unfair comment on Messiaen's *Turangalila Symphony*. In the case of Schnittke's First Symphony also, that 'little more' is present and sufficient—the colossal drive that fills a big space, a huge orchestra, a red-hot programme, fuelling these masterpieces of release and splurge, breaking barriers of taste and inhibition to manifest liberating benefit: the Road of Excess sweeping straight into the Palace of Wisdom by the great front gate.

But it's not a journey that can bear repeating. Messiaen's output subsequent to *Turangalila* shows this with dazzling inventiveness (though admittedly he fell into formula and self-replication in his old age). Schnittke's later music relies constantly on the same ploys; resource becomes recourse, returns sharply diminish; techniques that even at best and most necessary were never innately musical lose their surprise and turn routine; disgust supervenes, then boredom, finally indifference.

55

Russian jamboree

Kostomuksha is a new town in Soviet Karelia, twenty hours by slow train north of Leningrad through endless pine forests with occasional hamlets, close to the Finnish border and not so far from the Arctic Circle. Its prosperity is based upon iron ore; the grand canyon whence it is extracted (eventually to be some twelve kilometres long and 600 metres deep) and the gigantic plant where rocky debris is transformed into pure metal are close by. The town itself consists entirely of blocks of apartments, framing scrappy recreation areas interspersed with surviving strips of forest descending to a lake. There is, of course, no church; all cultural life centres upon a People's Palace with an excellent auditorium-cum-theatre.

An unlikely place for a music festival. Yet Kostomuksha has this year set up a sister to that already established at Kuhmo, just across the Finnish border. I was invited to attend early in the year; everything seemed completely forgotten, then suddenly it was all on. Last-minute uncertainty about visa and flights yielded finally to action. I went, it happened [August 1989], and I return still reeling from the sheer unlikeliness of the whole experience.

The concerts each evening resembled Victorian jamborees rather than the genteel, shapely affairs to which we have become accustomed. People turn up for entertainment and are willing, indeed eager, to be pleased with whatever is offered. A Karelian piano sonata, or something more sophisticated from Leningrad or Moscow, is placed alongside local children singing their self-composed tunes and interspersed with dance-band or baroque numbers from a brass quintet, a clever pianist improvising still further twists from the old Paganini Caprice, amiably idiotic musical jokes (farting bassoons, silly wrong notes). The occasional official modern music by the invited composers takes its place in these medleys, presented like a television show with jollying compère and commère, and takes its chance on an equal footing to appeal to the listeners' ignorant and generous avidity.

Not just listeners: for as well as containing an element of dance (with three appearances by a superb pair of professionals from Moscow and Leningrad, unfortunately to canned music that coated everything it touched with schmaltz), every evening ended with a different one-act opera, given with wit and style by the Leningrad Chamber Music Theatre. Two delicious little Donizettis, *Rita* and *La Campanella*, Musorgsky's *Marriage*, an *opera da camera* by Haydn, and *The Falcon* by Bortnyanski (hopefully dubbed 'the

Russian Mozart'), which replaced Hindemith's *Hin und Zurück*. The non-Russian pieces were translated into the vernacular, and all of them were adapted where necessary to modern circumstances, broadened in appeal without Philistine coarsening. The orchestra was amateurish, but the singing good, and the visual aspects—costumes and sets, individual movements, gestures, expressions, movements of the cast in ensemble—really first-rate.

I had brought with me a selection of my simpler chamber pieces with their performing materials (since no requests had been received by my publishers, and anything complex would not be rehearsable in the short time). So it was piquant to find that my *Serenade in E♭* turned out to be in a sense the Festival's climax, the final item in the final serious concert, which was an overlong affair devoted to all the invited composers together with a few extra local interest appearances—and a Yugoslav piano sonata (a flavourless mix of sub-Messiaen with sub-Rachmaninov), because one of the resident pianists was its composer's sister.

My Serenade, written to divert without lowering artistic sights, and with a glint of naughtiness in its play of tonal and melodic cliché against tight constructivism, had been trashed by most of the London critics at its première in 1985 as pastiche, nostalgia, cheap etc., and silently or vocally deplored by friends and colleagues. In Kostomuksha it was unquestionably the most complex music of the evening. Questions of style and quality apart, the sheer rate of events, play of irregularity on the short and the long scale, and the density of the more saturated passages made it anything but easy-listen music. And when the question of style is opened, the discrepancy is odder still. The players did find problems with tricky rhythms and so forth, but the main problems for Westerners, the post-modernistic 'cubistifying' of Haydn, Rossini, Bellini, Brahms, Strauss, Stravinsky, passed unnoticed. They played it absolutely straight—if lively, then lively, if expressive, then warm, sweet, affectionate, and so forth; and all without 'inverted commas'. It sounded indefinably but powerfully different from its excellent performances by English musicians; as if it were *real* music in a way beyond what I'd composed, even while I rejoiced to find that I *had*, after all, composed it, and meant it! And thus it was received by the audience. The problem for them, way outside the boring old avant-garde versus conservative polemic of the West, was concerned with simply holding on tight while a supposedly 'light' piece of supposedly 'modern' music actually surprised them into unexpected joy. And its composer too.

56

Stravinsky's self-concealment

A written-up version of a talk for the Sherrington Society at Caius College Cambridge given at some now-irretrievable date in the late 60s.

* * *

What is important for the lucid ordering of the work … is that all the Dionysian elements which set the imagination of the artist in motion and make the life-sap rise must be properly subjugated before they intoxicate us, and must finally be made to submit to the law: Apollo demands it.

Poetics of Music

'Subjugation' in Stravinsky's works on religious texts is conventionally taken to mean such things as the refusal to attempt 'expression' of the 'Et resurrexit' in the Credo of the Mass, or the awesome denial of depiction of or comfort from Stephen's vision of 'the heavens opened' in *A Sermon, a Narrative and a Prayer*. Nevertheless even in this ostensibly most impersonal branch of all his impersonal output, a pattern can be discerned by which self-expression is pursued and achieved. Stravinsky said '"In the beginning was the word" is, for me, a literal, localised truth.' I take him at *his* word, and examine his florilegia of religious texts in six major works, with just such a literal and localised intention.

The first movement of the *Symphony of Psalms* has words from Psalm 38:

Hear my prayer O Lord; with thine ears hear my lamentation; hold not thy peace. For I came as a stranger before thee, and a sojourner as all my fathers were. O spare me a little, that I may recover my strength before I go hence and be no more seen.

To this cry of distress the second movement (words from Psalm 39) is an explicit answer—patience and subjugation, suitably symbolised in a double fugue:

I waited patiently for the Lord and he inclined unto me and heard my cry: He hath brought me up out of the horrible pit and out of the miry clay, and ordered my goings. And he hath put into my mouth a new song, a thanksgiving to our God. Many shall see it and fear, and shall put their trust in the Lord.

The last movement is the 'new song' of which the second speaks, Psalm 150 entire, in a setting where tranquillity alternates with exuberance, the tranquillity raised finally into an austere ecstasy of timeless contemplation.

Even so cursory a glance as this shows a pattern of key-words and the emotions behind them, ordered into an analogue of experience which, once elicited, can be seen in all Stravinsky's other works setting a florilegium of religious texts. The pattern here is: a cry of distress, for mercy; subjugation of distress (in music of intensified technical concentration) and the supervention of patience and obedience, by which order is achieved and out of which emerges not only renewed strength, but a vindication—'many shall see it and fear'; and finally, a reversal of the first condition, an expression alternately of praise and contemplation, winding down into stillness.

That is the bare outline of the Stravinskian analogue of religious experience. The *Symphony of Psalms* gives it in generalised form; the central part of the *Canticum sacrum* makes it more specific, and, behind the gnomic quality of its utterance, gives it a marked personal intonation. After the opening dedication to Venice there has been a vigorous injunction—'Go ye forth into all the world and preach the gospel to every creature'—whose stuttering brass conveys homage to the traditions of S. Marco; and then a lyrical number from the *Song of Songs*. The work's central 'dome' contains the essential content. It is tripartite, each section devoted to one of the hortatory virtues. Stravinsky's order reverses St Paul's ('here abideth faith, hope and love; and the greatest of these is love'). For Stravinsky, Love comes first, Faith last, Hope remaining in between as mediator. This new position of seniority, as also the intensity of its setting, indicates that for Stravinsky Faith is the greatest, a preference carried over into the following number, a parable of faith offered as a demonstration—'go thou and do likewise'.

The greater discipline implicit in the increased strictness of serial writing has two complementary results in Stravinsky's latest music. It allows a still more scrupulous establishment of the 'order in things' whose establishment is, he says, music's 'sole purpose', and at the same time it acts as a release, allowing him to express with greater immediacy his personal religious concerns. This strictness is peculiarly fitted to an account of 'Caritas' presented in terms of obedience: 'Thou shalt love the Lord thy God with all thy heart and with all thy soul and with all thy might.' Stravinsky's ingenious scheme for the economical despatch of these words (a three-part canon) does not work so well for the second text fitted to the same music: 'Beloved, let us love one another, for love is of God, and everyone that loveth is born of God and knoweth God'—where no natural tripartite division is possible.

'Spes' juxtaposes two texts, the first an expression of trust: 'They that trust in the Lord shall be as Mount Zion, which cannot be removed but standeth fast for ever.' The second is: 'my soul doth wait, and in his word do I hope. My soul waiteth for the Lord more than they that watch for the morning.' Stravinsky's 'Definition of Hope' is different from Crashaw's

Sweet Hope! kind cheat! fair fallacy, by thee
We are not WHERE nor what we be,
But WHAT and WHERE we would be. Thus art Thou
Our absent PRESENCE and our future NOW.

— or surely, for that matter, anyone's? Stravinsky's Hope is subjugated to the point where it can only be defined in terms of patience and obedience. His 'Fides' is more idiosyncratic still: 'I believed, therefore have I spoken; I was greatly afflicted.' This verse's context in Psalm 116 must be given to show how unparticular it is:

8. ...thou hast delivered my soul from death, mine eyes from tears and my feet from falling.
9. I will walk before the Lord in the land of the living.
10. I believed, therefore have I spoken; I was greatly afflicted.
11. I said in my haste, All men are liars.
12. What shall I render unto the Lord for all his benefits toward me?
13. I will take the cup of salvation, and call upon the name of the Lord.

The emphasis given to verse 10 by so curiously isolating it from its context and presenting it as an instance of Faith—that is, of the greatest of the hortatory virtues in Stravinsky's scheme—is compounded by the setting of it. The first half is sung to a flexible wail, the chorus unison against segments of the row on four trumpets; the second half, however, is the climax of the Canticum's system of increasingly complex contrapuntal schemes: eighteen bars of canon producing the greatest harmonic density in the work, with excruciatingly unconsonant harmony and harsh scoring exacerbated by the deliberately inert rhythm.

So Stravinsky's Hope is drab; though we are to 'love the Lord with all our heart' his version of Love is not inspiriting; and his Faith is the most dismal of all—that one do one's duty, and believe, with no sense of being anything other than unworthy, or that belief is anything other than a burden. 'I believed, therefore I have spoken; I was greatly afflicted.' To believe is to suffer: neither rhetorically nor stoically, but in submissive obedience. This is the 'meaning' implicit in this crabbed and curiously gauche music; this indeed is what its tightness of construction and harshness of sound are expressive of. Such expressivity is of course very different from the norms of espressivo ('moi, je deteste l'Ausdruck'), but it is expressive, in a very unusual way, and the expression is a self-expression.

The following movement is an illustration at once of the lesson (compressed almost to the point of incomprehensibility) contained in the treatment of Faith as a hortatory virtue, and the lesson (similarly elliptical) it held for Stravinsky's style. 'Jesus said unto him, If thou canst believe, all things are possible to him that believes. And straightway the father of the boy cried out, and said with tears, Lord I believe, help thou my unbelief.' The subjugation here of music's powers of expression results in a poignant intensity not to be realised by any more overtly pathetic means. After this, the first movement returns in retrograde as the last and resumes the theme (the Virtues assimilated) of spreading the gospel: 'And they went forth and preached everywhere ... the Lord working with them and confirming the word ... with signs following.' Vigour, cheerfulness and Venetian brass accompany the words; during the gaps the droning passages for organ arrest the momentum, giving a glimpse of the rapt monotony which ended the song of praise in the *Symphony of Psalms*.

Taking the *Symphony* and the *Canticum* together, Stravinsky's pattern becomes clearer. An initial condition of suffering and unworthiness is resolved by converting it effortlessly, through the stringencies of ever greater and ever more 'impersonal' technical discipline, into the exercise of patience, comprising the three hortatory virtues of Love, Hope and Faith. Then Vindication—'many shall see it and fear' in the *Symphony*, 'confirming the word with signs' in the *Canticum*; and after justice is done, a renewal of energies and ultimately a translation into eternity.

This pattern is paralleled in the more explicit themes of Stravinsky's stage-works on classical subjects: *Oedipus rex*, 'the archetypal drama of purification', *Apollo* with his deification, *Orpheus* with his disobedience and lack of faith but final apotheosis, and *Persephone* with its promise of renewal down the ages 'if the grain consent to die'. Impersonality is achieved in these works by the loss of self-expression in the objective realisation of a given story. The works on religious texts, on the contrary, are 'made-up' works whose apparently impersonal themes are in fact idiosyncratic and profoundly self-expressive. It is as if Stravinsky has used the Vulgate in order to speak the more intensely with his own voice. The pattern of associations into which his choice of words always leads him is at once compulsive and magnificently conscious.

In *Threni* a further advance in technical strictness has enabled Stravinsky to complete his mastery over his especial territory. Part I is set in deepest abjection and contrition:

How doth the city sit solitary, that was full of people ... she weepeth sore in the night ... her enemies prosper; for the Lord hath afflicted her for the multitude of her transgressions ... Behold O Lord, for I am in distress; my bowels are troubled, my heart is turned within me, for I have grievously rebelled.

Again it is in the central area of a work with an odd number of movements that Stravinsky employs his pattern. The three movements of the *Symphony of Psalms* and the tripartite central dome of the *Canticum sacrum* are reproduced with essentially the same associations and significations in the middle movement of *Threni*, which is also tripartite, consisting of 'Queremonia' (Complaint), 'Sensus spei' (Perceiving Hope) and 'Solacium' (curiously given as Compensation, rather than Solace).

Here are the salient verses of 'Queremonia':

I am the man that hath seen affliction by the rod of his wrath; He hath led me and brought me into darkness and not into light; Surely he is turned against me; he turneth his hand against me all day ... And thou hast removed my soul far from peace; I forgat prosperity; And I said, my strength and my hope is perished from the Lord.

At the end comes anticipation of hope:

Remembering my affliction and my misery, the wormwood and the gall, my soul hath them still in remembrance, and is humbled within me: this I recall to mind, therefore have I hope.

'Sensus spei' is the longest section and the most complex in form; the theme is gratitude at the Lord's repeated mercies even in his anger. I give the verses which recall salient words in the *Symphony of Psalms* and the *Canticum*:

Great is thy faithfulness; The Lord is good unto them that wait for him; It is good that a man should both hope and quietly wait for the salvation of the Lord.

Then another of those submissive-beyond-stoicism utterances—'It is good for a man that he bear the yoke in his youth'—that reach (like 'I believed; I was greatly afflicted') into the heart of Stravinsky's self-expression. This one actually employs the metaphor of the yoke that gives life to the use of the word 'subjugation'. Then six verses concerned with disobedience and God's anger, in which the long-buried violence of the earlier Stravinsky, last heard in the bacchantes' dance in *Orpheus*, momentarily flickers up: 'We have trespassed and have rebelled; Thou hast not pardoned.' Then nine of affliction and neglect: 'Thou has covered thyself with a cloud, that our prayer should not pass through ... Waters flowed over my head; then I said, I am cut off' and a final three of renewed petition: 'I called upon thy name, O Lord, out of the low dungeon', and trust: 'Thou hast heard my voice ... Thou drewest near in the day that I called upon thee; thou saidst, Fear not'—with which compare the many parallels in the *Symphony*'s first two movements.

Vindication, hitherto comparatively inconspicuous in Stravinsky's pattern (though once heard, the setting of 'videbunt multi, videbunt et timebunt' will never be forgotten), comes into its own in the last section, 'Compensation', and in the most curious fashion. The whole text is needed to show why:

58. O Lord, thou hast pleaded the causes of my soul; thou hast ransomed my life.

59. O Lord thou hast seen my wrong.

60. Thou hast seen all their vengeance and all their imaginations against me.

61. Thou hast heard their reproach O Lord, and all their imaginations against me.

62. The lips of those that rose up against me, and their device against me all day.

63. Behold their setting down and their rising up: I am their musick.

64. Render unto them a recompense, O Lord, according to the work of their hands.

65. Give them sorrow of heart, thy curse unto them.

66. Persecute and destroy them in anger from under the heavens of the Lord.

In the rest of *Threni* Stravinsky has followed his usual practice of selecting verses from often quite widely separated passages and giving them a new context of his own making. Here, exceptionally, he has—with some relish—set nine consecutive verses of Lamentations III except for one tiny omission, the latter half of verse 59: the words censored by Stravinsky's *pudeur* are 'Judge thou my cause'.

This insistence on righteous anger seems to me to reflect something of the arrogance of artistic certainty confronted with the follies of critics, commentators, virtuosos, star-conductors and all the other musical superfluities which provoked Stravinsky's wit and contempt throughout his life. Omission of three words from a Latin text, in the work of a composer so reserved and austere, seems to me as revealing as for a more autobiographically exhibitionistic composer to give to a comic pedant in one of his operas the name of his principal hostile critic. But perhaps I claim too much. What is certain is that Stravinsky's magnificent *superbia* ('a nose is what it is, with no further question; and thus with my music') is the counterpart of his humility and sense of worthlessness before God, as also before the law and order of his musical material. Their connection is intimate—'I regard my talent as God-given and I pray to Him daily for the strength to use it'. *Here* he is obedient and humble.

Stravinsky's justified pride goes together with considerable aggressiveness, whose presence in his music proceeds from direct violence in the early ballets, through a sublimation via the 'Russian' works, especially *Les noces*, into the uniquely anti-downbeat vitality of his maturity. His last music in which the old ferocity was to be heard with full impact was the *Symphony in Three Movements*, illustrative of, or inspired by, aspects of the war. After this the Dionysiac strain dies down; its final home is in the element of Vindication in the works on religious texts.

There is a curious episode in which Stravinsky's arrogance expressed itself inwardly towards God rather than in aggression towards his enemies. Discussing the sense in which the music of *Oedipus rex* might be said to be religious, he recounts a miraculous healing of an abscess, and a request to God for a sign:

I made a pilgrimage to Padua for the seven-hundredth anniversary of St. Anthony. I happened to enter the basilica just as the Saint's body was placed on exhibition. I saw the coffin, I knelt, and I prayed. And I—my terrible ego—asked for a sign of recognition when and if my prayer were answered. As it was answered, and with the sign, I think of that moment of recognition as the most real in my life.

This anecdote perhaps reveals too much; for when the article on *Oedipus* reached one of the conversation books it was omitted, just as the words in the Lamentations which too overtly require God to vindicate are omitted from the 'Compensation' in *Threni*. 'Schoenberg was a cabalist of course,' remarked the Stravinsky who proclaimed his own belief in 'the Person of the Lord, the Person of the Devil, and the Miracles of the Church'. Such superstitiousness lies at the heart of the music Stravinsky wrote for his own collections of religious texts. While Schoenberg bared his soul in poems about the hardships of being the Chosen One, Stravinsky was more secretive, and infinitely more tasteful, but hardly more 'objective'. His music embodies his superstitions and gives them artistic sanction.

The last movement of *Threni* picks isolated verses from the last chapter of the Lamentations in order to represent the permanence which allows for perpetual renewal: 'Thou, O Lord, remainest for ever: thy throne from generation to generation. Turn thou us unto thee, O Lord, and we shall be turned: renew our days as of old.' As befits a lamentation, the exuberant thanksgiving of the final stage is absent—or rather has been subsumed into the Vindication—and the tranquillity and richness of the final eternity is all the more moving after so much indignation has been vented.

The last three works to be considered all show aspects of the same overall pattern which, taken together, endorse and amplify its presence. The words of the *Sermon* in *A Sermon, a Narrative and a Prayer* are a further exposition of the familiar link between Hope and Faith, this time from St Paul. This is the first occasion in these works where Stravinsky relinquishes the marble and secrets of Latin in favour of the vernacular:

> We are saved by hope; but hope that is seen is not hope, for what a man sees why does he yet hope for?

Its second half introduces the equally familiar motif of patience:

> If we hope for what we see not, then do we with patience wait for it.

The dry glumness of these words is mitigated by the fluid lightness of Stravinsky's latest style, and counteracted by the sentences acting as a refrain to both halves:

> The substance of things hoped for, the evidence of things not seen, is faith. And our Lord is a consuming fire.

Here is a new element in the pattern of faith by affliction and patience—God-given revelation, illuminating the drabness of Stravinsky's spiritual habit with a glance of momentary ecstasy. Compare the lines he set later from *Little Gidding*:

> We only live, only suspire
> Consumed by either fire or fire

— but in *The Dove Descending* dinginess has returned. In the setting of St Paul the music conveys a tremor of muted excitement.

The *Narrative* tells the story of the martyrdom of St Stephen, 'a man full of faith and of the holy Ghost ... full of faith and power', and above all, 'obedient to the faith'; all phrases retained in Stravinsky's highly compressed version of the story from Acts VI and VII. Stephen, having proved his obedience, is awarded the oddly disconcerting vision of 'the heavens opening'. Such patent Vindication infuriates the people who cast him out of the city and (with a further flicker of the old violence) stone him. After Stephen's death eight exquisite bars of epilogue recall the apotheosis of the god in *Apollo* and of the martyr-hero in *Orpheus*. Finally the *Prayer* (words from Dekker), while submitting to God's will, puts in an unambiguous request for election:

> O My God, if it Bee thy Pleasure to cut me off before night ... Yet make me,
> My Gratious Shepheard, for one of Thy Lambs to whom Thou Wilt say,
> 'Come You Blessed' ...

and ends with Alleluias where the vocal counterpoint gradually coalesces into harmony (as with 'renew our days as of old' at the end of *Threni*) whose winding down into rapt stillness takes us back further, to the end of the *Symphony of Psalms*.

The *Flood*, written to a text drawn from *Genesis* and miracle plays, is a scrappy work, often surprisingly maladroit, lacking either the granite implacability of *Threni* or the fluid lightness of the *Sermon* and *Prayer*. The interesting aspect here is the work's dramatisation of the Stravinskian pattern. Noah is Obedience personified. God says to him

> Noah, as I bid thee, do fulfill
> Although thou has but little skill

and he replies

> O mercy, Lord! wouldst Thou take heed!
> I am full old and out of heart,
> So that I dare do no day's deed
> Without great mastery on my part.

God promises to succour Noah, and announces the flood as just punishment for the rest of mankind:

Noah, I shall guide thee in all thy work.
Destroyed all the world shall be
Save thou; thy wife; thy sons three
And all their wives also with thee
Shall saved be, for thy sake.

Noah overcomes his unworthiness—'Thy bidding, Lord, I shall fulfil'—and gets down to 'The Building of the Ark'. The pattern of distress (here compounded by age and sense of incapacity), obedience and work (with the necessary insistence on craft and mastery) is clearly reproduced.

If his election as the one man worthy to be saved from destruction were not Vindication enough, Noah receives further reward when the flood has subsided and God establishes a Covenant, put by Noah to his family like this:

Sons, with your wives shall ye be stead
And multiply your seed shall ye,
Your bairns shall then each other wed,
And worship God in good degree,
All beasts and fowls shall forth be bred,
And so a world begins to be.

'Renew our days as of old': the work ends with one of those shining diatonic discords that characterise the Stravinskian translation into timelessness, from the ending of Les noces to the Postlude of the Requiem Canticles—and more specifically, the closing pages of the Symphony of Psalms, the organ drone in the first and last movements of the Canticum Sacrum, the four horns at the end of Threni, and the strings and tam-tams at the end of A Sermon, a Narrative and a Prayer.

The music of Abraham and Isaac recovers something of the impenetrability of the earliest serial works, while retaining the flexibility of the latest manner. Again the vernacular is dropped, and Stravinsky goes back beyond the Vulgate to the Hebrew (with a stipulation always to use it in performance). Thus the work gives an impression of secrecy, or erecting a still further barrier against a still more poignant personal utterance. For in this presentation of Abraham's sacrifice, the theme of subjugation in obedience is expressed with greater intensity than ever before. God says 'Take now thy son, thine only son Isaac, whom thou lovest ... and offer him for a burnt offering', and there is never a doubt in Abraham's mind that this is the proper thing to do. He simply 'rose up early in the morning and saddled his ass' and set off to perform his duty. Contrast Britten's Canticle on the same subject (which reappears in the War Requiem), where much is made of the 'human conflict' in Abraham between love for his son and obedience to his God. For Stravinsky this emphasis on sentiment not only does not arise, but actually could not exist in terms of his chosen expressive stance. (We recall the fourth movement of the Canticum sacrum.)

The words after Isaac's deliverance and the sacrifice of the ram are crucial:

By myself have I sworn, saith the Lord, for because thou hast done this thing, and hast not withheld thy son, thine only son;

That in blessing I will bless thee, and in multiplying I will multiply thy seed as the stars of the heaven, and as the sand which is upon the seashore; and thy seed shall possess the gate of his enemies;

And in thy seed shall all the nations of the earth be blessed; because thou hast hearkened to my voice.

Vindication appears in the words 'thy seed shall possess the gate of his enemies' but is lost in the abundance of the reward for such subjugation in obedience as Abraham's—the fertility of the stars and of the sands and of the peoples of the earth. So Vindication is now inseparable from renewal and eternity—a generous conclusion to what could easily enough have emerged as small-mindedness. After this moment of sublimely repressed exaltation the quiet mood of the final words and music is perfectly judged—'So Abraham returned unto his young men, and they rose up and went together to Beer-sheba: and Abraham dwelt at Beersheba.'

So the pattern of affliction, obedience, vindication and renewal is in *Abraham and Isaac* given its most compact and cogent form. As his technical means have become ever more stringent and his expression ever more withdrawn, so Stravinsky has penetrated more directly and more deeply into the meaning of these words. Satie said of him 'the lucidity of his mind has made us free'. These late works, still more than those which Satie knew, demonstrate the nature of that subjugation where service is perfect freedom.

In his idiosyncratic version of the communal religious experience, Stravinsky's impersonality is a personal utterance. The emphasis in these works on the same pattern of religious experience ('at once compulsive and magnificently conscious')—the music which embodies it no less than the words which say it—expresses 'a feeling, an attitude of mind, a psycho-logical mood' (and, one might add, in *The Flood* 'a phenomenon of nature'), everything which he has denied the power of music to convey. His personal utterance, however, is undertaken in terms of religious abstractions which by their nature and in their application are impersonal. Therefore his use of these generalities—patience, obedience, love, hope, faith—ostensibly accords with their universality. But in fact it is a private use; not 'cabalistic' but decidedly credulous, even superstitious. These words suggest no adverse judgement: Stravinsky's uses are artistic, and their objective truth is neither here nor there.

Denial of expression in Stravinsky's music is not the result of music's being 'essentially powerless to *express* anything at all'. Rather, it is *his espressivo*. The old party view (e.g. Ansermet—'Stravinsky, in response to some form of inner compulsion, does not make of his music as act of self-expression') shows Stravinsky as he would wish to be seen. In fact, like every other composer of modern times he *does* make of his music an act of self-expression, but his inner compulsion is twofold—to express himself, and to conceal his self-expression. This concealment must surely be understood in terms of a stylistic predilection. Sonorous autobiography, self-expression as understood by Wagner, Tchaikovsky, even Schoenberg ('music expresses all that is within us') are incompatible with the moderation, balance and self-restraint of Stravinsky's Apollonianism. Yet the vehemence of his commitment to these qualities indicates that the Apollonianism is an essentially romantic assumption. Thus, words like 'mask', 'heiratic', 'ritual' are misleading indicators of the nature of Stravinsky's concealment. More helpful is a quotation from the composer himself which might have been written to help his listeners over the question of style. He praises *Wozzeck* while deploring certain sensational aspects of its appeal:

> 'Passionate emotion' can be conveyed by very different means than these and within the most 'limiting conventions'. The Timurid miniaturists, for example, were forbidden to portray facial expressions. In one moving scene, from the life of an early Zoroastrian king, the artist shows a group of totally blank faces. The dramatic tension is in the way the ladies of the court are shown eavesdropping, and in the slightly discordant gesture of one of the principal figures. In another of these miniatures, two lovers confront each other with stony looks, but the man unconsciously touches his finger to his lips, and this packs the picture with, for me, as much passion as the *crescendo molto* in *Wozzeck*.

In Stravinsky's music, expression is achieved by just such a sublime sublimation of the romantic tradition of expressive subjectivity, and in the works I have been discussing the communal religious experience is the vehicle of a concealed and a profoundly personal utterance. From exposure of the internal chaos 'we are saved by style'; and through the ethos of law and order, the life-sap rises and 'a world begins to be'.

57

Stravinsky's spiritual son

Robert Craft's hard road to dignity

It must have been difficult all along for Robert Craft. Widely regarded in the early years of his association with Stravinsky as an obsequious yet pushy stooge; resented for coercing the old master into alien techniques, even opinions; to be then, in the years since the composer's death (1971) and his widow's (1982), surrounded by a palpable aura of failure because of his apparently stubborn refusal to produce the masterpiece of monumental biography for which he is uniquely informed; while, closer to home, this spiritual son, who manifestly served the composer more kindly and was more warmly loved than the composer's natural heirs and their spouses, has had to defend himself from their jealous hatred and active litigation.

His career 'without' Stravinsky is ambiguous too. Craft did not shine at concerts. His achievement as a conductor is based largely on the recording studio; the pioneer LPs of Gesualdo and Schütz, Boulez and Stockhausen, the second Viennese school (above all the famous first ever complete Webern) remain historically interesting rather than aesthetically attractive. Powerful intellectual grasp and pragmatic miracles achieved with *ad hoc* bands, minimal money, minimal time characterise these ventures; beauty of sound, depth or intensity of interpretation are rarely found. The same goes for the current series of Stravinsky re-recordings,[1] except that here sheer lucidity (together with privileged access to correct texts) can go most of the way. He is also an accomplished, fertile and often masterly journalist, and very various in subject-matter.

Yet he still exists principally as the ghost of the great man. The passing decades have been dominated by attention to him: the textual complication of the five volumes of collaborative *Conversations* are now (apparently) being resolved in a new variorum edition;[2] there have been three volumes of letters, copiously annotated, several picture-books by no means deficient in text. And

---

[1] Music Masters Classics.

[2] No, it's not variorum: rather, a puzzling and perverse further fiddling with already dubious texts, omitting in the process many remarks originally attributed to the composer whose pungent wit has over the years given them quasi-proverbial status (Faber, 2003).

much of the journalism, collected in several volumes, has also been devoted to aspects of Stravinsky; outstanding among it are an essay on the children as riveting in its way as a Compton-Burnett fiction, an account of the first wife so sensitive, and a vindication of his own role so acute, that it is as much on these subtler qualifications as on the length of the association itself that hope for one of the great biographies has been based.

The portrait in *Stravinsky: Chronicle of a Friendship*[3] is full-length and frank. Above all, it shows the animal in Stravinsky: the image inculcated by earlier publications now known to be ghosted—wholly intellectual, severe, rational, objective, theological—is complemented in this diary by a sensory creature, wary and superstitious, supercharged with an egotism at once adamantine and capricious. Food is relished equally to be smelled, ingested, digested and excreted (with exhaustive critical commentary on every stage); alcohol flows freely; dreams are noted and obeyed; the tough lean body exercises with rigour, then relaxes in the 'mammary utopia' of the opposite sex.

The powerful mental and emotional traits evinced by this creature of instinct are observed by Craft with equal sympathy: for instance, an unprecedented moment of near-collapse in March 1952 when the strong man 'seems ready to weep' as he fears he can no longer compose; and the fine balance of distance and astonishment with which he reports Stravinsky's deeds and words ('I regret ... that I was not here to help the new Soviet Union create its new music') during the return to Russia ten years later. And the composer's artistic personality is caught by off-the-cuff *obiter dicta* scattered throughout these pages. Almost at random: 'music is the best means we have of digesting time'; 'One composes a march to help men march, and it is the same with my Credo. I hope to provide some help with the text. The Credo is long. There is a great deal to believe'; among many down-to-earth basics, 'it doesn't give me an erection' is a favourite; 'Tradition carries the good artist on its shoulders as St Christopher carried the Lord'; 'I despise mountains. They tell me nothing'; the little exchange in Seville Cathedral with an avid padre who has heard that Stravinsky has just been awarded a handsome prize, ending 'peut-être je suis riche, mon père, mais je suis très avare' (his immediate response when asked by a journalist a few days before what he would do with the money, was 'I will try to sell it to Calouste Gulbenkian', then stationed next door in the same Lisbon hotel).

He finds 'power' not the *mot juste* for Beethoven—'I don't like it because it really means "use of power". Say "might", rather' (this prompts Craft to remark how little the *Conversations* as published show Stravinsky's 'cunning with words, his many-sided apprehension of them, and his sense of their aptness and weight'). Recalling a childhood schoolmate saying a cat was skilful in catching fish, 'The word "skill" impressed me, and I have paid attention to it ever since'; further, 'One has a nose, the nose scents and it chooses, and the artist is simply a kind of pig snouting truffles'. After tapes of dire Soviet compositions at the Leningrad Composers' Union, 'that was

---

[3] Revised and expanded edition (Vanderbilt Universithy Press, 1994).

the real *rideau de fer*'; during a documentary filmed in his eighty-fourth year, 'In the morning we think differently than in the evening. When I come to a difficulty, I wait until tomorrow. I can wait as an insect can wait.' Amid the harrowing mortifications of intensive care, he explains in answer to a doctor's question that 'time is a matter of speed, and rhythm is a matter of design' (on the same day, he can also say 'I want to be more exact in my thoughts', yet beg for 'a more powerful pill, so that I will not have to think any more tonight'). Two-and-a-half years iller (aged nearly ninety), he is encouraged to compose 'even two notes': 'But they must be the right two'. No wonder that Craft sums up this day by saying 'he betrays not the slightest opacity of mind, and knows exactly what he wants, whether word, object, or action.' When was it ever otherwise *chez* Stravinsky?

Craft's ability to evoke character with or without its environment (domestic, studio, restaurant) is by no means confined to his principal subject. Especially memorable is the portrait of Schoenberg in the last year of his life: 'the pained, sensitive face, difficult to look into and impossible not to ... he sits in the gravy-coloured *fauteuil*, on the edge of the cushion and without repose ... his voice is soft, but as pained and sensitive as his face, and almost unbearably intense.' Two-timing for several years in alien Hollywood between the incompatible poles of twentieth-century music, living a stone's-throw from each other in frozen antipathy, Craft is able to compare the incomparable, and to witness the survivor's prompt reaction by telegram to Schoenberg's death in July 1951. Stravinsky did not attend the funeral, 'believing his presence could only be seen as ironic'. (The compositional consequences, gradual but momentous, are taken in due course.)

Later come memorable vignettes of faces in their settings so diverse as— among many others—Forster in King's, David Jones in Harrow, Giacometti in mid-facture, Glenn Gould at rehearsal, Marianne Moore making swift decisions over verbal niceties for the text of *The Flood*. There are two more fully rounded-out memorial tributes to friends of long standing on hearing of their deaths—Aldous Huxley and Baroness d'Erlanger (in whose house Craft resided for some years, to whom he read aloud 'entire shelves of books, and some authors *in toto*'): 'characters' worthy of Harold Nicolson. Outstanding for sustained artistic interest is Stravinsky's conversation, running over several days of September 1961, with Ingmar Bergman. It circles around Bergman's celebrated production of *The Rake's Progress*, but is rich in *aperçus* about stage, opera, film, music in general, practical and ideal, from these two supreme old hands. A constant presence is the camping culture-prattle, now witty, now plain silly, of the opera's co-librettist. They first meet in the opening pages, back in March 1948, when Auden's delivery of the text to the Stravinskys in Washington coincides with Craft's first appointment; and, twenty-three years later almost to the day, Auden is the first visitor to the New York apartment which they moved into only nine days before the composer's death. (In general, I've not thought it of much interest to split hairs about the textual differences between this new volume and its earlier editions; but I must advise the curious reader that the discrepancies in the account of Stravinsky's actual death are marked and disconcerting.)

Craft's brilliance of phrase can sometimes rise to the master's ('this is architecture without furniture' of Webern's String Quartet), and sometimes seems to be taking the advice of another mentor (Auden) about unfamiliar words too nearly (of the air flight over the north of the globe: 'even the ocean is frozen—frazil [sic] ice and vaggy ice'). But he comes into his own in longer set-pieces—Russian Easter among the expatriates of Hollywood; the interior, and the religious motions, of the Blue Mosque in Istanbul, together with the incongruities of its furniture (grandfather clocks presented by Queen Victoria, exciting Stravinsky's interest because of 'clock-time in a place of prayer'); the dress, figure and gestures, as well as the conversation, of the Patriarch of Venice two years before his elevation to the pontificate as John XXIII; a sensory exercise worthy of Virginia Woolf's diaries describing the Palermo market. One's main reservation touches the oft-made comparison with Boswell, in particular, his extraordinarily convincing ear for speech. No one can know how Burke, Goldsmith, Reynolds *et al* phrased their sentences. Boswell's simulacrum reads well irrespective of the content of what's said. With Craft's reported speech, it's mostly the other way round; content-level is high (how could it fail to be with such a cast?), but the attributed words are not imbued with the feeling of a living tongue. If this can sometimes be true even of 'Stravinsky' himself, how much more so for a one-off like St-John Perse, St-Jean Cocteau, the sainted Eliot, Genet, Camus?

Nevertheless this speech-defect, though endemic, is only a small blemish on the vital part of the book where Craft is writing up things seen and heard. Its vein of sheer badness is a different matter. It would be unfair to concentrate on the embarrassments in a book conspicuous for its *richesses*. The author's vulnerability is already its own punishment. Nevertheless, since an element of self-presentation is a significant extra in this new edition, it has to be mentioned. On several occasions, Craft favours us with poems in the making ('Pleistocene shapes, still struggling as they drowned' etc.); when lovesick, he indites fourteen ways of looking at his pain by way of half-baked *pensées*. Accounts of lusts ungratified or (infrequently) fulfilled are squirm-making (whereas Boswell's feckless fornications don't cause any trouble—beyond a dose of clap); while the tone taken towards more elderly specimens of the *Ewigweibliche* is difficult to gauge ('what a great lady!' of Nadia Boulanger; the same adjective is used for Craft's mother when he quotes from her exceedingly prosaic letters during times of stress). Pious or sarcastic? Certainly sickly is the tribute to Vera sent by an old associate the first name-day after her death, and included by Craft as speaking for itself: 'Vera Arturovna was one of the most beautiful women who ever lived. She was not only born beautiful, but she inspired beauty, created beauty, and lived to make the lives around her more beautiful.' Yet such awful moments lead towards the heart of Craft's personal dilemma. Wounding diffidence and self-distrust ('why does the sight of my name in print, of a photograph of myself, of any kind of publicity concerning myself ... upset me so much?') cannot be assuaged by anything, let alone crumbs from the famous (Boulez's congratu-lations on the Webern records, included among many other 'testimonials'), the unknown, or Mr Great and Good himself ('letter of condolence from Isaiah Berlin [after the composer's death] saying that nothing will ever be the same for me again'). Even the master's affection, conveyed in birthday greetings or messages on soiled table-napkins, lovingly kept and reproduced among the photographs, does not appear to suffice. And the source of the insecurity is plain. As early as October 1953, he can say, 'I have changed families and at a terrible cost substituted my ideal for my real one.' Thirteen years later, the exchange has become, for some purposes, one of roles; the *New York Times* commissions from Craft two articles, 'one about I. S., ONE BY HIM!!!!'

Former accusations of brashness and crudity must yield to such confes-sions as these; traces of self-pity and callowness to remain, subsumed into a hard-won dignity. But the old charges of snobbery and ostentation cannot be dropped. The latter is the more venial—flamboyant vocabulary and look-at-me displays of culture are the forced blooms of a style whose essence, in spite of some successful purple passages, is not dandiacal. The snobbery is more serious and on the face of it less forgivable. Less simple, too. Evidence is only implicit; it's more a question of a ubiquitous tone that gives rise to suspicions of tuft-hunting and manipulation. The sheer turnover of famous figures is so rapid! Naturally this criticism does not apply to the composer's old friends and new colleagues. Elsewhere, the sense of going for the Right People (as, in the Conversation-books sometimes, the right opinions) smells bad. There are also some weirdly inapt conjunctions, where the giant pandas so laboriously brought together fail to mate. Throughout the book there is a sense of Craft as major-domo / naturalist / marriage broker, who then rushes back to privacy to write up the result. Moreover, he has his cake and his breadcrumbs, presenting cosmopolitan cultural exchange as desirably glamor-ous, yet at the same time indulging the pangs of diffidence and shame. Yet such snobbery (if this be the word) is an essential ingredient in the book's fascination. If we underprivileged latecomers can meet this cast of thousands, and Stravinsky himself, only via the medium of this reporter, then so be it.

One page (141) can focus the feeling. On it Stephen Spender writes to Craft that Francis Bacon 'would be thrilled' to paint Stravinsky: 'we see a lot of Chester and Wystan' he adds, as their opera with Henze approaches Glynde-bourne. Sir Isaiah writes, not looking forward to this event. Balanchine visits. Dinner with the Stravinskys at the Varèses'. Lunch with Stravinsky, Varèse and Elliott Carter—descending before the master, Craft finds himself in the lift with the Hindemiths. Such conjunctions—admittedly this is an extreme instance—suggest nothing so much as Jennifer's Diary. The difference is that these pages are peopled with creative immortals rather than socialite butterflies; the sense of 'don't you wish you were there' is identical.

Yet such passages can suggest the texture of the whole book, so rich and rapid in faces, so far-flung in places. Its peak is Stravinsky's return to Russia, after an exile of nearly half a century, in the autumn of 1962. The year had begun with the Kennedys' invitation to dinner in the White House, followed by days in Paris (Beckett, Cocteau), an African tour followed by Rome, Hamburg, ten days in Israel, a few days in Venice, Paris again before and after the Russian visit, succeeded by Rome again, then South America, New York and Toronto—all of them for work not play—before returning home to Hollywood in early December. The breathlessness of this *résumé* is not, this time, that of the original. At sixty-three pages, 1962 is the most generously detailed year, with gold plentiful and dross minimal, while the account of Stravinsky's three weeks in his native land is indescribably absorbing. One welcome addition to this volume is the series of annual postscripts added from the vantage-point of 1994. In that for 1962, Craft sums it up thus: 'Stravinsky's first year as an octogenarian was marked by more public exposure than he had ever had ... But in spite of the globetrotting, he finished *The Flood* ... and wrote a considerable portion of the new and very different music of *Abraham and Isaac*.' Underneath the flurry of busy surface what matters most remains constant—the composer's creativity.

The absolutely unique aspect of the Craft–Stravinsky friendship, and by far the most important, is the influence of the admirer and factotum on the actual creative output of the ageing master to whom he became attached. For this I can think of no parallel anywhere. Creative genius is of its nature avid at all times for stimulation and subject at all times to mysterious sterilities. Both, obviously, will increase as the artist ages. The impulse to compose can tire, grow mechanical and self-repetitive, gutter slowly out or altogether stop short. Renovation (unless it fails) can grow from within or also be fed by sources from without—a surprise, artistic or personal, a new challenge whether technical or expressive, a change of angle, an alteration in the light.

Stravinsky's works of the 1940s—his sixties—show vitality and productivity undiminished, in some ways indeed enhanced by changed circumstances: a new country, language, marriage and the need to consolidate. But their quality is patchy. Such pieces as *Scènes de ballet*, *Babel* and the Concerto for Strings verge on the epigonic. The most ambitious orchestral work, the *Symphony in Three Movements*, falls before one's unwilling eyes into its unreconciled constituent parts, though smaller works also deriving from unused film-scores succeed in their more modest aim. *The Rake's Progress* is desiccated and irritating, with wonderful things, especially as it proceeds. The Mass and *Orpheus* alone are both major and flawless; but they are masterpieces of mannerism. With hindsight, this decade is extremely prophetic, 'in the cracks' (so to speak) of the familiar: certain moments of the Symphony's finale, the dissonant linearity of the *Ode*'s opening and the *Orpheus* interludes, the weird string quartet prelude to the graveyard scene in the *Rake*.

But only with hindsight. Around 1951, it could easily have seemed like the end of the road, to be followed only by self-recycling or dignified silence. Instead, within a few years, Stravinsky, adapting to his own ends an idiosyncratic version of Viennese serialism, had re-made his musical speech. The earliest results are a bit wonky. With the epic-miniature canzona in memory of Dylan Thomas (1954), the touch is certain. With *Agon* (begun before, but not completed till 1957) comes a dazzling milestone, with a genuinely popular life thanks to its success as a vehicle for Balanchine's choreography. Thereafter, interspersed with some marvellous transcriptions of his own and other music, comes the precious body of late instrumental and choral works. Not destined (because of its extreme concentration and austerity) for *Petrushka*-like fame, this music is nevertheless widely regarded by connoisseurs as the crown of his *œuvre*. In these same years Stravinsky was once again in wide demand as a conductor, and found a completely new role (from around 1956) in the interviews eventually collected in five indispensable volumes of *Conversations*.

The precise balance of impulses, motifs and personalities is difficult to determine, but Craft played an essential role in this late flowering. Take 1954. In this year Craft suggests to Stravinsky two compositional projects which are both realised—to set the Dylan Thomas poem and to orchestrate Bach's organ-variations on *Von Himmel hoch* (his reward is its dedication); during the same period he is recording Gesualdo and Webern, the sessions attended by Stravinsky on whom, manifestly, nothing was lost. But such fertile give-and-take was already established, and continued to the end. Craft has documented it all in a dignified apologia. He was not so much a muse as a provider of surprises, shocks and plentiful raw material. He was the right man at the right time, and the chemistry was right. No one else could have done it; the rest is history.

Which makes the present book, together with the earliest and the best of the Conversation/collaborations (volumes 1–3) and the cornucopian scrapbook *Stravinsky in Pictures and Documents* (1978) the most important body of words about music since the war. It performs for twentieth-century music what Cosima Wagner's Diaries do for nineteenth; and is more comprehensive, more extended in time and place, imcomparably more diverse in population and (it must be added) far more fun. Forget Adorno! Here is the real thing, direct from its human source, the century's typical composer (though there is nobody like him), who is also the artist most central to the modern spirit in all its guises. Moreover, the fact that it is also a first-class travel book, a treasury of brief glimpses *à la* Aubrey, a sort of *Aspern Papers* crossed with Balzac crossed with *Cancer Ward*, gives it a hybrid vigour that is eminently in keeping with Stravinsky's own genius.

58

Customised goods

Beginning as a review of Richard Taruskin's magnum opus *(so far!) and extending in inadvertent imitation of its object way beyond the wordspace offered by the* New York Review of Books *to end up as an essay on Stravinsky himself and his dominant position athwart the twentieth century (and beyond). The* NYRB *naturally found the length a bit much, but shilly-shallied so many months over reducing it that I lost patience, withdrew the endeavour intact and offered it to the* Musical Times, *who to my delight took it on without demur, running it over three successive issues like a Victorian novel—hence the cliffhanger endings to the first two parts.*

*   *   *

i

Richard Taruskin's *Stravinsky and the Russian Traditions*,[1] an exhaustive study of the first two decades or so of Stravinsky's composing (1675 pages of main text, generous with musical examples, rich in photographic illustration, plus a good index and bibliography, a helpful guide to pronunciation and an indispensable glossary of key terms kept in play throughout the argument, the whole both handsome and reader-friendly in spite of its weight) effects a Russian Revolution. Commentators on Stravinsky will surely have to think Before and After Taruskin from this moment on! It will not now be possible to be vague, let alone ignorant, about the sources for the first third at least of Stravinsky's long creative life; and by implication of its remainder, in which these sources are diffused, disguised, transformed and (on the face of it) dispersed. Yet like all revolutions it consists as much, or more, in a realigned angle upon what was already there, than in the discovery of entirely new matter. Taruskin's industry and learning are beyond praise, yet the upshot is to substantiate, with an astounding range of detail, masterfully marshalled, authoritatively interpreted, what has long been intuited by Stravinsky's countless progeny of enthralled followers. With completeness sometimes obsessive, intellectual probing sometimes Talmudic, lightness of touch that, occasionally facetious or knowing, is more usually elegant, witty, and can often elicit outright laughter, Taruskin tells how a green young composer,

---

[1] University of California Press, 1976.

from a provincial backwater grown distinctly brackish, only modestly endowed with musical talent as understood in that epoch of musical culture, grew by dint of a colossally forceful willpower and a collocation of happy accidents, including a predictable shift in the collective stylistic Zeitgeist, to become the representative composer of modern times.

Taruskin subtitles his study 'a biography of the works through *Mavra*'—a journey from student exercises of the early 1900s, via the three famous triumphs from Diaghilev's pre-war Ballets Russes and the products of the wartime years spent in Switzerland, to the little *opera buffa* that, baffling its first audience in 1922, still remains its composer's least-appreciated work, and the première in 1923, after some nine years of experimentation with its instrumentation, of *Svadebka* (*Les noces*), which restored his admirers' faith in his intrinsic Russianness. In some respects the subtitle is a fair description. Biography and character-study are not the prime objects, though they emerge between the lines and in the footnotes on virtually every page. Nor does Taruskin provide what we have come to value in the best studies of great creative figures, the 'growth of a poet's mind' first adumbrated by Wordsworth, where interior events—dreams, visions, fears and joys, sorrows and ecstasies—comingling with family, friends, travels, schooling, loves and hates—fuse with the unfolding of developing tastes, techniques, self-realisations to form the unique individual who conceives and executes the artworks. All this is deliberately disavowed by Taruskin's exact subtitle which nevertheless doesn't do justice to his book's richness of content. For what he does give, even if involuntarily, is the account of one particular composer's road to the top, not just in the acquisition of skills but in such crucial traits as sizing up obstacles, seizing the moment, winning over or winnowing the rivals, using everything to hand in life, books and music, turning it to his own purpose with the raw opportunism of genius. It is appropriate that this biography of an *œuvre*, not of its creator, be presented as a conscious construct rather than the organic development by which the romantic artist grows in soul, mind, sensibility. Stravinsky's music, like his career, is selfmade in a wholly new way, to which this vast accumulation of context, charting concurrencies of opinion and taste, crosscurrents of polemic, accidents and designs within his native Traditions (note the plural in Taruskin's main title) is exactly attuned.

Taruskin's qualifications for the complex task he has accomplished are several. He is a skilful historian, copious with documentation, lucid and scrupulous in its use. Perhaps the better word would be antiquarian. He relishes the past, loves its surprises as well as its inevitabilities, takes infectious pleasure in winkling out forgotten facts and bringing them to life in new collocations of relevance. One instance among too many to enumerate is the twelve-page subsection on *L'affaire 'Mountjoie!'* (pp.995–1006). It comes in the context of Stravinsky's adoption, around the time of *Petrushka* and *The Rite*, by the intellectuals associated with the *Nouvelle Revue Française*. For the most part rejected in his native land, these great amalgams of folklore and modernity were recognised in France for what they are—classics of a new era; 'he wants to enunciate everything directly, explicitly, and concretely', wrote Jacques

Rivière. That the composer's later course was influenced if not indeed formed by such clairvoyant descriptions is one of Taruskin's typically bold glosses. Yet alongside such august praise came its slapstick parody in a short-lived journal called *Mountjoie!* whose hyperbolic enthusiasm must surely have brought a blush to the sallowest cheek. From the dual experience (documented with pictures and wry twists of narrative hilarity) Stravinsky learnt two interrelated lessons from which he profited for the rest of his career: the need for high-class intellectual company both to formulate and even provide his aesthetic positions, then give them an imprimatur; and for the ghost writers or conversation-partners to be the media of its articulation, all the way from the 'autobiography' and the Harvard lectures to the celebrated series of interviews with Robert Craft.

The antiquarian's goal is to capture from a vanished world every nuance that can possibly tighten our hold on the most important body of artworks it produced. And some of the most trivial too—not the slightest flick of the composer's pen escapes, be it only a tiny valse for children in a French news-paper, or the contemptuous *Souvenir d'une marche boche* written for a war-time charity-volume edited by Edith Wharton. When the work concerned is a *Petrushka* or a *Rite*, a whole river-system is traced, showing how via the single 'impersonal' channel of its named creator (and grudgingly-named col-laborators, their contributions sometimes retrospectively diminished or elimin-ated altogether) an entire culture, emanating from an entire folk, has been poured. 'Punch into *Pierrot*', the 118-page chapter on the sources and the making of *Petrushka*, can stand as example (though every major work is covered in such salient detail). More than relish, there is *joy* in this lucid unravelling of a brightly-coloured tangle of traditions primitive and sophisti-cated, rustic and urban, immemorial yet freshly-slanted, concerning the Petersburg Shrovetide Fair. There is also relish, if not joy, in the blow-by-blow exposition of the many rancorous cross-currents in the ballet's making and after, principally in the sordid fact that Stravinsky in a 1929 lawsuit tried but failed to write Alexandre Benois out of his due for the major part in its scenario, derived largely from his beautiful memoirs of childhood thrills amidst the smells, sights, tastes and sounds of the great festivity. The combin-ation of zest and acid resembles the multi-stranded masterpiece itself, fusing the entire cornucopia of source and circumstances into an unforgettable com-posite.

So Taruskin is an historian for whom the past lives in an antiquarian's insatiable appetite for its intricate nooks and crannies. Then there is Taruskin the lawyer—a *comprimario* rather than a leading role, but not one that he shirks. He appears for the defence and the prosecution, presenting with even-handed fairness behaviour and motivation that range from equivocal or pusillanimous to the frankly deplorable. He is moreover judge as well as counsel. Distasteful truths are given unpalliated, then verdicts are passed without axe-grinding. Stravinsky, originally trained for the law and remark-ably litigious throughout his adult life, is often hoist with his own petard.

Litigation and attempted elimination have already raised their ugly heads. A hard case of manipulating and distorting the truth is encountered when Taruskin comes to discuss Stravinsky's relation with Scriabin, the compatriot whom, when living, he most revered and sought to emulate. 'Every word Stravinsky ever published on the subject is false and biased and must be dismissed from consideration' (p.791). From student-days to at least the end of 1913 Stravinsky was a tremendous admirer. Their acquaintance in St Petersburg had been slight, but after an accidental encounter at the Warsaw rail-station in the autumn of that year (they both awaited the train for Switzerland) Stravinsky pressed Scriabin to visit him in Clarens (where he was on holiday); when this proved impossible he called on Scriabin in Lausanne (where he lived), and in the course of a long visit heard parts of the newest piano sonatas (nos. 8 to 10) with enthusiasm attested in a letter written soon afterwards. Peeved to learn on this occasion that Scriabin knew nothing of his recent work in spite of the noisy *Sacre* scandal only a few months before, he would have been appalled to discover from his host's letter to his mistress the next day that he had probably stayed too long: '...yesterday what prevented me from communing with my darling was Stravinsky (a composer), who is staying here in Switzerland. He came at 12 and sat till 7'—(nowadays all this would go straight down the telephone and we'd never know the extent of Stravinsky's humiliation!). When Scriabin's reactions to *Petrushka* and the *Sacre*, given the ensuing winter, were published in 1925, they were condescending in the extreme. He found in the first 'the usual Rimsky-Korsakoffery ... only a bit more ingenious, less naïve' (though he praised the depiction of the coachmen's boorishness); and the primeval sacrifice was dismissed as merely 'mentalistic ... *minimum* creativity'. The fact that this last comment was according to Taruskin a catch-phrase with Scriabin, 'applied to all and sundry', makes pretty bleak comfort. And in his next footnote (no.60 on p.797) Taruskin rubs salt in the wounded pride, retailing a quarrel between Stravinsky and his mother when in 1922 she arrived from Soviet Russia to join her family in the West, bringing with her a nimbus of old-style Scriabin-worship.Stravinsky, almost weeping with rage, at last admitted his detestation, to which his mother answered 'Now, now, Igor! You have not changed in all these years. You were always like that— always contemptuous of your betters!'

All in all, a story of unrequited love—hate with issue only in revenge. And Stravinsky's music of these years is permeated with the senior figure's influence, not just in the obvious connecting-link, the mystic cantata *Zvezdoliki—The King of the Stars* (1912), whose discussion provides the occasion for Taruskin to raise the subject and so thoroughly to sort it out; but in all three of the famous ballets too. No wonder the latter excoriation was so drastic—his only relief, to loathe. By no means the only, it is probably the most revealing and the saddest of the bad human stories which lurk in Taruskin's text and notes.

Such all-too-human ugliness uncovered and unwhitewashed in these volumes is disconcerting enough; and again it squares with what has been suspected before (or known, notably from some nobly unflinching accounts by Robert Craft). Although biography is declaredly not his aim, Taruskin's incidental sidelights on character, behaviour, machinations will necessitate important re-evaluations in the life of a composer who was such a recomposer of history. Not since Ernest Newman's monumental biography of Wagner has a great musician's tissue of mendacity, pettiness, smears, revenges, sins of commission and omission been exposed so wholescale. To present such mean traits in the makeup of a great man without apology or (for the most part) moralising yet also without belittling the stature is not the least of Taruskin's achievements.

But his greatest is, I think, as pure analyst. From the accumulation of cultural debris and human activity that goes into every work's 'biography', he moves naturally into a highly-wrought analysis of its technical clockwork. Since the subject is Stravinsky's 'Russian Traditions', these analyses ramify far back into the forebears—that specifically Russian line of empirical harmonic usage (though Schubert, Berlioz and Liszt are also involved) associated most often with representing the supernatural, the colourful, the exotic. By the period of Stravinsky's first appearance these usages had developed, then ossified, in the work of his teacher Rimsky-Korsakov, into a round of routines and formulae, fetishistic symmetries, shallow tricks and paradoxes handled with cunning virtuosity, held in Petersburg circles to represent true progress as opposed to the erosions of Debussy and the abominations of Strauss ('By God, I'd be ashamed even to play that in front of my maid,' Rimsky cried to his class one day, hurling the score of *Salome* to the floor; 'she'd think I'd lost my mind'—p.55). How Stravinsky found the further resources in these apparently moribund sleights of hand to do what he did and, incidentally, refresh and rejuvenate the course of music, is the book's principal and stirring subject. The non-technical reader will probably find Taruskin's passages of close analysis hard-going, and must be prepared to sink or skim: for the 'profession' they are crucial. Analysis of music has often enough been a dead exercise casting no light beyond delight at its own self-referential virtuosity. The analyses here are models of intelligibility and relevance, giving precise definition, straight out of the music, to the broader omnicultural themes. Their elegance and acumen provide chapter and verse, down to the tiniest minutiae, for the workings of one of the most conscious and conscientious craftsmen who has ever practised his calling.

Take Taruskin's *pièce de résistance*, over 100 pages on *Svadebka*. To condense this chapter would be as absurd as to reduce a building stone by stone. Taruskin has made a map on the scale of the actual terrain. But extracting a few nuggets can hint at the size of the whole hoard. On p.1338, as an indication of the traditional material's beauty and prodigality, Taruskin writes of an episode that could not be included: 'the *druzhko* ("wedding-jester") taking a skillet in one hand and axe in the other ... places three stones in the skillet and, after walking twice around the perimeter of the groom's house and reciting the Creed, makes the following incantation on the third go-round:

Be thou witch, be thou lizard, or be thou dungeon-dweller, only then wilt thou take my wedding when thou hast gone to Jerusalem-town and hast opened the coffin of our Lord and looked Him in the eye: and thou canst not go to Jerusalem-town and thou canst not unseal the coffin or see the Lord, and therefore thou canst not accomplish the deed. And there lies over a whirlpool, in the ocean, on the island of Buyan, a white stone; and when you find that stone, there you will find my wedding, and only then will you take it.

Then the *druzhko* strikes the stones with the butt of the axe and says, "As these stones have crumbled, so shall you evil spirits scatter".'

On p.1342 Taruskin writes of a tension, already felt in the earliest stages of amassing such material, 'between the archeological accuracy of the plan and the irrepressible fantasy of the execution'; by p.1363 he amplifies: 'In his basic approach and in his deviations alike, the composer followed authentic and highly specific customs, and ended up with settings closer both to the letter and to the spirit of Russian folk song than any Russian composer in the literate tradition had come before' (or, he might have added, was to achieve subsequently). Stravinsky, temporarily exiled from his native land for the duration of the war, and permanently after the 1917 Revolution, is creating in its image 'Turania', the land of lost content, the ideal Russia of his dreams. (Taruskin's special adoption of this portmanteau of Europe, Asia and the Russian Orient to baptise Stravinsky's wartime *œuvre* is explained and justified earlier in the book.)

The analytic strands reach their climax in an important description on p.1403: '*Svadebka* is a fundamentally monodic, or at best [*sic!*] a heterophonic composition ... its most quintessentially Turanian feature and its most significant departure from the norms of traditional Western practice'. This bald but crucial statement is amplified by the page opposite, my favourite of all the book's two-thousand-odd pages, a diagram compressing the entire 'musical space' of *Svadebka* into a single plane of modal/scalic symmetries/asymmetries whose intellectual beauty strikes as deep as the work's joyous physicality and the stirring realities within its formalised presentation of the fundamental facts of human fertility.

After this, the 'official' climax at the chapter's end can only seem bitter. Though Taruskin rightly sees *Svadebka* as the ultimate crown of Russian nationalism, this view was not shared by the new state whose people and their traditions it celebrates. So late as 1948 the high-placed music-bureaucrat Tikhon Khrennikov could write contemptuously that it uses some elements of Russian life to mock Russian customs and to please the European spectator by the express emphasis on Russian 'Asianism', 'crudity, animal instincts, sexual motifs'. A bizarre final twist from this same closing page (p.1422) is that one of Stravinsky's most sustained bouts of labour in all the work's tortuous compositional history had been in 1917 when, charged-up with patriotic feeling—none the less fervent for being so short-lived—he wrote in a telegram to his mother (once again the involuntary instrument for recording one of his drastic changes of mind) 'dans ces inoubliables jours de bonheur que traverse nôtre chère Russie liberée'. The chapter ends with a comprehensive Appendix summarising 'ethnographic sources, action, and musical themes'.

The glorious hunk of riveting synthesis—historical/antiquarian, anthropological/ethnomusicological, critical/analytic—elicited by the work Taruskin himself calls 'The Turanian pinnacle' is the high point of his study. There are several further outstanding moments, above all his account of the *Symphonies of Wind Instruments* (a clumsy title that Taruskin would replace with the still-worse *Concinnities*!), a masterpiece which had developed by 1922 out of a two-page chorale in memory of Debussy to become, all twelve minutes of it, the century's most influential single composition with the *Rite*—albeit after long decades of an obscurity never shared for a moment by the limelit ballet. Then comes a complex change of emphasis, shifting the Russian Traditions towards wholly different native idioms: Petersburg Italianate (*Pulcinella*) and *petit-bourgeois* formality (*Mavra*); and, as it became clear that the old Russia was lost forever and the new had no place for him, a neo-Imperial nostalgia whose presiding deity is Tchaikovsky. Then comes an Epilogue: a long dying fall, selecting for illustration such manifestly Russian-inspired pieces from the later years as the liturgical choruses of 1926–34 and the two-piano Sonata and *Scherzo à la russe* of the early 1940s, together with some selected works whose native inflection, if less quantifiable, remains unmistakable, from the Mass of the late 40s to the *Requiem canticles* of 1966, wherein the old faithful who had wavered throughout Stravinsky's years of idiosyncratic serialism gratefully recognised the Russian master latent within the apparently alien technique.

This Epilogue contains the one major work over which I'd venture to disagree—*Le baiser de la fée* (1928), the full-length ballet paying homage to Tchaikovsky not only by its scenario, an allegory of his life and muse, but in being made entirely out of Tchaikovsky's own material. From Taruskin's Turanian Pinnacle this later vision of a very different Russia must inevitably appear merely replicative and, as such, unacceptably bland ('no dislocation, no defamiliarisation': p.1614), Stravinsky's end-product all-too-congruent with its slender salon originals. This music, born of its composer's nostalgia for the vanished *ancien régime*, actually becomes his means of elevating himself retrospectively to its aristocracy. Yet for some Stravinskians *Le baiser* is a very special score; with his usual sedulous care he has tried, and effected, something different which, as always, is rich in hints of further possibilities not taken up by their discoverer.

All in all, then, and in spite of ending on a conscious decrescendo, this study is a marvellous achievement; the century's paradigmatic composer has been accorded the attention he demands and deserves.

But ...

ii

Auden in his obituary tribute called Stravinsky the representative artist of modern times. Whatever might be thought as to the claim's universality it is certain that he has become by now the century's mainstream composer. There was a seismic shift, and he made it; there was a battle and he has won. He is the air we breathe; or to use a grosser metaphor originating with Stravinsky himself (see p.1128), he inseminated the epoch, and the peculiarities of his physiognomy stamp his descendants unto the third and fourth generation.

His victory is to defeat the long hegemony of the Austro-Germanic musical culture, so mighty, so manifestly holding all the greatest figures from Bach to Brahms (to go no further back or forward) that every other felt itself inferior, subservient or marginal. By the turn of the modern century this tradition was decadent, although astonishingly fecund in its decay. A rating *circa* 1880 would still have been 'supreme': Wagner, Brahms, Bruckner, three giants at the height of their powers. Yet decay ran alongside: what is latent in the gods grows explicit in the succeeding demigods, the generation of the 1860s—Mahler, Strauss, Wolf—and the 70s—Reger, Schoenberg. These composers, heirs to a wealth of resources used with complete technical mastery, tend towards excess in all things—length, performing forces, volume (and later, exaggerated brevity, barely audible dynamics from a tiny group of players inside or without an enormous orchestra). Nervous intensity is the expressive goal; head and heart alike are liable to explode with approaching over-cerebration and overkill. A suitable motto for this era of *espressionismo* is 'means over ends', instantly evinced by its worst period-pieces—*Sinfonia domestica* in which Strauss blares the intimacies of married bed and breakfast to an indifferent audience, for instance, or Mahler's 'Symphony of a Thousand' (about which the young Stravinsky sardonically remarked, having first described its colossal apparatus, 'all this, you see, to prove that 2 + 2 = 4'). But whereas Stravinsky had 'Turanian' reasons to detest Teutonian romanticism in its terminal agonies, we can enjoy more freely the general stylistic ambience, and yield ourselves wholly to the particular strains in it that are supreme of their kind, alongside the bombast and slag. Our sense now is, 'What a wonderful way to go!'—feasting, debauchery, fireworks, squandering the savings of centuries in a riot of conspicuous consumption; sunsets and love-deaths by the dozen, nightmares and blasphemies, heads on dishes and corpses under the bench, self-projection of the artist as hero or martyr against a background of Alps, or Resurrections, or Jacob's Ladder, while the Great Bell of Midnight from *Zarathustra* clamours 'bimm-bamm'; decadent indeed, but still inexhaustibly interesting in its vitality, invention, expressive daring.

With the next generation—Schreker, Korngold, Webern, Berg—decadence becomes explicit and flagrant. *Entartete*—'degenerate'—was how the Nazis branded this music in the end: an exact aesthetic description, however deplorable in context. Thus by the 1920s 'Teutonia' was in dissolution. Wolf, Mahler and Reger had died relatively young; Strauss retained the *de luxe* pre-World War I manner right through and after the Second; Schoenberg by a mighty effort of 'mentalism' invented a language to ensure, in his notorious words, 'the supremacy of German music for a hundred years to come'. Degeneracy had overshot its zenith (probably to be located at the simultaneous premières of the twenty-three-year-old Korngold's *Die tote Stadt* at the end of 1920, soon followed by some eighty further productions); and a new generation headed by Hindemith, later made melodious by Weill, was busily engaged in cleaning out the rot in much the same spirit that Stravinsky (popular in progressive German circles throughout the decade, and in the 30s moving over to a German publisher) had already indicated. The altering political climate, the dispersal by exile, suppression, more war, complete the fragmentation. And the post-war regeneration is, by comparison, a sorry simulacrum: an *ersatz*-Bruckner/Mahler in the symphonies of Hartmann, an *ersatz* Strauss in the operas of Henze, in Stockhausen, neo-Wagnerian ambitions unmatched by the necessary talent; all-in-all a story of decline within one lifetime from musical hegemony to but one culture, by no means the most distinguished, among many.

The lifetime in which it came to pass is of course Stravinsky's own. And it was his authentic, instinctive loathing and fear of the endlessly uncoiling python of Teutonic expression that was instrumental in dealing it the *coup de grâce*. His attitude was not merely personal. Contempt and indifference were in the air. Well before World War I brought explicit anti-Boche sentiment into Debussy's music, he had deplored Germanic formulae, teased Strauss in print, walked in person out of a Mahler symphony, and writhed in subtle gyrations to escape the seductive wiles of Wagner. Debussy, the living composer to whom Stravinsky acknowledged (for once) his principal debt, had absolutely no use for the Teutonic forms or techniques from Bach to Brahms. Stravinsky's own stance, already formed, was perhaps confirmed by the edgy relationship with Debussy, and surely consolidated by friendship with the more congenial Ravel, younger, and frankly cheeky towards the horrors of the Huns, abominating Beethoven's *Missa solemnis*, preferring Chabrier to *The Ring*.

But Debussy and Ravel were, merely in this respect, no more than especially sensitive harbingers of a change in the climate. (Paradoxically both owed their liberation to fresh currents from earlier phases of Russian nationalism that Stravinsky was determined to supersede.) The hostility so radical that it needed to blow the tottering edifice to bits is Stravinsky's. The heat of his cultural and political enmity is unmistakable; the little *marche boche* already mentioned (with its lampoon of Beethoven's Fifth) makes a small musical parallel—more substantial, the outrageous Lutheran chorale-parodies in *The Soldier's Tale*—to what he declared in forceful unambiguous words. Equally unmistakable is the personal rage of the individual character, a rage that, exteriorised into acts of music, exerts so powerful an influence that one Russian provincial's quirky stance becomes the focus of the new aesthetic tendency of an entire epoch of composition, sweeping the stables clean of Germanic *Dreck*—and not just its decadent latter end but the whole world of romantic Teutonia, its sublimity, sensibility, soulfulness, seriousness and musical style.

All the evidence shows that, measured by these, Stravinsky's intrinsic compositional gift was puny. What is not puny is an enormous will to write music. If one is drawn by magnetic ambition to compose but knows one is capable only of featureless mediocrity when composing 'by the book', the solution is to make the book contemptible, out-of-date, no longer worth mastering. Send it up, push it over, burn it, reveal its feet of clay, dance upon its grave. Then do otherwise: *your way*, however perverse; indeed the more artificial and against the grain and nature of music as currently understood, the better. If you cannot join it, beat it.

What Stravinsky could not do and therefore disdained and subverted, was Teutonia at its apex: Wagner and Brahms. It's true that his immediate cultural enemy is the work of their living descendants, his older contemporaries, Brahms fatty-degenerated into Reger, Wagner dissipated into Mahler and Strauss. But behind them stand the Great-Grandfathers who represented the standard of Germanic music under which he grew up. His comprehensive re-slanting of the way to listen, to hear, the way music ought and ought not to be, the way music intrinsically is, is a rejection of the healthy centre as well as its disintegrating edges. Initially polarised in factitious polemic, Brahms and Wagner were revealed by the end of the old century as a complementary unity; they are equal tributaries in forming the composer who came to be seen, with a different kind of absurdity, for the first half and beyond of the new century, as Stravinsky's arch-antithesis: Arnold Schoenberg.

Of the two Teutonic giants, Wagner, on the face of it the more immovable impediment, can in fact be disposed of more easily, by the denigration born of genuine artistic distaste. Cutting Bayreuth down to size was as old as Bayreuth itself; the groundswell of hostility was given intellectual thrust in Nietzsche's polemics of the 1880s, and by 1900 or so, even as the musical world at large, and some of its best practising composers (Strauss, Mahler, Elgar, Delius), remained within the sway, the wave of reaction was almost a commonplace among young Turks as different as Debussy and Sibelius. The fascinating conjunction of ego-type and influence linking Wagner and Stravinsky, making each the composer who gives his voice to the entire epoch they dominate—the swing of the pendulum from the Wagnerian to the Stravinskian age—could make a detailed study on its own.

But Brahms could never be dismissed (like Wagner) as a hyperbolic adulterator of artistic genres who then elevated the poisonous brew into a bogus religion with his own glory inextricably bound in (the substance of Stravinsky's objections, common currency by the time they reached his Harvard audience in 1939–40). Brahms is less destructible than Wagner because he presents a smaller target. As the most recent embodiment of the Austro-Germanic continuities, he is subtly pervasive rather than crudely invasive. Brahms can represent the Teutonic type at its most normal—a craftsman and grammarian of musical usage at its peaks of culture, learned in a language rich in inherited resonance, affiliated to this heritage with unquestioning loyalty, bringing to it, so late in its life, a conscious consummation and subsumation. He gathers in a ripe harvest whose conspicuous emotional warmth is inextricably fused, by mastery of every technical means, with powerful brainwork. The result was criticised in his lifetime and still is—for lapses into cosiness and sentimentality, over-squareness that can become muscle-bound, lack of gaiety and lightness of touch, an unphysicality of movement, especially in the absence of a dance-element (apart from the glutinous Viennese waltz); and for limits of emotional range born of his very reverence for the past, showing that intensive cultivation can, sometimes, have its disadvantages. But of course Brahms survives such sniping (of which Stravinsky's own paper dart, deploring the later Schoenberg's stiffness of rhythm 'rooted in the most turgid and graceless Brahms' is a fair specimen), just as Wagner has survived the heftier ammunition turned upon him. Between them they fill out each other's alleged deficiencies, and the composite, with Brahms as the norm and Wagner the perpetually extraordinary, is impregnable. Together, they are the culmination of a musical language that comes with 'instructions' as to how it is to be heard and apprehended; how its listeners are to be moved. This is music as food—nourishment spiritual and ethical, though in a medium of almost carnal richness of textures; aimed at the deepest and highest spaces in the hungry human soul.

So what does Stravinsky provide instead? The nature of his alternative is of course not clear at first. Taruskin has charted the zigzags by which a genius for being different is gradually realised in compositions of equivalent worth. First come laboured attempts to be a dutiful Russian nationalist— Tchaikovsky for sentiment, Rimsky for orchestral magic, Brahmsian grasp of form and procedure dulled into the Petersburg academicism of Glazunov. (Glazunov is another victim of Stravinsky's long but selective memory. Taruskin unpicks the demonisation at the appropriate point in his first volume.) A whiff of Scriabin proves delusive and so for the moment do savours and scents from Paris (compatible with the vestiges of Russianness because in large part inspired by them). This brings us up to *Firebird* (1910). With *Petrushka* the next year comes the dawning of light. The ingredients of this work that so wonderfully dramatises its composer's fury and frustration remain the same (save only the use of 'found' material, for which a royalty had to be paid after every performance!); but the attitude towards them— subversion, mockery, malice, impudence, sarcasm, irony—alters everything; and so do the conjoined techniques of montage and collage, fragmentation and reassembly, dissection and destruction. From being slavishly obedient to his models, Stravinsky is from now on the most tyrannical of slave-drivers, brooking not the slightest impulse in his material to pull out of turn. The *difference* is at once total, yet oddly minuscule, like a change in the light that transforms all the colours, or the slip of a pen putting plus rather than minus in an equation, a not into a sentence, a nought on the end of a cheque. And of course an enormous talent for music-making is apparent after all, in this simple but drastic shift. It's like the tiny nick in Peer Gynt's eye that would enable him to see loveliness and grandeur rather than ugliness and squalor when imprisoned in the Troll-King's mountain fastness. Writing 'proper' music Stravinsky was derivative and weak. But in subversion lie strength, power and the possibilities, rapidly exploited, of a new rationale to substitute for the old.

The results are audibly primitive when placed in juxtaposition to the musical culture they aim to dislodge. Taruskin characterises 'Turania' in general when he adduces 'the tough, aggressive modernity that has not mellowed with age' for the peasant nonsense-songs of Stravinsky's Swiss years. 'It is not their Russian archaism but their belligerent rejection of Europe—the denial of "panromanogermanic" common practice—that has remained their most conspicuous feature' (p.1167). Ditching the depths and heights of Teutonian expression involves ditching the old-style master, learning, culture of the language which contained it. Yet what is done instead is done with consummate finish, a clarity and accuracy of aim that remain dazzling after eighty years and more. From *Petrushka* to *Svadebka* an exact balance of means and ends is restored to music by a barbarian from the East exactly when, at the centre, it seems to have been abandoned for good.

It is after this, where Taruskin leaves the mainline for his Epilogue with its long glance into the future, that the problems begin. Without this voluminous and erudite guide, the urgent questions that pressed upon the composer's subsequent trajectory at the time rise up again and clamour for answer. No doubt they were urgent questions for Stravinsky himself. Perhaps the crashingly obvious answer is also the true one—that he found himself, just turned forty-one at *Svadebka*'s première in 1923, to be, though famous and very experienced, as short of innate natural abundance as at the start of his journey. The 'Russian Traditions' had run out. In an artist so rigidly disciplined, self-replication was not permitted. So from now on every new direction became an ingenious feint, yielding a single work or a group of similar pieces before it, too, dried, and continuing again became problematic. 'Neoclassicism' (for continued want of a better phrase—I'm sure Taruskin could provide it!) seemed to require a fresh blood-transfusion from an as-yet-untried source for every further endeavour. Though the artist was never silenced, something vital was silenced in the music. Even now, as the best pieces from these decades harden into core repertoire, it is possible to admire, even to love, while still feeling the absence of some essential constituents. The former virtues of economy, exactness, directness, now feel like constriction, the self-denials (Stravinsky at work—'fretting, pacing, erasing, muttering "*pas de pitié*" the while'; p.1229) now seem to deny the music's actual substance. Moreover, its accompaniment of vindications, special pleadings, ever-more-bellowing Papal Bulls enjoining order, discipline, submission to the laws of Apollo, tends to drown the exiguous melody. Taken together, they amount to an aesthetic position that deliberately narrows music's scope. It becomes illegitimate for music to be anything other than what he himself happens to be writing. The completeness and rapidity of his early success seem to force him to go beyond a triumph-dance, to require the defeated enemy to embrace the victor's philosophy. And it is this philosophy, located more compellingly within the authority of the composer than in the borrowed mouthpieces uttering the aesthetic prescriptions, that has effected the seismic shift between the Age of Wagner and the Age of Stravinsky.

iii

When 'Teutonia', the 'panromanogermanic' alliance of head and heart for expressive utterance, is replaced by the composer as maker, organiser, or as Stravinsky described himself on his passport, 'inventor' of sounds, the main emphasis shifts into lucidity and patterning in deployment of the *materia musica*. The aim is order achieved through rigour; and the attitude resembles a naturalist's, an accountant's, a lawyer's, a bureaucrat's. *Circa* 1900 none of this would have seemed suited to music in any way: music's very nature, unquestioned whether the result was high art or low kitsch, was to be moving, rendering all human life to its extremes of turbulence and exaltation. But in earlier centuries, music had indeed been understood to be craft, and was categorised as a branch of knowledge, even a science. So Stravinsky's new attitude, counter-current in its time, is consonant with a wider historical perspective more fully appreciated nowadays. As always, he was ahead of the game. Indeed the later twentieth-century predilection for medieval, Renaissance and Baroque music runs loosely parallel to the altered notion of what music is for, Brought about by his aesthetic stance; and Taruskin has written persuasively elsewhere upon a more quantifiable alignment between the 'objectivity' of his neo-classic scores and the goal of authenticity in performances of early music.

But really there is no contradiction between the 'expressive' and the 'invented'. All great composers are concerned with making order, pattern, logic of construction; even Teutonia at its high-romantic apex. Who is more fetishistically careful over the small print, or more compelling in the architectural massing, than Wagner? Who more logical and lucid, almost to the point (sometimes) of laying out a self-analysis, than Brahms? And this remains true even as Teutonia disintegrates—the drowning of Wozzeck, the murder of Lulu, Salome and the Baptist's head, the green-faced chorus peeping through purple velvet curtains in Schoenberg's *Glückliche Hand*, the convulsive pulse and heartbeat that permeate the course of Mahler's Ninth Symphony first movement are classics of *espressionismo* by virtue of their technical and formal exactness, even as they abrade the nerves, churn the stomach and make the flesh creep.Stravinsky's orderliness, placing the emphasis upon logic, construction, obedience to laws and rules, is an indispensable element of all great art. The question is, whether his banishment of its other elements has left enough behind for subsistence.

It would be absurd to tax Stravinsky with an absence of what he can't do, therefore doesn't want to. What he *can* do, and therefore *does* want to, and therefore does, and is, are what matter. And in the interaction of positive and negative, definitions arise characterising the characteristics and qualifying the qualities of the epoch's dominant musician.

His muse is double-faced. On one side gaiety and wit prevail; in this he is unique among the twentieth-century masters (*angst*-ridden to a man). In divertimentos he is elegant, stylish, vivacious, at a pretty consistently high level. But there is nothing trivial in this ideal. The high spirits of a fable like *Reynard* or a morality like *L'histoire du soldat* are intellectual as well as

playful; the audience is likely to be as exhausted as stimulated by this strenuous entertainment; and the same goes for such later displays of athletic wit
as the Octet for winds, *Jeu de cartes* and *Agon* (ballets inspired, respectively,
by a game of poker and a formalised contest between male and female
dancers), or the orchestral Variations, his last purely instrumental work.
Though shadowless, the composer's divertimento-side is not shallow; which
is the cue for the serious face to appear. Not his most scathing adversary
could fail to sense the numinous in Stravinsky. His religious expression is the
antithesis of 'Protestant', eschewing any confessional witness to a 'personal'
saviour. Breast-beating or wrestling with the angel are equally alien. It
speaks, rather, by way of ritual observance, whose profundity resembles the
grave accusing indifference of a Byzantine Pantocrator. This aspect, like the
divertimento, was present nearly from the start—the first survivor is the third
of the three string quartet pieces of 1914 (newly entitled *Cantique* when
orchestrated in 1928); it surfaces soon after in the abortive project for a
Liturgy-ballet (documented by Taruskin with his usual fascinating detail) and
in the process whereby the aforementioned *Symphonies of Wind Instruments*
symbolically renders the Orthodox Burial of the Dead in memory of its great
dedicatee. Gestures like this when similarly placed in otherwise 'secular'
works (often enough divertimentos) can be understood by analogy as liturgical, from the end of the Octet (again) to that of the *Symphony in C* (1940).
The *Symphony of Psalms*, an unimpugnable Byzantine masterpiece, comes at
the very middle of the divertimento-era (1930), and the Mass completed in
1948 foretells the final period in which the great majority of pieces are
religious in inspiration, though never liturgical in function, even when the
text is drawn from the Catholic Requiem.

   Divertimento and Ritual unite in the core of major stage works where all
Stravinsky's principal sources—Russia primitive and sophisticated, Greek
mythology, Christian Orthodoxy—reveal a corporate core; for the theme is
always a variant upon sacrifice, cleansing, propitiating God, or the gods, or
the forces of nature, to ensure the continuity of renewed fecundity—*The Rite
of Spring* (where a virgin is sacrificed), *Svadebka* (where the victim is her
maidenhood itself), *Oedipus rex* (a blinding in order to see clearly, bloody
acts to purge evil blood-relations that have corrupted the body-politic),
Perséphone (the seed must consent to lie annually in the underworld of quasi-
death, that it may be reborn each spring and renew the earth as of old).

   And meanwhile beauty, expelled by the back door for sins of romantic
excess, is admitted in the rational light of noon by the Greek portico hastily
run up at the front. The impulse here is Apollonian; the genre is ballet (the
core of his *œuvre*, providing the idiom for many pieces not originally designated for dancing); the subject, disciplining the body's tensions and aggres-
sions into grace, moving communally in ordered symbolic pattern; an elo-
quence of bodily gesture rather than an expression of internal feeling, an art
of measure and stylisation, with strong sympathetic alignment to the rhetoric,
figures, metres of verse.

Stravinsky can scarcely be faulted! He effects an enormous liberation and refreshment of the musical language, in a large (but not redundant) output. Flawless in facture, delicious in entertainment and diversion, it does not abhor some broader humane themes, and succeeds better than any other of its time with the religious. So how can one complain?

An answer can begin in a round-up of some previous reservations. An early line that can still be heard now and again, especially in England, would see in Stravinsky mainly something cold and clever (a term of disapproval), lacking heart and naturalness, brilliant in colour and energy, short on content, cynically attuned to changing fashion (even when in earlier phases it set the styles) all the way from modernist folklore, via Cubist baroque, Verdi, Mozart, to neo-Webern. Teutonia's counter-attack has more to it and can command heavier artillery: for instance Adorno, with his notorious dismissal of Stravinsky's classicism as 'music about music'. This is one of those backhanded phrases whose apparent significance melts away the more one thinks about what it might mean and how it might apply. What else is the vast majority of Bach and Haydn (to take only the two clearest instances) but music about music, spun from its own substance, essentially made out of its own processes? Schoenberg's graphic metaphor of a naked savage sporting a bowler hat suggests better the serious Teuton's contempt for what must seem, from their angle, the merest cod and faking, ineptly executed ('Stravinsky can't hear below middle C'), sprinkled with wrong notes whose function—for grammatically they are functionless—is to provoke outrage or giggles. Paraphrased, this anti-Stravinsky line says that he is compelled, for lack of grounding in the loamy musical culture of central Europe, to borrow or steal the material that he then subverts, emptying out meaning, retaining only husks and shards.

Direct refutation of these old charges would be otiose so late in the day. Stravinsky has won, his wrong notes are right, his subversions are brilliant, and his way of putting music together from what lies to hand is (almost) everybody's way. And no-one, surely, would any more call Stravinsky cold, or fail to feel how he *burns*. Not with *espressionismo appassionato*, of course. His passion is for exactness and order, he burns to consume the waste, and to reach the essence, be it of an occasional trifle or a major project. For him the precise delineation of a musical object is an all-sufficing aim. But the husks and shards rejected in the process are those aspects of music that matter most to most of its lovers. Ask any average 'lay' music-lover what music means to him, and he will almost always grope after something vaguely romantic, inchoate but deeply-held, concerning the feelings and the emotions. This is by no means incompatible with strong unconscious recognition of the patterns, the construction, even the grammar, by which musical emotion works. But the prime purpose is always this emotion—a fact that the professional musician, especially the academic, tends to forget.

Music's power to move is by no means extramusical; not only is it absolutely intrinsic—first codified in classic times, most memorably encapsulated in the first neo-classic era (Dryden's 'What passion cannot music raise or quell?')—but it is, properly seen, the most important and wonderful thing about it. The 'ignorant' popular view is not vulgar: it is right; and the entire history of the art has been towards the locating, defining, releasing, extending, refining, of 'Musick's Empire', giving it ever-fuller scope to embrace and contain still more of human experience. The endeavour is risky: the incomparable equipoise of effects and causes in Bach, Haydn, Mozart is endangered by Beethoven's heroicism and pathos even as he also takes inwardness of expression to unheard-of heights and depths. The growth of romanticism throughout the nineteenth century can be measured in terms of loss and gain, but who, weighing the wealth of the achievement from Schubert to Berg (say), would care to count the cost?

Its motto could perhaps be 'from the heart, may it go to the heart', attached by Beethoven to the score of the *Missa solemnis*. And its view of music's role is none the less valid for being a bit squashy when put into words (but words are of course not its medium; it shouldn't *need* to be put into words). Music as mental refreshment and spiritual nourishment, solace in loneliness, depression and grief; music as shaper of fantasy and stuff of dreams; music as joy and sweetness. Also as the coursing of the blood, the surge of the libido, the free representation of the inner life of the dynamic imagination even as the outer circumstances of the industrial, the modern, the technological world contract into complete banality. It is an affair of the heart, warm, expressive, charged with sensibility in all things secret and intimate—'the private parts of the spirit'; or 'music's smile' (of sentiment not amusement, though amusement is part of it), expressive of tenderness and delight—the *petite phrase* that, as in Proust, unlocks the past and, as Cosima Wagner said of her Richard's Porazzi-melody (a fragment of *Tristan*-material unused in the eventual work) 'brought back the most secret incidents of her soul'. Music as balsam for aching heart, head, hand; and from this, music as guide to, or goal of, the deepest places of spiritual searching—music that not only exposes and forms and stimulates into utterance the innermost recesses of feeling, but seems to actualise a Platonic idea of human existence—thought, feeling, senses—rendered into a palpable reality. And thence to the most devastating and overwhelming effects of ecstasy and intoxication—the power of music to unite millions as one in a 'Kiss for the whole world' (Beethoven again, but this time setting Schiller).

All this redefines the role of the composer from its earlier incarnations as craftsman or quasi-scientist. A composer's music is born of the whole person—the physiological constitution, the physical characteristics, the identifying voice, gestures, walk; the individual tempo (why is Rossini naturally *allegro*, Bruckner *adagio*?); the personality as revealed in things both trivial (Schoenberg claimed that even the way Mahler tied his cravat was expressive) and vital; the cast of mind and temperament; the intellectual interests; the concerns social, cultural, spiritual, sexual.

Piquantly, Stravinsky is as clear an instance of all this as any composer one can think of—even down to his natty and self-revealing choice of cravats! But he would have outlawed the very idea of the composer as vehicle through which one individual's unique angle upon things, his especial sensitivity, acuity, depth of feeling, is realised by the nature of an equally particular musical gift into musical statements that can be communicated to others, and therefore shared, entered, possessed. And thence back from the composer to the attempted sketch of music's scope. All, all is forbidden: everything that music is able to do more efficaciously not only than any other art but than any other resource known to mankind; what music seems not merely to be *for* (if there has to be a function) but intrinsically to consist *of*: the life of the spirit rendered in sounds, giving wings to cumbersome body and invisible soul, uttering everything that cannot otherwise be uttered, or heard. All this, which those who love music as the world's most precious invention find the most precious of its properties, is ostensibly made illegitimate by the Stravinskian stance which, sweeping all before it, has become the very air we breathe. At first fresh and new, this attitude by now clips the wings and chokes the voice, limiting domains so rich and hard-won, stunting the idea of music in its very essence.

This essence, though permanent and indestructible, is nevertheless at a loss when under attack. Having no defences, it exposes the soft flabby frailty of human nature. Insistence on the soul, the smile, the heart, sounds so woolly! When they are invoked as the measure, silliness, even absurdity, are risked. They've become shaming, so their mocker encounters not resistance, but half-willing collusion from within. For who wants to appear wet and exposed in a posture of abasement; the heart and soul laid bare haven't a leg to stand on! So the attack is bound to hit the spot; embarrassment and self-betrayal are deflected by an affectation of detachment and cynicism. Stravinsky's idiosyncratic stance, born of personal and artistic limitation, has, because of his compositional prowess and the colossal authority born of it, cut music down to his own shape and size and put its larger, less concrete aspects out of court.

The principal weapon is 'irony', a word so ubiquitous nowadays as to merit an attempt at its explosion. Whatever it signified originally—a technical term in Greek drama involving 'speaking by contraries' (Johnson's *Dictionary*)—the idea developed into something both supple and subtle, a play of equivocation that, using the oblique to attain the direct, could penetrate to the core of a character, a situation, a thought, a feeling. Johnson's prime definition 'a mode of speech in which the meaning is contrary to the words' is the mere grit on which this pearl of European consciousness formed. But nowadays it is hard to find a term of comparable richness so trivialised and overworked; it has grown so vague and dilute as to mean virtually nothing. Colloquially it stands for something like 'tongue-in-cheek', odd, coincidental, mildly strange or amusing. Its more 'thinking' use is a careless commonplace in discussion of all the arts, a package containing sarcasm, mockery, parody, pastiche, spoof; disguise by quotation or allusion of the direct statement of explicit feeling and overt engagement; a parrying motion of the reflexes to keep such things at bay; guardedness towards the sublime, the sincere, the heartfelt, the naïve, the ingenuous. Defence against those is certainly required when they're bogus, but defensiveness in the face of the real thing reveals frigidity or cowardice. So irony is a bastion against the too-revealing vulnerability of impulse and spontaneity, a satirical instrument poised to mow it down. From this, its development as a desideratum inevitably follows; it builds upon fear, wariness, knowingness, evasion, to congratulate itself upon, even to rejoice in, unfeelingness.

But at the bottom irony has something to hide, and its guilty secret is the unchanging facts of human weakness, the quivering heart, the distresses of hope, desire, love, illusions and delusions, tenderness and feebleness, the corruptions of sympathy and empathy, and corrosion of compassion: all these poor human characteristics, seen with contempt rather than charity. Stripped of the protective armour of 'speaking by contraries', men and women are revealed in all their pathos—human, all-too-human. From which an escape can be found in the elevation of personal authority and *terribilità*, with its impersonal laws, rules, orders, over the hapless incoherence and muddle of humanity *en masse*. Yet the strength of irony is a false strength; its bristling bastions of defensiveness cannot conceal the internal collapse whereby head, heart, body, hand, are no longer integrated as an organic whole.

What might be called an 'irony' in one of its many debased senses deserves to be reasserted as an evident truth: that music's innate emotional content and message-bearing power can only be achieved through the discipline of construction and technique that the Stravinskian stance claims to be music's sole *raison d'être*. Bach, by common consent the greatest master of pattern and geometry ever known, is also saturated in a language of affective symbolism so harmonically rich as to stand closer to Wagner than to any contemporary or predecessor. Nor can Beethoven and Haydn, the master builders of development and argument, be charged with emotional dryness, except for brief spells of temporary desiccation before a newly-acquired technique has been assimilated and given blood. Contrariwise, the greatest masters of overflow and charged-up expressions—Schubert, Bruckner, Wagner—reveal an astonishing power to find formal and grammatical vehicles, even a geometry, for content that on the face of it would seem to have no chance of achieving organised utterance. Compared with these, Stravinsky, with a body of work, central to the modern spirit, whose consummate brilliance it would be stupid not to admire and rejoice in, seems exiguous. The sanctions he imposed on the name and nature of music bite most sharply at their source. Running right through his glittering yield is a vein of meagreness, perversity and acid. He has composed into his own music his own anti-musicality.

Of course, all great art is born of a collusion between its creator's limitations and strengths, knowing and using both, deriving one from the other. In music the clearest instance is Wagner who, manifestly not much of a melodist by nature, invents 'endless melody' by which unprecedentedly vast spans evolve out of brief pregnant motifs. Stravinsky also exemplifies the old truism well. The evident limits are short-windedness; frugality that can turn mean, and orderliness so exaggerated that it can become mere tidiness. But he also gives the truism an unprecedented twist, in his conspicuous absence of a fount of original, primal musical inspiration. Yet even this apparently devastating limitation can be turned to advantage too, as can be seen in comparison with related figures more generously endowed by nature: Bartók for instance, a *musikantisch* Brahmsian type at the start, only to arrive by remorseless rigour (in emulation, 'ironically' of Stravinsky himself) at self-made deserts of fearful symmetry; or, still nearer home, Prokofiev, over-flowing with natural fecundity, more tuneful, more human, more loveable, but indiscriminate, artistically unscrupulous, self-squandering. Stravinsky, with the careful management that *is* one of his most genuine traits, makes a shorter talent go further than either.

That the other deficiencies are converted to benefits is easier to discern. Shortwindedness becomes the basis for a brusque terseness of articulation and punctuation, a gestural authority, closely related to bodily charisma, unrivalled before or since (Balanchine claimed that he could choreograph every note Stravinsky wrote). This, extended in duration, builds an architecture of interlocking strata and juxtaposed blocks that has become twentieth-century common practice as surely as the polyphony, continuo, sonata (and so forth), of previous epochs. Frugality (or just meanness) and orderliness (or just tidiness) underlie the economy, elegance and precision of every move, and a self-observant self-consciousness permits no smallest detail to pass unexamined, evading cliché, banality and routine even where the sylistic surface makes naughty play with the most used-up materials. Wrong notes become his right notes; he has the courage to sound them in the first place, then relish them, sense and appreciate their strange qualities, and stick to them with single-minded obstinacy. Every scrap and nugget of perversity is worked with rigorous concentration till it becomes a new thing with a new validity. All this is personal indeed, with a sharpness of character born of the intelligence, acuteness, and sheer peculiarity of the ears, which have gradually become the ears by which the entire era hears. But it is the lack of anything fundamental of his own, clearly described in the opening chapters of Taruskin's book, that twists him into complete originality. He must be less gifted for music than any great composer in its history! The absence of an inner well of spontaneous naturalness compels him to forage, from the Folk, from the Past, from contemporaries senior and junior, making himself up out of whatever he cares to hunt down and devour. A new possibility, technical and stylistic, opens out around his every act of theft, rapine and murder; and the musical world, unto the third and fourth generation, has leapt into the outrage and made itself a home.

Can the deliberate emotional hobbling also be seen as a virtue in reverse? The party defence-line (beginning with his apologists in the 1920s and 30s) is that his anti-*espressivo* becomes an absent presence, wherein the music glows with the repressed strength of what it doesn't care to state full-frontally. Such 'suppressionism' clearly hasn't impeded the consistent energy and vitality of the wit, the gaiety, the ceaseless intellectual curiosity. (Compare Webern, where a comparable tendency towards self-pruning clearly results in self-mutilation.)

'Less is more.' But thinking of lost Teutonia, with its fabulous beauty and depth of expression inseparably fused into its technical glories, and all rendered by the loveliness of its undoubtedly right notes, I'm not so sure. Maybe another swing of the pendulum is due.

Stravinsky effected a necessary, timely, and inevitable purge. He was right by gift, by birthplace, and angle upon the art—the primitive onslaught from the East slashing with super-sophisticated weaponry into the bloated body of Austro-Germanic high culture, then piecing together a culture of its own, which substitutes 'Byzantine' impersonality and 'merciless' geometry for heredity and warmth, facture for fracture, in a series of masterpieces almost arrogantly perfected, celebratory, high-spirited, and instinct with religious observance. In all this he is a liberator; yet he is also a constrictor by inhibitions and prohibitions which, arising from individual necessity, harden into Laws as subtly inflexible as those of Schoenberg or Boulez are visibly repressive. In as much as he has permeated twentieth-century usage, one might say as Keats did of Milton that 'our language sunk under him'. But this isn't quite right. Our *language* rose like leavened bread. Having purged the bloated body, he refreshed the words of the tribe by a dose of salts, in a music where every element permitted to survive has been newly thought out. But the sacrifice is grave—it amounts to jettisoning what is so indispensable a part of music's gradual entry into the fullness of its powers that the old-fashioned *Musikant* would call it simply music itself. What music is for, what it can do, what it is, have been enormously curtailed by Stravinsky's particular sense of these things, and to the extent that he has become the air we breathe, our *century* has shrunk rather than sunk under his influence into something tighter, smaller, dryer. The age of Wagner choked the art one way; the age of Stravinsky chokes it another. Yet, paradoxically, this limited notion of musical creativity is hitched to a creative drive of colossal force, that has changed the general sense of what the art can do.

None of this is on Richard Taruskin's agenda, I have to add! I've hung upon a notice of his marvellous book the attempted revisionist account of its subject it has suggested; the composer as a whole, and his whole overwhelming and ambiguous legacy. The very completeness with which Taruskin gives the workings of the *œuvre* in its earlier phases, the cultural cross-currents and individual impulses which go into the making of these ever gleaming pieces and the all-too-human drives that fuel their composer's constructive/destructive trajectory not only add to the wonder but inspire the attempt to carry its story further. Only one man can do this properly. Were Taruskin willing to undertake the two-thousand-odd pages of a sequel covering the biography of Stravinsky's works 1923–71, musical scholarship and the wider world of cultural studies would be still more heavily in his debt.

59

Complex Oedipus

Now that the English National Opera has staged Busoni's *Doktor Faust* and Opera North Dukas's *Ariane et Barbe-bleue,* there remain three twentieth-century operas I long to see well staged in this country, and after seeing them die happy. Two, Fauré's *Pénélope* and Pfitzner's *Palestrina,* are firmly rooted in their own culture however infirmly in ours. The third, George Enescu's *Oedipe,* is homeless.[1] Though composed in French, in the 1920s, largely in Paris, it does not belong there any more than to Enescu's native Rumania. Its accidental displacement makes bitter mockery of a work whose universality is unsurpassed in the music-drama of modern times.

A complete recording coincides this month [November 1990] with the publication of a biography and work list, the fullest in English, by Noel Malcolm.[2] The fruit of the author's patience, care and learning lightly borne, together with the two fine CDs of the opera from EMI, will substantially lift a reputation that, when fully measured, will, I believe, reroute the clichéd highways of received modern-music history.

Perhaps an idiom so unfamiliar can be best defined by its antithesis. The obvious comparison with *Oedipe* is Stravinsky's treatment of the same subject in *Oedipus rex.* Both these 'outsiders' from the east of Europe, born within the same twelve-month and settled in Paris, tackled Sophocles in the same decade. But here the similarities end. Stravinsky uses only the central action—the plague, the hero's vainglorious promise of deliverance, the process of revelation and fall by which it is fulfilled. This 'telegrammatically' brusque abridgment is emphasised by the music's manner: tight, grim, severe. A 'cubist' assemblage of stolen goods ranging from Bach to Offenbach is held in a masterfully stylised vice; the whole is then distanced by an alienating spoken narration and 'turned to stone' (Stravinsky's own phrase) by the Latin language.

The resulting masterpiece combines liturgy and catharsis to unforgettable effect. It would be absurd to use it to knock Enescu's opera, or vice versa. What *Oedipe* has that *Oedipus rex* abjures is the humanistic breadth to encompass the entire story from the protagonist's birth, his confrontation with

[1] 2003: *Palestrina* has now reached Covent Garden, but the other two seem remote as ever.

[2] George Enescu: his Life and Music (Toccata Press, 1990).

the riddle of existence and his triumphant answer; and, after the grisly core, to add a further act of sublimely acquiescent apotheosis.

Nor can Enescu's version be so easily placed in its musical manner. Stravinsky's is characteristically flagrant; he seems to be saying, 'Look what I can get away with!' *Oedipe* is entirely devoid of neo-classical references and only vestigially resembles the possible sources for antique subjects in his adopted culture. The touch of Mantovani in Strauss's Sophocles-opera *Elektra* is never in question. Wagnerian leitmotifs are employed but Wagner himself is absent from the actual sonority and the large-scale rhetoric. Apart from a remarkable foretaste—in the scene where Oedipus encounters the Sphinx—of Messiaen at his most numinous, Enescu's music presages a future that has still not happened rather than recalling the past that has.

There is absolutely nothing cheap or showy in this work by a composer who was also one of the foremost virtuosos of his time. Here the comparison is with Busoni, who, also a lofty idealist, is not free from vulgarity when he tries to broaden the base of his appeal. Both lack the frank tackiness of Strauss, the inverted-comma sleaziness of Mahler, Berg, Weill, or Ravel's naughty commerce with the shopsoiled. But, unlike all these, Busoni's 'common touch' is unsuccessful, which both spoils the attempt to reach the folk and impugns the elevated stance. This Enescu retains, while never becoming tediously grey and high-minded. *Oedipe* achieves something very rare—distinction (in both senses) of utterance which at the same time is charged with tremendous visceral directness.

What of the rest of his output? His music reveals a gradual rarefication, over some five decades, from recognisable beginnings in late German romanticism, French impressionism, Fauré and his native folkstrains (those *Romanian Rhapsodies* that dogged his later life) into something utterly strange. The closest parallel would be as if Bartók, after his prodigious early flowering, had not for the most part grown schematic and mechanised. A comparable heritage, *chez* Enescu, continues to burgeon with ever-increasing suppleness and luminosity. It is 'difficult' music in a sense quite different from the usual problematic strains of contemporary composition. Its passion is sublimated into dispassion, its tortuous processes, sometimes so subtle as to defy direct perception, in the end emerge crystalline. The overall effect is of rhapsodic improvisation yet the notation is obsessively meticulous. The later chamber works especially are at once simple yet complex, straightforward yet elusive, inevitable yet unpredictable; and at their frequent best seem to me to belong easily with the century's highest compositional flights.

60

Expressive sources and resources in Janáček's musical language

An essay to preface Janáček Studies, *a symposium edited by Paul Wingfield (CUP, 1999).*

*   *   *

Broadly speaking either composers want primarily to make shapes, patterns, forms, journeys, buildings, tables, gardens, mud-pies or they want primarily to utter what wells up from within themselves, or from what is suggested within themselves by the impact of things from around them. If Haydn is the ultimate instance of the 'pure' composer writing 'music about music' (though manifestly not deficient in humanity), Janáček can surely be seen as the ultimate composer of *Affekt* in whom music becomes the medium for expression so immediate as to transcend the linguistic metaphor to become in itself the thing that feels and moves.

Suppose, when traversing the back routes of his loved and hated native land by coach or train, a vast pang of inarticulate emotion swells up around the composer's heart—'my country'; suppose, thinking of his parents, his earliest memories, impressions, motivations, sensations, thoughts—'my childhood'; suppose, reliving the deepest, tenderest, most painful intimacies, their mixture of harsh and delicate, tender and cruel, guilty and carefree, blighted and flowering, dampened and burning—'my life'; suppose, then, the composer would seek to 'express' these feelings, to capture the unutterable, as music purportedly can, in a chord-sequence, in a turn of phrase, a rhythmic gesture, a timbral combination, how would he do so? *What* chords, intervals, rhythms, timbres? They would need to be precise, notated without ambiguity (let alone mistakes) as performance instructions to players; also accurate containers of the complex of emotions and sensations, to be conveyed to the listeners so that they understand aright. It would be Janáček above all, and in some respects Janáček alone, who would be able to show how such things might be done.

But only if the means were sonorous—utterance, articulate or inarticulate, though not necessarily verbal. His *raison d'être* for writing music, and his main source of material with which to, is the sound of a human being in a condition of body and soul that compels such utterance. The human sound, whether heard or imagined wrung from the depths, or casually observed in, as it might be, the vocal intonations of two girls chatting as they wait for a man who doesn't turn up.Here with something concrete to start from, Janáček speculates about their characters, their lives, their futures; notates their converse as if collecting a folksong, finds the clue to its rhythmicisation and pitching; and eventually from these, the harmony and coloration that will realise its latent musical life:

> Perhaps it was like this, strange as it seemed, that whenever someone spoke to me, I may [not have] grasped the words, but I grasped the rise and fall of the notes! I knew what the person was like: I knew how he or she felt, whether he or she was lying, whether he or she was upset. As the person talked to me in a conventional conversation, I knew, I *heard* that, inside himself, the person wept ... I have been collecting speech melodies since 1879; I have an enormous collection. You see, these speech melodies are windows into people's souls—and what I would like to emphasise is this: for *dramatic music* they are of great importance.[1]

The same eager appetite to record is applied to birds, beasts, the mosquitoes of Venice, even the waves on the seashore at Vlissingen: there he is, note-book in hand, pencil poised, ears pricked. One feels he could have understood the language of 'rocks and stones and trees' and given contour to 'what the wild flowers tell me', so long as they spoke in noises not signs.

Thus far it could almost be the attitude of an ethnologist, a naturalist, even a speech therapist. But not quite. Janáček, in being after all a composer, can take the idea further: 'Identical ripples of emotion compel rhythms of tone which accord with rhythms of colours and touch. This is the secret of the conception of a musical composition, an unconscious spontaneous compilation in the mind.'[2] After conception, however, the problems begin: continuation, for a start, then continuity into whatever forms and organisations such material will suggest and be able to sustain. The empirical approach—'successive minute touches linked together by instinctive clairvoyance', as Debussy in characterising Musorgsky also characterised himself—is all very well, but there has to be coherence and direction, however spontaneous, and logic, even grammar, however wayward or erratic. Janáček of course knew all this, and here too his solution is typically extreme. Strange though it is to think of him as a theorist of music, he attacked the aesthetic and linguistic problems with all his wonted assiduity, fervour and oddness for most of his life, alongside the composing or, more usually, in unconscious prophecy of it. The almost impossibly elusive current of utterance mooted above, equally

---

[1] Janáček in an interview (8 March 1928) for the Prague literary fortnightly *Literárni svět*, translated in Mirka Zemanová, ed. and trans., *Janáček's Uncollected Essays on Music* (London: Marion Boyars, 1989), pp.120–4 (pp.121–2).

[2] From Janáček's feuilleton 'Sedm havranů' (Seven books), first published in the Brno daily *Lidové noviny*, 30 November 1922, and translated in Vilem and Margaret Tausky, eds, *Leoš Janáček: Leaves from his Life* (London: Kahn and Averill, 1982), pp.101–4 (p.103).

with the prosaic chit-chat of daily life, and every shade of feeling in between, as it emanates in sound, were for him deliberated theoretical goals as well as artistic starting points of tingling immediacy. He wishes by his notions of 'percolation', 'interpenetration' etc.,[3] to elaborate a thoroughgoing quasi-scientific dossier of affective usage wholly congruent with, indeed inseparable from, his 'enormous collection' of human and animal sounds. Old Janáček hearsay—'a chord that bleeds', 'a chord that makes you wring your hands' and so forth—can now be substantiated from what amounts to a composing-kit, however sketchy and in some obvious ways absurd. For Janáček even the most ordinary chord-connections contain an explosive emotional potential. Thus the 6/4 is 'like the swallow flying which almost touches the ground, and by that refreshing, lifts into the heights', and the 4–3 'ruffles' and the V^7–I cadence 'as a breeze ruffles the surface of a fishpond'.[4] If these bedrocks of tonal cliché can evoke such fantasy, the idea that more complex dissonances can cut, or be cut into, with a knife, like a knife,[5] suddenly ceases to be so preposterous.

The aim is for music to achieve its purpose, the intense utterance of feeling, via the startling physicality of its every sonorous constituent. Together, they reach the auditor direct, circumventing formalist routines and play of conventions. Music's innermost meaning lies 'above', 'behind', 'beyond' the working relationships of its notes that make its intrinsic, non-referential grammar.

This sense of what music can legitimately and naturally do leads inevitably to claims still more ambitious. Janáček would, one senses, have endorsed with enthusiasm these questions from the Shostakovich–Volkov *Testimony* that resounds with his own Slav urgency:

> Meaning in music—that must sound very strange for most people. Particularly in the West. It's here in Russia that the question is usually posed: What was the composer trying to say, after all, with this musical work? What was he trying to make clear? The questions are naïve, or course, but despite their naiveté and crudity, they definitely merit being asked. And I would add to them, for instance, Can music attack evil? Can it make a man stop and think?

---

[3] These terms are both attempts to render into English different connotations of Janáček's concept of 'prolínání'; further details can be found in Michael Beckerman, *Janáček as Theorist* (Stuyvesant, NY: Pendragon Press, 1994), pp.72–9.

[4] See ibid., p.115. '4–3' refers here to the intervals formed in a perfect cadence by the seventh of chord V^7 and the third of chord I in relation to the tonic (e.g. F–C and E–C in C major). Janáček's theory of harmony in fact rests on the hypothesis that in chord progressions all the notes in both chords relate to the bass note of the second chord.

[5] See Janáček's employment of the term 'zářez' (incision) in relation to certain types of voice-leading (ibid., pp.66–7).

Can it cry out, and thereby draw man's attention to various vile acts to which he has grown accustomed? To the things he passes without any interest?[6]

'All these questions began for me with Musorgsky', Shostakovich continues. They are equally germane for Janáček. The problem is how, with such views of music as essentially a humanistic moral agent, can it be composed as an art, disinterested, uncommitted, as organisation into grammar and form of pitches and durations and timbres?

Composers who put the *cri expressif* before all else usually have an internal music-machine to turn the wheels, which flows, courses, surges, spins: a force they can drive or be driven by—Schubert, Wagner, Tchaikovsky, Mahler. But when the utterance-type lacks this inner stream, or cannot reach it easily, cannot swim, or finds it dammed, choked, frozen—Schumann, Brahms, Berg are instances—schemes and artifices are needed: games, codes, constructivistic manipulations of material not 'naively' born from music in its primeval state. Though their eventuality appears spontaneous, its making has been contrived, even arbitrary. And when the utterer by instinct is by technique a stutterer—whether because the need for scaffolding or game-playing denies in its defiance of naturalness the utterer's 'from the life' directness, or through sheer lack of musical skill, or even talent, to match the sensitivity of the vibrations and the intensity of the vision—then there are radical problems for which only radical solutions will suffice. Examples of this are Musorgsky again, and Janáček, and indeed Shostakovich too, were it not for his being cursed, contrariwise, with one of the most facile music-machines ever seen. (Instances of vision outweighing skill or talent would include very obviously a Gurney or a Satie, rather controversially a Delius or an Ives.) What all these composers have in common, however different and mutually incomparable, is the primacy of expression. Each has his unique 'letter to the world', or, as Wordsworth said of the poet, he 'rejoices more than other men in the spirit of life that is in him'; he has a message and will burst if it is not delivered. They all stand at the polar opposite from the Stravinskian position which objects in sheer self-defence to music's capacity to say anything whatsoever outside itself.

It is not immediately clear how Janáček relates to these fellow-utterers. To Musorgsky for passionate commitment to naturalism, the expression of emotional truth via truth to human speech. But Musorgsky's manifest deficiencies in compositional technique and miraculous capture, in a handful of songs and some moments of opera, of exactly what he was after—exquisite musical precision in the teeth of incompetence—are like Janáček only in the upshot. For Musorgsky despised learning and training, whereas the youthful Janáček could not get enough. His bottomless craving for discipline is touchingly evoked in the early pages of Michael Beckerman's *Janáček as Theorist*.[7] Then

---

[6] Solomon Volkov, ed., *Testimony: the Memoirs of Dimitry Shostakovich*, trans. Antonina Bouis (London: Faber, 1979), p.181.

[7] Beckerman, *Janáček as Theorist*, pp.1–14.

came the revealing moment (possibly apocryphal) when his youthful work was deemed 'too correct'; a judgement inconceivable *chez* Musorgsky, notoriously 'corrected' by an overseer who mistook empirical genius for ignorant ineptitude or wanton perversity. (The truth being in Musorgsky's case a bit of all three.) The mature Janáček offers a comparable mix, which has again involved well-meant and sometimes well-made improvements to scores wherein brilliance and clumsiness are often juxtaposed and sometimes combined. He was determined, clearly, that his music could never again incur the same charge!

The middle category can be discounted. Janáček did not need scaffolding or schemes to unbind utterance. He is, rather, the most urgent of all composers. Once he found himself, in late middle life, his sheer impetuosity precludes Schumannish letter-and-word-play as much as Brahmsian note-play, let alone the sedulous ramifications and sophistries of a Berg. What he shares with this composer-type is a more personal trait, the obsessive fixation upon an unattainable muse to whom every aspect of his art is referred. Yet while his mature musical speech is nothing if not obsessional, the two fixations do not go hand in hand. He would never chain in codes the fetishistic initials or names or events: blurting directness, not swathed secrecy, is his intonation. But neither does he contain a mighty machine like Schubert, nor the infinite interweave of Wagner's leitmotivic procedures, nor the melodic fertility (and sequential shamelessness) of Tchaikovsky, nor the improvisational splurge of Mahler. The native endowment is song-and-dance length, Dvořák as prototype, manifested in modest, blameless Slav-nationalist successes like the *Lašské tance* (*Lachian Dances*, 1893) or the faded lyricism of the *Idylla* (*Idyll*, 1878) and the Suite (1877). When he gets into being himself the lengths remain brief and the units become tiny, but the shapes are large, and the powers of driving continuity inexhaustible.

The problem is to discover just how music as such can be reconciled with an aesthetic of unmitigated expression grounded in human utterance and guided by such peculiar theories (however well they worked for him in practice). His getting into being himself is a matter first of finding the right genre to take these overriding preoccupations—opera; then of finding what can be done with opera that squares with them, what can be put in and left out, what it can, when radically deconventionalised, astonishingly turn out to be able to do. The crucial leap, precipitated by the harrowing illness and early death of Olga, comes between *Jenůfa* (1894–1903; rev. 1906–7) and *Osud* (Fate; 1903–5; rev. 1906, 1907), the first a masterpiece in a received mould (Smetana not so far behind, except in stature), the second a Confession, of the utmost artistic oddity, an apparently unworkable maverick which, as it happened, prognosticates his late flowering into total idiosyncrasy. Once opera could be made wholly odd, other genres followed: song cycle, string quartet, piano sonata and lyric (here alone are precedents, for this is what the small piano lyric had always been for), all the way to 'Concerto' (the two bizarre works of 1925–6), 'Symphony' (*Sinfonietta*, 1926) and 'Mass' (*Glagolitic*, 1926, rev. 1927).

'Unmitigated expression': Janáček places a higher premium upon this dangerous weapon than any composer before or since. Not that music before him had lacked the desire or the means not just to be freely expressive but to encapsulate emotion within a sonorous image so fully that one has to say that this music means, or says, this thing. Its pre-Romantic history lies in tropes from madrigals and lute songs, onomatopoeia and charged-up rhetoric from Monteverdi to Purcell, Charpentier, Rameau, the entire charter of Baroque *Affekt* and its individual intensification in the hands of J. S. Bach. Nietzsche's notion of a 'lexicon' in Wagner of the most intimate, decadently perfumed, *telling* fragments, the miniaturist in him who palpitates with expressive life whereas the colossal remains stillborn, simply brings into the open what had been achieved with consummate success in countless unflawed gems of Schubert, Schumann, Chopin, and was to flower further in Brahms, Fauré, Wolf, Webern.

As this latter list shows, it is a gift that lies at the opposite end of music's spectrum from opera. The phrase that speaks low, bearing a secret caress or a private message, is a creature of small spaces and small forces—song, solo piano, music for the chamber. Opera is, obviously, a collective genre that needs to raise its voice to cross footlights and be heard in the upper circle. The illusion of intimacy is one of its resources. That it can whisper was well known to such professional masters of the caress as Puccini or Massenet; their desired reaction is corporate, a unison 'oooh!' throughout the house. At the other extreme, the most famous whisper in all opera, the declaration of love in *Pelléas*, is overheard not shared. Janáček's intimacy is as guiltless as Debussy of titillation, but otherwise resembles neither extreme. He is doing something else. Each individual within an attentive audience must feel that this music's utterance is directed to him alone. Even in communal scenes this tendency can be sensed; in the monologues it is undisguised. In Wagner's monologues or duologues the audience is witness to a situation and its participants—this Wotan or Sachs, these two lovers, or two squabbling brothers, or two contrasted sisters (and so on). The presentation is detached, indeed objective, for all the nudging commentary in the orchestra's tissue of leit-motifs and the heated immediacy of the musical language in general. Whereas Janáček compels every hearer to identify with the single figure—the Forester, say—and with every person in a group as his turn comes—the circle of regulars at the village inn, or badger, vixen and dogfox, owl in the forest. Nothing could be further from the various ways in which opera usually proceeds; different though they already are, Janáček is in contra-distinction to them all; he makes verismo and Wagnerismo seem as stylised as aria and cabaletta. Music in Janáček's operas is his means of dissolving the distances and boundaries of convention, not of establishing them. And inasmuch as the same goes for his concert music, thus far does he differ from all other composers.

Auden declared that in *Pelléas* Debussy flattered the audience, meaning (presumably) that, being given so little in the way of the usual vocal delights, their only compensation is the glow of cultural refinement their sacrifice has won them. Yet *Pelléas* is for the most part lovely to hear, if a little washy and deficient in dramatic momentum. These particular criticisms clearly do not apply to Janáček! But he is still more deficient than Debussy in grateful voice-centred lyricism, and can often be harsh, insistent, obsessive, tedious; even his brevity can seem aggressive because so foreshortened and brusque. Whole stretches and one or two whole works could fairly be called repellent for all his growth straight out of Dvořák and Smetana, and his non-relation to any of the commonly hated veins of 'ugliness' in twentieth-century music. He neither 'flatters' the specialised susceptibilities of the refined, nor wows his audience *all'italiana* to bring down the house. In this genre of music more posited than any other on pleasing, he does not try to please. More often, he stings, shocks, burns. His music to go with the whipcracks and chain-bearing in *Z mrtvého domu* (*From the House of the Dead*, 1927–8) renders physical pain that makes the hearer wince; crueller still is rendition in sound of mental and spiritual anguish. Compare the lashing in *Elektra*, the crushing in *Salome*, the torture in *Tosca*, or even such deeper expressions of psychological distress as the Kiss and its outcome in *Parsifal*, or Tristan's delirium. The audience writhes in its plush-covered seats with a groan of satisfaction. These places are protected, and distanced, by music, as surely as the padding and plush separate the soft body from the hard frame. Only such exceptional moments as Boris with the vision of the murdered boy, Golaud twisting Mélisande by her hair, Katerina Ismailova's song about the black lake, the music for the hanging of Billy Budd dare go so naked as Janáček does by habit. While *Wozzeck*, enthusiastically hailed in the last year of his life ('a dramatist of astonishing importance, of deep truth ... each of his notes has been dipped in blood'[8]), can seem altogether too well-dressed, in interesting, absorbing, intricate, richly inventive *music*. And in *Lulu* the discrepancies between its gorgeous sonic opulence, its intellectual fascination and the moral then physical degradation of its characters can often be hard to bridge.

Be it unbearable physical pain or mental torture; or quivers, ecstasies, visions, desires, delusions; or merely some equivalent of the two girls waiting for the man to arrive (like the tiny cameo for the engineer and the young widow in *Fate* Act I), Janáček's unique grip upon utterance, from mind and spirit, in the body, via the voice, produces this 'intimate letter' from individual to individual that, so far from pleasing—flattering, wooing—his audience, is an exposure of them as much as of his characters. He strips the warm clothing of protective safety to reach naked empathy. To get 'into the skin' of, say, Kát'a's religio-erotic outpourings or Emilia Marty's 337-year-old weariness, he puts every auditor there too; singly—there is no plural.

Also there is no space between the state of being and his rendition of it, whether it be just a flock of silly hens or the repartee of visitors at a summer spa—but it might equally be the farmer's decent son suffused with desire and shame, excitement and compunction—and correspondingly, no space between the music and its recipient. The only thing he does not express is *himself*; the

---

[8] Janáček in his 1928 interview for *Literární sv t*, translated in Zemanová, *Janáček's Uncollected Essays*, p.123.

absence of romantic egotistic self-projection is remarkable. So too is the complete avoidance of preachiness; no judgements are made, no moral is drawn. The incentive is generous but by no means soft. Hard, if anything. Also furious and provocative; shocking in rawness; rude, embarrassing, button-holing, speaking too close in your face in public places; as excruciating, or as boring, as it would be in reality—the mad mother's accusations and leap from the balcony, the breakdown at the piano, the night of illicit romance and the subsequent admission wrested from guilt by the conniving elements, the night of icy sex in exchange for a much-desired document, the three prisoners' successive slow-motion monomaniac monologues for the first yet umpteenth time. 'Realism'—not so much an art-historical term, as something the dog brings in, mangled and disgusting, a tribute yet also a victim, for its unwilling owner to share—see, feel, smell, taste, with its own keen senses; added to which, the wholly human sense of what everything *means*.

Yet it is not so much an appeal to pious *Family of Man* humanity ('from the heart, let it go to the heart' as its facile motto), still less a compassionate weepie of emotive blackmail anticipating tendencies all-too-familiar now-adays. 'Janáček is, if anything, hard.' He presents documentation of people observed, caught, notated, collected. The truest alignment lies with the photo-document, akin to the work of August Sander, who plonked a specimen of 'businessman', 'architect', 'composer', 'peasant', 'artiste' before his camera, squeezed the bulb, and gave the world the dispassionate image that makes the viewer weep.It's worth remembering that Janáček too began as a 'human naturalist' in observations from the 'field' that claimed quasi-scientific objectivity. For him this employment is without retirement. The humanity is boundless; the attitude towards its all-too-human-manifestations is ardently unsentimental, most of all in its refusal to stereotype.

To achieve all this his actual music itself, if not exiguous, ought at any rate not to be given first place. In the old operatic debate *prima la musica, poi le parole*, Janáček would award the *pomo d'oro* to expression, rendered by natural human utterance. Which would imply that music as such must be thinned out—the Monteverdi/Musorgsky/*Pelléas* aesthetic rather than the Mozart/Wagner/*Wozzeck*. In fact it is anything but: rather, it is vehement, assertive, busy, gesticulatory, frantic, emotive, and sometimes violently un-restrained. Simply on the practical level the orchestra has often to be curbed in order that the sensitive *parlante* of the voices that it ostensibly supports can be heard properly. Another kind of convention is at work, surprising but necessary, in this recasting of the genre that throws formality to the winds; for music undoubtedly comes first, possibly in spite of Janáček's wishes. He is in the end a composer, odd though this sometimes seems, and the composer in him cannot be prevented. It's not simply that the music is every bit as close-up as the life it renders—this is the first characteristic to strike every newcomer. It is something about his music itself. It can often be insufficient as such, yet it is the only medium that can carry his 'enormous collection' of human intonations, so spontaneously affixed to subjects and characters that it seems he might have collected these, too, at the bus stop or in the fishmonger's. It is the medium for his simultaneous detachment from and involvement with them all, and for his urgent concern to confront each single recipient in a physical encounter with what he has apprehended so acutely. It is the medium through which his recourse to the 'exotic and irrational' genre of opera (though his recasting of it is just as bizarre) can be rationalised and used, and its artificialities made real. It is the medium through which he can utter human speech. As this, it becomes great music like any other—albeit unlike any other in its premises and procedures.

Because Anglo-Saxon culture came quite late to Janáček, some potentially prohibitive problems of interpretation, in every sense, have been largely avoided. From pioneering productions, mainly by the old Sadler's Wells, the operas have become standard repertory in the other principal companies. Our chamber musicians play the chamber works, our tenors sing *Zápisník zmizelého* (*The Diary of One Who Disappeared*, 1917–19, rev. 1920) in Czech, our orchestras pitch bravely into the orchestra pieces and our choirs into the Mass. And with the benefit of outstanding scholarship both historical and textual (its first fruit lies in the series of superlative recordings under Mackerras) the chaos over 'versions' that stood so long in the way of authentic Musorgsky, and can still bug authentic Bruckner, has been largely obviated. Thus the Anglo-Saxon embrace of this initially so localised music has given a picture true enough to need little or no exegesis. What we hear and admire is exactly what there is. His strangeness and extremity have become normative, his obliqueness direct, his foreignness native.

This makes him difficult to write about further. His reception is both ardent and on-target; he is not misunderstood, and no longer a cause. The next steps, alas, are academic appropriation and universal establishmentarianism. That he remains resistant to analysis one discovers when banging one's head against his music in vain. He lays his materials and his processes, however eccentric, so squarely and clearly that there is nothing that cannot be followed, and description or unknitting seems more than usually futile. Monumentalising him is more attractive and more damaging. He has become the unlikely but perfect candidate in an epoch of fragmentative, alienating experiment, deliberate renunciation, even spurning, of liberal-humane themes, for music's continued concern with and expression of them without recourse to the bankrupt debris of late-romantic *espressivo*. He is in his own freaky way a Modern, who retained pre-modernist values while driven to 'make it new' in idiosyncrasy and isolation.

Such is human nature that the moment anything revolutionary shows signs of settling into marble, an impulse of reaction sets in. Perhaps an attempt to work it out can help towards further definition of this strange and wonderful figure. The qualms begin with the element of wilfulness, deliberate mannerism, even affectation—the perversity, cussedness, going-against-the-grain, in all that he does. It is consciously contrary—he seems to be saying 'look how peculiar I can be'. Which is of course inseparable from his genuine strangeness whose authenticity and ardour cannot be mistaken. The choice of way-out subjects goes with the choice of way-out instrumental registers, voicing and spacing, odd habits of momentum and eccentric notations of both pitch and rhythm. It is as if burning sincerity *depended* upon being peculiar. When it works, his idiosyncratic vision carries music's empire into territory hitherto unsuspected. When it does not work, the result is merely eccentric without illumination.

And there is no difference. His manner is so all-pervasive that the stretches where he is tedious are indistinguishable from the stretches where he is electrically inspired. The pressure is as consistent as if he wrote always in *italics* or CAPS. Thus, initially at least, discrimination is disarmed. Recognition of the co-existence of inferior material indistinguishable from superior material, with plenty of infill between the two, is compounded by the unfamiliarity of the idiom as well as its gestural consistency. And that all of it is equally aimed at the utterance of burning human intensity makes it still more difficult. When everything depends upon the throb of committed subject-matter, making secondary the calibre of the materials and their workmanship, then tendentiousness looms. Because Janáček is manifestly as artist and as exalted spirit far above any low emotional blackmail, it seems mean to hold artistic scruples concerning the protagonists of a Makropulos affair or amidst the denizens of a prison-house. Like holding one's nose and passing by on the other side; like denying that in every living creature is a spark of God. But one has to acknowledge that, in taking on such subjects and treating them with such all-out sincerity, Janáček has deprived his listeners of their options.

Fate near the start of his maturity, *Věc Makropulos* (*The Makropulos Affair*, 1923–5) and *From the House of the Dead* at its end show the difficulty most clearly. Between them comes the bulk of his mature achievement with its exact match of idiosyncratic music to the subject it sets, from the most intimate—*The Diary of One Who Disappeared* and the two programmatic string quartets (1923, 1928) drawn respectively from fiction and from life with equal immediacy—to the most public and ceremonial—*Sinfonietta* and *Glagolitic Mass*; not forgetting such joyous divertimenti as *Mládí* (Youth, 1924) and the *Říkadla* (*Nursery Rhymes*, 1925; rev. 1926). But the triumphant vindication of theory and practice alike, in all their peculiarity, comes in the two central operas, *Kát'a Kabanová* (1920–1) and *Příhody Lišky Bystroušky* (*The Cunning Little Vixen*, 1922–3). Their greatness silences reservations; the human tragedy with its blight upon happiness, tenderness and ardour crushed beneath the pitiless tyranny of propriety, and the animal comedy with its ecstatic cycle of endless renewal circumventing the vicious circle of ageing and death, are manifest high peaks of the century's artistic endeavour, good deeds in wicked times, vindicating humane themes in an epoch of cynicism and mechanisation.

So too are the three more awkward pieces, where greatness is flawed by his peculiarities outstretching their limitations, the inescapable obverse of his chosen manner. In all of them situations of extreme boldness are matched in music that appears to be on the point of fraying through sheer stress of wear. Sonorous images of unforgettable originality and intensity lie alongside stuff that sounds as if it was the first thing that came into his head in his tearing haste to get it down on paper.

In some ways *Fate* is musically the most satisfying. It shines with unforced surprise at what the new techniques can release, above all the way that the speech intonation of the voices grows into instrumental texture and thence into a continuity which can shape a whole act. Both in the 'photographic' rapportage of its places—the sunny day at the animated spa, the storm raging while the apprehensive students gather round the piano to rehearse their master's opera—and in the 'reports' from a terrain of private anguish shot through with twisted disturbed states of being—Janáček is pushing to the ultimate from two opposing yet fused positions, the avid theorising and the lacerating poignancy of his daughter's words notated as she lay dying.

Yet the artistic catalyst was Charpentier's *Louise*, that talent-free piece of cheap tat! Like many a child of its time, something in it, lost to later comers, sufficed to fertilise a work that completely transcends it. But *Fate*'s deeper kinship is rather with such adjacent theatrical adventure as Strindberg (for the painfully private pushed into public exhibition), Pirandello (for its extraordinary games of life *vis-à-vis* art in the work's own workings), Chekhov (for acute human observation, told by implication and ellipsis), and Maeterlinck (poetic suggestiveness in meshes of repetition and echo). Of course it is in such company vitiated by its amateurishness—the inept stage mechanics, the arty language, the inartistic ambiguities as opposed to those that function. Livid, red-hot content, clumsily handled, into which sensitive production can breathe the convincing theatrical life given it by the music, every page of which is infused with the passion that forced it into being. *Fate* is the first opera ever in the difficult new area, set up by Janáček, where the music, though vehemently present, could not exist as such without the pressure of what has caused it, without which it would simply disintegrate. Which is more of a tribute than a qualm.

And *From the House of the Dead* is the last. (It is worth remembering that he neither saw nor even heard either work.) Every discovery so fresh and vivid in *Fate*—speech intonation filling out the entire instrumental fabric, violent foreshortening, quasi-cinematic flashback, intercutting, montage— here reaches the end of its tether. The three acts are articulated through sonorous imagery of unforgettable simplicity, sometimes sweet, sometimes exalted, more often naked, gawky, awkward, and frequently pulverising in its ferocity. The simplest and most memorable idea of all, the *Urklang* that, like the *Tristan* chord, brings the whole work before one's eyes in a flash, is a chord of only three pitches but so spaced and voiced as to verge upon the physical pain it depicts.

This sound dominates Act I in an orchestra of squeals, squawks, shrieks up high, and growls, lurches and scrabbling down below, presenting a claustrophobic *huis clos* of oppression, lashings, privation that makes *Billy Budd* seem snug as a captain's cabin. Between piercing acridness and menacing snarl the 'stuffing'—the orchestra's middle range of warmth and support—

has been kicked away, replaced only by the clash of chains and the furious orders of a military drum. The shafts of ardent tenderness in the course of Luka's Lujza-narrative provide pain of a different kind. In Act II the bare start—a *Bohème* Act III, with chains—then the brilliant success in the risky endeavour of presenting bell-sounds by real bells as well as their instrumental imitation, then the unwonted gentleness of Skuratov's monologue all yield to the riot of crazy energy discharged into the holiday double-bill—cheeky, coarse, vulgar, parodistic, cubist Dvořák crossed with x-ray instrumentation *à la Renard* (the nearest comparison in burlesque folkloric puppet theatre), littered with 'the right wrong notes'; real 1920s impertinence but entirely his own, all the more remarkable within an idiom that however stretched remains fundamentally euphonious and Czech.[9]

The first part of Act III presents in the piteous tale told by Shishkov a perfect instance of Janáček's 'manners' as distinct from his mannerisms. Its villain–hero, unrecognised, is nearby, dying. Coughs, spasms, death-gasps, are rendered, but not the actual moment of death—not a nudge, let alone a symphonic elegy, simply a stage direction at an arbitrary turn of the narration, which itself is equally non-expressionistic. The agonising tenderness of the scenes with Akulina, so long ago, so immediately relived, is not exuded by the haunting beauty of the accompanying string-phrase but contained within it— the ultimate example of Janáček's 'concordance' (so to speak) hurting more, wringing more from its hearers, than the most excruciating of dissonances or the most swooning *espressivo*. Yet it is during the later stages of this same monologue that inspiration flags and monotony sets in which is not intended and does not contribute to the artistic impact. Instead, it is accidental: the music, going on just as before, goes off the boil to become not the suggestive minimum that permits a closer proximity to emotional truth, but merely, actually, scrappy. A dividing line that cannot be drawn has nevertheless been passed. Once discerned, it can never be ignored.

And thus the closing stretches stir up contrary reactions into a profoundly disturbing ambiguity. A wild priapic character infuses this music; it is 'possessed' in Dostoyevskyian fashion, driven by demons, written in speed and chaos, faster than it can be composed, written as if 'each of its notes has been dipped in blood'.[10] This churning brew of simultaneous upsurge and

---

[9] Like all great originals he was anxious to appear unbeholden, but he has to wear borrowed garments boldly because the personality within is incapable of disguise. Strauss and Debussy, as well as Puccini, figure unmistakably yet wholly translated. The remarkable parallels with Sibelius are presumably the result of affinity rather than knowledge (some of the most striking, the 'Janáček' in the *Kullervo Symphony* written when Janáček himself was still writing 'Dvořák', he couldn't possibly have heard or seen since the work lay withdrawn and unpublished after its first performance in 1892 till well after Sibelius's death).

[10] And reminding one of a still-more-physical metaphor: 'then I'll paint with my prick,' said Renoir ('*really* vulgar, just the once', his son comments), when his hands were threatened by crippling arthritis.

down-tread produces extraordinary emotional turbulence. A clear comparison again comes from *Billy Budd*, where the fomenting mutiny after Billy's execution is drilled back into order (Janáček provides the visceral thrust, Britten the fudge). A longer shot might be to find it akin to the feelings of the elect, among the audience revelling in the Hymn to the Leader, who share the unspeakable secret that by this music Stalin is excoriated. But in sheer musical calibre—and what else is there?—the ideas cannot take the strain. The power, incontrovertible and in its way beyond compare, comes from everything else. This is great *something*—Electricity, Intensity, Strangeness, Compassion, Uplift, Humanity—the actual notes are second to whatever in Janáček's version of the operatic equation comes *prima*.

The *Makropulos Affair* shows such worries more plainly. The electricity and shock inherent in story and situation go without saying. They produce awed astonishment at the boldness of treatment and breadth of understanding. But cavilling cannot be sopped. One is aghast at the really poor musical ideas upon which so much depends, especially the big primal melodic gesture manifestly intended to be the clue to the opera's dizzying subject; most of all when it is given in the fullest blaze of his orchestral heat an apotheosis that it cannot bear. Not even recourse to wordless off-stage voices (unforgettable for the seduction in the *Diary*, wonderfully atmospheric as soul of the Volga in *Kát'a* or the spirit of the forest in *Vixen*) can save the scene of Elena's rejuvenescence and disintegration which, by virtue of its extreme singularity, leaves the listener aghast anyway. The chorus in the third act of *From the House of the Dead* falls just the right side of emotional manipulation to be heartstopping, but it's a near thing. Its use in *Makropulos* is not so much manipulative as by rote, an 'effect', synchronised with the surreal lighting, disconcerting in a composer who, unlike Wagner, would seem to have no truck with such old tricks.[11] Elsewhere, *Makropulos* surpasses all his other stage works for variety, quiddity and unexpected wit—the 'Spanish' vignettes, for instance, which encompass a tiny world of quaint, touching vulnerability; though it also has, overall, the highest proportion of routine, humdrum and (dare one say) note-spinning. Often one wishes he had never happened upon the whole-tone scale or the ostinato. In really bad moments one can even regret the whole doctrine of speech-inflection upon which his art is based.

Such qualms, reservations, scrupulous attempts to sift chaff from grain, attempts to pinpoint the weakness with the greatness, are all very well. Then one hears Janáček again and falls to one's knees. He pulls and pulls your ears till you scream with the pain. Your art and your life fly about you in demented fragments; you are 337 years old and life has dried within you; you have murdered an officer, and a man who came between you and your girl, and then your sweetheart herself. You are exposed in all your human baseness. Yet you are not just told about the spark of God in every creature, you are

---

[11] It's true that Janáček wanted the *Diary* to be performed in a ghostly 'half-dark' lighting; but the work does not *depend* upon such an adventitious effect: here, as always when at his best, he's got the emotion into the notes.

made to feel its actual presence. You rejoice not with the stoical wriggle of the cut worm who forgives the plough but with the soaring flight of the freed eagle. Janáček, musical theorist, human ethnographer and composer, has brought all this about. There has never been anything like it, with or without music. 'What's music to do with it anyway?' Though, more often than not, the music is fully up to the insistent demands he makes upon it.

61

'Use your ears like a man'

This year's [1996] choice by the BBC of an individual twentieth-century composer for their annual January retrospective is Charles Ives, who died forty-one years ago and was born eighty years before that. Yet Ives seems like a contemporary still.

In part, this is fortuitous: his principal outburst of creative activity was concentrated into a couple of decades or so at the start of the century; they coincided with a strenuous and successful career in the insurance business. Some obscure breakdown of health and morale in the early 1920s brought both activities to an end, and he lived his final thirty years in wealthy reclusion, financing publication of a small part of his vast output, but seemingly uninterested in pushing it for performance. Disinterested too, preferring to forward the radical juniors who often remained ignorant of the fact that his own unvaunted discoveries had predated and sometimes pre-empted their own.

This meant that the chief impact of his work came late in his life, then posthumously—a time-bomb in a time-capsule. Problems abounded. Two of the most radical scores required a great deal of reconstruction. The astonishing Fourth Symphony was first played under Stokowski in 1966; further deciphering of Ives's labyrinthine hieroglyphics have led to later versions which compound the complexities to an almost unimaginable level. Its successor the *Universe Symphony* has only been realised for performance, to the extent that its fragmentary state permits, in the last few years. And though his largest work for solo piano, the *Concord Sonata*, was engraved in his lifetime and has entered the repertory of pianists bold enough to confront its transcendental difficulties, scarcely a season passes without the discovery of further variants that put a definitive text for ever out of reach.

These are extreme cases. But Ives's strangeness embraces even the few pieces which have become more or less established on the margins of standard orchestral fare. It is difficult to imagine that familiarity will ever blunt the best known: *Central Park in the Dark*; *Three Places in New England* and—most famous of all—*The Unanswered Question* (this also providing a well-chosen overall title for the BBC season). The bizarre mixture of intrepid exploration, visionary utterance, humour sometimes quirky but more often abrasive, with musical materials of the most prosaic homeliness will always remain surprising.

The mix doesn't always fuse. Ives would doubtless say, in his no-nonsense way, what the hell? 'What has sound got to do with music? Use your ears like a man!' But the truth is that, writing with such profuse abandon, he had no use for niceties either genteel or in the deeper sense whereby works of art achieve coherence even as they render the bewildering chaos of daily experience. Some of his seething stews of undigested collage give a queasy turn to the robustest appetite.

But when it does work it is without parallel. Take one of his highpoints, the *Holidays Symphony*. It dedicates each of its four movements to an American national festival—Washington's Birthday, Decoration Day, Thanksgiving and The Fourth of July. Each of these celebrations, lovingly evoked by adult recapture of a boyhood vantage-point, is made from an accumulation of folkloric *bric-à-brac*—barn dance and parlour-song, parade marches and circus polkas, hymnody and church bells—perceived in a hyper-real present, rough rustic and sweaty, which is simultaneously distanced with the most intense nostalgia down the tunnel of the years, and also overlooked *sub specie aeternitatis* as if from some lone star twinkling remote and unhuman in outer space.

With pieces of this order—they include the *Three Places* (with its wonderful effect of two regiments marching at different speeds, and then the glowing evocation of the Housatonic River in autumn) and its sequel the *Second Orchestral Set* (whose final panel unforgettably renders the spontaneous communal reaction of the New York rush-hour crowds to the news of the torpedoed *Lusitania* in 1915)—Ives is unambiguously among the great composers. The unflawed masterpieces also include many songs with piano and some fascinating miniatures for ensemble, where experimentation, visionary beauty and weird jokiness are expressed with a delicacy and intimacy at first surprising when one has heard only his glorious splurging orchestral writing. And even when his weirdness doesn't fully come off, the results remain fascinating.

For every aspect of Ives, from the tiniest to the vastest, the most refined to the most raucous, the most outré to the most homespun, has been important. First his modernism, prophetic of so much that followed generations later; and now its complement, the wholesale ingestion and transformation of the vernacular, is an equally potent example. Uniquely, he got these things together rather than holding them in separate pigeon-holes. Born in 1874, Ives is still our contemporary, and indeed our future.

62

'But is it art?'
Gershwin in a classical context

Essay for the programme-book of a Gershwin-Fest at the Barbican Hall marking the fiftieth anniversary of his death in 1987.

* * *

It is difficult properly to evaluate George Gershwin, the twentieth century's most popular composer. The most direct comparison is with his compatriots and music for stage and screen: the delights of Irving Berlin, Cole Porter, Richard Rodgers are many and various, and while Jerome Kern can dig deeper, it is evident by now that Gershwin remains unsurpassed in musical substance by these or subsequent musicians in the same line. Talents are more equally matched when he is placed with the three masters of nineteenth-century operetta: Offenbach and Second Empire Paris, Johann Strauss and the palmy days of imperial Vienna, Sullivan and the high-Victorian London whose tone was already Edwardian, Gershwin and glitzy Broadway and Hollywood shows of the 1920s and early 30s. All are period-pieces perfectly evoking the culture from which they sprang, local in inflection, universal in popular appeal, achieving the status of folklore. And then there is the music that, whatever its origins, has become core pops-repertoire. Gershwin's concert pieces clearly belong here, and bring him without incongruity into contact with the lighter side of some weighty composers.

None the less these direct comparisons somehow fail to get Gershwin right. He is different, and bigger. How does he stand in relation to the 'serious' achievements of his own epoch? Comparison now becomes sullied by the awkward question of popularity: Gershwin is far more widely enjoyed than even the best-known modern masters whose work, historians agree, has changed the course of music. Consider the century's crucial radical composer, still contentious unto the third and fourth generation, Gershwin's friend and admirer Arnold Schoenberg. At the time of Gershwin's meteoric rise to fame, Schoenberg reorganised musical grammar so drastically that it still hurts. The result remains as unassimilated by the average music-lover as when it was new. Scholars can trace a soundless echo of the performances it receives neither in the concert hall nor, as Schoenberg touchingly wished, on the lips of whistling errand-boys. Other kinds of musical experimentation have also proved generally unacceptable. Is it their fault? Is Gershwin better because of his enormous appeal? How is Success weighed against Importance?

Such polemically poised questions tend to invite Philistine answers, whether culture-bashing or elitist. It will be more fruitful to describe the four principal classical composers of recent times who really tried, and managed, to touch the popular pulse.

The boldest of these composers is Kurt Weill. Beginning as an 'ivory-tower' artist, he answers the internal call that his music communicate burning social and political issues by adopting the features of the American dance music which in the late 1920s was sweeping across Europe. Unless the cure is to fail, the medicine must reach the malaise, so its taste must attract. Weill's decision to debase his style is responsible and admirable; but his real power lies in the consequent release of a musical allure that corrodes the pill it was intended to coat.

Aaron Copland, though not initially, had become by the early 1930s a difficult composer understood only by a sophisticated minority. His subsequent stylistic simplification shows that the wish to reach a large audience is sincerely compatible with a sensitive response to public events, from Depression through to New Deal. Music greets the Common Man and the career prospers. By rigorous essentialisation, with Stravinskian irony and un-Stravinskian warmth, the raw materials of the American past, wild West or plain East, are slanted into a genuine vernacular, soon recognised and treasured as such.

Dmitri Shostakovich, however, begins modernistic in the last years when the Soviet State still allows it. Once the Golden Age is over he is told what he ought to write, not by sympathetic vibration with the times but by orders from above. Compulsory accessibility lasts until he is too eminent to be harried, and returns to the bleak final fulfilment of his youthful subjectivity, which, ironically enough, also touches a popular nerve.

Benjamin Britten does not have to de-modernise, when prompted by the atmosphere of England in the late 1930s to 'Advance Democracy', since he was gifted from the start with simplicity of utterance. Rather it is his achievement, in the operas of his prime, to turn this directness of appeal towards normalising highly personal themes in such a way that they work viably and successfully for audiences the world over.

The compulsion (whether from without or within) to broaden their style was beneficial for all these composers. In each case the spirit of the age has forced into flower an individual genius for popularity, with enormous benefit to musical culture at large. They contrast interestingly with Prokofiev and Poulenc, the only other recent art-composers of manifest stature and popularity, both of them accessible not because of ideology or unconscious opportunism, but because they can't help it.

Gershwin of course is also a 'naïve' composer (in Schiller's sense of being at one with his nature and his gift); there is no political mission and no crisis of style; for low commercial purposes he copiously yields high calibre music, which, immensely appealing to enormous numbers of people immediately and ever since, is problematic only in the attempt to define and evaluate it. Having set him in context I want now to start again, this time from the premise that Gershwin is a great composer, and see what follows.

The claim is based principally upon the songs from the shows (always provided that his own original harmony is unbowdlerised). His work here is at its most commercial, obedient to the genre with its given lengths, received range of sentiment and level of stylistic suitability. There is no sense that he wants to transgress these conventions, no discrepancy between what is expected of him and what he delights to give. Here he produces his most inventive, intense and distinctive music. So he is, in Hans Keller's phrase, 'a major master of minor forms' (but why should a song be called a minor form?): like, say, the Chopin of the Mazurkas or the Wolf of the Italian Song Book (for both of whom, as for Gershwin, the basic type is already given) or the Webern or Grainger of tiny forms that they have evolved for themselves. This category, of course, overlaps with the miniature masterpieces of composers who are also masters of 'major' forms—say, Bach's smallest chorale-preludes, Schubert's songs, Tchaikovsky's dance-numbers, Brahms's late piano pieces. The ideal behind all such music is the intense lyric utterance formalised and distilled, the brief duration filled with ideas both unmistakably personal and worked with a scrupulous precision that explores and expands all their possibilities.

These are exalted comparisons: for me Gershwin's best songs can sustain them. Insubstantiable claims arise only with his more 'artistic' endeavours. The concert-works contain splendid song-material, many touches of mastery and tons of vitality, but are damaged by formal stiltedness, exposing itself in padding, shortcircuiting and overblown rhetoric. That he was growing into bigger sizes is shown by *An American in Paris* (where the working-out between the 'hits' is more inventive); in the *Cuban Overture* and *I Got Rhythm* variations, where the whole is surer but the actual material is less distinctive. Only the *Second Rhapsody* gets the balance right, till its 'applaud loudly now' conclusion. But all-in-all, Gershwin's concert-works reveal, beneath the bravado, a character both vulnerable and naive: the best reply to his anxious quest for approval, demonstrated by his insatiable desire for high-class composition-lessons, is Ravel's 'Why be a second rate Ravel when you can be a first rate Gershwin?'

Porgy and Bess is a different matter. Its inspired fusion of Broadway and Hollywood with Negro Spirituals, Shouts and Blues puts the whole endeavour onto a different plane; for all its manifest lapses it stands with Berg's *Wozzeck* and Britten's *Grimes*, Janáček's *Katy'a* and Shostakovich's *Lady Macbeth*—the outstanding operas of compassion for the social outcast, breaking down barriers of style, class, and race.

But if it is to be the songs on which the main claim rests, what about the vulgarity, or downright ignobility, of their content? The subject is almost always romantic love, normative and sentimentalised; the tone oscillates between ardour and wryness, the emotional accent is commonplace. The lyrics, deftly crafted and delicious, hardly plumb the depths; the shows as entities put two-dimensional characters into plots consisting of little more than pretexts for a set-piece of song and dance. This is mass entertainment, that must appeal at once, or flop.But the musical ideas Gershwin finds are far superior to what is needed. His music seizes the true feeling that underlines every banality, intensifying it, as far as it can bear, with the Russian–Jewish fervour of melody, and especially harmony (that link him, after all, with Weill and behind him Mahler), and the physical vitality of rhythm and metre that, more obviously, connect with Copland, and hence Stravinsky.

This suggests that familiar situation where a cheap text on a sublime subject is transfigured by inspired music. But with Gershwin, because he is in tune with his subject and its level of utterance, the usual escape clause is not needed. A low style and content is fully integrated with musical gifts of a very high order; the emotional charge of one of his great love-songs is primal, going to the basis of pleasure more freely and directly than anything else in the whole range of music.

Pleasure—the very word is like a knell, closer-allied to pain than enjoyment, not least in our approach to the advanced culture of twentieth-century music. We sweat through *Lulu*, we fight through *Die Soldaten*, we must rise to *Moses and Aaron* and submit to *Donnerstag* or *The Mask of Orpheus*. Contrariwise, there is shame in the easy enjoyment of uncomplicated music—especially when, like Gershwin's, its sensuality is so frank. The prevailing imagery of our time puts indulgence in grossly seductive foodstuffs against the bran, iron, and vitamins that are good for us; pleasure counters with 'naughty but nice', the slogan 'can damage your health' incites dangerous thrills, to be curbed in turn by a regimen of cold baths, workouts, and all the rigours of the natural life. Artistic attitudes are still fundamentally puritan: pleasure is guilty, virtue grows as predilection and appetite are denied, enjoyment is a veneer upon Victorian Improvement. The ways of cultural self-deception are devious but they all end in hypocrisy.

Yet real unguarded desire will always, like water, find its level. Witness the ever-rising reputation of those serious composers—for instance Puccini, Berg, Tchaikovsky, Mahler, Strauss, Messiaen—who, in whatever ways, subvert once-received canons of good taste, compelling our 'lenience' to what had formerly been considered 'weakness'. Gershwin, being so completely commercial and vulgar, has a harder time. But eventually the directness of its appeal to all that is lowest in us, and the warmth and energy of its expression, dissolve snobbery whether direct or inverted. It is base and low, richly tasty and utterly tasteless, sexy and juicy—all this with both passion and tenderness and an ease of manner, a good-humour and happiness that is out of phase with the general tendency of modern culture. Everything is on the sleeve and below the belt; no faked-up seriousness, complexities, anxieties, rebarbarations, abstractions stand in the way of what everyone wants. 'Ain't got no shame, Doin' what l like to do' (as the chorus sing in *Porgy*).

And paradoxically, for all this robust vulgarity, Gershwin's musical means are remarkably pure. He is one of nature's grammarians, with an exactness in gauging chromatic inflections in tonal contexts surpassed only by

Schubert and Chopin. In all three composers there is a classic simplicity of harmony: a compositional essentialness, as in a Schenker analysis, lies behind the details and the individual traits of style.

Many very different great composers, then, can be mentioned, either in direct comparison or by oblique affinity, in an attempt to focus Gershwin's greatness more clearly. They are not demeaned by the contact, nor is he elevated in ways that do his cause disservice. His content lies in his notes, and the notes cannot lie. With characteristic naïve pride Gershwin asked Alban Berg why he so loved his songs; the answer was simply, 'Music is music'.

Aaron Copland

A review, turning towards a general appreciation, occasioned by Howard Pollack's biography which appeared from Faber in 2000 to coincide with the hundredth anniversary of the composer's birth.

* * *

Copland's music is oddly difficult to encapsulate. The *œuvre* is shapely and reasonable, virtually every genre is represented, the talent fully used; its trajectory is clear, from 'roaring twenties', via radical thirties, patriotic forties, fifties where renewed experiment fuses or alternates with demotic American in fine consolidation, succeeded by spare sixties, and in the seventies, dilution and dearth. Then the sound itself, whatever the stylistic vicissitudes, unfailingly frugal, lucid, exact, so shadowless and unambiguous as to be paradoxically elusive. Expression is not expelled with menacing pitchfork *alla* Stravinsky nor repressed *à la* Ravel (to take the two composers who make the clearest comparison). Within the hard flat brightness unmistakable for any other music—brazen, clangorous, metallic, glassy, strident, gaunt— lies the equally unmistakable Copland tenderness, oddly wistful (a favourite word), shy, stammering, vulnerable. Beyond both lies the seer, visionary lawgiver of such places as the declamatory close of the *Symphonic Ode* and *Music for a Great City*. Yet unlike his friend Benjamin Britten there is no self-expression via choice of subjects, motifs, texts, and unlike Mahler (an unexpected but fruitful influence from first to last), absolutely no musical autobiography.

So what about his actual life? Copland seems always to have known his own worth and who he was, understanding and embracing his exemplary standing as the first all-American professional composer. From the very beginning he evinced the sedulous care that had at the end of a long busy life accumulated 'approximately four hundred thousand items', varying from the MS scores to trivia and ephemera, all ready for the Library of Congress. His life is a model of integration and balance: like the music, there is nothing in excess, nothing wasted; precise without dryness, tight without costiveness, it flourishes within a harmonious relationship of public and private, conspicuously elegant and sober, for all the abandon; devoid of illusory goals, lurching embarrassments, painful agonisings, self-reproaches, guilt and compunction. Even when some twenty years before his death at ninety the life's *raison d'être* began to diminish before ceasing altogether, his attitude was calm and stoical. Then the depletions and humiliations of 'senile dementia' (this hideous technical term corresponds ill with the personal sweetness that never wavered in domestic contexts as I and countless others can remember) were worn with the same casual grace with which he habitually drsssed and the same bemused shrug with which anything ugly—the McCarthy persecutions; or painful—the troubles with Victor Kraft and later lovers—had always been accepted and accommodated.

Howard Pollack has produced a biography to match—the Official Record, first fruit of a laborious and scrupulous overview of those 400,000 items in the Library of Congress (together with many new interviews and personal communications), even-handed, neither whitewashing nor blackening, hagiographic nor demonising. Comprehensive, orderly, exhaustive, it could hardly have been better done.

The character is astutely assessed and the work-habits described, before we move off into lineage, early life and influences, the Boulanger-training, the penurious first years back home—setting out to make a living by composing took courage, and it's quite a shock to realise that only with the film scores from 1939 on was he able to support himself by his own creative efforts (but he was born knowing what money meant and how to handle it!). Artistic and intellectual background is somewhat ploddingly covered, and we move more freely into consideration of friends, associates, supporters, patrons, peers, performers, lovers. It is remarkable how the frequent pattern whereby a promising but vaguely troubled young artist was helped on his career in exchange for sex somehow doesn't seem to involve exploitation and bad-blood—a tribute to Copland's warmth and responsibility; and the moral weight occasionally exerted here recalls Bernac's authoritative call-to-order of the distraught and demoralised Poulenc.

The educational endeavours and writings about music are all duly slotted in, and the politics covered—the thirties, good solid left-wing stuff (not just the expected Group Theater and workers' songs, but actual speeches to real farmers at the grass roots); then its nightmarish postwar rebound in the bad years of UnAmerican Activities (Copland! UnAmerican?). The gradual development of his ambassadorial role is described, interlinked with his conducting career and its lively, disinterested repertoire. The composer is considered as Jew, as homosexual, as American, with a neat fusion of the three; the late years are sympathetically handled, and a judicious summary closes the proceedings. Every piece he wrote is put into context and adequately described, though the technical discussion is (deliberately) limited and (not so intentional) the critical tone is bland, allowing flavour and essence to escape.

But it would be churlish to complain. Nor do I! Yet something is missing from these fair full pages (555 of them, with another 106 of often invaluable notes). As with the equally indispensable but comparably disappointing two-volume compilation of reminiscences, interviews, recycled programme-notes, cameos by colleagues etc. that Vivian Perlis put together with the composer's

collaboration (vol. 1, Faber, 1984; vol. 2, Marion Boyars, 1992) the overall
effect is very slightly tedious. Pollack cannot be accused of the earlier effort's
prudishness, and indeed he 'tells all' without sensationalism. While wholly
sympathetic and, where needed, reverential without obsequiousness, he fails
to attain inwardness with the 'boy from Brooklyn' (and not so far behind,
from the Pale of Settlement) who by dint of hard work, high intelligence and
innate self-discipline extended a slender compositional talent to major
proportions, with such effect that he can truly be said, with Stephen Daeda-
lus, to be 'forging in the smithy of his soul the uncreated conscience of his
race'; in music and, because of the very nature of such an achievement, not
just in music alone. The clearest suggestion as to what this book fails to
illuminate comes when it quotes Bernstein detailing Copland's grandeur,
delicacy, severity, rage, bite, howl (etc. etc.; I've omitted all the adjectives
and some of the nouns!) before proceeding 'None of which corresponds with
the Aaron we loving friends know; it comes to us from some deep mysterious
place he never reveals to us except in his music'. No doubt the relationship
between creator and creation will for ever remain mysterious at best, and
ultimately unknowable; but it can be explored to good purpose, and it behoves a book like this to make the attempt.

Meanwhile, a more modest trawl through the *œuvre* could have its uses,
not least in laying out its full range: for all the undying popularity of a handul
of best-belovéds, Copland's output predominantly consists of neglected
treasure. The first two orchestral works (preceded only by juvenilia and a
graduation passacaglia for piano) are remarkable for their assurance. Both are
rich in potential for his later courses; neither has quite made it into the
repertory. *Grohg* (1922–5) as a venture into middle-Europe expressionist gothic
is most uncharacteristic, an extravaganza never to be pursued. But as an
exercise in dance-types, scoring and sheer composing, already so surefooted
as to have needed only minimal adjustment when, recast as the *Dance
Symphony* (1929), it sets the precedent of a lifetime. The *Organ Symphony*
(1924), his first actual commission, is still more prophetic, in actual sonorities, techniques, compositional personality. A withdrawn introductory first
movement unobtrusively setting up the material for an obtrusive extrovert
finale; between, the scherzo, brilliantly establishing at first go the basic
texture, material, momentum of the constructivistic minimalism that began to
flourish some fifty years later, in both its simplistic variety (no names) and its
compound (as e.g. the layered polyrhythmic heterophony of the earlier David
Del Tredici). To have put together such opposites as wilful understatement/
brazen rumbunction; to have dared play intricate games with material
teetering on the edge of sheer imbecility—required original conception and
courageous execution.

The Piano Concerto (1926) sustains a similar provocative stance. The
cool irony whereby the naïve on-heat passion of Gershwin's two piano-and-
orchestra successes (the *Rhapsody in Blue* of 1924, the Concerto of 1925) is
replicated 'in aspic', and bombastic *Schelomo*-schlock placed cheek by jowl
against splintery dessication; the wicked exuberance with which 'jazziness' is

x-rayed and dangled in tweezers for detached appraisal, evince extraordinary juvenile self-possession, calculated yet unwitting, knowing yet innocent. And the best work from this Adolescent's Corner, *Music for the Theater* (1925), enjoys superior material and a better attitude to it. Parody, slapstick, ribaldry are more closely tied-in to sheer un-awkward affection for the popular models. Its 'withdrawn' music also (the central interlude) is less guarded; and the veiled chorale-like passages in the prologue, returning in the epilogue, both times following on the nervy aggression of the stuttering trumpet summons, prophesy the utter simplicity of such mature, unstuttering utterance as the prayerful string music just before the end of *Appalachian Spring*. It shows Copland's later hommage to the common chord to be no affected *simplesse*, but powerfully affective simplicity.

Satire and sentiment adjoin in one of the neglected two pieces for violin and piano (also 1926). *Ukelele Serenade* is an ingenious, good-natured counterpart to the devilish wit of the *Soldier's Tale* dance numbers. The *Nocturne* is something more: warmly expressive in itself, and its principal phrase proves astonishingly pregnant and protean, yielding almost all the material for the summit and masterwork of Copland's early phase, indeed one of his greatest works *tout court*, the *Symphonic Ode* (completed in 1929). To the native strains of jazz and vaudeville, boldly stylised in primary colours and modernist cross-cutting, is added an unexpected and crucial element which lifts the music on to its imposing public plinth—the rhetoric, the strenuous ardour, the orchestral sonority at once piercing yet rounded, and the mighty paragraphing, of Mahler.

The resulting amalgam is one of the great celebrations of nationality in music. It ought to be up there representing its country like *Finlandia*, *Vltava*, 'Nimrod'. (Instead, it is a rarity.) Despite the eclecticism it bellows America from every bar, hard-edged and metallic or deep-pile-driven with juddering tenths into alluvial mud. And no special demotic was needed to do this. The Americanness is bigger than style (and individual in particular place and time): it is a Proclamation, with *Amériques* and the comparable aspects of Ives and Ruggles (not to mention Dos Passos, Thomas Hart Benton and other heirs of Whitman) celebrating the great land, its awe-inducing natural wonders and the mind-boggling upward thrust of its cities, its vibrant racial crucible, its larger-than-life abstractions that culminate in the notion and the actuality of Freedom. All this, palpable for the work's admirers, was probably not in its composer's mind. 'Ode', he said, is not an ode to anything in particular, 'but rather a spirit that is to be found in the music itself'. Perhaps if such heroic hymnic patriotism had been proposed, the sarcastic young firebrand of the Piano Concerto (etc.) would have jibbed. Or cynically produced a sort of *Grand Canyon Suite* (Ferde Grofé's famous movielogue was first heard in 1931, the year before the *Ode*'s much-delayed first-and-last). As it is, he steps into this colossal grandeur with the same cool quizzical unwitting that produced the flagrant provocations that preceded it.

But the grandeur was not the way to the immediate future (and when it was again specifically called for it was possibly never again so convincing).

The future had been prefigured in *Vitebsk* (1928), the excoriating movement for piano trio on an old Jewish melody, with its searing quarter-tone cantillation and skirling folkloric euphoria, Copland's only work to stylise his ethnic origins rather than his naturalised nationhood. In the next step the gaunt concentration with which this material is treated becomes the music's principal subject, by exploration of a set of pitches on the face of it as abstract as a Bach fugue-subject or a building motif in Haydn or Beethoven. The Piano Variations (1930) crucially discover that the constructivistic rigours eventually christened and codified as 'serialism' needn't be slave to a strict ordering of the notes. Rather, the notes make a pool of pitch-resources, a highly-characterised clench of harmony fused into itself or separated out into intervals forming a repertory of shapes, a sonorous image-cluster with the material and its total potential locked into a nugget of heavy-density plutonium.

Which above all needn't or even shouldn't consist of all twelve notes. The obsession with the twelve shows a misplaced exhaustiveness hanging-over from the nice artificial compromise of equal temperament, its authoritative canonisation by Bach, and the gigantic consequences for Western music ever since. For composer and listener here, less is more: more memorable, assimilable, audible, manageable, both by the composer who manipulates and by the ear that perceives. This is true whether the aim is to purge the sound of tonal implications, or (implicitly or explicitly) to employ them, or any stage intervening. The fact that Copland's five-note 'series' in the Variations and comparable cluster-clunches in subsequent pieces do preserve a strong quasi-diatonic/tonal identity—a major/ minor blues-tang with a predilection for a flattened second and a sharpened fourth—is seminal for the technique as, more important still, the actual sound with which some twenty years, a World War, and a cultural revolution later, the century's principal diatonicists all began, about the time of Schoenberg's death, to explore however shyly his technical legacy. Their means, and their results, are continually prophesied in Copland's tightest works of the 1930s; the greatest of them, Stravinsky, most particularly. Some passages in the *Short Symphony* (1932–3) take the listener from the Stravinsky-sound of the interwar decades, obviously its main starting-point, to the sound of *Agon* in the mid-fifties; while in the Symphony's version for sextet (1937) the span goes from the sound of *L'histoire du soldat* (especially in the comparable sonority of the 1919 suite for clarinet, violin, piano) through to Stravinsky's 1953 Septet at least. Copland's principal European debt is paid back, obliquely and ahistorically, in a fascinating three-way-bind whose detailed unravelling would be worth a doctoral dissertation one of these days. Then as both composers moved from the later fifties onwards towards a fuller chromatic serialism, this area of memorable sonic consensuality around the major/minor clench diverged totally (though never towards Vienna).

Copland's debt to Mahler survives in the marvellous slow movement of the *Short Symphony* where the long laden lines, burning with unStravinskian *affekt*, are straitened into a searing climax of Mahlerian intensity with unMahlerian terseness. Later, Mahler's sweetness and nostalgia, eschewed here, is permitted for moments of all three great ballets, flowers in the first movement of the Clarinet Concerto (1947–8) and turns to ice-crystals in *Inscape* (1967). Meanwhile the next important work of the thirties, the equally-neglected *Statements* for orchestra (1933–5), is a study, as the title implies, in varied intonations, wherein sentimental and bombastic rhetoric, and their parody, continue a ghost of the Mahler-lineage. For the audience that relishes the parody-element in early Britten and Shostakovich, 'Militant', 'Dogmatic' (with its sly insertion of the theme from the Variations in its 'note-row' form) and 'Jingo' offer a classier version of this typically thirties mood; 'Cryptic' and 'Subjective' dig deeper into the 'withdrawn' territory present from the very start; while 'Prophetic', the final *Statement*, reveals a further aspect of Copland as seer, visionary, law-giver of Mosaic power.

The pivotal work in Copland's output is surely *El Salon Mexico*. This is reflected in the protracted composition of a brief, apparently simple portrait of the favoured nightspot via the affectionate deconstruction and cross-copulation of its typical musics—four years, on and off (1932–6, years that included the *Short Symphony* and *Statements*, as well as the odd, somewhat perfunctory 'political' ballet *Hear ye! Hear ye!*, a score never revived in the composer's lifetime though as usual he frugally reused its best bits elsewhere). For *El Salon* despite its modest aim achieves something bold and new. It might well have seemed like a one-off without issue till its manifest quality was endorsed for the first time in his career by a spate of high-level performances, transforming his image from an esoteric specialist addressing a cultivated minority to a national figure poised on the brink of international popularity. Its success both inner and outer must have changed the way he viewed his talent and its course.

The great leap forward is the total reliance for every element in a piece upon popular melody, whether as here a lucky *trouvaille* or, as later, sedulously researched for the particular appropriate ends of subject, period and place. Whatever the virtues of his output heretofore, Copland could certainly not be called a melodist. His continuity, for all its command of an unStravinskian breadth of paragraph, is equally with Stravinsky made up of small units, ostinatos endlessly reiterated, varied, newly juxtaposed and realigned. Only *Vitebsk* had taken folk-material before, a use born of special circumstances, its inspiration in a production of *The Dybbuk*. But the plasticity, suppleness, inventive freedom with which the Mexican tunes are intercut, almost interbred, goes beyond the obvious origin in the opening and closing tableaux of *Petrushka*—almost, in its tender unsatirical purity, through the Stravinsky all the way back to Glinka's *Kamarinskaya*. This loss of personality in an identification with the foreign idiom so selfless that it becomes native, gives the cue for all the later feats of stylisation—the Wild West ballets with their ballads, sentimental ditties, dances etc., and the Gentle East whose hymnody infuses *Appalachian Spring* and the *Lincoln Portrait*. And thence the whole range—from loving literal arrangement as in the two sets of *Old American Songs* (particularly loving in the subsequent orchestral versions) to the distilled spirit of this language without its letter—the core of his mature style and his most beloved works, the sonorous incarnation of his country.

Thus Copland joins the glorious company of twentieth-century masters who need material given or taken from outside themselves to work on—be it folk-strains from their own immediate culture or from their own or other collectors' wide-wandering ethnic gatherings: not because of inferior endowment (the list after all includes Grainger, Bartók and above all Stravinsky) so much as self-formation through some element extra to that self, chiming with what is innate. The salient questions with all such composers are, what is the innate endowment? how far can it go before its limits are reached and/or it runs out of steam? what is right for it, that will provide the juice to recharge the engine and extend the journey? The answers given by Copland's two closest *vraisemblers* to this third question make an absorbing comparison. Ravel's was willing submission to a long succession of models, sometimes as a challenge to his prowess, more often from a sort of amorous wish to merge with and become indistinguishable from the adored original. Stravinsky's was the avid appetite of the lean kine to swallow up the fatness of whole fields of culture, giving him sustenance in the form of plentiful matter to reshape. Both lose themselves to find themselves; Copland too. The difference is the absence in him of any sense of dressing up, disguise, stylistic or technical *tour-de-force*. No matter that the boy from Brooklyn with his Paris training and Manhattan career is utterly remote from the wild west and the quietist east: the gift first revealed in *El Salon Mexico* is for cultural permeation and absorption so easy, natural, total as to disarm all intimations of artificiality. His stylistic and ethnic assumptions are his body not his clothes. Before, he was only a skeleton (though, remembering the Variations, and Cézanne's remark about Monet, one has to add, but what a skeleton!).

The difference between his work employing received material and work free of it can be appreciated at once by comparing the generic attractiveness of a nice friendly socially-serviceable school-orchestra workout, stamped New Deal Americana on every bar, like the *Outdoor Overture* of 1938 with *Billy the Kid* from the same year, with its absolutely specific focus, through its employment of the just-right borrowed material, upon a period, a place, a society, in all its moods from violence to tender elegy, from impersonal landscape to human community. Similarly, the dutiful school-opera of 1936, *The Second Hurricane*, and its resourceful but ultimately unmemorable sequence of genres and types, with the ostensibly 'grown-up' grand opera three-acter of 1952–4, *The Tender Land*, where the musical language has been washed through with this artificially-invented, wholly-naturalised American inflection—glowing, radiant, authentic, saturating the lame text and stilted situations, the two-dimensional characters, the knock-kneed dramaturgy. (Admittedly because of all this the orchestral suite, yielding the vision, without embarrassments, in all its freshness, is much preferable.)

The twelve years from Billy to Emily (the *Dickinson Songs* of 1950) are Copland's prime: his most prolific, popular, perfected. The earlier achievement is not surpassed.[1] The loss, if loss it be, is more than compensated for in the greater maturity, depth and breadth that result from the chosen language's deliberate extension of range and tone.

From now to the end of his composing life an oscillation-principle is loosely in play whereby each move towards expansive accessibility is counter-balanced by a complementary turn towards meditative, abstracted calm. That *Quiet City* (1939) comes between the two Westerns is fortuitous, since this haunting piece began life in incidental music for a play; but the Piano Sonata (1939–41) is a deliberated study in ascetic withdrawal before the festive raucousness of *Rodeo* (1942). Thus the astonishing chastity of the Violin Sonata of 1942–3 (Ravel's style *dépouillé* and Sibelius' 'glass of cold water' passed through the Satie-mirror and out the other side: Copland seems here to take up his own challenge 'I wanted to see how simple I could be without losing my personality' more radically than in *The Second Hurricane* which actually occasioned the wish, and far more successfully) runs concurrent across 1942–3 with the fabulous acridity, pungency, humour and metrical kick of the *Danzon Cubano* for two pianos, and the celebrated pieces of wartime uplift, *Lincoln Portrait* and *Fanfare for the Common Man*. Unique in their day for attaining imaginative utterance (*Statements*, continued) with a genuine populist charge unsullied by condescension or vulgarity whether English Imperial or Sovietsky Bathetic, their purity of diction and severity of technique not only saving them from such pitfalls but preventing the willingly-stirred auditor from even thinking about the potential tackiness (except when an overzealous narrator sends *Lincoln* over the top).

This overschematic view should of course be nuanced by enjoyment of the beautiful use of raucous/quietist contrasts within individual works: in *Rodeo*, the 'corral nocturne' between its extrovert neighbours, in the Piano Sonata the shifting, hesitant, then clangorous scherzo between its 'Quaker' outer movements: a favourite sequence would be the passage in *Billy* from night-scene, via gunfight, and Billy's death, to open out again on to the wide empty prairie with which the story began.

The impulse to cleanness, freshness, frankness, simplicity, precision informs both the inward- and the outward-directed music of this time. *Appalachian Spring* (1943–4), still the *locus classicus* (more particularly in the sparer, less shiny sound of the original thirteen-instrument scoring) of a particular hard yet tender, soft yet stringent vision of American Pastoral. This triumph of hard-earned intonation yields a procession of successors, gradually diluting and turning very slightly towards the habitual. Still at the top comes the *a capella* chorus *In the Beginning* (1947), a model of luminous choral layout that, beneath its appearance of gobbling up the long text of the

---

[1] Nor, maybe, equalled; it's interesting that its two highpoints are both revisited later as the prime begins to turn: the *Ode*, virtually unheard since its première, recommissioned in 1955 with orchestration at once slightly curbed yet slightly filled-out, the Variations orchestrated 1957 without revision, but compromising the specifically pianistic qualities—resonance and attack—that give the original its unforgettable impact.

seven days of creation from Genesis as prosaically as possible, succeeds through sheer wide-eyed straightforwardness in inducing awe at the miracle better than could a more elaborate pose. And the twelve Dickinson songs are a wonderful *summa* of all the composer's accents, compacted, intensified, deepened: 'nature, death, life, eternity' as he succinctly puts it. The contrasts here of bright/dusty, hard/sweet, burning/melting surpass those within or between any other music of this phase: take the final succession, from the pounding darkness of the 'funeral in the brain', the plain mellifluous old-world 'organ talk', the sprightly scherzando of the trip to heaven so poignantly shading off into wry connivance at the older folks' delusion, to the hallucinatory journey past the playing children, the fertile fields, the setting sun, and then the grave and the timeless consciousness beyond; taking up and into its quietus the cycle's climactic midway setting of the death-vanquishing declamatory 'Sleep is Supposed to Be', in its fusion of naked with full, deep calm with brittle bell-like clangour and crashing wide-spaced resonation the quintessence of the Copland vision at its most perfected. Then the vein flows a little perfunctory in the viol-fantasia scherzo centre of the string Nonet (1960), where the reward lies in the gorgeous jammy harmony (new adjectives for this composer!) of the slow opening pages and their somewhat protracted return at the end. Finally in the Duo for flute and piano (1971) it has grown too dilute for the intensity to hold. Here, at last, the white is too pale!

Meanwhile the adventure with serialism counterpoints the slow decline of pastoralism. One's reaction to this nowadays, long after the 'historical moment' that seemed so imperative has passed, is slightly regretful: not from a doctrinaire standpoint; just because Copland the scrupulous, counting 'the note that costs', mean by instinct, training, experience, simply doesn't seem to need it. But perhaps, as with Stravinsky and Britten, even Poulenc and Frank Martin, there was a sense that a well-practised language required refreshment and surprise. As Copland said, experimenting with twelve-tone organisation 'I began to hear chords that I wouldn't have heard otherwise'. It certainly makes a direct link with the earlier phases from which the American adventure—East, West and Latin—had been a detour. But this return to constructivistic modernism has its disadvantages. Put the tingling specificity of the pitches in *Vitebsk* beside the relative unmemorability of the texturally similar Piano Quartet of 1950 which occasioned the pious remark about new chords; put the compelling inevitability of the Piano Variations and Sonata beside the masterfully laboured gawkiness of the vast architectonic Piano Fantasy (1952–7), the nearest approach in these years and in this idiom to a compositional *summa*. Compare above all the glorious overreaching ecstasy of the slow music in the *Ode* and the tense athletic exhilaration of its allegro, with the steel-plated rhetoric and allegro-by-rote of the equivalent places in *Connotations* (1962). A remarkable acuity of ear has weighed the late work's dense sonorities—Copland would not 'professionally' be capable of the carelessness obscuring much of the century's atonal music before, contemporary with (and persisting). The loss is not of skill, vigour; precision;

inevitable decline in sheer exuberance is made up by the bracing challenge of the craggy new crunches and crashes. Yet something difficult to formulate fair-and-square has disappeared from this music; for want of a more ambiguous phrase it could be called inner necessity

The need is, rather, an aspiration at least partly extramusical, in the Quartet to align with the then-irresistible serialism; in the Fantasy to consolidate and surpass a consummate earlier achievement; in *Connotations* to make the ultimate Statement for a Solemn Occasion. The deficiency is unmissable with a potboiler like *Canticle of Freedom* (1955), a second-brew from the fresh leaves of *Lincoln Portrait*; far harder to distinguish in the three works under discussion; and notoriously divisive with the Third Symphony with its dead-central position in his life and output (1944–6). This large, noble score is not just patchy but positively slippery. Its meditative movements (first and third) are withdrawn to the point of secrecy but lack the magic inner concentration of such moods in *Statements* and *Quiet City* (etc.), while the high spirits of the intervening scherzo seem, just for once, blatant and patronising rather than popular and liberating. Then in the finale, after the heroic magnificence of the famous *Fanfare* and its equally convincing transformation, after the infamous dissonant crisis, into unexpected pastoral delicacy steers perilously close to the bombast of a Shostakovich apotheosis without (so far as one can tell) any rumour of (un)mitigating irony.

But another rather deliberated piece, his final work of size and emotional scope, gets together pastoral simplicity and the craggy modernistic, makes a farewell, and effects in its dedication to Charles Ives a hommage that elegantly celebrates the past, serves the present and salutes the future—*Night Thoughts* for piano, of 1972. Last thoughts too: after this the music's cessation, long in coming, set in for good (for one can't count the quasi-posthumous gleanings issued during the seventies and eighties, most of them written well before; and the two *Threnodies* (1971 and 1973) even sound like ghosts). 'I must have expressed myself sufficiently. I certainly don't feel tortured or bitter, only lucky to have been given so long to be creative.' Though, as often, this fine stoicism has a slight tinge of the press-release, his grateful admirers can only agree.

Howard Pollack's solid biography, and still more a trip down the noisy city streets and the quiet country lanes of the output (and the looked-for spread of centenary performances that shouldn't be confined to the centenary) focus the gratitude in pleasure, delight, and deep simple feeling that Copland evokes, transcending country, race, and gender, in the 'common man' whom he has reached, to whom he has given utterance in a 'serious classical' language complementing the demotic commercial genius of Gershwin, Kern, Berlin *et al*. Not, like them, a song on every common man's lips: *speech*, rather, or better, *idiom*; a stylised vernacular invented with scrupulous cunning and *savoir faire* from indigenous folklore. A narrow vein compared with Europe and Russia, more out of books than the living throats of cowboys and shakers; a sort of Ives (throwing in the West to join the East) that takes a chaos of nostalgia *bric-à-brac* 'cubisticised' *à la* Shrovetide

Petersburg, and tidied into eminently non-messy lucidity through the Franco-Russian training (Stravinsky curbed by Fauré; Fauré primitivised by Stravinsky) whose combination manages miraculously to avoid genteelising the natural American flamboyance and razzmatazz.

Then the gratitude (pleasure, delight, feeling) of the *cognoscenti* (and, alas, the 'academic community') for the austere, inscaped, unforgivingly essentialised modernist, who composes as if there was not a common man, a leaf of grass, a democratic vista, in sight. Yet this music in its clarity, unambiguity, ineffable physicalisation of cerebral intensity, is listener-friendly too, however rebarbative or withdrawn in its refusal to cosset the palate with pralines and the body with cushions.

So in the end neither strain nor wishfulness is needed to hear him integral and integrated—which is what he always claimed. With Copland, uniquely among the twentieth-century masters, there is 'no problem'.

64

Ralph Shapey's *Trilogy* in Chicago

The main celebration for Ralph Shapey's sixtieth birthday [March 1981] was a complete performance of his *Trilogy* on the *Song of Songs* (Part I, composed 1978–9, had already been played several times; Parts II and III, composed 1980, were being heard for the first time). This concert on 24 April 1981 in the Mandel Hall of the University of Chicago was given under the auspices of the Fromm Foundation, long and consistent champion of this maverick composer. He conducted his devoted Contemporary Chamber Players, and the demanding vocal parts were sung with effortful perseverance by Paul Kiesgen and with untroubled radiance by Elsa Charlston. Paul Fromm was present and afterwards presided genially over the distribution of a handsome birthday-cake. But Shapey's music remains as uncomfortable as ever; most of the audience emerged stunned and glassy-eyed after some 100 minutes of heavy labour.

Part I of the *Trilogy* (soprano) presents the Shulamite and her songs to her Lord, the King Solomon. Part II (bass) is Solomon's celebration of the Shulamite's beauty, and ends with a loud and passionate cry for her return. Part III begins with the same cry; she returns; and both singers combine in duet what they have already sung singly, concluding with the work's core: 'Set me as a seal upon thy heart; for love is strong as death.' The overall effect is of a three-sided monolith which very slowly rotates, exposing different facets while remaining essentially unchanged. Fearful symmetry is everywhere evident, in detail and in the whole. Nevertheless there is a real sense of lyric–dramatic progression, through a balance between rigidity and subtle deviation from it as fine as that which allows a huge weight to be moved by a light touch.

The monolith is made up of individual lumps of instrumental sound (Shapey's favourite 'graven images'), which also rotate, hardly changing in themselves while locking and cogging into each other in ever-varied superimposition. Submerged in this instrumental process are the two singers (who require amplification to be properly heard, even though their parts are frequently doubled by instruments). Only rarely are the voices the central focus of interest; the words, rather than immediate surface, are more like a leaven working secretly within the dense texture. A further element is a four-channel tape which runs alongside the soloists, singing or speaking in up to three voices, and just before the end of each Part taking off for a four-voice 'a cappella' chorus. The unsatisfactory sound, together with the exasperating difficulties of balance and synchronisation, suggest that this tape (whose pitches and rhythms are exactly notated and abjure special effects) is an exigency substitute for a chamber choir.

Construction with pre-made blocks, first singly then superimposed in endless repetition, recalls Messiaen, particularly such works made out of more radically 'thing-like' material as *La Transfiguration*. But even when most implacable there is always a juiciness in Messiaen's chords—and of course he is by no means implacable all the time! Shapey's harmonic norm is leaner and harsher, and the purple–orange–*volupté* range is altogether alien to him. In actual sound this music really does not resemble any other composer. Above all in its frank abandonment to ugliness! The harmony is the harshest I have ever heard, and it is exacerbated to extremity by the grotesque scoring and spacing. Then the texture is usually dense and the movement always slow, the repetition obsessive, the intensity searing. Shapey's desire is to overwhelm by raising these things to a pitch of religious ecstasy; some fervent observance is grinding away, rapt and self-absorbed in its incantatory duty; indifferent to anyone who happens to overhear, let along to an audience with its shallow corporate goal of 'pleasure'. Yet once accustomed to such a norm of unremitting rebarbaration, the listener can find this music spell-binding, so much so that any slackening of intensity seems like a kind of palliation. Thus the frequent little instrumental monodies irritate by betraying the norm of dense exultation (the fact that they are compositionally feeble is less important). The true oases here are just as intense as the living desert all around them. There are moments which render rapt sensuality in an extra-ordinarily inward manner quite without sensuous beauty, as previously under-stood; and with familiarity one recognises the reciprocity of such tender-burning withdrawal with the more usual harsh-burning exclamation. The general effect is of an achieved and sustained vision of the Ugly–Sublime.

There is always the danger that such perpetually incandescent, hyper-charged music will repel its listeners at the least, and at worst bore them off altogether. Shapey doesn't care—'You may hate it, but you're not going to forget it.' The trouble is that his superb indifference to his listeners' endur-ance or enjoyment coincides with real compositional limitations. The melodic sparseness, the rhythmic stiffness, the perpetual slow tempos, the fact that there is only one contrast of dynamic and texture, and only one mode of feeling—these things do seriously narrow the range of his music, even while one has to acknowledge that they are inseparable from the powerful positive effects he produces. Above all there is something self-defeating and unheard (for all the ear's acuteness) in the density of the more all-out passages of superimposition—the spirit would see the intended vision, but the carnal ears protest the rioting congestion; and they are right. Yet even in these passages the effect is very different from the welter of such a grand and in its way impressive Ugly as Stockhausen's *Trans*. The difference is one of musicality —i.e. using the accepted means of notation and its resulting sounds to recognisable expressive effect. The *Trilogy* shows this most clearly in the ubiquitous use (there is scarcely a page without several) of the Italian turn. Naturally not for allusion; rather by sheer isolation and insistence Shapey turns what was originally the prettiest musical ornament into (via Schumann, Wagner, above all the last movement of Mahler's Ninth Symphony) the most burdened. It is crude, bold, surprising, and it works; after so much battering, the cadence in the last bars of Part III which at last lays this much-used figure to rest is extraordinarily moving in its finality.

Ralph Shapey is a difficult composer to evaluate, all the more so for his determination to be a square peg without a niche. The phrase 'radical conservative' which he is fond of quoting as the *mot juste* for his music seems rather unhelpful; a concept so general will be true for virtually every great composer and many minor ones too. Shapey belongs to a much smaller category—with figures of painful but creatively benevolent paranoia, the composers who flourish on misunderstanding, contempt, and neglect, of whom the greatest examples are Schoenberg, whose art and life are audibly warped by it, and Beethoven, whose *art* at least—at most rather!—emerges unscathed. (It is instructive to hear Shapey's characteristically intemperate defence of the *Grosse Fuge* as the greatest music ever written.) Whatever differences of achievement and style, Shapey is the same *kind* of composer; and in his case the connection between the hostile environment and the internal flowering is particularly clear. The outward story is of slights, insults, involuntary cruelty, damning with faint praise; the result, the opposite of a 'success'. Yet the man is hardly a failure who can realise with great completeness an extremely idiosyncratic personality in a catalogue of over seventy works. He knows this; and there is something triumphant even in his appearance of a humble late Rembrandt self-portrait, let alone in the magnificent burnished ugliness of the sounds he constructs with so much painstaking, pain-making joy. Such integrity flourishes upon abrasion; he has succeeded where it matters to succeed.

65

Two on David Del Tredici

i Adventures Underground

In an attempt to focus the unique phenomenon of David Del Tredici I offer a
thumbnail sketch of a musical ancestry. His work is 'all-American' by three
generations. With Ives and Ruggles as grandfathers, Copland, Carter and
Babbitt as fathers, the generation of composers currently gaining their full
stride is likely to show exceptionally strong traits of character and physiognomy. One has only to compare England—grandfathers Elgar, Vaughan
Williams, Delius; middle-heirs Walton, Tippett, Britten; flourishing prime of
life, Crosse and Maw, Bennett and Wood, the Manchester troika—to register
the emphatic individuality of the Americans, and their communal indepen-
dence of outside influence. For all the Germanic training of the earliest
generation and the Franco-Stravinsky orientation of the next, the results
could hardly be more idiosyncratic. The second generation is less rugged,
more alert, polished and clever than the pioneers; but the all-Americanness is
just as unmistakable. Del Tredici is the most striking representative of the
third generation, inheriting both the boldness and exuberance of his grandfathers and the technical accomplishment of his fathers; together with a
strong element of that sheer weirdness that, as with other American originals,
seems to have no ancestry or progeny, is just a pair of sharp predatory ears in
an untouched desert of sounds.

This is hard to see because the style, of the *Alice* pieces at least, consists
of progressively more extravagant inroads into the cliché material common to
all musical cultures. In *Pop-Pourri* (1968) 'Es ist genug', and in *Vintage
Alice* (1972) 'God Save the King' are subjected to splintering and dislocation,
augmentation and diminution in different keys and registers, scored in the
most bizarre fashion imaginable. This is knife-edge play, both in taste (one
slip and your palate is cleft) and in interest; the effect, with the characteristically extreme-as-norm vocal writing, is of a single prolonged manic
scream. One can admire the supreme cleverness while finding the strained
high camp and the solipsistic jokiness almost unbearable. It leaves me only
half-amused, and wholly puzzled. Why all this fuss and expenditure on a
couple of nonsense-books for Victorian children? What is he *doing*?

For me the turning-point—the yielding in taste that allows a whole new
area of predilection to be recognised and flourish as it wants to—came with
first hearing *Final Alice* (1976). This is on a different plane: the cliché

material is now a tune of the composer's own, and the huge blow-ups, absurd repetitions, cadence-delays, general twists, teases and tortures to which it is subjected achieve comic magnificence—the most, perhaps the only, successful musical surrealism that I've ever heard. Most surrealism in music is accidental; one gets the giggles at involuntary shortcircuitings and ineptitudes, and relishes the shame of the cliché caught *in flagrante* as the conscious mind labours to attain the obvious. But nothing is accidental in *Final Alice*: the jokes are all so musical and composed with such mastery as to silence narrow-gutted querulousness about content. They are the content. The subject-matter is perfect timing of a cadence-delay, or the amplest super-Strauss/Respighi orchestration of a common chord. The ear is flawless, the sensibility bizarre, the invention original-*through*-clichés, and the overall effect overwhelmingly funny and beautiful.

Comic generosity of this order (as if MacGonagall were written with Brahmsian mastery, thoroughness and warmth) makes the pastiche and parodistic elements in modern British pieces, and the cliché-blow-ups and cosy horrors of the new Viennese MOB/ART music appear simply puerile. In sheer professionalism this is obvious enough; more important, the poetic intelligence is incomparably more interesting. *Here* the only parallel is with *Le grand macabre*. I would think (my knowledge is unfortunately confined to the concert suite of Ligeti's opera) that Del Tredici surpasses Ligeti as musical surrealist, because his effects are achieved by purely musical means with no need for funny noises and gooning. Of course (and leaving apart the rest of his output) Ligeti achieves moments and whole stretches of seraphic beauty with no hint of cliché and parody. But use of popular material is one of Del Tredici's strengths and a central strain in his American ancestry; he descends from the great Impurists, Ives via Copland, not from those who need to give every chord the 'test of time', or to 're-think the medium' in order to write a piano piece. Above all it enables him to realise so fully the mixture of demure and mad, parody and heartfelt, nonsense and logic, in the *Alice*-books themselves. The vindication of his every move is that it captures some further aspect of the essential spirit, if not the letter, of the original, in a way inconceivable to an English composer to whom—questions of inhibition apart—the books are so normal. He shows just how strange and wonderful Carroll is.

The European première of the revised version of *Adventures Underground* (Amsterdam, Concertgebouw, 13 April 1980) confirms and extends these impressions. Since I had never heard the original I can't say to what extent it's been changed (the composer is reported as saying that the old version sounded like 'constipated chamber music'); but can confidently report another stunner, worthy of a place beside *Final* in the *Alice* series. Part I, 'The Pool of Tears', is permeated by one of those insanely memorable cliché-phrases that affect one like the ancient hymn, getting 'within, behind, beside, beneath, above'—all but inside-out. Part II, 'The Mouse's Tale', is more striking still—surely the best orchestral scherzo written in all these decades without 'genuine fast music', its fantastic speed and glassy lightness over the entire timbre and compass of a large orchestra leaves the listener as breathless as Alice after her run with the Red Queen. The score of this movement[1] will become a *locus classicus* for 'eye-music', in its exhaustive rendition in musical notation of Carroll's famous typographical joke, but really of course because it is such good ear-music. Eye-music mostly means that you see (as it might be) a mass of clearly designated polyphonic parts, or an excitingly black passage of textural complexity, but hear an indistinguishable and meaningless mess. Here the perpetually diminishing zigzags of the mouse's tail are a triumph of genuine audio-visualisation—seen and heard simultaneously, as pattern, as speed of note-iteration, as rate of harmony or non-harmony. It's minimal, and it's a conceit; as with Donne or Cleveland it requires brilliance to bring it off—one false move and it would be silly; and once brought off, stands as its own *raison d'être*. Del Tredici makes no mistakes; the infallible ear and utter technical mastery ensure the maximal working of his minimal material, all in the service of a deep dangerous poetic sensibility, realised without forcing or masking, without let or scruple.

The concert, conducted with his customary grace and fire by Michael Tilson Thomas, began with Ives's Second Symphony, a piece of dull Americana whose pious inclusion was justified only by the effect of its outrageous last chord on the lethargic Sunday afternoon audience, and ended with *Suntreader*, where the admirable but staid orchestra was roused to a tense fury of sound, except for the obstinately phlegmatic cymbal-player. *Adventures Underground* suffered from technical shortcomings in amplifying the folk-band and soprano (Phyllis Bryn-Julson in terrific form, knocking up top D♭s like a cash register). The speed of the scherzo left singer, players and audience alike holding on for dear life. But the golden acoustic, so right for the Ruggles, muffled the lethal cleanness of Del Tredici. Moreover for such a *tour de force* of eye-music the décor was equally improper, with its pastel distemper, fustian garlands, plush curtains and gilded names of great composers. Zweers and Dopper must have shivered in their graves—any one of this concert's three Americans could replace them at a moment's notice.

ii   All in the Golden Afternoon

David Del Tredici continues to live dangerously, disgusting the academic composition establishment, delighting his audiences, and giving evaluative criticism a tricky task. A mere description of *All in the Golden Afternoon* (first performances 8 and 9 May 1981 by Benita Valente with the Philadelphia Orchestra under Eugene Ormandy) would make it appear to be the same kind of enterprise as *Final Alice* or *Adventures Underground*. But the sound of this new work is very different: its starting-point, rather than the diatonic tags and cadence-delays of heretofore, is a composite of fin-de-siècle deliquescence, the clichés of a style that, however exalted its origins, has come down to be the stuff of a million miles of romantic muzak. Into these turgid

---

[1] Now (2001) published by Boosey and Hawkes for all to *see*: I wish we could *hear* it once in a while!

and treacherous waters Del Tredici moves with characteristic exuberance, freedom and bad taste.

At thirty-five minutes it can stand singly as a concert item; nevertheless comprehension is enhanced by knowledge of its place in a larger scheme. This whole-evening event, *Child Alice*, alternates extravagant settings of slender Carrolliana for amplified soprano and large orchestra with three size-able interludes for orchestra alone, each entitled *A Tale is Told*, which take off from the basic vocal material into sheer fantasticality. Part I, 'In Memory of a Summer Day', sets 'Child of the pure unclouded brow' (the dedication poem for Alice Liddell on the manuscript of her *Adventures in Wonderland*); its *Tale* is an extended march and trio. Part II contains 'Quaint Events' and the second orchestral 'Tale', a tour-de-force of fugal technique and orchestral speed entitled 'Happy Voices'. This leads into Part III (newly heard at Philadelphia): its text is the prefatory poem (beginning 'All in the golden afternoon / Full leisurely we glide') to the published *Alice in Wonderland*; its tale is a Fantasia for orchestra, and its character is consummatory and valedictory.

Thus *Child Alice*, though still setting only his words, takes the endeavour beyond Carroll's two classic stories (plus the additional material in *Alice's Adventures Underground*). There are no longer any events, and the prim-spirited little girl is expanded, diffused, projected into a wholly original area of musical evocation. Only a composer with special powers of empathy could find in these fustian peripheral texts a vehicle for authentic feeling. Del Tredici is that composer. His programme note for the première speaks warmly of Carroll's 'simultaneity of rapture and regret', and recalls an ecstatic infantile memory of his own. 'Musical identification of such feelings seemed to me natural, inevitable—to join together, as only music can, a feeling and a text.' After all, there is ample precedent for the musical impulse altogether to overwhelm the poem that occasions it! And on a wider front, the urgency of his preoccupation compels us to accept the fact that this composer has for the time being made *Alice* into a working-convention as well as a subject—like Degas his dancers or Morandi his bottles.

All in the Golden Afternoon falls into four main sections. The 'Aria' sets the entire poem with frequent interruptive glosses (as when the word 'nonsense' inspires a musical nonsense of delightful waltzing and birdcalls) and some Tredician games familiar from previous pieces (passages which go berserk over a phrase of text and music, sending it into an hysterical spin of ascending diminutions). An orchestral link makes prolonged play with con-flicting pivot-notes (the one passage which requires its context in the complete *Child Alice* to make full sense), before opening up into the 'Tale'; here invention pours forth in profusion unchecked by the remotest responsi-bility to the words. Notable in this Fantasia is a marvellous passage called 'Bagatelle–Burlesque' which superimposes different speeds and characters in a manner recalling *Pop-Pourri* of 1968 but altogether less scholastic; and towards the climax there are some grand thematic combinations in the manner of Berlioz's 'Witches' Sabbath' or 'Romeo at the Feast of the Capulets'.

The ensuing 'Lullaby' returns to stanzas already set—'Thus grew the tale of Wonderland'—whose retrospection now flowers fully in the exquisite setting of 'and now the tale is done'. A climax of anguish culminates in a cadenza of wildly impassioned parody vocalises on the single name 'Alice!'. The soprano sings for Alice herself, crying her name aloud to prove it still is she (not, for instance, *Mabel*) as her childhood passes irreversibly from her; and as it were in the composer's own voice—'I want *never* to grow up!'—as he reluctantly puts away girlish things; and as it were for everyone—'She—all youth, beauty, past—is reft from me; I want her now, unchanged, still as she always was.' A further climax *con gran disperazione* (he is good at climaxes) sinks at last into tranquillity; 'In Conclusion' returns to the poem's first line, repeated over and over like the 'ewig ... ewig' of Mahler's 'Abschied', in a ravishing technicolour dream, the suspended harmony finally fixed even as it melts away, no longer suggesting cadence let alone wanting it; all passion spent.

(After such a farewell as this Del Tredici will *have* to find a new subject!)

Harmony is the *raison d'être* of this music, and gorgeous orchestration its blooming surface. The voice-part drifts in and out of both, only rarely dominating the essential movement. Even the 'Lullaby', a concentration of the work's melodic and harmonic bases, is not exactly a self-contained tune; the norm is comparable to Wagnerian arioso (like Venus in the Paris rewrite of *Tannhäuser* or Kundry's 'Ich sah das Kind' in *Parsifal*), vocal prose floated upon a magic carpet of richly-woven instrumental texture. The harmonic vocabulary of romanticism past its vigour and very sweetly moving towards decay is obviously apt for rendering what Del Tredici calls 'the nostalgia-impulse'. Such vibrant colours so headily used again tend to obliterate the faded little poem, whose keywords (however inert) are seized upon, taken literally and blown up in explosions of great local intensity that quite destroy overall verbal sense.

But the sense of this piece is in the chords not in the text. This harmony is redolent by association: of Palm Courts, of Theosophy, of Paradise Garden and Florida orange groves, of Dehmel and Klimt, of pink bonbons stuffed with Norwegian snow, of gift-wrapping and expensive scents from the *belle époque*. These associations, while not underlined and pedalled as a more knowing composer would, are certainly not anaesthetised; they set up an iridescent haze of overlapping stylistic echoes essential to the total effect. The very uncleanness of this harmony, though enjoyed at first for its *frisson* of forbidden fruits ('don't touch it dear, you don't know where it's *been*'), ends up as a compositional resource. It brings to mind Reger's modulation manual where every possible key-connection (including such academic conceits as Cb minor to B major) is made in moves at once deft, correct and succulent. Del Tredici, like the bad poet who 'tortures one poor word ten thousand ways', subjects his already luscious chords to the still more exhaustive treatment their greater complexity implies. The brilliance of his puns and paradoxes, timing of harmonic delay or release, instinct for when to do a new thing or confound with what has been already heard, is more startling than ever. And fused with this pedantic comprehensiveness are two qualities that raise it into creative expression. First, the infectious relish with which these skills are shown off; and second, the beauty revealed in the process. How else is expression made but by relish and skill in manipulating patterns of sound to form their most beautiful arrangements for the purpose in hand?—equally so when every sound comes laden with past associations ('where they've *been*'), whose resonance is part of how they are being used in the present.

New composition with old musical clichés would seem to require different aesthetic criteria for its evaluation. At its purest, it desires to parallel the eighteenth century's wide repertoire of formulae for all functions. But even when a modern composer uses received material with an unforced mastery in its manipulation, self-consciousness is unavoidable; it is impossible not to be aware that this material is, frankly, in its raw state, worn-out rubbish. Moreover, most usage is so far from pure as actually to need this trashy quality for its appeal to a particular aspect of sensibility whose extremest form is the ultimate camp—'bad *ergo* good'.

Del Tredici's music of the last decade or so is finely poised in this difficult area. *Child Alice*, especially, glows with an unmistakable feeling of homecoming—a lowering of ingestive inhibitions, free entry into a kingdom of spontaneous license—'fay ce que vous voudrez'. Equally unmistakable is a thrill of discharge—late romantic slag is being purged from the system with vehemence and relief. Both attitudes are excessive and even violent; accumulated provision is squandered or gobbled with reckless audacity and obsessive single-mindedness. This *is* indeed composing dangerously; and when the nature of the material used to realise an undertaking of this scope is recalled, the likelihood of its succeeding seems remote. Yet it triumphantly comes off. And it is very strong. Beneath the utterly enjoyable, in an obvious way 'self-indulgent' gorgeousness, lies rigorous severity, which pushes violence and excess to extremes of Robespierrean logic. The old criteria for quality *do* still apply with all their old force; the aesthetic of 'bad *ergo* good', if it is to qualify by more exalted standards, has eventually to show the flint and iron beneath the velvet.

However it would be a bad mistake to attribute these intellectualisings to Del Tredici himself. He is a Natural, and his attitude to the stylistic implications of his chosen method and manners can afford to be unselfconscious. For most of us 'you don't know where it has been!' is a lie; we do know, and take subtle pleasure in our knowledge. Del Tredici unaffectedly doesn't—'if I knew these chords had been used before, I'd not dream of using them myself; I must believe that they are fresh—that I'm the first person to handle them'. Thus speaks the Schillerian *naïf*, who composes his ostensibly sentimental pieces with such an intensity of musicality, such a rage to order (and such a talent for composition) that anything dubious in the enterprise is overtaken by a surprising directness; real love of these clichés for their beautiful sound, real warmth and joy in eliciting their powers of expression, and real mastery in exploiting their possibilities for complex organisation.

Moreover he shows that, in its capacity to reach the depths of our nostalgia, this commonplace material is not merely banal or empty or silly—any more than are the feelings themselves, though what touches them off may well be. In this light, Carroll's stilted verses can assume the visionary quality of Blake's *Songs of Innocence* and Wordsworth's *Immortality Ode*. Only a positive lack of crippling good taste is able both to see this and to do something about it. Further, Del Tredici achieves a strange effect of 'nostalgia for things to come', reversing the flow of the nineteenth century by using the idiom of the famous late-Romantic sunsets of Delius, Strauss, *Gurrelieder*, to evoke a pristine vision of the child, 'trailing clouds of glory', at Romanticism's dawn. His range, at first sight narrowed by such drastic specialisations of taste, is constantly widening. The command of technique and tone grows in proportion; and each greater challenge to a contemporary-historical view of the likely and proper makes more and more centrally for the longing of audiences that music do what it always did in the good old days; what it can do; what it ought to do; what it is *for*.

His envious compatriots think that this is to truckle and pander—transparent confession of their own failure to communicate. The reverse is true; this is a ferocious individualist who refuses to do anything except what he wants. And in the end it's the power and originality of his invention that compels admiration. Each piece, whatever the foul rag-and-bone shop of its basic material, depends less on a play of vagabond sensibility, becomes closer to 'real music' by 'proper composers' like Brahms. It's 'all about' the same thing—establishing relations between real life and fantasy, moving through abstraction and the disinterested fascination of making, and out again into the human arena, an amalgam of imagination and experience, transsubstantiated into an expressive artefact for its audience's delight. I can think of no composer currently active who does it better.

* * *

Such admiration for D.D.T.'s 'middle period' splurges now strikes me as a bit excessive. It was an excited reaction to this music's generosity and lack of costiveness at a time of almost-universal stylistic meanness. But actually, with the passage of years, the 'meanness' of his own earlier work is what appears to have saved it from the rot courted by the later work's over-ripeness. The trajectory from the best of his James Joyce period culminating in Syzygy *(1966), via* The Last Gospel *(1967) and the earliest in the* Alice *period—*Pop-Pourri *(1968), the* Alice Symphony *(1969–75),* Adventures Underground *(1971),* Vintage Alice *(1972)—still seems to me, whenever I hear any of these pieces, one of the most brilliant and startling of any since WW II, well up there with the most daring and accomplished of his compatriots, Carter, Nancarrow, Feldman.*

Part III

'Think pieces'

66

The search for a sound aesthetics

Accepting the TLS*'s invitation to review Bojan Bujić's* Music in European Thought 1851–1912 *(CUP, 1988) was an act of masochistic self-improvement—'nasty but good for you'. Having hankered in vain since student days for help or insight from aestheticians and philosophers of music, this of all its epochs seemed likely to vouchsafe them. Five successive drafts, each far shorter than the previous (Monty struggling with the Python) ruined the summer of 1988. The upshot was this relatively succinct record of renewed disappointment with the barren desert masquerading as an oasis.*

* * *

Can philosophy, as straitened into aesthetics, unlock the old problems of musical expression; above all, the vexed question of what music means? Everyone interested in an answer—all the combinations and overlaps of composer, academic, performer, listener—harbours the nostalgic hope that the art so precious to them can actually be explained; it is to such an anthology as *Music in European Thought 1851–1912* that they will turn for guidance.

The writers in it are presented in a user-unfriendly classification by chronology, country and type; for the general reader they can be more simply divided into three broad categories. First, composers and other figures whose theorising grows out of current or projected creative concerns, and their criticism from explicit or implicit self-definition. Next, scientists: naturalists and anthropologists interested in origins, physicists and physiologists interested in causes. And third, academics investigating the nature of aesthetic phenomena, a pursuit which in the epoch covered by this volume becomes a branch of learning in its own right.

Most of the writing in the first category centres on Wagner, *pro* and *contra*. Berlioz reviewing Wagner's 1860 Paris concerts asks of his music 'more invention, less research', and gives a balanced opposition-view founded on the cultural values of Rome and France. Baudelaire's famous essay 'Richard Wagner et "Tannhäuser" à Paris' (1861) presents the thrill of a great artist recognising in another medium, however different and however misapprehended, a correspondence that enables him to realise his own genius. On this showing Baudelaire is the most intelligent observer, the most subtle critic, the profoundest aesthetician in the anthology. His prose-poems on the preludes to *Lohengrin* and *Tannhäuser* are more than ecstatic rendition of the music's effect; they suggest a moral vision, transcending the merely aesthetic, of the power of art to animate good and evil. The underlying drift of these lacerating self-revelations is that music successfully achieves its unambiguous aim to grasp 'all that is excessive, immense, ambitious, in both spiritual and material man'. Music—in context Wagner's, by extension (with suitable qualification and redefinition) all music—expresses 'all that lies most deeply hidden' in the heart of humanity.

Nietzsche, another great non-musician thoroughly penetrated by the art he can replicate so well in words, would not have disagreed. Not the young Nietzsche anyway, represented here by extracts from *The Birth of Tragedy*, where the bardic power of the Apollo–Dionysus dichotomy remains stirring even though the philosophic value is small. A few late ravings from *Der Fall Wagner* show him almost over the edge. This diatribe remains valuable for another well-known polarisation, the brilliant sketch poising the 'damp' North against the 'African' sensuality and life-death-force of Bizet's *Carmen*. As a psychological document—the gleefully injudicious wounding of what is most loved—it is merely painful.

So to the *Meister* himself. In the welter of theories and notions with which Wagner surrounded his uniquely audacious body of work, brilliant flashes of intuitive insight can be discerned that quite possibly could not have occurred to a properly schooled mind. His discussion of the 'thinking memory' is latent Proust, the passage that follows, pre-emptive Freud; examples might be multiplied of equally searching moments he lacks the power or the discipline to explore and clarify. Out of his depth he may be, but depth it is. Even in the extract from *Beethoven*, which is mainly mawkish, tub-thumping and turgid, there are flickers of sense and sublimity.

Some resounding names in nineteenth-century science concerned themselves peripherally with music, both the question of how it arose and the question of what it actually is in purely physical terms. Helmholtz, whose great study (undervalued by this book's editor, Bojan Bujić) on *The Sensation of Tone* (1863) was a sideline to his principal life-work in physics, doesn't pretend to find an 'explanation' of music. But he says with justice that any aesthetic system whatsoever will need to be grounded upon proper acoustical investigation, every aspect of sound *not* mentioned in textbooks of Thorough-Bass or The Beautiful. Pitches, scales, triads, tonality are thus for the first time given their basis in acoustic fact. The paradoxical result is to show that they are as much the product of culture as of nature in the raw. As for music's origins, Darwin and Herbert Spencer agree they are primarily vocal. Spencer prefers the human aspect—sounds loud and soft, high and low, are moved alike by painful or pleasurable feelings achieving an utterance that is then intensified, formalised, idealised into artistic shape. Darwin favours the primeval—all vocal sounds in the animal world, from the spider's stridulation ('sometimes pleasing even to the ears of man') up to the gibbon with his octave of semitones and manifest excitement after performing upon it, are purely functional, developed and perfected for the better fitness of propagation. What Darwin and Spencer both miss is the evolution of music as an art—the vast distance it has grown from these putative origins, the extension of possibility brought about by instruments, notations, conventions, techniques that utilise to the maximum effect the physical and physiological bases so well described by Helmholtz.

Some subsidiary figures in this second category do not really earn their inclusion here. But real cavils begin with the third, the writers on the aesthetic of music itself. One figure of calibre is represented, the isolated and impressive Edmund Gurney, by his book *The Power of Sound* (1880). Gurney makes what in this context is a quiet revolution: the first actual music example! Though his approach is fundamentally academic, he writes the excellent late-Victorian English of the scientist, the historian, *The Times*, with such spirit that there is no danger of stultification. Short-circuitings are caused more by his brisk eagerness than by any deficiency of concentration. Gurney's is the acutest mind to be encountered among these official aestheticians, the one who comes closest to describing if not explaining what actually happens as music is perceived and taken in.

Of the remainder, Eduard 'Beckmesser' Hanslick still reads well; it seems unfair that this lucid if shallow mind is best remembered for Wagner's cruel caricature of him in *Die Meistersinger*. Gratitude rises for his fluent urbanity as one grapples with the monstrous regiment of professional (and usually professorial) aestheticians and their increasingly tortuous attempts to plumb the depths.

The subject's aspirations loom ever bolder as it becomes more autonomous, the modest achievement of scholarship and practical technique explodes into *Geisteswissenschaft* and *Künsterswissenschaft*. By far the larger proportion of the book is devoted to such writers. I won't name names; some are famous, and of course there are a few passages worth having (the two by no means go together). But on the whole this tradition combines the features of a bog and a desert without the hope of mutual alleviation, nor a good view once they're traversed. Relief comes only at the very end with five brief extracts from another composer, Busoni, and his luminous little *New Aesthetic of Music* (1907), easily available elsewhere in full.

The editor's preface gives a fair idea of his aims and criteria; his own angle (if I read aright the somewhat opaque key passage on pages xiii–xiv) is that music is best seen as *ancilla philosophiae*, philosophy's handmaid. Such piety is oppressive, and even by Bujić's own standards there is a prejudice in favour of obvious dead ducks, a nostalgia for dusty tomes that should remain on the shelf or in the stacks. And where is the *music*? An imaginary visitor from another planet, who had only this collection to go by could never know that these years cover the maturity of Verdi as well as of Wagner, of Brahms, Bruckner, Dvořák, Tchaikovsky, Mahler and Elgar; Fauré and Wolf; the young Strauss and the young Sibelius (to draw the line before the start of the great Moderns for obvious reasons).

Access is needed to a much wider range of sources than the editor admits. Diaries and letters (not only of composers); poetry, fiction and drama; memoirs, biography, anecdotes from aural tradition; not least, durable high-grade music journalism. All these, sometimes at length, more often in brief hints, come nearer the heart of music, in this epoch as in any other. The criterion for selection would, obviously, be intrinsic interest and quality in whatever mode. Such an anthology could constitute a real 'Music in European Thought 1851–1912'. That under review is not only limited in scope and crippled by academicism in the pejorative sense; it is also, for all the manifest hard labour, intellectually lazy, lacking in cultural depth and breadth, and all too narrowly focused on the questionable discipline of musical aesthetics. For one begins to doubt the actual existence of this subject. As presented here it forms a kind of gigantic metaphor, independent of and superior to music's historic course and intrinsic substance. Audiences, players, instruments, compositions, composers, sounds themselves are scarcely considered worthy of close attention. Yet the aesthetics of music must be a vague and abstract affair unless it overcomes this scorn of the art's specifics. The pride of this subject—that it can sit on equal terms with the sciences and humanities as a branch of learning—stems surely from uneasy acknowledgement of its parasitic nature. Music's being is completely realised in an eternal triangle between composer, performer and listener; to this, music aesthetics is at its rare best dispensable, and at its frequent worst quite useless.

67

Models of invention:
old music with a new ear

An essay in the programme-book for a concert series at the Barbican Hall in October 1993. The choice of particular examples was often geared to the repertoire being heard, but the general points remain clear.

* * *

i

Music, the art that most purely consists of its own materials and procedures, has in most epochs reworked its actual substance to make more. Polyphony depends upon plainsong; successive masters cannibalise their own or their predecessors' motets to make new mass-settings. In the Baroque era a common stockpot of motifs, usages, forms, produces a well-received international language. Handel's notorious thefts (as for example *Israel in Egypt*), so shocking to the mind that places a premium upon original inspiration (and still, maybe, to the modern age when a composition is both intellectually and commercially a protected property) were not so much exceptional as exceptionally flagrant. Moreover the medium itself was flexible, so Bach (sometimes considered more unworldly than his contemporaries) could refashion concertos, convert secular into sacred and carve a Passion out of cantatas, or remould cantatas into a Passion.

Shared conventions and free give-and-take bind together the great composers of the 'classical style' (despite their enormous differences) and plentiful minor ones. Already in early Schubert, even in the young Beethoven, we find what has to be called 'neo-classicism', a tendency to turn to the model that grows throughout the Romantic epoch whenever a composer essays the classical forms. Mendelssohn and Schumann spring to mind, and of course this tendency culminates in Brahms. But in Brahms the relationship to the model becomes so intense that he can be seen as a direct herald of the modern atti-tude. Not only is his past longer and more populous, embracing Schütz, Couperin, Scarlatti, Bach, Handel, as well as the classics, and the early Romantics from whom he directly began—but more of it is at work in his output than ever before. Whereas full appreciation of Wagner required patient labour at a new aesthetic (together with a willingness to be immersed, perhaps drowned), full appreciation of Brahms required high musical culture. His work is defined, even enhanced, by audible relationship to predecessors who are also models. And so it is with the still more demanding works that grow out of the same tradition, with Brahms as catalyst and Wagner thrown in, whether 'conservative' like Elgar, Reger, Schmidt, or radical like Schoenberg, Webern, Berg.

Just as prophetic, but very odd, is Debussy's relationship with his sources. The oddness can be shown by comparing Ravel who, disavowing originality, advised young composers to copy slavishly, thus acquiring a technique, and to discover their individuality (if any) by 'unwitting deviation' from the chosen model. Ravel's own *hommages* are explicit—Satie, Chabrier, Liszt, Balakirev, Saint-Saëns, to name but a few; Stravinsky's 'kleptomania' is already in sight. Debussy, equally eclectic, is secretive. He *does* value originality and greatly desires not to appear beholden to anyone. Plenty of Massenet and Franck survive into Debussy's maturity; when he recognised something he liked in contemporaries—Satie, the young Stravinsky, Ravel himself—he took it in; and he was profoundly transformed by the three most important influences on his style, Wagner, Musorgsky and gamelan-sounds. The difference is enormous between Debussy, 'self-made' from heterogeneous objects linked only by the sensibility that finds them attractive and can put them fruitfully together, and Brahms who with no choice inherits a mantle so venerable as, at first sight, to leave him little chance of unimpeded motion. What they share, however, is 'this-ness'; each is wholly himself, characteristic down to the last semiquaver, even when what they are made out of is laid bare. Somewhere between the two the modern attitude to models and invention is born.

This new attitude towards sources born with Brahms and Debussy fuses with the turn-of-the-century impulse towards democratisation of banal and trivial strains from popular music. Such vulgar material had always 'known its place', namely salon, café, street and park, fields and barracks, the ballet orchestra and the *banda* in Italian opera; and it is the stuff of operetta, especially in Vienna and Paris. But it could always be changed, even ennobled, by a different context. Berlioz uses a valse and a march in the *Symphonie fantastique* to render episodes in his opium-dream; when Brahms slips a brief waltz-dream into the stern chaconne of the Fourth Symphony (and an entire *Liebeslied* into the *German Requiem*) or Tchaikovsky insinuates ballet-material into the workings of a symphony first movement, no illustration is intended, nor for that matter provocation: the light popular vein is a natural part of their musical speech. And when 'vulgar' material is so beautifully composed as in *L'Arlésienne*, or *España*, or *Caprice italienne*, or *Neue Liebeslieder*, or *Dolly* (let alone a collection of ultra-refined mazurkas and polonaises) it stands unimpugned in its own right—as much *art* as any requiem or symphony.

All this lies behind the sudden liberation of attitude towards the demotic that has persisted ever since. The common impulse in some very diverse music *ca.* 1890–1910 is inclusiveness, smudging distinctions, breaking decorum, lifting limits, allowing 'everything' access, to jostle down together in new juxtapositions that produce surprising new expressive possibilities. 'Everything' is what Mahler notoriously urged that a symphony should contain. His use of ready-made material ranges from purely atmospheric (distant fanfares in legendary woods), to expressive (deep sentimental nostalgia for what was and what never was), to expressionistic (disruptive, shocking, traumatised, at once burlesque, histrionic and genuine). Next stop the marching soldiers and crazed drunken waltzing in *Wozzeck*; end of the line, the commercialised *angst* of a horror-movie score.

But Mahler's inclusiveness can also be celebratory, as in the fantastic 'May-Day' rabble-rousing of the Third Symphony first movement, charged up with workers' songs and student ditties. Here he touches hands briefly with Ives. But the American's inclusiveness is fundamentally different. His kaleidoscopic pile-ups of remembered material are drawn from a far wider range of demotic than Mahler would acknowledge, and are more drastically and comprehensively used. It's as if the nostalgic tribute to his own culture's minutiae, timed and placed at the point—boyhood—most acute for him, was guaranteed authentic because actually made out of the same old débris and riffraff—the stuff of memory—that it so movingly evokes. Something of the same urge to preserve the shards of a vanishing culture—in this case to catch the demotic of the entire planet before it's forgotten—fires the *œuvre* of Grainger, whose marvellous little pieces are in a sense 'all arrangements' as Ives' are 'all quotations'.

Richard Strauss, untinged with such complicating aspirations, is just plain vulgar, and wonderfully liberating as such. When he uses the Viennese waltz to render (among many others) the ultimate embodiment of Nietzsche's Superman, the triumphal revenge and ecstatic death of Elektra, and the bedroom canoodlings in a Vienna before the waltz actually existed, he sweeps away inhibition about appropriateness and good taste. Kitsch is used straight—which, of course, produces new aesthetic problems in itself. Yet Strauss's suite drawn from the more extensive score for Hofmannsthal's version of *Le bourgeois gentilhomme* is in fact unwontedly elegant, transparent, indeed *tasteful*. As well as the characteristic warmth of sentiment there is a wit and freedom in his way with these ancient airs and dances which brings the endeavour strangely close to Stravinsky's *Pulcinella*. Coming quite close in date from antithetical cultures and artistic personalities, they perform a comparable act of recognition to the past with a comparable aim—in Stravinsky's words, to make something they love their own.

Stravinsky's *Petrushka*, written a few years earlier, exemplifies another aspect of democratisation that turns out to be extremely prophetic. Against a background of folk and popular song, it uses scraps of tinsel and sweet-papers (musically speaking) to bring the street-scene to life, and to portray the puppet-ballerina in all her vacancy. The new quality here is the irony—sometimes playful, sometimes naughty, malicious, disdainful, always affectionate but always detached—with which these waifs from the gutter and scraps from the wastepaper basket are manipulated, cut off, intercut, drolly coloured and accented, juxtaposed and superimposed, in a quasi-mechanical cinematic montage. However different, Ives and Mahler were never deadpan about their borrowed riffraff; they *love* it, and it can be the container and transmitter of the intensest feeling. Stravinsky's cool is new; and it is via Stravinsky that the era is formed when it becomes normal frankly to model, steal, make what you love your own, possessing it in active practice rather than respecting it on its plinth, in its frame—or in its shop-window or its owner's strongbox. *Pulcinella* itself is a crucial starting-point; Stravinsky's own well-known remarks announce it 'the epiphany through which my later music became possible'. A less-bruited epiphany at around the same time is equally important—his orchestration of a couple of numbers from *The Sleeping Beauty* for Diaghilev's celebrated 1921 revival. This also elicited a letter of homage to Tchaikovsky that, with the dedication of *Mavra*, marks an official change of aesthetic direction; and audibly provided a more copious stock of materials and routines for the future than the one-off 'Pergolesi' job.

Direct modelling on and stealing from the past provides grist for Stravinsky's busy mills for the rest of his life. For 'Neo-classicism' itself the sources are diverse. Bach is vital, most explicitly in the 'Brandenburg Concerto' *Dumbarton Oaks*. So is Tchaikovsky—by imitation in *Apollo*, by actual annexation and conquest in *Le baiser de la fée*, his influence remains unmistakable in such later scores as *Danses concertantes* and *Scènes de ballet*, and can still be heard in such 40s works as *Orpheus* and *Ode*, where a new world trembles on the brink, and *Agon*, where Webern as well as Renaissance dance-patterns and the English virginalists have joined the team. Many other sources could easily be added down the decades, whose watershed is a full-length operatic tribute to *Così fan tutti*, with a plot out of Hogarth and *Don Giovanni*, and many a touch of Donizetti, Handel, Russian folksong, Broadway etc. After which comes a re-orientation as radical as that of 1921, which opens up to him some hitherto alien aspects of modernism itself as models of invention.

While Stravinsky is the principal thread, he by no means stands alone. The interwar years see also the energetic no-nonsense 'back-to-Bach' of the young Hindemith (another 'Brandenburg', the *Kammermusik no.1* is a good example); the 'back-to-Brahms' of such Schoenberg works as the two concertos and the orchestral variations; Weill's wholescale incorporation into a background of Hindemithy–Busoni-ish Baroque of the idioms of commercial American dance bands; and the saucy thieving of that ultimate magpie Francis Poulenc. This is to name some only of the music that has survived its period. There are plenty of 'fellow time-travellers' sharing in all its guises the same general tendency, who can serve to measure the calibre of what has come to stay. That it *has* come to stay is by now incontrovertible; the old Adorno-style dismissals make bizarre reading in the face of such manifest compositional seriousness as this whole venture produced. A permanent work that remains something of a maverick is the Falla Harpsichord Concerto. In an aesthetic tending toward the playful this gaunt little masterpiece will not make so many friends as Poulenc's *Concert champêtre*. But its inner mightiness belies its slender forces and the outer movements' initial impression of neo-Baroque chatter. The slow movement, drawing upon hymnody and bell sounds to evoke a liturgical procession, sets it closer in spirit to the *Symphony of Psalms* than to *Jeu de cartes*.

ii

Already a way of life before the second war, modelling and stealing have taken on new directions and added vehemence in the decades since, with an explosion of allusion, pastiche, quotation, parody, stylistic game-playing, involving all shades of party-colour from avant garde to reactionary, that make the 20s and 30s seem in retrospect positively decorous. A few instances from the hundreds possible will suffice: the fusion, by a personal brand of serialism, of Japan, Bali and plainsong, in Britten's church parables; the enigmatic confrontation in Shostakovich's Fifteenth Symphony of sparky Rossini with solemn intonations from Wagner; the apocalyptic orgy of quotations with which Zimmerman blows western culture to bits at the end of *Die Soldaten*; the mordant mockery and *joie-de-vivre* with which Berio puts it together again in the celebrated Mahler-montage movement of his *Sinfonia*; David Del Tredici's reconstitution of turn-of-the-century vastness with minimalist means; the minimalist's expansion of little moments of Satie, Stravinsky, Copland, to become total texture, procedure, duration; the Henze of *Voices*—'if it moves, put it in!'—the list could be endless, and very diverse. Much of it has been silly and will sink without trace; enough is good to ensure that it will be remembered as, at the very least, the prevailing tendency of these decades, whose common intention, not withstanding individual composers' particular aims, is surely towards an eventual reconstitution of a shattered musical grammar.

Indeed one aspect can be seen as the conscious pursuit of lost coherence —taking an extant work not so much as a source of musical material as the ground-plan for musical structure, often with no discernible resemblance of style. It is interesting that what used to be a discipline whereby a young composer learnt the craft—as in Elgar's juvenile exercise on Mozart's G minor symphony—has moved into place as a creative venture in its own right. Several Beethoven-based endeavours come to mind, Robert Simpson's three 'Razumovsky' quartets, and the *Metamorphosis/Dance* that Alexander Goehr derived from the proportions and rhythmic relationships of the variations in the last piano sonata. Theo Verbey's *Triade* is one of the latest in this fascinating line; adhering faithfully to the shapes and phrase structures of Mozart's 'Prague' Symphony, he has filled them out with fleecy textures and a volatile momentum that owe nothing to the source.

Knussen's *Ophelia Dances* has certain analogies but moves off in directions of its own. The debt to Schumann is threefold: to his skill in building complex wholes out of little nuggets of song and dance; to the play of cipher and enigma in *Carnaval*, whose famous pitch-sphinxes are perpetually re-ordered in fantastical metamorphoses (*lettres dansantes* indeed!) to make the entire musical frabric; to the tender poetic spirit with which Schumann evokes in a thumbnail sketch a Chiara, Estrella, Ernestine etc., inspiring this full-length rendition from within of Ophelia in her madness. The picture is then characteristically enriched by a further level of allusion. Her delirious alternation of grave and gay recalls Debussy's *Gigues*, first entitled *Gigues tristes*, whose prevailing rhythm, delicately capturing both ends of the paradox, is worked into the material whose pitches derive from the Schumann.

My own approaches in the *Fantasy Pieces* on Schumann's Heine *Liederkreis* is perhaps more superficial, certainly concerned more with surface resemblance. I want the originals to be always wholly recognisable (an intention that can be assisted by the optional inclusion of the entire song cycle in its original form). The transformations and expansions to which they are then subjected are an intensification, by way of loving homage to a musical style and its expressive content that seemed at the time of (re)composition to be both forbidden by prevailing winds and lost beyond recall. Yet there is an element of the 'in-depth' approach in, for example, the way the quotations from further Schumann songs that flicker subliminally in the adagio are then woven organically into the texture of the finale; the phrase from *Dichterliebe* is still clearly audible in the coda as an exhausted afterglow when the hard work is over; and underneath, the opening chords of *Frauenliebe und -leben*, cadential in themselves, seek a variety of resolutions from the multiplicity of keys so untonally employed, before focusing in on a pure A major from which all alien notes have been gradually composed out. In theft begin responsibilities, artistically speaking: it's never a question of blithe 'smash, grabbit and run'.

Another way with quotation and montage—the expressionist, involving distortion, irony, alienation—leaves me personally rather cold (probably a tribute to its queasy power). The line from Mahler runs via such moments as 'Ach du lieber Augustin' in Schoenberg's Second Quartet and the bitter wrong-right-note passage in Bartók's fifth, to Shostakovich and Schnittke. Górecki's *Kleines Requiem für eine Polka* belongs in this awkward area. 'Is it over-the-top clowning, or absolutely serious, or both?' asks Adrian Thomas. The answer is, does he make it matter, does he make it meaningful, does he make it work?

iii

Nothing is new. Recycling its past by imitation, stealing, eating, transformation, is absolutely normative, and always has been. Pure originality is the unusual thing; to be without models of invention is almost unknown amongst the great composers. It produces at best the oddball genius who gets away with it (Berlioz, Musorgsky); more often just eccentricity or a private *Volapük* (Langaard, Hauer, Satie, Partch). Even the twentieth century's most radical figure, Webern, was adamant about his place in a great tradition whose every device is inherited to be used again, and all his later work has a model behind it, sometimes explicit.

Nonetheless there *is* something new. Somewhere between Brahms and Debussy, Ives and Mahler, Ravel and Stravinsky, 'human nature changed', musically speaking, in respect to the laws of property. And now, after a century or so given over to re-creation, this altered impulse has developed laws of its own (albeit little suggestion of common practice). So how does a composer within an aesthetic of re-using still contrive to 'be himself' and make something new? And what is the value of work so dependent upon transfusions from the past? These questions are difficult to answer in theory, though actual achievement should long have made them redundant. The repudiation of self-expression that emanates from Stravinsky, Eliot and the general move towards impersonality after the First War has not sunk very deep. Most young composers nowadays would neither take nor be offered Ravel's advice. To hell with Saint-Saëns they want to be *themselves*. And most grown-up composers, whether they subscribe to old or neo avant-garde positions that demand a wholly new start for each new undertaking, would say they try to hear and capture a sound they've not heard before, a sound they'd like to hear, missing from the music around them, as yet non-existent, needing *them* specifically to make it. The appraising consensus, critics, academics and impresarios, is still fixated upon newness, so an aesthetic of quotation and re-using, unless melodramatically drastic, is in theory impermissible. Especially vulnerable is sheer continuity with the past, which (in theory) hasn't got a leg to stand on as it bravely takes to the middle of the open road.

But all this gets the wrong words and the wrong values. What does originality actually consist of, when it's not a rare stroke of audacity whereby something is done, and seen in the end to make sense, that had not been done before? Certainly since the 'alteration of the property laws' it has been a matter of the angle from which a given or taken source is viewed. The ingenuous testimony of Prokofiev's son—'first my father writes music like everyone else, then he Prokofievises it'—can be amplified by Stravinsky's derogatory comment on the same composer, that he evinces only 'biological personality' rather than a fully-rounded artistic persona. Taken together these two apparent negatives can help towards a positive definition. For who has ever displayed more 'biological personality' than Stravinsky himself? A composer's music is born of the whole person—the physiological constitution; the physical characteristics; the identifying voice, gestures, walk, the individual tempo; the characters as revealed in things both trivial and vital; the cast of mind and temperament; the intellectual interests; the concerns social, cultural, spiritual, sexual. So Stravinsky's particular music will inevitably contain his particular amalgam of all these things, be the occasion an *Oedipus rex* or a ballet written in tongue-in-cheek olden style, and the materials to make it a motley garment of tropes and clichés begged, borrowed or stolen from Bach to Offenbach. He has 'Stravinskified' the lot. We value his work because he is who he is, because of what he's done and how he's done it, because it is what it is.

Eclecticism and kleptomania are totally compatible with originality—think of Elgar, Mahler, Ravel, Britten, Stravinsky himself. Moreover a lifetime's dependence upon a *donnée* or *volée*, whether as starting-point or as the work's substance, is hardly an admission of creative impotence when the witnesses include Ives, Grainger, Copland, Bartók and Stravinsky again. The individual angle from which the received ideas or stolen goods are viewed is the angle from which the modeller manipulates the clay and the sculptor attacks the stone, working the received material till it makes a new shape that gives satisfaction. The attitude to the model is ultimately an attitude to the job in hand. This requires invention—specific gifts and skills, functioning at a high level informed by biological personality in the fullest sense—the uniqueness of the individual, doing what it uniquely can, making its unmistakable mark in sound. And as for value, the criteria are really just the same as those by which 'proper music' is judged—the music by the masters of the past before the change in the property laws. Let me come clean and say that this, too, is proper music. It's not so different, after all, to begin from a Schumann sphinx or song or the ground-plan of a Mozart symphony, as it was to make masses, fugues, concerti grossi, symphonies, entire operas, out of borrowed tags, clichés and formulae.

The whole ancient topic is still an unresolved problem, and the specifically modern end of it is a minefield. But one thing is clear: the diverse and numerous composers along this path have been guided by intuition and surprise. The Fux and Rameau, let alone the Schenker, will follow later. They will have the benefit of comprehension; the creative thrust itself has been made in the dark.

68

Business as usual

Its arts columnists were invited in 1998 to report on the state of their art over the then 170 years of the Spectator's *existence. Though no-one could accuse him of insensibility to the twentieth century's music, Michael Tanner's response, after an exaltation of the preceding era with which few could disagree, was dispiritingly downbeat about everything since. I'd not be a 'practising composer' if I were to hold so depressed a view of my contemporaries, my great fathers and grandfathers, my juniors and indeed myself! Hence this vigorous countermove.*

* * *

I can't resist a positive riposte to the dying fall of pessimism which closes Michael Tanner's piece on the terminal (as he sees it) 170 years of Western music. No complaints about his nineteenth century (save the omission of such commanding figures as Liszt, Tchaikovsky, Musorgsky, Dvořák). But when he claims that the musical achievement of the twentieth is 'surely dismaying' in comparison I have to demur, not merely to defend the honour of my profession, so much as with the sharp knowledge, in head, heart and gut, that it isn't true.

His reason—that the finest music of the last ninety years (despite its 'magnificence') can be recognised only against a background of the previous hundred—doesn't stand up.Music has since its origins recycled and transformed its own constituents, enriching or refining, altering emphases, tending here towards euphony and perfection, there towards gargoyles of mannerism and strangeness, all in the pursuit of expressive and formal intensity. In the past, be it mediaeval, Renaissance, baroque, classical, such continuities were called Tradition: copyright didn't exist, the Deadly Sins didn't include plagiary.

The classical epoch is a clear instance. Even the extremist Beethoven is measured with and against a norm of Haydn–Mozart to which is added in later life the profound influence of Bach, Handel and older church music. Even the formal and expressive outbursting of Schubert in 1828 is rooted in a classical tonality of which in some ways it remains the purest usage. And not just the overtly nostalgic Brahms but the radical Wagner, the visionary Bruckner, the expressionist Mahler, flow equally if differently from these twin sources (as well as many others). A constant across the twentieth century's dizzying contrasts is the continuation of this immemorial practice, imbued now with a self-consciousness that attempts to hide, or to disavow, or if to acknowledge, uses metaphors taken from crime (theft: Eliot) and pathology (kleptomania: Stravinsky). But it is the same practice in a new guise.

A simplified bird's-eye view of Western music perceives three epochs where the going textures and procedures drastically change: the replacement of choral polyphony by an instrumental style with chordal accompaniment built up from the bass; the replacement of the Baroque at its zenith (Bach, Handel, Rameau) by classical sonata style; and the fragmentation after the impact of Wagner is fully assimilated. With the first two, the initial result is all loss. How thin the twangling continuo and single declaiming soprano after the glories of Byrd, Victoria, Palestrina and their long procession of predecessors! How trivial the scraps of comic opera cliché that serve Haydn to construct a string quartet! Yet these revolutionary changes contained the seeds of greatness. Within a few years of the first, Monteverdi, within the century, Purcell: of the second, the astonishing achievement that gives the classical style its name and standing. The difference with the third is that Wagner's sheer width and depth liberate an explosion of such richnesses as have never been heard before or since. Music is still shuddering in the fall-out, or the reaction to it, or the reaction to the reaction.

Beethoven and Schubert are so manifestly classical that, if we want to sophisticate the periods, we can say the romantic nineteenth century runs from 1829 to 1914. To its (strictly speaking) twentieth-century years belongs the most of Mahler, Debussy, Scriabin, Sibelius, Puccini; the greatest of Ravel, Elgar, arguably Strauss and Delius; as well as the shattering early success of the big moderns—Stravinsky, Ives, Bartók, Schoenberg, Webern, Berg. By further date-twisting we can claim that the nineteenth century lasts so long as its last great figures are still writing on top form: which prolongs it to Fauré and Janáček in the 1920s, Rachmaninov and Strauss in the 1940s. Such games with chronology are piquant and sometimes helpful; but of course *all* this is modern music really; the 'old-fangled' idioms of these composers richly overlaps and interact with the accredited 'advanced' idioms all around them, making simultaneity more diverting than successiveness, as well as more accordant with fact.

The fragmentation since (in the 'adjusted' twentieth century, beginning *ca.* 1920 and giving no sign of closing down in 2000) is clearly comparable to the confusion, lawlessness, eclecticism, dither, ambiguity of previous eras of prolonged transition. I am 'biologically' convinced that the innate inventive mother-wit of humankind will see it through into new territories; contingent upon, contiguous with the old, as usual. The delusion is to look for a Messiah, be it a gigantic synthesiser like Bach or a 'world-historical figure' like Wagner, rather than to the innate potential of the art itself in these exceedingly interesting decades.

We should rejoice in what has been added to music since classical dialectic and the romantic sublime. One ideal emerges in particular—concentration upon colour, timbre, texture, the *image sonore* (in Copland's phrase), an essence that didn't exist previously as an isolated concept, more as an inevitable given, of sound itself. If this appears trivial to the lover of Bach fugues, classical symphonies and the Love/Death/Transfiguration of high nineteenth-century Romanticism, just listen to the notes! The burning imaginative exactitude of the greatest in Debussy, Ravel, Varèse, Messiaen, Carter, Boulez, Ligeti shows content displaced and replaced into music's sonic intrinsicality. 'Who could ask for anything more?' The B minor Mass, the *Choral Symphony*, *Tristan* are not to be involved in the factitious comparisons resulting from category-confusions. The works themselves don't call for such treatment.

And this is but one path—the purest—across the incomparable diversity and fertility of the modern epoch. Others would invoke the opening up of horizons; the democratisation of style, idiom, function; the experiments (some of them unsuccessful) to replace or recharge eroded formulae; the fun and malice (not just existentialist desperation) to kick over defunct spiritual ideology. They are all matters that Nietzsche would have understood, endorsed and relished.

69

Keller's causes

This memoir and critique was commissioned by the London Review of Books *as a review of Hans Keller's* Essays on Music, *ed. Christopher Wintle (CUP, 1994).*

* * *

In his heyday, from the late forties to around the start of William Glock's regime at the Third Programme (afterwards Radio Three), Hans Keller's vehement presence was a force for the good in English musical life. He represented at a high level old-style modern values—not exactly cosmopolitan (an important reservation to which I shall return) but emphatically not insular. In general he ground a Freudian axe, and his angle on his own specifically musical repertoire—the Austro-German sonata tradition from Haydn to Brahms, with opera in the back seat, and lieder almost out of sight—was fervently Schoenbergian

Not that the classical tradition had been exactly ignored or unappreciated here. Donald Tovey, dying in 1940, had built up since the turn of the century a body of commentary covering exactly the same field, and comparable, too, in being predominantly occasional—programme notes, encyclopedia entries, contributions to symposia and so on. Tovey's work lacked a Grand Unified Theory, yet even now yields to none in profundity of understanding. But Keller's personal accent was new; he also emphasised some older names which, still peripheral at that time to English taste, were, equally with the moderns, commanding subjects for major campaigning—Bruckner and Mahler above all, with Franz Schmidt and Hans Pfitzner as second strings. He was also involved with the post-Schoenbergian arm of the avant garde, crusading for worthy figures like Skalkottas the Greek, Dallapiccola the Italian, Mátyás Seiber the anglicised Hungarian, and such native-born composers who ventured to take up the twelve-note system (dead ducks, as it turned out). This is all-of-a-piece; amidst it there is one surprise, the feverish championship of Britten, no dead duck for sure, but not at first glance related to the other concerns.

All this meant whamming into the then home-culture of the country that had taken in the refugee from Nazi Austria. Someone had to counter the flab and dead wood, and there was at that time no denunciation from within. Nevertheless, it's possible to feel that the energy of aggression, the sheer blood-lust, was in excess of the necessary. There is a parallel with Leavis: an outsider (though native-born) equally uncompromised by tolerance or catholicity, who flayed shoddy thought and lowbrow values with a purifying zeal and high moral purpose that could be seen as censorious, even destructive.

Most of Keller's causes have been resolved by now, and there is an inevitable air of datedness about these old battles. Polemic that remains readable after the issues are dead survives on its calibre as sheer writing—as 'literature'. Such is the happy fate of Bernard Shaw, whose copious music criticism from the mid-1870s to the mid-1890s makes another interesting comparison. Shaw's demolition of Victorian musical gentility and amateurism, alongside his mission to promote Wagner (not to mention his fight for acceptable standards in the performance of Mozart and his expert appraisal of Italian opera) remain timely, or timeless, though the occasions have passed. Shaw, like Keller, is aggressive, provocative, an unashamed self-presenter (in Shaw's case self-promoter too, though of course not as musician); both are outrageously biased and flamboyantly exhibitionistic. The differences are that Shaw is wide-ranging, intellectually curious, humanly rich, sound in sense and judgement beneath the preaching, hectoring and banter; he is also exceedingly amusing. The spent causes live again because the writing lives, a classic of the genre. The appearance from a learned press of this handsome volume of Keller's essays makes, implicitly, the same claim. I believe it cannot be sustained. The man's magnetism was almost wholly personal; and I would like to evoke and celebrate it before turning in more detail to the book which so regrettably fails to enclose it.

During my teens and student days Hans Keller was already an established fact, stimulation personified, with an authority that seemed to emanate, via Freud and Schoenberg, from the Burning Bush, which made him vastly appealing to anyone possessing the juvenile desire to be told what to think. The unforgettable voice, ubiquitous in print and on the air, posed paradoxes, puns and provocations. 'Hans Killer', oft-quoted in Pseud's Corner, became a sort of household name, if only as the current embodiment of a national stereotype, the intense, weird foreign genius, familiar as Herr Klesmer in George Eliot's last novel and Otto Silenus in Evelyn Waugh's first, not to mention cartoons in Punch from George du Maurier in the 1880s to 'Pont' and The British Character (of which Keller fused at least three—'Importance of Not Being an Alien'; 'Importance of Not Being Intellectual'; 'Failure to Appreciate Good Music'). His stance was certainly designed to invite hostility. But Pseud he was not. Even when (frequently) the manner and matter gave hostages to fortune, the underlying passion for things of the mind and spirit was unmistakable. And in one celebrated broadcast the drive towards clarity wholly subdued the tendency towards bossiness, just as his emphatic enunciation overcame a latent stammer, to produce a moving account of his escape from Nazi Vienna all the more effective for its dispassionate tone and the final lesson derived for a lifetime's benefit from an early experience so terrible: 'if, against all realistic expectations, I was going to survive, I would never again be in a bad mood ... Whenever there is motivation for a bad mood, it is enough for me to remind myself of this thought, and the attendant emotion comes back with it, the result being a grateful elation about being alive.' It can be seen even from this brief instance that he made himself a master of exact English usage.

My personal recollections of him at this time are vivid. I had long admired the public provocateur in print, on the air, and at guru-sessions on the lawn during long sunny afternoons at the Dartington summer school. Grinding to a halt as composer in my mid-twenties, I applied to him for help. As with Leavis, public bellicosity disguised personal courtesy and attentiveness to the individual, however unimportant. He always had time and advice to spare. The preliminaries to our meeting were not propitious. I forget whether I'd lost my glasses before or after passing out, from sheer nervous tension, in a West End department store (to enjoy all the embarrassing pleasure of attendance from a nursing staff with not enough to do). When I wobbled off to keep our appointment in a BBC pub I was beside myself with apprehension. Keller couldn't have been kinder or more solicitous; perhaps secretly amused by such juvenile fragility, but taking its every manifestation to heart. Many musicians must have received comparable treatment. At the end came a diagnosis ('Brahms') and an invitation to work with him prefaced with a characteristic challenge: to write anything and everything that came into my head with no censorship on grounds of quality or taste, nor even, necessarily, any attempt to 'compose' it—simply, in my own good time, to make a mess, then return to him with it *all*; and he'd be ready. Such terrifying freedom was unbearable. I strained, and squeezed out only wretched fragments of stilted inhibition. Then, somehow, the knot dissolved; I began to compose more freely, tentative at first, then more confident, then suddenly in spate. So the pages of free association were never produced. By a marvellously simple strategy his intervention had all by itself done the trick.

Some years later we *did* work together, to sort out a five-minute talkette for Radio Three, of which he himself was a past master. I submitted two proposals. The second, which contravened his favourite notion (of which more later) that music proceeds through meaningful contradiction of expectations, he understandably rejected. The first, a gangling attempt at a compositional credo, he took on board so long as it was rethought from top to toe. His help with this shows his mind so sharp—or blunt—in sureness and acumen that I cannot forbear to quote. The first inspissated draft bears brusque editorial comment ('non sequitur', 'no need to be incomprehensible' etc.) and a distinctive formulation: 'Nature and art: you don't define the fundamental difference. The one only communicates if you project meaning on to it; the other communicates.' After several rewrites I received a letter making nine precise staccato points with, elegantly placed at halftime, the inevitable challenge: 'if I can't write a clear summary of your talk, who can? I bet you (£5, even bet) you yourself can't. Will you accept the challenge? You would be the judge.' 'If you wish', the letter concluded, 'we'll meet and start knocking it into shape (repeat: shape). It will take hours.' Who could resist such a call to order? We met; it *did* take hours; and the eventual result is probably not worth the expenditure of his brilliance on my alluvial mud. But this, too, was a lesson, efficacious and unforgettable, which opened up, as deftly as its precursor had composition, a potential for writing about music that I have followed ever since.

So I turned with personal gratitude as well as disinterested desire for excellence to this first posthumous collection of Hans Keller's voluminous writings. What is left twenty-odd years after the heyday, when the fighting is done, the causes won (or sometimes lost) and the lustre of a charismatic personality has departed? Thirty-nine articles (oddly designated 'chapters') are gathered, centring on twenty-one about individual composers—several each on Schoenberg and Britten, and one-offs on, *inter alia*, Haydn, Beethoven (the *Choral Fantasia*), Brahms (resistances to), Wagner ('*Tristan* and the Realism of Adolescence'), Elgar (the Progressive) and Stravinsky. This central section is framed by five grouped together as 'Criticism', and followed by another thirteen called 'Towards a Theory of Music'. These are Christopher Wintle's categories, and his Preface remarks 'a continuity' within Keller's thought: 'the concerns of one essay often lead into those of the next'. This is certainly true but turns out to be an ambiguous advantage. Keller's 'continuity' could also be seen as obsessional and narrow; in particular, the endless recourse to the same examples diminishes the initial impression of wide horizons.

But the reservations go far deeper than this. The first essay, 'Problems in Writing about Music', is unfortunately prognostic. The impression it gives, confirmed throughout with little alleviation, is of factitious verbal precision, logic-chopping, a word-wasting that belies the oft-declared economy, all busily fussing at an awfully small nugget of paradox or provocation, and more often than not couched in psychoanalytic jargon that by now seems as dated as wax fruits under glass. When we have a mind of acknowledged brilliance assiduously devoting itself to a small core of central repertoire we look for insights, whether sustained or in aphoristic flashes; and more, for the power to encapsulate the essence of a composer's or a piece's individual personality, heart and brain, what the music communicates and how it does so. Take three characteristic samples.

> Tchaikovsky's music is, in fact, the opposite of ego-centric; it's id-centric and superego-centric, and often concentrates on the conflict between these two centricities. As a result, where the music sounds most personal, most intensely charged with emotion, it is, in fact, at its most impersonal: so far as our ids are concerned, we are basically pretty much alike, and the question of personality no longer arises—or does not yet arise.

This on the 'Schubert snob' (who 'pretends he likes' the composer's repetitions, replacing the 'anti-Schubert snob who used to turn up his nose' at them):

> The snob, any snob, is spontaneously convinced that repeatability is proportionate to the complexity of what is being repeated. His instinctive criterion, after all, is his own unconfessed incomprehension: as soon as something is difficult to understand, it deserves repetition. Inevitably, therefore, the Schubert snob who has to like Schubert's repetitions points to an illusion—the complexity of Schubert's deceptive simplicity: genuine simplicity is the one thing which

he—like his predecessor, the anti-Schubert snob—can't take, depending as he does on understanding what you can't.

And this, on resistances to Brahms:

> Since ... the sensitive, but resistant listener or player is aware not only of Brahms's identification with Beethoven, but of his self-therapeutic identification with Bach, he proceeds to blame Brahms for both not being a Beethoven and not being a Bach. The fact is that Bach and Beethoven apart, there are very few composers around who are either—few, at the same time, who get anywhere near Brahms's monumental genius. It follows that it is Brahms's genius he is reproached with, and nothing else.

The work on Mozart brings out something more irksome than this, because it *is* concerned to crunch notes not words (interestingly, all the Mozart essays appear in the 'Theory' section). Here Freud and Schoenberg join hands in unlucky collusion: the master's petty accidents and slips of the pen are heavily interpreted along the lines of *Psychopathology of Everyday Life*, in a general aura of look-at-me cleverness. I feel I know less about Mozart, understand him more imperfectly than ever, after raising a bruised head from such a hammering. Schoenberg *solus* predictably elicits the tone of conspiracy and private ownership—together with sermons and exhortations to the Great Unwashed—which, beyond his advocates, has still not been dissipated by any wider enjoyment of his music. Schoenberg and Mozart collide to bad effect in the once-notorious 'Strict Serial Technique in Classical Music'; forty years on it fails to convince. Two subjects likelier to bear fruit, 'Key Characteristics' and 'Knowing Things Backwards', are sketched in with disconcerting superficiality, for all their strident orchestration.

And so it goes on. The nuggets of wit and wisdom that truly gleam gold are few and far between. Indeed, most can be quoted here: passing remarks that arrest the attention and continue to ramify in the mind until they become part of one's understanding of artistic matters in general. Glazunov, 'helped by his detailed and delicate knowledge' (of the violin, evinced in his concerto), 'and his ruthless lack of emotional inhibitions'. 'When I first heard the music' (the Harry Lime theme) 'I at once detested it—as if it were important enough to be detested. As soon as I detest something I ask myself why I like it.' 'Confidence and doubt—this is the truly creative conflict. Amongst the false, you find neither confidence nor doubt, but arrogance and insecurity.' 'The music of the greatest composers has always evinced the greatest sylistic impurities; in fact, in our musical culture there seems to be only one composer of genius who has a pure style—Gluck; and the purity of his style seems to be the only thing that is wrong with his music.' 'To show mastery is to be as clear and short as possible (which may be long).' It is good to learn from the editor's introduction that 'the papers in the estate contain a large number of delightfully focused aphorisms', since this is clearly what Keller did best.

Behind the specific topics—binding them together on common ground with shameless self-repetition—lie a couple of wider theoretical 'laws'. I've referred already to the first, that musical communication consists in the meaningful contradiction of expectations. This idea, at first impressively all-embracing, becomes more puzzling the more one reflects, and eventually casts as much darkness as light. For there is at least as good a case for saying that music fulfils what it sets up, in whatever style or epoch, be it Machaut, Handel, Bruckner or Boulez. The listener might be all at sea the first time, but even by the second (or with another work by the same composer heard for the first time), expectation gives something to go on, something which can be clung to as guide for comprehension, and which can only increase with mounting familiarity. And if this is true for the music of romantic individuality and contemporary idiosyncracy, how much more so for the epochs of common practice, and above all for the area of sanctified Austro–German classics from which Keller's First Law derives. It's not just that we know for certain that a Haydn string quartet will not contain Bartókish effects, any more than it will break its contemporary code of stylistic practice. Nor, in a classical symphony, is a singer going to pop up after three instrumental movements to sing a song for the finale. (Moreover, when the expected conventions *are* broken—as in the first ever irruption of vocal into abstract in Beethoven's Choral Symphony—such an event, if 'meaningful' and not merely freakish, can achieve expectedness in the end, to become a new resource, sometimes special, sometimes becoming the basis of new conventions, as when Mahler takes it up.) But the point lies deeper: the initial *Gestalt* comes with its future latent within it; the movement's, or indeed the entire work's subsequent course being a matter of detailed exploration of implications, fulfilling expectations with maximum inventiveness, making potential actual. This is as true for a tight worker (Haydn, say) as for a discursive (Schubert) or a mould-filler (Dunstable) or process-maker (Reich). The combination of relevance and fantasy in a Haydn working-out follows from the nature (and the particular *donnée*) of what he sets up, just as the rhapsody of the Liszt Sonata follows from the character of his themes and the metamorphoses to which they are then subjected, and the unrolling weave of Wagner's leitmotivic texture follows from his evident, explicit intentions, embodied from the outset in his chosen kind of musical material.

The same reservations, with a different emphasis, apply to Keller's other law, for whose demonstration he devised the once notorious 'Functional Analysis'. This idea is characteristically logical. Music being a wordless language of highly-elaborated abstract usage which expresses its whole content in terms of itself, verbal exegesis can only be approximate, either off-puttingly technical or belletristically adjectival. Musical analysis should be conducted within the medium of music. Words are employed in discussing a poem; so why not use a musical work's own notes as the means of dissecting its structure? And here Keller always has the explicitly Schoenbergian aim of showing the hidden unity behind apparent contrasts, whose integration is as much what makes the masterpiece as its 'meaningful denial of expectation'.

Hence the fourteen Functional Analysis scores (hardcore Viennese classics except for a Brandenburg and a Britten), in which the original is played complete, with analytic links between its movements, the whole then framed within an exegetic prelude and postlude. All the extra material is fashioned out of the original, re-angled to bring out relationships both direct and oblique, across the span of several movements which on the face of it couldn't be more differentiated. F. A. is a fascinating idea; also a creative one, betraying in Keller the frustrated composer who couldn't (any more than Adorno and for rather the same party reasons) have practised what it oddly resembles, the tendency in twentieth-century music to dislocate and re-assemble, mock and love, x-ray, devour, possess a style from the past and sometimes an actual piece or group of pieces. Out in the open with Stravinsky (after such widely discrepant precursors as Brahms, Mahler, Debussy, Satie) this avid cannibalism has by now become a commonplace, whose artistic results range from the sublime to the abject. By now it can be better understood than in its early days, as a more historically panoramic version of what music has always done—remake itself out of the same fundamentals, simultaneously recycling yet evolving. It used to be called tradition and be handed down with pious reverence; now it's called polystylism or Post-modernism, and implies cheek and insouciance. But there was rudeness enough in the old—subversion, rapine, pillage; and the new if scratched can reveal love and homage as well as naughtiness.

Functional Analysis resembles all this; also another more specialised venture of our time, the restoration of torsos, whether in scholarly 'performing versions' such as (to mention only comparatively modern works) Mahler's Tenth, Schoenberg's *Jakobsleiter*, Ives's *Universe*, Act III of Berg's *Lulu*, or, in a more fantastical and freewheeling way, exemplified in Busoni's *Fantasia Contrappuntistica* (on Bach's unfinished *Art of Fugue*) or Berio's play with the fragmentary material of Schubert's Tenth Symphony. But F. A., which might work well as Free Association, too, comes out instead as laboured, pedantic and obvious. If only Keller had had the courage of his quasi-creative insights and written with the economy and clarity of his best English. I've played carefully and obediently through the sample included in this volume (of Mozart's A Minor Piano Sonata K.310), to be in the end stupefied at something so patiently, patently trivial. The connections made are not in the slightest profound; it's all puns and accidents—silly ones, *not* the stuff of 'Everyday Life'. (And now a more demotic connotation of the two letters comes to mind!)

The trouble lies in Keller's poor view of what the listener can take out from music, as well as what the composer can put in. High-calibre composing in any idiom is achieved by an artist's intensive concentration, however subconscious, on his own procedure, even when the Schubert, Rossini, Wolf in question is habitually in a burning hurry. A specified clot of material is in play, much of it stereotyped and formulaic. Naturally it will be germane to itself, and throw up contrasts (if contrasts are needed—they aren't obligatory) that are pertinent, not arbitrary. 'Unity' can be laid on with a trowel, but is more often supple and organic, and sometimes evasive, even fugitive. Its appreciation is a matter of intuition as much as knowledge—one feels 'this is right, here; that's a good twist; that's really neat' (etc., etc.—gormless phrases for complex processes of pleasure and perception). It can be interesting to have such delicate apprehensions explored and confirmed by sensitive analysis; though if they are not already nascently perceived, the music is not being fully heard. But of these intimate relations between composer and listener, Functional Analysis shows not a trace. A very few elementary connections are underlined with crashing obviousness, while the subtle truths escape. In all cases the original work flings its contrasts around more freely and integrates them with greater audacity, disdaining pun and paradox except where they, too, have aesthetic and expressive value.

The failure both of the grand formulations and of their practical demonstration can be attributed to Keller's lack of respect for music's history; his shortsighted (not to say chauvinistic) repertoire; his narrow conception of what music is for and what it can do; and an underestimation of its listeners (and also his readers) so marked as to be fairly called condescending. These are grave indictments; Keller-like, I will amplify them one by one.

History for him is mediocre, pedantic, dead facts on dusty shelves. No more than he would I advocate the advancement of bores and precursors in the general move to raise the wrecks, rightly sunk by time, that has become still more prevalent since his heyday. But recognition of and respect for the vital importance of convention in the great masters of his canon is another thing—it's respect for the facts of life. These composers are not post-Schoenbergian. Even when Beethoven breaks the moulds and Schubert floods over into new lands, elements of usage are paramount; elsewhere they are quintessential, and this music would not exist without them any more than architecture without its laws and orders. The classical style in both is a balance of pattern and formula with idiosyncrasy and individual inventiveness. It follows that interconnections, recyclings, resemblances, relationships will be normative rather than exceptional. But because Keller seems not to acknowledge this evident truth (ordinary though it is), he attributes overweening importance to material and procedures that are in fact formulaic (indeed 'expected'), reading into them significances that cannot be sustained. In his anti-historic stance—born of a hangover from the High Romantic premium on uniqueness induced by Wagner, Mahler, Schoenberg, not to mention Strauss, whom he so disdained—Keller simply doesn't want to see this at all, let alone to see it as fundamental.

His repertoire is almost parodistically Teutonic, apart from the special prominence in the pantheon of Britten. Tchaikovsky and Glazunov figure briefly, and Elgar's covert progressiveness is used as a stick with which to tease his English reputation. Shostakovich, Gershwin and Stravinsky are all present, though the essays ostensibly concerning them manage to be as much about Schoenberg as anything else. Robert Simpson and Peter Maxwell Davies are given such occluded treatment that one might be forgiven for not recognising them at all.

But it is the holes that I deplore. Bach is a pious shadow rather than a solid substance; the rest of the Baroque is altogether absent. So are whole centuries of glorious polyphony, and among much else the entire musical cultures of Italy and France. Now of course Keller doesn't set out to cover all music, and says that he won't write about what he doesn't understand. Chauvinism is therefore not explicit. But the stance is so excessively omnisicient that any omission has the force of an accusation. By implication Monteverdi and Verdi (say), and Dvořák and Debussy and Musorgsky and Sibelius—the list could be endlessly extended—because they aren't understood by Hans Keller, aren't worth understanding. This wouldn't matter if the essays on canonic figures offered greater value. Schenker and Tovey concentrated on a comparably compact repertoire (though they did include Chopin); and a more recent example of a study tilling the same endlessly interesting field to rich effect— Charles Rosen's *Classical Style*—has joined its precursors to become classic in its own right. But simply to mention these writers is to lay bare the impoverished yield of Keller's pen for all its activity. He is too proud to descend to mere helpfulness and too impatient to work his theories out into responsible and comprehensive form. And if the Keller essays here reprinted represent 'understanding', then one can after all be grateful for the xenophobia which considers the musical achievement of entire epochs and races not worth its attention.

The next point, Keller's narrow conception of music's aims and possibilities, follows from all this. He exemplifies a 'pure Puritanism'—I remember his objection to my using 'crisp' as an adjective to characterise a snatch of Stravinsky, because it was a metaphor from food. Luscious writing can certainly be awful; he had to combat a nation of purple-patchers, and we are still confronted with plenty of 'creamy' sopranos and 'beefy' brass-playing. But the purist attitude can deny a legitimate part of delight in art. Moreover, it can cut off the living metaphor whereby music is indeed mental refreshment; spiritual nourishment; solace in loneliness, depression and grief; not to mention its unique power to embrace communal rejoicing and effect communal catharsis. The narrow view eschews diversion high and low. But it wasn't only the despicable Poulenc, Ravel and Fauré who devoted some parts of their not inconsiderable gifts to entertain or to tickle in hedonistic bliss. The culture of classical Vienna also pursued and attained musical joy, all the way from the *gemütlich* to the celestial (often enough within the same work). With the Romantics music can also become the licensed vehicle for fantasy, escapism, ecstasy, nirvana. But Keller's prohibitions extend to the so-called 'extra-musical' with which the art has always shown so productive an affinity, whether in song, ballet, opera, tone-poem, or in the intrinsic language of laughter and tears, tension and release. Literature, the visual arts, nature, for all their manifest overlapping with music, are conspicuous by omission. Keller's remark about Gluck, quoted earlier, could boomerang here: his purity is that of an antiseptic chamber, airless and sterile, wherein music, divorced from the circumstances of humanity through which it lives, dwindles into an etiolated abstraction.

And, 'fourthly', the condescension. Keller's stance is flagrantly *de haut en bas*. He speaks as One Who Knows and Has Been There (Vienna, where he played in a string quartet alongside someone who knew a man whose brother-in-law had once shared a railway compartment with Schoenberg's great-aunt—I exaggerate the circumstances, but not the tone). This desiderated figure then comes to tell the benighted English what they've missed, and how things ought to be—which, being suckers and born to inferiority-complexes in matters cultural, they lap up like dogs. His tone disdains modesty and straightforwardness. He insults the general listener's capacity to hear, or his particular reader's to read him, and alternates between emphasising the obvious and emitting hot air that, for all Keller's flawless mastery of English, is very difficult to read—the jocularity is especially painful. Hectoring, bullying, patronising, indulging ferocious Functional Aggression under guise of truthtelling and Clapham Omnibus plain speech, it makes all in all an unedifying spectacle. Time brings in its whirligigs, and twenty years later all this is 'public as Wembley' to anyone who can disinterestedly distinguish between vinegar and wine.

It is also a very sad spectacle. For the vainglory, the narrowness, the contempt, the prevailing sense Keller exudes of futile discord and sterile ingenuity come cheek-by-jowl with outstanding gifts and a generous humanity, spirituality too, that, unlike the negatives, can scarely be recognised in his printed words. He effected a dent in our musical consciousness that still smarts. What he might have achieved if his positive side had, like the destructive, been given its head, doesn't bear conceiving.

70

Tovey

Today the rising generation may still remember to have spoken with people who were married before Beethoven died.

(1915)

We have every reason to rejoice in the great educating and inspiring influence that, in close friendship with Brahms and Joachim, has seemed to bring Schumann as a living personal influence down to the present day.

(1906)

[German music] attains a beauty as cogent and all pervading as has ever been attained by the human mind.

(1915)

The name Donald Francis Tovey (always, even if one omits the knighthood, given rather pompously in full) used to typify, before career musicology swept all before it, the broadly cultured rather than narrowly scholarly writer on music, sometimes browbeating and always unashamedly didactic, avid to improve his readers' minds, popularising without condescension or dumbing down.

He had begun as a pianist of outstanding gifts in an alternative late nineteenth-century tradition of high seriousness as opposed to bravura: and remained all his life an aspiring composer, keeping up mainstream Teutonic forms, procedures and idioms with Quixotic ardour, in a world eroded (as he saw it) by feckless and meretricious experimentation. But he was best known in his lifetime and after for the seven volumes of programme notes, preponderantly on standard classics, six of which were published from 1935 onwards as *Essays in Musical Analysis*; the seventh was on *Chamber Music*. These notes range from elaborate early pieces (whose mandarin density caused resentment or mockery at the time), written as much to inform taste as to introduce the works in his own youthful London concerts, to casual affairs dashed off for the orchestral seasons given mainly under his own baton with the band he founded on taking up the chair of music at Edinburgh in 1914.

In the mid-decades of the twentieth century no music bookshelf would have been without these volumes, in which occasional bursts of facetiousness and patches of Edwardian–Georgian man-of-letters fustian run alongside intellectual strenuousness and extraordinary powers of explanation and illumination. It is sad to realise that his is no longer a (middle-class) household name. This popularising suggests in flickers what his more formal essays, decidedly not written for the general music-lover, achieve with mastery: an overview of the language and workings of classical tonality that remains unequalled in lucid profundity for all that it was never extended into an elaborated theory.

Tovey's musical universe is founded on a line from the summit of Baroque (Bach, Handel); to Viennese Classicism, the triumph of tonality and the sonata principle (Haydn, Mozart, culminating in Beethoven); its expansion and decline alongside wonderful new possibilities in Schubert; its dilution and academicisation in Mendelssohn; new romantic and affective impulses from Weber and (mainly) Schubert, into Schumann; their fusion with classical models in Brahms. To this long line can be added a preliminary, in his profound appreciation of the golden age of polyphony from Josquin to Victoria and Byrd; and a coda in an equally profound appreciation of the superficially subversive and unassimilable musical aims and language of Wagner. As my initial quotations suggest, far from being simply historical, his feeling for all this is charged with an almost familial sense of belonging: a matter of inheritance over and above mere nationality and blood-ties, of immediacy irrespective of the passage of time, of idealism almost religious in its fervour.

Such writing can never date. Its ramifications—historical, technical, stylistic—can be and have been drawn out at length; it has to be extended to cover epochs unknown to him, or alien, or inimical, or (inevitably) subsequent. But its golden core ensures Tovey's permanent place as one of the greatest of all writers on music. And because his more accessible work, despite a tincture of jocularity and oracularity, never descends into middle-brow simplification, it is charged with the same quality.

All this can be readily ascertained from his already published output; so what does this stout new collection of 'talks, essays and other writings previously uncollected'[1] add to Tovey's scope and standing? Some 250 pages of programme notes can now join the seven familiar volumes, plugging conspicuous gaps and extending coverage of the great masters, alongside surprises—'Casta Diva' from *Norma*, Walton's *Crown Imperial* march, exquisitely appreciative introductions to Debussy's *L'Après-midi d'un faune* and Mahler's *Kindertotenlieder* (the prose résumés of Rückert's poems bring tears to the eyes); a few characteristic lost-cause dead ducks; a handful of long forgotten Celtic Twilighters performed in local piety (*The Riders of the Sidhe; Springtime on Tweed; Caristiona*); some misplaced efforts at accommodating alien modernity (including a wildly incongruous *rhapsodie nègre*).

Of least value are book reviews, tributes, obituaries, marginalia (sometimes virtually hackwork), from the span of Tovey's working life. One wearies of the coercive propaganda on behalf of a conservative aesthetic already moribund even as he wrote—Julius Röntgen, the 'Dutch Brahms'; the repressive figure of Joachim—though it does help one to understand the

---

[1] *The Classics of Music*, ed. Michael Tilmouth, completed by David Kimbell and Roger Savage (OUP, 2001).

shock-waves caused by Richard Strauss, rocking the boat with solecisms, crudities, reckless infringements of instrumental propriety, general vulgarity and callowness, all this troubling to Tovey the chaste grammarian and self-appointed guardian of the sacred Teutonic flame. (But he doesn't follow through the consequences to his rueful acknowledgement of Strauss's overriding compositional energy.)

Some passages from this mainly dull material are well worth revival. The composer entries for the *Encyclopaedia Britannica*, which were omitted from the 1944 volume which collected his masterly genre-definitions for the *Encyclopaedia* (including the classic forty-page piece on 'Music'), have their moments. An attempt in 'Permanent Musical Criteria' to define the meaning of 'progress' in six extremely different composers from Monteverdi to Wagner provokes reflection. The date—1915—of a long account of 'German Music' points to an unspoken cultural wastage alongside the human carnage, equally tragic for both sides in a conflict between enemies with so much held richly in common. Some passages in it deserve to become standard: for instance, the encapsulation of Germanic *Innigkeit* ('inwardness'), from Schütz to *Tristan*, that quality so strongly sensed but almost indefinable, more fundamental than the conventional divisions of Baroque/Classic or Classic/ Romantic (and, indeed, Romantic/Modernist). The essay exhibits command of a wide historical sweep that Tovey never again attempted, though it is implicit in the fluency of later dashed-off writing, and justifies its magisterial offhandedness.

Tovey's prewar style had been stodgy, even constipated. Its habitual effortfulness recalls still more youthful striving: 'it was one of my naïve undergraduate ambitions to make a contribution to aesthetic philosophy by a systematic review of music.' And from one of these earlier efforts comes a severe dictum that puts the tone in a nutshell: 'the key to musical and all artistic experience is *the maintaining of a correct attitude concerning the works of a mind greater than your own*'. His italics, his priggishness, his impossible self-abasement and impossible highmindedness! Such inordinate goals, and their inevitable disappointment, are the indispensable basis for all his subsequent achievement. In the course of this new volume, as in his previously available work, we can chart the growth from this stiff juvenile idealism into a mature humility that nevertheless remains conscious of its own powers and not merely obsequious in the proximity of greatness.

This transformation goes hand in hand with the emergence of his later style, in which the early stodginess is leavened and made more supple by his teaching at Edinburgh. The move into colloquial spontaneity recalls the easy naturalness of Johnson's *Lives of the Poets*, coming at the end of a lifetime of conversation, compared with the studied constructivism of the *Rambler* and *Idler*. Though he is not built on the same scale, there is something of the Great Cham about the later Tovey. All this is shown in the most valuable and important sections of the new volume: its elaborate reconstruction of two lecture series delivered in the 1920s, together with a selection, by way of appendix, of his 1930s broadcast talks.

Even so, the second of the lecture courses (Glasgow, 1925) begins with the fussy garrulousness that gives hostages to his detractors. Especially irksome is the continued recourse to the same examples. Yet the series almost visibly improves as it proceeds. By about the sixth lecture (out of ten) it takes wing, as he defines, then—above all—demonstrates at the piano with masterful memory, technique and relevance, the textures, procedures and underlying grammar of some of the basic musical shapes. Its upshot, that such things are more a matter of phrase-length, proportion and key-relationships than of themes and their evolution, has never been more clearly put. And from here on he is on course, with an excellent account of the balance, and contradictions, between form and content, and a persuasive description of how what would have seemed puerile to Bach becomes the *Ursprung* of Haydn's material, where its handling is so far from childish. Here he anticipates Charles Rosen's *Classical Style*, which has always seemed to be a brilliant codification and tidying up of the rich overview implicit in Tovey's sprawling *œuvre*, in which extraordinary hints and insights are thrown out to left and right in the most hurried and occasional contexts. And the penultimate stretches, concerning, *inter alia*, the power, *in parvo* (of a composer, of an idiom, of music itself)—the *Miserere* of Victoria, Mozart's commercial dance music turned out by the yard—are new as well as good. Despite beginning in huff and puff the series ends on a high, even though nothing is tied up and perhaps couldn't be.

The same reservation applies to the sampling from Tovey's talks for the BBC. He had difficulty in staying within the allotted time (and keeps tediously saying so): his voice, manner, tendency to a rush of hot air and—alas—the advancing rheumatism that furred the once pellucid mastery of his piano exemplification, evidently became liabilities. At their start these twenty-minute talks show an admirable grasp of the tone and level best suited to a radio audience. His impassioned fundamentalism answers questions that occur to all music-loving 'laymen'—recognisability and intelligibility of tonal relationships without technical knowledge or perfect pitch; how memory functions and hence why recapitulations work; the functioning of counterpoint, but why classic polyphony is 'unmemorable'. Then the verbal fussing sets in, its high-flown diction affording ammunition not just to Tovey-dislikers but to more general anti-intellectual prejudice.

The first of these lecture courses, eight on Beethoven delivered (probably in Edinburgh) in 1922, is on a different plane, full of new matter on the composer central to Tovey's sense of what music essentially *is* and is essentially *for*, and already the subject of much of his previously available work (there is some overlap). Outstanding here, amid much else, is the comparison in the second lecture of Beethoven and Schumann (with its unusual emphasis on the lyric and epigrammatic aspects of the Thunderer); the discussion of tonality and key-relationships in the third; and in the eighth, of the absoluteness of Beethoven's musical language and the compellingly clear-cut account of the *how/why* intrinsicness of music's way of being and doing what it is and does. These precede and follow on from the climax of the series, the titanic go at the *Eroica* first movement that occupies most of the seventh. Truly evoking the physical, intellectual and emotional power of what it describes and indeed explains, this lecture must have left its audience flabbergasted, not so much like a great performance of the symphony as a naked encounter with the same forces that brought it into existence. By way of an encore come a couple of further pages devoted to another of Beethoven's 'miracles with contradictory keys', this time tender and intimately expressive rather than muscular and heroic, in a local rather than global context: a single changed harmony in the final variation of the 'Archduke' Trio's slow movement, and its wonderful consequences. 'These mighty passages in Beethoven are really amongst the most sublime things that have ever been achieved in music, and we must leave them at that.' It is the glory of Tovey that he can make this bald assertion of defeat after bringing his listener/reader close to the mountain top through faithful observance of the small steps whereby sublimity is brought about. The offbeat ending to the last lecture, opening up into that awkward stumbling-block *Fidelio*, is so pregnant in suggestion as to make one wish for another eight given over entirely to opera.

The volume ends touchingly, with Tovey's ardent advocacy right at the end of his life for Haydn's authorship of a newly discovered symphony. An editorial footnote on the very last page condoning the 'excess of zeal' with which he rushed to make the mistaken attribution (the great Joseph wrote only the finale, the rest was by his middling younger brother Michael), and adding the testimony of a German refugee doctor to whom the by now mortally sick Tovey confided his favourite composer ('he became serious and concentrated on what he was going to say: and he said "the older I grow, and especially recently, I feel more and more it is Haydn"'), is typical in its elegance, scrupulousness, erudition and generosity of the overall approach of this edition. Tovey's Edinburgh successor Michael Tilmouth had put it together, with introductions and annotation almost complete, before his own death in 1987: two colleagues have taken another twelve years to carry it through to publication; and Oxford has produced it beautifully.

Tovey's musical universe is hardly a 'forgotten planet', but it can appear forbiddingly remote. The humanistic stance and the vocabulary with which it is expressed are alien to today's thinking and speech. Although the music he values as without question the best remains timelessly vital and his illumination of it perpetually relevant, perceptions have shifted. Yet whatever later commentators might add by way of amplification, sophistication or repudiation, Tovey's grasp of the essential homogeneity of what he deals with remains paramount. Every other comparable writer—Schenker, Keller, Rosen —notwithstanding individual flashes or sustained flights of equivalent insight, seems partial after Tovey, whatever his deficiencies. No one reaches so deep down into the wellsprings of music itself.

So what does Tovey miss; where is he limited, and possibly flawed? For obvious reasons the modern epoch is the main absentee—not because he died in 1940, but for reasons of temperament and culture. A spiritual child of Brahms and Joachim would by definition be unable to follow the radical directions of pre-1914 Paris, even when Debussy, Ravel and the Stravinsky of the early Diaghilev ballets were already positively popular. Nor was there comfort from the contemporary strains in the Austro-German culture that formed Tovey's natural habitat. I've already noted his doubts about Strauss (even before *Salome* and *Elektra*). How would it be for *Erwartung* and *Pierrot lunaire*?

Webern figures in the index of this book, but only as an early musicologist, one of the three editors of the Isaac edition consulted to write the 1915 article on German music. Schoenberg and Scriabin occur once, *en passant*, unnamed but identifiable, where three suspect moderns, the first being Strauss, are hit by one stone ('names his works after Nietzsche, claims his inspiration from theosophy, even writes a harmony book'). Ravel elicits a few non-committal remarks in a note for the BBC orchestra's visit to Edinburgh with the second suite from *Daphnis* in the programme; some facetious remarks by Satie are quoted with misplaced scorn, without attribution (save the editor's); Stravinsky, Prokofiev, Bartók, Janáček, Berg, all of whom had peaked, and in some cases died, well within Tovey's lifetime, are absent. The permitted moderns, here and in his writings in general, are Sibelius above all (held to have solved the problem failed by Bruckner of reconciling Wagnerian size with classical momentum); Vaughan Williams and Hindemith for their robust practicality and manifest aversion to meretricious mod. cons; Walton—once juvenile sauciness mellows via Hindemith into classic craft, via Elgar into warm romanticism—occasions real enthusiasm, missing in the dutiful promulgation of Dame Ethel Smyth (probably exacted at umbrella-point). Otherwise, his heart is in Bantock, Röntgen and Adolf Busch.

The maddening thing is that we'd willingly exchange most twentieth-century 'specialists' for a few paragraphs of Tovey-type commentary on, for an obvious start, the classicising works of Bartók and Schoenberg in the 1920s and 1930s; then (admittedly, a difficult leap of the imagination) Stravinsky's neo-classicising works from the same epoch. Maybe a time will come when this music is grasped as Tovey grasps Bach-to-Brahms, but it hasn't happened yet. And what would this sane, forthright, grammar-wielding yet poetic mind make of Britten, Messiaen, Nancarrow, Ligeti? He'd surely be able to sort out the tangle of ideology, biography, fire slag and ash in Shostakovich? Tovey on Adams, Stockhausen, Birtwistle? We *need* it.

His limitations in earlier epochs are also those of his culture and generation, though compared to their norms he emerges as relatively enlightened. Archaic, ancient and ethnic musics leave him largely indifferent. He understands the Greek system of course, and shows a fine sense of the qualities of folksong and plainchant, and positive relish for *Sumer is icumen in*; but there is no awareness of the riches from Africa, America, Oceania, Asia. Overall, it's Dark Ages until the burgeoning of vocal polyphony, with Josquin as 'the first unmistakably great composer' (it took originality and percipience to print, entire, Josquin's lament for Ockeghem in a general encyclopedia in 1906). He is ardent in appreciation of the Golden Age, literate and learned (the footnotes testify to his vigorous annotations throughout volume after volume of collected editions), yet way ahead of his time in practical application, preparing his own versions for a choir in Edinburgh especially to bring out the cross-rhythmic life of the lines.

This informed advocacy precedes his only real deaf spot, a blankness towards the entire epoch of *seconda prattica* emanating from Monteverdi, so out of tune with its present-day status as to be quite disconcerting. Again and again the same viewpoint is voiced and varied: in the *Britannica* entry for Monteverdi himself, again in Gluck's, again in one of the accounts of how tonality evolved, again in the account of what 'progress' in music means, finally in the essay on German music. His principal scorn is vented on mannerism and *bizarrerie*; thus Gesualdo receives short shrift, as also anything perceived as perverse, malformed, incoherent—precisely what later generations have come to love for its bold peculiarity. But the whole epoch until the next classic peak of Bach and Handel is for a grammarian like Tovey a chaos in which language gropes in darkness and disarray. He compares it with the confusions arising out of late Wagner, the recklessness of Strauss in particular, and prophesies the slow birth of a new coherence towards the end of the twentieth century. It's a cogent point of view, consistent with the centralising normalcy of his grasp of modality, then tonality. (Is it so wildly wrong?)

Tovey's high Baroque is decidedly deficient, too. He is always marvellous on Handel and Bach; other masters of the epoch are only shadowy. The *Britannica* entry on Couperin *le grand* is kindly but patronising: it mentions the superior genius of Rameau but he's not referred to elsewhere, and the wonderful Charpentier was not yet recovered. (Tovey's love of Purcell shows that this stylistic terrain was by no means inaccessible to him.) Then one realises that the triumph of the Baroque, from the tiniest *pièce de clavecin* to the most monumental *opéra-ballet*, the restitution of Vivaldi, Scarlatti, Telemann, Lully (to name but four)—above all, *L'Incoronazione di Monteverdi* and the radical revaluation of Handelian opera—has been the greatest adventure in musical taste and awareness since the Second World War. One can return from it with an enhanced sense of classic tonality as understood by Tovey, more exactly defined in itself, and more interestingly and variously related to wider ramifications of artistic endeavour that needn't be outside the pale.

In later styles his deaf spots are more apparent than actual. It's odd to read in the Berlioz fan-literature of Tovey's supposed antipathy, when one remembers the balance of humour, acute observation and sheer relish with which he copes with a maverick genius whose output will by its nature remain forever divisive. Such figures are better served by judicious astringency than vacuous hype, and the proximity in Berlioz of absurdity and ineptitude to unique strokes of poetic delicacy or power has never been better handled. Bruckner is a different case. Full awareness of his astonishing sizes and shapes has grown slowly, producing a reversal whereby what was first seen as incompetent, even impotent, is now what is most revered. Tovey's few notes for this composer always recognise the innate sublimity even while, conditioned by Brahmsian terseness on the one hand, and on the other by Wagner's self-evident control of a new vastness, he inevitably fails to measure originality—bolder than either, and perhaps greater—that seemed at first merely cranky. He was so sympathetic to Schubert for facing and partially solving the problems of classic procedures expanding under the pressure of new expressive content that one feels he ought to have got Bruckner right. Which he certainly, surprisingly, managed for Mahler. The long introduction to the Fourth Symphony (in one of the familiar programme-note books) pays warm-hearted tribute to this work's riotous inventiveness; Tovey's canny recognition of its interdependent contradictions—elegant and tasteless, rustic and urban, sentimental and exalted, copious and economical—make an important pioneering contribution to a universal Mahlermania which he couldn't possibly have foreseen or shared.

Other outsiders to his main Teutonic line are often treated with special sensitivity. Dvořák, of course, as Bohemian country cousin to Brahms; Chopin, Tchaikovsky, Verdi are highly and accurately valued too, with many points of individual illumination the more telling for coming at an angle. Elgar has never been so lovingly etched in. And there is sometimes a particular felicity in coping with composers or works for which he confesses a soft spot despite their clear shortcomings. The essay on the Franck Symphony is a favourite example: the indulgence of its lapses, the intuitive sympathy for its struggles, the generous endorsement of what's noble in it, the ability to draw, from all this, aesthetic generalisations full of human insight, show a perfect command of tone.

With the absence of other nineteenth-century nationalists, Musorgsky especially, the threshold of the twentieth is reached, where it is clear that his universe comes to its outer edges. The feeling for the beauty of Debussy is keen, the apprehension of what he does technically is highly suggestive, but whatever it is in L'Après-midi d'un faune that caused Boulez to say 'modern music begins here' passes Tovey by. Later stages of the Franco-Russian revolution by which the Austro-German hegemony was demoralised, dissolved and disintegrated leave him cold, and leave him out. Nor did he know, nor could he have known, that this is what was happening. What with hindsight is absolutely obvious was for him, there and then, simply not possible within the scope of what he understood and loved. He couldn't have seen in the 1920s that Röntgen, Busch and indeed he himself in his own compositions no longer possessed what they had seemed to, and that Stravinsky, Schoenberg, Bartók had it instead, or something else, or both.

Its many insights and some sustained stretches of brilliant illumination make this new volume indispensable despite a proportion of chaff, gas, replication and ponderous laying down the law. Even so, the supreme things in Tovey, all of them contained in the long out of print 1949 *Essays and Lectures on Music* (Oxford should be urged to make it available again), are not matched here. For all the excellence of his impromptu style, formal writing-up at maximum pressure suits him better still: such fully elaborated pieces as the essay on 'Some Aspects of Beethoven's Art Forms' and the two on Schubert are in my 'deliberate but not dogmatic' opinion the most outstanding writing on music there has ever been.

Particularly as his reputation has sunk into depression, and since (despite reassuring evidences of a turning tide) this kind of writing on the arts in general has become so unfashionable, it's worth trying to say why. Big woolly words like wisdom, humanity, depth, breadth, poetic sensitivity, spiritual insight etc. should answer, but have become debased. And supposing them restored to gold-standard, what have they to do with the *notes*? Everything and nothing. Even if a purist reaction rejects the humanistic paraphernalia as otiose, sentimental, unquantifiable, what remains *chez* Tovey is the antithesis of waffle. On his chosen ground, by common consent 'the best that has been thought and said' in the art, he is a great master—via total understanding, expressed with masterly cogency, of its grammar and language—of music's *how*.

The principal comparison is with Heinrich Schenker (his elder contemporary who died in 1935, aged seventy-six), the celebrated arch-classicist analyst whose theories and methods cowed American *academe*, thence British, from the 1950s onwards. Schenker undoubtedly probes more intricately the workings of harmonic structure in tonal music. His notorious limitation is neglect of the detailed surface, of the way the fundamental processes are enlivened by caprice, invention, surprise; and of the rhythmic parameter that makes them breathe, their articulation in time. Far more disabling is his implicit snobbery, which, selecting only accredited 'masterworks' for examination, refuses to distinguish and evaluate quality; and the quasi-scientific rigour which declines to acknowledge and accommodate emotional content. Here, in just what matters most, in just what is so difficult to discuss usefully that the purist makes it out to be beside the point, is where Tovey, acknowledging the power of the big woolly words, transcends the technical supremo. As well as the *how* Tovey aims to reach the *what* of music: what it is, what it's saying, what it means, why it's good. He aims to reach the emotional core, expressed in a coherent organic/grammatical structure, embodied in a medium of sensuous physical immediacy and superimposed on / counterpointed with real time in a time-scape of its own: all the complex interdependent actuality of a communicative experience so important to music-lovers that we want more and more of it again and again, always the same, yet different, infinitely renewable.

It's not a matter of rules (though no one has understood them better). Creative freedom, with Schenker, is imperilled by theoretic rigidity which, if obeyed as compositional goal, could only result in idle and sterile pedantry. With Tovey the rules emerge from within the composition itself: there are no generalisations, everything is specific to the unique expressive and technical life and the chosen *matière* of the individual work of art, whether it is one of dozens or a one-off.

In the end the greatness of Tovey's work is the greatness of the man: the two are fitful, fugitive and inextricably fused. Again Dr Johnson comes to mind: they share a darkly serious view of the Vanity of Human Wishes, equipoised with an exalted or utopian hope for the life to come. Also Johnsonian are Tovey's weight within the superficial ponderousness, lucidity behind superficial tortuosity, wit and humour within superficial facetiousness, warmth behind shyness. All these qualities are scattered throughout his copious pages, sometimes in such surprising contexts that it's difficult to remember how to locate them, so intimately intertextured is his view of life, humanity, art, with the here-and-now details of a particular work's workings. And whatever the ultimate fate of Tovey's actual compositions (I fear, for all one's desire that they be as good as he deserves, that they remain, like *Irene* and *Rasselas*, noble still-births), it is surely because his principal ambitions were creative that, together with the powerful verbal and conceptual gifts not normally granted to creative artists and not normally needed by them, he was able without vainglory to achieve feats of empathy with the greatest musical creators.

'hab' Dank!'

Alexander Goehr, my revered composition teacher and later longstanding boss in the music faculty at Cambridge, was always snooty about writing on music that was anything less than exalted: 'colour supplement' and 'record-sleeve culture' were favourite hates, and the shudder of disdain was summed up in one withering phrase: *belles-lettres*. Stimulated early by colour supplements, owing most of what I know about music to record sleeves (and their successors, the stocky blocks of info in CD packs), and often diverted as well as edified by *belles-lettres*, I've long wanted to put the opposite case, and in doing so to repay some ancient debts.

Principally to that masterpiece of the idiom, *The Record Guide*, written originally by Edward Sackville-West and Desmond Shawe-Taylor, with further help in later editions from William Mann and Andrew Porter—this last still happily keeping up the standard elsewhere, nearly fifty years after the first version of the *Guide* first appeared. Obviously this venture's practical value is by now virtually nil. What survives, and gives the hefty volume its classic status, is, secondarily, many a sharp-eared comment, treasurable as such though its occasion has long since passed, characterising performances from abysmal to superlative (for which back in the 1950s two asterisks sufficed) and, mainly, its marvellous initial and evocative introductions to individual composers.

I'm not sure that these stylish epitomes have ever been surpassed, even by Tovey in the composer-entries he wrote for the *Encyclopaedia Britannica*, recently reprinted by Oxford University Press. Tovey, magnificently weighty, beyond all taint of *belles-lettrisme*, covers only a handful of the greatest names. Whereas the *Guide* has no choice: if a composer's work was recorded, she or he has to have an introduction. And its authors' style is anything but weighty—rather, grateful and graceful in best *belles-lettres* tradition, somewhat literary but eschewing preciousness. Words such as gentleman-amateur, connoisseur, even butterfly, could be applied, not unfairly, so long as the grip within the glove is also acknowledged. These flowers are grounded in wide and profoundly comprehending appreciation of European music and its culture, worn lightly enough yet strong and durable, with stringent judgement and taste transcending mere aestheticism to edge over, albeit unobtrusively, into a moral category.

Again and again as I idly dip for pleasure, I'm surprised by the perfect formulations, impeccably expressed, that have proved starting points for exploring all kinds of music, starting points, that turn out, when expanded by experience, to be some kind of arrival point too. Then the authors' quizzical insights—e.g. Beethoven's identification with his Leonora, Tchaikovsky's with his Tatiana; the distinctions between Debussy and Ravel; the word-transcending music of Wagner; the *splendeurs et misères* of Strauss (to name but a few, for there is scarcely a page without illumination, glancing or dead-centre)—have proved uncannily fertile in suggestion and stance, whatever their readers' later accretions or divergencies. Secondhand copies remain quite frequent; and once owned, it's not willingly yielded.

My other principal debt is still larger and more fundamental. Perhaps *belles-lettres* are not the *mots justes* for Wilfrid Mellers's style, in his half (Haydn to the present) of a two-author history entitled *Man and his Music*, for it was born of the Cambridge severity that stood steadfast against grace and elegance. Unlike *The Record Guide* I don't return to Mellers for nips of delight that its continuous format and unabashed didacticism aren't intended to yield. Rather, an initial lump of red-hot leaven, taken in via adolescent absorption in its pages, has saturated the whole system ever since. One is fashioned by such influences even while what they've fashioned is transformed into something quite other.

Though he does not abhor the occasional purple patch, Mellers could never be charged with fine writing: its qualities are more important—urgency and missionary zeal in communicating what matters so. And continues to, for he is still at work, bubbling into the new century, more than forty years after *Man and his Music* first appeared, and sixty since his pioneering studies of Mahler, Fauré and late Debussy first appeared in Leavis's *Scrutiny*. There have been full-length studies of Bach, Beethoven, Vaughan Williams; slim volumes on Poulenc and Grainger; and copious essays, some collected. All are euphoric with energetic enthusiasm; but never recapture the focus of the big, bold canvas.

Such individual overviews have long been unfashionable (though the world of music awaits with desire and trepidation the latest one-man survey of its history, by the formidable Professor Taruskin of Berkeley). Instead, there is a splintering specialisation, requiring full-time attention merely to keep up, yet often enough too narrow to be enjoyable even for the fellow-specialists who comprise the principal readership. The sheer bravura of trying to hold it all together invites hubris. When it succeeds (like Gombrich's comparable *Story of Art*) something is effected which could happen no other way. *The Record Guide* succeeds beyond its ostensibly humble aim, suggesting via a useful dictionary of introductory cameos a coherent picture of Western music, without recourse to historical continuity or an explicit aesthetic. *Man and his Music*, with greater ostensible ambition, attempts both: its higher leap is thoroughly vindicated by the integrity and intensity of its message. They couldn't be more different. Yet both are equally rooted in the wish to share and spread joyous involvement in a musical culture broad-based and humane.

Sources

The Spectator: 'Robust masterpiece', 19 Nov. 1988; 'The great mutilator', 28 Jan. 1989; 'Unobtrusive conservative', 25 March 1989; '*La vie en rose*', 27 May 1989; 'Russian jamboree', 19 Aug. 1989; 'Bach betrayed', 23 Sept. 1989; 'Gingerbread artistry', 23–30 Dec. 1989; 'Schubert's songs recorded', 10 March 1990 and 30 Dec. 2000; 'Rott stopped', 22 Sept. 1990; 'Complex Oedipus', 24 Nov. 1990; 'Henze's law', 26 Jan. 1991; 'Dutch treat', 15 Feb. 1991; 'Mozart: redundant genius', 23 Nov. 1991; 'Mengelberg's *St Matthew Passion*, 25 April 1992; 'Purcell's diligent muse', 24 Oct. 1992; 'An original magpie', 23 July 1994; 'Fulfilling every desire', 13 May 1995; 'Best of British', 18 Nov. 1995; '"Use your ears like a man"', 20 Jan. 1996; 'Batting for Bruckner', 26 Oct. 1996; 'Love abideth foremost', 26 April 1997; 'Love abideth foremost', 26 April 1997; 'A noble nature', 20/27 Dec. 1997; 'Remembering two composers', 31 Jan. 1998; 'Homage to Elgar', 28 Feb. 1998; 'Business as usual', 25 July 1998; 'Poulenc centennial', 27 March 1999; 'Celebrating Strauss', 30 Oct. 1999; 'Humanising Wagner', 29 April 2000; 'Shostakovich horrors', 26 Aug. 2000; 'Recovering from Schnittke', 27 Jan. 2001; 'Ravel's struggles', 26 May 2001; 'Britten 25 years on', 24 Nov. 2001; 'hab' Dank!', 29 Dec. 2001; 'Chabrier's songs', 26 Oct. 2002; 'Oliver Knussen at 50', 30 Nov. 2002

Tempo: 'Stravinsky's Self-Concealment', 1974; 'Two on Weill', 1975, 1997; 'Britten memorial piece', 1977; 'The complete *Lulu*', 1979); '*Adventures Underground*', 1980; '*All in the Golden Afternoon*', 1981; 'Reports from the U.S.', 1981; 'Stockhausen's *Inori*', 1982; 'Debussy and the theatre', 1983; '*Die Frau ohne Schatten*', 1992; 'Thoughts on the 50th anniversary of Strauss's death', 1999; 'Schoeck the evolutionary', 2001

The Musical Times: 'Sugar and spice', Nov. 1993; 'The Kraken Wakes', Dec. 1994; 'Master of hearts', Aug. 1995; 'Revival of the fittest', Nov. 1996; 'Smiling through', Dec. 1996; 'Customised goods', Oct., Nov., Dec. 1997; 'Howard's way', July 2000

Times Literary Supplement: 'The search for a sound aesthetics', 31 March – 6 April 1989; 'A world of private meanings', 23 Aug. 1991; 'Splendid but silly', 27 Sept. 1991; 'Strange victory', 13 Nov. 1992; 'Stravinsky's spiritual son', 24 March 1995; 'A colossal drive to create', 8 May 1998

Cambridge Review: 'Britten – The Sentimental Sublime', 30 May 1964; '*Lulu*', 2–4 June 1979

Music and Musicians: 'Strauss's last opera', 26–8 June 1973; 'The writings of Debussy', 1978

London Review of Books: 'Keller's causes', 3 August 1995; 'Empathy', 8 August 2002

The Listener: 'The man and his toys', 17/24 Dec. 1987

BBC Music Magazine: 'Scriabin: the *Poem of Ecstasy*, March 1999

Observer: 'An artist of interpretation', 6 April 1986

Independent: 'Beware the pitfalls of sincerity, 14 Oct. 1989

Programme Book for L.S.O. Gershwin Series (1987): '"But is it Art?" Gershwin in a classical context'

London Sinfonietta programme book: 'Models of invention', Oct. 1993

The Music of Alexander Goehr, ed. Bayan Northcott (London: Schott, 1980): 'Towards a critique—the music of Alexander Goehr

The Britten Companion, ed. Christopher Palmer (London: Faber, 1984): 'The church parables (II): limits and renewals'

Twilight of the Gods, ed. Nicholas John (London: ENO/ROH Guide 31, 1985): 'Motif, memory and meaning'

Parsifal, ed. Nicholas John (London: ENO/ROH Guide 34, 1986): 'Experiencing music and imagery'

Richard Strauss: Elektra, ed. Derrick Puffett (Cambridge: CUP, 1989): 'The orchestration of *Elektra*: a critical interpretation'

Richard Strauss: Salome, ed. Derrick Puffett (Cambridge: CUP, 1989): '*Salome*: art or kitsch?'

Haydn Studies, ed. Dean Sutcliffe (Cambridge: CUP, 1998): 'Haydn: the musicians' musician'

Janáček Studies, ed. Paul Wingfield (Cambridge: CUP, 1999): 'Expressive sources and resources in Janáček's musical language'

Nexus Institute Proceedings 29 (2001): 'Some thoughts about *Tristan*'

Index

This index cannot hope to be comprehensive. I've highlighted every main subject in bold; more or less extended discussions come next, with some indication of their content; then come passing references ranging from single (e.g. Col Porter, Sir John Stainer) to the composers whose names are in constant play throughout the collection (e.g. Brahms, Stravinsky, Mahler, Britten, Wagner, Debussy). Often with these I've given a page number to refer to a work whose composer's name is in context taken for granted (e.g. *Tristan, Jeux*); there are also occasional references that are more glancing or oblique (e.g. the source of a remark in conversation). When these pages are successive, discussion of the recurring composer is discontinuous. And there are many names (usually poets set, librettists, performers, editors) mentioned so fleetingly that I've not indexed them at all.